HTML 4.01 Programmer's Reference

Stuart Conway
Gary Damschen
Cassandra Greer
Dan Maharry
Simon Oliver
Sean Palmer
Jon Stephens
Chris Ullman

Wrox Press Ltd. ®

HTML 4.01 Programmer's Reference

Published by Wrox Press Ltd,
Arden House, 1102 Warwick Road, Acocks Green,
Birmingham, B27 6BH, UK
Printed in the United States
ISBN 1-861005-33-4

Trademark Acknowledgements

Wrox has endeavored to provide trademark information about all the companies and products mentioned in this book by the appropriate use of capitals. However, Wrox cannot guarantee the accuracy of this information.

Credits

Authors
Stuart Conway
Gary Damschen
Cassandra Greer
Daniel Maharry
Simon Oliver
Sean Palmer
Jon Stephens
Chris Ullman

Additional Material
Alex Homer
Christian Jarolim
Rita Ruban

Technical Architect
Peter Morgan

Technical Editors
Howard Davies
Richard Deeson
Phillip Jackson
Sarah Larder
Chris Mills

Additonal Editing
Nick Manning

Author Agent
Marsha Collins

Project Administrator
Vicky Idiens

Category Managers
Sonia Mullineux
Dave Galloway

Technical Reviewers
Maxime Bombardier
Natalia Bortniker
David Emery
Damien Foggon
Howard Freckleton
Chrissy Gureski
Brian Higdon
Martin Honnen
Sing Li
Sean Palmer
Imar Spaanjaars
Jon Stephens
Andrew Watt

Production Coordinator
Tom Bartlett

Index
Michael Brinkman

Diagrams
Paul Grove
Shabnam Hussain

Cover
Dawn Chellingworth

Proof reader
Chris Smith

About the Authors

Stuart Conway

Stuart Conway is a Web Engineer currently working at Redmond Technology Partners LLC in Bellevue, WA. He develops Internet and intranet business applications for outsourced client development efforts. These applications include Intranet Communications, Advertising Sales, Sales Development, Knowledgebase, Collaboration Tools, B-2-B Web Applications, and others using ASP, XML/XSL, and JavaScript. He spends most of his free time with his wife and kids, but usually manages to carve out enough time to keep on top of technological advancements in the web technology arena.

I would like to thank the Wrox staff for all the support for a new author. I'd also like to thank my wife and kids for their patience with me as I undertook this effort. Finally, I'd like to thank my mother, without whom none of this would have been possible.

Gary Damschen

Gary Damschen is a Lead Programmer Analyst for Kelly Services, Inc. His love affair with computers began in high school, when he wrote his first program on a TTY terminal and saved it on paper tape. Although he spent many years in a successful career in Radiation Safety, computers always found their way into what he was doing. Finally, he succumbed to the siren call and became an IT professional after teaching himself HTML and starting a web consulting business. He now develops online training delivery systems and courses. Gary now resides in California with his wife, daughter, cat, dog, and four computers.

Special thanks to my wife, Marilyn, and my daughter, Charlotte, who have supported me through all my projects and went to town for the day so I could make my deadline. I love you both.

Cassandra Greer

Cassandra Greer is currently Documentation Queen at Mozquito Technologies in Munich, Germany. She spends her days running around after programmers and W3C people trying to figure out what the heck they are trying to do. She spends her nights writing down what she figured out during the day. Her goal is to write it (whatever it is) so that normal people can understand it. When she's not at work (which is not often), Cassandra likes to solve puzzles, watch science programs, fiddle around with her iMac, cook, and occassionally pretend she's in the Middle Ages with her SCA group.

Special thanks to Bob Lojek and Josef Dietl, the editors at Wrox for the invaluable technical support in writing my chapters, and to Peter Morgan for talking me through a few dark patches.

Daniel Maharry

Daniel Maharry currently lives in Birmingham, UK, where he has worked for Wrox Press – both there and in India – for three and a half years as an itinerant editor and diarist with a penchant for the obscure topics that never sell many books. With any luck, this tome will see him starting to come out of that particular malaise. If you can't find him online, you're likely to find him either in the cinema or somewhere near loud music, if he's not making any himself. At some point, he will take the under construction sign off hmobius.com and put something there of note.

Daniel would like to thank his family and friends for being there, Pete for being suckered into letting him write something, and you the reader for boosting his CD collection. Congratulations to Lou for passing her M.Phil. and thanks for the cheque, Aunty Julie.

Simon Oliver

A graduate of Cambridge University, Simon is currently responsible for eCommerce Strategy and Technology at a NASDAQ-listed specialist pharmacy company. His track record in commercial software development stretches back almost 20 years, and he has been professionally involved in internet technologies and online application development since the mid-1990s – including 15 months as a technical lead on the award-winning FedEx.com web site.

Having moved from England to Memphis, Tennessee in 1998, Simon is having a blast, living there with two puppies, three cats, and a wonderful wife!

My contribution to this book is a result of many years' personal and professional growth. Belated thanks to my late parents for all their love and encouragement, and also to my wife, Lisa, for being there for me throughout the hard times and long hours. A handful of true friends have sustained me along the way – thanks especially to my former business partner Jeff, alongside whom I first learned so much of the material I have shared in this book, and to Ed, for his enthusiasm, and for being such a good friend, for so long.

Sean Palmer

Born in England in 1982 (and an undergraduate at the time of writing), Sean is an invited expert in three W3C Web Accessibility Initiative Working Groups, currently concentrating on accessibility applications of the Semantic Web, and the XML Accessibility Guidelines. Music and television aside, he also dabbles in and occasionally develops RDF, XHTML, URIs, and World Wide Web architecture in general, as well as being a Working Group member of the recently founded Semantic Web Agreement Group (SWAG).

Sean can be contacted at sean@blogspace.com

Jon Stephens

Jon Stephens was a freelance web developer/consultant for 4 years, until recently accepting a position with the Micro-Cap News Network, doing JavaScript and DHTML GUI programming and maintaining PHP/MySQL-based backends for MCNN's sites. Previously, Jon worked with digital production and broadcast automation systems. He studied mathematics at East Tennessee State University, computer science at Northeast State Technical College, and is a Certified Master JavaScript and HTML Programmer. He is a long-time participant in the Builder Buzz developers' site, where he serves as a volunteer community leader. In his spare time he enjoys driving his van around the Arizona desert with the radio turned up very loud.

I would like to thank all the editors and project managers at Wrox Press with whom I've been privileged to work, and who've offered me a great deal of encouragement over the last two years as a reviewer and now as an author. Thanks are also due to those "Buzzzers" who've provided me with invaluable feedback during the writing process: Jonny Axelsson of Opera Software and Jody Kerr of RMI Consulting.

Chris Ullman

Chris Ullman is a Computer Science graduate who came to Wrox five years ago, when 14.4k modems were the hottest Internet technology and Netscape Navigator 2.0 was a groundbreaking innovation. Since then he's applied his knowledge of HTML, server-side web technologies, Java, and Visual Basic to developing, editing, and authoring books.

When not trying to reconstruct the guts of his own PC or trying to write extra chapters in a hurry, he can be found either playing keyboards in a psychedelic band, *The Beemen*, tutoring his cats in the way of eating peacefully from their own food bowl and not the one next to theirs, or hoping against hope that this is the year his favourite soccer team, Birmingham City, can manage to end their exile from the Premiership.

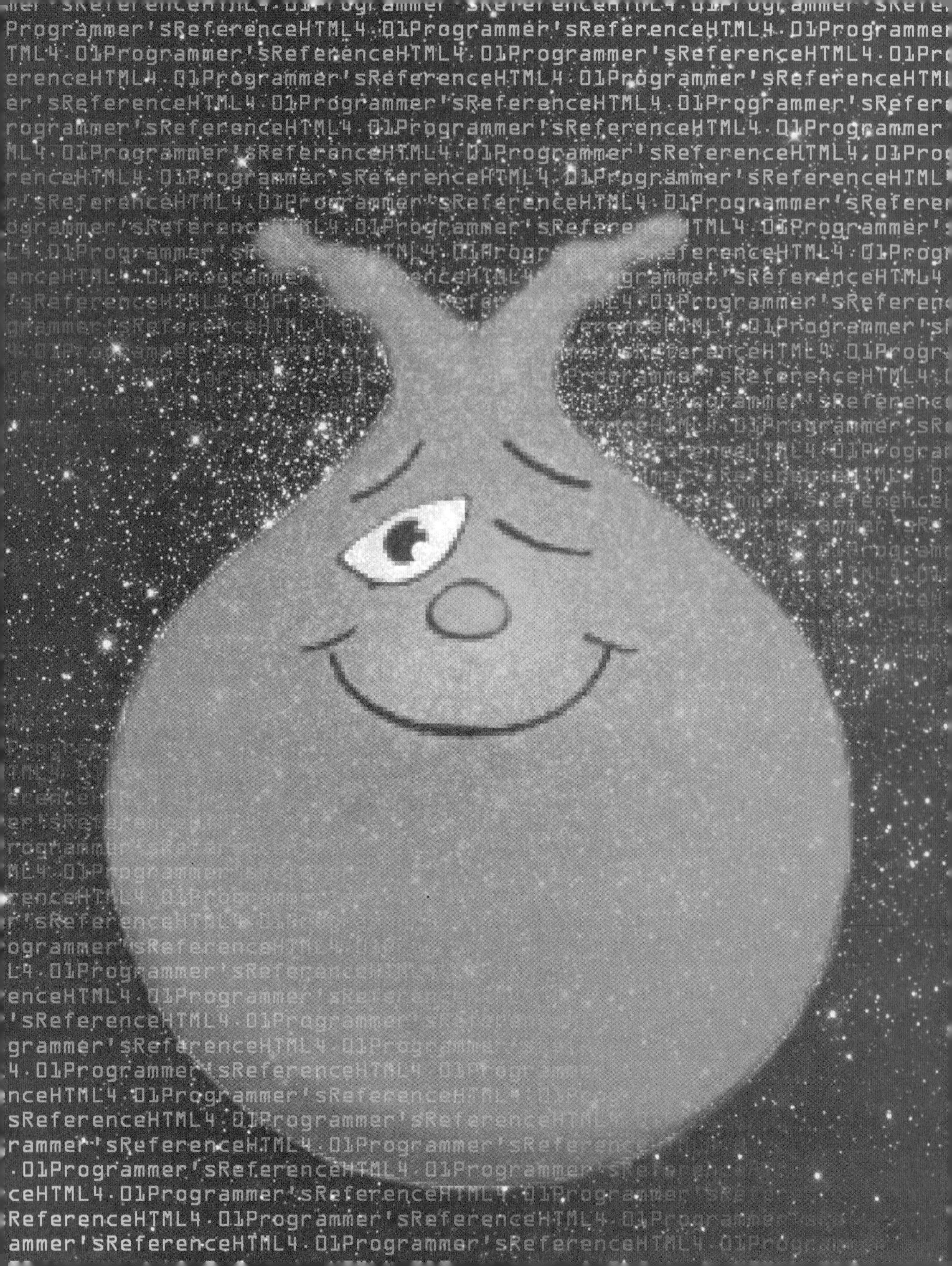
Programmer'sReferenceHTML4.01

Table of Contents

Table of Contents

Table of Contents

Table of Contents

Table of Contents

Table of Contents

Table of Contents

Table of Contents

Table of Contents

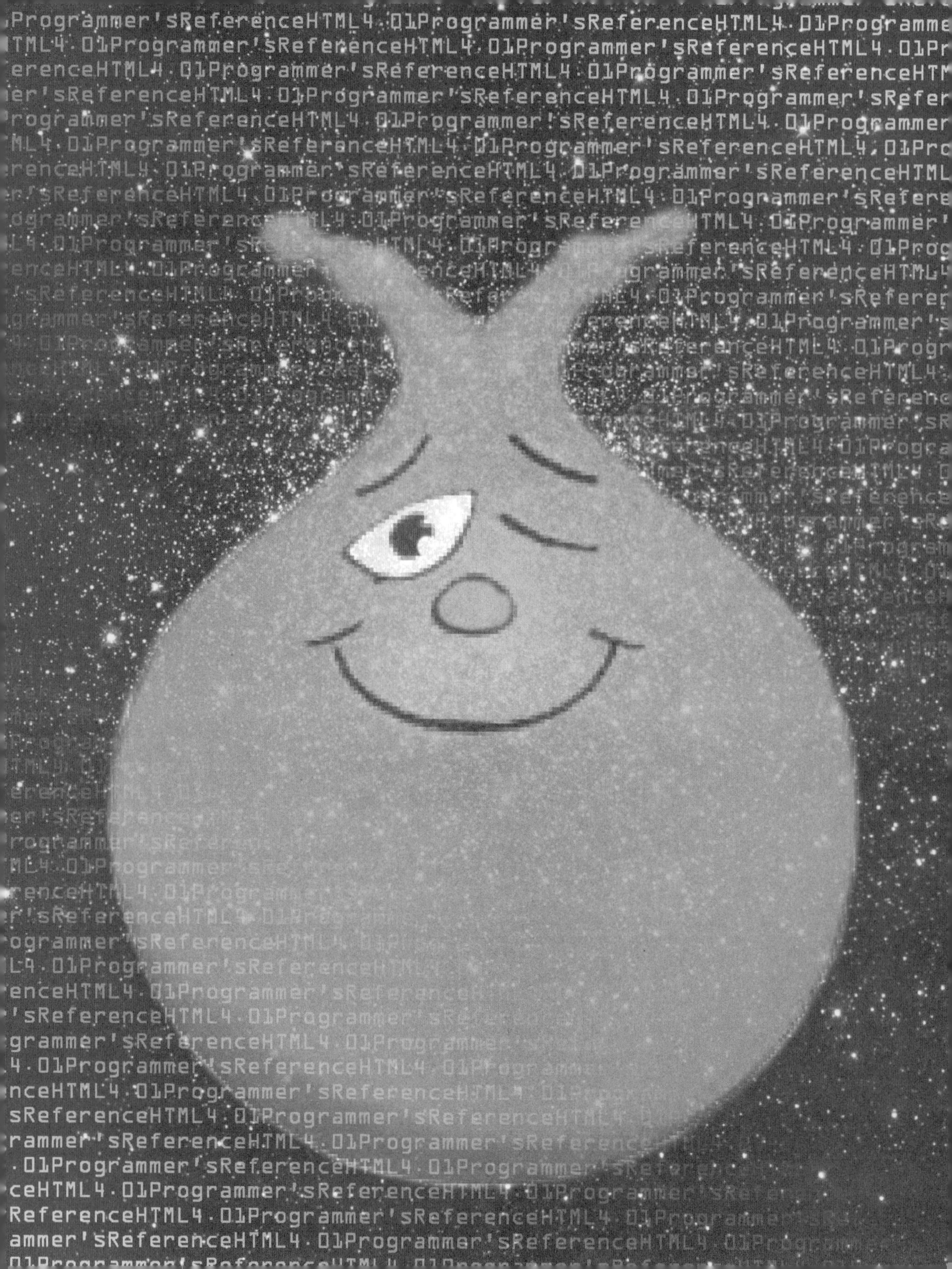
Programmer'sReferenceHTML4.01

Introduction

HTML, or **HyperText Markup Language**, has dominated the World Wide Web as its publishing language for many years since its release circa 1992 (the web itself first being conceptualized in 1983 in the CERN laboratories, Geneva). In recent times, some alternative standards that allow delivery of content have appeared, such as **Wireless Markup Language** (**WML**) for mobile devices (which is soon to be replaced by **XHTML basic** anyway), and **XML**, which can hold data for (among other uses) publication on the Web (but which has no display capabilities of it's own, and instead must rely on further steps, such as transformation to HTML via **Extensible Stylesheet Language Transformations** (**XSLT**)).

So, there are not really any alternatives to HTML out there, even after all this time. This is because, as you will see over the course of this book, HTML is a very simple language to get to grips with – anybody can write a simple web page, given an hour, a computer, and an HTML book (such as this one!).

However, things are changing in the world of HTML, and more changes will come in the future. The most important change is the drive towards using XHTML, which is simply a reiteration of HTML 4 as XML, and therefore has the strict well-formedness rules of XML attributed to it. The aim of this is to try to get rid of some of the bad programming practices that have sprung up among HTML authors (as you will see later, many HTML browsers will parse and display HTML which technically contains illegal syntax), which can cause web sites to be inaccessible by certain web browsers, or slower to load than they should be. If we accept and start to abide by these strict rules, the web will be a better place for everyone. Other changes include the modularization of XHTML, and XHTML events, which you will learn about later in this book (see Chapter 21).

The specifications for these technologies are held at the **World Wide Web Consortium** (W3C) web site. The W3C is a standards body supported by 512 different companies and organizations that consists of different working groups that uphold technology standards such as HTML 4.01, and CSS 1, 2 and 3.

Further References

To learn more about:

❑ XML and XSLT: Pick up a copy of *Professional XML second edition*, by Nik Ozu et al. (ISBN: *1-861005-05-9*).

❑ WML: Check out *Professional WAP*, by Charles Arehart et al. (ISBN: *1-861004-04-4*).

❑ Alternatively, go to the W3C web site at http://www.w3.org for the latest specifications of technologies covered in this book, and look at http://www.webstandards.org for more on the drive for web standards.

Who is This Book For?

This book is for anybody who programs web pages, right from the inexperienced novice who wishes to get to grips with the basics, through the moderately experienced HTML programmer who is comfortable with HTML and wishes to get into scripting, embedding, and CSS, right up to the seasoned web developer who wants a comprehensive HTML reference, and wants to get right up-to-date with the latest standards, features, and browsers.

This has been made possible by our use of informative tutorial sections, and theory based chapters, alongside the usual wealth of comprehensive reference material, including the Ultimate HTML Reference (see Appendix A).

Why a New Edition?

Instant HTML Programmers Reference 4.0 Edition (ISBN: *1-861001-56-8*) covered the fundamentals of the HTML 4.0 standard in a quick reference style, including HTML basics, scripting, DHTML, Embedding, and Cascading Style Sheets. We felt that it was time we updated our reference for a number of reasons: Firstly, the W3C released the full recommendation of the new HTML 4.01 specification (a sub-version of HTML 4) on 24th December 1999. Now, this sounds quite old, but it is only recently, with the release of the new versions of the major browsers (such as IE 6 and Netscape 6) that there has been any kind of reasonable support for some of the important new features, such as the <object> element (which had no support outside of IE until recently).

There has also been a recent lift in support for some of the most important W3C specs related to HTML. For example, the CSS 2 spec is now starting to see significant support in newer browser versions, and people have started to take notice of XHTML. Consequently, we have stuck strictly to XHTML rules (see Chapter 1) in our examples, to make the book more future-proof.

Lastly, with the new drive in recent times to make the Web a more accessible, more functionally sound, happier place for all, we felt it was important to cover the main web standards, and accessibility and interoperability issues, and how to get round them.

What does the Book Cover?

For the most part, this book covers the entire scope of HTML and CSS, also touching on more advanced topics such as DHTML/Scripting, Cross Browser and OS coding, Accessibility and Interoperability etc.

We have tried to do this in as browser- and platform-independent a way as possible, and we kept this strongly in mind, especially when writing the code examples. However, it would have been impossible to cover every eventuality, so we settled for fully supporting the three major browsers (see the *"What do I Need to Use this Book?"* section for more details).

The book **doesn't** give much coverage to proprietary or deprecated/obsolete web technologies – while we thought it was important that we mentioned them (for example, Internet Explorer- and Netscape-specific HTML, and deprecated/obsolete HTML get a chapter each – see below), we have strongly tried to discourage their general use, because it goes directly against what the new web standards authorities are trying to achieve.

How is the Book Structured?

This book involves a hybrid of styles: Most of the chapters, with the exception of some of the later design-oriented ones, feature tutorial style sections that explain how to use the elements, attributes, properties, etc. covered, alongside more traditional reference sections that offer a comprehensive reference of the material. In addition, the appendices offer even more compact reference lists. The book is formed as follows:

❏ Chapters 1 and 2 cover the basic fundamentals of programming HTML web pages, including how the web works, an outline of the main web standards, creating a basic HTML document, HTML Doctypes, XHTML rules, and the all encompassing <head> and <body> elements.

❏ Chapters 3 to 8 cover the basic HTML elements and attributes needed to format text, create links, tables, and forms, and embed images and use frames in your HTML pages.

❏ Chapter 10 carries on where Chapter 5 left off, going deeper into the area of embedding objects into web pages, using the <object> element. As well as images, this can be used to embed a whole host of much more exciting and complex objects, such as MP3 audio files, Quicktime movies, Excel spreadsheets, Flash animations, and Java Applets. The <object> element is set to become the standard for embedding in web pages.

❏ Chapters 11 to 13 cover Cascading Style Sheets, looking in turn at the fundamentals of the CSS language, then at Character Styles (including downloadable fonts), before finishing up on CSS positioning and packaging, involving positioning elements, and styling lists and tables.

❏ Chapters 9 and 19 offer a more theory-based look at the concepts involved in the use of Scripting in web pages, including DHTML, Events, and Document Object Models (Including CSS 2 DOM and Events). These chapters are not supposed to provide an exhaustive scripting reference; to do so would take several volumes more on it's own. Instead, they are intended as an introduction to scripting and what is involved in it, along with some simple examples, and a whole host of useful references for the interested reader who wishes to delve deeper into this exciting area of modern web design.

❑ Chapters 15-17 deal with some of the issues you need to consider if your HTML pages need to be compatible with older browsers, and/or across multiple browsers. The first of these deals with the deprecated/obsolete elements and attributes of HTML that you should ideally stop using, as they are marked for eventual removal from the standard, but might want to use in certain circumstances, for example, a company intranet built on Internet Explorer 3. The next chapter deals with proprietary elements and attributes supported only by Internet Explorer or Netscape, which are obviously a bad choice if you want to achieve cross-browser compatibility. The third of these chapters looks at other issues faced with cross-browser and cross-OS coding, including browser, OS, object and DOM detection, and problems these can help to solve.

❑ Chapters 14, 18, 20, and 21, on the other hand, deal with some of the very newest technologies and issues concerning web development that have surfaced in recent times. Chapter 14 looks at the concept of aural style sheets, a currently very little supported technology that will become very important to the goal of universal web accessibility. Chapter 18 looks at internationalization, and the importance of making the World Wide Web truly World Wide. Chapter 20 looks in-depth at accessibility and interoperability, following up some of the concepts first explored in Chapter 14. Finally, Chapter 21 offers a look at the future of web standards, and some of the most nascent web technologies.

What do I Need to Use this Book?

Reading about a language won't make you an expert in it; you also need to try it out and learn from your own experience. We suggest that you try out the examples in this book, but more importantly, we hope that you are inspired to try out examples of your own.

You can download all the code for the worked examples from the page of this book at http://www.wrox.com on the ·   *click on Html Then title of book*

HTML, CSS, JavaScript, and the other technologies featured in this book are all text based, so to run most of the examples all you will need is a text editor, and an Internet browser – but which ones?

Microsoft's very own **Notepad** comes free with Windows, and is the text editor that we've been using during the creation of this book (I'm sure you will have a text editor within easy reach, no matter what OS you are using). However, other editors that we would like to recommend are as follows:

❑ **Programmer's File Editor** (**PFE**), available from various archive sites including: http://www.simtel.net/pub/simtelnet/win95/editor/pfe101i.zip

❑ **Editplus** is a very useful text editor that has additional advantages: it recognizes and provides templates for HTML files, and various other languages (C++, Perl, Java), and even allows you to browse web pages within its confines. You can download an evaluation copy from http://www.editplus.com/.

Note: We must suggest that you don't use a dedicated HTML authoring package such as FrontPage when working with our code, or your own. This is because these packages add extra lines of code in (as timesaving mechanisms) that you don't need, and which may cause confusion.

On the subject of browsers, we have made supreme efforts to ensure that this book fully supports all but the most ancient versions of **Microsoft's Internet Explorer** (5.5 and 6 beta downloadable at http://www.microsoft.com/windows/IE/), **Netscape** (go to http://www.netscape.com and follow the link to download version 6), and **Opera** (download at http://www.opera.com – latest version is 5).

Other browsers that we will mention include:

❏ **Mozilla**: Version 0.9 out at the time of writing; go to http://www.mozilla.org/releases/ to download it.

❏ **Amaya**: The W3C's own browser, purported to be compliant with pretty much all of their standards – download it at http://www.w3.org/Amaya/.

❏ **Lynx**: A text-based browser popular amongst Unix users, Lynx can be downloaded from http://www.trill-home.com/lynx/binaries.html

We should make it clear at this point that not all of these browsers will successfully run all of the code in this book, due to the differing levels of browser and OS support for the different technologies we will cover. You will find out all about these levels of support throughout the course of the book; in particular, refer to Chapter 17, "*Cross*-Browser and Cross-OS Coding".

To run scripts, other embedded code (such as a Java applet), or embedded multimedia in your browser of choice, it must support the particular technology you are using:

❏ Support for different scripting languages can differ wildly between browsers. For example, VBScript is not supported in non-Microsoft browsers without the aid of plug-ins. JavaScript is more widely supported.

❏ Embedded code and multimedia support differs too. See Chapter 10, "*Embedding Objects*", for full details.

Conventions

To help you get the most from the text and keep track of what's happening, a number of conventions have been used throughout the book.

Code examples that you have not come across before are generally highlighted like this:

```
<html>
<head>
    <title> A Simple Example <title>
</head>
<body>
    <p> This is some text </p>
</body>
</html>
```

If the example is repeated again, for example, if it is updated with some new code lines, the sections you have seen before will no longer be highlighted:

```
<body>
    <p> This is some text </p>

    <p> This is a new line </p>

</body>
```

As for styles in the text:

❏ Important terms, when first introduced, are highlighted as follows: **important words**.

❏ Filenames, and code within the text appear as: dummy.xml .

❏ Text in user interfaces, and URLs, are shown as: File/Save As...

❏ Keys that you may be required to press are indicated like this: *Ctrl, Alt, Ctrl-z, F12*.

In addition:

> **These boxes hold important, not-to-be forgotten information, which is directly relevant to the surrounding text.**

While the background style is used for asides to the current discussion.

Customer Support

Wrox has three ways to support books. You can:

❑ Check for book errata at www.wrox.com

❑ Enroll at the peer-to-peer forums at p2p.wrox.com

❑ E-mail technical support a query or feedback on our books in general

Errata

You can check for errata for the book at our web site www.wrox.com; simply navigate to the page for this book where you will find a link to the list of errata.

P2P Lists

You can enroll in our peer-to-peer discussion forums at p2p.wrox.com where we provide you with a forum where you can put your questions to the authors, reviewers, and fellow industry professionals. We suggest that you go to the "Web Design" section, which contains the following relevant lists:

❑ **beginning_xhtml**
Getting to grips with XHTML

❑ **browser_compatibility**
Don't look a fool: make sure your pages work on every browser

❑ **flash_programming**
Creating and programming Flash movies

❑ **html_code_clinic**
Need help making your HTML display correctly? Post your problems here!

❑ **javascript**
Putting dynamic client-side code in your web pages

❑ **multimedia**
Troubled by multimedia issues? Discuss general topics here

You can choose to join the mailing lists or you can receive them as a weekly digest. If you don't have the time or facility to receive the mailing list, then you can search our online archives. You'll find the ability to search on specific subject areas or keywords. As these lists are moderated, you can be confident of finding good, accurate information quickly. Mails can be edited or moved by the moderator into the correct place, making this a most efficient resource. Junk and spam mail are deleted, and your own e-mail address is protected by the unique Lyris system from web-bots that can automatically collect newsgroup mailing list addresses.

E-mail Support

If you wish to point out an errata to put up on the web site or directly query a problem in the book with an expert who knows the book in detail, then e-mail support@wrox.com. A typical e-mail should include the following things:

❑ The name of the book, the last four digits of the book's ISBN, and the page number of the problem in the Subject field

❑ Your name, contact info, and description of the problem in the body of the message

Tell Us What You Think

The authors and the Wrox team have worked hard to make this book a pleasure to read as well as being useful and educational, so we'd like to know what you think. At Wrox we are always keen to hear what you liked best and what improvements you think are possible. We appreciate feedback on our efforts and take both criticism and praise on board in our future editorial efforts. When necessary, we'll forward comments and queries to the author. If you've anything to say, let us know by sending an e-mail to:

feedback@wrox.com

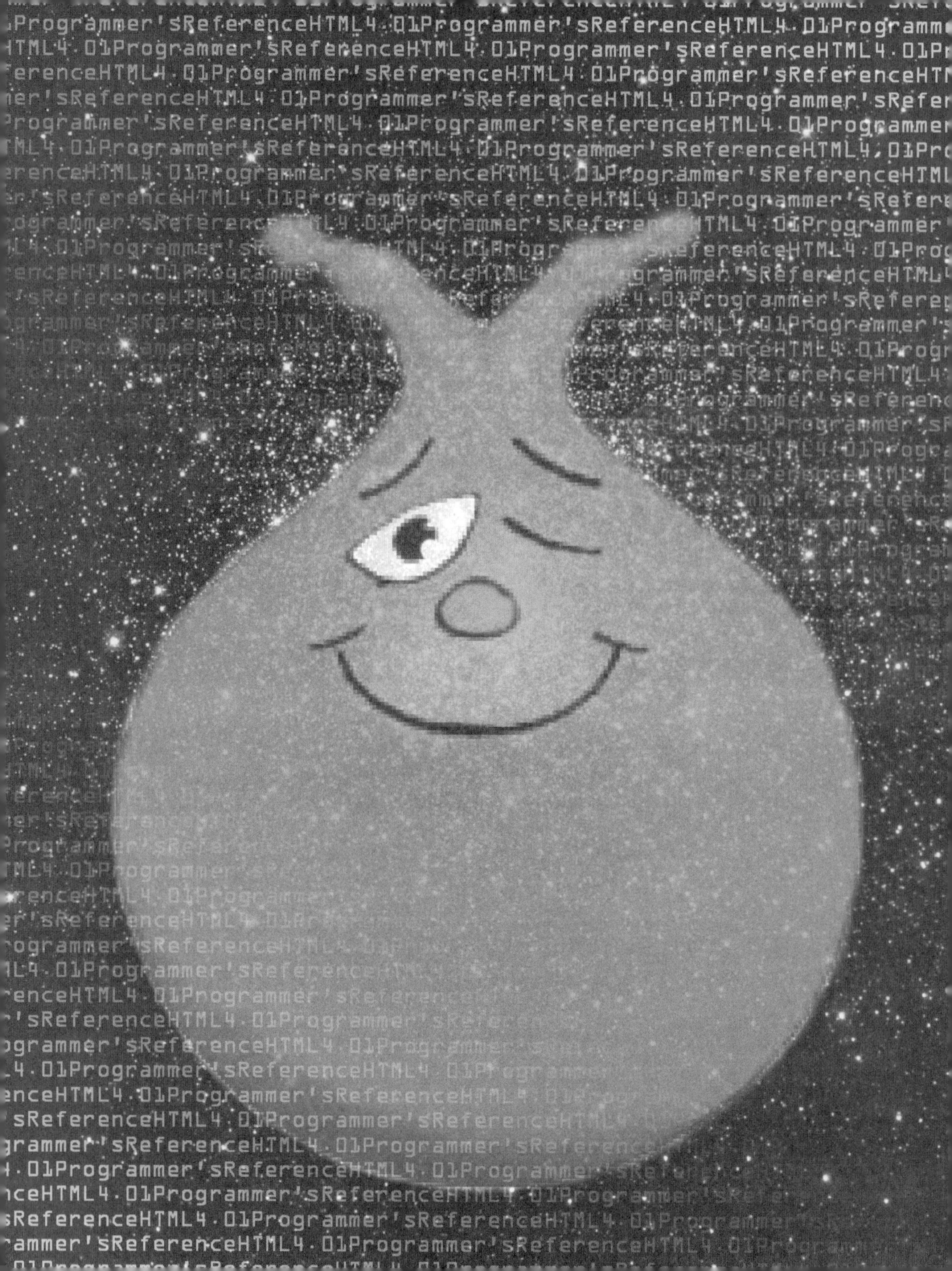

1

The HTML Document

HTML stands for **HyperText Markup Language** and is the main publishing language of the World Wide Web.

The concept of the World Wide Web, or simply the Web, first came into being in 1983 at the CERN (European Organization for Nuclear Research) laboratory in Geneva, when Tim Berners-Lee was looking for a way of disseminating information in a friendly, but platform-independent, manner. The scheme he devised was placed in the public domain in 1992, and the World Wide Web was born.

Most of the activities in developing the many standards and technologies that go into making the World Wide Web function have now been transferred from CERN to the World Wide Web Consortium (W3C). Its web site at http://www.w3.org/ is always a good starting place for discovering more about the Web.

We're going to take a look in this chapter at what goes to make up an HTML document and how it is transported across the Web. Although strictly speaking, when creating an HTML web page you don't need to know that much about the process of accessing a web page, there are two areas in HTML that we'll look at later in this book, notably forms and the element for storing meta-information about an HTML document, which require some background knowledge of the process.

We'll start by discussing the method of transfer of the document, and then go on to consider some of the standards used to ensure that the methods for accessing and creating web pages are uniform across the Web. Lastly, we'll look in more detail at what needs to go into an HTML document according to the standard.

The important topics discussed in this chapter are:

❑ The process of viewing a web page

❑ The client-server model

❑ The different web standards relevant to web developers

❑ The basic building blocks of an HTML document

How the World Wide Web Works

In this book, we won't spend a lot of time examining how the World Wide Web works, but it is important to understand the basics of the technology that makes it possible. There are three parts that enable a user to browse a web page:

❑ The **web server** that holds the information

❑ The **client** that is viewing the information

❑ The **protocol** that connects the two

Documents, including text, images, sounds, and other types of information, are held on a remote web server, viewed on a client, and transferred between the two using the **HTTP (HyperText Transfer Protocol)**. There are other protocols involved, as we shall see, but it is HTTP that handles the physical transfer of information between the server and clients.

Viewing a Web Page

When a client (the computer, workstation, or other device being used by the person that wishes to view the document) makes a request to the server for a web page (the machine that the information sought is stored on), it uses the HTTP protocol across a network to request the information – in the form of a **Uniform Resource Locator (URL)** – from the server.

> *A URL is a way of specifying a web page, or more accurately speaking, a resource. It consists of a protocol name, a colon (:), two forward slash characters (//), a machine name, and a path to a resource (using / as a separator). For example, the Wrox Press home page can be found at http://www.wrox.com. URLs are the way that all resources are specified on the Web. Note that URLs can specify more than just web pages. For example, to retrieve a text document using the FTP protocol, we could specify ftp://www.myserver.com/example.txt. URLs are often embedded inside web pages, to provide links to other pages, as we shall see later.*

The server processes the request and, again, uses the HTTP to transfer the information back to the client. As well as transferring the actual information, the server must tell the client the type of document being returned. The client must then process the information before it presents it to the human viewer (or passes it to an application, or whatever).

It is the job of a web server to make web pages available to all and sundry. A web server is a software package that resides on the server machine, whose job it is to process requests, and return the correct responses to the client. Another job of the web server is to provide an area (typically in a directory or folder structure) in which to organize and store web pages or whole web sites.

There are many commercial and freeware web servers available, but two web servers predominate with over 70% of the market according to http://www.netcraft.com/survey. The two products are **Apache**'s web server and Microsoft's **Internet Information Server (IIS)**.

> *For more information on Microsoft IIS and Apache, visit:*
> *http://www.microsoft.com/windows2000/guide/server/features/appsvcs.asp and*
> *http://httpd.apache.org/, respectively.*

When we use a web browser to view a web page, we will automatically be making contact with a web server. The process of submitting a URL is called making a **request** to the server. The server interprets the URL, locates the corresponding page, and sends back the page as part of what is called the **response** to the browser. The browser then takes the code it has received from the web server and interprets it, producing a viewable page from it. The browser is referred to as a **client** in this interaction, and the whole interaction as a **client-server relationship**.

Client-Server

This term describes effectively the workings of the Web by outlining the distribution of tasks. The server interprets requests and distributes data, and the client accesses the server to get at the data. From now on, whenever we use the term client, we are just referring to the browser (used to view a web page, for example).

To understand what is going on in greater detail, we need to briefly discuss the workings of the Internet itself.

Internet Protocols

We won't go through the entire history of the Internet here; the important point is that it is a network of interconnected nodes (a node is a point at which connections originate or upon which they center). The Internet is designed to carry *information* from one place to another. It uses a suite of networking protocols (known as **TCP/IP**) to transfer information around the Internet. TCP/IP itself is a layer for a set of protocols such as a Data Link Protocol, but we don't need go any deeper than TCP/IP for the purposes of this book.

> *A **networking protocol** is simply a method of describing information packets so that they can be sent down your telephone, cable, or T1 line from node to node, until they reach their intended destination. They are for general networking, and not just for Internet communications.*

One advantage of the TCP/IP protocol is that it can re-route information very quickly if a particular node or route is broken or slow. When the user tells the browser to fetch a web page, the browser parcels up this instruction using a protocol called the **Transmission Control Protocol** (or **TCP**). TCP is a transport protocol that provides a reliable transmission format for the instruction. It ensures that the entire message is packaged up correctly for transmission (and also that it is correctly unpacked and put back together after it reaches its destination). The TCP protocol actually uses a suite of protocols, such as HTTP for web pages, FTP for files, SMTP for e-mails, as a way of describing information packets so that they can be sent down a telephone line, cable, or T1 line and such like across the Internet. The IP section of the name is short for **Internet Protocol**, and this provides for the transmission of data between source machines and destination machines, where both source and destination machines are identified by unique fixed-length numerical addresses (known as IP addresses).

Before the parcels of data are sent out across the network, they need to be addressed. So another protocol called **Hypertext Transfer Protocol (HTTP)** puts an address label on them, so that TCP/IP knows where to direct the information. HTTP is the main protocol used by the World Wide Web in the transfer of information from one machine to another – if we see a URL prefixed with http://, we know that the Internet protocol being used is HTTP. (Other common prefixes we may see are ftp:// for file transfer protocol and https:// for secure HTTP.) We can think of TCP/IP as the postal service that does the routing and transfer, while HTTP is the stamp and address on the letter (data) to ensure it gets there.

The message passed from the browser to the web server, containing the URL, is known as an **HTTP request**. When the web server receives this request, it checks its stores to find the appropriate page. If the web server finds the page, it parcels up the HTML contained within (using TCP/IP), addresses these parcels to the browser (using HTTP), and sends them back across the network. If the web server cannot find the requested page, it issues a page containing an error message (in this case, the dreaded Error 404: Page Not Found) – and it parcels up and dispatches that page to the browser. The message sent from the web server to the browser is called the **HTTP response**.

Here's an illustration of the process:

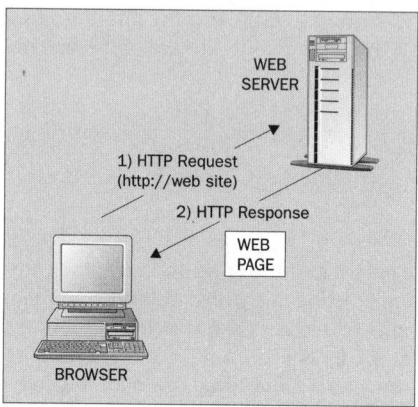

The HTTP Protocol

There is still quite a lot of technical detail missing here, so let's dig further down and look more closely at exactly how HTTP works. When a request for a web page is sent to the server, this request contains more than just the desired URL. There is a lot of extra information that is sent as part of the request. This is also true of the response – the server sends extra information back to the browser. Most of the time we don't need to know anything about this extra information, but as we will see in later chapters there are a couple of situations that demand it.

Every HTTP message assumes the same format (whether it's a client request or a server response). We can break this format down into three sections: the **request/response line**, the **HTTP header**, and the **HTTP body**. The content of these three sections is dependent on whether the message is an HTTP request or HTTP response – so we'll take these two cases separately.

The HTTP Request

When the browser sends the HTTP request to the web server, it contains the following:

The Request Line

The first line of every HTTP request is the **request line**, which contains three pieces of information:

❑ An HTTP command known as a method

❑ The path on the server to the resource that the client is requesting

❑ The version number of HTTP (like HTML, HTTP has different versions and the number indicates which version of the protocol is being used – a different method of dealing with the information might be used in a different version)

So, an example request line might look like this:

```
get /testpage.htm HTTP/1.1
```

The method is used to tell the server how to handle the request. Here are three of the most common methods that might appear in this field:

Method	Description
get	This is a request for information residing at a particular URL. The majority of HTTP requests made on the Internet are get requests. The information required by the request can be anything from an HTML page, to a JavaScript source file, or some other executable. You can send data to the browser, in the form of an extension to the URL.
head	This is the same as the get method, except that it indicates a request for the HTTP header only and no data.
post	This request indicates that data will be sent to the server as part of the HTTP body. This data is then transferred to a data-handling program on the web server. This is the protocol that the majority of forms use.

There are a number of other methods supported by HTTP – including put, delete, trace, connect, and options. As a rule, these are much less common; they are therefore beyond the scope of this discussion. For more information about these, take a look at RFC 2068, which can be found at http://www.rfc.net/rfc2068.html.

> An RFC (Request for Comments) is, despite its misleading title, a document detailing a protocol definition or convention. Most protocols that the Internet is based on are defined in RFCs.

The HTTP Header

The next bit of information sent is the HTTP **header**. This contains details of what document types the client will accept back from the server like the type of browser that has requested the page, the date, and general configuration information.

An example HTTP header might look like this:

```
Accept: */*
Accept-Language: en-us
Connection: Keep-Alive
Host: www.samplesite.com
Referer: http://webdev.samplesite.co.uk/samples/SampleList.htm
User-Agent: Mozilla (X11; I; Linux 2.0.32 i586)
```

As can be seen, the HTTP header is composed of a number of lines; each line contains the description of a piece of HTTP header information, and its value.

There are many different lines that can be part of an HTTP header, and most of them are optional, so HTTP has to indicate when it has finished transmitting the header information. To do this, a blank line is used.

The HTTP Body

If the `post` method was used in the HTTP request line, then the HTTP request **body** will contain any data that is being sent to the server – for example, data that the user typed into an HTML form (we'll see examples of this later in the book). Otherwise, the HTTP request body will be empty.

The HTTP Response

The HTTP response is sent by the server back to the client browser, and contains the following.

The Response Line

The **response line** requires three items of information:

❑ The HTTP version number

❑ An HTTP request code that reports the success or failure of the request

❑ A short message describing the status of the request

An example response line might look like this:

```
HTTP/1.1 200 OK
```

This example returns the HTTP status code 200, and the message "OK", which corresponds to the error code 200. This denotes the success of the request, and that the response contains the required page or data from the server. You may recall that we mentioned the status code 404 a few pages ago – if the response line contains a 404 then the web server failed to find the requested resource. Error code values are three-digit numbers, where the first digit indicates the class of the response. There are five classes of response:

Code class	Description
100-199	These codes are informational – they indicate that the request is currently being processed.
200-299	These codes denote success – the web server received and carried out the request successfully.
300-399	These codes indicate that the request hasn't been performed, because the information required has been moved. It also indicates usually that further action is required, which is usually performed by the browser, to receive the information requested.
400-499	These codes denote a client error – that the request was incomplete, incorrect, or impossible.
500-599	These codes denote a server error – that the request appeared to be valid, but that the server failed to carry it out.

The HTTP Header

The HTTP response **header** is similar to the request header, which we discussed above.

Once again, the header consists of a number of lines, and uses a blank line to indicate that the header information is complete. Here's a sample of a header (including the response line), with the name of each line down the side:

```
HTTP/1.1 200 OK                                    – the status line
Date: Mon, 1st Apr 2001, 16:12:23 GMT              – a general header
Server: Apache/1.3.12 (Unix) (SUSE/Linux)          – a response header
Last-modified: Thu, 29th Mar 2001, 12:08:03 GMT    – an entity header
```

The first line we've already discussed, the second is self-explanatory. On the third line, "Server" indicates the type of software the web server is running, and as we are requesting a file somewhere on the web server, the last line of information refers to the last time the page we are requesting was modified.

> The header can contain much more information than this, or different information, depending on what is requested. More information about the different types of information contained in the three parts of the header can be found listed in RFC 2068 (Sections 4.5, 7.1, and 7.2), available online at: http://rfc.fh-koeln.de/rfc/html/rfc2068.html.

The HTTP Body

If the request was successful, then the HTTP response **body** will contain the HTML code, and any other data, such as image data, ready for the browser's interpretation.

Now we've have a good idea of the process by which HTML pages are transported from browser to client, it's time to take a look at the language itself, which goes to make up our web pages.

Standards and Specifications

HTML isn't an out of the box product like Visual Basic or C++. Internet Explorer and Netscape both support their own variations of the language. Each browser supports the same core functionality, together with the browser vendor's own custom extensions. To make sure that the core functionality doesn't differ too much on each browser, each browser's version of HTML is expected to conform to a central standard. As we mentioned at the beginning of this chapter, the organization that looks after the HTML standard is the World Wide Web Consortium, or W3C for short.

The most recent recommendation from W3C is HTML 4.01. The HTML standards (and indeed all standards that W3C look after) typically have to go through four stages before they become standard and can be officially termed **recommendations**.

The first stage is the **working draft** (although there can occasionally be a pre-working draft stage, called a note), where the proposals are made public and are open to large-scale review and change. After a last-call working draft has been accepted, and necessary changes made, the document then becomes a **candidate recommendation**. During this period it is expected that the standard will be put into practice by leading companies and developers, and any experience and feedback is used to alter the recommendation. Once these proposals have been available for a sufficient length of time, during which people have used it, the recommendation moves forward and, after more potential modifications, becomes known as a **proposed recommendation**. During a 4-week period a W3C advisory committee decides on whether the recommendation should be adopted as the final standard.

It is possible for the committee to accept the standard fully, to accept it with minor changes, to return it to any of the prior statuses for further consultation, or to reject it completely. If the vote is for one of the first two options, then the standard becomes a recommendation (after any minor changes have been made) and is finally adopted by W3C.

Why Do We Need Web Standards?

The HTML and HTTP specifications are both subject to this process, and each new set of updates to these specifications yields a new version of the standard. To see why we need standards, we will start by looking at the three main aims of W3C:

❑ To provide universal access to web technologies (such as HTML), so that anybody can use them

❑ To develop a software environment to allow users to make use of the Web

❑ To guide the development of the Web, taking into consideration the legal, social, and commercial issues that are raised

The process we've just outlined for creating a standard sounds a very painful and laborious method of creating a standard format, and not something you'd consider as spearheading the cutting edge of technical revolution. Indeed, the software companies in the mid 1990s found the processes involved too slow, so they set the tone by implementing new innovations themselves and then submitting them to the standards body for approval. Netscape started by introducing new tags in its browser, such as the `<font>` tag, which added presentational content to the web pages. This proved popular, so they added a whole raft of tags, which enabled users to alter aspects of presentation and style on the web pages.

When Microsoft entered the fray, it was playing catch up for the first two iterations of its Internet Explorer browser. However, with Internet Explorer 3 in 1996, it established a roughly equal set of features to compete with Netscape, and so was able to add its own browser-specific tags. Very quickly the Web polarized between these two browsers, but the problem was that pages that were viewable on one browser, quite often wouldn't appear in a readable form on another. One problem was that Microsoft had used its much stronger position in the market to give away its browser for free, while Netscape still needed to sell its own browser, as it couldn't afford to freely distribute its flagship product. Although, Netscape was available as freeware for many people (geared towards academics and such) as well as shareware for the others, Netscape depended partly on the revenue from corporations and ISPs that used its browser. To maintain a competitive position it needed to offer new features to make the user want to purchase its browser rather than use the free Microsoft browser.

Things came to head with both companies' version 4 browsers, when dynamic page functionality was introduced. Unfortunately, Netscape did this by the means of the `<layer>` and `<ilayer>` tags, while Microsoft chose to use a full document object model and style sheet positioning. The W3C consortium needed to take a firm hand here, since one of its three principle aims had been compromised – that of universal access. How could you guarantee this aim, if you needed a particular vendor's browser to be able to view a particular set of pages? It decided on a solution that used existing standard HTML tags and Cascading Style Sheets, both of which had been adopted as part of Microsoft's solution. As a result, Microsoft gained a dominant position in the "browser war". It hasn't relinquished this position since with subsequent version 5 and version 6 browser releases, while the Netscape browser has only recently undergone a significant upgrade with the release of Netscape 6, jumping directly from version 4, after a gap of over 2 years. Current usage statistics hover between 70 vs. 30 percent and 90 vs. 10 percent in Microsoft's favor, depending on which browser statistics sites you visit.

The HTML standard itself has gone through several versions. The versions 1.0 and 2.0 of HTML were simple enough small documents, but when W3C came to debate HTML version 3.0, it found that much of the new functionality it was discussing had already been superceded by new unsanctioned additions made to the version 3.0 browsers such as the `<applet>` and `<style>` tags. Version 3.0 was discarded, and a new version 3.2 became the standard. However, a lot of the features that went into HTML 3.2 had been introduced at the behest of the browser manufacturers and ran contrary to the spirit of HTML – it was intended to solely define structure. The new features, stemming right back to the `<font>` tag, just confused the issue and added unnecessary presentational features to HTML. These features really became redundant with the introduction of style sheets. The version 4.0 of the HTML standard was left with the job of sorting out this chaotic mess, and marked a lot of tags up for **deprecation** (removal) in the next version of the standards. It was the largest version of the standard and included features that linked it to style sheets, the Document Object Model, and also added facilities for the visually impaired and other much unfairly neglected minority interest areas. Finally, minor updates were made to HTML 4.0 in the last version of the standard, 4.01.

With a relatively stable version of the HTML standard in place with version 4.01, boasting a set of features that will take a long time for any browser manufacturer to implement completely, development continues apace in other areas of the Web. A new set of standards was introduced in the late nineties governing the methods of presentation (style sheets) and the programmatic creation and manipulation of HTML documents – the **Document Object Model (DOM)** – that linked into the HTML 4.01 standard; however, they are still being updated. Other standards emerged, such as **XML (Extensible Markup Language)**, which offers a common format for representing data in a way that gives and preserves its structure. We'll take a look now at the main standards that have been created, and learn a bit about what each of the technologies does.

Associated Standards and Technologies

We're going to have a brief look now at the technologies and standards that have an impact on HTML and give a little background information about each. A trip to the W3C web site, http://www.w3.org, will reveal a huge number of standards in varying stages of creation, dealing with a lot more technologies than just HTML. Not all of these standards will concern us, and not all of the ones that concern us can be found at this web site. However, a lot of standards that are important to us can be found there.

HTML itself is actually defined in terms of another standard, known as SGML; we'll look at that first.

SGML

SGML is the abbreviation for **Standard Generalized Markup Language**. This language, or more accurately, meta-language, was defined in 1986 by International Standard **ISO 8879:1986**.

At the time it was developed, there were several "markup languages", none of which were particularly portable between platforms or even software packages. The purpose of SGML is simple – to allow a formal definition of markup languages that can then be used to give complete flexibility and portability of information display between applications and platforms.

It is tempting for the newcomer to SGML to view it as a markup language in its own right – defining a set of tags, etc., and providing meanings for those tags. This is not the case. SGML is a theoretical language (that is, one that you can't program in or compile – it only exists in paper format) for describing other languages. What SGML *does* do is describe the relation of components within a document. As such, SGML is not a competitor with the likes of TeX or Postscript, which define such things as layout, but a way of describing what the document "is", rather than how it should be "rendered".

A markup language consists of a set of conventions that can be used to provide a way to encode text. A markup language must also specify what markup is allowed, what markup is required, and how the markup is distinguished from the text of the document. SGML does all this – what it doesn't do is specify what the markups are, or what they mean.

XML

XML is a standard for creating markup languages (along the lines of HTML, but don't get this confused; HTML **isn't** a subset of XML – see below). XML has been designed to look as much like HTML as possible, but that's where the similarities end.

HTML is actually an application of the meta-language SGML, which is also a standard for generating markup languages. SGML has been used to create many markup languages, but HTML is the only one that enjoys universal familiarity and popularity. XML on the other hand is a direct subset of SGML. SGML is generally considered to be too complex for people to be able to accurately represent it on a computer; XML acts as a simplified version for this purpose.

XML's main purpose is for the creation of customized markup languages, which are very similar in look and structure to HTML. The main use of XML is in the representation of data. Whereas a normal database can store information, databases don't allow individual stored items to contain information about their structure. XML can use the tag structure of markup languages to represent any kind of data, from mathematical and chemical notations to the entire works of Shakespeare, where information contained in the structure of the data might otherwise be lost.

XML is also cross-platform, since it contains just text. This means that an application on Windows can package up the data in this format, while a completely different application on UNIX should be able to unravel it and read the data, although admittedly text has the UNICODE format and not all platforms can read UNICODE, so it isn't 100% cross-platform.

XML is more complex than HTML, as you might imagine. Whereas the average browser will take HTML code, interpret the relevant details, and display the corresponding web page for you without any intervention, applications of XML will usually require extra steps.

As we're creating the markup language ourselves, we need to first create a set of rules via which the language will be run. The main two ways of doing this are by **XML Schema** or by a **DTD** (**Document Type Definition**). Both of these are used to draw up rules, such as which tags we can use in our markup language, what attributes these tags take, and what kind of data these attributes are expecting. These aren't the only two ways by any means, however they are the ones in most popular usage. Other ways to create these rules exist, such as **SchemaTron** and **Trex**.

Secondly, once you've written your XML document in your new language, it must be checked against both the syntax rules laid down for XML documents and the rules in the schema or the DTD to see if the code conforms. This is done by an XML parser, which is built into the browser (the latest versions of both Internet Explorer and Netscape have XML parsers), although it can also be done externally. Then it is ready for use by the browser.

XHTML

XHTML is where the XML and HTML standards meet. XHTML supercedes HTML, and the XHTML 1.0 standard is just a re-specifying of the HTML 4.01 standard as an XML application. The advantages of this allow XHTML to get around some of the problems caused by a browser's particular interpretation of HTML. More importantly, the formulation of HTML as an XML application lets developers write an XML parser once and use it for XHTML as well as other XML applications like WML, MathML, etc. This is in turn means that you only need one application, which can run on your PC and equally as well on handheld computers, mobile phones, or any software device that might be connected to the Internet (perhaps even your refrigerator!).

It also offers a common method for specifying your own tags, rather than just adding them without first properly defining them. You can specify new tags via a common method using a ruleset (such as an XML schema) and an XML **namespace** (this is a way of identifying one set of tags uniquely from any other set of tags). This is particularly useful for the new markup languages such as WML (Wireless Markup Language), which are geared towards mobile technology and require a different set of tags to be able to display on much-reduced ability interfaces.

Having said that, anyone familiar with HTML should be able to look at an XHTML page and understand what's going on. There are differences, but not ones that add new tags or attributes.

The main differences between XHTML and HTML are that:

❑ We have to provide a DTD declaration at the top of the file referencing the version of the DTD standard you are using, be it your own creation, or a previously created recognized standard.

❑ XHTML allows an optional XML declaration at the top of the file: `<?xml version="1.0"?>` (in HTML 4.01 it is non-standard).

❑ We must include a reference to the XML namespace within the HTML tag.

❑ We need to supply all XHTML tag names and attributes in lower case, as XML is case-sensitive.

❑ The `<head>` and `<body>` elements must always be included in an XHTML document.

❑ Tags must always be closed and also nested correctly. In the cases where only one tag is required, such as line breaks, the tag is closed with a /, for example `<br/>`.

❑ Attribute values must always be housed inside quotation marks.

This set of rules makes it possible to keep a strict hierarchical structure to the tags, which in turn makes it possible for the Document Object Model to work correctly. This is the route that HTML is currently taking, and all future HTML standards will be XHTML standards. You should now be creating your HTML documents according to the rules specified above. If you do so, you will find the job of writing pages that can work on all browsers, and work in the way they were intended, much, much easier. Also, in the dim and distant future, your web pages will require fewer changes when the day arrives that browsers no longer support "HTML" and pages must be coded in XHTML.

Scripting Languages

Scripting languages were in existence long before web browsers, but they only concern us since their introduction into browsers, from Netscape 2.0 and Internet Explorer 3.0 onwards. Before their introduction into browsers, web page content was essentially static, and originally all HTML could display was graphics and text. With their arrival, browsers could react directly to user interaction, update web pages dynamically, and offer much greater control over the layout and manipulation of the web page.

Netscape had originally developed a scripting language, known as LiveScript, to add interactivity to its web server and browser range. It was introduced in the release of Netscape 2 browser, when Netscape joined forces with Sun and in the process, they changed its name to **JavaScript**.

JavaScript

JavaScript is the original browser scripting language, and is not to be confused with Java. Java is a complete application programming language in its own right. JavaScript borrows some of its syntax and basic structures from Java (which in turn borrowed ideas from C), but has a different purpose – and evolved from different origins (LiveScript was developed separately from Java).

For example, while JavaScript can control browser behavior and content, it isn't capable of controlling features such as file handling. Java on the other hand can't control the browser as a whole, but it can do graphics and perform network and threading functions. They make a useful combination, but JavaScript is much simpler to learn. It is designed to create small, efficient applications that can do many things – from performing repetitive tasks, to handling events generated by the user (such as mouse clicks, keyboard responses, etc.).

Microsoft introduced its own version of JavaScript, known as **JScript**, in Internet Explorer 3.0. It has only minor differences from the Netscape version of the language, although in older versions of both browsers the differences were originally quite a lot wider.

VBScript

In Internet Explorer 3.0, Microsoft also introduced its own scripting language, **VBScript**, which was based on its Visual Basic programming language. VBScript was intended to be a direct competitor to JavaScript. In terms of functionality, there isn't much to choose between the two, it's more a matter of personal preference. Visual Basic developers sometimes prefer VBScript because VBScript is, for the most part, a subset of Microsoft's Visual Basic language. However, it enjoys one advantage that makes it more attractive to novice programmers, in that unlike JavaScript, it isn't case-sensitive and is therefore less fussy about the particulars of the code.

The biggest drawback is that there isn't a single non-Microsoft browser that supports VBScript. For a short while there were some proprietary plug-ins for Netscape that provided VBScript (and also ActiveX control) support, but these never took off. You'll find that JavaScript is much more widely used and supported. If you want to do client-side scripting of web pages on the Internet then JavaScript is the only language of choice. Indeed Microsoft itself has replaced VBScript in its .NET framework, with the VB.NET and JScript.NET languages. VBScript should only be considered when working on intranet pages where it is known that all clients are IE on Windows.

ECMAScript

JavaScript itself has followed a similar trajectory to HTML. It was first used in Netscape and then added to Internet Explorer at a later date. The Internet Explorer version of JavaScript was christened JScript, and wasn't far removed from the version of JavaScript found in Netscape. However, once again there were differences between the implementations of the two and so when writing script for both browsers a lot of care had to be taken.

It was left to Netscape to send JavaScript to the **European Computer Manufacturers Association** (**ECMA**) to decide on a standard specification. This didn't appear until a few versions of JavaScript had already been released. Unlike HTML, which had been developed mostly under the guidance of the W3C consortium, JavaScript was purely a proprietary creation. Microsoft and Netscape both agreed to use ECMA as the standards vehicle/debating forum, because of its reputation for fast-tracking standards and perhaps also because of its perceived neutrality. The name ECMAScript was chosen to avoid bias to either vendor's creation, and also because "Java" of JavaScript was a trademark of Sun licensed to Netscape. The standard, named ECMA-262, laid down a specification that was roughly equivalent to the JavaScript 1.1 specification.

> To obtain a copy of the current ECMAScript language specification, go to
> http://www.ecma.ch/ecma1/STAND/ECMA-262.HTM.

All current implementations of JavaScript are expected to conform to the current ECMAScript standard. While in the version 3 browsers there were quite a few irregularities between the Microsoft and Netscape dialects of JavaScript, they're now much closer together in the latest versions of the browsers, although perhaps not quite identical enough to yet be considered the same language. The Opera browser also supports and offers the same kind of support for the standard. However, ECMAScript governs only the core JavaScript language. ECMAScript does not govern the individual browser and document-object-model objects, and this is where Netscape, IE, and Opera differed and still differ most.

Although this is a good example of how standards have provided a uniform language across browser implementations, there is still a feature war, similar to HTML, albeit to a lesser degree, that applies to JavaScript, as only core features are covered by the ECMA standard.

Which Language to Use?

This is a book about HTML, so we're looking primarily at this language. However, there are elements that enable us to use scripting languages in our pages. So we will, in later chapters, be looking at how the different languages link together. For the time being, all we need to consider is HTML.

HTML

The first thing we need to consider is what actually makes up a typical web page or to give its proper name, HTML document. Go to the http://www.wrox.com web page for example:

and then view the source code; you will see something like the following:

```
<html>
<head>
<!-- #BeginEditable "doctitle" -->
<title>wrox.com - Programmer to Programmer</title>
<!-- #EndEditable -->
<meta http-equiv="Content-Type" content="text/html; charset=iso-8859-1">
</head>

<body bgcolor="#FFFFFF"  leftmargin="0" topmargin="0" marginwidth="0" marginheight
<!--<basefont size=2 color="#000000"  face='Verdana,Verdana,Arial, Helvetica, sans
<table width="100%" border="0" cellspacing="0" cellpadding="0" align="center">
  <tr valign="top" align="center">
    <td align="center">

<table width="775" border="0" cellspacing="0" cellpadding="0">
    <tr>
        <td width="111" height="62">
            <div align="center">
                <img src="/Includes/images/newwroxlogo.gif" border="0" alt="wrox "
            </div>
        </td>
        <td width="668" height="62">
            <div align="right">
                <img src="/Includes/images/newwroxhead.gif" alt="Programmer to Pro
            </div>
        </td>
    </tr>
</table>
```

Note: on the Wrox.com page you will have to scroll down a bit to get to this section of code.

The document is composed of a series of HTML **tags** and text. Tags are easily recognizable because angled brackets surround them. They are typed in lower case typically, but as browsers are case-insensitive, you will find on many web sites, that they are typed in upper case, as it makes them easier to read. In fact, you can freely mix the upper or lower cases as you please. However, HTML 4.01 recommends using lower case, because this often allows better compression of the document, as the content is likely to contain more lowercase than upper case text. Also, the XHTML standard specifies that they should be in lower case, so throughout this book we will be using lower case and recommend strongly that you do the same.

Start and End Tags

In HTML, there are two types of tags: **start tags** and **end tags**. Both are placed inside angled brackets, for example: <h1>. End tags are the same as start tags, except that they are preceded by a forward slash, for example:</h1>. The combination is used to indicate where the effects of the tags start and finish.

For example, type the following code into a text editor:

```
<html>
  <head>
    <title>HTML 4.01 Programmer's Reference</title>
  </head>
  <body>
    <h1>An Introduction to Tags</h1>
    In HTML tags are used to format plain text.
  </body>
</html>
```

then save it as a file with an .htm extension (or .html if the system isn't constrained by the 8.3 naming convention) and view it in a browser via the File | Open menu options. This should be the result:

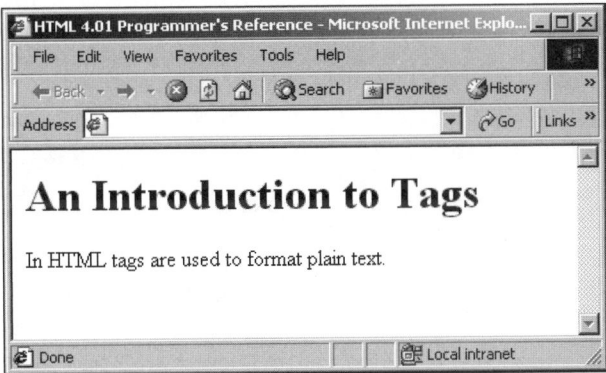

The whole combination of start tag, contents, and end tag is termed an **element**. Most elements can contain further elements or nodes and therefore have a start tag and an end tag, but there are also so called empty elements too. For example, the <img> element (image) does not require a corresponding end tag, and the use of one is forbidden by the HTML 4.01 standard. We will mention throughout the book where this is the case.

Think of the end tag as "switching off" the start tag, and it will seem logical. Elements with both start and end versions are often referred to as **enclosures**. Except for tags such as <img>, tags should always be correctly closed. Some people treat tags such as the <p> tag as not needing a closing tag, however it does have one and it should always be used. Unless specifically mentioned otherwise, assume that all tags we will discuss have end tags.

The reasons for always closing tags are:

❑ Browsers might not correctly render the page – the browser will always make an effort to render the page – however, if you don't close tags properly, it might produce unexpected results, such as not all elements being rendered.

❑ Scripting languages won't be able to use the Document Object Model – while we haven't looked at scripting or the DOM, to be able to use the DOM, the elements in the HTML page must be correctly closed, and fully nested inside one another, otherwise it will generate errors in the script.

❑ If we're using XHTML, then we will actually generate an error. As mentioned in the XHTML section, XHTML is a "strict" version of HTML in many ways.

So while the last two points don't concern us at the moment, hopefully you can see why careless HTML coding can cause immediate problems.

Nesting Elements

Most elements can be nested. In other words, we can have elements inside other elements. The order of nesting is important. For instance, this is legal:

```
<b>This word is <i>emphasized</i></b>
```

but this isn't:

```
<b>This word is <i>emphasized</b></i>
```

Although the above line of code is illegal, most browsers will still render the text – it makes the code harder to understand though and once again it will prevent the DOM from being able to represent the page, and cause errors in XHTML.

Attributes

Attributes allow us to extend the capabilities of elements, and are placed within the opening tag. We can use attributes to control fonts, border spacing, text alignment, etc. For example, the <h1> element, which prints text on a separate line and in a larger font (as a level 1 heading), has an align attribute, which affects the positioning of the heading on the screen.

So, as might be expected:

```
<h1 align="center">An Introduction to Tags</h1>
In HTML tags are used to add special effects to plain text.
```

will result in the heading being aligned centrally:

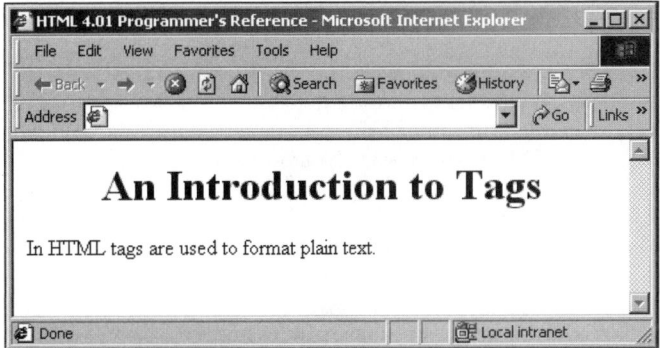

The syntax for attributes is as follows:

```
<tagname attribute="value">
```

Note that if the value contains only letters, numbers, hyphens, or periods, it is possible to omit the quotes. However, to ensure that all browsers render the code correctly, and more importantly, that the XHTML standards are adhered to, we should always use quotes. If there are any other types of characters included in the attribute value then it must be contained within quotes.

Creating an HTML Document

When writing HTML, the first thing we need to understand is that it is almost impossible to format a page so that it will look exactly the same in every client (or browser). Indeed, the original HTML idea was specifically based on not telling the client exactly how the page should look.

There are several good reasons for this:

❑ Different people use different browsers, and even different operating systems and devices. We can't guarantee that the font we've chosen for the page is present on another computer, nor can we guarantee the resolution – our system may be set to a resolution of 800 x 600, and the page may be viewed by someone with a computer set to 640 x 480, or if our page is WAP-enabled, we may get users browsing it on a wireless device – for example, the Nokia 7110 has a useable screen size of 96 x 65 pixels!

❑ The user of the browser has complete control over aspects such as default font type, link colors, whether or not to display inline images, etc. Bearing this in mind, the users should be advised to set their browsers to the default settings. At least that way, the majority of people will see web pages as their writers intended.

❑ There are some tags that will have different effects on text; depending on which browser they are viewed with. For example, one browser may use italics for emphasis, while another may use bold type. Always check your HTML pages on as many different browsers as possible.

❑ Different browsers support different non-standard browser-specific extensions to HTML. We'll talk more about these in later chapters, but what it means is that if you want your pages to be readable to as wide an audience as possible, you should stick to the standard syntax. Compromise is the order of the day! Staying with the standard tags and attributes will mean that as many people as possible will be able to view your pages.

Having said all this, HTML's great strength lies in its flexibility. For instance, if a browser is incapable of displaying an image, then providing the HTML has been properly written, text describing the image can be shown instead; likewise, static images can be shown in place of video, etc.

When an HTML viewer is presented with a tag it doesn't understand, it usually just skips past that tag. This means that it's possible to use vendor extensions to HTML, providing you ensure that your document still looks reasonable with other browsers. The best approach to ensure the widest possible audience for your HTML is to stick to the standard.

There are several elements that should be included in all HTML documents. These define the structure of the document and allow browsers to correctly interpret the content. Have a look at this code:

```
<!DOCTYPE HTML PUBLIC "-//W3C//DTD HTML 4.01//EN"
        "http://www.w3.org/TR/html4/strict.dtd">

<html>

  <head>
    <title> A description of the page </title>
    Other head elements
  </head>

  <body>
    Body elements go here
  </body>

</html>
```

This is the basic form that every HTML document should take. Let's have a look at each constituent part.

The <!DOCTYPE> Declaration

First thing to note is that despite its similarity to other HTML elements (namely the angled brackets surrounding it), the <!DOCTYPE> declaration isn't an element at all. It doesn't require closing and it is denoted entirely in uppercase as well. The <!DOCTYPE> declaration is used to declare what Document Type Definition (DTD) is being used to describe the current HTML page. The DTD's purpose is to define the legal productions of a particular markup language.

As we have already touched upon in the "XML" section, a simple DTD would do nothing more than, say, define a set of rules stating what tags and attributes can be used by a particular markup language. The HTML 4.01 standard, however, consists of three formally defined SGML DTDs – strict, loose, and frameset – more about these below. In other words, the definition of HTML 4.01 is itself specified using the SGML meta-language. This allows HTML specifications to be rigorously defined.

To fully define HTML 4.01, two different specifications are required. The first is the relatively small SGML definition that defines general features, such as the character set and size limits. The main information is contained in the DTD, which defines the detail, such as the tags and attributes, which we will learn more about later.

The <!DOCTYPE> declaration should be the first item in any proper HTML document. This is most useful for parsers, as it declares what version of HTML the document is written in, and thereby allows the parser to interpret the coding correctly. A rigorous HTML-checking program will reject any document that does not include it, but most browsers are not so fussy, and so most of the documents on the web do not include it, even though it is required by the HTML 4.01 standard. However, when using XHTML, it is a good idea to include this in your HTML pages (although not compulsory as browsers will still display XHTML without it).

As mentioned above, there are actually three different legal declarations for documents that conform to the HTML 4.01 standard. The first is the **strict** declaration:

```
<!DOCTYPE HTML PUBLIC "-//W3C//DTD HTML 4.01//EN"
          "http://www.w3.org/TR/html4/strict.dtd">
```

HTML pages that conform to the strict DTD cannot use frames and also cannot use elements marked as deprecated. The Strict DTD is for documents that strive to achieve clean, XML-like markup that is free from any presentational formatting. Any presentational formatting on a document using the Strict DTD is achieved through style sheets (see Chapter 11 for more on these). This is also the default DTD to use, if none is specified in the document.

If we wish to use deprecated elements and attributes (such as the <font> element) then we can use the **loose** (or transitional) DTD, which will permit them:

```
<!DOCTYPE HTML PUBLIC "-//W3C//DTD HTML 4.01 Transitional//EN"
          "http://www.w3.org/TR/html4/loose.dtd">
```

Use this DTD to take advantage of HTML's presentation features to ensure backward compatibility for software that does not yet support Cascading Style Sheets. It also allows use of the <iframe> element. It still doesn't allow us to use frames however. If we wish to use all of the deprecated elements and use frames as well then we will need to use the **frameset** DTD.

```
<!DOCTYPE HTML PUBLIC "-//W3C//DTD HTML 4.01 Frameset//EN"
          "http://www.w3.org/TR/html4/frameset.dtd">
```

Although this tag is required by the HTML standard, if our document includes vendor-specific extensions or deviates from the standard in any other way, it should be left out. Otherwise, you may get unpredictable results.

If we wish to use the XHTML equivalents, then these are the DTDs we should use. For the strict DTD it should be:

```
<!DOCTYPE html PUBLIC "-//W3C//DTD XHTML 1.0 Strict//EN"
          "http://www.w3.org/TR/xhtml1/DTD/xhtml1-strict.dtd">
```

The transitional DTD is as follows:

```
<!DOCTYPE html PUBLIC "-//W3C//DTD XHTML 1.0 Transitional//EN"
          "http://www.w3.org/TR/xhtml1/DTD/xhtml1-transitional.dtd">
```

The frameset DTD should be as follows:

```
<!DOCTYPE html PUBLIC "-//W3C//DTD XHTML 1.0 Frameset//EN"
          "http://www.w3.org/TR/xhtml1/DTD/xhtml1-frameset.dtd">
```

We'll look at the role DTDs play more actively, when we consider XHTML in later chapters. However, in HTML 4.01 the <!DOCTYPE> doesn't play any active role, although in the Netscape 6, Internet Explorer 5 for the Macintosh and Internet Explorer 6 on Windows, the content of the declaration is used by the browser to decide whether to use quirks or standard compliant layout mode.

The <html> Element

This element signals the beginning of the HTML document. Although the <!DOCTYPE> declaration appears first, the <html> tag defines the beginning and end of the HTML content, and encapsulates everything that is supposed to be parsed as HTML. Closing this tag with </html> ends the document – anything appearing afterwards is supposed to be ignored by browsers.

From HTML 3.2 onwards, this tag was no longer required, but its use is strongly recommended. You will find that older browsers that do not understand the <!DOCTYPE> declaration will act strangely if you don't include <html> tags.

The <head> Element

The part of the page denoted by the <head> element is known as the document header. In the document header, information comes in various forms of differing non-document content, such as the title of the HTML page, the base URL of the document, the keywords needed to index the page with search engines, and refresh information. It can also contain presentational information contained within style sheets or even scripts needed to dynamically render your page. Only the title of the page, as specified in the <title> element, which is discussed in the next chapter, is considered compulsory.

Although the HTML 3.2 standard specified that it was no longer strictly necessary to include a <head> element, it is still a prerequisite for HTML documents in the HTML 4.01 standard. Also, most browsers will behave oddly if you omit it, so we advise using it at all times. We look at the <head> element itself in detail, and all the legal elements that can go in it, in the next chapter.

The <body> Element

The body section is where the meat of the HTML goes. The <body> and </body> tags mark the beginning and end of the body section. Here, we add the text we want displayed in the main browser window, tags and attributes to modify that text, hyperlinks to other documents, etc. We can also set the color of the text, background, etc., for our document. We can place just about every element in this section, and with a couple of exceptions we shall see later, every HTML element should go in the either the body or the head of the HTML document.

Which specific elements can go in the <body> element is the subject of discussion for the rest of this book!

Summary

This has been a quite a theoretical introductory chapter. We started by outlining quickly how HTML requests are passed from client to server, and how the server replies with the requisite HTML page, looking briefly at the HTTP protocol that underlies this. We then moved on to a discussion of the standards body that governs both HTTP and HTML. We then looked at the technologies and standards associated with HTML, to give you a clearer idea when we came discuss the purpose of some of the core features of an HTML document (such as the DOCTYPE declaration).

We looked at the building blocks of HTML – the tags and attributes – and outlined the elements that contain the meat of the HTML document, <body> and <head>. We didn't go as far as looking at what was contained inside these elements, but rather we concentrated on giving an overall idea of the structure of a typical HTML document.

In the next chapter we will look at the elements we can typically place within the <body> and <head> of a HTML document.

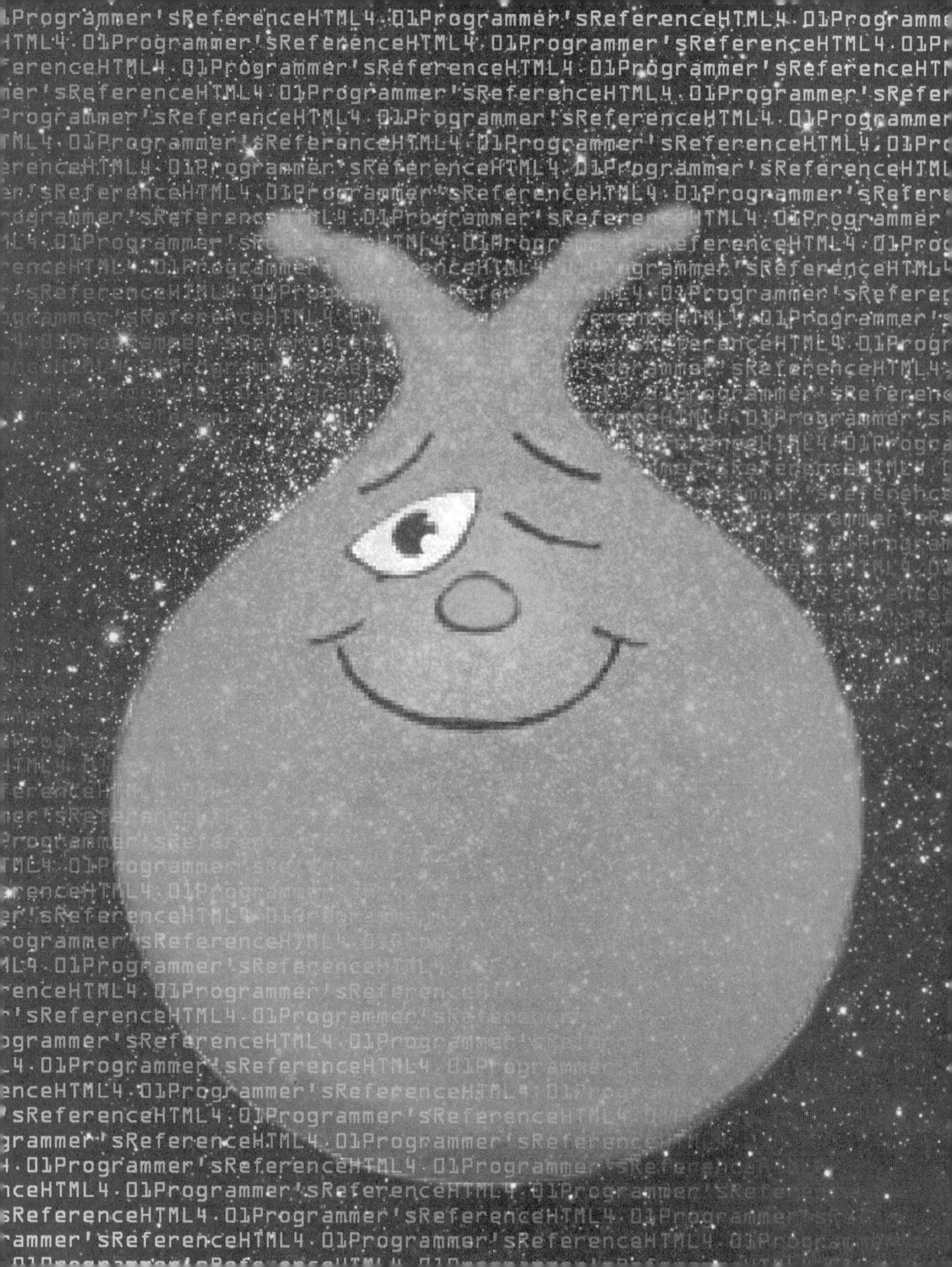
Programmer'sReferenceHTML4.01

2

The Document Body and Head

There are two basic parts to any HTML document: the **body** and the **head**.

It is in the document body that the actual content for display is found. This is where any text, images, links, forms, tables, and the like should be placed. The HTML 4.01 standard likens the document body to an artist's canvas when used with a visual browser, but in an audio-assisted agent, this content could just as easily be spoken as rendered visually. Whichever, this is the place where the lion's share of the HTML document is likely to end up.

In the document head, information comes in various forms of differing non-document content, such as the title of the HTML page, the base URL of the document, any keywords provided to index the page with search engines, and page expiry information. The head can also contain presentational information contained within style sheets or even scripts that dynamically render parts of the page.

Both body and head consist of **HTML elements** that can contain further elements. Each structural part of the document is referred to as an element. In this chapter we will consider the different elements that should go in the document head, but first we will look at some of the different types of element that can be used to group content within the document body. The topics discussed will be:

- ❑ The `<body>` element
- ❑ Grouping Elements
- ❑ Headings
- ❑ The `<head>` element
- ❑ Meta content
- ❑ Linking to external resources

The <body> Element

The <body> and </body> tags mark the beginning and end of the body section. It is here that you should add the text you want displayed in the main browser window, along with tags and attributes to modify that text, hyperlinks to other documents, and so on. You can also set the color of the text, background, and other components of your document.

There are many attributes available to use with the <body> element. These have been broken down into three categories each described in turn: HTML 4.01 standard attributes, deprecated attributes, and browser-specific attributes.

The HTML 4.01 <body> Attributes

The HTML 4.01 standard defines a further subdivision here in that there are two distinct sets of attributes that the <body> element supports. Both sets are common to the majority of HTML elements. The first set of attributes we'll consider are referred to by the standard as the **core attributes**:

```
id      title      class      style
```

Although there are no truly universal attributes that *all* elements share, the four core attributes mentioned here are used by the vast majority of elements. Some of these universal attributes have particular functions, which we will examine later in the book – particularly the style and class attributes, which are used by style sheets. We will describe the basic function of each of these attributes here. Later, when describing elements that share these attributes we will not repeat the explanations here, unless something is different about them.

In addition there are two attributes known as the **i18n (internationalization)** attributes. The rather obscure sounding name refers to the document draft in which these were first defined, draft-ietf-html-i18n. Incidentally, the 18 indicates the number of characters that appear between the first i and last n of internationalization, and the two i18n attributes are these:

```
dir      lang
```

These two attributes are also common to most elements, although once again not to all elements. There are also occasions where we find the core attributes are supported by an element, but the i18n attributes are not. Hence this clear distinction between core and i18n attributes. However, as the majority of elements support both sets of attributes, we shall refer to the core and i18n attributes collectively as **universal attributes**.

There is one further attribute of the body element, language, which is said to be universal, but is only found in IE, and not in the HTML 4.01 standard. This attribute sets the default scripting language for the page, as either JavaScript or VBScript. The script interpreter will use this attribute if a <script> tag is included with no language attribute.

We'll look briefly at each attribute here. More details about how to use them can be found with the individual elements in later chapters.

The Core Attributes

Here are the four core attributes in detail:

id

Specifies a unique name or identifier for an element in a page or style sheet. The syntax is:

```
id="string"
```

The string specified must begin with a letter (that is, the range A-Z a-z) and can be followed by any number of letters, digits (0-9), hyphens ("-"), underscores ("_"), colons (":"), and periods ("."). For example a legal identifier for an <h1> element might look like this:

```
<h1 id="First_Heading">This is the lead article</h1>
```

title

This gives an advisory title for the element in which it is set. This information is often displayed as a tooltip, in a help query, or while the element is loading. The syntax is:

```
title="string"
```

class

Specifies the class of element, and is used to associate an element with a style sheet. The syntax is:

```
class="classname or space-separated list of class names"
```

We'll look at how to specify classes in more detail in later chapters.

style

Specifies style information for the element, in the form of a property or set of properties. The syntax is:

```
style="string"
```

Style information is specified in the following way, between quote marks, for example:

```
<h2 style="font-family:arial">This is a heading</h2>
```

We'll look at how to specify style information in more detail in the style sheet Chapters 11 and 12.

The I18N Attributes

The i18n attributes aren't supported by as many elements as the core attributes, but there are elements such as `<frameset>`, where the standard doesn't specify them (probably because the element has been deprecated), but where Internet Explorer allows them anyway as browser-specific extensions. However Netscape doesn't add them, so this is something to bear in mind if you wish to use these attributes, listed below, with deprecated elements.

dir

This specifies a direction for text to flow in, when surrounded by elements of text which flow in differing directions. The syntax is:

```
dir="ltr | rtl"
```

This notation indicates that you can either use `ltr` (short for left to right) or `rtl` (short for right to left). The | symbol will be used to mean 'or' whenever we discuss syntax in the book.

The `dir` attribute can also specify the direction of flow of text in a table. The `dir` attribute is inherited from surrounding elements, although this can be overridden.

lang

This specifies the ISO (International Standards Organization) code for the language of the element. The syntax is:

```
lang="language-code"
```

The language information can be useful in many circumstances, such as helping spell-checkers, assisting search engines, assisting speech synthesizers, and deciding on the correct forms of punctuation or hyphenation for a particular language.

Typical language codes are "en" – English, "en-us" – American English, "fr" – French and "de" – German. You can find a list of all of the possible language codes and how they may be combined in Appendix C.

Intrinsic Events

In addition to the above attributes, there is a set of events that may be defined for many of the HTML elements. For such elements, events – known as intrinsic events – can be programmed using a portion of scripting code, typically JavaScript or VBScript, and associated with an element using the appropriate event-name attribute. The list of all intrinsic events, together with their function and the elements that support them in HTML 4.01, is as follows:

Event name	Description	Elements Supported
onload	Occurs when the window or all of the frames in a window have loaded	`<body>`, `<frameset>`
onunload	Occurs when a document has been removed from a window or frame	`<body>`, `<frameset>`

Event name	Description	Elements Supported
onclick	Occurs when a mouse button (or similar) is clicked when over an element	Most elements
ondblclick	Occurs when a mouse button (or similar) is double- clicked when hovering over an element	Most elements
onmousedown	Occurs when a mouse button (or similar) is first pressed (or held) down when over an element	Most elements
onmouseup	Occurs when a mouse button (or similar) is released while hovering over an element	Most elements
onmouseover	Occurs when a cursor (or similar) is moved onto an element	Most elements
onmousemove	Occurs when a cursor (or similar) is moved whilst hovering over an element	Most elements
onmouseout	Occurs when a cursor (or similar) is moved away from an element it was hovering over	Most elements
onfocus	Occurs when an element receives the focus from the cursor (or similar) or via a tab movement	<a>,<area>,<label>, <input>,<select>, <textarea>,<button>
onblur	Occurs when an element loses the focus from the cursor (or similar) or via a tab movement	<a>,<area>,<label>, <input>,<select>, <textarea>,<button>
onkeypress	Occurs when a key is pressed and released over an element	Most elements
onkeydown	Occurs when a key is pressed and held over an element	Most elements
onkeyup	Occurs when a key is released over an element	Most elements
onsubmit	Occurs when a form is submitted	<form>
onreset	Occurs when a form is reset	<form>
onselect	Occurs when the user selects some text within a text field	<input>,<select>, <textarea>
onchange	Occurs when a field on a form loses focus and has had its value changed as well	<input>,<select>, <textarea>

A typical intrinsic event is declared using the above event names as attributes. The attribute must specify either some lines of script as the attribute value, or the name of a script function name, that should be applied when that event occurs. For instance if we wanted to display a message if the user clicked at any point on the web page, we could use the onclick event attribute of the <body> element as follows:

```
<body onclick="alert('You clicked somewhere on the web page');">
```

We supply it a single line of JavaScript, which pops up a simple message box. We could also link it to a function name as follows:

```
<body onclick="display()">
...
<script language="JavaScript">
  function display()
  {
    alert('You clicked somewhere on the web page');
  }
</script>
```

We are not going to be talking much more about intrinsic events here, as more detailed discussion of these can be found in the scripting chapter. However for each element we discuss later in the book, we list the set of events it supports as well.

The intrinsic events supported by the <body> element are as follows:

onload	onunload	onclick	ondblclick
onmousedown	onmouseup	onmouseover	onmousemove
onmouseout	onkeypress	onkeyup	onkeydown

As all but two (onload and onunload) are common to most elements, the other 10 events are referred to as **common events** throughout the rest of the book. The HTML 4.01 standard refers to them rather unhelpfully as just **events**, unlike a separate distinct naming that we have decided to adopt. Just to recap, intrinsic events refer to *all* events, while common events refer only to the last *ten* events listed above, from onclick through onkeydown.

Deprecated Attributes of <body>

Some attributes are specified as **deprecated** in the HTML 4.01 standard. Deprecated attributes are those that are still present in the standard, but have been marked for removal and will disappear in later versions of the standard. This is generally because there are alternative and better ways of achieving the same effect, either with other attributes or style sheets. We briefly consider the issue of deprecation in conjunction with style sheets in later chapters. The deprecated attributes in <body> are:

background	bgcolor	alink	link
vlink	text		

background

This specifies a background picture. The syntax is:

```
background="url"
```

where `url` is the address of the picture to display. The picture is tiled behind all images and text.

bgcolor

This sets the background color of the page. The syntax is:

```
bgcolor="#rrggbb | colorName"
```

where `rrggbb` are pairs of hexadecimal numbers for the red, green, and blue content respectively (for example, `FFFFFF` would be white, and `000000` would be black; we'll discuss this in detail a little later).

Alternatively, `bgcolor` can be set to any of the HTML standard 4.01 color names by substituting any of: `black`, `green`, `silver`, `lime`, `gray`, `olive`, `white`, `yellow`, `maroon`, `navy`, `red`, `blue`, `purple`, `teal`, `fuchsia`, and `aqua`, for `colorName`. We look at color in more detail in the next chapter.

`bgcolor` can be used in conjunction with `background`. If the background is a large image, we might set the color of the page using `bgcolor`, so that the browser will display this color while the image is loading. This is useful if, for example, we are using light text over a dark background image: set a dark background color so that the text is visible even before the image loads.

alink

This sets the color of an active hypertext link. A hypertext link is active only while the mouse remains clicked on the link. The syntax is:

```
alink="#rrggbb"
```

where `rrggbb` are hexadecimal values for red, green, and blue. Some browsers do not provide an active state for hypertext links

link

Sets the color of hypertext links that have not been visited. The syntax is:

```
link="#rrggbb | colorName "
```

where `rrggbb` are hexadecimal numbers describing the red, green, and blue components of a color.

vlink

This sets the color of visited hypertext links. The syntax is:

```
vlink="#rrggbb | colorName "
```

where `rrggbb` are hexadecimal numbers relating to the red, green, and blue intensity of the color.

text

This sets the color of normal text on the page. The syntax is:

```
TEXT="#rrggbb | colorName "
```

where `rrggbb` are hexadecimal numbers relating to the red, green, and blue intensity of the color.

Internet Explorer Extensions to <body>

There are also six extensions to the <body> element found in Internet Explorer, but which are not supported as attributes by Netscape:

```
bgproperties    bottommargin  leftmargin
rightmargin     topmargin     scroll
```

bgproperties

This sets a watermark. The watermark is the background picture, previously set with the `background` attribute. It remains 'fixed' in place and doesn't scroll with the rest of the page. The syntax is simply:

```
bgproperties="fixed"
```

bottommargin

Specifies the bottom margin for the page. The syntax is:

```
bottommargin="n"
```

where n is a numeric value expressed in pixels. If n is set to 0, the bottom margin will be on the bottom edge of the page.

leftmargin

This specifies the left margin for the entire page. The syntax is:

```
leftmargin="n"
```

where n is a numeric value expressed in pixels. If n is set to 0, the left margin will be exactly aligned with the left edge of the page.

rightmargin

This specifies the right margin for the entire page. The syntax is:

```
rightmargin="n"
```

where n is a numeric value expressed in pixels. If n is set to 0, the right margin will be exactly aligned with the right edge of the page.

topmargin

This specifies the top margin for the page. The syntax is:

```
topmargin="n"
```

where n is a numeric value expressed in pixels. If n is set to 0, the top margin will be at the top edge of the page.

scroll

This turns the scrollbars on and off on the screen. The syntax is:

```
SCROLL="yes|no"
```

Netscape Extensions to \<body\>

There are also two attributes that Netscape adds to the \<body\> element that are not supported by Internet Explorer. In place of the `topmargin`, `rightmargin`, `leftmargin`, and `bottommargin` attributes, Netscape specifies its own variants to provide this functionality.

marginheight

This specifies the margin height for the page. The syntax is:

```
marginheight="n"
```

where n is a numeric value expressed in pixels

marginwidth

This specifies the margin width for the page. The syntax is:

```
marginwidth="n"
```

where n is a numeric value expressed in pixels.

Inside the \<body\> Element

While it just isn't possible to cover every possible element that goes in the document body in this chapter, there are some interesting elements that can be used to organize information and discussion of them is pertinent.

Block Level and Inline Elements

Within the \<body\> element there are said to be two particular groups of element: block-level elements, and inline elements. The distinction between these types of element is that block-level elements can contain inline elements and other block-level elements, while inline elements can only contain data and other inline elements. Generally block-level elements are started on a new line while inline elements aren't. We can use style sheets to specify whether an element is specified as block-level or inline, but the HTML 4.01 standard doesn't recommend this.

Examples of block-level elements are the \<p\> element and the grouping element \<div\>. Inline elements are elements like the \<b\> (bold) element, the \<i\> (italic) element, and the grouping element \<span\>.

Grouping Elements: The <div> and <span> Elements

We have just mentioned the grouping elements, but we haven't come across them before. The <div> and <span> elements offer another way of adding structure to our HTML pages, and can surround other elements on the page – they have no direct influence on the presentation of the page whatsoever.

The <div> element is the document 'division element', and is a block-level grouping element. The <span> element is the inline version of the <div> element. While <div> creates a block, <span> only applies to the text it spans, and doesn't create a new line after it. They both take the exact same attributes shown here:

```
id       class     lang      dir
title    style     align
```

In other words, they both support the four core attributes, the two i18n attributes and the deprecated `align` attribute. They also support the common intrinsic events.

align

The `align` attribute has been deprecated under HTML 4.01 and text should now be aligned using style sheets instead. The `align` attribute aligns the text in position starting at the left or right margin of the browser, or in a central position, depending on which value is specified:

```
align="left|right|center"
```

The default here is `left`.

Internet Explorer-Specific Attributes

There are actually quite a few IE-only attributes added to the grouping elements by the IE browser, as listed below. Note that the `disabled` attribute is unique to the <div> element.

```
accesskey       atomicselection      contenteditable
datafld       , dataformatas         datasrc
disabled        hidefocus            nowrap
tabindex        unselectable
```

In addition, IE 6.0 also introduces a number of attributes for <span> and <div> based on the SMIL 2.0 (Synchronized Multimedia Integration Language) specification from the W3C, discussion of which is unfortunately beyond the scope of this book. They are: `begin, end, syncmaster, timecontainer`.

Similarly, IE 6.0 also contains a number of `iframe` *attributes based on the HTML + TIME extension to SMIL, which are, again, beyond the scope of this book. They are:* `systembitrate, systemcaptions, systemlanguage,` *and* `systemoverduborsubtitle`.

We will run briefly through these attributes now.

accesskey

Sets or retrieves the accelerator key for an object. When the *Alt* key is pressed with another key (termed the **accelerator key**), then this particular element will receive the focus.

```
accesskey="string"
```

For example if the `accesskey` is set to 1:

```
<div accesskey="1"> This is the first selection of code.</div>
```

then pressing *Alt* and *1* simultaneously would select this element

atomicselection

`atomicselection` specifies whether the grouping element and its contents must be selected as a whole.

contenteditable

This attribute sets or retrieves a string, to determine whether the or not the content of the grouping element can be edited by the user.

```
contenteditable="inherit | false | true"
```

`inherit` means that the `true` or `false` setting is inherited from the parent element.

datafld and datasrc

`datafld` and `datasrc` are used when the grouping element is connected to a client-side or server-side database during data-binding. They are briefly described in Chapter 19.

dataformatas

This attribute sets or retrieves whether the data contained by the grouping element should be displayed as text or HTML.

```
dataformatas="text | html | localized-text"
```

The `localized-text` setting that was introduced in IE 5.01 indicates that the text is customized according to the particular locale setting.

disabled (Applies to <div> Only)

Sets or retrieves whether the grouping element is shown 'dimmed' and unable to respond to user input.

hidefocus

`hidefocus` allows us to determine whether or not the browser will indicate on screen that the frame is the page element currently in focus.

nowrap

This attribute sets or retrieves whether the browser should automatically perform word-wrapping within the grouping element.

tabindex

By specifying a value for `tabindex`, we can set the order in which elements on our page come into focus when the *tab* key is pressed.

unselectable

This specifies whether or not an element can be selected:

```
unselectable = "off | on"
```

If we specify `off`, then the element is selectable, otherwise if we specify `on`, then it isn't. Note that specifying `off` doesn't guarantee that the element will be selectable. Other circumstances might prevent it being selected (such as setting the `visibility` to `hidden` in a style sheet).

The `<div>` element works in the following way. The following code saved as `division.html` file:

```
<html>
  <head>
    <title>the document division element</title>
  </head>
  <body>
    <div>This is the first selection of code.</div>
    <div>This is the second selection of code.</div>
  </body>
</html>
```

results in this this:

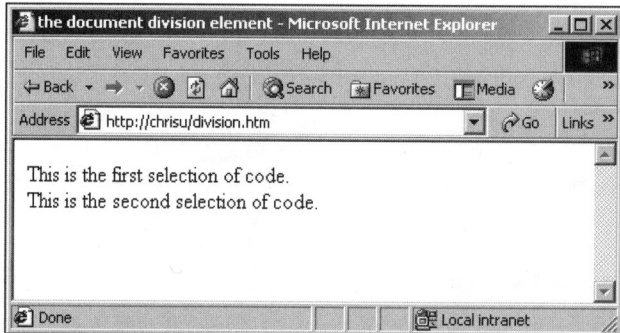

This is consistent with any block-level element. However, no other presentation is added to the text. This is ideal for when we come to look at style sheets. The idea is we use these elements to surround text we wish to style, and then use the `class` attribute to group blocks of content that are to be rendered in the same fashion.

Let's return to the sample, change the code as shown below, and save it as `span.htm`:

```
<html>
  <head>
    <title>the span element</title>
  </head>
  <body>
    <span>This is the first selection of code.</span>
    <span>This is the second selection of code.</span>
  </body>
</html>
```

The only visible effect is that the text is now bunched up:

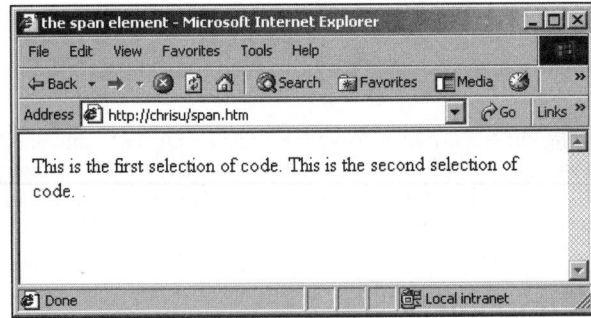

This is consistent with an inline container. In fact this is the only difference between the two elements in terms of their intrinsic effect on text. The other note to remember is that block-level elements are allowed to enclose other block level elements and inline containers, while inline containers may only contain data and other inline containers. Both of these elements will be heavily used in the chapters on style sheets later on.

Headings

There are six levels of headings. They can all be defined via the <hn> element.

The <hn> element

n is being used here to denote any number from 1 through 6 to specify the heading 'level', where level 1 typically uses the largest text and level 6 the smallest. So in other words there are six legal <hn> elements, which are: <h1>, <h2>, <h3>, <h4>, <h5>, and <h6>. The <hn> element is used to define topic sections and also to break up web documents and organize them, in such a way that the browser can construct a table of contents. Generally, the more important the heading, the larger the size it will display it in.

However, some browsers will display some of the headings as the same size, so don't be surprised, for example, to find that another system shows a level 1 heading at the same size as a level 3 heading on your system. The corresponding end tag </hn> must be used.

```
<H2>This is a second level heading</H2>
```

Under HTML 2.0, headings had no associated attributes, under HTML 3.2, only the `align` attribute was permitted, but under HTML 4.01 there are now a total of seven permitted attributes, in addition to the common intrinsic events.

```
align       class       dir       id
lang        style       title
```

Six of these are universal, so they won't be discussed further here.

align

The `align` attribute has been deprecated under HTML 4.01 and text should now be aligned with the use of style sheets instead. The attribute aligns the text in position at the left or right margin of the browser, or in a central position, depending on which value is specified:

```
align="left|right|center"
```

The default here is `left`.

> *It's possible to create different size headings using the `<font>` tag, but be warned – not all browsers will display the attributes of `<font>`, so there is a risk of headings not appearing as desired on some users' systems. Also, some search engines use words that appear in higher-level headings as items to index.*

The <head> Element

The document head is contained within the `<head>` element. The `<head>` element is often unjustly neglected, because the elements it contains aren't generally rendered for display. However, it's perhaps a little lazy to ignore this element, as the elements it contains are made use of in other ways by the browser, or by external agents such as search engines.

Although the HTML 3.2 standard declared that it was no longer strictly necessary to include a `<head>` element, it is once more a prerequisite for HTML documents conforming to the HTML 4.01 standard. Also, most browsers will behave oddly if it is omitted, so we advise using it at all times. The `<head>` element can take three core attributes:

```
dir       profile       lang
```

Internet Explorer also adds the following attributes, which aren't actually specified in the HTML 4.01 standard, although all these attributes are already used for other elements and they should be familiar to you:

```
class       id       title
```

The `title` attribute appeared briefly in IE 4 and has since been omitted in IE 5.5. All of these attributes, despite being non-standard, are also supported in Netscape 6 as well.

Attributes of <head>

<head> has six possible attributes in total. As five of the <head> attributes listed above are universal (although three of them are not strict HTML 4.01), they are already explained in previous sections, and this only leaves one more to discuss.

profile

This specifies the location of a **metadata profile**. This is used in conjunction with the <meta> element, which is discussed later in this chapter. A metadata profile is used either as a globally unique name (which a browser can assume things about and perform activities for, without the actual profile being accessed), or as a link where the browser can actually use properties defined within the profile.

```
profile="url"
```

We can add multiple URLs here if we wish and separate each of them with a space. Despite being present in the HTML 4.01 standard, this attribute is only supported in the IE 6 and Netscape 6 browsers. Netscape 6 does support it and makes it available to the document object model, but doesn't actually use it any further.

Child Elements of <head>

The set of elements that <head> can enclose is more interesting than its attributes. The elements that <head> supports in HTML 4.01 are:

```
title     base      link       script
style     meta      object
```

There are also a number of elements that can appear in the <head> element that are specific to one particular browser. The following elements are specific to Internet Explorer:

```
bgsound      nextid
```

There is also one element that has been deprecated from the HTML 4.01 standard

```
basefont
```

This last element can be used in both IE and Netscape, although it only has very limited functionality in Netscape 4, and has since been removed from version 6. We cover it in the next chapter when looking at the related <font> element, and so won't be discussing it further here.

We'll look at each of the rest now.

The <title> Element

Strictly speaking, every HTML 4.01 document must have a <title> element according to the standard, and is usually displayed in the browser title bar. Note, however, that we can't include any other HTML inside the <title> element. If we do, the tags will appear on-screen, rather than being applied as styling for the title. The title should be a meaningful description of the page, since it is usually the title that is used as a bookmark by browsers. <title> takes two universal attributes, lang and dir, and one IE only attribute, id.

> *Bookmarks* (or *Favorites* as they are known in Internet Explorer) are used to build up a list of sites and pages that are visited often. We can normally bookmark any page that we are currently viewing, and come back to it later.

A typical <title> declaration within the head might look like this:

```
<html>
  <head>
    <title>The Namllu Corporation home page</title>
  </head>
  <body>
    ...HTML code here...
```

This would be displayed as follows in Internet Explorer 6:

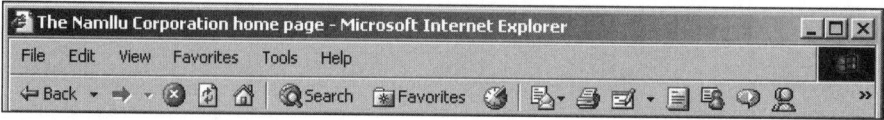

Another good reason for having a <title> element in our web pages is that it is useful for users with slower links, as the <title> element is among the first things to be rendered in the page, and often before the actual document content. With such sites, while the user is waiting for a page to load, the first sign that they have made a successful connection and that the requested page actually exists and content is being downloaded, may be the title information shown in the browser's title bar.

The <base> Element

This element defines the base URL, or original location, of the document. Without <base>, if the document were to be moved, relative links (that is, links that do not include the complete server and directory path) may no longer work. This is because the true URL for such links would be derived from the new, current URL of the document. The <base> element is not compulsory, but is advisable when using relative URLs.

If <base> is included, the URL it specifies is used to create absolute addresses for any relative ones. <base> takes the following attributes:

```
href      target
```

It also takes the non-standard attribute id (for this element), which is supported both in IE and Netscape.

href

This attribute specifies the entire URL of a linked file as a string. The syntax is:

```
href="url"
```

An example is:

```
<base href="http://this-server.org/inthisdir/filename.html">
```

target

This specifies the window or frame where a new page should be loaded, any time the user clicks a link taking them out of the page. The syntax is:

```
target="window_name | _parent | _blank | _top | _self"
```

Note that some older browsers do not support the use of <base> though others will use it as the URL to "bookmark". We look at the target attribute more fully when we deal with frames in Chapter 8.

> In Chapter 4, we shall cover the concept of relative and absolute addresses, or URLs, in greater detail.

The <meta> Element

The <meta> element is used to provide information about the HTML document. This **meta-information** can be extracted by web servers and by search engines to identify, index, or perform other specialized functions. For example, we can add keywords, which can be used by search engines to describe our page, or use <meta> to force browsers to automatically load a new page at a specified interval. We can also add details such as who the author of the document is, and when the document should expire. The <meta> element can be used in conjunction with the metadata profile set up in the <head> element. Properties defined by the profile can have their values set in subsequent <meta> declarations.

The <meta> element also doesn't have a closing tag, as the information needed is contained within the attributes for the element. To keep within the XHTML standard, which specifies that all elements must be closed, we'd need to close the tag with the requisite back-slash, for example:

```
<meta name="description" content=" Wrox Press Inc - computer book publisher.
    Programming books, written by programmers for programmers."/>
```

There are seven attributes for the <meta> element:

```
dir     lang     title       scheme
name    content  http-equiv
```

Three of the attributes dir, lang, and title are universal, the other four are specified in the HTML 4.01 standard for the <meta> element.

Internet Explorer also formerly supported the following attributes.

```
charset        url
```

`charset` was only supported by IE 3, so we won't discuss it further. The `url` attribute specifies the address in the `<meta>` element and was removed in IE 5 after being present in IE 3 and IE 4, and also merits no further discussion.

We'll concentrate on the `name`, `content`, `http-equiv`, and `scheme` attributes, as they can add quite a bit of functionality to our web pages that is often overlooked.

name and content

These attributes are used to specify the name and value of a property for our web page, such as author, date, company, keywords, etc. These are the two attributes that search engines will use to index our site with. The syntax for `name` is as follows:

```
name="metaName"
```

The `metaName` can be set to anything; it isn't restricted by the standard or by the browser. However most browsers will only actually make use of the information, when specified with a set of predefined keywords.

The most common keywords that `metaName` can be set to be are `description` or `keywords` (it can also be set to `robots` which we will look at separately). It should always be used in conjunction with the `content` attribute. `content` specifies the value for the `name` property. The syntax is:

```
content="metaContent"
```

It doesn't matter whether we set the `name` attribute to either `description` or `keywords`, as it always has to be followed by the `content` attribute. This attribute will list either the description for the site that should appear on a search engine hit, or a set of keywords that should return our site, when supplied to a search engine, depending on what value was supplied to the `name` attribute.

A little bit more explanation is called for here. The `description` and `keywords` values help make our site more visible, add extra information about it, and also determine for some search engines, under which circumstances our site will be listed in a response to a query. Some search engines use the `description` attribute to display a short description of a site. It should be a maximum of 200 characters, although some search engines (such as Google) will only display the first 100 characters. If considerably less than 100 characters are used, then we risk not using our free advertising space (so to speak). A typical description might look like this:

```
<meta name="description" content=" Wrox Press Inc - computer book publisher.
    Programming books, written by programmers for programmers.">
```

If we ran a search for "Wrox Press" on the AltaVista search engine, then we'd find that the content supplied in the `description` attribute provides the sum total of the information displayed by the search engine, as in this screenshot:

Without it, no Wrox entries would appear.

See errata

The keywords attribute will then supply the list of keywords that a search-engine will index our site with. This means if someone types in the word, or a combination of words contained within this attribute, the search engine may return our site. This alone will not guarantee a hit, as the search engine will use this as an aid to help index our site, along with the actual words contained on our site, and other criteria chosen by that particular search engine. So, for the Wrox Press web site (at http://www.wrox.com) a typical set of keywords might look like this:

```
<meta name="keywords" content="Books, Programming Books, Programming, Web
     Developer, Community, Visual Basic, JScript, JavaScript, XML, IE,
     Internet Explorer, Navigator, Netscape, Browser, Internet, Intranet,
     Java, IIS, IIS 4, IIS 5, NT, Windows 2000, W2K, SQL, Access, Oracle,
     Microsoft, VB, Wrox, Computer, Developer, Professional">
```

We can also set the words with the lang (for language) attribute so that our page will be returned when searched for in different languages. For example if we wished to translate travel agent information into three different languages, we could do the following:

```
<meta name="keywords" lang="en-us"
      content="vacation, Greece, sunshine">
<meta name="keywords" lang="fr"
      content="vacances, Gr&egrave;ce, soleil">
<meta name="keywords" lang="de"
      content="feiertage, Griechenland, sonnenschein">
```

We have no guarantee that our page will be returned at the top of this search, although most search engines have an option allowing us to pay for this privilege. If we don't wish to pay, then in general the more words that are matched, the better the likelihood of being returned higher up in the list. Plus, the more words we supply, the greater the likelihood we have of generating hits from a wider range of search strings. However, if we supply words that have nothing to do with the content of our web site, or their use is tenuous then this is considered spamming. If discovered you can find yourself removed from the directories of particular search engines. There is a limit to the number of words we can supply; it is dependent on the search engine, but usually less than 1000 characters is a good maximum guideline. If we supply more than 1000 characters to most search engines, then this is likely to be considered tantamount to spamming and may also result in your removal from a search engine listing. If we are running short of space, we can remove the commas from the content listing; however, this can reduce readability of the contents.

We can test to see whether we've set up our meta tags correctly, and whether we're making most efficient use of them via several popular freeware programs. One such program META-medic can be located at http://www.northernwebs.com/set/setsimjr.html.

Some search engines, such as Google, will aid matters by returning the words from our search, highlighted, along with the text they are surrounded by on the page:

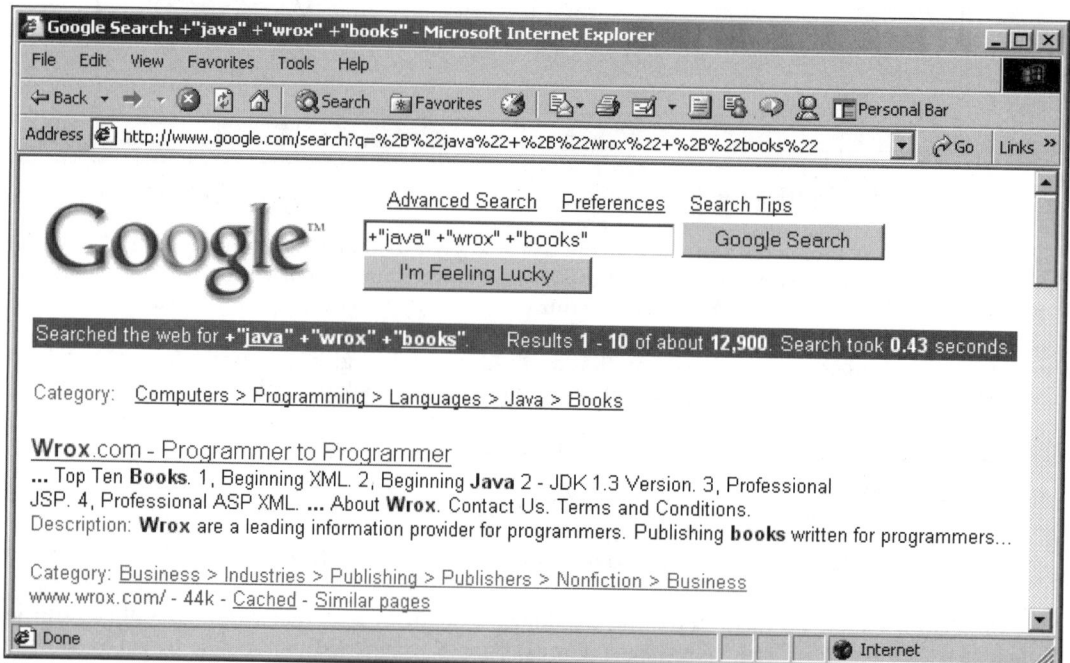

It is ultimately down to the individual particulars of the search engine involved as to how it uses the words contained within the content to index the page. If we submit our site manually, then this often means that the site will be categorized more effectively, and result in more site visits. A web site's effectiveness is often measured by the number of visitors, although in recent times the revenue it generates has become an equally, if not more important, statistic.

Other search engines such as Yahoo and Lycos don't rely on the <meta> element information and instead rely on manual categorization of web sites. This generally means that we have to submit the URL of the web site to them, and they will then place our web site information under an appropriate section in their web site, which can take anywhere between a couple of weeks and six months.

Some search engines don't support the <meta> element at all, and if we wish to supply a description to the engines that don't, then we need to supply the contents of our `description` attribute within a set of comment tags as well:

```
<!-- Wrox Press Inc - computer book publisher. Programming books, written by
programmers for programmers. -->
```

Getting On Search Engines

We've now answered one query about how to go about getting our web site on search engines – we go to the search engine involved and submit our URL manually. However not all sites works like this. Some search engines will automatically index our site if we've correctly set up our <meta> tags with the requisite `description` and `keywords` tags; we just have to wait for a couple of weeks. How do they do this?

Many search engines send out what is known as a **web crawler**, which generates an index of all the pages on a site. A web crawler is in this context simply a piece of software that sucks up all the different URLs given on a site for indexing by a search engine. It will then follow the links on the site, and go to other sites and index other sites in this way. Some search engines will only send out a web crawler after we've registered our home site URL manually with them, though, so we shouldn't wait to be indexed, as we might be waiting a long time for some search engines. Web crawlers are case sensitive as well, so make sure that the case used in the links and the actual web page names concur.

Also, when manually notifying search engines about a new site, we should only do it once and wait about a month before doing it again. Over-listing is also considered spamming and once again the web site may not get listed at all. It is fine to notify search engines if we have made numerous changes to the site so the new changes can be indexed though.

For information on individual search engines and the policies they use for ranking sites, look at http://www.beldamar.com/search_a.html, which has a neat little overview of how many of the most popular search engines rank our pages.

Robots.txt

There is the disadvantage, especially on large web sites, that every page will be indexed. Some pages might form part of a frame and be useless without the other frames (such as banners), so we won't want these pages indexed. To prevent this from happening, we can set up a file called `robots.txt` on our web site, which can disallow access to specified parts of the site by web crawlers. Here's how it works.

There can only be one occurrence of a `robots.txt` file and it must be located in an `htdocs` folder in the root of our web server. The syntax of `robots.txt` is as follows:

```
USER-AGENT: web crawler name (* means all)
DISALLOW: /folder name/
```

The `USER-AGENT` directive specifies which search engines we want affected. Here we need to specify the robot's name for a particular search engine. Fortunately an up-to-date list of active web crawlers/robots is kept at: http://www.robotstxt.org/wc/active/html/index.html.

The `DISALLOW` directive specifies the folder name we wish it to ignore. Although web crawlers are case-sensitive, if we specify `/asp/` for example then the web crawler will assume that we also wish to disallow access to `/ASP/` as well. If we're working on a UNIX system then we may wish to specify both cases explicitly as we might have two folders called `foldera` and `FOLDERA`.

So a typical `robots.txt` file might look like as follows:

```
USER-AGENT: *
DISALLOW: /asp/
DISALLOW: /cgi-bin/
USER-AGENT: WebCrawler
DISALLOW: /private/
```

All this file says is, 'disallow access to the contents of the `asp` and `cgi-bin` folders to all search engines, and disallow the web crawler search engine from accessing the private folder as well'. Lastly, as we don't know when a web crawler will visit our site, if we don't put this file up right from the start with a new site, it may be too late to keep the folders we want disallowed from being scanned.

Restricting Access with the meta Element

It is also possible as we said earlier to set the `name` attribute to the value `robots`. We can also disallow access to our whole site by setting the `<meta>` element as follows:

```
<meta name="robots" content="noindex, nofollow">
```

The `noindex` setting of the `content` attribute indicates that the document should not be indexed. The `nofollow` setting indicates that the web crawler shouldn't follow any links on the document.

The `content` attribute can be set to any of the following values:

```
all      none      index      noindex      follow      nofollow
```

By default, our site will be set to, `all`, `index`, and `follow`, allowing web crawlers to follow any of the links and index all pages.

A final word of caution, `robots.txt` is not a guarantee that our site will be indexed correctly or not indexed. It is not a requirement for a crawler to take this file into account, so be careful when storing any sensitive content that you do not want listed by search engines.

http-equiv and content

The http-equiv attribute of the <meta> element maps the attribute and its respective name to an HTTP response header for processing. HTTP response headers were discussed in the previous chapter. The initial data in the HTTP response is called the "HTTP header block". The header gives the browser information, which may be useful for displaying a particular HTML document. The http-equiv attribute usually controls the actions of the browser and can be used to further enhance information provided by the actual headers. http-equiv attributes are designed to affect the browser in the same manner as normal HTTP response headers (so whatever the header does, the http-equiv and content attribute set will also do).

The syntax for setting http-equiv is as follows. Once again when using the http-equiv attribute, we also need to set the content attribute as well:

```
http-equiv="string" content="http-header value"
```

We don't have room to discuss all possible values of http-equiv (in other words all possible HTTP response headers). The most common values of http-equiv are refresh, expires, pragma, set-cookie, window-target, and pics-label and we'll consider each of them in this section.

One very common application of the http-equiv attribute is to refresh the page or redirect the user to another page.

Refreshing the Page

If the <meta> element http-equiv attribute is set to refresh as in the example below, and the URL is set by the content attribute to the page to refresh with:

```
<meta http-equiv="refresh"
      content="5;URL=http://www.server.org/currentpage.html">
```

then the above has the effect of the browser refreshing the page after five seconds. The time set in seconds, and the URL of the page to be refreshed, are both specified within the content attribute. This is very useful if we change the location of the page, because it will automatically be loaded from the new location.

Using a Refresh to Redirect a User to a Different Page

We can use the refresh setting to redirect the user to a separate page to the one they are currently on, by sending them to a different site in the content attribute. Perhaps the most popular application of this type of meta refresh is with users who have purchased their own domain name and wish to point it at free web space they have with an ISP such as Geocities, Yahoo, or Tripod. We might have purchased the domain name such as http://www.chrisullman.com and wish to direct it on to some free space, which has the following format: http://members.cheapncheerfulisp.com/~chris_ullman. Rather than purchasing a whole site from the people we purchased the domain name from, we can set up a single page with the <meta> element redirecting it to our free web space.

The HTML required to do this is as follows:

```
<meta http-equiv="refresh"
      content="0;URL= http://members.cheapncheerfulisp.com/~chris_ullman ">
```

This works by telling the web server to redirect the user when it receives a URL for a particular domain, by passing another URL back to the browser instead.

Specifying the Expiry Date

If we wish to make sure that a user doesn't always load a cached copy of a web site when browsing then we can set the http-equiv to expires:

```
<meta http-equiv="expires" content="Tue, 17 Apr 2001 23:59:59 GMT">
```

This ensures that if the user reloads the page after the expiry date, a fresh copy is fetched from the server, rather than the browser displaying a locally cached copy. This is useful if we want to ensure our readers get the latest version of our documents.

Preventing a User from Caching a Page

It is also possible to prevent a user from caching a page locally using the <meta> element, if we set the http-equiv attribute to pragma, and the content attribute to no-cache, as follows:

```
<meta http-equiv="pragma" content="no-cache">
```

Versions of Internet Explorer from 4 onwards refuse to let this instruction go ahead and cache the file regardless, so this isn't a foolproof method of doing this.

Specifying Ratings

The <meta> element can also be used to declare a rating for our page. If we don't include a rating, certain browsers may prevent access to our site. These ratings are invisible to the user, but the browser will pick them up, without the aid of any specialized software. The way that it does this depends on the particular browser.

The method of associating labels with the content of a web page is known as **PICS (Platform for Internet Content Selection)**. Originally PICS was designed for use by parents and teachers to effectively control what minors could view on the Web, while protecting everyone's right of free speech. New uses for PICS are, however, being developed all the time, including privacy and code signing. PICS does not provide a rating system itself, it merely provides the ability to apply ratings to content. Comprehensive information on the PICS specification can be viewed at http://www.w3.org/PICS/.

The actual rating information is known as the **rating label**. The label appears in a web document as part of the HTML code and each part of the content that is rated has its own label. We must first obtain a ratings label in accordance with the guidelines specified by the **Internet Content Ratings Association (ICRA)** – see http://www.icra.org.

Once we have a label from ICRA, then to include ratings within our code, we specify the rating as part of the <meta> element in this general form:

```
<html>
  <head>
    <meta http-equiv="pics-label"
          content="(PICS-1.0
        The ICRA identifier: http://www.icra.org/ratingsv02.html
        The ICRA ratings parentheses: r (cz 1 lz 1 nz 1 oz 1 vz 1)
        The RSACi identifier: http://www.rsac.org/ratingsv01.html
        The RSACi ratings parentheses: r (n 0 s 0 v 0 1 0)">
  </head>
```

The ratings label splits down into four separate sections, an ICRA identifier, the ICRA ratings parentheses, the RSACi identifier (RSACi being the old Acronym for ICRA and standing for the Recreational Software Advisory Council for the Internet) and the RSACi ratings parentheses. The ratings parentheses accord with the guidelines specified on the ICRA, so for example the above RSACi ratings according to the ICRA site means nudity: 0, sex: 0, violence: 0, and bad language: 0. Check out the ICRA site for more details.

Setting Cookies

We can use the `<meta>` element to set cookies in the browser, by setting `http-equiv` to `set-cookie` and then supplying a cookie name, a value and expiry date in the `content` attribute as follows:

```
<meta http-equiv="Set-Cookie" content="cookie_name=cookie_value;
      expires=Tue, 17 Apr 2001 23:59:59 GMT">
```

If we don't set an expiry date, then the cookie will expire when the browser is shut down.

Setting the Author Name

The http-equiv attribute can also be used to specify author information for a particular document:

```
<meta http-equiv="author" content="Chris Ullman">
```

Some search engines will also pick this up.

Setting the Character Encoding

With many web pages character encoding is often left undefined and we don't have to worry about it. However, in earlier versions of HTML, the character encoding was supposed to use ISO-8859-1 if none had been specified. There were many browsers, though, that used a different default, so you couldn't rely on ISO-8859-1 being the default. In fact the HTML 4.01 standard says that if the character encoding isn't specified, then any character encoding can be used.

How does this affect us? Well sometimes we do need to specify the character encoding, because if the web server doesn't have a default, then it can't tell which characters are special. To set it, we set the `http-equiv` attribute to `Content-Type` as follows:

```
<META http-equiv="Content-Type" content="text/html; charset=ISO-8859-15">
```

We've set it to `ISO-8859-15`, as this is actually a corrected version of ISO-8859-1, and supports some characters that ISO-8859-1 missed out.

Setting the Default Style Sheet Language

We've not looked at style sheets yet, and while we are only going to be considering the cascading style sheets language within this book there are also other style sheet languages that can be used. To specify that we are using cascading style sheets we can set the `http-equiv` attribute as follows:

```
<META HTTP-EQUIV="content-style-type" CONTENT="text/css">
```

This subject is further discussed in Chapter 11.

Setting the Default Scripting Langage

If we wish to specify a default scripting language across the whole page, so that we don't have to keep constantly setting the language attribute in script elements across a page, then the <meta> element can be used as follows (for JavaScript and VBScript respectively):

```
<meta http-equiv="Content-Script-Type" content="text/javascript">
<meta http-equiv="Content-Script-Type" content="text/vbscript">
```

This subject is further discussed in Chapter 9.

Preventing a Window from Appearing in a Frame – IE 4 only

Lastly an old IE 4 tip, which unfortunately doesn't seem to work on N 4, IE 5.5 or Opera 5. If we don't want a new window to appear in a frame when the page is loaded, we can set the http-equiv attribute to window-target. Then within the content attribute we can specify the target frame where we want our new window opened. To set it to be the topmost window and therefore ensure that it won't be opened within a frame you could set it as follows:

```
<meta http-equiv="window-target" content="_top">
```

We discuss target settings in more detail in Chapter 8.

scheme

The scheme attribute will be used to specify a scheme, which will be used to interpret the property's value. The syntax is as follows:

```
scheme="string"
```

This is mainly of use when we are trying to interpret data held in an ambiguous format. A good example of this would be date/time formats. For example, the European and American date formats are different – in the US it is mm-dd-yy while in Europe, it is dd-mm-yy. We can reflect this in the scheme attribute as follows. In the USA you would set it as follows:

```
<meta scheme="usa" name="date" content="04-17-2001">
```

while in Europe you might set it as follows:

```
<meta scheme="europe" name="date" content="17-04-2001">
```

The possible scheme values can be set in the profile attribute that we mentioned earlier. However, as profile isn't widely supported currently we won't go into further detail on the scheme attribute. The reason that it isn't supported is that much of the meta-information of this kind is yet to be standardized. There is an initiative that is looking after "the development of interoperable online metadata standards", which is the Dublin core profile. You can find further information about its efforts at http://dublincore.org.

The <link> Element

The <link> element enables the current document to link to other documents. Unlike the <a> (anchor) element, which also specifies links and which we will be looking at in Chapter 4, the <link> element can only be used in the <head> element. Also unlike the <a> element, <link> has no closing tag.

The <link> element also has no content, but it can be used to convey relationship information between documents to be used in different ways – such as to create a toolbar with a drop-down list of links, or a glossary or index of links. It can also be used to specify the way to navigate through a web site or set of sites. For example, we might have a set of pages 1 through 10. We could specify page 1 as the home page, and page 2 as the next page. On page 2, we'd specify a <link> element setting page 1 as the previous page, and page 3 as the next page that a user can navigate to. It can also be used to specify links to standard pages such as a home page, a help page or a contact information page.

The <link> element is not in general usage for much web navigation though, as these aspects of it aren't supported in the major browsers (IE and Netscape) and only in small browsers such as Lynx and iCAb (a web browser for the Macintosh). This is because the browser has to determine the way in which it will convey the link information to the user. Lynx does this without any problems as it is a text browser, however Netscape and IE would need to render it graphically and for the most part, the browser's forward and back buttons are considered to provide this functionality.

To see an example of <link> in action for this kind of navigation we need to use Lynx. A quick example looks like this:

```
<!DOCTYPE HTML PUBLIC "-//W3C//DTD HTML 4.01//EN"
          "http://www.w3.org/TR/html4/loose.dtd">
<HTML>
  <HEAD>
    <TITLE>Page 2</TITLE>
    <LINK rel="Index" href="../index.html">
    <LINK rel="Next"  href="page3.html">
    <LINK rel="Prev"  href="page1.html">
  </HEAD>
  <body>
    Test link page 2
  </body>
</html>
```

While the major browsers (IE, Netscape, and Opera) all ignore the <link> element in this context and won't display anything, if we run this page in Lynx, the links are displayed as follows:

The `<link>` element is set to become more important for XHTML and there are details of how to use the navigational aspects of `<link>` with the Lynx and iCab browsers at http://www.euronet.nl/~tekelenb/WWW/LINK/.

This isn't to say that the `<link>` element is irrelevant in the major browsers either; it is used to provide more limited (but nonetheless important) functions such as links to style sheets or to icons within the browser, as we shall see shortly.

Here is a list of attributes that the `<link>` element can contain according the HTML 4.01 standard:

```
charset      class      dir      href      hreflang
media        id         rel      rev       style
target       title      type
```

There are no browser-specific attributes for `<link>`. Descriptions of each non-universal attribute follow.

charset

Specifies the **character encoding** of the resource designated by the link, so the browser can render text it receives using the appropriate character set.

```
charset="charset"
```

href

Contains the entire URL of the linked file, as a string. The syntax is:

```
href="url"
```

hreflang

Specifies the language of the resource designated by `href` and can only be used when `href` is also defined. The syntax is as follows:

```
hreflang="langcode"
```

There is a list of all of the possible language codes in Appendix C.

media

Indicates the output device to be used for the document. The syntax is:

```
media="screen|tty|tv|print|projection|handheld|braille|aural|all"
```

❑ `screen` – Intended for non-paged computer screens

❑ `tty` – Intended for media using a fixed-pitch character grid, such as teletypes, terminals, or portable devices with limited display capabilities

❑ `tv` – Intended for television-type devices (low resolution, color, limited scrollability)

❑ `print` – Intended for paged, opaque material and for documents viewed on screen in print preview mode

❑ `projection` – Intended for projectors

❑ `handheld` – Intended for handheld devices (small screen, monochrome, bitmapped graphics, limited bandwidth)

❑ `braille` – Intended for Braille tactile feedback devices

❑ `aural` – Intended for speech synthesizers

❑ `all` – Suitable for all devices

rel

The 'forward' relationship between this document and the one specified by the `href` attribute. This is also known as the "link type". The syntax is:

```
rel="relationship"
```

where `relationship` can be:

Keyword	Description
alternate	Defines substitute versions for the document in which the link occurs
stylesheet	References an external style sheet; see Chapter 3 for details
contents or toc	References a document serving as a table of contents
index	References a document providing an index for the current document
glossary	References a document providing a glossary of terms for the current document
copyright	References a copyright statement for the current document
start	Points to the first document of a series of documents
next	Points to the next document to visit in a guided tour
prev or previous	Points to the previous document in a guided tour
help	Points to a document offering help; this is aimed at helping users who have lost their way
chapter	Points to a document that acts as a chapter in a collection of documents
section	Points to a document that acts as a section in a collection of documents
subsection	Points to a document that acts as a subsection in a collection of documents

Table continued on following page

Keyword	Description
appendix	Points to a document that acts as an appendix in a collection of documents
bookmark	Provides a means for orienting users in an extended document; several bookmarks may be defined in each document
shortcut icon	Points to a small graphic file used in shortcuts; this last one is IE-specific

We can use the `<link>` element to link to a lot of external resources. A common example of this would be to link an HTML page to an external style sheet (this method of style sheet linking only works in IE 4+, Opera 5, and N 6):

```
<link rel="stylesheet" type="text/css"
      href="http://servername.com/style.css" title="style">
```

We will revisit this particular usage in more detail in the style sheet chapters.

Another way to use it, is to link to `favicon.ico`.

favicon.ico (Favorites Icon)

One forgotten backwater of the Web is the favorites icon for use with Internet Explorer, to accompany the text description in the favorites listing. Not all sites supply one, but it's a good way of making a site stand out in from other favorites. For instance the `favicon.ico` for Jungle.com looks like this:

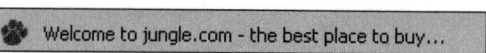

The `favicon.ico` is just a small graphic/icon that is downloaded automatically when we bookmark a site, and was introduced as a feature of IE 5.0. It works because IE will download an icon, if available, to represent a site when we add it to our list of "Favorites". The file that is requested is `favicon.ico`, and it is formatted just as any other Windows icon.

We can link our site to a favorite icon as follows:

```
<link rel="shortcut icon" href="http://www.yourservername.com/favicon.ico">
```

We need to place this icon in the same directory as the file added to favorites or otherwise in the root directory on our web server to make sure that this works as intended. If we wish to edit our own favorites icon, then we can go to the web site http://www.favicon.com, which has a neat Java applet for creating icons. Be warned though, IE 5 contained a bug which allowed a hacker to create an icon file in such a way as to break into the web-browser, but this has since been rectified.

rev

Defines a "reverse" relationship, that is, the relationship between the document specified by the `href` attribute and this document. The syntax is:

```
rev="relationship"
```

where `relationship` can have the same values as the `rel` attribute.

target

Specifies the window or frame where the new page should be loaded. The syntax is:

```
target="window_name|_parent|_blank|_top|_self"
```

type

Specifies the MIME type for the link. The syntax is:

```
type="mime-type"
```

We look at MIME-types in Chapter 10, and a full list of MIME types can be found in Appendix E.

The <style> Element

The `<style>` element plays a vital part in styles and style sheets, by providing the web page author with a means of including style sheet information within the head of an HTML document. A style sheet is essentially a set of display rules. If a browser doesn't support the `<style>` element, then its contents must be hidden from the browser.

The `<style>` element supports the following attributes:

```
dir      lang      media      title      type
```

In addition, the following two non-standard attribute are supported:

```
id       src
```

Both Internet Explorer and Netscape 6 support the first attribute, while only Netscape 6 supports the second.

The `src` attribute is supplied as a method to link to an external style sheet, as prior to Netscape 4 the `link` element didn't work with style sheets. However the `src` attribute also didn't actually work correctly in Netscape 4 and only functions properly in version 6. The `link` element is the correct way to link an external style sheet. An example of the `style` element in use inside the `head` element now follows:

```
<html>
  <head>
    <style type="text/css">
      h1 {color: red}
    </style>
  </head>
  <body>
    <h1>This is a red heading</h1>
  </body>
</html>
```

This would turn all occurrences of the <h1> element in the page red. Style sheets are a hefty topic in their own right and are discussed in Chapters 11-14.

The <script> Element

The <script> element is used to place script within a document. Scripts can be specified within the head or body of an HTML document or in an external file. They can even be placed outside the HTML elements completely. The advantage of placing them in different locations is that they will be processed at different times by the browser. Script placed in the <head> element will be processed first. We can specify more than one script, throughout the head or body.

The <script> element has the following five attributes:

```
charset       defer        src        type        language
```

The language attribute is still in the HTML 4.01 standard, but is marked for deprecation (removal). Properly, the type attribute should be used in its place.

IE adds the following extra attributes:

```
event        for        id        lang
```

Netscape also supports the following non-standard attributes:

```
archive        class        id
```

An example of script in action inside the <head> element looks like this:

```
<html>
  <head>
    <script language="JavaScript">
      alert("Hello world!");
    </script>
  </head>
  <body>
  </body>
</html>
```

We're using the deprecated method of specifying a language, as using the type attribute isn't yet commonly supported in browsers. Scripting is an extensive topic in its own right and will be looked at in detail later on. We will also discuss the meaning of the different attributes involved. We'll look at scripting and the <script> element in Chapter 9.

The <object> Element

Microsoft originally introduced the <object> element for the inclusion of Microsoft **Component Object Model** or **COM** objects (such as ActiveX Controls and a wide variety of different media types and plug-ins). Internet Explorer introduced this tag with support for ActiveX controls, and Microsoft has continued to develop around it, but it has now been accepted by the W3C and incorporated into HTML 4.01. We can use it to insert anything from Java applets and Flash animations to images and our own customized components. See Chapter 10 for a detailed discussion of this element.

Browser-Specific Elements that May Appear in the <head> Element

There are also several elements not specified in the HTML 4.01 standard, but that may be placed in the document head. The first is the <basefont> element, which is discussed in the next chapter.

The <bgsound> Element

The <bgsound> element is an Internet Explorer-only element that specifies a background sound to be played when the page is first loaded. The <bgsound> element doesn't have to appear in the document head, it can appear anywhere within the document, but as it isn't rendered visually, the head is the logical location for it. It is discussed more fully in Chapter 16 on browser-specific elements.

The <nextid> Element

This last element is a non-standard element that can only be found in Internet Explorer browsers. It creates a unique identifier that only text-editing software will pick up on.

It takes the following attributes:

```
atomicselection     class       id
inselectable        lang        language
```

Summary

The information contained within the document head is diverse and wide-ranging and often unfairly overlooked. We considered all of the elements that are allowed within the <head> element, in particular the <meta> element, which specifies important information for search engines to index our pages on, the link element, which allows us to link to external resources, the <title> element, which specifies information for the browser title bar, and also touched upon the <style> and <script> elements covered more fully in later chapters. Although other elements can be included within the document head, such as <isindex>, <bgsound>, and <nextid>, these elements are deprecated or non-standard and don't merit the same amount of attention.

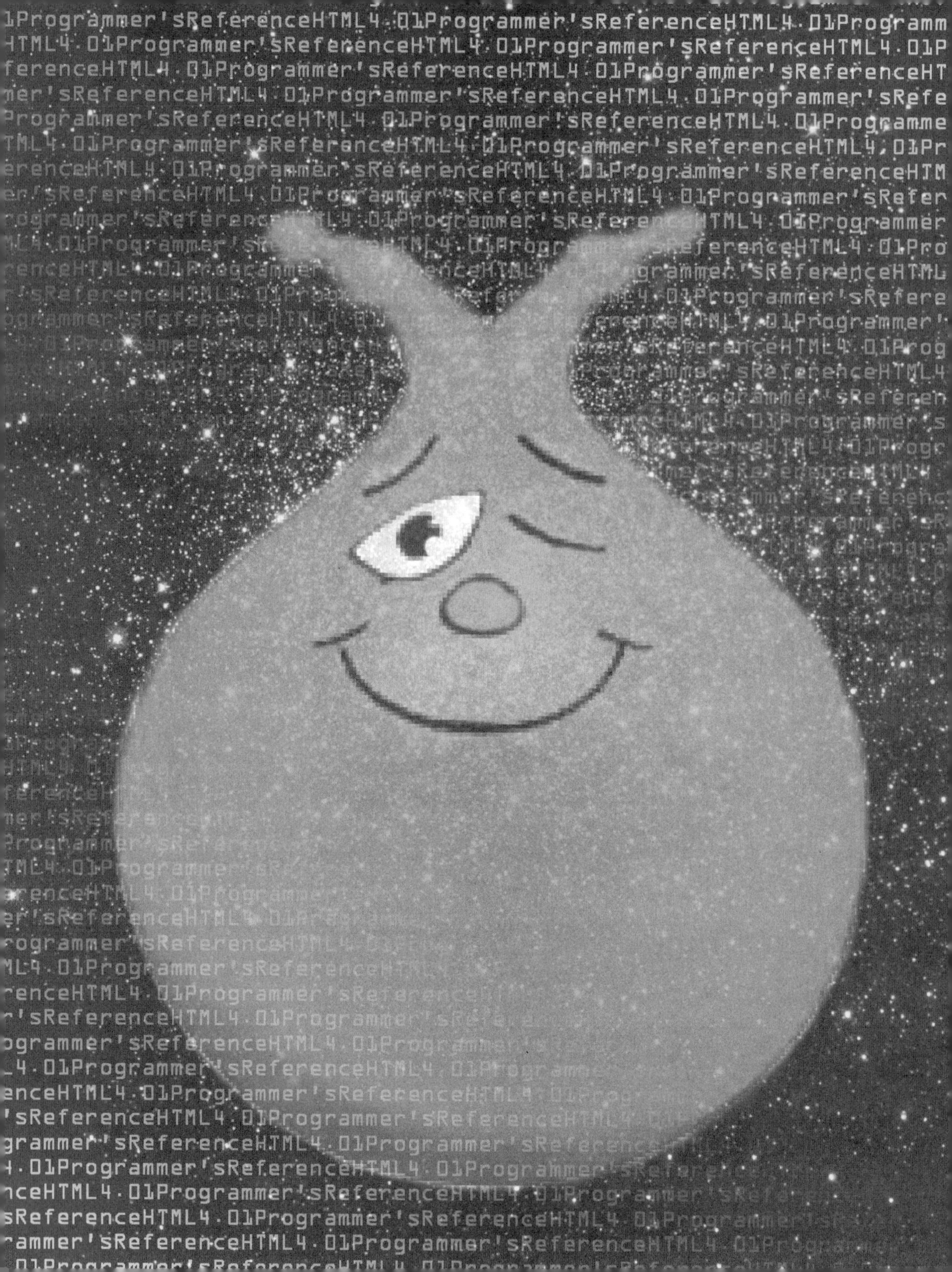
Programmer'sReferenceHTML4.01

3

Text Formatting

The basis of any HTML document is the information you are trying to get across. More often than not, this comes in the form of text. One way of enhancing the text on your page is to lay it out well, so that the user can easily follow what's written. You can do this by breaking the text up into paragraphs and sections, by grouping related information together in lists, and by breaking the information up into separate pages where appropriate. We will look at the elements that do this first.

We will also look at how you can manipulate the text of your document to use styles and colors, alter layout, and add special effects. However we won't linger on many of the elements that do this, as style sheets (which we look at later in this book) have mostly superceded them. Lastly, we will consider how you can annotate your HTML code effectively without worrying that your comments will be rendered as part of the web page's display.

In this chapter we will consider:

❑ White space

❑ Line Breaks

❑ Lists

❑ Fonts

❑ Physical and Logical Styles

❑ Colors

❑ How to annotate and comment your HTML code

Breaking up Text

We'll start by considering how you can use spaces within HTML to pad out a sentence. Despite being a relatively innocuous concept, it's actually more difficult than might be expected.

White Space

We need to use special white space characters in HTML to pad out a line, because if we use several spaces characters as follows:

```html
<html>
  <head>
    <title>White Space Example 1</title>
  </head>
  <body>
    This is a line broken        by white space.
  </body>
</html>
```

We find that these aren't rendered by the browser:

White space characters are legal characters recognized by the browser that denote one blank space, albeit one that can vary in size. In the HTML 4.01 standard, there are four allowable white space characters:

❑   ASCII space (` `) or (` `)

❑   ASCII tab (`&#09;`)

❑   ASCII form feed (`&#10;`)

❑   Zero-width space (`&#32;`)

Each one is followed by a code that you can use in HTML to create the white space. In fact, the one mostly used is the first ASCII space. To get the HTML code to space out the sentence as expected, we must use the explicit ASCII code as follows:

```html
<html>
  <head>
    <title>White Space Example 2</title>
  </head>
  <body>
    This is a line broken    by white space.
  </body>
</html>
```

Then we will get the desired effect:

It's a similar story with line breaks too.

Line Breaks

We can't use carriage returns to create new paragraphs or to break lines in HTML. See what happens if we try to use carriage returns, by having a look at the following code:

```
<html>
  <head>
    <title>Examples of line breaks</title>
  </head>
  <body>
    <p>This line has a carriage return here,
    but it is ignored by the browser.</p>
    <p>This line, however, has a line break element here, <br/>
    so it is on two lines.</p>
  </body>
</html>
```

The carriage return after the word here isn't rendered and is effectively ignored by the browser. It's the width of the window that determines where lines break:

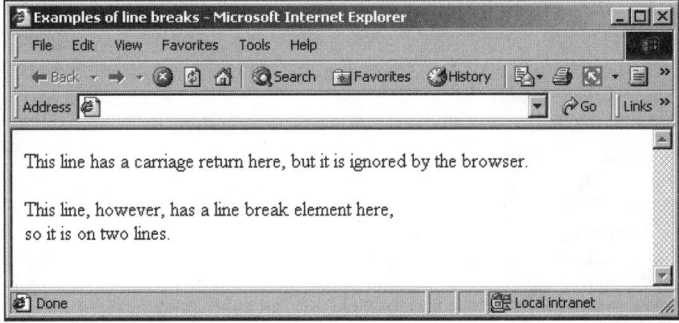

In fact, carriage returns are actually treated as white space characters by browsers, so carriage returns can't be used as line breaks. Also, they shouldn't be used as white spaces either; we should use any of the other white space characters specified above!

So to break lines, instead of using carriage returns, we have to use the
 (line break) element.

The
 (Line Break) Element

The <br /> element does nothing more fancy than start text that follows an occurrence of the <br /> tag on the next line of the browser's display.

With some browsers, including Internet Explorer and Netscape, we can use consecutive <br /> elements to space out blocks of text:

```
<br/><br/><br/>
```

The <br /> tag takes five attributes. Four of them are universal, so have already been discussed in Chapter 2.

```
class        clear        id        style        title
```

clear

The clear attribute can be used with the <br /> tag to extend the wrapping options of text around images. When clear is used in text that's wrapped round an image, it ensures that any subsequent text begins below the image.

```
<html>
  <head>
    <title>Example of the "clear" attribute</title>
  </head>
  <body>
    <img align="left" src="wrox_logo100.gif">
    This text would normally continue to wrap around the right hand side
    of the image, but the clear attribute here,<br clear="left" />means
    that text will continue here instead.
  </body>
</html>
```

This code, has the following effect:

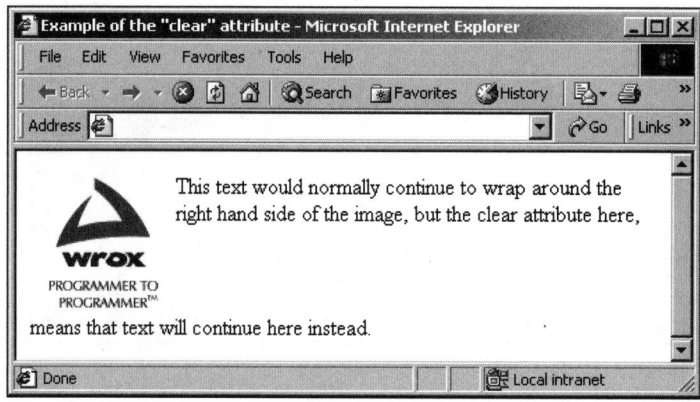

The syntax is:

```
clear="left | right | all | none"
```

left means that the text will appear at the first clear left margin position. right means the text will appear at the first clear right margin position. all means that both margins have to be clear before text will appear. none is the default value when the attribute is omitted.

If, on the other hand, we don't want a line of text to be broken, we can use the Netscape extension <nobr>, like this:

```
<nobr>Here's a line of text we don't want broken ... here's the end</nobr>
```

The <nobr> element works in both IE and Netscape, but isn't and never has been part of the HTML standard.

The <p> (Paragraph) Element

Paragraphs are defined with the <p> element. The <p> element, unlike <br/>, has an opening and closing tag. The <p> element is used to group sections of text and provide some space formatting, similar to that provided by line breaks.

Some people use the <p> element, to actually break lines, however it isn't valid HTML to use consecutive <p> elements to break lines. By definition, a paragraph can't be empty. If you do use consecutive <p> elements, some browsers will add the space, some will ignore all but the first <p>, and some will complain about the use of invalid HTML. This is because the <p> element hasn't been correctly closed, and even if we close the tag it can't be empty.

<p> has seven attributes:

```
align      class      dir      id
lang       style      title
```

Again, six of these are universal, so won't be further discussed here.

align

The align attribute has been deprecated under HTML 4.01. The syntax is:

```
align="left | right | center | justify"
```

The <hr/> (Horizontal Rule) Element

Horizontal rules are used to break up sections of a document from each other. A horizontal rule is placed using the <hr/> element. As this isn't a container element, no end tag is required or allowed.

Allowable Attributes

Allowable attributes for <hr/> are:

```
align      classdir      lang      noshade      size
style      title         width     id
```

align

This specifies the position of the rule. The syntax is:

```
align="left | right | center"
```

The default value is center. This attribute is deprecated under HTML 4.01.

noshade

noshade means the rule is displayed without any 3D shading effects. This attribute is deprecated under HTML 4.01.

size

This sets the height of the rule. The syntax is:

```
size="n"
```

where n is the height in pixels. The default value is 2. This has been deprecated in HTML 4.01.

width

This sets the width of the rule across the browser window. The syntax is:

```
width="n"
```

where n is the width, either in pixels, or expressed as a percentage of the window's width. To express the width as the latter, add %, for example, width="50%". This has been deprecated in HTML 4.01.

Internet Explorer-Specific Attributes

IE also supports two non-standard attributes; color and src.

color

This specifies the color that the rule is displayed in. The syntax is either of:

```
color="#rrggbb"
color="colorName"
```

where #rrggbb is a hexadecimal number defining the amount of red, green, and blue that makes up the color, and colorName is one of several preset color names. The default color is based on the background.

src

This specifies the external graphic file to use as a source for the element.

```
src="url"
```

This only works in versions of Internet Explorer prior to 5.x.

Using Horizontal Rules

Have a look at the following example:

```
<!DOCTYPE HTML PUBLIC "-//W3C//DTD HTML 4.01//EN"
          "http://www.w3.org/TR/html4/loose.dtd">
<html>
  <head>
    <title>An example of a horizontal rule</title>
  </head>
  <body>
    <hr align="center" size="5" width="70%">
    <hr align="center" size="10" width="80%">
    <hr align="center" size="2" width="50%" noshade>
  </body>
</html>
```

This produces:

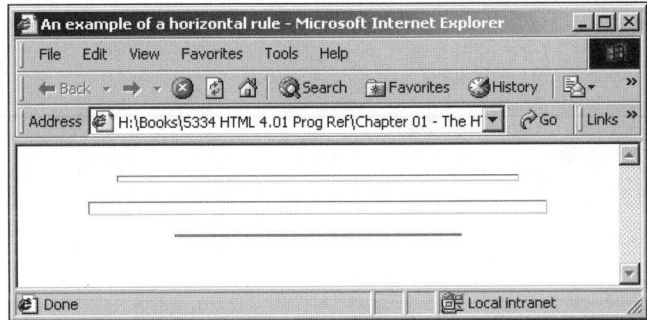

Note that the first two horizontal rules appear in 3D, whereas the last example is flat, because we've used the `noshade` attribute. This is particularly useful when the background color is very light, as the 3D shading won't show up very well.

Lists

Lists are used to organize information in a clear and easily understood format. There are three main types of list that you can set up in a document:

❏ Unordered, or bulleted lists (using <ul>)

❏ Ordered, or numbered lists (using <ol>)

❏ Definition lists (using <dl>)

<ul>, <ol>, and <dl> are the tags that define the type of list. They are all container tags – in other words, they must have a corresponding end tag. The list entries themselves are defined by <li> tags in bulleted and numbered lists, and by <dt> and <dd> in a definition list.

We can add a list header to any type of list using <lh>, although it should be noted that not all browsers will start a new line after the closing </lh>. Netscape will give you the results you would expect, but many other browsers won't.

The <ul> (Unordered List) Element

The purpose of <ul> is to produce an unordered list, which is the same as a bulleted list that we would use in a word processor. The syntax for unordered lists is:

```
<ul>
<li>first list item</li>
<li>second list item</li>
<li>third list item etc.</li>
</ul>
```

To output a simple list such as the one above, we could use the following code:

```
<html>
  <head>
    <title>Example of the "li" and "ul" elements</title>
  </head>
  <body>
  <p> Using unordered lists</p>
  <p>
    <ul>
      <li>first list item</li>
      <li>second list item</li>
      <li>third list item etc.</li>
    </ul>
  </p>
  </body>
</html>
```

The list would then be displayed as follows:

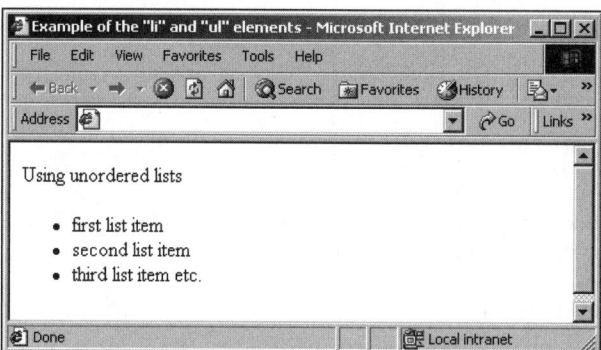

The <UL> tag has eight attributes, six of which are universal, so won't be discussed here:

```
class      compact      dir      id
lang       style        title    type
```

compact

This tag has been deprecated under HTML 4.0. compact tells the browser to fit the list into a smaller space. This is usually achieved by removing white space from between each list item. However, the browsers that don't support compact will just ignore it.

type

The `type` attribute allows the appearance of the bullets to be changed.

```
type = "circle | disc | square"
```

This attribute has now been deprecated in HTML 4.01.

The <li> (List Items) Element

The `<li>` element is used with the `<ul>` and `<ol>` elements to define a list item. If `<li>` is contained inside a `<ul>` tag, it defines a bullet point, but if contained inside an `<ol>` element, then it defines some list number. It can also be used with the `<dl>` (description list) element, which we also consider shortly. It can take eight attributes (two, plus the universal ones):

type	value	class	dir
id	lang	style	title

type

The `type` attribute specifies the type of ordering used. The syntax is:

```
type="n"
```

where n is one of the following:

- ❑ 1 – Arabic numerals (1, 2, 3); this is the default
- ❑ A – Capital letters (A, B, C)
- ❑ a – Small letters (a, b, c)
- ❑ I – Large roman numerals (I, II, III)
- ❑ i – Small roman numerals (i, ii, iii)

This attribute has been deprecated in HTML 4.01.

value

Specifies the number of the current list item, even if the current list item is non-numeric.

```
value="n"
```

This attribute has been deprecated in HTML 4.01.

Using <ul> and <li>

The following fragment encodes a compact, unordered list with square bullets (the full code can be found in the download as `squarebullets.html`):

```
...
<p> Using square bullets </p>
<ul compact type="square">
  <li>First list item</li>
  <li>Second list item</li>
  <li>Third list item</li>
</ul>
...
```

In Netscape 6, it looks like this:

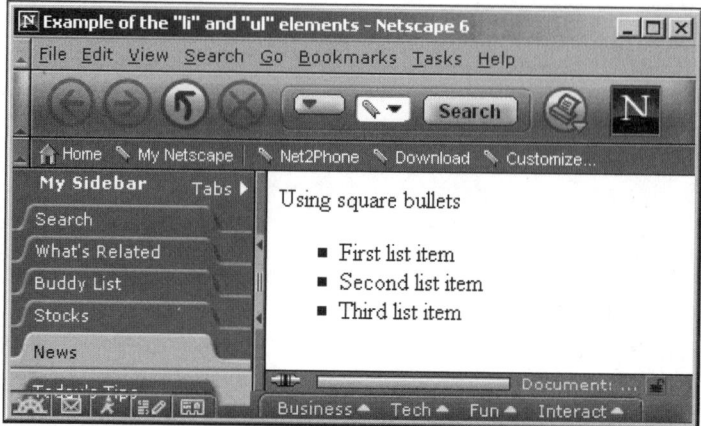

The <ol> (Ordered List) Element

`<ol>` will produce an ordered list numbered in a style of your choice. The default style is 1, 2, 3, but you can choose various other styles such as a, b, c, or i, ii, iii, etc. By using the `type` attribute, the default style can be changed. The syntax is:

```
<ol>
<li>First item</li>
<li>Second item</li>
<li>Third item etc.</li>
</ol>
```

To output an ordered list such as the one above, we would insert the above code fragment into an HTML document in a similar fashion to what we have seen already with the `<ul>`/`<li>` examples above. See the file `orderedlist.html` in the code download for a full example – this is displayed in IE 5 as:

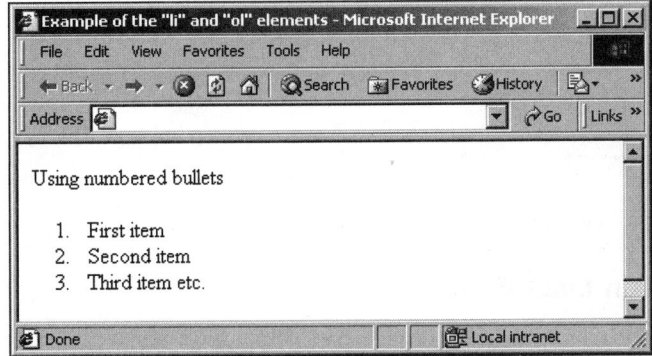

Note how the browser has inserted the numbers for us. Allowable attributes for <ol> are:

```
class     compact    dir    id       lang
title     start      type   style
```

compact

This tag has now been deprecated under HTML 4.01. compact tells the browser to fit the list into a smaller space.

type

The type attribute specifies the type of ordering used. The syntax is:

```
type="n"
```

where n is one of the following:

❑ 1 – Arabic numerals (1, 2, 3); this is the default

❑ A – Capital letters (A, B, C)

❑ a – Small letters (a, b, c)

❑ I – Large roman numerals (I, II, III)

❑ i – Small roman numerals (i, ii, iii)

If this attribute is set in the <li> element – then it overrides what is set in <ol>. This attribute has been deprecated in HTML 4.01.

start

Alters the number/letter that the list starts with. The syntax is:

```
start="n"
```

where n specifies the new start number/letter, for example, 3, C, c, III, or iii. This value will always be numeric, so if you are using capital letters for ordering, and the value of n is "3", the start letter will be "C". However, we don't need to have the start 'type' being the same as the list type. For example the following is also valid:

```
<ol type="a" start="5">
```

This attribute has now been deprecated in HTML 4.01.

The <dl> (Definition List) Element

Definition lists are used to include a short text description for each list item. Allowable attributes for <dl> are:

```
class     compact     dir     id
lang      title       style
```

compact

This tag has now been deprecated under HTML 4.01. compact tells the browser to fit the list into a smaller space.

The <dt> (Definition Term) Element

This is used to define a term with a <dl> element. <dt> is restricted to in-line content. Allowable attributes for are <dt>:

```
class     dir     id     lang     title     style
```

The <dd> (Definition Description) Element

This is used to specify a description within a <dl> element, and can be indented from the list. Allowable attributes for <dd> are:

```
class     dir     id     lang     title     style
```

Using <dl>, <dt>, and <dd>

You could use a definition list to produce, for example, a glossary of terms, using <dt> for the definition term and <dd> for the description:

```
<dl>
  <dt>HTML</dt>
    <dd>HyperText Markup Language</dd>
  <dt>HEAD</dt>
    <dd>The first part of an HTML document</dd>
  <dt>BODY</dt>
    <dd>The main part of an HTML document</dd>
</dl>
```

This would be displayed as follows (see the file `dl_dd_dt.html` in the code download for a full code example):

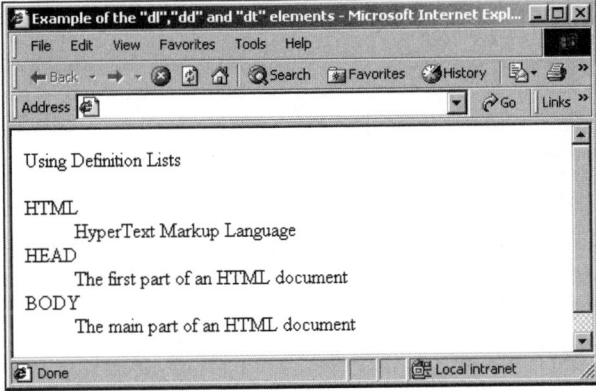

Nesting Lists

Lists can be **nested,** as can most elements within HTML. Nesting means placing a set of tags or elements inside another set. The nested list is independent of the outer list, so if it is numbered, it will start again from 1 (unless you explicitly change this).

```
<ol type="i">
  <li>first list item</li>
  <li>second list item</li>
  <li>third list item</li>
  <ol type="i">
    <li>first sub-list item</li>
    <li>second sub-list item</li>
    <li>third sub-list item</li>
  </ol>
</ol>
```

A nested list would be displayed as follows (see the file `nestedlist.html` in the code download for a full code example):

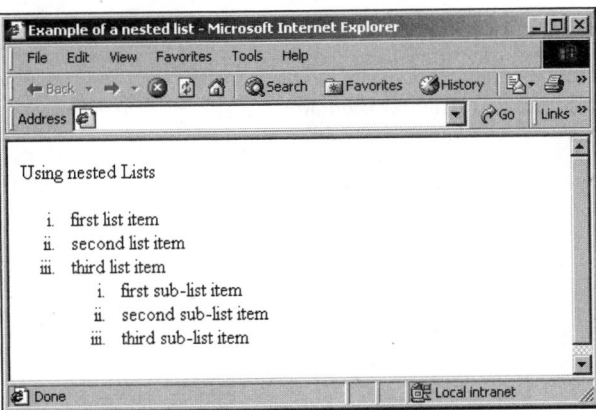

Other Types of List

As well as the types of list discussed above, we can also use <menu> and <dir> for lists. The <menu> element is designed for use in single column menu lists, while the <dir> element is designed for use with multiple column directory lists. We can use <li> with both, and each will indent the items in the list. These tags have been deprecated in HTML 4.01 and are pretty much obsolete as menus are now created by a vast array of other technologies; from scripting languages to Flash animations, and directory lists can be created by server-side technologies, so we won't discuss them here.

Text Emphasis and Style

There are many different tags for emphasizing and styling text. One of the major methods of doing this is to change the font of a piece of text. We'll now look at how this can be done.

Fonts

Most documents on the web are in the default font, which can be set by the user of the browser. Until the mid 1990s, it wasn't possible to define the font in a web document. The main reason for this is that we can't guarantee that the font we define for the text is installed on the user's system. However, with the current rate of advance in computers and software, this is becoming much less of issue. Most platforms have several standard fonts such as Arial, Courier, or Times New Roman.

Microsoft and Netscape have both worked on the embedding of fonts into web documents. This means that the font is transferred to the user's system at the same time as the rest of the page downloads. In Netscape this technology is known as dynamic fonts. IE 4 onwards also allows for the possibility of downloadable fonts. We need to use style sheets to embed them, and this is covered in Chapter 12, "*Character Styles*".

However, for specifying the font type without messing around by downloading fonts, the most popular method is still the <font> tag.

The <font> Element

This element and each of its attributes have become deprecated under HTML 4.01. Nevertheless it is still, perhaps, the commonest way on many web sites to apply a font. It has become deprecated mainly due to the introduction of **style sheets**. Style sheets are a list of display rules that can be applied to different HTML elements. They are the recommended way to apply fonts and styles. We will look at style sheets in later chapters.

The tag defines the appearance of the text it encloses. Allowable attributes are:

```
class     dir     id      size      face
color     lang    style   title
```

size

Specifies the size of the lettering. The syntax is:

```
size="n"
```

where n is a number 1 through 7; 1 is the smallest font size, 7 the largest. If a value outside of 1 – 7 is specified then the value is cropped at the min/max value.

The actual size of the font is determined in relative terms, by the `size` attribute of the `<font>` element. `size` can also be used to set font settings relative to the previous font size using the '+' or '-' modifiers. `size="+2"` would make the font two sizes larger; `size="-1"` would make the font one size smaller.

face

Specifies the font, or list of fonts, that we want to use. The syntax is:

```
face="fontname1, fontname2, fontname3"
```

When `face` is used to specify a list of fonts, if the first font in the list isn't present on the user's system, the second will be tried, and so on. If none of the specified fonts exist on the user's system, the browser default font will be used.

Microsoft recently announced a list of special TrueType web fonts, which anyone can download from its web site. The idea is that pages are coded with the relevant fonts, and then a link placed to Microsoft's site so that the user can download the fonts for use on their system. To check the latest details on this, go to http://www.microsoft.com/truetype/fontpack/win.htm

> *If you're wondering which fonts to use, a general guideline is to use sans-serif fonts (like Arial) for headlines and serifed fonts (like Times) for large portions of text.*

color

`color` specifies the color that the font will appear in. This can be displayed as a hexadecimal number or a color name.

Some interesting typographical effects can be achieved with these attributes, for example:

```
<!DOCTYPE HTML PUBLIC "-//W3C//DTD HTML 4.01//EN"
          "http://www.w3.org/TR/html4/loose.dtd">
<html>
  <head>
    <title>An example of the "font" element</title>
  </head>
  <body>
    <p>
      <font size="5" face="arial" color="blue">T</font>he first letter of
      this sentence should be three sizes larger than the rest of the
      sentence. The first letter should also be displayed in blue rather
      than black.
    </p>
  </body>
</html>
```

The result of this code is as follows:

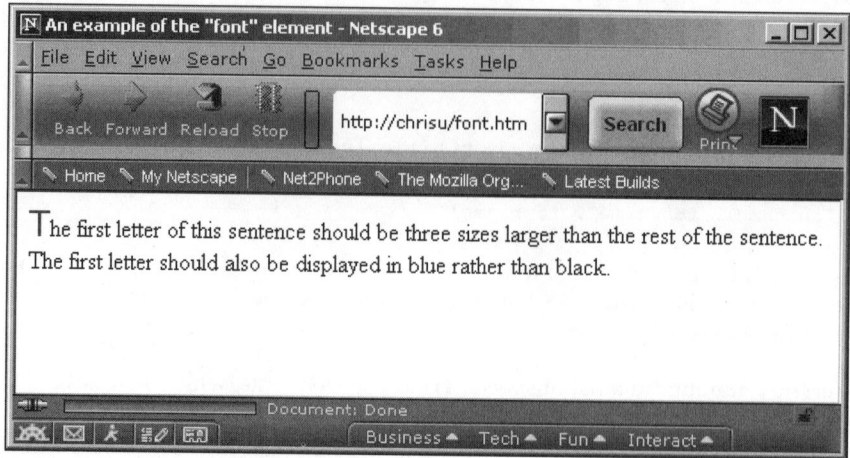

Netscape-Specific Attributes

There are two attributes particular to Netscape 4/6 that aren't part of the HTML 4.01 standard. These are `weight` and `point-size`.

weight

Specifies the weight of the font used to display the text. It can only be a number and not the word "bold", which you might expect to be able to set it to also. It has the following syntax:

```
weight="number"
```

This number can range from `100` to `900` (in steps of 100).

point-size

This attribute specifies the size of the font in points (absolute only – to specify a relative size use the `size` attribute).

```
point-size = "string | number"
```

Note that points are an absolute unit of measurement that refers to typeface points, of which there are 72 in an inch. We look at units of measurement in closer detail in Chapter 11, "Style Sheet Fundamentals".

The <basefont> Element

If you want to set a default font-size for the whole document, then you can use an element called `<basefont>`. This element sets the default attributes for any text that has not been formatted with the `<font>` element or a style sheet. This element is not supported at all in Netscape 6, and only the size attribute of it is supported in Netscape 4. This has also been deprecated under HTML 4.01. Allowable attributes are:

```
class      size      face      color      id      lang
```

The `size`, `face`, and `color` attributes all function in the same way as for the `font` tag. The values for the attributes are the same as for `<font>`. The default value for the `size` attribute is 3. The value for the `<font>` size attribute can be specified relative to the `<basefont>` size, like this:

```
<!DOCTYPE HTML PUBLIC "-//W3C//DTD HTML 4.01//EN"
          "http://www.w3.org/TR/html4/loose.dtd">
<html>
  <head>
    <title>Relative font sizes</title>
  </head>
  <body bgcolor="#F9FFFF">
    <basefont size="4" face="arial">
    <p>
       This text is the basefont size.
    </p>
    <P>
      <font size="-1">This text is one size down from the basefont
      size.</font>
    </p>
    <p>
      <font size="+2">This text is two sizes larger than the basefont
      size.</font>
    </p>
  </body>
</html>
```

The result of this code is:

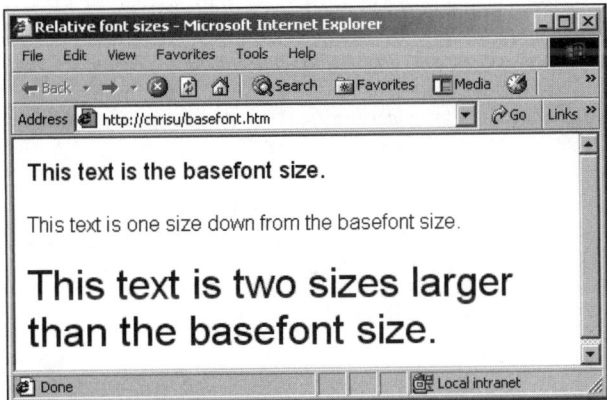

By simply prefixing a minus or plus sign before the value, the size becomes relative to the `<basefont>` size attribute. Unfortunately, we are still constrained to the 1 is smallest, 7 is largest limit. Choosing values outside this range won't work; once again they are cropped at the minimum and maximum values:

```
<!-- This is acceptable -->
<basefont size="1">
<font size="+6">This will work as 1 + 6 = 7 </font>
```

```
<!-- This is wrong. The font size will only change to 7, the maximum -->
<basefont size="2">
<font size="+6">This won't work as 2 + 6 = 8 </font>
```

When a '+' or '-' is used, the `<font>` size attribute is always relative to the `<basefont>` size attribute, not the last `<font>` size, assuming there is a `<basefont>` element included in the page.

Physical and Logical Style Tags

Fonts aren't the only way we can affect the appearance of a piece of text. There are many different tags, which can be used to italicize or embolden the text. These tags can broadly be split into two categories:

- ❏ Physical tags
- ❏ Logical style tags

HTML distinguishes between two groups of character-formatting tags: logical character-attribute tags and physical character-attribute tags. It may help to think of physical character-attribute tags as closely related to the direct formatting you could apply to text from a word processor, such as "bold". The appearance of HTML text formatted with physical character-attribute tags is more likely to remain constant from one browser to another. Logical character-attribute tags in HTML can be thought of as like "styles" in a word processor – the appearance of text formatted with a style, in a word processor, depends on how the style is defined in that word processor. Similarly, the appearance of HTML text formatted with logical character-attribute tags depends upon the browser's interpretation of that logical character-attribute tag.

> *The idea behind logical styles is that they can be rendered in the best way for that particular platform. For example, if you want to emphasize a word, `<em>` might produce italics in a browser, but on a text-to-speech system, it could be rendered by increasing the volume slightly. In this application, if you used an `<i>` tag it would have no associated meaning, and the text-to-speech system wouldn't know how to render italics. (How do you speak an italic?)*

Physical Tags

Physical tag styles do not vary from browser to browser, or in the case of browser-specific tags then browser version to browser version. They include:

- ❏ `<b>`   Bold
- ❏ `<i>`   Italic
- ❏ `<u>`   Underline – deprecated under HTML 4.01
- ❏ `<tt>`   Typewriter
- ❏ `<s>`   Strikeout – deprecated under HTML 4.01
- ❏ `<blink>`   Blinking text (Netscape specific)

and are rendered as follows:

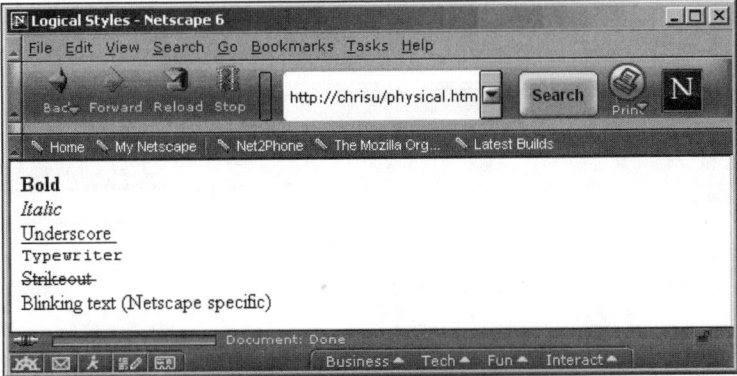

Logical Tags

One of the things you should remember when building web pages is that HTML was designed to specify the relationships between the different parts of the document. Many tags are logical tags, and HTML does not specify how they should be represented. Logical style tags take on the preferences set for them within the browser, as well as being rendered differently depending on the browser vendor. For example, many browsers will let the user specify which size and shape of font will be used to display the <h1> tag. It will usually be larger than the <h2> tag, but you can't even be sure of that! Logical tags include:

- ❏ <H1> to <H6>   Headings
- ❏ <em>   Emphasis (usually italic)
- ❏ <strong>   Strong (usually bold)
- ❏ <address>   Usually italic
- ❏ <cite>   Used for quoting text (usually italic)
- ❏ <code>   Monospaced font (usually Courier)
- ❏ <samp>   Monospaced font (usually Courier)
- ❏ <kbd>   Monospaced font (usually Courier)
- ❏ <blockquote>   Denotes a quotation in text, Usually a paragraph or more.
- ❏ <big>   Makes text one size larger
- ❏ <small>   Makes text one size smaller
- ❏ <sup>   Renders text as superscript
- ❏ <sub>   Renders text as subscript
- ❏ <abbr>   Logically denotes abbreviations and acronyms
- ❏ <dfn>   Definition
- ❏ <q>   Denotes a short inline quotation
- ❏ <var>   Denotes a variable name, usually rendered in italics

`<code>`, `<samp>`, and `<kbd>` (keyboard) are particularly useful if your document contains actual code that you are trying to explain to your reader.

When viewed in Internet Explorer, relative tags appear as follows:

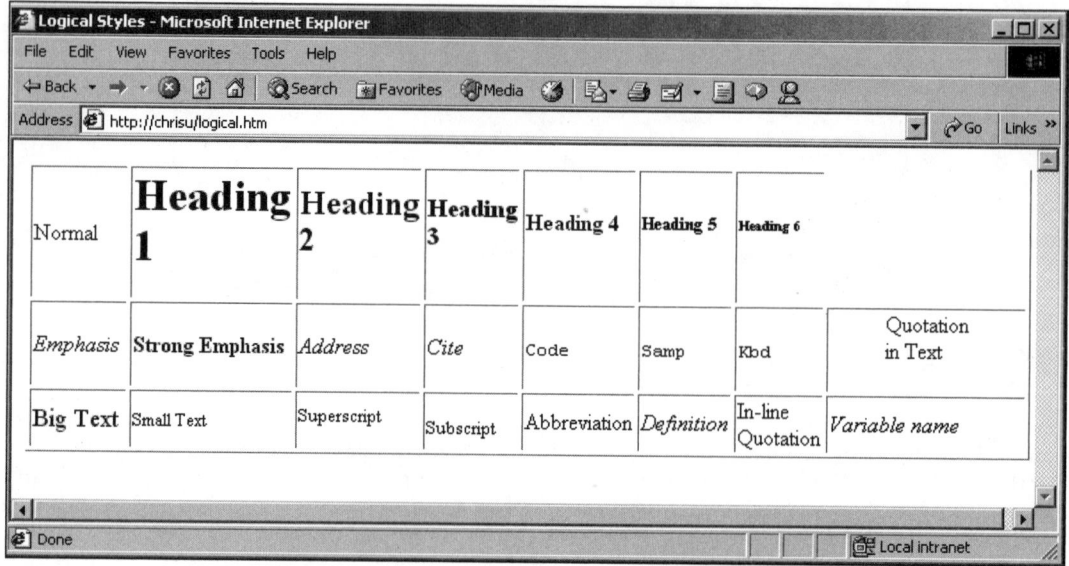

Note that the above style types have all the universal attributes associated with them. The `<h1>` to `<h6>` tags also allow the `align` attribute too.

When deciding which type of tag to use, bear in mind that while it's easier to stick with the physical styles – at least that way you can be sure that the page will be viewed as you intended – we should be using logical tags, as our page might be translated to different media, such as aural style sheets, which we look at in Chapter 14.

The `<marquee>` Element

Finally one interesting, but definitely non-standard element that Internet Explorer supports is `<marquee>`. This is used to produce scrolling text messages, which otherwise might require complex scripting or Java code.

If you have Internet Explorer installed on your system, you can try the following example:

```
<marquee direction="right" behavior="scroll" scrollamount="10"
        scrolldelay="200">
  This is a scrolling marquee!
</marquee>
```

This element is covered in Chapter 16, "IE- and Netscape-specific Tags and Styles".

Colors

When creating web pages, we will want to use colors to make the page attractive, and to draw the user's eye to certain parts. With HTML, one way to express the color we want to be displayed is as a six digit hexadecimal value, which represents the individual red, green, and blue components of the color (the other way is using a color name).

The first two digits are the red component, the second two are the green component, and the last two are the blue component. Setting a value to 00 means the component is "off"; in other words, it has an intensity of zero. A value of FF means the component is fully "on", that is, is at full intensity. Different colors are achieved by "mixing" different intensity levels of the three components. White is all three components fully "on", represented as #FFFFFF; black is all components fully "off", represented as #000000.

> Note that hexadecimal RGB colors are exactly the same as the RGB colors used in most graphics editing programs – the only difference is that they are expressed in hexadecimal, not decimal.

As an example, to display normal text in red, we would use the text attribute of the <body> element:

```
<body text="#FF0000">
```

If you're confused by hexadecimal notation, don't worry. There's a much easier way of defining the color you want. Both Netscape and Internet Explorer support the use of color names: we can replace the hexadecimal value with a name – which is somewhat easier to remember:

```
<body text="midnightblue">
```

The HTML 4.01 standard introduces the following color names:

HTML Color name	Hexadecimal equivalent
black	000000
silver	C0C0C0
gray	808080
white	FFFFFF
maroon	800000
red	FF0000
purple	800080
fuchsia	FF00FF
green	008000
lime	00FF00

Table continued on following page

HTML Color name	Hexadecimal equivalent
olive	808000
yellow	FFFF00
navy	000080
blue	0000FF
teal	008080
aqua	00FFFF

However there are actually over 200 color names supported by both Netscape and Explorer. These color names are also consistent between the two browsers. A full list is supplied in Appendix D.

An Example Page

Let's put some of this into practice. Type the following into your favorite text editor:

```
<!DOCTYPE HTML PUBLIC "-//W3C//DTD HTML 4.01//EN"
          "http://www.w3.org/TR/html4/loose.dtd">
<html>
  <head>
    <title>Welcome to The Global Coffee Club</title>
  </head>
  <body bgcolor="#FFFFEA" text="#0000A0" link="#FF0000"
      vlink="#808080" alink="#008040">
    <h1>The Global Coffee Club welcomes you to its Web-Site!</h1>
    <h2>We hope you enjoy your visit</h2>
    News flash! You can now
    <a href="taste.html">taste our range of beans on-line</a>
  </body>
</html>
```

The `<a href="...">` tag defines a hypertext link. We'll be looking at this in more detail in Chapter 4, "Links". Save the file as global.html and view it. It should look like this:

If your page doesn't look exactly as above, don't worry. There are many reasons why your browser may be rendering the page differently, as we'll see throughout the course of this book. What you should see, though, is that all the text is in blue (with the exception of the hypertext link, which should be red), and the background is off-white. At the moment of course, the hypertext link doesn't lead anywhere, because we have yet to create the `taste.html` document. Clicking on the link may result in an error message, or maybe nothing at all: it depends on your browser.

Let's look at this example more closely. The first few lines are all familiar from the last chapter. It's in the document body that we start setting color information. The `<body>` tag is where we set the color attributes for the rest of the document.

```
<body bgcolor="#FFFFEA" text="#0000A0" link="#FF0000"
      vlink="#808080" alink="#008040">
```

Note that we could just as easily (in fact, more easily) have used color names instead of the hexadecimal numbers. The rest of the code looks like this:

```
<h1>The Global Coffee Club welcomes you to its Web-Site!</h1>
<h2>We hope you enjoy your visit</h2>
News flash! You can now
<a href="taste.html">taste our range of beans on-line</a>
</body>
</html>
```

The first two lines format the text to be rendered as different sized headings. Then comes some ordinary body text, in which we specify a hypertext link. We're getting a bit ahead of ourselves here, but don't worry, it's just been included to make the usage of the `<body>` element's color attributes clearer. The code ends by closing the body section of the document and then the HTML document itself.

Annotating HTML Code

Annotation doesn't concern the formatting of the text in an HTML document, it is used to add documentation to HTML code, to highlight insertions and deletions or add comments to code that don't show up in the final web page. It is possible to annotate HTML code in several ways, as in the following methods.

Insertions and Deletions, the <ins> and <del> Elements

The HTML 4.01 standard specifies two elements that can mark text that has been recently inserted or should be deleted from a document. These are the `<ins>` and `<del>` elements.

They both take the following attributes:

```
id       class    lang        title
style    cite     datetime
```

There are only two non-universal attributes; these are `cite` and `datetime`, which we will briefly look at now.

cite

The `cite` attribute is used to specify a source document, explaining why the information has been amended. It has the following format:

```
cite="url"
```

datetime

The `datetime` attribute specifies the date and time of the change. It has the following format:

```
datetime="datetime"
```

We've separated these two elements out, because they are unusual in HTML in that the standard specifies that they can serve as either inline or block-level elements. Further to this, though, they cannot be used to contain block-level elements when they are acting as inline content. The easiest way to explain this is to look at a couple of quick examples.

The first is the correct way to use the element.

```
<html>
  <head>
    <title>Correct way to use the insertion and deletion elements</title>
  </head>
  <body>
    <p>Sales Target for 2002:    <ins>50,000</ins><del>30,000</del> units</p>
  </body>
</html>
```

This will display the following in the browser:

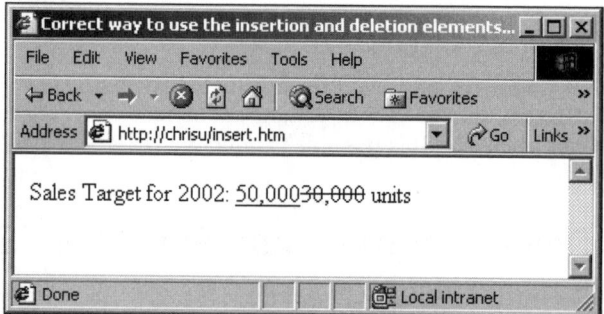

The inserted text is underlined, while the deleted text is struck through. This is partly the reason why the `<s>` strikeout and `<u>` underline elements are deprecated in the HTML 4.01 standard, but not the other physical style elements.

However, it's not possible to use the `<ins>` and `<del>` elements inline to insert or remove block-level content, such as other elements:

```html
<html>
  <head>
    <title>Incorrect way to use the insertion and deletion elements</title>
  </head>
  <body>
    <p>Sales Target for 2002:
      <ins><div><img src="newsales.gif"></div></ins>
      <del><div><img src="oldsales.gif"></div></del>
    </p>
  </body>
</html>
```

The browser isn't capable of applying styles to block-level content such as that given above.

Adding Comments

Adding comments to documents is as good an idea in HTML as it is in other languages. Comments allow the author to re-acquaint themself with the code when they come to alter it months later. Anything between the `<!--` and `-->` tags will be ignored by the browser, and forms a comment:

```html
<!-- This text will be visible only to someone viewing the
source code -->
```

Note that this comment spans two lines – comments can be multi- or single-line; the browser will still ignore them.

Preformatted text

The `<pre>` element, short for preformatted, is a deprecated element in HTML 4.01 that allows you to send of "hints" to the browser on how wide a particular block of text should be. In practice this means that text rendered in between the opening and closing tags will be rendered in a fixed-width font, such as courier.

```html
<pre>This is some preformatted text</pre>
```

You should use style sheets now in preference to this element.

Revision Dates

In keeping with general programming practice, it's a good idea to add revision dates to all documents. The majority of visitors to sites want to know when the last revision was made, and it's common practice to add the current date to the bottom of a document. Many authors just put something similar to the following:

```html
<p align="right">Last Revision : Apr 25 2001 by Chris Ullman</p>
```

Remember that the World Wide Web is a global entity. Avoid using country or regional-specific syntax such as 04/25/01.

89

Summary

In this chapter we looked at text formatting, and in particular we saw how to break text up into manageable sections using white space characters or by using line breaks, paragraphs, and horizontal rules. We then looked at the different lists available in HTML and how we could organize our text in a logical and clear manner.

Next we looked at how to apply styles to make particular words or phrases stand out. However as we have hinted, all this changes with the introduction of style sheets (which we look at later). There are many different tags and attributes that can all be used to apply the different/conflicting styles. The advent of style sheets may achieve a uniform way for specifying style information. So, while many of these tags and attributes work now, in future XHTML standards we won't able to find tags such as <font> as they have already been deprecated in HTML 4.01 and will probably be omitted.

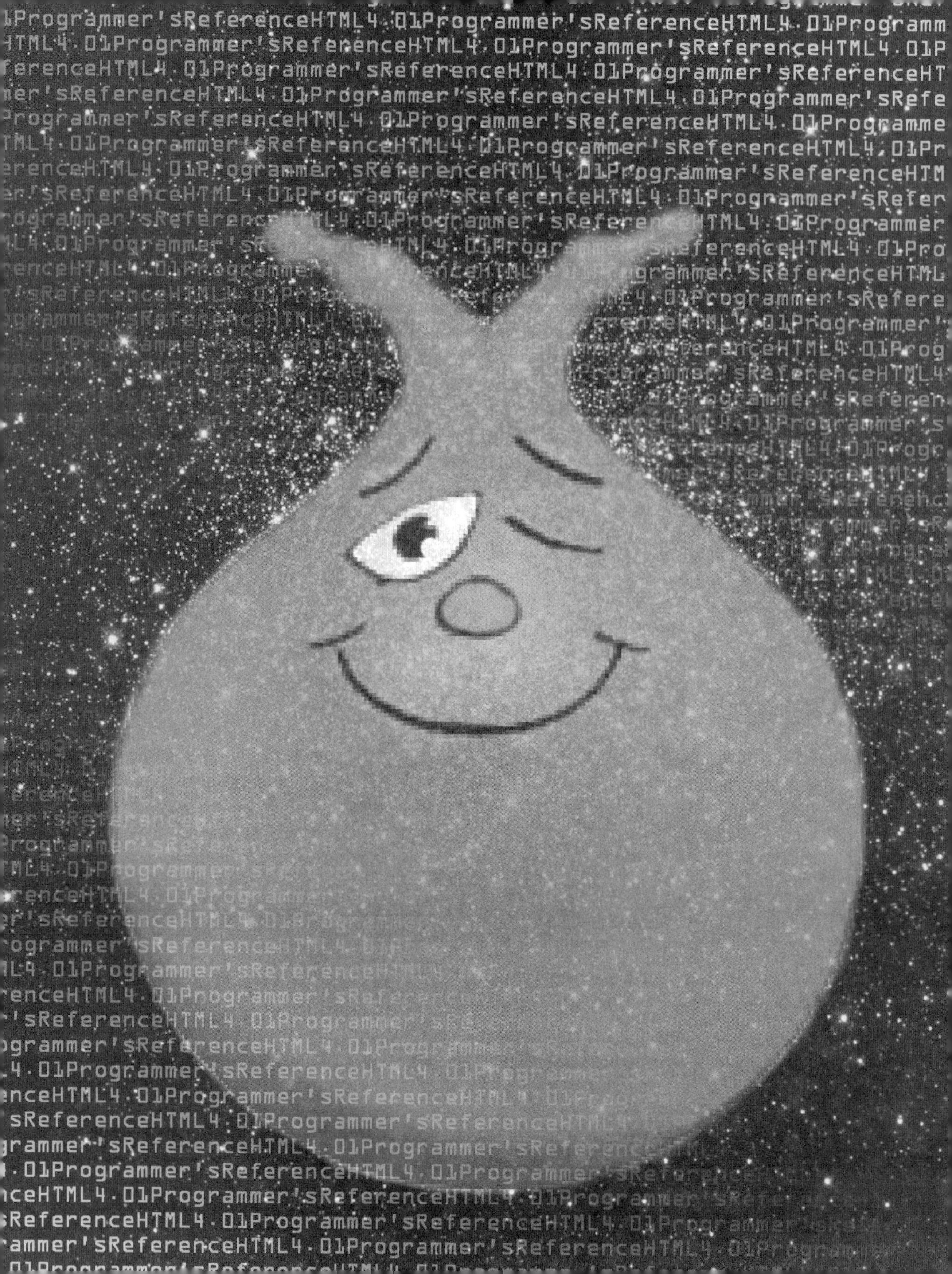
Programmer'sReferenceHTML4.01

4

Links

Right from the earliest days of the Web, the power of the medium has lain primarily in its use of **hypertext links** – the mechanism by which documents are connected together within and between sites. This allows vast virtual libraries of information to be assembled, which visitors can navigate through by simply clicking on a word, phrase, or graphic on a page in order to be taken to a related document.

Even as the standards have evolved and browser technologies improved, the basic mechanisms of page-to-page text links have changed very little. This chapter explains the HTML elements that are used to provide those links, and then goes on to consider the use of graphics as links, using the "imagemap" construct. In that area at least, as we shall see, the HTML standard has evolved from earlier versions to favor enhanced browser capabilities.

Finally in this chapter, we will discuss some of the common pitfalls, tricks, and tips of link usage, which can help you to get the best from these fundamental Web technologies.

It is worth noting that the concept of a link in a web page as we discuss it here relates specifically to a clickable "hotspot" within a document that allows the viewer to open a related file or page. HTML does allow for other types of linkage between files, however, and one of the most important of these is the ability to embed graphics within a page, which is the subject of Chapter 5. Also of increasing importance are the logical links between documents, which can be encoded using the <link> tag, discussed in Chapter 2, "The Document Head and Body".

URLs: Identifying the Target of a Link

In order to create a link, we have to understand how to uniquely specify the page, file, or other resource that we want to link to. This is in the same format as is used to enter the address of a web page into a browser – the **Uniform Resource Locator**, or URL.

> *If we look at the HTML Specification and other similar standards documents, we can see they refer to URIs – **Uniform Resource Identifiers**. This is a generalized term, which includes the everyday URL and an alternative format, the **Uniform Resource Name**, or URN. In practice, URNs (which all begin with "urn:") are not used, so the terms URI and URL can be thought of as interchangeable.*

Understanding the format of a URL

Although you are probably familiar with any number of URL's for your favorite web sites, it is worth taking the time to understand exactly how a URL is formed, and what some of the required and optional elements are. In general, a URL can be broken down into a number of sub-components, like this:

```
<scheme>:<credentials>@<host>:<port><filepath><other_specifiers>
```

In the above, each set of angle brackets represents a different component of the URL, and should be replaced with the appropriate information. Most of the components are optional, and indeed it is unusual for all of them to be used at once.

In the sections that follow, we will look at each component in turn, referring back to this generic example above.

1. Scheme

The first part of the URL identifies the precise type of the URL and, by implication, how the resource should be retrieved from the network. The most common examples are:

❑ **http://** **Hypertext Transfer Protocol** is the protocol normally used to communicate with web servers on intranets and the Internet.

❑ **https://** A special secure version of http://, which authenticates the identity of the server by reference to a digital certificate, and encrypts the data exchange using SSL (**Secure Sockets Layer**).

❑ **ftp://** **File Transfer Protocol** is an older protocol for exchanging files between clients and servers. Although it is more efficient for large file transfers than http://, the latter is increasingly used with web sites because it provides better integration with most browsers and is less likely to be affected by security firewalls.

❑ **file://** This is used to indicate that the resource is a local file and should be accessed from the client's local file system – either from the local disk, or from a shared directory on the LAN.

❑ **mailto:** This is not really a true protocol, but a way of indicating to the browser that it should invoke the user's e-mail client. When used in a link, this type of URL usually causes the e-mail client to create a new blank e-mail with the recipient address pre-filled, ready for a message to be entered. (It can also be used with forms, as described in Chapter 6).

❑ **javascript:** This is also not used to represent a communication protocol, but rather to tell the browser to execute the rest of the URL line as JavaScript code. This can be used to create a link that runs some code that creates the target page on the fly – without sending any data back to the server – when the link is clicked. (See Chapter 9 for more information about scripting).

There are several other schemes defined, and others are likely to be added over time. However, the vast majority of URLs used in web pages are covered by the examples above. Details of specific schemes are given in the **RFC** (**Request for Comments**) documents published by the IETF. See the IEFT web site (http://www.ietf.org) for further details.

2. Credentials

Although rarely used, the specification of a user name and password in the form `username:password` is permitted in a URL. This was originally used for ftp:// URLs, but can also be used for password-protected http:// connections, in which case the supplied user name and password will be used to log the user in automatically, rather than bringing up the dialog box that would normally appear.

For instance, the URL below references a password-protected web page on a hypothetical server, and supplies the necessary user name and password – `exampleuser`, and `itsasecret`, respectively:

http://exampleuser:itsasecret@myserver.mydomain.com/securedpages/index.html

If the credentials are not given, the '@' sign is omitted from the URL.

3. Host

This identifies the server, and can be given either as a fully qualified domain name, such as www.wrox.com, or as an IP address such as 204.148.170.161. When a domain name is used, then the client will have to perform a DNS lookup in order to find the associated IP address. However, using host names in URLs is generally preferred as it is a more user friendly form, and the lookup step allows the client to be sure it has the most current IP address.

> *Note that although web servers' host names often start "www", there is no technical reason why they have to; that name is not significant to the protocol. Rather it is the "http://" designation itself at the start of the URL that tells the browser that it will be connecting to a web server. The use of "www" in the name is simply a convenient tradition for users and system administrators alike.*

4. Port

Referring back to the example URL that we are working through in this section, the next component that can be specified is the port number.

This is used with the host's IP address to identify which server to connect to. Frequently, a host will have several different server programs running on it – each listening on different IP port numbers.

If the port is not specified, the default one for the protocol is assumed. For http://, the default is port 80 – and for https:// it is 443.

For instance, to reference a file called `index.html` on a web server, running on port 8080, the following URL could be used:

http://myserver.mydomain.com:8080/index.html

If the port is not specified explicitly in the URL, the colon that is used to separate the port from the host is omitted.

5. File path

The file path begins with a slash, and consists of one or more directory names separated by slashes, and optionally having a file name on the end. For instance, a file path might be:

/mysite/books/htmlref/chapter3/index.html

6. Other Specifiers

These are scheme-specific additions that allow a URL to either target a resource more closely, or supply additional information such as search criteria.

In the case of http URLs, there are two common additions after the file name:

❑ `#<anchor name>` – a **fragment identifier**, specifying a particular subsection of the page to link to (see the section *Creating Hypertext Links*, below, for more information).

❑ `?<name=value>` – **path arguments**, used to pass "name=value" argument pairs in to CGI scripts and other server-side logic (see Chapter 6, "*Forms and HTML Controls*", for more information).

Absolute and Relative URLs

An **absolute URL** is one that includes all the elements necessary to uniquely identify a particular resource out of all the ones available on the Internet. In particular, it specifies the host and the protocol to be used to connect to it, plus the full path to the file in question.

This format can be used within a Web page, but is also suitable for use outside one – such as being typed manually into a Web browser to connect to a specific page on a specific server, or being used as a bookmark. See below for examples of absolute URLs.

A **relative URL** is only suitable for use inside a web page, since it does not specify the full location including server name and protocol, but rather just expresses the location of the required resource relative to the current page. The protocol, credentials, host, and port information are assumed to be the same as for the page containing the URLs.

Since relative URLs make no explicit reference to the host on which the pages reside, they allow collections of pages to be moved from one host to another – for instance when moving between testing and production servers – without having to change the links between the pages. Largely for this reason, relative URLs are almost always used within a site, with absolute URLs used for references between sites.

> **Browsers always use absolute URLs to communicate with web servers. Therefore, relative URLs are converted to the equivalent absolute URLs by the browser before the referenced resource is requested.**

Special Notation in Relative URLs

There are a number of abbreviations that can be used in relative URLs, which draw on the syntax used in Unix systems – which were both the servers and clients in the pioneering days of HTML.

In order to see how this works, let's consider an example of a hypothetical page located at this absolute URL:

http://www.mycompany.com/books/htmlref/chapter3/index.html

Files in the Same Directory

These can be referenced in a relative URL by just using the name of the file. For instance, from our example page, the relative URL "`authors.html`" would be equivalent to this absolute URL:

http://www.mycompany.com/books/htmlref/chapter3/authors.html

Files in a Subdirectory

These can be referenced by giving the path from the current directory. For instance, the relative URL "`examples/ex1.jpg`" would be equivalent to:

http://www.mycompany.com/books/htmlref/chapter3/examples/ex1.jpg

Files in a Parent Directory

These can be referenced using the notation "`../`" to indicate a parent directory. More than one can be used, if you need to go up more than one directory level. Once you have navigated up the tree, you can then add on additional subdirectories to start navigating down a different branch of the directory tree. For instance, in our example, the relative URL "`../../javaref/index.html`" would be equivalent to this absolute URL:

http://www.mycompany.com/books/javaref/index.html

Root-Relative URLs

Web servers typically have a "server root directory". This is the directory that contains the home page for that server, and all of the subdirectories and files that server can publish onto the Internet. In our example scenario, it would contain a directory called "books", which in turn would contain all of the other files in that part of our site.

It is important to recognize that the server root directory is usually not the root of the local filesystem. On a Windows NT server, for instance, the server root directory might be: d:\inetpub\mysite. If this were the case for our example site, then the index page for Chapter 3 would actually reside at this location on the hard drive:

```
d:\inetpub\mysite\books\htmlref\chapter3\index.html
```

There is a shortcut available to reference files in, or under, the server root – that is to start a relative URL with a slash character. When you do that, the path that you give is relative to the server root directory. For instance, the relative URL "/images/heading.gif" is equivalent to:

http://www.mycompany.com/images/heading.gif

The root directory itself is indicated by a single slash character.

> *Note that properly secured web servers should prevent the serving of files other than those intentionally made accessible under the server root directory, in order to avoid serving up configuration and password files to would-be hackers. In particular, the " . . / " notation should not be allowed to traverse up above the server root directory. Some early web servers allowed this to happen, but this was soon recognized as a security flaw, and the behavior was fixed.*

Default Files

Most web servers include a feature that allows them to provide a default file if the URL requested goes to the directory level, but does not specify a particular file within that directory. By convention, the file is named `index.html`, although the name can vary, depending on the server configuration.

For instance, this is how a web page can be returned to you when you specify just a protocol and host in your web browser. If you send a request for http://www.mycompany.com/ then the server will see this as a request for the server root directory "/", and so return the default page – for example, `index.html` – to the browser.

However, if you request a directory without a trailing slash, then the situation is a little more complex. In the first instance, the browser cannot tell that you are requesting a directory rather than a file – it is purely convention that dictates that file names have to have an extension of around two to four letters at the end. For instance, this URL is ambiguous:

http://www.mycompany.com/books/htmlref/chapter3

A browser will first request the URL as entered – asking for a file called `chapter3` in the /books/htmlref/ directory. Now, the server will realize that this is not a file, but a directory, and could return the default page in that directory. However, that would then break relative URL links within that page. Why? Because the browser would think it was displaying the file that it asked for – one called `chapter3`. Therefore, it would interpret a relative URL in the page it received, such as a link to `authors.html`, as being for a file in what it thinks is the current directory, in this case /books/htmlref/. Hence it would interpret that relative URL as pointing to

http://www.mycompany.com/books/htmlref/authors.html

Rather than what the author intended to reference, which was the `authors.html` file inside the `chapter3` subdirectory.

In order to avoid this, the standard behavior for a server when a directory is requested without a trailing slash on it is to return a redirection message, telling the browser to instead request the original URL, but this time with the trailing slash on it. This time, when the request is sent, the server can safely return the default `index.html` page, and the browser will be in no doubt that the content it receives is coming from within the `chapter3` subdirectory – thus ensuring that relative URLs continue to work.

You can see this happening; try typing the following incomplete URL into your web browser:

www.wrox.com

After the connection is made, the URL line in your browser will change to read:

http://www.wrox.com/

and the Wrox Press home page will be displayed. Several steps have happened here: first, your browser did a DNS lookup on the host name, to find its IP address, then it assumed the protocol was http://, and requested an empty file path from that server IP address.

The server interpreted this as a request for the root directory, but lacking the trailing slash. It therefore issued a redirect to the client, telling it to send the request again, with the trailing slash. The browser did this, updating the URL it displayed back to you, accordingly.

Finally, the server then saw this second request as a properly formed request for a directory, and so returned the default page to you.

As this example demonstrates, you should always include the trailing slash on URLs that only specify a directory: if you do not, you will put an unnecessary extra load on your servers, and slow down the response time for visitors to your site.

An Alternative Base for Relative URLs

As discussed above, the most usual case is for relative URL's to be expressed relative to the location of the current file. However, as discussed in Chapter 2, you can use the <base> element within the header of an HTML page to specify an alternative URL from which reference point relative URL's should be evaluated.

Two situations where this can be useful are as follows:

❑ When the HTML page does not have a URL of its own – for example, when it is embedded in an e-mail. In that case, relative URL's will not work without a defined <base> URL.

❑ When a page has been moved to a different server, but you still want the links within the page to point to the original location, not to the new server. In that case, the <base> URL can be set to be the old location of the file, causing the relative URLs to be interpreted relative to that.

Example URLs

To complete this overview of URLs, we give some examples of other types of URL that you might come across.

Standard Web Connections

As we have discussed above, the normal connection method for the Web is http. URLs using this protocol might look like these examples:

http://www.mycompany.com/index.html
http://www.mycompany.com:8080/index.html
http://server.mycompany.com/books/
http://fred:xyzzy@private.mycompany.com/

The first of these is a standard request for a web page. The second is similar, but specifies a non-standard port where the server is listening for connections. The third example points to the default page within the "/books/" subdirectory. The final one points to a password-protected home page on the server called private.mycompany.com, and includes the username and password to be used to log in.

Secure Connections

Secure connections use **Secure Sockets Layer (SSL)** to encrypt the data flowing between client and server. This is generally indicated in the browser with a message and a "lock" symbol in the status bar.

    https://www.mycompany.com/order.htm

This URL specifies the https:// protocol, which is used to make http connections using SSL. It will use port 443 – the default for such connections – since another port is not specified explicitly. The client and server will have to be running SSL-capable software, and the server will need to have a valid digital certificate attesting its identity in order for this connection to succeed.

Note that once the user has navigated to a secure site, the URL's within the page can be relative ones, and do not need to explicitly reference the https:// protocol: since the enclosing page uses that protocol, relative URL's will be assumed to use it as well. Indeed, in order to ensure the security of the page, browsers will typically display warning messages if the HTML page itself was served using SSL, but some of the content it references – such as images – are accessed using non-https:// URLs.

Server-side Scripts and Applications

These URLs specify pages that are not normal HTML files. They are generally scripts or applications that will be executed on the server, and which dynamically produce a page that is sent back to the browser.

    http://www.mycompany.com/scripts/processorder.pl
    http://www.mycompany.com/cgi-bin/weathermap.asp
    https://www.mycompany.com/cgi-bin/appserver.exe

The file extension normally indicates the type of file, such as .pl for a Perl script, .exe for an executable, and .asp for an Active Server Page file. Note that these can be used with http:// or https:// protocols.

Files for Downloading

If the server has the ability to provide a File Transfer Protocol service, the browser can download a file using this service by specifying the ftp:// protocol:

    ftp://ftp.mycompany.com/pub/interesting.zip

This causes the server's FTP service to send the file interesting.zip back to the client machine, where it is stored as a file on the local system.

As noted above, many sites use http:// instead for transferring files, in order to avoid running into problems caused by visitors' firewalls not allowing ftp:// connections.

    http://www.mycompany.com/pub/interesting.zip

In this case, the web server will be configured to recognize zip files, and report them to the browser as having a certain MIME type (application/zip, in this case). The MIME standard provides a mechanism by which clients and servers can agree on the type of certain files, and hence how they should be handled – for a more detailed discussion of MIME types, see Chapter 9, "*Embedding Objects*"). The server reports the type to the client, which then chooses how to handle the file. In this case, the browser will normally download the file to your hard drive, or open it with a suitable helper program, rather than trying to display the file's contents within the browser window.

Sending E-mail

You can provide a hypertext link in your pages that is used by the viewer to send e-mail. This depends on the browser having a suitable mail application installed, but generally works fine on most modern browsers:

```
mailto:feedback@wrox.com
```

Notice that there are no double "slashes" in the address this time, because it is not a protocol, just an instruction to the browser to open the e-mail application and insert the address after the colon into the To box.

Creating Hypertext Links

Now that we have explored how URLs are formed, and therefore how we can refer to the resources we want to link to, we can look at the mechanics of including links in HTML pages.

HTML links have a source and destination, known technically as **Anchors** – hence the use of the <a> tag to encode them.

Source Anchors – The href Attribute

A **source anchor** is the technical term for what people normally think of as a "link" on a page – that is, a piece of text or a graphic that when clicked causes a new page to be loaded. The active text of the link is included between the opening and closing <a> tags, and the target URL that the browser should load when the link is clicked is given using the href attribute.

For instance the following code creates a link, which causes the file chapter4.html to be loaded when the word "here" is clicked on. Note that this uses a relative URL – and so will load the destination file from the source web page's own directory.

```
...
To go to the next Chapter, click <a href="chapter4.html">here</a>.
...
```

When embedded in a suitable HTML code framework, the above line will be displayed like this:

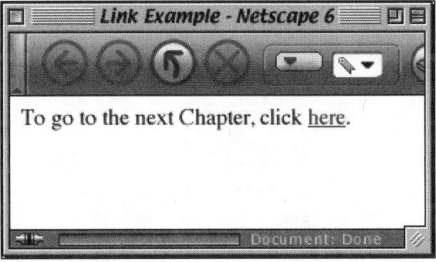

By default, when a linked page is loaded, the page is scrolled all the way to the top, so that the start of that page is in view in the browser. However, this can be controlled using another form of the <a> element – the destination anchor.

Destination Anchors – The name and id Attributes

A **destination anchor** is used to give a name to a section of a page so that source anchors can point directly at that section of the page by name. A destination anchor can be referenced from within the same document – such as "back to the top" link that goes back to the top of the current page – or from a separate document – as in the case of an index entry linking over to a specific part of a different page.

Destination anchors are set in two ways: either by using the name attribute of the <a> tag or, in HTML 4.01, by specifying the id attribute in any other tag. We will look at both mechanisms, starting with the original mechanism – the <a> tag's name attribute.

For instance, imagine that we had an HTML version of this chapter, and wanted to link directly from the Index page to this current section on "Destination Anchors". The HTML for this section might start like this:

```
...
<h2><a name="anchor1">Destination Anchors</a></h2>
...
```

Note that this use of the name attribute in an <a> element does not turn the "Destination Anchors" heading into a link – that is, a source anchor – but rather, gives the name "anchor1" to that section of the page, so that we can link straight to it.

In HTML 4.01, the alternative way to specify a destination is to use the id attribute of any HTML element in the page, and then link to that. For instance, the code snippet above could be re-written as follows:

```
...
<h2 id="anchor1">Destination Anchors</h2>
...
```

This has the same effect of designating a position within the document named "anchor1", which can serve as the destination of links.

Destination Anchors are used by using a special form of URL including a **fragment identifier**. In practice, what this means is that you end the URL – whether absolute or relative – with a hash character, #, followed by the name of the destination anchor.

For instance in the index.html file in the same directory as this chapter's page, we might have a link like this one:

```
...
Click <a href="chapter3.html#anchor1">here</a> to find out more about destination
anchors.
...
```

This link will cause the chapter3.html file to be loaded and then scroll directly to the destination anchor named "anchor1" that we defined in the previous code snippet. This is a great way to produce tables of contents or indexes that allow the user to jump directly into the middle of larger documents.

As well as linking to named destination anchors in another document, you can also use them within a page – this is a good way to provide a summary at the top of the page, with links to separate sections of content below. When both the link and destination anchor are in the same page, the filename can be omitted completely in the target URL, using the hash sign and the anchor name, as follows:

```
This page includes information about links and how to set named
<a href="#anchor1">Anchors</a> within your page.

...
<h2><a name="anchor1">Destination Anchors</a></h2>
...
```

This uses the same format for the destination link that we saw above, but links to it from the top of the page, simply by specifying href="#anchor1" within the link tag.

As you might expect, if you use both the name (or id) and href attributes within one <a> element, we get both behaviors – creating a link and also providing a named anchor at that point in the document for other source anchors to link to:

```
<a href="ch5.html" id="ch5summary">Chapter 5</a> covers the following topics:
```

Here we make the phrase "Chapter 5" be a link to the page ch5.html, and at the same time, we identify it as a destination anchor with the id of ch5summary.

Other Attributes

The <a> element supports several other attributes. As well as the href, name, and id attributes discussed above, and the common HTML 4.01 attributes class, title, style, dir, and lang described in Chapter 2, <a> also supports several more attributes:

accesskey	charset	coords	hreflang	rel
rev	shape	tabindex	target	type

We will now look at these in turn.

accesskey

This attribute specifies a keyboard character that can be pressed to activate the link. Some browsers will simply focus the link, allowing the user to press the return key to follow the link. Others will actually go ahead and follow the link automatically, and load the resource it references. The syntax is:

```
accesskey="key"
```

where key is the keyboard character, such as "J", which is pressed in conjunction with the *Alt* or *Control* key (depending on the client system). The value key is case-insensitive.

charset

This attribute defines the character encoding of the document that the hypertext link references; that is, the page that will be loaded. The syntax is:

```
charset="character_set"
```

where `character_set` is a character set identifier string, such as `"ISO-8859-1"` – the Latin set. See Appendix C for a list of supported character set codes.

coords

If the element is used with an image, this attribute defines an area within the image and the URL it will reference when clicked. The syntax is:

```
coords="coordinates_list"
```

where `coordinate_list` is a string of x and y coordinates that define the shape within the image.

❑ For `shape="rect"` (or `shape="rectangle"`, in the browsers that support it) the syntax is:
   `coords="left_x,top_y,right_x,bottom_y"`

❑ For `shape="circle"` the syntax is:
   `coords="center_x,center_y,radius"`

❑ For `shape="poly"` (or `shape="polygon"`, in the browsers that support it) the syntax is:
   `coords="x1,y1,x2,y2,...etc"`

   (that is, a series of coordinate pairs that define the shape. If the last coordinate pair is not the same as the first, then the browser will infer an extra coordinate pair that is the same as the first, in order to close the polygon.)

We'll look at using images with links later in this chapter.

hreflang

Specifies the language of the resource designated by `href` and can only be used when `href` is also defined. The syntax is:

```
hreflang="langcode"
```

where `langcode` is one of the language codes listed in Appendix C

rel

Specifies a relative forward relationship between this document and the resource specified in the `href` attribute. The syntax is:

```
rel="relationship"
```

where `relationship` is a string value defining how the two documents are connected. For more information on using relationships, refer to the `<link>` element in Chapter 2.

rev

Specifies the reverse relationship, in other words the opposite of `rel`. The syntax is:

```
rev="relationship"
```

where `relationship` describes the way that the two documents are related. For more information on using relationships, refer to the `<link>` element in Chapter 2.

shape

If the element is used with an image, this attribute defines the shape of an area that forms the link. The syntax is:

```
shape="shape"
```

where `shape` can take the values `rect`, `circle`, or `poly`. The default is `rect`.

In addition, you can use `shape="default"` to provide a default target when a location outside any of your mapped shapes is selected. Some browsers also accept `rectangle` and `polygon` as a value for `shape`, in place of the shorter standard forms.

tabindex

Indicates the position within the tabbing order of the page for this hypertext link. The syntax is:

```
tabindex="number"
```

where `number` is the relative position in the tabbing order from 1 to 32767. When the user presses the *Tab* key, the input focus normally moves through all the elements that can receive it in turn, in the order they are declared in the HTML source. By setting the `tabindex` value, you can change this order, such that the page elements with positive `tabindex` values are iterated through first, in ascending order of `tabindex`, followed by the elements without a tab index set (in the order they appear in the HTML source).

target

Indicates that the document referenced by the `<a>` element should be loaded into the specified window or frame. The syntax is:

```
target="window_name"
```

where `window_name` is the name of a browser window or existing frame. See Chapter 8 for a discussion of using frames, and the special reserved names `"_blank"`, `"_parent"`, `"_self"`, and `"_top"` that can be used with this attribute.

type

Specifies the MIME type for the link. The syntax is:

```
type="MIME-type"
```

where `MIME-type` is a standard content-type, such as `text/plain`. The HTML 4.01 standard includes this tag so that browsers have the option of treating the link differently if it points to a media type – such as audio – that the client cannot support.

Using Images as Links

Although text links are a vital part of almost any web site, most sites make some use of images as links to provide attractive buttons, and other navigational elements.

At the simplest level, an image can be used as a link just by placing the source anchor tags around the <img> element that is used to include a graphic in your page (See Chapter 5 for more on the <img> element):

```
...
<a href="chapter4.html">
    <img src="/images/ch4button.gif" border="0" alt="Go to Chapter 4"></a>
...
```

In the above example, the image located below the document root at "/images/ch4button.gif" will become a clickable link that will cause the browser to load the file "chapter4.html" when the link is clicked.

Image Borders

When an image is used within a source anchor tag, as in the above example, then by default browsers will show the image with a border around it, in the same color as is used to underline text links.

This is largely a legacy from early days of the web when VDU s offered limited resolutions and colors, page layouts were unsophisticated, and users were not as familiar with the graphical conventions of GUI furniture such as buttons. This outlining of images is generally undesirable for most modern web pages – far better to make the graphic look like a button, or find some other way to draw the users attention to it, rather than simply draw a blue box around it. Fortunately, this default behavior can be suppressed, by the simple expedient of setting the attribute border="0" on the image element.

Image Maps

Quite sophisticated graphical navigation bars and menus can be built up simply by juxtaposing several images on the page – perhaps by using a table to control the placement of the separate images – and then making each image a separate link as necessary.

However, for more complex layouts, containing abstract shapes, HTML offers an alternative mechanism – the **image map**. An image map allows several links to be associated with one image, with each link applying to a certain area of the picture. Each area is defined in terms of the pixel coordinates of the vertices of the shape, with the top left corner as the origin.

Fortunately, you no longer have to calculate the coordinates for an image map by hand – most graphics and web authoring tools can do it for you, and a search online will turn up any number of freeware or shareware tools.

Server-Side Image Maps

Originally, image maps were implemented using server-side CGI scripts, which processed the coordinates of the user's click on the image, and returned a redirect to the appropriate destination URL. An extension to the `<img>` element, the `ismap` attribute, was used to indicate to the browser that it should send the coordinates of the click back to the server, as part of the request for the image map handling CGI.

This required an additional connection to the server for each click on an image-mapped image, and also had other limitations, such as requiring an online connection to the server in order to process the image map.

Client-Side Image Maps

Due to the limitations of server-side image maps, a standard for handling image maps on the client-side soon emerged. By embedding all the necessary information in the page itself, the reliance on the availability of the server to interpret the user's choice is broken. The client is able to provide more meaningful feedback to the user – such as showing the destination URL or associated tooltip as the cursor hovers over an image.

The HTML 4.01 standard recommends only using client-side image map technology, but provides two ways in which it can be done. Using `<map>` elements, or the newer, more generic `<object>` element.

Using <map>

The older and more widely supported mechanism for client-side image maps is to use the `<map>` element, containing one or more `<area>` elements to define the coordinates of the hotspots within the image. For example:

```
...
<img src="Imagemap.gif" usemap="#Map" border="0">
<map name="Map">
    <area shape="circle" coords="99,28,27" href="home.html"
          alt="Return to the Home Page"/>
    <area shape="poly" coords="5,10,75,10,69,27,75,50,5,50"
          href="chapter2.html" alt="Go to Chapter 2"/>
        <area shape="poly" coords="122,10,191,10,191,50,122,50,127,31"
              href="chapter4.html" alt="Go to Chapter 4"/>
</map>
...
```

The only attribute of the `<map>` element itself is the name of the map. This map is then referred to by that name from the `usemap` attribute of the associated `<img>` element. In the example code above, the name of the map we are using is, imaginatively enough, "Map".

The <area> Element

Inside the `<map>` element, are the `<area>` elements defining the hotspots. In the example above, three areas are defined – two polygons and one circle. Note also the use of the `alt` attribute for each area. Most browsers render this as a pop-up tooltip message when the cursor hovers over the area. You can see the result of combining this code with a suitable graphic, below.

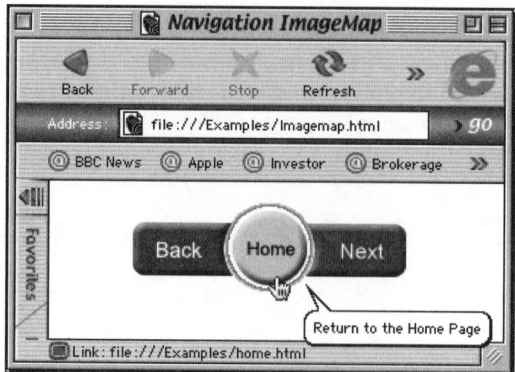

The <area> element supports many of the same attributes as the <a> element, described above, including accesskey, shape, coords, href, tabindex, and target. Additionally, it has the following attributes of its own:

    alt   nohref

Now let's look at both of these attributes:

❑ **alt** specifies the descriptive text to associate with the area. The syntax is:

    alt="text"

where text is the word or phrase to display.

❑ **nohref** indicates that this area is not an active hyperlink. The syntax is simply:

    nohref

When this area is clicked, the browser takes no action. It can be used to overlay inactive areas on top of other active ones (by defining it first in the list of areas), to provide finer control of the image map operation.

> **If the areas you define overlap, the browser searches sequentially through the list of <area> elements in the map and uses the first one listed.**

Using <object> Elements

HTML 4.01 promotes the use of the <object> element for embedding files within an HTML page – including graphics. This is discussed in more detail in Chapter 10.

The <object> element has its own syntax for creating image maps. The reason that <a> elements and <area> elements share so many attributes is that those elements were added to the anchor element to allow more consistent use of that element to represent links in image maps. Instead of a <map> element, we simply embed <a> elements within the <object> element that represents the image, and use the same attributes as before to define the hot spots.

Thus the previous example would be reworked to look like this:

```
...
<object data="Imagemap.gif" type="image/gif" usemap="#Map" border="0">
   <map name="Map">
      <a shape="circle" coords="99,28,27"
         href="home.html">Return to the Home Page</a>
      <a shape="poly" coords="5,10,75,10,69,27,75,50,5,50"
         href="chapter2.html">Go to Chapter 2</a>
      <a shape="poly" coords="122,10,191,10,191,50,122,50,127,31"
         href="chapter4.html">Go to Chapter 4</a>
   </map>
</object>
...
```

Note that this time there is no need to use the `alt` attributes to render help text – instead, the standard requires that the contents of the `<a>` elements be used. While this approach to using `<a>` elements is more consistent with the emerging standards, the support by the major browsers is still *very* poor. Therefore, it makes more sense to use the `<area>` element unless you have a tightly controlled audience for your site and can be sure that their browsers will support it.

More information about this approach to image maps can be found in Chapter 13 of the HTML 4.01 standard, at http://www.w3.org/TR/html401/struct/objects.html.

Useful Tips

When creating links in pages be sure to watch out for the following:

❏ Everything inside an `<a>` element gets rendered as a link: including any white space around text or images. Be sure there are no spaces or new lines between the end of the link text and the anchor tags themselves, or stray areas of untidy underlined space will be left.

❏ `<a>` tags should always have a closing `</a>` tag, and should contain some content, but not other nested `<a>` tags. While the HTML 4.01 standard allows for anchor tags with no contents (for example, `<a name="emptylink"></a>`), not all browsers support it properly, and may fail to find the named destination when linking to it.

❏ Destination anchors should be unique within a page. However, when linking to a named destination anchor, standards-compliant browsers should do a case-sensitive match on the name. To be safe, and avoid confusion, pick a naming convention for your anchors, and stick to it.

❏ When setting a destination anchor in a subsection of a long page of text, it can often be a good idea to set the destination in the white space area immediately above the area that the user will view. This can be more visually pleasing than having the text appear tight up against the top of the window. Given the above advice to always enclose some content inside the `<a>`...`</a>` tags; putting a non-breaking space (` `) often works well.

❏ Remember to provide descriptive `alt` attributes for any graphics that have links, in case the user's browser is unable to render the graphics, or does not want to wait for the page to load.

❏ Many sites, which use complex graphical navigation links on their pages, will offer simple textual version of the links elsewhere on the page. This makes the pages more accessible to people with browsers that cannot render the graphics, who have graphics turned off in their browser, or who are unclear how to use the graphical navigation system for whatever other reason. Although graphics are eye catching, frequent or heavy users of your site may prefer to use the faster loading, easier-to-assimilate textual links.

Summary

In the first part of this chapter we covered URL's in some detail, since they are crucial to understanding so many aspects of HTML markup. As we shall see in subsequent chapters, graphics, forms, and, in fact, almost all aspects of HTML and web site design are founded on a solid understanding of URLs.

We then went on to look at the use of the <a> element for creating text links, and setting destination anchors, and explored some of the other attributes of the element.

Finally we considered the various ways in which links can be attached to images. While we touched briefly on the older server-side image map techniques, we concentrated mostly on the use of the <map>, <area>, and <object> elements to create standard client-side image maps.

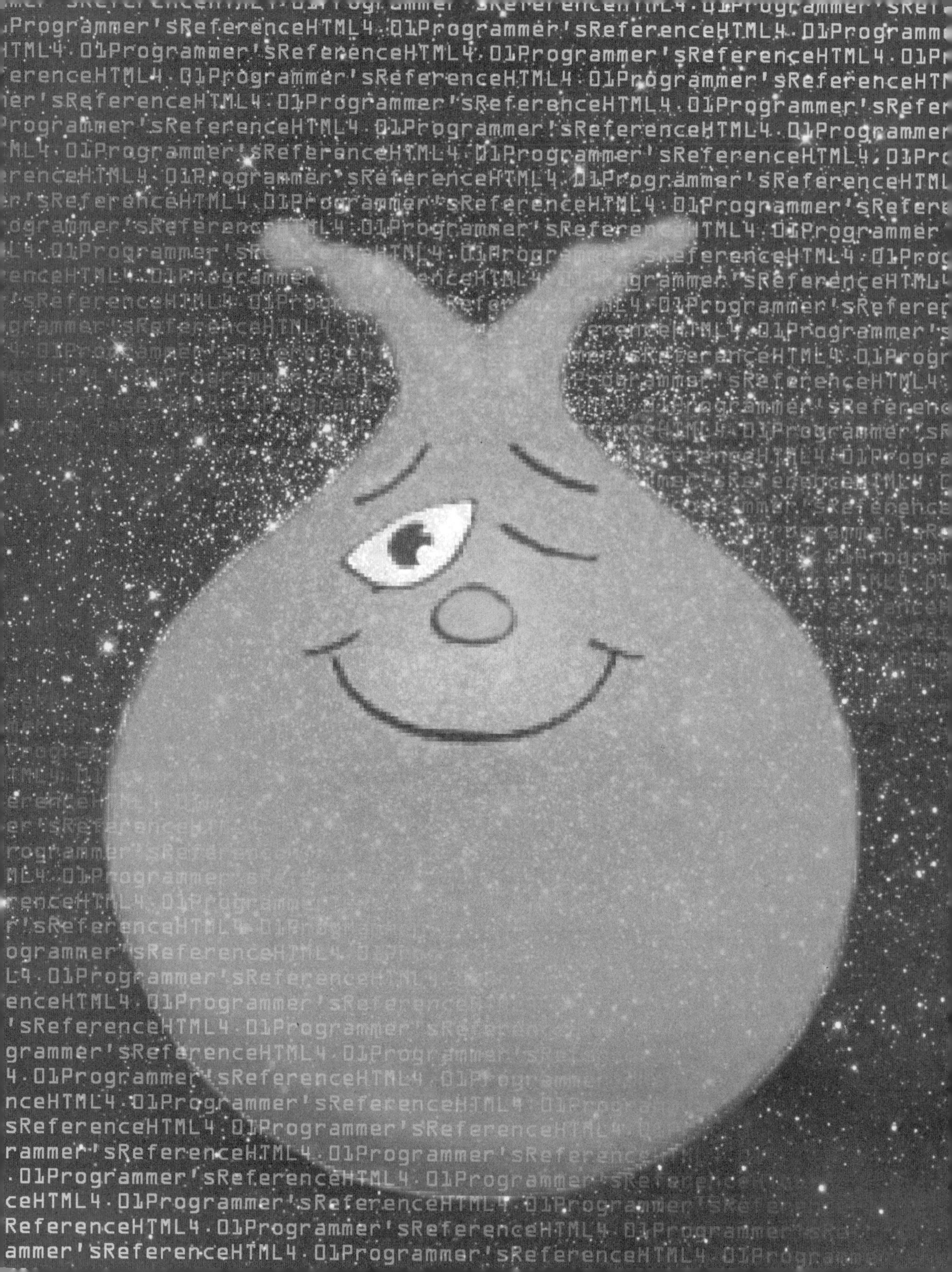
HTML4.01Programmer'sReference

5

Images

Although the earliest web browsers were text based, the ability to include and display "inline" images within the page soon became widely used to increase the visual appeal of web sites, and provide more user-friendly navigation tools. However, like all other HTML capabilities, images offer the opportunity for misuse, which can severely impair the user experience that visitors to your site enjoy.

In this chapter, we look at the three types of bitmap image formats that are widely used in HTML documents, and explore the mechanics of including images in your pages. With the basics out of the way, we then turn our attention to some of the issues and pitfalls connected with using (and abusing) web graphics, and show some examples. Finally, we recap the key points and offer some handy tips for getting the best out of graphics on your web pages.

Bitmapped and Vector Graphics

Broadly speaking, images can be divided into two major groups: **bitmapped** and **vector** graphics. The former type divides the entire picture into a regular grid of cells, known as **pixels** (a contraction of the phrase "picture elements") and then specifies the precise color of each cell across the entire image area. By contrast, vector images break the picture down into a logical collection of components such as lines and filled shapes, and store the image in terms of the coordinates and colors of these geometric figures that can be used to recreate the scene.

Bitmaps are typically used for photographs, scans, and computer rendered scenes – all of which are likely to feature subtle graduations and nuances of color and shade. On the other hand, vector graphics are often used for drawings and line art (especially illustrations drawn on a computer) and typically feature high-contrast areas of flat color.

Since vector graphics are a logical arrangement of geometric shapes, they can be scaled to a wide range of sizes without reducing image quality, since all that is required is to scale up the coordinates, and redraw the lines and shapes at the larger size. They are also well suited to use in animation, since a wide range of effects can be achieved efficiently by simply scaling or moving the individual components within the scene.

By contrast, bitmap images scale less well, since at larger sizes the individual pixels become noticeable, creating a blurred or blocky effect. Bitmaps also tend to be larger files, since they store tens or hundreds of thousands of color values per square inch, rather than just the coordinates of the edges of the component shapes. However, it is precisely because they store so much additional data that bitmaps are so well suited for capturing the subtle shades of high quality photographic images.

For a long time, the web was largely the preserve of bitmap file formats – and indeed, that is what we will concentrate on in this chapter. However, there are a couple of vector image formats, which we will mention in passing.

Vector Image Formats

Precisely because vector formats are so good for illustrations and animations, many different proprietary vector formats and their associated viewer plug-ins were developed during the second half of the 1990's.

However, the *de facto* standard for vector images has now emerged as Macromedia's **Flash** format. This is a powerful format, which incorporates scripting capabilities that allow it to be used for everything from simple logos and animations up to extended cartoons and complex interactive user interfaces – all while retaining the benefits of cross-platform deployment and relatively small file sizes. Although Flash requires a browser plug-in in order to view files, it is widely and freely available.

By contrast, an emerging standard is the **Scalable Vector Graphics (SVG)** format. First released as a draft in 1999, and with the backing of numerous major industry players and the W3C, SVG is well placed to emerge as a powerful new open standards tool for vector graphics and animations online. SVG is an XML-based language designed to represent two dimensional vector graphics. It allows for animation and user interactivity, and because it integrates into the document object model used by XML and related technologies such as HTML, it allows for the elements within the image to be controlled by scripts within the web page. Numerous SVG viewing and editing tools are already available, even before SVG becomes a formal standard.

Because they are later additions to the web repertoire, there are no specific HTML elements for vector-based images. Instead, they are included in a web page using the <object> element. See Chapter 10 for further details of this.

HTML does, on the other hand, have a specific element for use with bitmap image file formats – the <img> element, which we will look at in greater detail later in this chapter. Because standards for vector formats are relatively new, a wide range of capabilities and facilities have been developed around using bitmap images within web pages, and it is these that the remainder of this chapter will explore.

Bitmap Image Files and Formats

While browsers typically support a range of bitmap graphics formats, some generic and others platform-specific, there are to all intents and purposes just three universally supported formats, which are used for virtually all bitmaps on web pages. These are known by their acronyms: GIF, JPEG, and PNG. Pretty much all graphics programs can save images to these formats – especially GIF and JPEG, which have been available longer than the newcomer, PNG, which only dates from the mid-1990's.

Early web designers had to make do with a hodge-podge of commercial and shareware tools for creating, optimizing, and saving good quality, compact graphics for use on the Web, but these days there are lots of good quality integrated tools available, which not only help you design great looking static images, animations, and interactive "rollover" images, but also build the necessary HTML and associated scripts for you.

The Importance of File Size

Throughout this chapter, we will be concerning ourselves almost above all else with the size of the image files that we will be using. The reason for this is simple: despite the gradual spread of high throughput "broadband" connections at home and work, bandwidth is still physically limited and/or expensive for most Internet users. When many users' connections are restricted to 56k bits per second or less, poorly designed web pages can take an inordinately long time to download – and embedded graphics are the single biggest culprit for this.

Bear in mind that while a closely-typed page of text can pack a lot of information into about 3k bytes of ASCII character, a single badly-compressed half-inch square graphic can take up just as much file space, and hence download time, while conveying little or no additional information to the reader. In fact, on most web pages, 90% or more of the total download time is spent retrieving images, which may look pretty, but probably offer very little useful information to the user.

As web designers, there is one question that we should always be asking when adding a graphic to a web page: "Is this image really worth the download time to the user?". Often, we may decide that the answer is, realistically, no. In that case we have two choices – either replace the image with textual alternatives, or find ways to make the file as small as possible without compromising the quality so much that it becomes a waste of bandwidth, no matter how small the file. Often, it is a delicate balancing act!

The GIF Image Format

GIF, short for **Graphics Interchange Format**, is arguably the most established file format on the Web, aside from HTML itself. Pronounced either "gif" or "jif", depending on personal preference, the format has been around since 1987 when CompuServe introduced it for use with their proprietary dial-up service.

The format was revised in 1989 to add some extra features, most notably support for simple animations, and the ability to designate parts of the image as transparent. As the Web took off in the 1990's, GIF was quickly adopted as the *de facto* standard for (bitmapped) web graphics.

The GIF format offers a number of technical features that make it well suited to use online, where, as we noted above, small file sizes are still an important design goal.

Variable Palette Size

The first thing to note about GIF is that it is an "indexed color" format – meaning that it allows each image to pick its own selection of up to 256 colors from a full range of over 16 million. Rather than storing the full color information for each pixel, the file includes a color lookup table, and the pixels within the image specify their color by referencing the detailed entries in that table.

The number of bits-per-pixel – from 1 to 8 – is known as the color depth of the image. For instance, an "8-bit GIF" contains 2^8=256 colors, while a "4-bit GIF" contains 16 colors, but only uses half as much storage for each pixel. In fact, all things being equal, a 4-bit rendition of an image will take less than half the storage of an 8-bit one, as the color lookup table will also be shorter, containing just one-sixteenth as many entries.

It is important to note that while the image overall is limited to 256 colors, each of those colors can be taken from a full 24-bit palette. This limited number of colors certainly means that GIF is not well suited to storing photographic images, but JPEG is far better for that anyway (see below). For non-photographic images, such as line art, interface buttons, logos and other pictures containing large areas of flat color, GIF works well, and can produce relatively compact files.

Even with a highly restricted number of bits per pixel, quite subtle effects can still be created using dithering techniques, that is, interweaving pixels of two or more different colors, to create the visual effect of a third color. Typically, most graphics programs will perform the dithering for you automatically when saving a full-color image as a GIF file. As noted below however, dithering can affect the compressibility of the image, and so make the final file larger, as well as reducing the quality compared to a non-dithered rendition.

Transparency

A major advantage of GIF files is that they allow you to specify one color to represent a transparent background. Wherever that color is found in the image, the browser allows the background of the page it is placed on to show through.

This can be used to present graphics that are not regular rectangles, even though the actual image files themselves are just that – straight-sided rectangles. Alternative shapes – from simple rounded-corner buttons up to intricate cutouts – can be simulated within GIF images by specifying a transparent color. This allows the background color or image to bleed in from the edge of the rectangle right up to the edge of the foreground image.

There is one major caveat when using transparent GIFs, however: it is not true "alpha-channel transparency". This means that there are no "degrees of transparency" to give subtle smoothed edge effects. Each pixel is fully opaque, unless it is the designated transparent color, in which case it is fully transparent. There is nothing in-between. This requires careful planning ahead when using transparent GIFs over colored backgrounds – see the "*Useful Tips*" section below, for a further discussion of this.

Loss-less Compression

GIF files are compressed, using a run-length-encoding compression technique known as LZW (named after Lempel, Ziv, and Welch – the three people who developed it). In essence, this compresses the files by scanning the rows of the image, looking for sequences of identically colored pixels, and replacing them with a code which effectively says "insert X pixels of color Y, right here".

The first thing to note about this type of compression is that it is "lossless" – that is, no data is discarded – the reconstructed image is identical in every respect to the original, and thus there is no loss of quality.

On the other hand, based on the description above, you may notice a weakness in GIF's approach to compression. It relies on finding sequences of identical adjacent pixels, and there are certain obvious cases where this is unlikely to happen, so the compression will be relatively poor.

The first weakness is experienced when dealing with photographic-quality images. Precisely what gives those images their high quality and realistic appearance is that there are very subtle shadings and graduations of color within the image. Consequently, adjacent pixels are generally unlikely to have exactly the same color. The colors may be so close in hue as to be indistinguishable to the human eye, but if the color values are not exactly the same, then the GIF format will not be able to compress them. Indeed, since there has to be a slight overhead introduced into the file in order to support the compression coding, a GIF file that is poorly suited to compression might actually end up larger than before compression.

The second case where GIF can prove inadequate is where the palette has been reduced significantly – perhaps down to just 16 or 8 colors, and dithering has been used to improve the visual quality by mixing together adjacent pixels of color to give the impression of a greater number of colors. Even though there are very few colors being used, the intermingling of color values across the image again tends to reduce the runs of any one single color, and so once again the compression ratio is reduced, possibly outweighing the benefits of cutting the number of bits per pixel in choosing a smaller palette.

Interlacing for Faster Viewing

A further advantage of GIF for use over slow dial-up connections is that it supports **interlacing**, a very useful feature that was not originally provided by image processing software or web browsers. Interlacing means storing the lines in the image out of sequence, so that every eighth row is stored (and hence downloaded) first, before filling in the intervening rows. This means that a rough view of the image is downloaded quickly and then the detail fills in as the download proceeds.

The practical benefit of this depends on how the image in question is being used, and how familiar the user is with the content. Small detailed images and text may not be easily recognizable until the download is almost complete, but larger, familiar images – such as a large-scale map or a logo – may be very quickly comprehended when interlaced. This rather usefully acts as a kind of "Work in Progress" measure, and in addition, allows the user to click the appropriate link and navigate onwards through your site without waiting for the image download to complete, if wished.

Animation

Another benefit of GIF images that web designers were quick to adopt was the ability to produce simple animations, by including multiple frames within one GIF file. The compression used for these images is reasonably efficient, with only changed blocks of pixels within each frame needing to be stored, along with details of precisely where to overlay them over the previous frame. The designer can also specify how many frames per second to show, and how often to repeat the animation – just showing the sequence once, looping through it indefinitely, or repeating some finite number of iterations in between those extremes.

Animations can certainly be used to good effect to attract visitors' attention to an important part of your site. However, they need to be used with caution, as they can easily become distracting, or very large in size, slowing down the download time – something we were trying to avoid in the first place!

What is GIF Good For?

As outlined above, GIF is the workhorse of web graphics. It is well suited for computer-generated graphics and line art, containing a limited number of colors in flat areas of single shades. Navigation buttons, logos, and typography all are strong candidates for using GIF files. It is also the natural choice for simple animations and where transparency or non-rectangular edges are required.

However, GIF is less well suited to rendering highly colored, naturally textured scenes such as photographs, paintings, or other natural media artwork. For those, JPEG is an ideal candidate, as we shall see below.

The JPEG Image Format

JPEG is pronounced "jay-peg", and takes its name from the **Joint Photographic Experts Group** – a committee established by the ISO and ITU-T standards bodies to develop a standard for storing and compressing **continuous-tone images** – such as photographs – that contain a wide range of subtly graduated colors.

In fact, the title of this section, and the common use of the term "JPEG file", is something of a misnomer. Technically, the term "JPEG" as such refers only to the algorithm used to compress and recreate the image. The actual file format used to store that image on disk is technically known as "JFIF" – the **JPEG File Interchange Format**.

Lossy Compression

JPEG does an excellent job of compressing full color photographic images, reducing the file size by as much as 99% with little or no discernable loss of quality in the final image. It is able to achieve such high rates of compression because it is tuned to the workings of the human vision system, and actively discards some of the data that people would not normally perceive – such as minute changes in color. The outcome of this however is that the final image is not identical to the original one before it was compressed: some data has been irretrievably lost: the technique is said to be "lossy". Compare this to the lossless compression that GIF uses.

A significant advantage of JPEG is that it allows the person encoding the file to specify how much compression to use, depending on their requirements. This is typically expressed in terms of the final image quality. A "high" quality setting might reduce an image to 20% or less of its original size, and generate an image that is to all intents and purposes indistinguishable from the original. A lower quality setting will create even smaller files – achieving compression ratios exceeding 100-to-1 – but at the expense of introducing discernable errors in the image. Known as "artifacts", these typically take the form of ghosting or banding of colors around high contrast areas of the image.

The precise level of compression that can be achieved at any given quality setting, and just how good the resulting image will look, depends on each individual image – some degree of trial and error is required to find the optimal settings for each image and circumstance.

Comparison to GIF

The source materials that JPEG and GIF were designed to work on are really quite different. There is normally not much overlap between the two formats, so you should not normally find yourself faced with a choice as to which format to use; one or the other will usually be a natural choice, for reasons of image quality or file size.

Nonetheless, it is useful to note that JPEG implementations were expanded in the mid-1990's to support interlacing (see the "*Interlacing for Faster Viewing*" section above, for more on this), with the "Progressive" JPEG. This format allows an initial "blocky" view of the image to download first, with greater detail filling in as the rest of the image is retrieved.

However, JPEG does not support transparency or animation, so if you need those capabilities, you will need to use GIF, or one of the vector formats discussed above (for example, Flash or SVG).

Limitations of JPEG

JPEG is designed for a very specific purpose: compressing continuous-tone "photo-realistic" images. It is not well suited to the sort of limited-palette illustrations that GIF is typically used for. Those images tend to have high-contrast hard edges, with crucial fine detail – such as the shape of lettering. Only at the very highest quality settings will JPEG be able to capture the necessary detail in these sorts of images, and then typically the resulting file size will be much larger than when the same image is rendered as a GIF.

The PNG Format

The **Portable Network Graphics** (**PNG**) format was developed in the second half of the 1990's in response to a number of intellectual property and technical issues that were identified with the GIF format, the most significant of these relating to the LZW compression scheme used in GIF files. It emerged that the said scheme was covered by a patent owned by Unisys, and that developers of software for creating or viewing GIF images are required to license the technology in order to use it. This offended the sensibilities of the fledgling Internet community, with its emphasis on free access and open standards, and the search began to find a replacement file format that was unencumbered by such restrictions.

> *The users of LZW-based software – including web designers on the one hand, and web surfers on the other – are not required to pay license fees: just the developers of the tool they use. Nonetheless, the licensing requirement was an issue for many small, independent developers such as shareware authors.*

PNG, pronounced "ping", was specifically designed to fit this need. At the same time, the authors introduced some new capabilities intended to address the perceived technical shortcomings of the GIF standard. We will now look at these new capabilities.

Improved Progressive Display

The first of these technical improvements was that GIF's line-by-line interlacing mechanism was replaced with a two-dimensional sampling of pixels that enabled the browser to begin displaying a rough image when just $1/64^{th}$ of the file had been downloaded – 8 times less data than GIF requires.

Support for True-Color Images

Secondly, PNG was expanded to handle not just the indexed-color model used by GIF, but also to provide lossless data compression for true color images with unrestricted palette sizes.

True Alpha Channel

PNG adds the ability to include a full pixel-by-pixel transparency map – commonly known as an alpha channel – allowing each pixel to have an associated level of transparency. This provides significant improvements over GIF, where there are only two levels of transparency: totally opaque, or totally transparent.

Gamma Correction

The reality of all monitors, printers, and other graphics-handling devices, is that color and brightness levels are not linear. In other words a 50% shade of gray, midway between black and white, *should* give off exactly half as much light as a solid white image would. In practice, however, this is not the case and the precise output levels for different color shades vary from device to device. Thus, all displays and printers have an associated "gamma" factor, which indicates how far their color handling differs from the theoretical norm.

Because different monitors can differ significantly in their gamma factors, shading and colors in images can look very different between systems. This is especially the case between MacOS and Windows systems, which are standardized at totally different gamma levels.

In order to achieve some sort of consistency between differing systems, there needs to be some sort of **gamma correction** process. This adjusts the colors within the image such that when the output gamma of the system is taken into account, the displayed image is as close as possible to the image as seen by the original creator.

PNG allows gamma profile information be included in the image file, so that the viewing software can take into account the gamma of the original creator's system when making the adjustment.

Improved Compression Ratios

The final benefit that PNG offers lies in its redesigned image filtering and compression algorithm. Depending on the particular quality of the image, a PNG file tends to compress better than the GIF equivalent.

Using PNG in Your Web Pages

Early browsers pre-dated PNG, but the standard was quickly phased into versions 3 and 4 of the major browsers, not least because of the legal and licensing advantages that it offered. Equally, the technical advantages that it offers make it a superior choice compared to GIF for many purposes. However, support for some of the more advanced features in the PNG format, including true alpha channel transparency, is still patchy, even in versions 4 and 5 of the major browsers.

Additionally, the original concerns about the licensing aspects of GIF really failed to capture the attention of web designers and users as the technology gained wider acceptance, and GIF remains the *de facto* standard for non-photographic bitmap images online.

Embedding Images

Now that we understand a little more about the types of image files we will be using on our pages, we need to look at the mechanics of adding images to HTML documents. There are two alternatives: the traditional use of the `<img>` tag, and the newer HTML 4.01 `<object>` element. We will look at these in turn, below.

The `<img>` Element

The `<img>` element supports a number of attributes, which we will discuss below:

```
src       alt       align     border    height    width
hspace    vspace    ismap     usemap    longdesc  name
```

plus the HTML 4.01 universal attributes `id`, `class`, `style`, `dir`, `lang`, and `title`, and the common events (see Chapter 2 for further details of these, and Chapter 9 for more on using the events). These events can be used to trigger script code to provide interactive animations – such as highlighting a graphical button when the mouse pointer hovers over it, using such attributes as `onmouseover`, and `onclick`.

src

This required attribute specifies the URL of the image file to include. The syntax is:

```
src="url"
```

where `url` is the absolute or relative path of the image file. See Chapter 4, "*Links*", for more information about URLs.

alt

This attribute specifies a text alternative for the image if the browser or application cannot display images. The syntax is:

```
alt="text"
```

where `text` is a word or phrase relating to the image specified by the `src` attribute. The importance of this attribute cannot be over-emphasized, and the HTML 4.01 specification makes it a required attribute.

Remember that people may have graphics turned off, or might be using a non-visual browser that cannot display them – such as a text-to-speech system. Many browsers will also display the `alt` text while waiting for the image to download, when printing, or as a tooltip when the cursor hovers over an image. The `alt` text should be a meaningful description of the graphic – not just the filename, or some other description that has no meaning to the user. For graphical buttons, it is often helpful to include the same legend that appears on the button image in `alt` text, so the user can still use the buttons to navigate, even if the graphic itself does not load.

align

Use this attribute to align the image within the page and the surrounding elements. The syntax is:

```
align="alignment"
```

where `alignment` is one of the following:

- ❏ `top` – the top of the image is aligned with the top of the current line of text.
- ❏ `middle` – the center of the object is aligned with the current text baseline.
- ❏ `bottom` – the bottom of the image is aligned with the baseline of the current line of text: this is the default.
- ❏ `left` – the image is aligned along the left edge of the containing window or element, and text and other elements flow around it to the right.
- ❏ `right` – the image is aligned along the right edge of the browser window or element, and text and other elements flow around it to the left.

There are several other values, which are not part of the standard, but which most browsers support, albeit with inconsistent results:

- ❏ `absbottom` – the image is aligned so that the bottom is in line with the absolute bottom of the surrounding text – that is, the bottom of the largest character descender.
- ❏ `texttop` – the image is aligned so that the top is in line with the absolute top of the surrounding text, including the height of the largest character ascender.
- ❏ `absmiddle` – the image is aligned with the middle of the image at the midpoint between the `absbottom` and `texttop` of the surrounding text.
- ❏ `baseline` – the bottom of the image is aligned with the baseline of the surrounding text.

The interpretation of all of these values varies between browsers, and between versions of the browsers. Furthermore, earlier versions of Netscape tended to only consider text that preceded the image on the line, when interpreting the alignment codes.

As of HTML 4.01, the `align` attribute is deprecated: you should instead use cascading style sheets for future compatibility. See Chapters 11 to 13 for more information on using style sheets for positioning.

border

This specifies the width of the border around the image. The syntax is:

```
border="n"
```

where n is a numerical value in pixels. The value 0 turns the border off. The default for images is usually 0, unless they are used as a hyperlink – see Chapter 3, "*Links*", for details. Note that this attribute is deprecated in HTML 4.0, and you should use style sheets instead. See Chapter 15 for more information on deprecated attributes.

height and width

Specifies the height and width that the image is to be displayed at. The syntax is:

```
width="x"
height="y"
```

where x and y are the width and height in pixels, or as a percentage of the available space in the containing element (in which case, the value should be denoted with a % sign after the number).

You can use the width and height attributes to specify the size of box that you want the image to fit into, and the browser will scale the image to suit. Also, using width and height with the <img> element helps the page to be laid out more quickly, because the browser can paginate the document using the declared dimensions of the image without having to wait to load the image in order find out its size.

> Note that although using **width** and **height** will scale the image size to the required dimensions, the image file size remains the same: the scaled image will still take the same amount of time to load as the unscaled version. Only after it is loaded is the image scaled in memory.

hspace and vspace

These attributes are used to control the white space around an image. The syntax is:

```
hspace="x"
vspace="y"
```

where x and y are numerical values in pixels. They specify the amount of white space to allow around the image – horizontally and vertically, respectively.

ismap and usemap

ismap and usemap are used with image maps, to indicate that the image can be clicked on to initiate a link to another page. ismap is used for the older server-side image mapping technique, and usemap indicates the name of a client-side image map. See Chapter 4, "Links", for details.

longdesc

This attribute was introduced in HTML 4.0 and allows the addition of a link to another document that describes the image in more detail. The syntax is longdesc="url" where url is the address of the other document or resource. This is intended for providing extra information about an image that the user can see if they wish, without cluttering up the page. It is also designed for use in non-visual applications. At the time of writing, the major browsers, such as Netscape 6, still do not support it.

name

This attribute is used to specify an identifier for the image, which can be used to reference it from within script code. The syntax is name="item_name".

Extensions to the <img> Element

There are a some non-standard attributes, which major families of browsers support. Both Internet Explorer (from version 4) and Netscape (all versions) support the lowsrc attribute, which can be used to specify the URL of a lower-resolution version of the image which can be loaded first to give the user a preview image while the full image downloads. This has largely been superceded by the interlacing capabilities of all the major graphics formats, and actually has the drawback of increasing the total time to download the page, since the initial preview version is a separate download in addition to the main image.

A few years ago, the lowsrc attribute was occasionally used for special effects, with two different images – one replacing the other as the page loaded. However, scripting and Dynamic HTML provide far better ways to achieve this, and as broadband Internet connections become more common, the images will tend to download so quickly that the lowsrc version might scarcely be seen before it is replaced.

Internet Explorer also adds other non-standard attributes such as dynsrc and datasrc for embedding movies and binding to client-side data caches, respectively. These are not supported by other browsers however, and should be used with caution – such as in a controlled intranet environment.

HTML 4.01 Alternatives

As discussed in more detail in Chapter 10, "Embedding Objects", HTML 4.01 supports the use of a generic <object> element to embed all types of media, including graphics. Version 5 and especially version 6 of the major browsers are now starting to support this newer way of specifying images, although implementation varies across platforms.

For instance, this is the traditional way to include an image (in this case my cat, Custard):

```
<img src="cat200.jpg" width="200" height="209" alt="Custard Cat">
```

And this is the alternative way, using the newer syntax:

```
<object data="cat200.jpg" type="image/jpeg" width="200" height="209">Custard
        Cat</object>
```

Here we specify the URL to the file using the data attribute, and also specify the MIME type of the file – a JPEG image in this case – for completeness. Also, note that in place of the alt attribute in the <img> element, we now specify the alternative description as the body of the <object> block. The HTML 4.01 standard specifies that the content of such a block should only be rendered if the object itself cannot be: exactly how an alt attribute works.

Unfortunately, given the current unpredictable implementation of the <object> element by virtually all browsers, it is probably safer to continue to use the <img> element to embed bitmap graphics.

Effective Image Techniques and Examples

There are a number of different ways we can use images to good effect within our web pages.

Background Images

The days of dull gray backgrounds of web pages have long gone, and we can add a lot of character to our pages by using small repeating images as a background texture within our pages or tables.

Adding a background texture is simple – we just need to be sure that the texture will tile seamlessly, and does not have any strong elements that will catch the eye on each repetition, forming a grid pattern – unless that is the effect that we are looking for, of course!

```
<html>
  <head>
    <title>Image Examples</title>
  </head>

  <body background="texture.png">

    <h2>Meet my Cat!</h2>

    <table border="1" cellspacing="10" background="moss.png">

      <tr>
        <td>

          <img src="cat200.jpg" width="200" height="209" alt="My Cat!">

        </td>
      </tr>
      <tr align="center">
        <td>
          <font size="4"><b>Custard Cat</b></font>
        </td>
      </tr>
    </table>
  </body>
</html>
```

In the example above, the first highlighted line sets a background texture for the page as a whole, the second line adds a different background for the table, and the third line includes the picture of the cat herself. The result is shown here:

Animations

Animations can be a very effective way to draw attention to key links or announcements on our site. There are no extra techniques to be learned either, as we can use the animation capabilities built in to the GIF format – we simply build the frames of the animation and set the parameters within the GIF file. Then, we simply include the GIF file within our code using an `<img>` or `<object>` tag. The client browser will recognize the file format, and begin to play back the animation.

At the same time, however, it is important to recognize that it is very easy to over use animations, and they can be counter productive. Large, rapidly moving, or jerky animations can very easily become annoying and distracting, making it hard to concentrate on other material on the page. Therefore, it may be better to avoid using animations in close proximity to one another, or to large blocks of text.

It is also important to recognize that animations unavoidably increase the file size to include all the separate frames, and the animation will not play back smoothly until all the frames are downloaded. If the animation is too large or complex, then the file size may be so big that users either do not wait for the page to finish loading, or else click through to the next page before they ever see the animation play.

Interactive Rollovers

Using a scripting language such as JavaScript, it is possible to build an event-driven animation system within our pages in order to respond to user actions such as rolling their mouse pointer over a button on the page. Not only do most users feel that this looks pretty slick, but it is also a good way to reinforce to users that the images within your page are clickable.

What we do is to load the default image in the normal way, and then attach a script to the image, which swaps the image for a second version when the browser detects that the mouse has moved over the image. This second version might display the button depressed, or lit up, or offer some other visual clue that the image is meant to be clicked. Similarly, when the mouse leaves the image, the initial image is put back again.

Inevitably, these techniques add to the total download time for the page, but a load-time script can be added to the page that goes ahead and downloads the alternative images behind the scenes, after the rest of the page has loaded. This means that the user can start to read and work with the page without waiting for the additional graphics to download. In addition, the images will most likely have been loaded by the time that the user actually gets around to interacting with the buttons, and hence the special effect will be ready to execute.

Such effects can be coded by hand, but most good web graphics and/or HTML layout tools can generate and embed the necessary code these days.

More details of the underlying scripting techniques can be found in Chapter 9, "*Scripting and Inherent Events*".

Slicing Large Images

A problem that sometimes arises in relation to the above technique is how to deal with large graphics – such as a complete one-piece menu bar with navigation buttons built in. Clearly we do not want to have to recreate and reload the entire graphic for each possible combination of rollover graphics – depressed buttons, lit up buttons, etc.

The workaround for this is to slice the image up into a number of smaller ones, and then reassemble them using an HTML table, with one graphic in each cell of the table. Then when we need to animate one particular part of the image, all we need to do is to change that one individual graphic.

Once again, page layout and graphic editing tools can be a big help in slicing the images up, and generating the necessary HTML tables to reassemble them: the precise measurements and nested tables can quickly get complicated!

This technique actually slightly increases the total amount of graphic data on the page, because of all the additional headers included in the separate graphics files. However, the user perception is of a faster load time, since thy can see lots of separate pieces arriving one by one, rather than waiting for the one large image to download.

An example of this approach can be found in Chapter 7's discussion of HTML Tables.

Transparent Shims

Perhaps one of the most controversial uses of images is the transparent shim, or "single-pixel GIF" technique – a way of gaining finer control over the layout of text, especially within tables, by using a totally transparent graphic as a placeholder.

How this works is that a small GIF is created (typically called "spacer.gif") – usually just 1 pixel, and it is set to be transparent. Then whenever we need an exact number of pixels of white space within our layout, we add an <img> tag for that image, specifying the height and width attributes to be whatever size we need. The browser retrieves the image, scales it to the precise size that we specify, and then displays it. Since it is transparent, all that the user sees is a precisely sized area of empty space.

There is no doubt that these shim graphics can occasionally be useful, especially when trying to create a demanding layout in such a way that it will display correctly on a range of browser versions.

However, they can also be the kiss of death for a web site. Depending on browser settings and behavior, the shim graphics may or may not be cached by the browser, and even if they are, the browser may still connect back to the server to check that the graphic is up-to-date. The net result can be that a significant extra load is placed on the servers, simply to dish out these single pixel graphics that the user doesn't even see. On high-traffic or limited-bandwidth sites, the extra connections can reduce the site's responsiveness and usability significantly.

It is important to remember that there are usually ways to achieve the same effects without resorting to inserting dummy files. Style sheet properties and DHTML can be used to get accurate positioning control for most elements in a recent browser, and even in older ones the desired effects can usually be obtained by working with nested table cells with size attributes set, and non-breaking spaces as the content.

Useful Tips

To get the best from your graphics, bear in mind the following hints that the author had to learn the hard way!

❑ When creating transparent GIFs, be sure to create the image with approximately the same background color that you will ultimately display the "cut-out" shape against. This is because the edge of your shape will be "anti-aliased", or smoothed, by filling in the edge of the shape with pixels midway between the foreground and background colors. The eye interprets these as a smooth edge to the shape.

However, because GIF can only code for the totally opaque pixels that get hidden altogether, these intermediary pixels will show up in the final image, and will be totally opaque. What is more, they will be the wrong color for any background other than the one originally used in the image.

Imagine that we have an image that is predominantly blue, and we create it on a white background. The edge pixels will be a light blue color – mid way between blue and white. Then we put it on our web page, and display it against a dark background. Now those edge pixels need to be a dark blue color – midway between the foreground and new background colors. But they're not, they're light blue, because that is the way they're saved in the file, and only the totally white background pixels turned transparent in the GIF file. So now our image has a jagged halo of light blue pixels all the way around it that make it look terrible against the dark background of the site.

The only cure is to create the image against the right background color to begin with, or to use a format such as PNG that supports true alpha channels, so that the edge pixels can also be partly transparent and let the background show through.

❑ Choosing the right format is crucial to making good use of graphics – that's why we looked at the different formats in relative detail above. The ultimate arbiter of what is the "right" format is the one that produces the smallest possible file size while giving an acceptable image quality. More generally, we will want to use JPEG on a medium-to-low quality setting for online photographs, and GIF, or perhaps PNG, for everything else.

❑ There is a tradeoff between quality and file size, and each case needs to be considered on its merits. As a rule of thumb, each page should be kept below a total size of 50kB to 70kB as an absolute maximum, including the HTML and all graphics. Most pages should be far smaller, if they are expected to have a lot of visitors on 56kb/s or 28kb/s modems. Try out different quality and size settings to see what works best for each graphic.

❑ Be ruthless about the standards you set for the graphics on your pages. Always ask yourself whether the image is of enough value to the user, in terms of information or entertainment to make it worth the time it takes them to download it. If not, you either need different image settings, a different graphic, or perhaps just a few lines of text instead!

❑ Interlacing is a good idea. Although it adds a little to the file size, it gives the user useful information more quickly during the download process. Progressive JPEG and PNG formats are especially good for this.

❑ The alt text attributes should always be given – the HTML standards require them, and they can enhance the user experience: not only for non-graphical browsers, but also to speed user comprehension as the page loads. Make the descriptions meaningful, but only use them where the graphic is significant to the user interface. If the graphic is merely padding – such as non-interactive areas within a larger sliced-up graphic, then it is acceptable to simply give an empty string for the alt text (that is, <img alt=" "...>). This produces less clutter on non-graphical browsers, and other access devices such as Braille or text-to-speech systems for users with disabilities.

❑ Get into the habit of always giving the `height` and `width` attributes on graphics; it speeds up the display of the pages significantly, since the browser can reserve space for graphic and then go on laying out the rest of the page while it waits for the graphic to load.

On the other hand, you should also always aim to display the images at their natural size. Scaling the images by setting these attributes to something other than the actual size of the image is not a good idea: the file size remains unaffected, so there is no benefit to the user in scaling the graphic down, and the image quality is likely to suffer when scaling the image – particularly by a small number of pixels. The image data needs to be redistributed across the new file size, and this will generally work better when done offline, using a dedicated image-processing package, and then re-saving the resulting image out at the new size, rather than relying on the browser to perform the conversion on the fly, using its own non-optimized code. Remember that users are taking the time to download the images – make sure they get the best possible return on that investment of time!

Summary

In this chapter we have considered several different types of images: both in terms of the underlying technology (bitmaps compared to vector graphics) and the particular file formats used to represent images – including Flash, SVG, GIF, JPEG, and PNG. We have paid special attention here to the bitmap file formats supported by the `<img>` element, and as we saw above, choosing the right format and quality settings is crucial to getting the optimal trade-off of image quality and file size, and so ensuring a good user experience.

Having considered the pros and cons of each format, we also turned our attention to the specifics of the `<img>` element, and also looked briefly at the less-widely supported <object> element, introduced by HTML 4.0.

Finally, we looked at a number of techniques and tips for getting the best out of online images, such as how to deal with background colors for transparent GIFs, and how best to use `height` and `width` attributes.

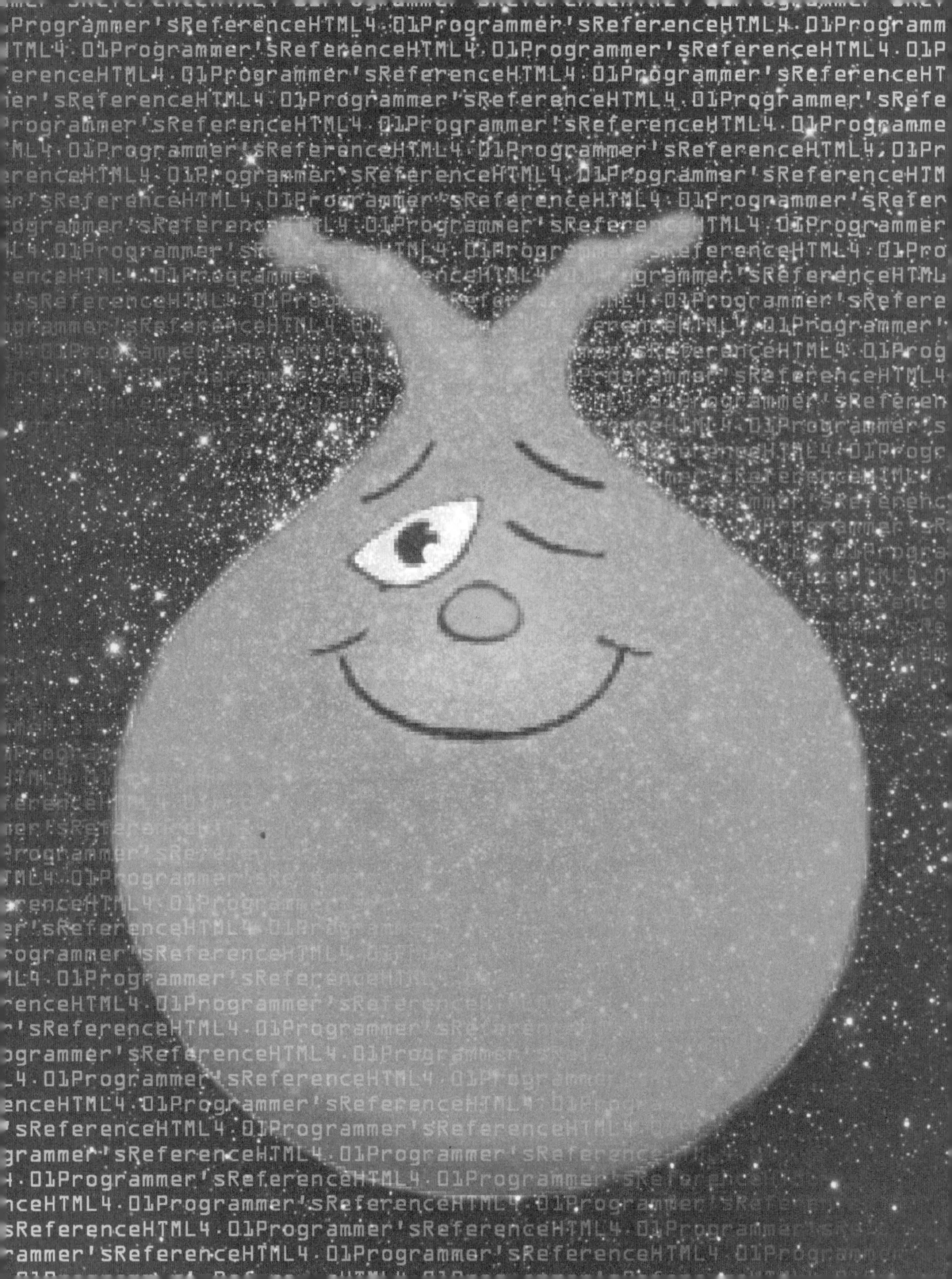
Programmer'sReferenceHTML4.01

6

Forms and HTML Controls

One of the key advantages of the Web over most other forms of media is the fact that it is truly interactive: allowing users to be presented with individually tailored content. Based on the information that the user enters into the site, and with the possible addition of a server-side data source such as a user account database, the server can build pages on the fly that offer a customized user experience.

Whether it's an online banking or brokerage site that shows the details of our own account, or an auction site that shows items we've recently bid on, or even just a weather site that remembers where we live and shows us the weather in our region, all are essentially doing the same thing: taking some information about us that we have entered into a form on their site, and then sending it to the server to be processed.

This processing typically takes the form of running a script or program on the web server itself (or on a dedicated application server) that validates the information we supplied, and either builds a page specifically for us, or chooses one from a pre-built list, and sends it back to our browser. Generally, this all happens so quickly that we don't even realize that any processing has taken place, and that we haven't in fact just gone to another static page that was just sitting on the server waiting to be surfed to!

The key to all of this functionality is the concept of the **HTML Form** – the mechanism by which a web page can gather responses to questions, and send them back to the web server for processing and storage.

The processing that occurs on the server side is relatively complex, and could be – and indeed *is* – the subject of many books in its own right. As such, we will only talk about that at a fairly high level. Instead, in this chapter, we will concentrate on the HTML elements that are used to present the forms themselves to the user, and assume that a suitable processing mechanism is already in place.

In fact, very often this will be the case: many web hosting services provide a range of standard server-side scripts pre-installed on their servers, which the sites they host can use – including feedback forms, simple surveys, guest books and shopping carts. If that is the case, we may be able make use of forms within our site, just by building the appropriate fields into the page, and sending the form information to those scripts.

For more complicated or custom applications, however, we will need to build our own server-side applications. The sections below on the client's and server's respective views of form submission and processing provide a stepping-off point for further exploration of this field, and include some references to other Wrox books that you might find useful.

How a Form Works

Before we dive into the details of forms, and look at some examples, it will be useful to consider the high-level aspects of how forms are used within a page. In fact, there are two ways in which they are used – although the first is by far the most common.

The Normal Client-Server Model

Forms are normally delimited using `<form>` and `</form>` tags to mark their beginning and end within the page. Between those tags, a form will usually contain normal HTML mark-up, used for formatting purposes, and at least one **form control** – the items such as text fields, checkboxes, and the like that are used to gather the information that we wish the user to supply.

Defaults may be supplied for the form elements, and they will be rendered initially with those values: however, the user will then typically be able to amend those values as they see fit, before the form is **submitted** to the server.

Submission is normally triggered by clicking on a submit button, but can also be triggered in two other ways. One is via a script action in the page (for example: when the user makes a choice from a menu item within the form – see Chapter 9 for details of scripting). Alternatively, using a convenience offered by many browsers, forms containing just one text field can be often be submitted by pressing the *Return* key within that field.

We discuss the mechanics of form submission in more detail below. However, it is important to recognize that once the browser has submitted the form, it is up to the server to process the information, and return the appropriate next page for the browser to display.

Client-Side Only Forms

There is one exception to the idea that forms should be contained in a `<form>` block. That is when the form elements are being used as part of a user interface that is supported by client-side script logic, and where the intent is not to forward the data captured by those elements to the server for processing at all.

For instance, we might have a fixed navigation menu within our page, which lists a number of subsections of the site, and links the user directly to that section when they make a choice. That can be done using a script embedded in the page, and triggered when the user makes a selection from the menu, as discussed above. However, instead of then sending the choice to the server, as we would in the standard model, we can instead process the choice entirely within the client-side script, and load the appropriate new page into the browser. Scripting is discussed further in Chapter 9.

> *In these cases, where the form data is not being sent back to the server, it is not strictly necessary to enclose the form components in a `<form>` block, and the HTML 4.01 standard requires that browsers should still render such components correctly. However, some browsers – including Netscape up to and including version 4.7 – do not adhere to this requirement, and will simply not display form controls outside of a `<form>` block. In view of this, even when the `<form>` element is not strictly necessary, it is a good idea to use one, and simply specify empty values for the attributes such as `method` and `action` discussed below, which are normally used to submit the form data to the server.*

Available Form Controls

Now let's turn our attention to the different data-capture items, known as **controls**, which can be used in a form. In order to do this, let's look at a simple example form that demonstrates them all:

```html
<html>
  <head>
    <title>Form Elements</title>
    <style type="text/css">
      <!-- .btn {  font-family: Arial, sans-serif; font-size: 10px}
      -->
    </style>
  </head>
  <body>
    <form action="/cgi-bin/test.pl" method="post">
      <table border="2" cellpadding="10" frame="box" rules="none">
        <tr>
          <td>Your Name</td>
          <td>
            <input type="text" size="30" name="yourname" />
          </td>
        </tr>
        <tr>
          <td>About you</td>
          <td>
            <textarea name="desc" cols="40" rows="5">
              Give a brief autobiography here...
            </textarea>
          </td>
        </tr>
        <tr>
          <td>Your sex</td>
          <td>
            <input type="radio" name="sex" value="f" checked /> Female
            <input type="radio" name="sex" value="m" /> Male
          </td>
        </tr>
        <tr>
          <td>OS's used</td>
          <td>
```

```html
            <input type=checkbox name="os" value="Win" /> Windows
            <input type=checkbox name="os" value="Mac" /> Mac OS
            <input type=checkbox name="os" value="Lin" /> Linux
          </td>
        </tr>
        <tr>
          <td>Knowledge of HTML</td>
          <td>
            <select name="knowhtml">
              <option value=""> Please select one...</option>
              <option value="0"> No knowledge</option>
              <option value="1"> Know the basics</option>
              <option value="2"> Fairly knowledgeable</option>
              <option value="3"> Very experienced</option>
              <option value="4"> HTML Guru</option>
            </select>
          </td>
        </tr>
        <tr>
          <td>Your photo (.gif file)</td>
          <td>
            <input type="file" name="photo" />
          </td>
        </tr>
        <tr>
          <td>Your password</td>
          <td>
            <input type="password" name="pass" size="10" maxlength="10" />
          </td>
        </tr>
        <tr align="center">
          <td colspan="2">
            <hr width="75%" align="center">
          </td>
        </tr>
        <tr align="center">
          <td colspan="2">
            <input type=submit name="s1" value="Submit Form" />  
            <input type=reset value="Reset Form" />
          </td>
        </tr>
        <tr align="center">
          <td colspan="2">
            <button type="submit" name="s1" value="prj" class="btn">
                  View related<br/>projects
            </button>
            <button type="submit" name="s1" value="wrox">
              <img src="wrox.gif" width="32" height="32" />
            </button>
          </td>
        </tr>
        <tr align="center">
          <td colspan="2">
            <input type=image name="navbar" src="Imagemap.gif" />
            <input type=hidden name="hiddenval" value="123" />
          </td>
        </tr>
      </table>
    </form>
  </body>
</html>
```

Internet Explorer 5.5 for Windows renders the form like this:

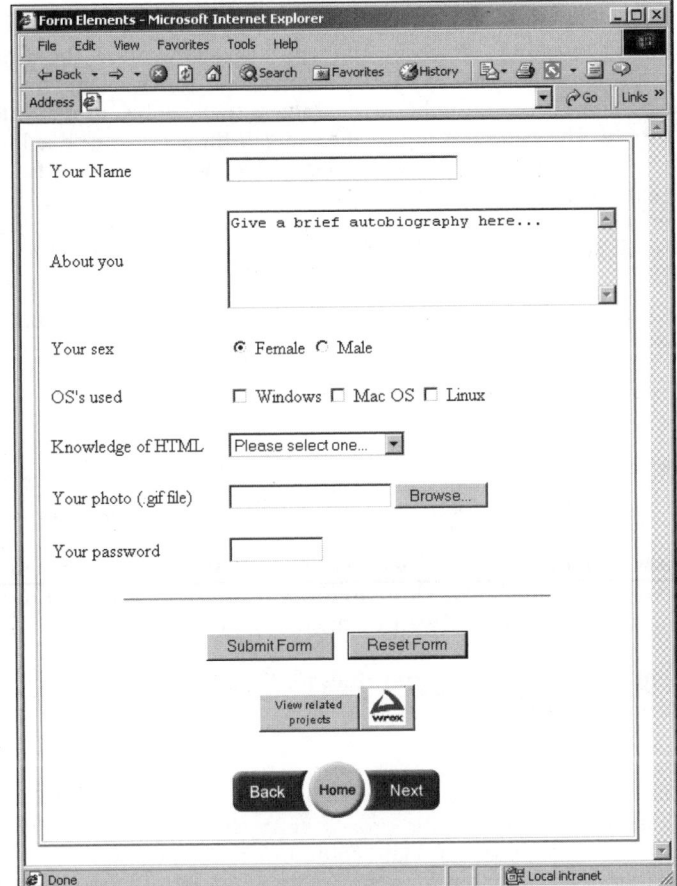

In the above code, the highlighted lines define the form and its controls. At this point, don't worry too much about the details of the elements and attributes – we will detail all of those later.

In the code above, we begin with the head definitions, including a stylesheet that we will use later, and then in the body of the page we have the <form> definition, wrapped around a <table> block that we use to lay out the form contents. The <form> element specifies an action attribute of "/cgi-bin/test.pl". This is the address of the server-side script that will handle the form data when it is submitted: in this case, we are assuming that there is a script written in the Perl language that has been written to handle our data, and placed in the /cgi-bin/ directory.

Both stylesheets and tables are discussed later in the book, in Chapters 11-14, and 7, respectively.

Note that each control (all the highlighted sections, excluding the first) has a name attribute, which is used to define the identifier that will be used for that field's value when the form is submitted. For instance, if the value fred is typed into the first field, which is represented by the name attribute identifier yourname, then the name-value pair yourname=fred will be sent to the server when the form is submitted. The mechanics of the submission process are discussed later in this Chapter.

Now let's walk through each important section of this code piece by piece.

Text Fields

The first item on this form is an example of the most widely used form control – the text field. It is created using an `<input type="text">` element, and is used to allow the user to type in a single line of text. It allows the page designer to specify an onscreen width for the field using the `size` attribute, and also the maximum number of characters that can be entered into the field, using the `maxlength` attribute. The two need not be the same: if the `maxlength` is longer than the `size` of the field, then the text will scroll as the user types in the later characters. If it is less, the user will still only be able to enter the smaller number of characters specified by `size`, and so the field as displayed will never be filled with text. In our example above, we simply defined a name and width for the field, with no maximum number of characters set:

```
<tr>
  <td>Your Name</td>
    <td>
      <input type="text" size="30" name="yourname"/>
    </td>
</tr>
```

A `value` attribute can also be given for a text field, in which case it is used as the default value.

Note that HTML form components (with the exception of buttons, which we will look at below) do not generate their own labels, and so we chose to put the text "Your Name" into an adjacent table cell, to explain to the user what data we wanted them to type into the field.

The `<input>` element is used with different values for the `type` attribute to represent several of the form controls, as we will see below.

Text Blocks

Multi-line blocks of text are rendered using `<textarea>` elements. These present a block for the user to type text into – the number of rows and columns can be specified using the `rows` and `cols` attributes. Note that there is no maximum on the amount of data that the user enters (other than any hard limits that particular browsers or servers might impose on the amount of data they can handle – and such limits are typically quite large). If the user enters more data than will fit in the box, then browsers typically add scroll bars to allow the user to navigate through the data.

```
<textarea name="desc" cols="40" rows="5">
  Give a brief autobiography here...
</textarea>
```

Note that unlike the text field we looked at above, a `<textarea>` is a container (is formed using two tags, not one), and the contents between the opening and closing tags are used as the default value for the control.

Also note that any white space between the `<textarea>` tags may have an effect on the formatting of your text in the box, so be careful about unnecessary white space!

Radio Buttons

Radio buttons are another of the controls that are defined with the <input> element. They allow the user to select one from a number of options, by clicking on the button next to the appropriate label text. Radio buttons are grouped using name – buttons forming a group are all given the same value for the name attribute, as can be seen in the code below. Whenever a radio button in a group is selected, any others that are already selected become deselected.

Each of the buttons has a distinct value attribute – it is that attribute for the selected radio button that is returned to the server when the form is submitted.

```
<input type="radio" name="sex" value="f" checked> Female
<input type="radio" name="sex" value="m"> Male
```

A default can be set for one of the radio buttons by specifying the checked attribute for that radio button. Also, note that a text label has to be given alongside the buttons, so that the user understands what each button represents. However, that description is solely for the benefit of the user, and is not part of the definition of the button, and is not communicated back to the server when the form is submitted.

Checkboxes

Checkboxes are similar to radio buttons, except that any or all of the buttons may be selected: there is no restriction that just one may be selected, as there is with radio buttons. For each button that is checked when the form is submitted, a name=value pair is submitted to the server.

```
<input type="checkbox" name="os" value="Win"> Windows
<input type="checkbox" name="os" value="Mac"> Mac OS
<input type="checkbox" name="os" value="Lin"> Linux
```

Menus

Menus are presented in HTML forms using the <select> element. This contains a number of <option> elements, each representing one row in a drop-down menu. By default, the item will allow one item to be selected from the list: when the multiple keyword is added to the definition, more than one selection can be made. When the form is submitted, the name associated with the <select> element is paired with the value attributes from each selected <option> element, to form the name=value pairs that are sent to the server.

```
<select name="knowhtml">
  <option value=""> Please select one...</option>
  <option value="0"> No knowledge</option>
  <option value="1"> Know the basics</option>
  <option value="2"> Fairly knowledgeable</option>
  <option value="3"> Very experienced</option>
  <option value="4"> HTML Guru</option>
</select>
```

For instance, in our example, if the user picks the "HTML Guru" option from the list, then the server will be sent the string "knowhtml=4" when the form is submitted. See below for more details about the <select> and <option> tags, and the way that form entries are submitted to the server.

File Selectors

Occasionally it is useful to allow the user to upload a file to the server as part of their form submission – for instance, as in our example, to allow them to upload a photograph of themselves for inclusion in a contact directory.

This is done using the `<input type="file">` element. Browsers typically render this as a text entry box, into which the user can type a file path specification, plus a "browse" button which brings up an OS-specific file selector dialog to help the user navigate to the file on their local file system that they want to upload.

```
<td>Your photo (.gif file)</td>
<td>
  <input type="file" name="photo">
</td>
```

When the form is submitted, the contents of the chosen file are uploaded as binary data, and the filename is stored in the value specified for the `name` attribute – `photo`, in this case.

Password Fields

Sometimes we want to ask the user for a password, or other secret information. To prevent people from prying over the user's shoulder as they enter it, we can specify the `type` attribute as "password", which will replace each character typed with an asterisk, dot, or other placeholder character as the user enters their information.

```
<input type="password" name="pass" size="10" maxlength="10">
```

In our example, we use the `size` and `maxlength` attributes to tell the browser to make the field ten characters wide, and allow at most 10 characters to be typed in.

Note that although `password` fields obscure the appearance of the password as the user types it in, the data that is entered is still submitted to the server in plain text. In order to provide security for data in transit, an encryption scheme such as SSL (Secure Socket Layer) needs to be used.

Submit and Reset Buttons

Forms normally need at least one button on them so that the user can submit the form. However, there are several different types of buttons that can be used: ranging from simple, generic buttons with text labels, to the visually more versatile button objects and clickable images.

A basic submit button is specified using `<input type="submit">`; when it is clicked, the form data is assembled and sent to the server for processing.

A second type of built-in button is the "reset" button. This causes all the controls in the form to be reset to the default values that they had when the page was loaded. This is specified using `<input type="reset">`.

```
<input type="submit" name="s1" value="Submit Form">  
<input type="reset" value="Reset Form">
```

In both cases, the `value` attribute specifies the text to appear on the button.

Button Objects

In early browsers, the simple submit and reset buttons outlined above were the only types that were supported. However, HTML 4.01 includes a <button> element, which has its contents rendered onto the face of the button – allowing greater design possibilities than the simple text buttons allowed.

Firstly, we can specify style attributes and formatting on the text within a <button> element, to gain full control over the text label that is rendered on the face of the button.

```
<button type="submit" name="s1" value="prj" class="btn">
  View related <br/>projects
</button>
```

Note that the code is shown indented here for readability, but in fact the white space before the button text in this example would be collapsed down to a single space, and rendered in front of the label, pushing the label text fractionally off center.

An image can be placed on the face of the button – either in place of, or in addition to text, by including an <img> element:

```
<button type="submit" name="s1" value="wrox">
  <img src="wrox.gif" width=32 height=32>
</button>
```

The type attribute allows us to specify that the button should behave like a submit button, as in our example, or as a reset button, or just a "button", which has no default behavior, but can be used with client-side scripting to trigger the execution of code. (See Chapter 9 for a discussion of scripting.)

Clickable Images

A clickable image combines a graphical submit button with the behavior of an image map, discussed in Chapter 5 (and indeed, you will recognize our clickable image in the first example as having been borrowed from Chapter 3!). Specified using <input type="image">, this sort of button acts as a submit button for the form, but also causes the coordinates of the click within the image itself to be sent to the server. This can be used to determine where in the image the user clicked, in order to take different actions. Normally this would be used with an image containing several different "button" graphics, as in our example, or perhaps another click-location sensitive image such as a map. In that case, we might process the data differently, depending on which city, state, or country the user clicked on in the map.

```
<input type=image name="navbar" src="Imagemap.gif">
```

Before support for the <button> element became widespread, this type of graphical submit button was often used to allow the designer to specify a more stylish submit button incorporating logos, specialized typography and so on. Often the graphic would contain just one button image, and the click coordinates would be ignored on the server side: the fact that the image had been clicked and the form submitted would often be all the data the server-side program required.

Hidden Values

The final type of form control is the hidden element. These are name=value pairs, which are not displayed within the UI (user interface), but are sent to the server when the form is submitted. These are often used to carry forward data from previous screens, so that when the form is processed, all the necessary information is available to the server. Often a unique user reference number will be stored in a hidden field, so that the server can tie the form data to the user's entries in a server-side database.

```
<input type=hidden name="hiddenval" value="123">
```

In this case, the string "hiddenval=123" will be sent to the server when the form is submitted.

Further Refinements

We looked above at the HTML form controls, and some of the basic attributes and their uses. However, HTML 4.01 supports a number of additional features, which make form layouts even more powerful.

Grouping Controls

Controls can be grouped together using the <fieldset> element to contain the fields in question. This causes the browser to group the fields together – typically by drawing a box around them, and also identifies a logical grouping of fields that may be exploited by non-graphical browsers.

A label can be provided for a <fieldset> group by using the <legend> element. For instance, the following form uses a couple of fieldsets:

```
<html>
  <head>
    <title>Fieldsets</title>
  </head>
  <body style="font-family:arial">
    <form method="post" action="/cgi-bin/formreader.exe">
      <fieldset>
        <legend>About you</legend>
        <table width="100%">
          <tr>
            <td>
              Your name:
            </td>
            <td>
              <input type="text" name="name1" size="20">
            </td>
          </tr>
          <tr>
            <td>
              Your age:
            </td>
            <td>
              <input type="text" name="age" size="5">
            </td>
```

```
          </tr>
        </table>
      </fieldset>
      <p>
      </p>
      <fieldset>
        <legend>Your pet</legend>
        <table width="100%">
          <tr>
            <td>
              Your pet's name:
            </td>
            <td>
              <input type="text" name="pname" size="20">
            </td>
          </tr>
          <tr>
            <td>
              Their favorite toy:
            </td>
            <td>
              <input type="text" size="20" name="ptoy">
            </td>
          </tr>
        </table>
      </fieldset>
    </form>
  </body>
</html>
```

IE 5.5 displays this form as follows:

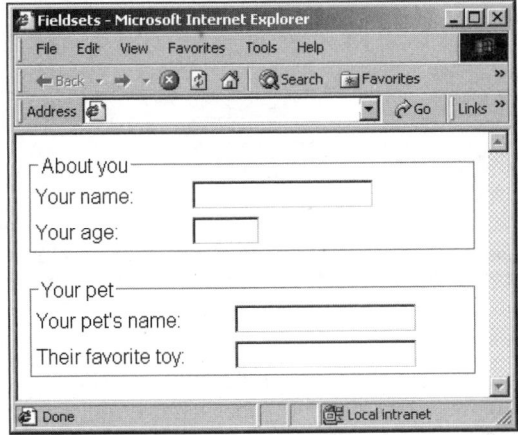

Labels

HTML 4.01 also includes a `<label>` element for specifying the labels that will be applied to individual fields. This is used primarily to logically associate the label text and relevant control, (in order to provide the browser with additional structure information), such as might be required when performing a text-to-speech conversion on the page.

A label can be associated with a control in two ways: either by including a single control within the body of the `<label>` element, or by using the `for` attribute to reference the `id` attribute of the appropriate control. The example code below shows both variations:

```
<html>
  <head>
    <title>Labels Example</title>
  </head>
  <body>
    <form method="get" action="cgi-bin/test.cgi">
      <label>
        Your name:
        <input type="text" size="20" name="yn">
      </label>
      <br/>
      <label for="field1">
        Your favorite color:
        <input id="field1" type="text" name="favcol" size="15">
      </label>
    </form>
  </body>
</html>
```

Note that the `<label>` element does not cause the enclosed label text to be rendered any differently, or at a different position within the document. It is shown on screen wherever it appears in the flow of the document, just as if the `<label>` tags were not present. In particular, the fact that a label is associated with a particular field does *not* cause that label to be automatically displayed adjacent to that field. In our example above, the labels only appear in the right place because each is defined next to the form component to which it refers – exactly where we want it to appear:

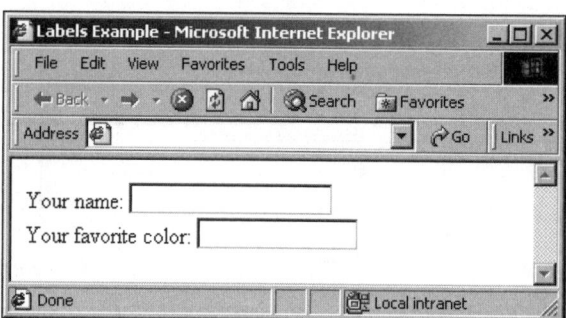

Focusing Fields

In order to enter data into a field, it has to be focused: that is, keystrokes have to be directed to that particular control. By default, there are two ways that a form field gets focus: either the user clicks in the field, or they press the *Tab* key enough times to work through the fields and get to the one they want to have focus.

The `tabindex` attribute can be used to specify the order in which the fields should receive focus when the *Tab* key is pressed, if different from the physical order in which the fields appear in the HTML. This attribute takes values between 1 and 32767 – with fields receiving focus in ascending order of `tabindex` each time the *Tab* key is pressed.

The user experience with long or complicated forms can be enhanced significantly by focusing the first field on the page for the user automatically, or by providing keyboard shortcuts.

Keyboard shortcuts can be set up using the `accesskey` attribute of the form element to specify a keyboard shortcut – in much the same way that shortcuts can be specified for links. The availability of shortcuts can be advertised to the user by either noting them explicitly in the page or associated help text, or by using some other convention such as underlining the appropriate letter in the field's label. For instance:

```
<u>D</u>og's Name:
<input type="text" name="dogname" size="20" accesskey="d">
```

will associate the keyboard shortcut *Alt-d* (or *Control-d* on a Mac) with that field, jumping the text cursor straight to that field when it is pressed.

Automatic focusing can be done by using a script to call the `focus()` method on the first form element within the page – typically as part of an `onload()` handler attached to the body of the page. See Chapter 9 for more details about scripting.

Disabled and Read-Only Controls

In HTML 4.01, form controls have two further attributes that can be used to mimic some of the concepts that we are used to seeing with desktop applications, specifically: **disabled** and **read-only** fields.

A control is marked as disabled by including the `disabled` attribute. This causes the field to be grayed out, and is typically used to indicate to the user that the field cannot be meaningfully completed, given other choices they have made. Any values in that control are not sent to the server when the form is submitted, and fields of this type cannot receive focus.

A read-only control is displayed normally, and can receive focus (for example, by tabbing to the field), but the user cannot edit the information. Specifying the `readonly` attribute causes this behavior. Unlike disabled controls, read-only control values are submitted to the server.

While using read-only controls can help prevent inadvertent changes to complex forms – for example, by requiring the user to select a specific "Edit" button before allowing them to make changes to a block of data – read-only fields suffer from a major disadvantage in that they do not usually provide the user with sufficient visual clues that the field is locked. Typically, it is better to render such "locked" fields using plain text, rather than form components – reserving the actual form components for occasions when the user can interact with and change the data.

For instance, the following code includes three fields. The first is normal, and so can receive focus, and be edited normally. The second one is read-only, so can receive focus, but can't be edited. The third and final one is disabled, so can't be interacted with at all:

```
<html>
  <head>
    <title>Disabled/Read-Only Controls</title>
  </head>
  <body>
    <form method="post" action="/cgi-bin/test2.pl">
      Name:
      <input type=text size=20 name="name"/><br/>
```

```
        Codename:
        <input type=text size=10 name="code" value="starling"
                readonly><br/>
        Termination Date:
        <input type=text size=10 name="term" value="none YET"
                disabled>
     </form>
   /body>
</html>
```

This displays as follows:

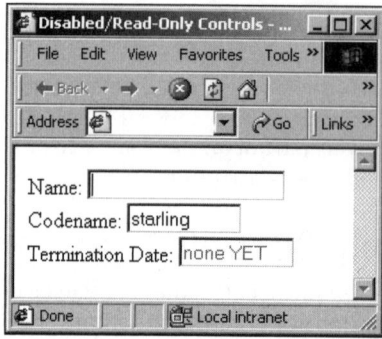

Hierarchical Menus

HTML 4.01 includes limited support for hierarchical menus, using the `<optgroup>` element to specify a header label for a group of subordinate selections: effectively producing submenus. This is designed to make it easier to navigate long lists of structured data, and also to provide improved support for non-graphical browsers.

For instance, in this code, the eight choices are divided up into three groups:

```
<html>
  <head>
    <title>Option Groups</title>
  </head>
  <body>
    <form method="post" action="/cgi-bin/test.exe">
      Make a Choice:
      <select name="test">
        <optgroup label="Level 1">
          <option value="1a">Choice 1a</option>
          <option value="1b">Choice 1b</option>
          <option value="1c">Choice 1c</option>
        </optgroup>
        <optgroup label="Level 2">
          <option value="2a">Choice 2a</option>
          <option value="2b">Choice 2b</option>
          <option value="2c">Choice 2c</option>
        </optgroup>
```

```
                <optgroup label="Level3">
                    <option value="3a">Choice 3a</option>
                    <option value="3b">Choice 3b</option>
                </optgroup>
            </select>
        </form>
    </body>
</html>
```

This code produces a layout that varies quite a lot on different browsers. For example, it looks like this in IE 5 on MacOS:

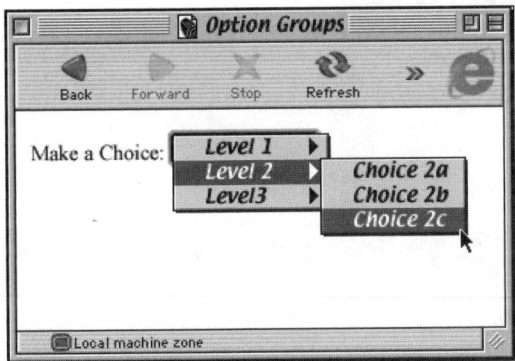

and like this on IE 5.5 for Windows (Opera 5 for Windows renders it virtually identically):

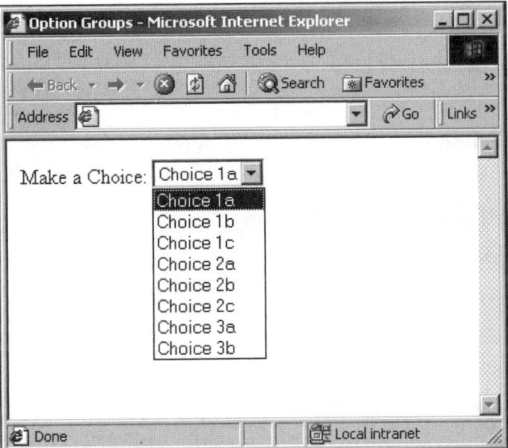

and like this on Netscape 6 for Windows:

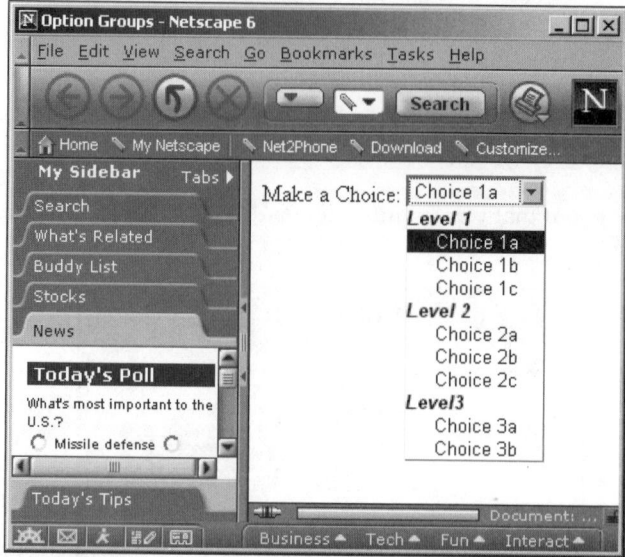

According to the specification, `<optgroup>` elements cannot be nested, although this is noted as an option for future versions.

The HTML Elements

Having considered the basics of HTML forms as well as some of the more advanced features, let's pull all of the information together as we take a detailed look at the different elements used to describe HTML forms.

Each element, and its associated attributes, are considered in turn.

The <form> Element

The `<form>` element accepts the following attributes:

accept	accept-charset	action	enctype
method	name	target	

plus the universal HTML 4.01 attributes `id`, `class`, `lang`, `dir`, `style`, and `title`, and the common events, as described in Chapter 2. Of particular note is the `onsubmit` handler, which can be used to trigger client-side validations of data prior to submitting the form to the server. This is discussed a little more at the end of this chapter, and scripting more generally is covered in Chapter 9.

accept

Specifies the MIME-type(s) that the server can support for the data submitted from the form. It can be a comma-delimited list if more than one type is required. This attribute is optional, and was added in HTML 4.0. Most browsers do not support it at present. The syntax is:

```
accept="mime_type_list"
```

where `mime_type_list` can be one MIME-type, or many in a comma-delimited list.

accept-charset

Specifies the character set used for the data from the form, and that the server must support. This attribute is optional, and was added in HTML 4.0. Most browsers do not support it at present. The syntax is:

```
accept-charset="character_set_list"
```

where `character_set_list` can be one character set, or many in a comma delimited list.

action

This required attribute is used to specify the URL that will receive the data when the form is submitted. The syntax is:

```
action="url"
```

The `url` does not have to be on the same machine as the one that hosts the HTML document, although it generally is.

We may also specify that the form data be e-mailed to a particular address, rather than passing it to a server script. This is easily accomplished, by using a `mailto:` URL (discussed in Chapter 4) as our `action`. In this case, the name=value pairs of data from the form will be passed off to our e-mail client, which will e-mail them to the requested address. Note that this is a particularly insecure way to send the data, and may not be particularly seamless to the user: in general, `mailto:` form submissions should be avoided.

enctype

This optional attribute is used to indicate the MIME-type (or Internet Media type) to be used when encoding the form data for submission when the `method` is `"post"`. The syntax is:

```
enctype="mime-type"
```

Unless otherwise specified, it defaults to `"application/x-www-form-urlencoded"`. For forms that includes files to be submitted, as well as form data, the type should be `"multipart/form-data"`. For a complete list of MIME types, see Appendix E.

method

This attribute defines the method used to send the data to the server. The syntax is:

```
method="method"
```

where method is post or get. If not specified, the default is get.

post is the preferred method, and will generally be used in most cases – unless we have a compelling reason for not doing so. This method sends the information to the server as a data stream within the body of the request.

get is an older method, and should normally be avoided. With this method, the data is appended to the URL itself after a question mark separator:

```
http://foobar.edu/cgi-bin/query?Name=Smith
```

The get method does have the advantage of allowing the form results to be book marked (useful in the case of searches), but has the disadvantage that the length of the data string is limited, since it is assigned to an environment variable on the server.

name

This attribute allows a name to be specified for the form. This can be used to refer to the form block by name within client-side scripting code. The syntax is:

```
name="form_name"
```

where form_name is the identifier for this specific form.

target

By default, the returned page is loaded into the same frame or window as the page containing the <form> tag. To have the returned page loaded into a different frame or window, we can use the optional target attribute to specify the frame or window name, just as we would for an <a> element. The syntax is:

```
target="window_name"
```

where window_name is the name of a browser window or existing frame.

The <input> Element

The attributes supported by the <input> element are:

accept*	accesskey*	align	alt*
checked	disabled*	ismap	maxlength
name	readonly*	size	src
tabindex*	type	usemap*	value

plus the universal HTML 4.01 attributes `id`, `class`, `lang`, `dir`, `style`, and `title`, and the common events, as described in Chapter 2.

The attributes above marked with an asterisk are new in HTML 4.01, and are generally not supported in older browsers. See Appendix A, *"The Ultimate HTML Reference"*, for further details of attribute support by browser version.

The `<input>` element can be used to create several different types of element, and the combination of attributes and events supported for each type is different.

accept

This specifies the MIME-type(s) that the server must support for the data submitted from the form. It can be a comma-delimited list if more than one type is required. See the section above, *"The <form> Element"*, for more details.

accesskey

Defines a keyboard character that can be pressed, usually in conjunction with the *Alt* or *control* key, to switch the focus directly to the control. It acts as a "hot-key" or short cut key allowing easier navigation. The syntax is:

```
accesskey="character"
```

See the above section, *"Focusing Fields"*, for more details.

align

Use this attribute to define how the text will be aligned within or in relation to the element. The syntax is:

```
align="alignment"
```

where `alignment` is `top`, `middle`, or `bottom`. These values have the same effect as with inline images. This attribute is deprecated in HTML 4.01 – style sheets should now be used instead.

alt

Added in HTML 4.0, and analogous to the similar attribute for use with inline images, this specifies the text that will be displayed for an `<input type="image">` control if the browser can't display the image itself. The syntax is:

```
alt="text"
```

Note that in some browsers (such as Internet Explorer 4, 5, 6), the `alt` text has a secondary purpose – when we move the mouse pointer over the image, the `alt` text will be displayed as a tool tip.

checked

Forces a checkbox or radio button to be selected (that is "on") when the form loads. The syntax is simply `checked`. This is useful for "presetting" certain values, in order to make them the default choice.

disabled

Added in HTML 4.0, this attribute forces the control to be disabled, that is, it is grayed out, and the user cannot change the value in it. The syntax is simply `disabled`.

This is often used in conjunction with scripting code, which can change the setting of the attribute to enable the control at appropriate times, based on other fields in the form, for example.

ismap

This attribute is used to indicate that an image type input element is intended for use with a server-side image map. The syntax is simply `ismap`.

Note that server-side image maps are little used today, having given way to client-side equivalents. See Chapter 5 for more information about image maps.

maxlength

This sets how many characters the user can enter into a text box. It does not set the actual size of the control. The syntax is:

```
maxlength="n"
```

where n is the number of characters. Care must be taken when setting this value, as we never know how much space a user will need for the data. However, `maxlength` may well be required if our server-side processing script or the database that will ultimately hold the information has a fixed field size for the data.

name

Specifies the name of the control. The syntax is:

```
name="name"
```

The `name` specified is sent to the server in a name=value pair, and used to identify the control.

readonly

Added in HTML 4.0, this attribute forces the control to be read-only, that is, displayed normally, but the user cannot change the value in it. The syntax is simply `readonly`.

size

This attribute specifies the size of the control, that is, the text box. The syntax is:

```
size="n"
```

where n is the number of characters. If the `size` attribute is set to a smaller value than `maxlength`, the characters will scroll. The actual on-screen dimension of the control depends on the client system's default font size, so will appear at different sizes on different machines, even with the same value of `size`.

src

Used with `type="image"`, to specify the image to be used. The syntax is:

```
src="url"
```

This attribute behaves in exactly the same way as for inline images (see Chapter 5 for more details).

tabindex

Added in HTML 4.0, this attribute allows the HTML author to set the order that the focus moves between controls when the *Tab* key is pressed. The default is the order of the controls in the HTML source. The syntax is:

```
tabindex="n"
```

where n is a number between 1 and 32767, indicating the relative position in the tabbing order.

type

Specifies which type of control to use. The syntax is:

```
type="type"
```

where `type` is one of the following:

❑ **text** – this is the default if `type` is not specified. It produces a single line text field for user input, and is used in conjunction with `maxlength` and `size`. Additionally, this type of `<input>` control should be used in place of the `<isindex>` element, which is deprecated in HTML 4.0 (see below for an explanation of `<isindex>`).

❑ **password** – this produces a similar control to the `text` type, except that text is not displayed as we enter it. The text is displayed as asterisks, so that people looking over our shoulder cannot read it.

❑ **hidden** – the user will see no field, but the value of the field (set by the `value` attribute) will be submitted with the form as text. This is useful for sending information to the server that we don't want the user to see, and can be used in a variety of inventive ways including passing data from one page to the next, depending on the application.

❑ **checkbox** – creates a checkbox control. Used to provide a "Yes" or "No" type of control.

❑ **radio** – creates a radio button control. Usually used to provide a selection of options from which only one can be chosen, by giving each button in the group the same value for the `name` attribute. The `value` attribute of the selected radio button is the only one to generate a name=value pair when the form is submitted.

❑ **reset** – creates a button that resets all the fields to their initial default values. Setting the `value` attribute will alter the caption on the button itself; the default is "Reset".

❑ **submit** – creates a button that submits the form to the server. Setting the `value` attribute will alter the caption on the button from the default, which is "Submit" for most browsers. If a value for the `name` attribute is provided, the button will generate a name=value pair that is sent to the server with the other form data, if that submit button is the one that is clicked.

❑ **image** – creates an image map that the user can click to submit the form. The coordinates of the selected point on the image are sent to the server along with the data from the form. The coordinates are sent to the server using two name=value pairs, where the names used are derived from the name attribute of the control by appending ".x" and ".y" respectively, and the values are the appropriate coordinates, in pixels, with the origin as the top-left corner.

❑ **button** – creates a button that can be linked to a client-side script, rather than directly submitting or resetting a form, like the submit and reset buttons.

❑ **file** – new in HTML 4.0, although has been supported by Netscape in the past, and IE as of version 3.02. This creates a control that is used to submit a file to the server. When the form is submitted, the file specified in the control is sent to the server as well.

usemap

This attribute specifies that the image in an <input type="image"> control is a client-side image map, which has area elements that define the value to be passed to the server. The syntax is:

```
usemap="map_name"
```

where map_name is the map to be used. See Chapter 5 for more information about image maps.

value

Specifies the default value for text fields; the value of a hidden field, or the value to be associated with a checkbox or radio button, when it is selected. The syntax is:

```
value="value"
```

The <button> Element

The <button> tag is an alternative way of creating command buttons. It is more flexible than the <input> element with type="button". It requires the closing tag </button>, and the contents of the tag are rendered on the button face. This means that images, even animated GIFs, can be displayed on the button face – as well as, or instead of, text.

The attributes supported by the <button> element are:

```
accesskey    disabled    name    tabindex
type         value
```

plus the universal HTML 4.01 attributes id, class, lang, dir, style, and title, and the common events, as described in Chapter 2.

accesskey

Defines a keyboard shortcut key: see the "*Focusing Fields*" Section for details.

disabled

Forces the control to be disabled, that is, it is grayed out, and the user cannot click it. See the <input> element for more details.

name

Defines a unique name for the element. See the `<input>` element for details.

tabindex

This attribute allows the HTML author to set the order that the focus moves between controls when the *Tab* key is pressed. See the `<input>` element for details.

type

Specifies the type of button to create. The syntax is:

```
type="button_type"
```

where `button_type` can be `button`, `reset`, or `submit`. This makes the control behave the same as an `<input>` element of the same `type`.

value

Assigns a value to the button. This is the value used for the control at submit time, if this particular button was clicked.

The <textarea> Element

This element produces a multi-line text box area for user input. The supported attributes are:

```
accesskey*      cols      disabled*      name
readonly*       rows      tabindex*
```

plus the universal HTML 4.01 attributes `id`, `class`, `lang`, `dir`, `style`, and `title`, and the common events, as described in Chapter 2. The attributes marked with an asterisk are new in HTML 4.0, and are generally not supported in older browsers. See Appendix A for an overview of features supported by each browser version.

accesskey

This specifies a keyboard shortcut key. See the `<input>` element for details.

cols

Sets the width of the text area. The syntax is:

```
cols="n"
```

where n is the width in characters. The actual on-screen dimension of the control depends on the client system's default font size, so will appear at different sizes on different machines even with the same value of `cols`.

disabled

Forces the control to be disabled, that is, it is grayed out, and the user cannot change the value in it. See the <input> element for details.

name

Gives the text area an identifying name. See the <input> element for details.

readonly

Forces the control to be read-only, that is, displayed normally, but the user cannot change the value in it. See the <input> element for details.

rows

Sets the height of the text area. The syntax is:

```
rows="n"
```

where n is the height in characters. The actual on-screen dimension of the control depends on the client system's default font size, so will appear at different sizes on different machines even with the same value of rows.

tabindex

This attribute allows the HTML author to set the order that the focus moves between controls when the *Tab* key is pressed. See the <input> element for details.

Extension to the <textarea> Element: wrap

Both Netscape and Internet Explorer support an extra attribute to the <textarea> tag: wrap. This defines how the text within the element is wrapped if the line is longer than will fit in the width of the control. Its syntax is:

```
wrap="wrap_value"
```

where wrap_value can be off (text is not wrapped in the control), hard (text is wrapped in the control, and carriage returns are inserted at the end of each line when the value is sent to the server) or soft (the text is wrapped in the control, but sent to the server as a single string with no extra carriage returns inserted).

The <select> Element

The <select> element is used, together with the <option> element, to produce a list box or a drop-down combo-box from which one or more selections can be made. The closing </select> tag is required in all cases.

The attributes it supports are:

```
disabled     multiple     name     size
tabindex*
```

plus the universal HTML 4.01 attributes id, class, lang, dir, style, and title, and the common events, as described in Chapter 1. The attributes marked with an asterisk are new in HTML 4.0, and are generally not supported in older browsers. See Appendix A for an overview of features supported by each browser version.

disabled

This attribute forces the control to be disabled, that is, it is grayed out and the user cannot change the value in it. See the <input> element for details.

multiple

Indicates that multiple items can be selected. If multiple is not specified, only one option can be chosen. Depending on the operating system, hold down the *Ctrl*, *Alt*, *Shift*, or command keys to click multiple selections. The syntax is simply multiple.

name

This defines a unique name for the element. See the <input> element for details.

size

Specifies the height of the list control, and therefore how many options are visible at one time. The syntax is:

```
size="n"
```

where n is the number of rows that will be shown at once.

If size="1", the control appears as a drop-down combo-box with only one option visible at once. When the control is clicked (or the button at the end of the control in some cases, such as Mac OS IE 5) it opens to display a list of options. If size is set to a value greater than one, it creates a scrollable list control with more than one entry visible at one time.

> Note that **size** does not set the width of the control, but the number of lines it displays. The only standardized way to specify the width of the control is to use the **style** attribute, and set the **width** property.

tabindex

This attribute allows the HTML author to set the order in which the focus moves between controls when the *Tab* key is pressed. See the <input> element for details.

The <optgroup> Element

The <optgroup> element allows web developers to group choices into a hierarchy. It creates a two-level, hierarchical, collapsible list of options, which the user can browse and select from. Browser support is currently limited to Internet Explorer 5 for Mac OS, and Netscape 6.

The attributes supported by the `<optgroup>` element are:

```
disabled       label
```

plus the usual HTML 4.01 attributes `id`, `class`, `lang`, `dir`, `style`, and `title`, and the common events, as described in Chapter 2.

disabled

The presence of this attribute keyword indicates that the item cannot be focused or submitted, and should be displayed as grayed-out.

label

Specifies the label for the option group. The syntax is:

```
label="text"
```

where `text` is the entry that is displayed for the group in the top-level menu. This attribute is always required.

The `<option>` Element

The `<option>` element is used to specify the individual entries that appear in a `<select>` list, and is only used in this context. A set of `<option>` elements are enclosed by the `<select>` and `</select>` tags, and an optional `<optgroup>` element. The text of the option is given within the `<option>` block.

The attributes supported by the `<option>` element are:

```
disabled       label       selected       value
```

plus the usual HTML 4.01 attributes `id`, `class`, `lang`, `dir`, `style`, and `title`, and the common events, as described in Chapter 2. The `disabled` and `label` attributes are new in HTML 4.0, and are generally not supported in older browsers. See Appendix A for an overview of features supported by each browser version.

disabled

This makes the control disabled, that is, it is grayed-out and the user cannot change the value in it. See the `<input>` element for details.

label

The `label` attribute is used to specify an alternative label for the `<option>`, to be used in place of the contents of the `<option>` element itself. The syntax is:

```
label="text"
```

selected

This specifies if this option will be selected when the form is first displayed. The syntax is simply `selected`.

value

This specifies the value that will be sent to the server if that option is selected. If more than one is selected (when the <select> element includes the multiple attribute), the values are sent as multiple name=value pairs, with the same name in each case.

The syntax is:

```
value="value"
```

If omitted, the text that follows the <option> element (and is displayed in the list) is used as the submitted value instead.

The <label> Element

This element provides a way to logically link a caption or label for an HTML control to that control. To explicitly link a <label> with another control, the for attribute is used; however, if we just want to implicitly link this element with a control, then we just add the chosen control between the opening and closing <label> tags.

The <label> element supports the following attributes:

```
accesskey       for
```

plus the universal HTML 4.01 attributes id, class, lang, dir, style, and title, and the common events, as described in Chapter 2.

accesskey

This attribute is used to define a keyboard shortcut. See the <input> element for details.

Note: pressing the shortcut key for a label causes the associated field to be focused, not the label itself.

for

This attribute provides the link between the label and the control. The syntax is:

```
for="control_name"
```

where control_name is the ID of the associated HTML form control.

The <fieldset> Element

This is used to group form controls together. Most browsers render this by drawing a box around the controls. See Appendix A for an overview of features supported by each browser version.

The <fieldset> control supports just the universal HTML 4.01 attributes id, class, lang, dir, style, and title as described in Chapter 2.

The controls to be grouped together are placed between the <fieldset> and </fieldset> tags.

The \<legend\> Element

This element is used in conjunction with a `<fieldset>` element, and provides a caption for the frame created by `<fieldset>`.

The `<legend>` element supports the following attributes:

```
accesskey        align
```

plus the universal HTML 4.01 attributes id, class, lang, dir, style, and title, and the common events, as described in Chapter 2.

accesskey

This attribute is used to define a keyboard shortcut. See the `<input>` element for details.

align

This attribute is deprecated, but can be used to define how the legend will be aligned with respect to the fieldset. The syntax is:

```
align="alignment"
```

where `alignment` can be: top, bottom, left, or right. These values have the same effect as when placing a caption with a table, and can place the legend at various places around the fieldset frame.

The \<isindex\> Element

This element is deprecated, but was one of the earliest supported form elements. It was typically used to provide a single field for entering search text. Similar, but enhanced functionality can be achieved using `<input type="text">` and so this element can safely be ignored for all practical purposes.

A Client-Server View of Forms

To conclude this chapter, we are going to briefly consider what happens when a form is submitted – firstly from the browser's perspective, and then, in the following section, from the server's viewpoint.

The Client Side

Once the submit button is activated on the form, the browser goes through a number of steps to get the data to the server.

onsubmit Processing

The first thing the browser does, is run any server-side script code associated with an onsubmit handler on the form element. This can be used to validate the data entered, before the form is sent to the server. If the code is present, and returns a value of false, then the form submission is abandoned, and the existing page continues to be displayed as if the submit action had never been initiated. Otherwise, it proceeds normally, as outlined below.

See Chapter 9 for a discussion of scripting techniques.

Successful Controls

The next thing that the browser does is to identify the **successful controls.** These are the ones that are eligible to forward their data to the server. Firstly, all disabled controls are excluded, and then all remaining text fields, password fields, and text areas are included. Next, any selected radio buttons, checkboxes, and selection items are added in, along with any file upload controls. Finally, the actual submit button that was activated is added to the list.

Form Encodings

The list of successful control names, and their associated values is then encoded. Typically this is done using an encoding called the **application/x-www-form-urlencoded** content-type. This concatenates all the name=value pairs using ampersand characters, then replaces every space with a "+" sign, and escapes certain non-alphanumeric characters using a "%" sign, followed by two hexadecimal digits representing the ASCII value of the character.

An alternative encoding, **multipart/form-data** is used for forms containing file uploads. This breaks the data up into sub-messages, each with a field-specific header: more details can be found in "Section 17" of the HTML 4.01 specification, at http://www.w3.org/TR/html401/interact/forms.html.

To use this encoding, it should be specified using the `enctype` attribute of the `<form>` element.

Methods

The encoded form data is then sent to the server, using the method specified by the `<form>` element.

For the `get` method, this involves appending a question mark to the end of the action URL, followed by the encoded data.

For the `post` method on the other hand, an http post transaction is sent to the server, with the encoded data as the body of the message.

Security Issues

Security is an important practical and user-confidence issue for forms-based web sites. As noted above, form data is sent in plain text by default, and so can be observed in transit. In order to avoid this, an encrypted data flow has to be used. This is done using the SSL capabilities of both the browser and server, to establish an https protocol connection for the form submission. This is configured on the server, and does not require any changes to the HTML, other than to ensure that the `action` attribute of the form points to the configured `https` server.

An in-depth discussion of security is way beyond the scope of this chapter, so for more information, look at the security content of *Professional JavaScript* by Nigel McFarlane et al (ISBN: *1-861002-70-x*), published by Wrox Press, the SSL chapter of *Professional Java Security* by Jess Garms and Daniel Somerfield (ISBN: *1-861004-25-7*), also published by Wrox Press, or look at http://www.verisign.com (Verisign is a company that offers web security services).

Field Edits: Validating Data Entry

Finally, in discussing the client side of the transaction, it is worth noting that by default, no processing or validation of the entered data is performed by the browser. The data is simply sent back to the server, and the server decides how to deal with it – for example, by returning an error page if the form entries are not valid.

It is possible to perform some basic validation on the browser before the form is ever submitted. This is done using embedded scripting code, such as JavaScript. The code is usually triggered when the submit button is clicked, by specifying an `onsubmit` handler attribute within the `<form>` element. This provides the necessary client-side script code to check the field values. Any errors are usually flagged to the user in alert dialogs, prior to programmatically aborting the form submission, and giving the user the opportunity to correct their mistakes.

Although the details of this approach are outside the scope of this book, further details about scripting can be found in Chapter 9, or in other Wrox books such as the aforementioned *Professional Javascript* by Nigel McFarlane et al (ISBN: *1-861002-70-x*), published by Wrox Press.

The Server Side: a 30,000ft View

When the form is submitted to the server, the first thing that has to happen is that the server checks to see if the resource identified in the URL knows how to handle the form data. If the form page was correctly set up then it should do, but if not, and if for instance, the form data was directed to a regular HTML page, then the server will usually return an error, indicating that it received data that it did not know how to process.

What Does the Server Do with a Form?

Assuming that the URL correctly pointed to a form-handler of some sort, the web server will hand over processing of the request to that handler. We will discuss exactly what that handler might be in a moment, but before that we need to look at the process that the handler goes through.

Firstly, the data that was sent is decoded and passed on to the dedicated program logic, which processes the data in whatever way is appropriate for the application. The standards really don't have anything to say at this point. The field names and data content are specific to the particular application, and so the application must parse out and react to it as it sees fit. Typically, this involves validating the fields, retrieving and storing entries in databases etc., and ultimately choosing or constructing the next page to be sent back to the user.

Types of Server-side Form Handler

There are an increasingly large number of choices for server-side web application logic. Originally these were likely to be C programs, or Perl scripts conforming to an early inter-application communication standard known as CGI – the **Common Gateway Interface.**

In fact, a lot of server-side applications still use the CGI standard, but other alternatives are now coming to the fore – most notably Microsoft's Active Server Pages (ASP), Java-based technologies such as Java Server Pages (JSP) and Servlets, open source technologies such as PHP, or dedicated Application Server environments such as Apple's WebObjects or BEA WebLogic.

If you want to develop your own custom server-side applications to interact with the forms on your site, you may want to take a look at other Wrox books such as *Professional ASP 3.0* by Richard Anderson et al. (ISBN: *1-861002-61-0*), *Professional JSP 2nd Edition* by Grant Palmer et al. (ISBN: *1-861004-95-8*), or *Beginning PHP 4* by Chris Ullman et al. (ISBN: *1-861003-73-0*).

Summary

In this chapter, we have looked at the different types of form components that can be used to capture user data within a <form> element. HTML 4.0 added a number of elements and attributes, although even by 2001 – nearly four years after the standard was published – many are not widely supported by mainstream browsers.

We worked through a detailed example of a basic form demonstrating most of the standard form controls. Next we looked at some of the more advanced formatting options that the HTML standard offers, before detailing all of the relevant HTML elements and attributes.

We concluded this chapter by considering briefly the mechanics of form submission, from both the client and server perspectives. However, the design and development of online applications to process form data is a major field of its own, and you may wish to look at some of the other books listed above to find out more.

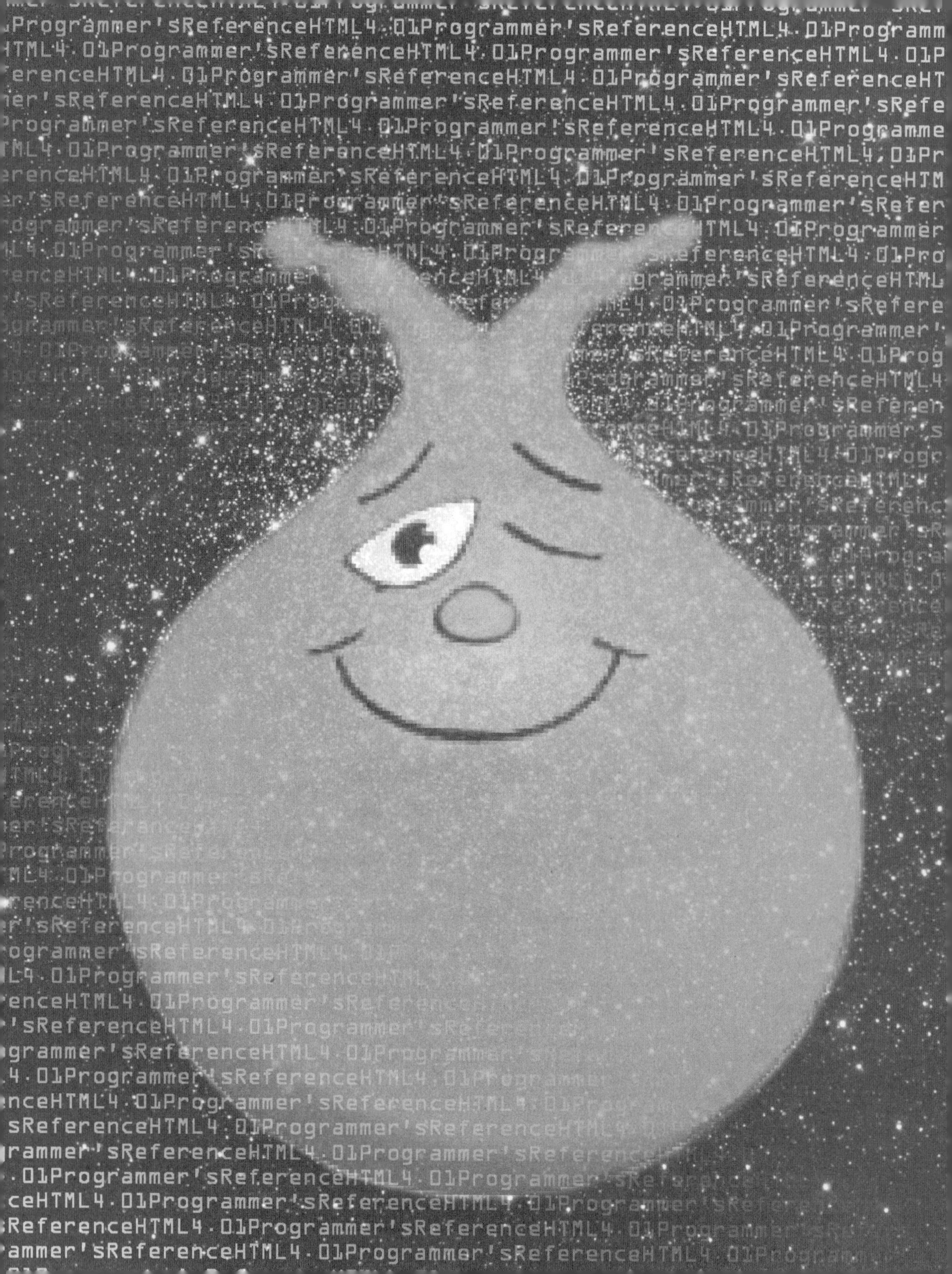
HTML4.01Programmer'sReference

7

Tables

Tabular layouts have become one of the most important tools in web design, allowing many useful layout effects to be achieved. Basic table formatting capabilities were among the earliest additions to the original web browsers, and all major browsers have supported the simplest table layout tags since version 1.1 of Netscape shipped in the mid 1990s.

Those original elements remain at the heart of contemporary HTML tables, but HTML 4.01 has added a number of additional capabilities – most of which are now starting to be implemented sufficiently well by the major browsers that they can be considered for general use. Most of these enhancements are concerned with providing additional logical structure to the table, such as a concept of headers and footers, as well as enhancing the formatting options that can be applied to tables.

Although originally intended primarily for laying out rows and columns of data, tables soon expanded their role as a technique for providing more precise control over screen layouts. Since individual cells in a table can contain almost any other HTML elements – including other tables – most complex web pages that one sees today make heavy use of tables to provide multi-column layouts of text and graphics that can be successfully viewed by virtually all browsers.

In this chapter, we start by looking at the logical structure of an HTML table. Then we detail all of the related elements and attributes, before turning our attention to some of the techniques for more complex layouts and formatting.

We conclude with an example that pulls together many of the different alternatives discussed in this chapter.

The Structure of an HTML Table

HTML tables are delimited by `<table>` and `</table>` element tags. Within this block, we use other tags to create the individual row and cell elements, specify how many columns and rows there are, what kind of cell each one is, and encapsulate the data in the cells themselves.

The following diagram shows the logical structure of a table. We will briefly discuss this structure now, before going on to look at the HTML syntax in detail in the section "The HTML Table Elements", below.

High-level Overview

At its heart, a table is composed of rows of cells. Each **table row** is indicated using the `<tr>` element.

The cells within the row are represented by either **table data** elements or **table header** elements. These are indicated by `<td>` and `<th>` tags, respectively. The latter are used to indicate column or row headers, and are typically displayed in bold, or with some other emphasis. All the data items that we want to display in our table are included inside either `<td>` or `<th>` blocks.

The original HTML implementation of tables did not go much further than these basic structures. However, the HTML 4.01 spec adds a number of further refinements, as shown in the diagram.

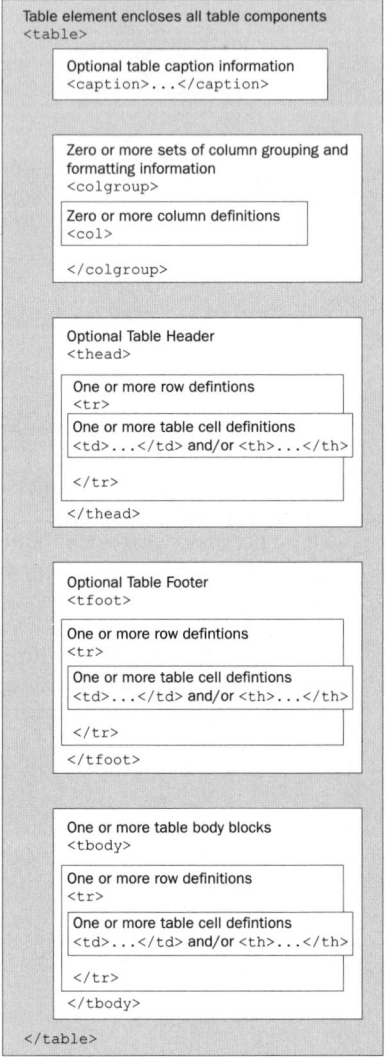

Table element encloses all table components
`<table>`

Optional table caption information
`<caption>...</caption>`

Zero or more sets of column grouping and formatting information
`<colgroup>`

Zero or more column definitions
`<col>`

`</colgroup>`

Optional Table Header
`<thead>`

One or more row defintions
`<tr>`

One or more table cell definitions
`<td>...</td>` and/or `<th>...</th>`

`</tr>`

`</thead>`

Optional Table Footer
`<tfoot>`

One or more row defintions
`<tr>`

One or more table cell defintions
`<td>...</td>` and/or `<th>...</th>`

`</tr>`

`</tfoot>`

One or more table body blocks
`<tbody>`

One or more row definitions
`<tr>`

One or more table cell defintions
`<td>...</td>` and/or `<th>...</th>`

`</tr>`

`</tbody>`

`</table>`

Caption

The `<caption>` element is optional, and is intended for providing a title for the table. By default, most browsers will display this title centered over the top of the table, but this can be controlled, as outlined below.

Column Formatting

As noted above, HTML tables are composed of explicitly defined rows of table cells: the column structure is not explicitly modeled at the data level – rather, it emerges from the alignment of the appropriate cells in each row.

While this approach facilitates row-level formatting, it can make it awkward to format a column of cells consistently. To address this, the `<colgroup>` and `<col>` elements are provided as a way to group columns together, and specify the formatting to be applied to a column of cells. These elements are discussed in more detail below, but it should be noted that support for these tags in browsers up to and including Netscape 6 and IE 5 is poorly implemented on most platforms.

Grouping Rows

After the caption and column data, the content of the table finally appears, optionally broken up into groups: a table header, table footer, and one or more table body elements.

The purpose of these blocks is to provide the browser with some additional structure information that it can use to display the table appropriately: for instance, printing the header and footer on each page of hardcopy output.

Each of these blocks, if present, contains a series of `<tr>` elements, each containing as many `<td>` or `<th>` elements as necessary to provide the data for all the columns in the table. As noted above, the only place that the actual renderable table cell content can appear is inside the `<td>` or `<th>` elements.

A Basic Table Example

The code below illustrates the basic mechanisms of setting up a table in HTML, using the components discussed, and a handful of additional formatting attributes, which we will explore in more detail below.

Note that although the HTML 4.01 standard does not require closing tags for table elements – such as `</td>` or `</tr>` – their omission can cause significant problems for many older browsers. Furthermore, it can make the code harder to understand, so we will include the closing tags in our examples in this chapter.

```
<html>
  <head>
    <title>Basic Table Example</title>
  </head>
  <body bgcolor="#FFFFFF">
    <table width="100%" border="3" cellpadding="5"
           bgcolor="#CCCCCC">

      <caption style="font-family:Arial; line-height:150%">
        A simple table layout
      </caption>
```

```
      <thead>
        <tr bgcolor="#EEEEEE">
          <th colspan="2">This is a header row for the table</th>
        </tr>
        <tr bgcolor="#EEEEEE">
          <th>Column 1</th>
          <th>Column 2</th>
        </tr>
      </thead>

      <tfoot>
        <tr bgcolor="#EEEEEE">
          <td colspan="2" style="text-align:center; font-style:italic;
             font-weight:bold">This is a footer for our table</td>
        </tr>
      </tfoot>

      <tbody>
        <tr>
          <td>(1,1)</td>
          <td>(2,1)</td>
        </tr>
        <tr>
          <td>(1,2)</td>
          <td>(2,2)</td>
        </tr>
      </tbody>

    </table>
  </body>
</html>
```

A browser that can implement HTML 4.01 tables, such as Netscape 6, or IE 5.5, renders the previous example as follows:

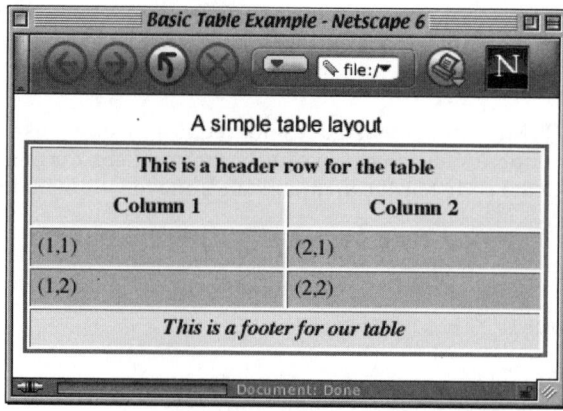

Looking at the code above, we see that we start the table definition with a table element:

```
<table width="100%" border="3" cellpadding="5" bgcolor="#CCCCCC">
```

This marks the start of the table, and specifies that the table should be the full available width of the browser window, with a 3-pixel border, and a medium-gray background color. The color is specified using HTML's hexadecimal notation: the value #CCCCCC sets each of the red, green, and blue values to CC – that is, 204 on a 0-255 scale. Setting all three colors to the same value gives a neutral gray shade. The `cellpadding` value specified for the table puts a 5-pixel margin inside each cell, ensuring the contents are not tight up against the cell borders.

(Note that with a width specified as a percentage, the table will grow and shrink as the user changes the size of the browser window, redistributing the available space between the rows and columns of the table.)

Next we declare the caption for the table:

```
<caption style="font-family:Arial; line-height:150%">
  A simple table layout
</caption>
```

Note that this browser defaults to placing the caption centered above the table. The `style` attribute for the `<caption>` element uses an inline style-sheet format to specify the style of the text. The use of style sheets is discussed in detail in the second section of this book, starting with Chapter 11.

Now we start to define the content of the table itself, starting with the two header rows:

```
<thead>
  <tr bgcolor="#EEEEEE">
    <th colspan="2">This is a header row for the table</th>
  </tr>
  <tr bgcolor="#EEEEEE">
    <th>Column 1</th>
    <th>Column 2</th>
  </tr>
</thead>
```

This `<thead>` element includes two table rows, corresponding to the two rows of the table header. The actual cells within these rows are defined using `<th>` elements, in order to signify that these cells are headers, rather than ordinary table data. As a result, the browser we used in our example emphasizes the cells by making the text bold.

Note that in the first row, the header cell is made to span across both columns by using the `colspan` attribute, with an argument equal to the number of columns that should be covered by the cell being defined – two in this case. (There is also a similar `rowspan` attribute, which works for vertical spans of cells, and is discussed below).

The `bgcolor` attribute is used on the `<tr>` elements to specify a lighter gray color for the cells in this row, in order to help clarify the distinction between header and body rows. Using different background colors is a good design technique to remember if we wish to help users quickly assimilate complex tables of data, and distinguish between rows or columns, which contain different types of information.

The table footer is defined next, using a `<tfoot>` element:

```
<tfoot>
  <tr bgcolor="#EEEEEE">
    <td colspan="2" style="text-align:center; font-style:italic;
        font-weight:bold">This is a footer for our table</td>
  </tr>
</tfoot>
```

Notice that even though this logically belongs at the bottom of the table, the HTML 4.01 Standard requires that it be defined between the header block and the body of the table. This is done so that the browser can interpret and present the body data in light of both the header and footer blocks. This can be particularly important for non-visual browsers, such as systems for reading web pages to visually impaired users.

This positioning of the `<tfoot>` block presents something of a quandary, as non-HTML 4.01-compliant browsers will typically ignore the `<tfoot>` tags, and so render what is intended as table footer between the header and the body rows. If this is likely to be an issue, given the target audience, then there are two alternatives. The first is to place the `<tfoot>` block after the `<tbody>` elements, which contravenes the standard but is widely supported – either by design or, in the case of older browsers, simply by default. The second alternative is to not use the `<tfoot>` element – simply adding any footer information onto the bottom of the body rows.

Notice that the footer again uses different background color for the row, and a `colspan` attribute to make it bridge two columns. This time, however, the `<td>` element is used rather than a `<th>`, since the cell does not contain descriptive header information. While the distinction between these two cell types is purely cosmetic in most browsers, it is useful to preserve this distinction in order to benefit non-visual browsers and other tools that parse the HTML and need to understand the underlying structure of the data.

Once again, we have used inline style sheet information to format the text in the footer block.

Now, at last, we get to the body of the table. Here we see straightforward `<tr>` and `<td>` elements, arranged as two rows of two columns:

```
<tbody>
  <tr>
    <td>(1,1)</td>
    <td>(2,1)</td>
  </tr>
  <tr>
    <td>(1,2)</td>
    <td>(2,2)</td>
  </tr>
</tbody>
```

Notice that it is the text within the `<td>` blocks that gets put into the cells of the table, working from left to right, and top to bottom. (However, HTML 4.01 does include capabilities to display languages that are written from right to left, with attributes such as `dir` to change the direction in which tables are rendered.) See Chapter 18 for more on the `dir` attribute.

Finally, we conclude the table with the appropriate closing tag:

```
</table>
```

Although tags such as `</td>` and `</tr>` are optional, `</table>` is required and its omission can cause problems; with some browsers it can result in a failure to display any of the contents of the table. So, if the table doesn't show up, be sure to check for the closing `</table>` tag!

Later in this chapter we'll look at some more complex examples of tables, and look in more detail at the formatting options. First, though, let's review the full syntax of the elements we've been working with.

The HTML Table Elements

To create more sophisticated tables, we need to be aware of the full set of attributes that we can use with the table elements. These are outlined below.

The <table> Element

We can specify the following attributes for the `<table>` element:

align	bgcolor	border	cellpadding	cellspacing
dir	frame	rules	summary	width

In addition, the universal HTML 4.01 attributes `id`, `style`, `class`, `title`, and `lang` can be used, as well as several event handlers that can be used in scripting. (See Chapter 9 for information about scripting.)

align

Defines the alignment of the complete table itself, relative to the page or element that contains it. The syntax is:

```
align="type"
```

where `type` is `left`, `right`, or `center`. If we use `align="left"` or `align="right"`, the table 'floats' against that edge of its available space, and text will flow round the table. To avoid this we should use: `<br clear="value">` after the `</table>` tag, where `value` is `left` or `right`. This variation on the simple `<br>` line break element causes the next line to begin where the specified margin – left or right – is clear of any floating objects – such as tables, or images.

By default, if the align attribute is not specified, browsers typically align the table to the left, but do not flow text around it – continuing with the next element underneath the table.

This attribute is deprecated in HTML 4.01 – style sheets should now be used to position elements on the page.

bgcolor

Specifies the background color for the table. The syntax is:

```
bgcolor="colorValue"
```

where colorValue is the color, expressed either as a standard color name such as lightblue or as a numeric value in the form #rrggbb where the hexadecimal values for the red, green, and blue components of each color are provided. Browsers offer varying levels of support for other numeric formats and color names, but for maximum compatibility use the #rrggbb format. It is deprecated in HTML 4.01; style sheets should now be used.

border

Draws a border round both the table itself, and each of the individual cells in it. The syntax is:

```
border="n"
```

where n is the width of the table's outer border in pixels. Setting border="0", or omitting the attribute, results in no visible border for either the table as a whole, or between the individual cells. Using border on its own, with no value, gives a border width of 1 pixel. This attribute is deprecated in HTML 4.01 and only supported for backward compatibility – style sheets should now be used instead.

cellpadding

Specifies the amount of space between all four edges of a cell and its contents. The syntax is:

```
cellpadding="n"
```

where n is the amount of space in pixels. For a percentage value append the % percent sign.

cellspacing

Specifies the amount of space between the borders of the individual cells in the table. The syntax is:

```
cellspacing="n"
```

where n is the amount of space in pixels. For a percentage value append the % percent sign.

dir

This specifies the text direction for the table. The syntax is:

```
dir="direction"
```

where direction is either ltr or rtl, for left-to-right (the default), or right-to-left (as used in some languages). Note that when applied to a table as a whole, it causes the cells on each row to be output from right to left, with the first cell defined on the right.

frame

Specifies which outer borders of the table are displayed, and allows more precise control than the `border` attribute. The syntax is:

```
frame="type"
```

where `type` can be one of the following:

- ❑ `void` – no outer borders are displayed
- ❑ `above` – displays the top border
- ❑ `below` – displays the bottom border
- ❑ `hsides` – displays the top and bottom borders
- ❑ `lhs` – displays the left border
- ❑ `rhs` – displays the right border
- ❑ `vsides` – displays the left and right borders
- ❑ `box` – displays a border on all sides of the table frame
- ❑ `border` – equivalent to `box`: displays a border on all sides of the table frame

The default is `void`. The `frame` attribute defines only the outer border around the table. If both the `frame` and `border` attributes are used, `frame` takes precedence. Using the `border` attribute with no value has the same effect as `frame="border"`, while `border="0"` has the same effect as `frame="void"`. At the time of writing, support for this in browsers such as Netscape 6 and Internet Explorer 5 is patchy and idiosyncratic. Note CSS2 style sheets now provide similar functionality, and the HTML 4.01 specification suggests they should be used instead.

rules

Specifies which inner borders of the table are displayed. The syntax is:

```
rules="type"
```

where `type` is one of the following:

- ❑ `none` – no inner borders are displayed; this is the default
- ❑ `groups` – displays inner borders between all table groups; groups are specified by the `<thead>`, `<tbody>`, `<tfoot>`, and `<colgroup>` elements
- ❑ `rows` – displays horizontal borders between all table rows
- ❑ `cols` – displays vertical borders between all table columns
- ❑ `all` – displays a border for all rows and columns

The default is `none`. The `rules` attribute defines only the inner borders of the table. At the time of writing, support for this in browsers such as Netscape 6 and Internet Explorer 5 is patchy and idiosyncratic. CSS2 is recommended as a replacement for this attribute in HTML 4.01.

summary

Provides a summary of the table's purpose and structure for browsers rendering non-visual media such as speech or Braille. Generally not rendered by mainstream browsers, but promoted by the Standard for accessibility reasons. The syntax is:

```
summary="text"
```

width

Sets the width of the table. The syntax is:

```
width="n"
```

where n is the width in pixels or as a percentage of the available space. If the table is not nested inside another table or element, then the available width will be the distance between the left and right margins of the window. If the table is itself inside a table cell or other element, then the available space is the width of the containing element. To set a percentage, a % sign must be appended to the end of the value.

Netscape <table> Extensions

Netscape supports other attributes for the <table> tag, including:

❑ background – specifies a background picture that will be tiled behind the content of all the cells. The syntax is background="url"

❑ hspace – defines the minimum horizontal distance, to the left and right of the table, between it and any surrounding elements. The syntax is hspace="n" where n is the number of pixels.

❑ vspace – defines the minimum vertical distance, above and below the table, between it and any surrounding elements. The syntax is vspace="n" where n is the number of pixels.

Internet Explorer <table> Extensions

Internet Explorer supports additional attributes for the <table> tag, including:

❑ background – specifies a background picture that will be tiled behind the content of all the cells. The syntax is: background="url"

❑ bordercolor – specifies the color of the table border. The syntax is bordercolor="color" where color can be a pre-defined color name or a set of hexadecimal values in the format #rrggbb

❑ bordercolordark and bordercolorlight – allow the specification of colors used, when a table is rendered with 3-D borders in Internet Explorer. By swapping the usual colors over, we can provide an etched appearance rather than the usual raised border.

The <caption> Element

This element is used to describe the contents of the table, and provides a caption that is displayed next to, above, or below the table. The element is optional, but if included there can only be one, and it must come directly after the opening <table> tag.

The <caption> element accepts the attribute align, plus the standard HTML 4.01 attributes id, style, class, title, dir, and lang. The <caption> element also provides several events that can be used in scripting. (See Chapter 9 for information about scripting.)

align

Specifies the position of the caption in relation to the whole table. The syntax is:

```
align="type"
```

where type can be one of:

❑ top – places the caption above the table

❑ bottom – places the caption below the table

❑ left – places the caption on the left side of the table

❑ right – places the caption on the right side of the table

Note: browsers often use the <caption> element in different ways from the HTML 4.01 proposals (see below).

Extensions to the <caption> Element

Current browsers generally use an extra attribute with the <caption> element, and implement the align attribute in a different way:

❑ valign – specifies whether the caption should appear above or below the table. The syntax is valign="vtype", where vtype can be top (the default) or bottom

In this case, the left and right values for align will only align the caption in relation to the width of the table, rather than placing it physically to the left or right of the whole table. The valign attribute is then included to control whether the caption appears above or below the table. Often the extra value center is added to the align attribute to center the caption in relation to the width of the table.

The <thead>, <tfoot>, and <tbody> Elements

HTML 3.2 introduced the concept of dividing a table into three sections, the head, body, and foot, and this has been carried forward in HTML 4.01. This division of the content of the table into sections allows the browser to lay out the table in special ways so that, for example, the body section can scroll while the header and footer rows are fixed. (Netscape 6 was among the first browsers to implement that particular capability.)

It also allows the browser to add appropriate header and footer sections to each page while printing the content as hard copy, or perhaps when exporting it to other applications. Above all, it also provides internal structure, which allows non-visual user agents or automated page readers to get information about the content. As noted above, the correct ordering of the elements in the HTML is to have the <tfoot> section before the <tbody> section. This helps the browser lay out the table more quickly.

The entire <thead>, <tbody>, and <tfoot> elements can be omitted if required, and in this case the table is assumed to consist of a single <tbody> element. Note that the optional end tag </thead> can only be omitted when the next tag is either <tfoot> or <tbody>. Likewise, the optional end tag </tfoot> can only be omitted when the next tag is <tbody>.

The <thead>, <tbody>, and <tfoot> elements support the following attributes, which are inherited by all the cells in that section unless over-ridden within the row or cell:

    align   char   charoff   valign

In addition, the standard HTML 4.01 attributes id, style, class, title, dir, and lang are supported. The <thead>, <tbody>, and <tfoot> elements also provide several events that can be used in scripting. (See Chapter 9 for information about scripting.)

align

Defines the alignment of the content of all the cells in this section of the table. The syntax is:

    align="type"

where type is one of:

- ❑ left – cell contents are left aligned
- ❑ right – cell contents are right aligned
- ❑ center – contents are centered horizontally within the cell
- ❑ justify – text content is justified to fill the cell
- ❑ char – cell contents are aligned horizontally around a specified character

The default is left for body cells, and usually center for header and footer cells. The individual rows and cells within that block inherit the value. When type is char, the text contents are supposed to be aligned so that the first instances of a specified character in each cell are placed vertically above each other – for instance to align the decimal points in a column of numbers. For more details see the char and charoff attributes below, but note that only Netscape 6 currently supports the justify attribute value, and neither Netscape 6 nor Internet Explorer 5.x support character alignment.

valign

Specifies the vertical alignment of the content within the cells in that section. The syntax is:

    valign="type"

where `type` can be:

❑ `top` – places the content at the top of the cells

❑ `middle` – centers the text vertically within the cells; note that some browsers use `center` as a synonym for this attribute value

❑ `bottom` – places the content at the bottom of the cells

❑ `baseline` – aligns the content so that the first line of text in each cell starts on the same horizontal line

char

Specifies the character that will be used to align the text contents of the cells in each column. The syntax is:

```
char="character"
```

where `character` is the **axis** character that will be used for the alignment (the comparison is case-sensitive). For instance, `char="."` will align the contents so that values line up on the decimal place – depending on the language specified for the page or element. Note that most browsers do not support this attribute at present.

charoff

Specifies where to position the aligned characters given by the `char` attribute. This is in terms of character widths, or a percentage of available space. For instance, with an alignment of `char="."` and `charoff="75%"`, a column of numbers would be aligned with the decimal points in line, three-quarters of the way across the cells.

The syntax is:

```
charoff="offset"
```

where `offset` is the number of characters to offset the axis character by. If a percentage of the text length is required as the offset, a `%` percent sign must be appended to the value. If the `char` attribute is present and this attribute is omitted, the contents are shifted so that the text before the axis character in all the columns is visible. Note that most browsers do not support this attribute at present.

Internet Explorer Attribute Extensions

Internet Explorer adds another attribute to the `<thead>`, `<tbody>`, and `<tfoot>` elements:

❑ `bgcolor` – defines the color for the background of the cells in that section of the table. See the `<table>` element for details

The <tr> Element

The <tr> element defines the start of a table row, which can contain either <th> or <td> elements. A complete table, or a <thead>, <tbody>, or <tfoot> section, consists of one or more <tr> elements. Anything between the first <tr> element and the next will be on the same row. The optional end tag </tr> can be omitted, although this may cause some browsers to display the table incorrectly.

The <tr> element supports five attributes that control the presentation of the content within the row, and are inherited by all the cells in this row unless over-ridden in the individual <td> or <th> elements. The attributes for <tr> are:

```
align        bgcolor        char        charoff        valign
```

The universal HTML 4.01 attributes id, style, class, title, dir, and lang are supported. The <tr> element also provides several events that can be used in scripting. (See Chapter 9 for information about scripting.)

align

Defines the horizontal alignment of the content of all the cells in this section of the table. See the section on the <thead>, <tbody>, and <tfoot> elements for details.

bgcolor

Specifies the background color for the row. See the section on the <table> element for details. This attribute is deprecated in HTML 4.01 and style sheets should be used instead.

char

Specifies the character that will be used to align the text contents of the cells in this row. See the section on the <thead>, <tbody>, and <tfoot> elements for details.

charoff

Specifies the offset to the first occurrence of the character in the char attribute. See the section on the <thead>, <tbody>, and <tfoot> elements for details.

valign

Specifies the vertical alignment of the content within the cells in this row. See the section on the <thead>, <tbody>, and <tfoot> elements for details.

Internet Explorer <tr> Extensions

Internet Explorer adds three more attributes to the <tr> element:

❑ bordercolor – specifies the color of the cell borders. See the section on the <table> element for details.

❑ bordercolordark and bordercolorlight – allow us to specify the colors used when the cells are rendered with 3-D borders. See the section on the <table> element for details.

The <th> and <td> Elements

The <th> and <td> elements define an individual cell within a table row. <th> elements are used for table headings, and the contents are usually displayed in a different way – generally in bold text and centered, whereas the default for a <td> element is usually left-aligned.

Both have corresponding optional end tags </th> and </td>, which can be omitted. Anything between one <th> or <td> tag and the next cell, or row is displayed in that cell. Note, however, that this may cause some browsers to display the table incorrectly.

The <th> and <td> elements have a set of attributes that affect only that cell. These take precedence over the same attributes set by the enclosing <tr>, <thead>, <tbody>, <tfoot>, and <table> tags.

The attributes supported by <th> and <td> are:

abbr	align	axis	bgcolor	char
charoff	colspan	headers	height	nowrap
rowspan	scope	valign	width	

The standard HTML 4.01 attributes id, style, class, title, dir, and lang are supported as are several attributes for events that can be used in scripting. (See Chapter 9 for information about scripting.)

abbr

Provides an abbreviated version of the cell's content, for use where there is little available space. The two major browsers don't support this at present. The format is abbr="text".

align

Defines the alignment of the content of the cell. See the section on the <thead>, <tbody>, and <tfoot> elements for details.

axis

This attribute provides a way of assigning a category name to a cell. The syntax is:

```
axis="categoryNames"
```

where categoryNames is a comma-separated list of names for the cell's category. This is intended primarily for programs that convert the page to speech, or otherwise process the data within the page. If omitted, the content of the cell is used as the axis.

bgcolor

Specifies the background color of the cell. See the section on the <table> element for details. It is deprecated in HTML 4.01; style sheets should now be used.

char

Specifies the character that will be used to align the text contents of the cell. See the section on the `<thead>`, `<tbody>`, and `<tfoot>` elements for details.

charoff

Specifies the offset to the first occurrence of the character specified in the `char` attribute. See the section on the `<thead>`, `<tbody>`, and `<tfoot>` elements for details.

colspan

This attribute specifies the number of columns of the table that the cell will span. The syntax is:

```
colspan="n"
```

where n is the number of columns to span. `colspan` allows us to join cells – providing a way to place a heading or content across several columns to provide richer layout.

headers

Identifies which cell contains the header that labels or describes the current cell's value. The syntax is:

```
headers="idrefs"
```

where `idrefs` is a space-separated list of the appropriate header cells' `id` attributes. Intended primarily for text-to-speech applications, this attribute is not widely supported.

height and width

These allow us to specify the size of an individual cell, either in pixels or as a percentage of the available space if the % sign is appended. The syntax is:

```
height="n"  or  width="n"
```

where n is a number of pixels, or a number followed by a percent sign. These are deprecated in HTML 4.01, and style sheets should be used instead.

nowrap

The `nowrap` attribute stops the text from wrapping in the cell. The syntax is simply `nowrap`. This attribute is useful for laying out text content that would not make sense if allowed to wrap to the next line, and also provides some control over the way the available page width is distributed between the columns in the table. Note that `nowrap` is deprecated in HTML 4.01, and supported for backward compatibility only – use style sheets instead.

rowspan

This attribute specifies the number of rows of the table that the cell will span. The syntax is:

```
rowspan="n"
```

where n is the number of rows to span. Like colspan, rowspan allows us to join cells, but this time spanning over adjacent cells vertically rather than horizontally. When a cell spans down into a row below it, the definition of the corresponding cell in that table row must be omitted. (See the example at the end of this Chapter for details of a sample layout with cells spanning multiple rows).

scope

Specifies the set of data cells for which the current header cell provides label/header information. Can be used in place of the headers attribute in simple tables. This isn't widely supported. The syntax is:

```
scope="identifier"
```

where identifier is one of row, col, rowgroup, and colgroup. For instance, scope=row indicates that this cell contains the header label for all the cells in the current row.

valign

Specifies the vertical alignment of the content within the cell. See the section on the <thead>, <tbody>, and <tfoot> elements for details.

Non-Standard <th> and <td> Extensions

Some browsers support other attributes for the <th> and <td> elements:

❑ background – specifies a background picture that will be tiled behind just this cell. See the section on the <table> element for details. This is supported by Internet Explorer, and Netscape 4 or later.

❑ bordercolor – specifies the color of the cell borders. See the section on the <table> element for details. Internet Explorer supports this.

❑ bordercolordark and bordercolorlight – allow us to specify the colors used when the cells are rendered with 3-D borders. See the section on the <table> element for details. Internet Explorer supports these.

Column Grouping Elements

The final two elements used in tables are <colgroup> and <col>. They provide a way of grouping adjacent columns together, and applying formatting to them as a group rather than having to format each column separately. They are generally used in more complex tables; where a set of adjacent columns contain similar types of information, while other groups of columns contain different types of information.

At the time of writing however, the major browsers' support for column grouping is limited.

The <colgroup> and <col> Elements

We can specify that a number of columns belong to a group using the <colgroup> element. We can then specify any different individual attributes for a particular column within a group or outside of one, by using the <col> element. The <colgroup> and <col> elements support the following attributes:

```
align        char        charoff        span        valign        width
```

In addition, the standard HTML 4.01 attributes id, style, class, title, dir, and lang are supported, as well as several events that can be used in scripting. (See Chapter 9 for information about scripting.)

align

Defines the alignment of the content of the cells within this group or for an individual column. See the section on the <thead>, <tbody>, and <tfoot> elements for details.

char

Specifies the character that will be used to align the text contents of the cells within this group or for an individual column. See the section on the <thead>, <tbody>, and <tfoot> elements for details.

charoff

Specifies the offset to the first occurrence of the character specified in the char attribute. See the section on the <thead>, <tbody>, and <tfoot> elements for details.

span

This attribute specifies the number of columns of the table that this group will refer to. The syntax is:

```
span="n"
```

where n is the number of columns to span with the attributes of the current <col> or <colgroup>.

valign

Specifies the vertical alignment of the content within the cell in this group or for an individual column. See the section on the <thead>, <tbody>, and <tfoot> elements for details.

width

Specifies the width of each column within the group or for an individual column. The syntax is:

```
width="n"
```

where n is the width in pixels. To specify a percentage of the available width, the % percent sign must be appended to the value. The special value "0*" means that columns will be the minimum width required to display all the contents.

A More Complex Example

Having looked at all of the table-related elements, we will conclude this section with an example that uses most of the features that IE 5 and Netscape 6 support.

In this example (available in the download as `starnav2001.html`), we will use a table to assemble a user interface panel, using a number of juxtaposed images. While most of the table cells will contain images, we will use two of the table cells to display text messages to the user. Indeed, one of the cells will, in turn, contain another table, allowing us to lay out out some numerical data.

Let's start by looking at the end result. The screenshot shows the finished layout. Most of the layout consists of graphics: the two text areas in the page are the area on the right detailing the 'current location', and the main central panel containing the columns of numbers.

The image for this example was created by drawing an outline of the main panel and the circular button arrangement using Macromedia Freehand, and then importing those into Adobe Photoshop. The images were superimposed and had embossed effects and text labels applied. The resulting image was then squared off into 'slices' using Adobe ImageReady, which also created the basic HTML table framework and measurements, and saved the individual graphics.

This page consists of one big table with multiple cells and spans in it, almost all of which contain graphics of pieces of the larger image. These fit together like a puzzle to make up the whole image. To get a better idea, let's see the same page, with a border added to the outer table, and a few pixels of cell spacing. This has the effect of moving the components apart, so that all the individual shapes can be seen. As can be seen from the following screen shot, there are 13 separate graphics which go to make up the page – plus the two table cells with colored backgrounds into which the textual content is written.

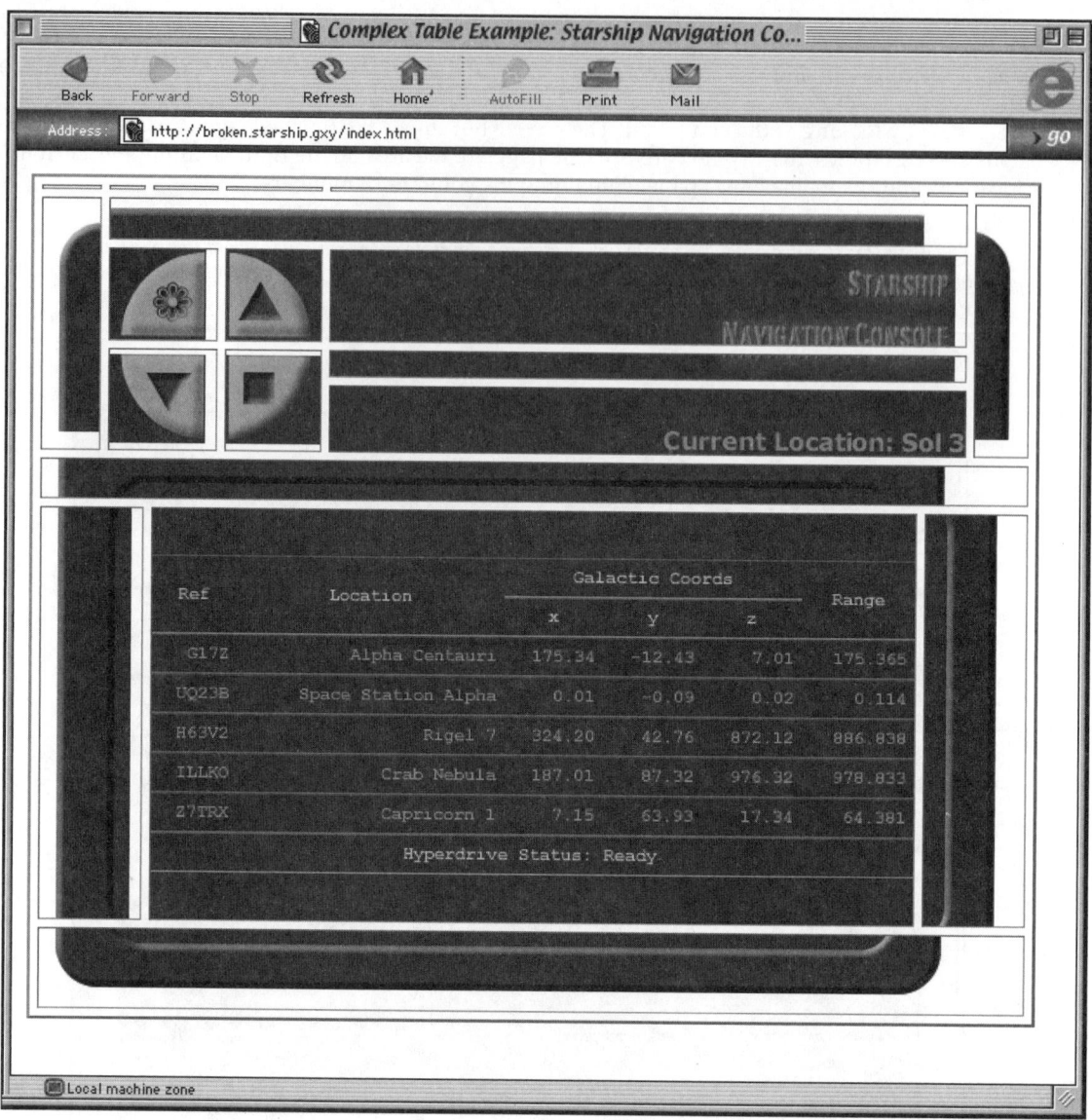

Next let's look at the code itself, and see how the page was assembled. The head block for the page is fairly standard, providing a title, and defining some styles that we will use later to format the text. (Style sheets are discussed later in the book; for now the details of these can be ignored.)

```
<html>
  <head>
    <title>Complex Table Example: Starship Navigation Console </title>
    <style type="text/css">
      <!--
        .location {  font-family: Verdana, Arial, Helvetica, sans-serif;
        font-size: 16px; font-weight: bold; color: #6699FF; text-align:
        right}.plainterm {  font-family: "Courier New", Courier, mono;
        font-size: 12px}.goodstatus { color: #66FF00; font-weight: bold}
        .destinations {  color: #00CC66; font-weight: bold; text-align:
        right}
      -->
    </style>
  </head>
```

Then comes the main table, which pulls together all of the individual images. Note that there is no border, padding, or spacing, so as to tightly abut the individual cells. The first row consists of seven cells, each containing a transparent single-pixel-high GIF. This spacing technique was discussed in Chapter 5, and here we are simply using it to establish the width of the columns that the rest of the rows will be lined up under. As noted in Chapter 5, purists sometimes frown upon single-pixel spacer GIFs, but this is one context where they are invaluable. The single-pixel spacer GIF establishes the widths of each column in the very first row, before the image itself is introduced. Without this device, the browser may struggle to select appropriate widths to meet the space requirements of the differently sized and interlocking images. By establishing the widths of the columns first, we provide a table layout that will be correctly reproduced by as wide a range of browsers as possible.

Since the images are of different sizes, and do not line up all the way through the image, we are going to use various combinations of colspan and rowspan to position the images. Calculating the necessary column widths can be tricky, and graphics or page-layout tools that can work out the geometry for us are a big help.

```
<body bgcolor="#FFFFFF">
  <table width="612" border="0" cellpadding="0" cellspacing="0"
         class="goodstatus">
    <tr>
      <td>
        <img src="images/spacer.gif" width="38" height="1">
      </td>
      <td>
        <img src="images/spacer.gif" width="22" height="1">
      </td>
      <td>
        <img src="images/spacer.gif" width="41" height="1">
      </td>
      <td>
        <img src="images/spacer.gif" width="63" height="1">
      </td>
      <td>
        <img src="images/spacer.gif" width="389" height="1">
      </td>
      <td>
        <img src="images/spacer.gif" width="25" height="1">
      </td>
      <td>
        <img src="images/spacer.gif" width="34" height="1">
      </td>
    </tr>
```

After this first row, we lay out the rows and columns of the table, inserting a graphic into each cell. Notice that we specify the width and height of each image to help the browser lay out the page quickly.

```
<tr>
  <td rowspan="4">
    <img src="images/starnav2001_01.gif" width="38" height="143">
  </td>
  <td colspan="5">
    <img src="images/starnav2001_02.gif" width="540" height="26">
  </td>
  <td rowspan="4">
    <img src="images/starnav2001_03.gif" width="34" height="143">
  </td>
</tr>
<tr>
  <td colspan="2">
    <img src="images/starnav2001_04.gif" width="63" height="59">
  </td>
  <td>
    <img src="images/starnav2001_05.gif" width="63" height="59">
  </td>
  <td colspan="2">
    <img src="images/starnav2001_06.gif" width="414" height="59">
  </td>
</tr>
<tr>
  <td colspan="2" rowspan="2">
    <img src="images/starnav2001_07.gif" width="63" height="58">
  </td>
  <td rowspan="2">
    <img src="images/starnav2001_08.gif" width="63" height="58">
  </td>
  <td colspan="2">
    <img src="images/starnav2001_09.gif" width="414" height="16">
  </td>
</tr>
```

Now we have reached the cell where we want to put the first piece of regular text. First, we set the background color of this cell to match the color of the surrounding images. Next we insert another spacer graphic to ensure the browser keeps this cell the right height, and then we include the actual content that we want. Note that we use the style sheet definitions from earlier (invoked using the class attribute) and the name of the style, to format the text.

```
<tr>
  <td colspan="2" bgcolor="#142F57" class="location">
    <p>
      <img src="images/spacer.gif" width="1" height="39">
        Current Location: Sol 3
    </p>
  </td>
</tr>
```

We then continue laying out a few more cells in the grid, until we get to the main body section of the layout.

```
<tr>
  <td colspan="7">
    <img src="images/starnav2001_11.gif" width="612" height="25">
  </td>
</tr>
<tr>
  <td colspan="2">
    <img src="images/starnav2001_12.gif" width="60" height="269">
  </td>
```

Now, in this central cell, we are going to embed another table. We start the table by specifying one of the styles we defined earlier, `plainterm`, for the table as a whole, and setting the background color to match the surrounding graphics, so making our table blend in to the images around it. We turn off the outer edges of the frame, but tell the browser to display the horizontal lines between rows, using the `frame` and `rules` attributes.

```
<td colspan="3" bgcolor="#333333">
  <table width="100%" border="1" frame="void" rules="rows"
         cellspacing="0" cellpadding="5" class="plainterm">
```

The header block for this table is fairly straightforward. We use another stylesheet to set the formatting for all the text in this section, and header cells to define the column headings. Note that we use a `rowspan` of two for most of the cells on the first row. This leaves room for the "x, y, z" labels on the second row under the "Galactic Coords" heading, which itself only spans one row, but three columns.

```
<thead class="goodstatus">
  <tr>
    <th rowspan="2">Ref</th>
    <th rowspan="2">Location</th>
    <th colspan="3">Galactic Coords</th>
    <th rowspan="2">Range</th>
  </tr>
  <tr>
    <th>x</th>
    <th>y</th>
    <th>z</th>
  </tr>
</thead>
```

Note that in the code above, in the second row of the heading we only had to specify three cells – the x, y, and z heading cells. The first two columns on this row were filled by the Ref and Location cells from the previous row that were defined with a `rowspan=2`.

Next we define the footer, using a combination of inline and predefined stylesheet information to provide the formatting.

```
<tfoot>
  <tr>
    <td colspan=6 style="text-align:center"
        class="goodstatus">
      Hyperdrive Status: Ready
    </td>
  </tr>
</tfoot>
```

And then finally we get to the table body block for our inner table! The text is formatted using a stylesheet applied to the <tbody> element, and the cells themselves are a straightforward arrangement of five rows of six columns of data.

```
<tbody class="destinations">
  <tr>
    <td>G17Z</td>
    <td>Alpha Centauri</td>
    <td>175.34</td>
    <td>-12.43</td>
    <td>7.01</td>
    <td>175.365</td>
  </tr>
  <tr>
    <td>UQ23B</td>
    <td>Space Station Alpha</td>
    <td>0.01</td>
    <td>-0.09</td>
    <td>0.02</td>
    <td>0.114</td>
  </tr>
  <tr>
    <td>H63V2</td>
    <td>Rigel 7</td>
    <td>324.20</td>
    <td>42.76</td>
    <td>872.12</td>
    <td>886.838</td>
  </tr>
  <tr>
    <td>ILLKO</td>
    <td>Crab Nebula</td>
    <td>187.01</td>
    <td>87.32</td>
    <td>976.32</td>
    <td>978.833</td>
  </tr>
  <tr>
    <td>Z7TRX</td>
    <td>Capricorn 1</td>
    <td>7.15</td>
    <td>63.93</td>
    <td>17.34</td>
    <td>64.381</td>
  </tr>
</tbody>
```

Finally we close this inner table, and the cell from the outer table that contained it.

```
      </table>
    </td>
```

Then we continue on with the last few cells to complete the image that surrounds our content and so gives the appearance of one seamless design.

```
      <td colspan="2">
        <img src="images/starnav2001_14.gif" width="59" height="269">
      </td>
    </tr>
    <tr>
      <td colspan="7">
        <img src="images/starnav2001_15.gif" width="612" height="51">
      </td>
    </tr>
```

Finally, we can close the outer `<table>`, `<body>`, and `<html>` elements.

```
    </table>
  </body>
</html>
```

As shown above, the results of this kind of sliced graphic and nested table approach can blend text and graphical elements together seamlessly, to make something quite eye-catching. However, these complex layouts can be prone to differences between browsers, which can sometimes introduce misalignments, or thin white lines into the arrangement. Furthermore, editing the content can be tricky: it takes very disciplined approach to avoid introducing unexpected changes into the surrounding pieces: just adding spaces or line breaks between elements can upset the alignment in some browsers.

Summary

In this chapter, we've looked at all aspects of creating HTML tables. We started with an example of a relatively basic table, before considering all of the attributes available for the HTML elements that are used in tables. We looked at how the formatting of individual cells can be affected, and how we can format an entire table and then override that format for specific cells. We also looked at the `<colgroup>` tag, and how this can be used to simplify column formatting. Finally, we looked at how nested tables can be used to format whole pages of graphics and text.

Bear in mind that table layouts are complex, and the browser often makes a number of sizing and formatting choices as it displays the layout. Usually this will be done in a transparent and consistent way, but occasionally, differences between browsers can manifest themselves: the more complicated we make our tables, and the more advanced features we rely on, then the more likely it is that our pages will break or look ugly on some browsers – even quite recent ones.

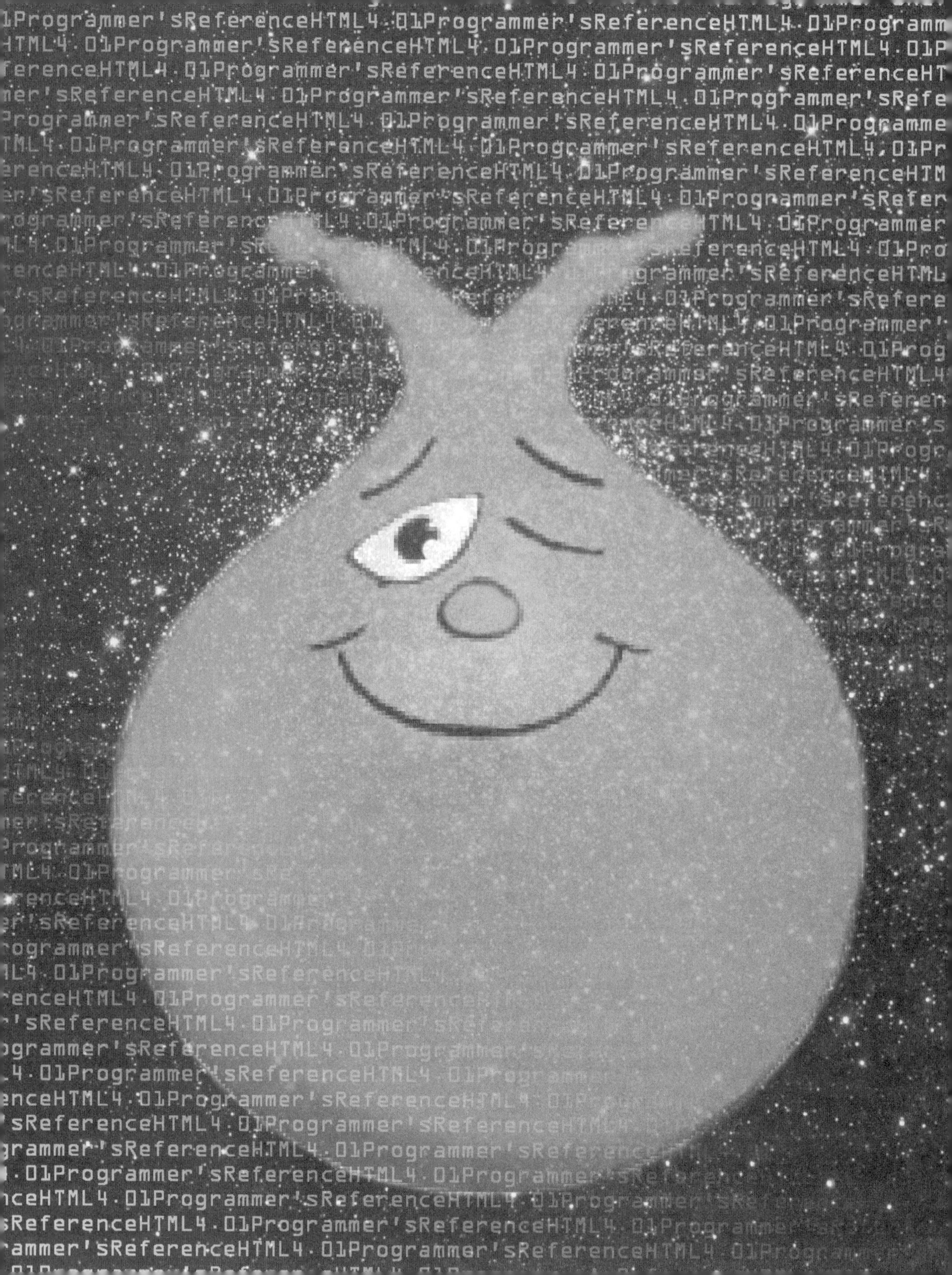
Programmer'sReferenceHTML4.01

8

Frames

Frames give the web page designer an alternative way to organize information that is more flexible than tables can offer. Using frames, you can specify areas of your page as distinct sections of your browser window that can then load or reload new pages of content into view – independently of each other. A classic use for this functionality is to make a standard set of features available to the user at all times no matter where they are on the site – for example, a central sitemap, menu, or reminder in one frame and the actual content in the other. This could contribute to a consistent look and feel for the site as well as making it easy to navigate.

Even though frames only made it into the official HTML Specification with the arrival of version 4.0, both major browsers have supported them for several years – since Netscape 2 and IE 3 in fact.

In this chapter, we'll look at:

❑ How to create a frameset

❑ How to create inline frames

❑ How to pick and choose between frames

❑ How to cater for those users whose browsers don't support frames

❑ Some effective examples of frames online

You can find the entire wealth of code examples found in this chapter in this book's code download, available from www.wrox.com.

Creating a Frameset

To create a web page that is divided into two or more frames, you need to make use of two new page elements, and be aware of a third:

❑ The `<frameset>` element defines the outline for your group of frames, how they will look and how they will divide up the page.

❑ The `<frame>` element defines how a single frame will look and what it will contain.

❑ The `<noframes>` element lets you display some content for those users whose browsers do not support frames.

For each `<frame>`, you specify another HTML page that will be its content. The page that defines how the frames are arranged within the frameset is often referred to as a **frameset document**. For example, in this screenshot from hotmail.com, the frameset defines two frames; the top frame is of a fixed height and contains its fixed message, and the other covers the rest of the browser window.

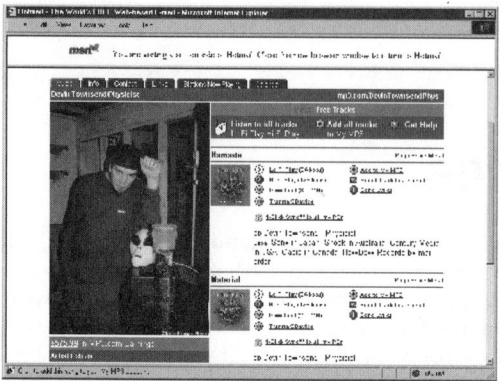
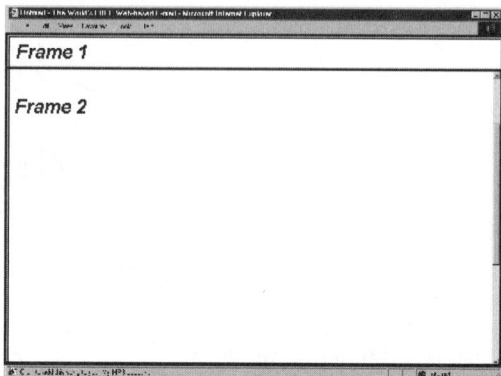

All things being equal, pointing your browser at the frameset document will first load that and then the HTML pages to populate the frames within. It may happen that a user's browser doesn't support frames, in which case it will display the HTML you've enclosed in the `<noframes>` tag that we'll see later, but, as we have already said, frames and framesets have been supported since Netscape 2.0 and IE 3.0, so the chance of this is growing smaller with the passing of days. Once you start using frames, it's very easy to get carried away and use them for everything: logo at the top, site map or menu down one side, adverts down at the bottom, and so on. Be sparing with your use of frames, and remember that not everyone is using the set-up you are: frames are rendered slightly differently on different browsers and not everyone may be using the same resolution on screen as you or have the same connection to the Internet. Don't forget either that each frame onscreen is another page the browser must download.

A Basic Frameset

A basic frameset document looks like this:

```
<!doctype html public "-//W3C//DTD HTML 4.01 Frameset//EN"
    "http://www.w3.org/TR/html4/frameset.dtd">

<!-- skeleton.html -->

<html>
<head>
<title>
This is a skeleton frameset document - nothing will appear
</title>
</head>

<!--the frameset definition must be first after head-->
<frameset>
    <frame />
    . . .
    <frame />
    . . .

<!--an optional noframes section,
    for older browsers that don't support frames-->
    <noframes>
    . . .
    </noframes>
</frameset>
</html>
```

As you can see from the top line, the makeup of a frameset document differs from that of any other HTML page, as it is defined by the HTML 4.01 Frameset DTD that it maps to rather than the Transitional or Strict DTDs you would usually refer to (as you will recall from Chapter 1, this is the DTD you *have* to use if you want to use frames).

It's not actually that scary though – the DTD simply declares the page to consist of a head element followed by a `<frameset>` and not a `<body>`.

According to the W3C spec, you should not put any other tag, with the exception of a comment, between `</head>` and `<frameset>` tags, like so:

```
</head>
```

```
<p> can u see this? </P>
```

```
<!--the frameset definition must be first after head-->
<frameset>
    <frame />
```

In this case, the frameset *should* be ignored and the content of those tags be displayed instead. This holds true in all versions of IE, and Netscape up to v4.8x, but this only applies in Mozilla for the case where the <body> tag is the first element after </head>. In the case of other tags, such as <p> in the above example, Mozilla ignores them and displays the frameset instead.

Inside the frameset element, a declaration is made for each frame to be rendered on screen and a <noframes> element can also be declared, giving some alternative content for those users whose browsers do not support frames or in which frame support has been turned off.

For those browsers that support frames, any elements within the frameset except for frames are ignored, as are any placed after the frameset.

The Frameset Elements

Let's look at each of the three frameset elements in turn – <frameset>, <frame>, and <noframes>.

<frameset>

The <frameset> element is used to declare how the browser window should be divided up into rectangular frames. It encloses the subsequent frame and noframe declarations within the document. It supports the following attributes

```
cols       rows
```

plus the HTML 4.01 universal attributes id, class, style, dir, lang, and title, and the common events (see Chapter 2 for further details of these). It also supports some IE- and Netscape-specific extensions, which we will look at later.

Note that there are no specific CSS styles related to the <frameset> element.

cols

Defines the number and size of the columns that will be used when dividing the frameset's parent element up among the frames. The syntax is:

```
cols="column_list"
```

where column_list is a comma-separated list of the widths of each column as seen from left to right, specified as one of:

❑   an absolute value in pixels

❑   relative widths between the columns

❑   a percentage of the width of the parent frame/frameset or browser window

❑   *, meaning the remainder of the parent frame/frameset or browser window not used up

Let's look at some examples:

```
cols="50%, *, 40%"
```

defines three columns as a percentage of the width of the frameset's **parent element** – sometimes called the **frameset's container**. This can be either the browser window that contains the frameset document, or the frame in which the frameset is nested (See section on "*Nested Framesets*" below).

The first column will be 50% of the width of the frameset's parent element and the third 40% of the width. The second column will take up the remaining space – 10% of the width in this case. Note that the width of each frame will be recalculated as the user resizes the parent element.

```
cols="1*,3*,2*"
```

The above line again defines three columns, this time using relative widths rather than percentages. The first is one sixth of the width of the frameset's parent element, the second takes up half (three sixths), and the third the remaining third (two sixths). As above, the exact widths will be recalculated as the user resizes the parent element.

```
cols="100, 350, *"
```

This also defines three columns, but this time as absolutes: the first column will be 100 pixels wide, the second 350 pixels wide, and the third will fill up the remainder of the screen, as indicated by the asterisk.

Browsers give columns of absolute width priority within their frameset. Should a user resize a frameset's parent element to be narrower than the sum total widths of those absolute values, they will try to show as much of those columns as possible to the exclusion of those given a relative width. The extent of this exclusion depends on the browser and where the particular columns are in the frameset – they may be given some minimum width or not be displayed at all. In the example above, a window 350 pixels wide would show 100 pixels of column 1, the leftmost 250 pixels of column 2 and none of column 3.

```
cols="1*, 100, 20%, 3*"
```

This example defines four columns using a mixture of the three methods we have seen above. Column 2 will be 100 pixels wide, and the other three columns will divide the remaining space between them. Column 3 will take 20% of the remaining width in the parent element while columns 1 and 4 will fill up the remainder of the width in the ratio 1:3.

It is perhaps a little unwise to mix value types like this though, as it can become difficult to predict what you'll see on screen – especially as the user resizes the frameset's parent element.

There are a few more traps to be wary of here:

❑ Make sure you give the right number of values for the number of columns you want frames for. If you specify, for example, four columns in your frameset, but only three frames, (that is, fewer frames than columns) the rightmost column becomes just blank space. If, on the other hand, you declare five frames but only four columns (that is, more frames than columns) then the fifth frame will be ignored.

❑ If you're giving column widths **only** as percentages but they total either more or less than 100, the browser will adjust each column width in proportion to fill the window exactly.

❏ Likewise, if you're giving column widths **only** as absolute values, but these total either more or less than the actual width of the frameset's parent element, the browser will adjust each column width in proportion to fill the window exactly. This resizing can be "remedied" by making sure you always have at least one column with a dynamic width – "*", for example. If you do not specify a set of values for cols, it will default to a value of "100%", that is, the frameset will contain just one column the width of the page.

rows

Defines the number and size of the rows that will be used when dividing the frameset's parent element up among the frames. The syntax is:

```
rows="row_list"
```

where row_list is a string containing the heights of each individual row from top to bottom, given in the same way and with the same caveats as col_list is given for the cols attribute above. For example:

```
rows="125, 60%, *"
```

will produce three rows in our frameset, the topmost being 125 pixels high, the middle row 60% of the remaining vacant height in the frameset's parent element, and the bottom row filling in whatever's left.

As with cols, the default value for rows is "100%", so by not specifying it, the browser will assume the frameset will contain just one row the height of the parent element.

> By not specifying values for either **rows** or **cols**, an HTML 4.0-compliant browser will assume you want a frameset one column wide by one row high, that is, your frameset will contain just one single frame, much like, but not the same as, a normal page.

Creating a Grid of Frames

By declaring values for both rows and cols in your frameset, like so:

```
<frameset cols="*,*" rows="*, 80%, *">
    <frame src="frame1.html" />
    <frame src="frame2.html" />
    <frame src="frame3.html" />
    <frame src="frame4.html" />
    <frame src="frame5.html" />
    <frame src="frame6.html" />
</frameset>
```

you can create a grid of frames for your frameset. The above example, for instance, generates this:

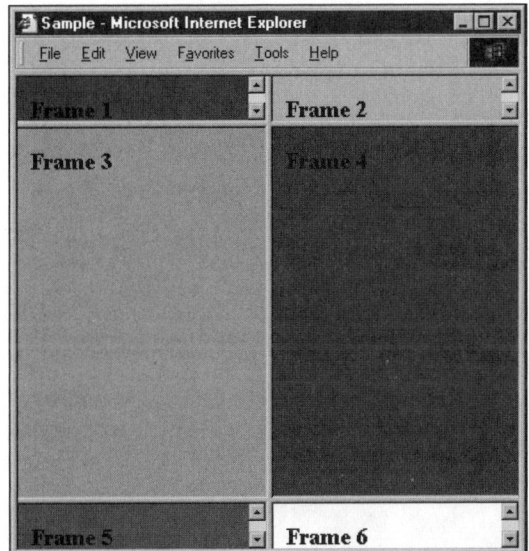

As you can see, the grid is populated starting with the top row from left to right, then the second row from left to right and so on down to the bottom right-hand frame. This approach is very simple to get the hang of, but allows only the creation of grids – with the same number of frames in each row (and each column) across the page. To get this to vary, we can nest framesets within each other in static HTML as discussed below, or dynamically, using script to load a frameset document into a frame.

Nested Framesets

Just like tables, framesets can be nested within each other, allowing you to create uneven divisions of space within your page. You can do this by declaring another frameset instead of a frame. For example:

```
<frameset rows="30%, 50%, 20%">
    <frame src="frame1.html" />

    <frameset cols="*,*,*">
        <frame src="frame2.html" />
        <frame src="frame3.html" />
        <frame src="frame4.html" />
    </frameset>

    <frame src="frame5.html" />
</frameset>
```

creates a frameset of three rows, and nests a second frameset of three columns within row two, as shown below:

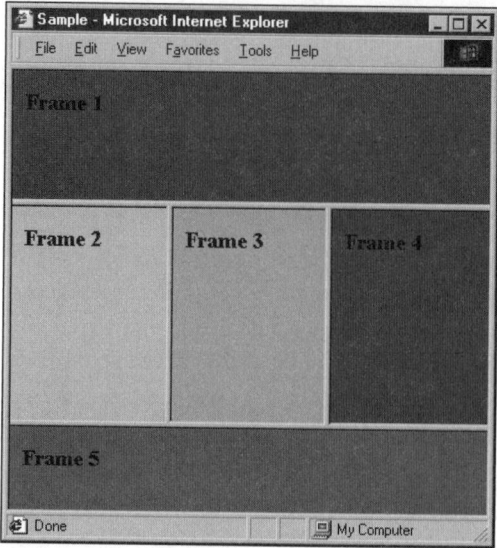

You can nest framesets within each other to any degree, although you run the risk of quickly losing track of what frame contains what page.

> While you are experimenting with frames, you may notice problems using the "refresh", option as some older browsers can only refresh the current frame. While this is appropriate when viewing a document across a slow modem link, it may not be what you want when experimenting with frame layouts. Look instead for an option to re-open the entire document.
>
> Most modern browsers make the distinction by having the reload/refresh option in the context menu to reload only the frame you right-clicked on to bring up the menu, while the reload/refresh option in the main menus reloads the entire frameset and frames.

Frameset Events

As we have already seen, the frameset element supports two scripting events under the HTML 4.01 specification – `onload` and `onunload`.

onload

The `onload` event fires when all the frames in a frameset have been accounted for, either by loading successfully or by returning errors to those frames whose contents cannot be downloaded. Take the following example:

```
<frameset cols="*,*"
          onload="javascript:alert('Frameset loaded');">
   <frame name="firstframe" src="http://lwn.net/daily" >
   <frame name="secondframe" src="http://doesntexist.com" >
</frameset>
```

Hopefully your connection is slow enough and the lwn page large enough to see that the alert box pops up only when your browser has loaded the page and returned the error page for the web site that doesn't exist.

In a more practical example, we can use onload with the body tag to force one frame to load only after another has finished loading first. If our frameset looks like this:

```
<frameset rows="*,*">
    <frame name="firstframe" src="frame9.html">
    <frame name="secondframe">
</frameset>
```

and frame9.html contains the line:

```
<body onload="parent.secondframe.location='frame10.html'">
```

then a browser will have to load frame9.html successfully into the first frame before frame10.html is loaded into the second.

onunload

The onunload event fires when the frameset is unloaded from its parent element. This could be the result of reloading the frameset document as a whole or a new page being loaded into the frameset's container, but it will not fire in the event of the contents of a frame changing for whatever reason.

To demonstrate, try using this frameset:

```
<frameset cols="*,*"
          onunload="javascript:alert('An unload occured');">
    <frame src="http://www.wrox.com" >
    <frame src="http://www.hevydevy.com" >
</frameset>
```

and once it is being shown in your browser, reloading the whole document – F5 is the usual shortcut. The event will fire as soon as F5 is pressed and before the browser actually reloads the page.

Browser Extensions to <frameset>

Microsoft Internet Explorer (IE) and Netscape (N) both implement several other attributes for <frameset>:

IE

atomicselection	hidefocus	tabindex
unselectable	name	framespacing
frameborder	bordercolor	border

Netscape

frameborder	bordercolor	border

We will now go through each of these in turn.

atomicselection – IE 5.5+ Only

atomicselection specifies whether the frameset and its contents must be selected as a whole or can be selected as individual elements – frames, text, graphics, etc. The synatax is:

```
atomicselection="boolean_value"
```

where boolean_value is either false (the default), or true. This attribute is relevant only to browsers with atomic selection mode on.

framespacing – IE 3+ Only

framespacing determines the amount of space, given in pixels, between frames in a frameset. The syntax is:

```
framespacing="spacing_in_pixels"
```

It does this by increasing the size of the border between frames. For example, the frameset below is set at framespacing="10":

```
<frameset rows= "30%, 50%, 20%" framespacing="10">
    <frame src="frame1.html">

    <frameset cols="*,*,*">
        <frame src="frame2.html">
        <frame src="frame3.html">
        <frame src="frame4.html">
    </frameset>

    <frame src="frame5.html">
</frameset>
```

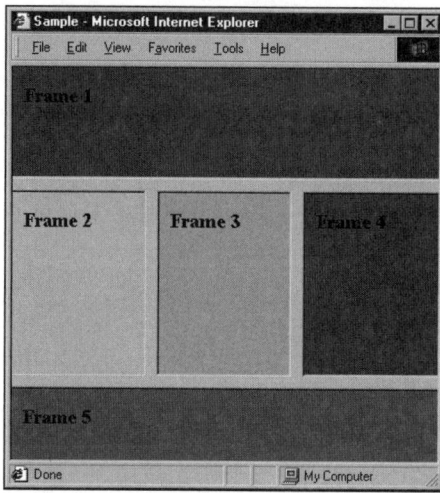

The default value for framespacing is 2.

frameborder – IE 3+, N 3+

frameborder determines whether or not a 3-D border is displayed between the frames. The syntax is:

```
frameborder="value"
```

where value can take four values:

- 1 (yes), which is the default, indicates that borders should be shown
- 0 (no) that they should not be shown.
- yes, which corresponds directly to 1
- no, which corresponds directly to 0

The values yes and no are not part of HTML 4.01, but are supported by both main browsers.

bordercolor – IE 4+, N 3+

bordercolor determines the main color of the 3D frame border, given as a color name or a #RRGGBB value.

```
bordercolor="colorname | hexadecimal value"
```

To demonstrate, let's look at the border around frame3.html in our example frameset.

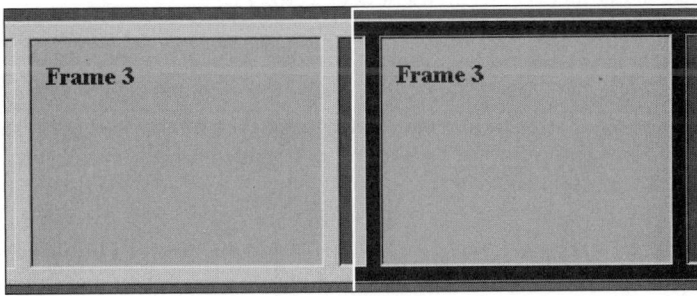

By default, with the frameset not specifying bordercolor, thus

```
<frameset rows= "30%, 50%, 20%" framespacing="10">
```

we get the left-hand side screenshot, the 3D frame getting its color scheme from the user's desktop. By saying that the frameset's bordercolor should be black, like so

```
<frameset rows= "30%, 50%, 20%" framespacing="10"
          bordercolor="#000000">
```

we get the screenshot on the right-hand side, the borders now being mostly black. The secondary color in the border to give it a 3D effect remains specific to the client's desktop, that is, there is no way you can change this second color at page level.

199

border – IE 4+, N 3+

Like `framespacing`, border sets a value for the width of the border, in pixels, between frames in a frameset.

```
border="spacing_in_pixels"
```

Navigator obeys this attribute without question, but in IE, if `framespacing` is also given, it overrides the value for `border` and follows that instead. Thus

```
<frameset rows="30%, 50%, 20%" framespacing="1" border="15">
```

produces frames a pixel apart in IE and frames 15 pixels apart in Navigator. However, IE and N "count" pixels differently, so if `framespacing` and `border` were both set to fifteen, it would appear that the frame borders were still of different size although as far as the browsers are concerned, they are not.

> To create a set of borderless frames in all browsers inclusive in IE 3+ and N 3+ with the same code, you need to explicitly set frameborder, framespacing, and border all to "0" in your frameset tag. This guarantees no borders across all those browsers. It is unclear how to guarantee this across *all* browsers however.

hidefocus – IE 5.5+ Only

`hidefocus` allows you to determine whether or not the browser will indicate on screen that the frameset is the page element currently in focus. The syntax is:

```
hidefocus="boolean_value"
```

By default, `boolean_value` is `false`, meaning that if in focus, the frameset is surrounded by a dotted rectangle (a "focus rectangle"). If `boolean_value` is `true`, the focus rectangle will not appear if the frameset is currently in focus.

name – IE 4+, N 4+

The name attribute allows you to give an identifying name to your frameset, allowing it to be easily referenced via script. The syntax is:

```
name="frame_name"
```

tabindex – IE 4+ Only

By specifying a value for `tabindex`, you can set the order in which elements on your page come into focus when the tab key is pressed. The syntax is:

```
tabindex="integer_value"
```

where `integer_value` can be a value between 0 and 32767 if you're using IE 5.0 and between -32767 and 32767 if you're using IE 5.01 or higher. Please refer to the *"Playing with Focus"* section below for more.

unselectable – IE 5.5+ Only

unselectable allows you to specify whether or not the frameset can be selected by the user.

```
unselectable="on |off"
```

By default, unselectable is set to off, meaning that the frameset can be selected

Playing with Focus – IE 4+ Only

We met this concept in Chapters 6 and 7. Now let's have a more in-depth look at the concept of focus, given that it is also very important to framesets.

Although we may not realize it, every GUI-based application on our PC makes use of the concept of focus. When two apps are running on your desktop, one window is active while the other is not. The active window is in focus while the other is not. On this scale, it's easy to distinguish between the two, as your window manager is likely to define a different color scheme for the window in focus against those not in focus to make it stand out. At a lower level however, color schemes are replaced by a **focus rectangle**. Consider a warning box that pops up if you close an app without saving your work:

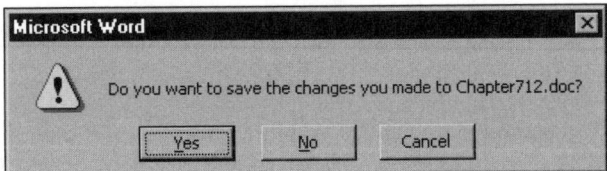

By default, if you press the return key on your keyboard, you will save your work because the <u>Y</u>es button is in focus, as you can see in the screenshot because the focus rectangle encloses the button. Now if you wanted to shift the focus to the <u>N</u>o button without using the mouse, the traditional method is to press the *Tab* key once, once more to focus on the Cancel button, and once again to return focus to the <u>Y</u>es button. The order in which the buttons come into focus is known as the **tab index**.

IE 5.0 introduced the idea of being able to set a tab index for a number of elements on a HTML page and not just the controls in a <form>, as specified in the HTML 4.0 specification. This should certainly aid those people who have difficulty in using a mouse or who prefer not to. It's perhaps easier to see this tabindex at work with some of the "larger" page elements, so the demonstration below takes the example of setting a tab index for cycling the focus around a frameset and its constituent frames.

Consider the basic frameset:

```
<frameset cols="*,*" rows="*,*,*">
    <frame src="frame1.html">
    <frame src="frame2.html">
    <frame src="frame3.html">
    <frame src="frame4.html">
    <frame src="frame5.html">
    <frame src="frame6.html">
</frameset>
```

Once loaded, you can switch focus onto each frame in turn by pressing the *Tab* key, and see that focus switch as the focus rectangle moves about the frames and elements in the frames.

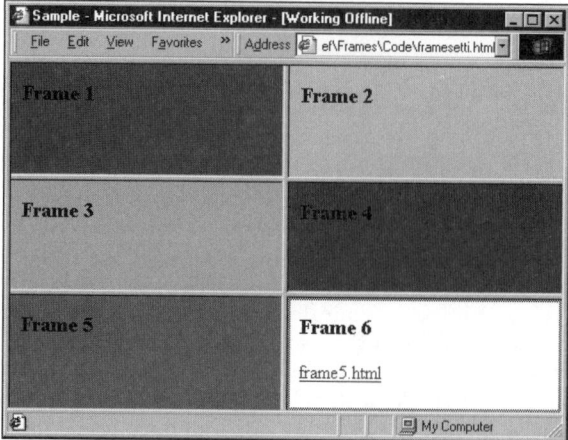

In the screenshot above, frame 6 is in focus. By default, the tab index around the elements of the page works in order of their creation – frame 1, 2, 3, 4, 5, 6, the link in frame6, the web address in the browser menu bar, and back to frame 1 again.

As you might surmise from the link in frame 6 being part of the cycle, if there are any subelements in a frame that can be focused on – links, forms, etc. – the focus will switch from the frame as a whole onto those elements, also in order of creation if tab index is not given. Once each subelement has been cycled through, the focus then moves onto the next frame in order.

We can override the default tab index for our frames by making use of the `tabindex` attribute. For example, by changing the frameset to read:

```
<frameset cols="*,*" rows="*, *, *" tabindex="4">
    <frame src="frame1.html" tabindex="5">
    <frame src="frame2.html" tabindex="4">
    <frame src="frame3.html" tabindex="3">
    <frame src="frame4.html" tabindex="2">
    <frame src="frame5.html" tabindex="6">
    <frame src="frame6.html" tabindex="1">
</frameset>
```

we alter the focus order to frame 6, then frame 4, then 3, then the frameset (which by default is not focused on), then frame 2, then 1, and finally 5. `tabindex` orders the focus from lowest number to highest, parents before children, children in order of creation, with any elements whose `tabindex` is not specified defaulted to 0.

We also have one last trick up our sleeve in the shape of the `hidefocus` attribute, which was introduced in IE 5.5. By default, when a page element is in focus, it is surrounded by a focus rectangle. By setting `hidefocus` to `"true"`:

```
<frame src="frame4.html" tabindex="2" hidefocus="true">
```

we can turn off the focus rectangle and thus hide the fact that that element is currently in focus – try it!

<frame>

The <frame> element is used to declare how one of the areas declared in a frameset will look, and what information it will contain. It supports the following attributes:

```
frameborder      marginwidth      marginheight
noresize         scrolling        longdesc
src              name
```

plus the HTML 4.01 universal attributes id, class, style, dir, lang and title, and the common events (see Chapter 2 for further details of these).

Note that there are no specific CSS styles related to <frame>.

frameborder

frameborder determines whether or not the borders of a specific frame are shown or not. The syntax is:

```
frameborder="value"
```

where value can take one of four values:

❑ 1 (yes), the default, indicates that the borders should be shown

❑ 0 (no) that they should not be shown

❑ yes, which corresponds directly to 1

❑ no, which corresponds directly to 0

The values yes and no are not part of HTML 4.01, but are supported by both main browsers.

The value of frameborder for each frame is inherited from the value of frameborder for the frameset as a whole. By specifying it as an attribute of <frame>, you override this inherited value only for that particular <frame>. If you'd like all your frames to either have or not have borders, assign the appropriate value to frameborder in the parent <frameset> tag.

marginwidth and marginheight

marginwidth allows you to specify, in pixels, the width of the frame's left and right internal margins between the 3D border of the frame and its contents. The syntax of marginwidth is:

```
marginwidth="width_in_pixels"
```

marginheight, correspondingly, allows you to specify, in pixels, the height of the frame's top and bottom internal margins between the frame border and its contents – its syntax is:

```
marginheight="height_in_pixels"
```

To demonstrate, let's take our 5-frame frameset from above and rewrite the second row's three <frame> declarations like so:

```
<frame src="frame2.html" marginwidth="0" marginheight="0">
<frame src="frame3.html">
<frame src="frame4.html" marginwidth="50" marginheight="50">
```

The middle frameset will now look like this:

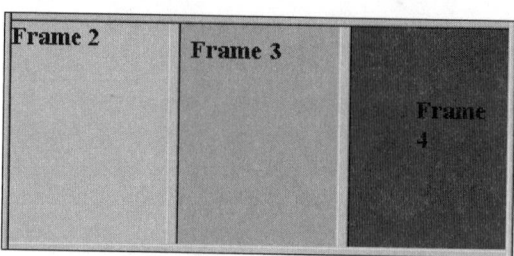

In frame 2, we specify the minimum values for marginwidth and marginheight, 0. Any negative values given for these attributes will be treated the same as zero. Note that even with a marginheight of 0, the frame's text contents still do not touch the top frame border. This does not apply to images, which do touch the top frame border.

Note that according to the HTML Specification, 1 is the actual minimum for marginwidth and marginheight and HTML-compliant browsers will reflect this with values of 0 and negative values being rounded up to 1. N 4 and Opera also operate this way.

In frame 3, the default values for marginwidth and marginheight are being used. The specification states that the default value for these may vary between browsers; in reality, this is true. The default is usually either 10 or 15 depending on which browser you are using.

In frame 4, the margins are both set to 50, causing "Frame 4" to wrap over two lines. Depending on your browser and how you have set the scrolling attribute for your frame, this frame could also contain a horizontal scroll bar.

noresize

By default, the frames on a page can be resized by dragging the borders to wherever is convenient for the user. However, this facility can be turned off by using the noresize attribute, the syntax of which is simply noresize.

Be careful with this attribute, as it is easy to freeze borders in your frameset when you don't want to. For example, in our five frames example above, if we wrote:

```
<frame src="frame3.html" noresize>
```

then we would not be able to move any of the borders on the page because they all touch frame 3, which is not resizable. However, if it was frame 2 we chose to noresize, then we could still alter the border between frame 3 and frame 4.

Again, be considerate of those users who may be viewing your pages at a lower resolution than you, and who may prefer to resize the frame rather than scroll up and down or left and right.

scrolling

Determines whether or not a frame will contain scrollbars or not. The syntax is:

```
scrolling="value"
```

where `value` is one of three possible values:

❑ `yes` tells the browser that the frame must always contain a set of scrollbars, regardless of size and content.

❑ `no` tells the browser that the frame must never contain a set of scrollbars, regardless of size and content.

❑ `auto`, the default value, tells the browser to include scrollbars within the frame when necessary, for example when user-resizing or when displaying content too large for the current size of the frame.

Note that there is little consistency between browsers as to how `scrolling="yes"` is implemented. For example, IE shows just the vertical scrollbar while Opera and Mozilla simply act as if scrolling has been set to `auto`.

longdesc

`longdesc` allows you to specify a link to another page that gives a longer description of the contents of the frame than would otherwise be possible using the frame's `title` attribute. The syntax is:

```
longdesc="uri"
```

where `uri` is the address of the document containing the alternative description. `longdesc` was added to HTML 4.0 for use in non-visual sites and also to make this extra information available without it cluttering up the page. Unfortunately, this attribute is not currently supported in any browser, although when this text was being written, Microsoft had suggested it would be supported in IE 6.

src

The `src` attribute tells the browser which source file a frame will contain. The syntax is:

```
src="url"
```

`url` can be written as either an absolute or a relative address. The target file does not have to be an HTML file. It could, for example, be a picture.

Note: It is illegal to have `src` point to an anchor link in the same page as the frameset that is defining the frame. The following is an example of this type of illegal code:

```
<frame src="#anchor_in_frameset_document">
```

name

The `name` attribute allows you to give an identifying name to a particular frame. The syntax is:

```
name ="identifying_name"
```

By identifying individual frames within our frameset, we can reference them specifically when instructing the browser which frame to send a page to. We'll look at this in detail in the "*Targetting a Frame*" section.

Browser Extensions to <frame>

IE and Netscape both support additional attributes for <frame>:

IE

lang	language	allowtransparency
application	align	atomicselection
bordercolor	datafld	datasrc
hidefocus	security	tabindex
unselectable		

Netscape

bordercolor	align

align – N 4, IE 3 Only

Sets the alignment of the frame's contents to either left, center or right. Both IE and N no longer support this attribute in favor of letting the frame's source page do it, preferably using CSS styles.

allowtransparency – IE 5.5+

In IE 5.5 and later, the allowtransparency attribute enables the web developer to create frames (and inline frames) with transparent backgrounds. The syntax is:

```
allowtransparency="boolean_value"
```

The transparency of a frame's background depends on two things:

❏ the background color for the frame's source document must be set to "transparent". You can do this in either of the two following ways:

```
<body bgcolor="transparent">
<body style="background-color: transparent">
```

❏ allowtransparency must be set to true for the relevant frame in the frameset document and the frame's background color must not be set in the frameset document.

To demonstrate these in combination, let's suppose we have a file called transparent.html, which includes the line:

```
<body bgcolor="transparent">
```

and a frameset that demonstrates these rules (frameset_trans.html):

```
<frameset rows="*,*,*">
   <frame src="frame1.html">

   <frameset cols="*,*,*,*">
      <frame src="transparent.html" allowtransparency="true">
      <frame src="transparent.html" allowtransparency="true"
             style="background-color: brown">
      <frame src="transparent.html">
      <frame src="transparent.html"
```

```
                style="background-color: brown">
    </frameset>

    <frame src="frame5.html">
</frameset>
```

From the screenshot below, you can see that frames 1 and 5 are control frames and work as normal, while in the middle row from left to right:

❑ The first frame is indeed transparent, showing through the color of the browser window behind it.

❑ The background color of the second frame is brown because it was set from the frameset document and overrode the `bgcolor` attribute in `transparent.html`.

❑ The third and fourth frames have a white background because `allowtransparency` is set to `false` (the default) and IE thus looks for a background color in the frame's source document, ignoring any color set in the frameset document.

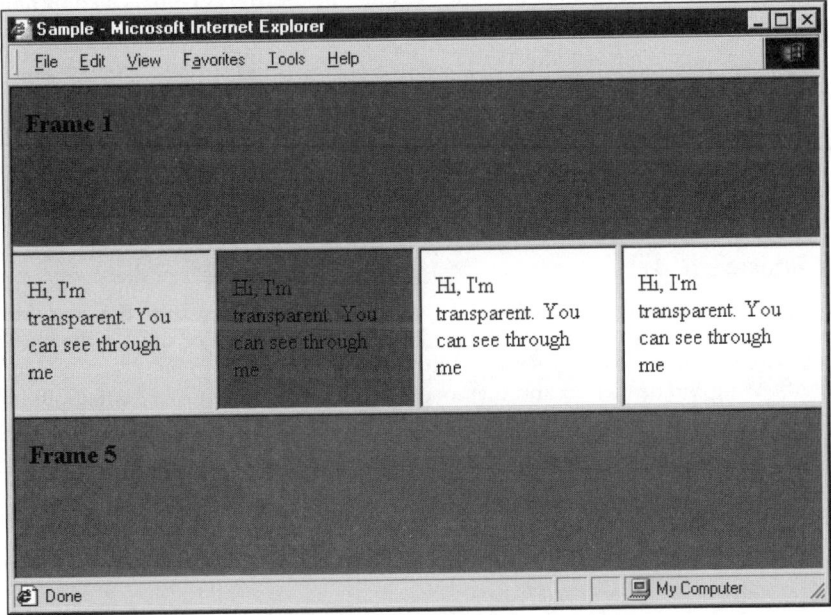

application – IE 5+

In IE 5, Microsoft introduced the concept of **HTML Applications** (HTAs) – fully-fledged applications written using HTML and script that used IE as a backbone but circumvented its security model or user interface. The `application` attribute states that the content of the frame, given by its `src` attribute, is an HTML application and not a normal page. Thus, the IE security model should not apply to it. The syntax is:

```
application="yes |no"
```

If a frame nested within another frameset contains the HTA, the container frame must also be set as `application="yes"`, else the default of `"no"` will be assumed and the contained frame's application attribute will be ignored. For more information on HTAs, go to:

http://msdn.microsoft.com/workshop/author/hta/overview/htaoverview.asp

atomicselection – IE 5.5+

`atomicselection` specifies whether the frame and its contents must be selected as a whole or can be selected as individual elements – frames, text, graphics, etc. The syntax is:

```
atomicselection="boolean_value"
```

where `boolean_value` is either `false`, the default, or `true`. This attribute is relevant only to browsers with atomic selection mode on.

bordercolor – IE 4+, N 3+

`bordercolor` determines the main color of the frame's 3D border, given as a color name or a `#RRGGBB` value, in the same fashion as the frameset `bordercolor` property. The syntax is:

```
bordercolor="colorname | hexadecimal value"
```

As with `frameborder`, `bordercolor` overrides the frameset attribute of the same name. However, be aware that there's no agreement between browsers or even versions of browsers on exactly which borders are recolored when you override the frameset's `bordercolor` setting. You'll have to experiment with this until you get a consistent result.

datafld and datasrc – IE 4+

Since IE 4.0, Microsoft has given web designers the ability to embed a **Data Source Object (DSO)** into a web page. This DSO identifies either a server-side data source or one on the client-side (such as a CSV file), which is downloaded as part of the object, and can then be referenced by various HTML elements using the `datafld` and `datasrc` attributes. The `datasrc` attribute identifies the DSO as the source of the information to populate the frame with, and the `datafld` attribute identifies which column in the DSO that particular frame should get its information from.

Let's consider a very simple situation (`dataframe.htm`):

```
<!doctype html public "-//W3C//DTD HTML 4.01 Frameset//EN"
    "http://www.w3.org/TR/html4/frameset.dtd">

<html>
<head>
   <object classid="clsid:333C7BC4-460F-11D0-BC04-0080C7055A83"
           id="Numbers" height="0" width="0">
      <param name="DataURL" value="data.csv">
      <param name="UseHeader" value="True">
   </object>
   <title>Data Sample</title>
</head>

<frameset cols="*,*">
   <frame datasrc="#Numbers" datafld="Odds">
   <frame datasrc="#Numbers" datafld="Evens">
</frameset>

</html>
```

We'll see more about the `object` element in Chapter 10, but for now, take it as red that this embeds a DSO in our page that points to a comma-separated file called `data.csv` (from the `DataURL` parameter) and which we can refer to as `Numbers` (from the `id` attribute). `data.csv` contains the following:

```
Odds,Evens
*\frame1.html,*\frame2.html
*\frame3.html,*\frame4.html
```

The left-hand column is called `Odds` and holds the addresses of `frame1.html` and `frame3.html`. The right-hand column is called `Evens` and holds the addresses of `frame2.html` and `frame4.html`. The asterisks above are not part of the code – replace them with the full web directory path to the files, for example, `myTestServer\myTestFolder`.

With the DSO loaded, our first frame looks in `data.csv` for the first non-header entry in the `Odds` column – the location of `frame1.html` – and the second for the first non-header entry in the `Evens` column – the location of `frame2.html`. In the case of frames, these entries are assumed to be the addresses of the frames relative to the root directory of the web server you are running the code on; the browser then tries to access the pages at those locations and displays them, if available, on screen:

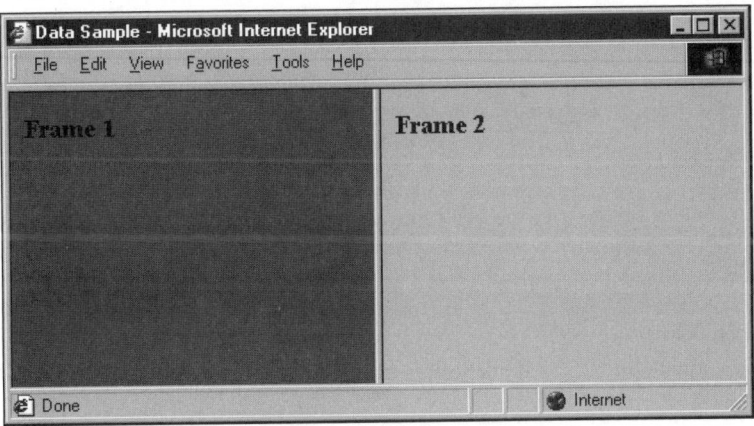

Not very impressive as such, but the power of data binding in this fashion comes from adding other elements to your page, allowing you to cycle and search through the various entries for each field. This however is beyond the scope of this book. If you'd like to investigate further, Microsoft's DHTML workshop site has a section devoted to data binding starting at:

http://msdn.microsoft.com/workshop/c-frame.htm?/workshop/author/databind/data_binding.asp

hidefocus – IE 5.5+

`hidefocus` allows you to determine whether or not the browser will indicate on screen that the frame is the page element currently in focus. The syntax is:

```
hidefocus="boolean_value"
```

By default, this is set to `false`, meaning that if in focus, the frame is surrounded by a dotted rectangle (a "focus rectangle") – if set to `true`, the focus rectangle will not appear if the frameset is currently in focus. See the *"Playing with Focus"* section earlier in this chapter for more.

security – IE 6+

Setting a frame's `security` attribute to `restricted` – the only value it can take – forces the frame to enforce the user's security settings (found in the Security tab of the Internet Options control panel) to that frame. The syntax is:

```
security ="restricted"
```

Setting `security` also enforces the following restrictions over and above those settings the user has set up:

- All links within the secured frame will open in a new browser window, regardless of the specified target.

- Links to `JavaScript`, `VBScript` and `about` "pages" will have their functionality restricted.

- All nested frames in the secured frame will also be secure.

Note that this was written before IE 6 was finally released, so the final implementation of this tag was not fixed. However, for more information, go to:

http://msdn.microsoft.com/workshop/author/dhtml/reference/properties/security.asp

tabindex – IE 4+

By specifying a value for `tabindex`, you can set the order in which elements on your page come into focus when the *Tab* key is pressed. The syntax is:

```
tabindex="integer_value"
```

where `integer_value` can be a value between 0 and 32767 if you're using IE 4 or between 5.0 and -32767 and 32767 if you're using IE 5.01 or higher. Please refer to the "*Playing with Focus*" section above for more.

unselectable – IE 5.5+

`unselectable` allows you to specify whether or not the user can select the frame. The syntax is:

```
unselectable="on_or_off"
```

By default, `unselectable` is set to `off`, meaning that the frame can be selected.

Targetting a Frame

As mentioned earlier, HTML 4.01 allows us to give each frame in our frameset an individual name, and also to send a new page to that named frame. We can do this by setting a `target` attribute to the name of that frame. Several HTML elements cater for a target attribute – `<a>`, `<link>`, `<area>`, `<form>` and `<base>`.

By default, a hyperlink within a frame loads the page or resource that it links to into the same frame. Say, for example, we have a very basic frameset, like so:

```
<frameset rows="50%, 50%">
    <frame src="frametop.html">
    <frame src="framebottom.html" name="bottomframe">
</frameset>
```

We can place a link in the page in the top frame (frametop.html) that loads another page (target.html) into the bottom frame that we've named bottomframe:

```
<a href="target.html" target="bottomframe">Go here</a>
```

If the top frame contained a <form>, we could target the result of submitting the form to the bottom frame using:

```
<form target="bottomframe" action="results.html">
...
</form>
```

The same syntax is used for the target attribute within <link> and <area> elements.

Setting a Default Target Frame

If you want to set a frame to which links send their contents **by default**, you can do this using the <base> element in the <head> section of your HTML page. For example, by specifying:

```
<head>
   <base target="bottomframe">
   ...
</head>
```

in a page, all hyperlinks will send their links to fill bottomframe unless the target attribute specifies otherwise inside the actual <a>, <form>, <link>, or <area> element.

Special Values for Target

The only rule given in the specification for naming your frames with the src attribute is that you should begin their name with a letter, upper or lower case. Beyond that, there is no reason why you can't name lots of frames the same thing, barring common sense, that is.

The only exceptions to this rule are the five pre-defined, case-sensitive special names for target:

- ❑ _self loads the page into the current frame. This is the default when there is no target attribute.

- ❑ _blank loads a page into a new browser window, effectively opening a second window of the browser. This has the same effect as using a name in the target attribute that doesn't already exist.

- ❑ _parent is used with nested frames. The frame is loaded into the parent window. In a simple frameset this is the main browser window. In nested framesets, it is the frameset that created this frameset – that is, if the current frame is a child frame the page loads into its parent frame.

- ❑ _top loads the new page into the main browser window directly, replacing any frames that are there at present.

- ❑ _search loads the new page into the browser search window. Note that it is only recognized as a special name by IE 5 and above.

Thus, when presented with a `target` value either in a link or the `<base>` element, the browser goes through several steps to determine where to send the link, in case there are several frames with the same name:

1. If the `target` value is one of the five special values given above, load the page as specified above.

2. If the `target` value provided by a link or by the `base target` attribute is the name of a frame within the same parent frameset, load the page in that frame.

3. If not in the same frameset, start from the top frameset on the page and perform a depth-first search through all the framesets on the page until the target frame is found, or you run out of framesets.

4. If not in the frameset in this browser window, search through any other open browser windows in the same manner as in point 3 until the frame is found or there are no more windows to search. (Note that browsers use different methods for determining the order in which windows are searched. This could cause some trouble if two frames in two different windows are named the same).

5. If a value for `target` is supplied, but it isn't the name of an existing frame or window, create a new browser window and load the page there. Assign the window the given `target` name.

If you use frames on your page, remember that all external links should have the `target` set to `_top` or `_blank` – otherwise the external document may be unintentionally loaded into a frame of the current document. This can produce some strange, and very undesirable, screen layouts! Watch also for your homepage to be loaded into `_top`. Again, recursive framesets do not look very pretty:

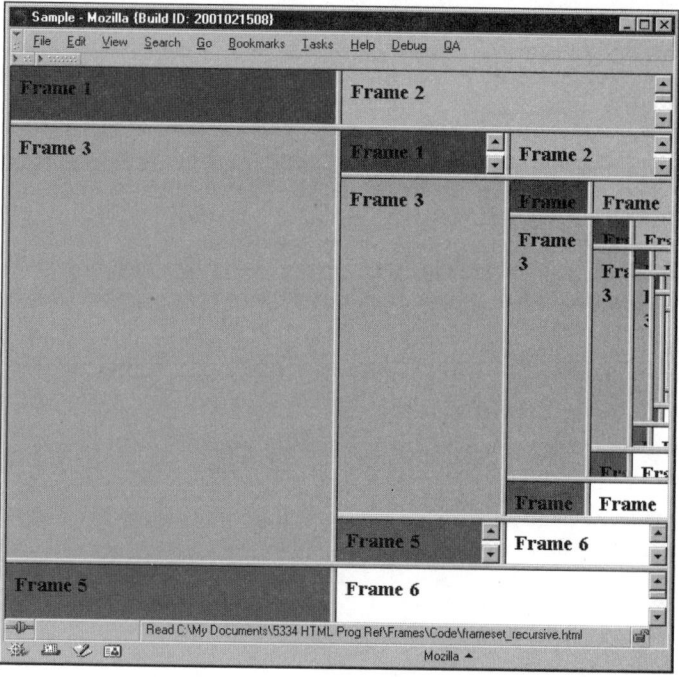

<noframes>

The <noframes> element is available to allow you to address those users whose browsers either do not support frames or have their support for frames disabled. By using a <noframes> element at the end of a frameset, you can present an alternative message to those users to switch on support or upgrade their browser. You can also use a <noframes> element inside a normal HTML page, which would be a frame's source page, for the same purpose:

```
<frameset rows="*,*">
    <frame src="frame1.html">
    <frame src="frame2.html">
    <noframes>
        Here's where you put your message to be seen by users
        in the case
        that their browsers don't support frames.
    </noframes>
</frameset>
```

<noframes> supports only the universal attributes and intrinsic events covered in Chapter 2. Note that there are no specific CSS styles or events related to <noframes>.

Neither IE nor N use any browser-specific extensions for this element.

Floating or Inline Frames

HTML 4.01 provides for a second type of frame for displaying separate documents within normal HTML pages – the **floating frame** or inline frame. These act in the same way as <img> elements do – non-text elements around which text can wrap, margins that can be defined, etc. – but instead of a graphic, a second independent file (HTML page, graphic, text file) is loaded into the space instead, allowing the addition of more interactive inline features. It is also targettable by links if you need it to be.

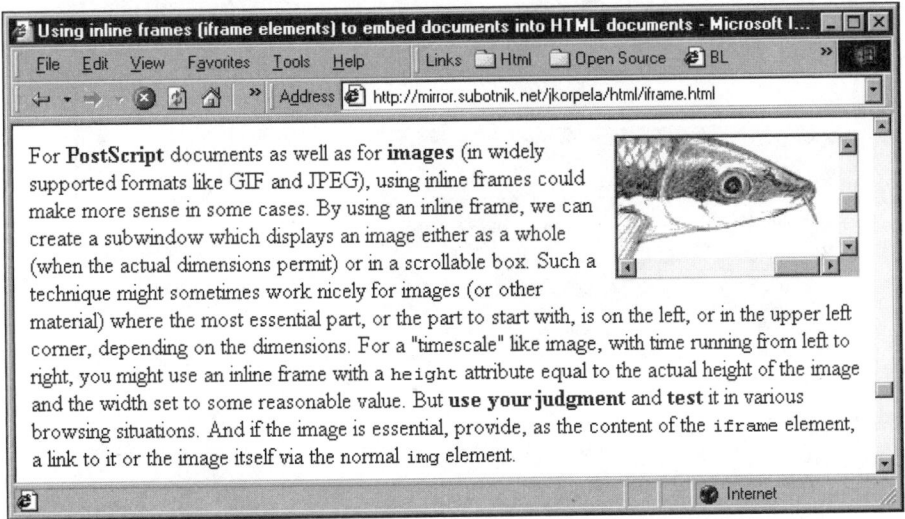

Floating frames, defined by the <iframe> tag, have been supported in IE since version 3, but only in Netscape since version 6.0. Previously, Netscape users could simulate <iframe>s using the non-standard <ilayer> tag (see Chapter 16), but that is not recommended, as both browsers now support the use of <iframe> and N 6 no longer supports the <ilayer> tag.

Floating frames are not part of the normal <frameset> container, but are just placed into a normal HTML page like any other HTML element – this is why they are termed inline frames.

For example, take a look at this code:

```
<!DOCTYPE HTML PUBLIC "-//W3C//DTD HTML 4.0 Transitional//EN"
         "http://www.w3c.org/TR/html4/loose.dtd">

<html>
<head>
   <title>Inline frame example</title>
</head>

<body>
   <p>What's in this one then - Crunchy Frog?</p>

   <iframe src="frogframe.html">
      Can't see the description? Our sales will plummet!
   </iframe>

   A bit tastier than Spring Surprise then.

</body>
</html>
```

In IE 3+, Netscape 6, and Mozilla, we get a page that looks like this:

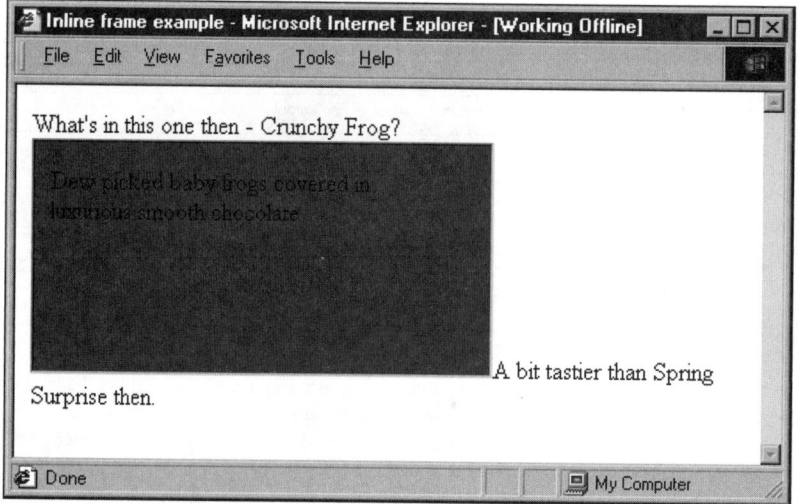

Just like with `<img>`, there is no automatic text wrap after floating frames, hence their alternative name, **inline frames**. Note how we can write text inside the `<iframe>` element that works as the equivalent to the `<noframes>` element for standard frames. This can lead to problems, however, if you don't remember to close the element with an `</iframe>` tag, as the remaining HTML on the page will not be displayed.

<iframe>

The `<iframe>` element supports the following attributes and events:

align	height	width
frameborder	marginwidth	marginheight
scrolling	longdesc	src
name		

plus the HTML 4.01 universal attributes `id`, `class`, `style`, `dir`, `lang`, and `title`, and the common events (see Chapter 2 for further details of these). Note that there are no specific CSS styles or events related to `<iframe>`.

align

Determines how the text outside the floating frame will be laid out with respect to the frame. `align` has been deprecated in HTML 4.01. See Chapter 15 for more on deprecated tags and attributes.

```
align="value"
```

where `value` can take one of the following five values:

- ❑ `left` aligns the frame flush with the left margin of the page and any text following it flows around it on the right.
- ❑ `right` aligns the frame flush with the right margin of the page and any text following it flows around it on the left.
- ❑ `top` sets the top of the floating frame inline with the line of text outside it.
- ❑ `middle` sets the middle of the floating frame inline with the line of text outside it.
- ❑ `bottom` sets the bottom of the floating frame inline with the line of text outside it. This is the default setting.

height and width

`height` and `width` allow you to specify the height and width of the floating frame. The syntax is:

```
height="n"
width="n"
```

where n is the height or width, either in pixels or as a percentage of the height/width of its parent document (in which case the value should be appended with a % sign). You can include one, both or none of these attributes in your `<iframe>` tag. If not included, a default value is used based on the size of the parent document.

frameborder

`frameborder` determines whether or not the borders of a specific frame are shown. See the above section on the `frameborder` property of the `<frame>` element for more details.

marginwidth and marginheight

`marginwidth` allows you to specify, in pixels, the width of the left and right margins between the 3D border of the frame and its contents. `marginheight`, correspondingly, allows you to specify, in pixels, the height of the top and bottom margins between the frame border and its contents. See the section on `marginwidth` and `marginheight` for the `<frame>` element for more details.

scrolling

Determines whether or not a frame will contain scrollbars or not. See the section on `scrolling` for the `<frame>` element for further details.

longdesc

`longdesc` allows you to specify a link to another page that gives a longer description of the contents of the frame than would otherwise be possible using the frame's `title` attribute. See the above section on `longdesc` for the `<frame>` element for further details.

src

The `src` attribute tells the browser which source file a frame will contain. See the section on `src` for the `<frame>` element for further details.

name

The `name` attribute allows you to give an identifying name to the inline frame. See the section on name for the `<frame>` element for further details.

Browser Extensions to `<iframe>`

Here is a list of the IE-specific extensions to `<iframe>` (there aren't any similar cases for Netscape):

allowtransparency	application	atomicselection
begin	border	datafld
datasrc	end	frameborder
hidefocus	hspace	lang
language	security	syncmaster
systembitrate	systemcaptions	systemlanguage
tabindex	timecontainer	unselectable
vspace	systemoverduborsubtitle	

Now we will look at each of these in turn.

hspace and vspace – IE 4+

hspace allows you to specify, in pixels, the amount of space between the left and right borders of the floating frame and the contents of the HTML page that contains the frame, including the edge of the page itself. The syntax is:

```
hspace="distance_in_pixels"
```

vspace, correspondingly, allows you to specify, in pixels, the amount of space between the top and bottom borders of the floating frame and the contents of the HTML page that contains the frame, including the edge of the page itself. The syntax is:

```
vspace="distance_in_pixels"
```

To demonstrate, consider the previous <iframe> example. If we change the previous <iframe> declaration to:

```
<iframe src="frogframe.html" vspace="30" hspace="30">
```

we'll get the following results:

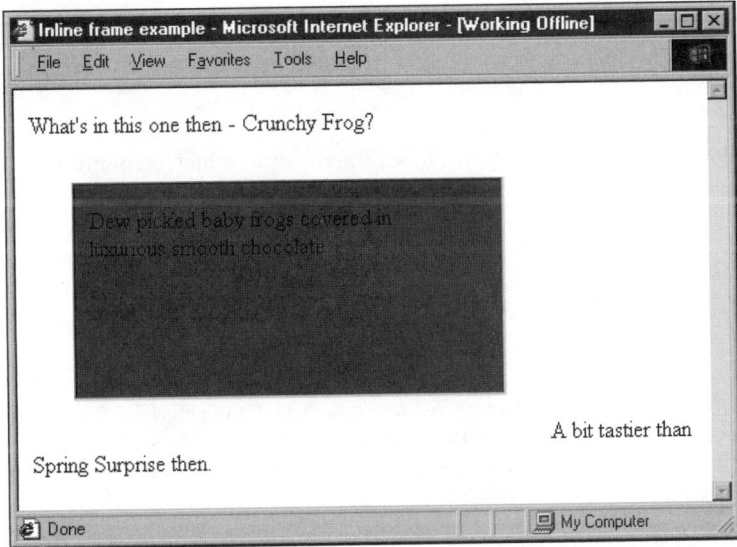

As you can see, an invisible margin of 30 pixels now surrounds the iframe and the following text, "A bit tastier..." begins on the "same" line as the frame, but 30 pixels to right of and down from the frame.

allowtransparency – IE 5.5+

In IE 5.5 and later, the allowtransparency attribute enables the web developer to create frames (and inline frames) with transparent backgrounds. See the above section on allowtransparency for the <frame> element for further details.

application – IE 5+

The `application` attribute states that the content of the floating frame, given by its `src` attribute, is an HTML application and not a normal page. See the above section on `application` for the `<frame>` element for further details.

atomicselection – IE 5.5+

`atomicselection` specifies whether the floating frame and its contents must be selected as a whole if either it or one of its contents are selected. See the above section on `atomicselection` for the `<frame>` element for further details.

datafld and datasrc – IE 4+

`datafld` and `datasrc` are used when the frame is connected to a data source during data binding. See the above section on `datafld` and `datasrc` for the `<frame>` element for further details.

hidefocus – IE 5.5+

`hidefocus` allows you to determine whether or not the browser will indicate onscreen that the frame is the page element currently in focus. See the above sections on `hidefocus` for the `<frame>` element and *"Playing with Focus"* for further details.

security – IE 6+

Forces the floating frame to enforce the user's security settings, found in the **Security tab** of the **Internet Options** control panel. See the section on `security` for the `<frame>` element for further details.

tabindex – IE 4+

By specifying a value for `tabindex`, you can set the order in which elements on your page come into focus when the *Tab* key is pressed. See the above sections on `tabindex` for the `<frame>` element and *"Playing with Focus"* for further details.

unselectable – IE 5.5+

`unselectable` allows you to specify whether or not the user can select the frame. See the above section on `unselectable` for the `<frame>` element for further details.

> *IE 6.0 also introduces a number of `<iframe>` attributes based on the SMIL 2.0 (Synchronized Multimedia Integration Language) specification from the W3C, which are out of scope for this book, but are noted here for completeness. They are:* `begin`, `end`, `syncmaster`, *and* `timecontainer`. *For more on SMIL, see Chapter 21*

> *Likewise, IE 6.0 also contains a number of `<iframe>` attributes based on the HTML + TIME extension to SMIL, which are, again, out of scope for this book. They are:* `systembitrate`, `systemcaptions`, `systemlanguage`, *and* `systemoverduborsubtitle`. *More information can be found on these attributes via:*

> *http://msdn.microsoft.com/workshop/author/behaviors/reference/timemisc_entry.asp*

Legacy <iframe> Attributes for IE 4 Only

When Microsoft first implemented <iframe> in IE 4, it gave floating frames the same extra attributes as <frame>. In IE 5+ however, it seems to have revoked these in favor of adhering to the HTML 4.01 recommendation more closely.

❑ bordercolor allows you to specify a top color for the border of a specific frame, given as a color name or a #RRGGBB value.

❑ framespacing specifies the size of the 3D border between frames on a page.

❑ noresize, if present, specifies that the user cannot resize the frame. Note that the HTML 4.01 standard doesn't allow floating frames to be resized anyway.

Examples of Frames

As you can see, frames are not difficult to get to grips with and it shouldn't be too difficult to come up with a really good design involving multiple nested framesets. However, you should consider several points when designing your frame-based site.

❑ For every frame, there must be a source file to populate it, so your file management needs to be that much tighter. Each new file could also be quite large, so keep in mind the people on a low bandwidth.

❑ Some browsers also have a problem printing out pages that contain framesets.

❑ The browser back button may not work quite as expected.

❑ Make sure you target your homepage to _top or _blank. Recursive framesets are not pretty.

❑ Consider designing your frames with border="1" even if that is not the desired end result, as it can be set to "0" on completion. This allows for faster development when working with framesets.

Some good examples of well-executed frame-based web sites actually use very simple frame-based layouts, as we shall now see:

Our first example is the default homepage for Microsoft's MSDN Library reference pages. You can find it at http://msdn.microsoft.com/library/default.asp.

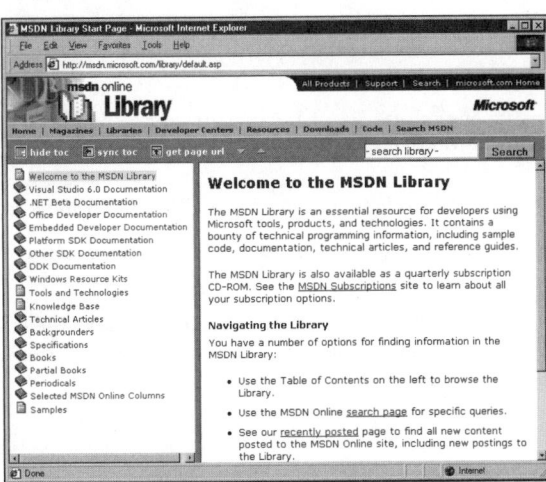

The library table of contents (an activeX control embedded in the frame) on the left is always in view and clicking on the page you want has it loaded in the right-hand side frame.

It is possible to navigate through most of this site without the table of contents, and so, with a neat piece of scripting albeit only for IE 4+, the user can choose to hide the left frame by clicking on the "hide toc" button. Once hidden, this button becomes a "show toc" button to allow you to retrieve it.

The second example is the HTML Frames version of the extended JavaScript Programmer's Reference by Wrox Press, which can be obtained on CD with the book itself (*JavaScript Programmer's Reference* by Cliff Wootton, ISBN: *1-861004-59-1*).

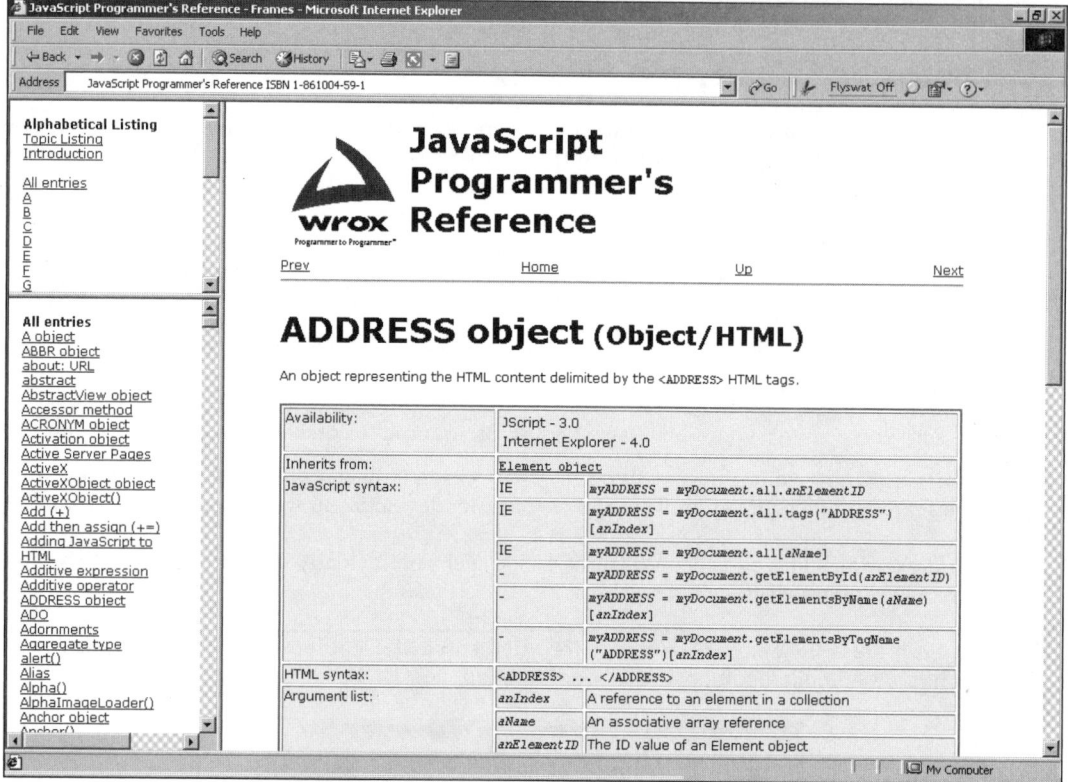

This page is a comprehensive encyclopedia of JavaScript, hence needs to be easy to navigate around the 3000+ entries. To help with this, there are 3 frames:

❑ The top-left frame allows you to navigate between the different alphabetical sections.

❑ The bottom-left frame drills down into the current section selected, allowing you to navigate the entries in each section.

❑ The main information panel (the right hand frame) is what displays the currently selected entry. On each entry page, there are links to allow you to go to the next or previous entry, plus all the entries that relate to the currently selected one.

Summary

In this chapter, we have seen how we can use a frameset document to divide up the browser window into several smaller, independent windows, each of which can host its own content, or be used to determine the content of another. All of this was made possible by the using the <frameset>, <frame>, and <iframe> elements introduced to the HTML recommendation in HTML 4.0. Under the frameset DTD, the frameset element describes the layout for a set of frames that are filled in based on instructions given in the frame tag. Alternatively, we can use the <iframe> element to place a floating, or inline frame in a normal HTML page.

With the frames set up, we saw that by using the target attribute in link-related elements combined with a frame's name attribute, we could direct the contents of a link to a specific frame, and we saw how the browser determined which frame the name referred to. Last but not least, we saw how to provide some alternative content for those users without a frames-enabled browser and a couple of examples of some popular frame-based web sites.

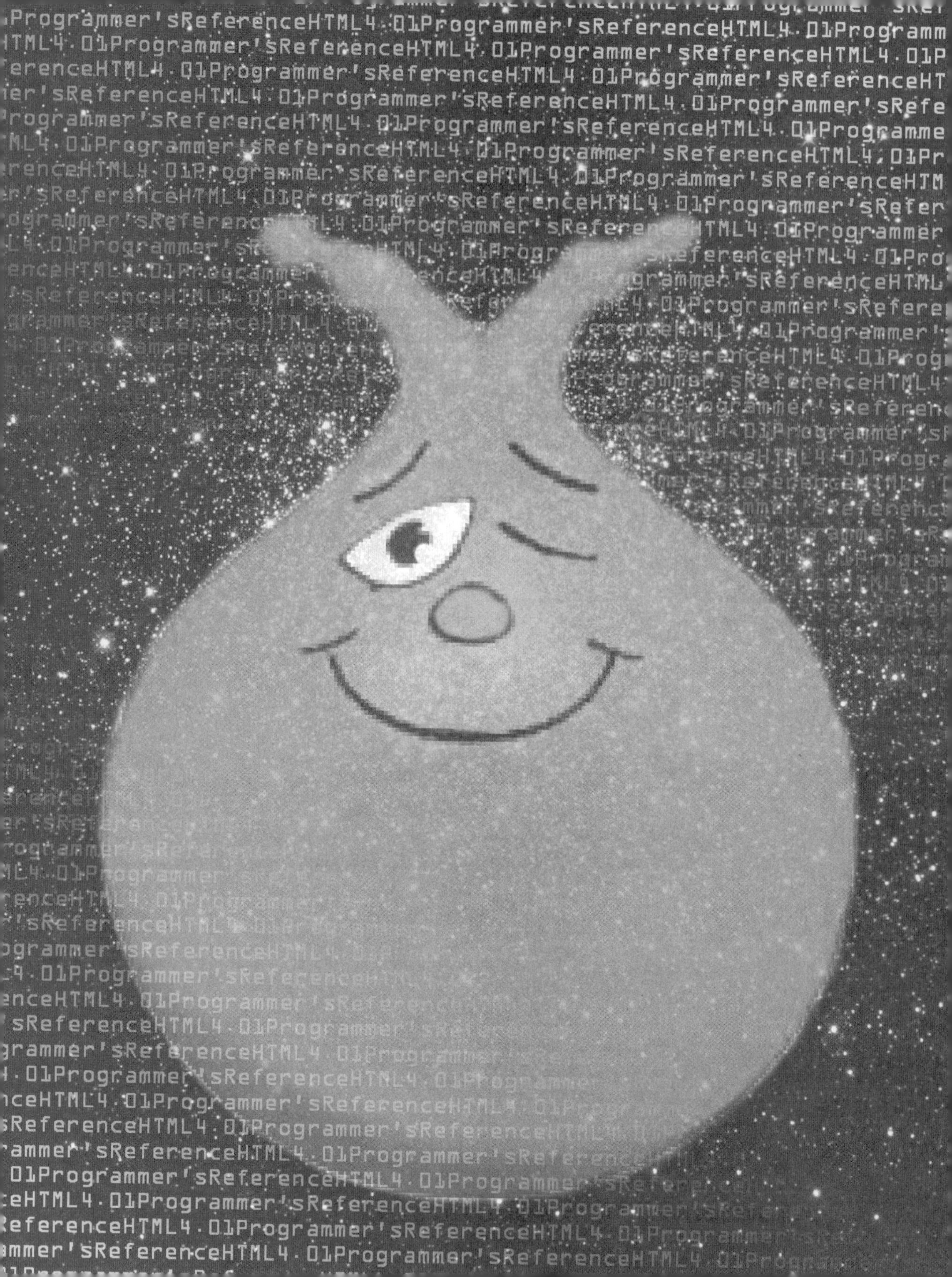
Programmer'sReferenceHTML4.01

9

Scripting and Inherent Events

In this chapter, we'll explore the use of **scripting** in our web pages. This is something that we've seen a few brief mentions of up until this point; now it is time to explore scripting further.

We'll define the term "script", both in a general context, and as it relates to HTML authoring specifically. We'll also discuss some of the capabilities that scripts can add to your pages, as well as some of the things that can't, or shouldn't be done with scripting.

We ought to now provide a few words about what this chapter **isn't**. What we present here is a very general overview of client-side scripting for web pages – we won't attempt to provide a complete how-to guide, as that would warrant enough material to fill another large book in its own right. In fact, it's filled quite a number of them, and we encourage the reader who wants to pursue this worthy area of endeavor to start with some of those works listed in the Bibliography at the end of the chapter.

Nor do we attempt to offer anything like a detailed explanation of the Document Object Model (DOM) or the browser object models that led up to it, deferring this discussion to Chapter 19, "*Dynamic pages: DHTML and the DOM*".

What is a Script?

A **script** is, in simplest terms, a type of computer program that runs within a specified environment, such as, embedded inside an HTML document inside <script> tags (more on this later, see the "*How Scripts are Deployed*" section). Before we go any further, let's look at the history of scripting, and it's rise to acceptance on the World Wide Web.

HTML and CSS aren't really programming languages at all – they are languages for describing, respectively, the structure and presentation of documents. In the earliest days of the World Wide Web, HTML pages were nothing more than documents that a user could read, and whose only claim to interactivity lay in the fact that they sported a means to call up other (presumably related) documents on demand via hyperlinks. Except for their ability to act as a conduit to and from server-side programs, they didn't provide for input or output of data. Nor did they provide for any sort of direct interactivity between a web page and the person viewing it.

By the mid-1990s, however, the dominant paradigm of the web page or web site was beginning to shift away from that of a flat document, or a collection of unchanging documents, to that of an application, that is, of an entity that responded immediately to user input and produced customized information or a desired action in response. This was first realized to some degree through the use of CGI (Common Gateway Interface) programs on web servers, by which users could make searches for particular pieces of information or documents.

In 1995, Netscape Communications released Netscape 2.0, the first web browser offering support for a scripting language. This language was initially called LiveScript, but quickly came to be known as JavaScript. This is something of a misnomer – while JavaScript in many ways superficially resembles Java, and the two are often confused, they are, in reality, quite different, Java being a standalone language allowing you to write independent applications, and JavaScript being a embedded language that allows you to apply more complex functionality within web pages and the like (see below for more about the differences between standalone apps and scripting languages).

We'll take a look at some of the facilities available to web page scripters shortly. Netscape continued to make improvements in its JavaScript implementation in successive versions of Netscape 2 and 3. Microsoft soon joined in the client-side scripting game with the release of IE 3.0, which offered not only support of JavaScript (actually Microsoft's own variant – JScript), but for a second scripting language as well, known as VBScript (short for Visual Basic Scripting Edition), based upon its popular Visual Basic programming language. Although differing from JavaScript/JScript in its syntax, it offered much of the same functionality. However, neither Netscape nor Opera (another browser vendor whose product first became commercially available in 1996) offers native support of VBScript in its browsers, nor does MSIE on the Macintosh platform, so JavaScript remains the client-side scripting language of choice.

At this point, it is important to mention ECMAScript – this isn't really a language in it's on right; it is actually a standardization of JavaScript and JScript, decided on by the European Computer Manufacturers Association (ECMA). For more details, see the "*Standards and Specifications*" section of Chapter 1.

Unlike a commercial standalone software product – such as, say, Adobe Photoshop, Microsoft Word, or Lotus 1-2-3 – a script runs "inside" a host program or environment. It works in much the same manner that a Word macro does inside Word and has no functionality apart from its host. Some other examples of scripting languages include Perl, Python, VBA, and Rebol. Each of these must be run within a host software application such as mentioned previously, or else within a type of application known as an **interpreter** or **scripting engine**, that translates the script code into machine language commands, which can then be executed by the computer's operating system and hardware.

Scripts also differ from standalone programs in that the script's source code is **interpreted**, not **compiled** – that is, the script code is delivered as the source text and translated into machine language at run time, whereas a standalone program's source is converted into machine language just once, as the final step of the software development process.

The distinction between a script and an executable program is not always hard and fast – for instance, applets, servlets, and applications written in the Java programming language require the presence of a Java Virtual Machine (JVM) in order to be run. However, we can't consider them scripts, strictly speaking, because the Java source code must first be compiled into a form compatible with the JVM before it can be run, unlike a script whose author is responsible, as it were, for delivering the source text only.

There are advantages and disadvantages to using each of these two packaging and delivery systems for applications. Scripts often tend to be smaller in file size than standalone executables, since much of their functionality and overhead is already taken care of by the host application – for instance, a VBA programmer can take advantage of the form functionality already provided in Word or the database-related features of Access.

In web terms, we need to make a further distinction between those scripts that run within the user's browser software (or client) and those than run on a web server. Server-side scripts are mostly outside the scope of this book (for more brief coverage, see the latter half of Chapter 6). We should mention in passing that server-side scripts are used to generate HTML documents and that it is very important that their output is syntactically and otherwise correct. However, we're chiefly concerned here with client-side scripts, which are included with or embedded within an HTML document, downloaded with it by the client, and executed solely on the client's machine.

There are numerous attributes of the browser, browser window, web pages, and the elements within those pages that are available to client-side scripters. In addition, there is a limited set of data concerning the user's operating environment that can be obtained and used. We'll look at some of these in greater detail, but before we talk about what can be done with a web document and the elements found within it using client-side scripts, we need to make a distinction between "simple" or "basic" scripting and what is known as "Dynamic HTML". This distinction arises largely from historical reasons that are likely to disappear over time as older user agents fall out of general use. We will not go into these in depth here, deferring this discussion until Chapter 19. For now, we simply ask that the reader keep in mind that much more is possible in terms of the number and types of page elements and properties that are accessible from script than we cover here.

What Can Scripts Do for My Web Documents?

JavaScript scripting allows for a number of dynamic features, which web authors can take advantage of. These include:

❑ Load-time determination of content or page display attributes

❑ Interaction with the user

❑ Processing and display of results in response to user-generated or other events

❑ Information about the client software and platform

Developers can use scripting to access information about the browser itself (as opposed to the document being displayed within the browser) such as the name and version of the browser, as well as the operating system it's being run on. It's also possible to find out the language version of the browser. In addition, information about the types of HTML elements that can be manipulated by the browser's scripting engine can also be obtained. Known as **object detection,** this technique is important because different browsers and different versions of the same vendor's browser may offer differing degrees of support: for example, neither Netscape 2.x nor IE 3.x can manipulate images in real time using script, but the succeeding generations of both browsers can do so readily.

In some cases, a given browser version may not support certain scripting language features necessary to the running of a particular script. Some scripts may be less than optimal when being run on a Mac as opposed to a Windows PC. Failure to detect these capabilities, and make provision for them can lead to scripting errors in non-supporting browsers, and thus to broken applications – as well as detracting from the user experience. (We'll discuss some of these concerns again later in this chapter.) Scripting can also be used for getting information about other environmental factors – such as the user's screen resolution and the color depth of the user's monitor – that can be very helpful in planning the layout and design for a web application's front end.

A number of interesting and useful properties of the browser window can be detected and manipulated via script. Among these are the window's width and height, position of the window on the user's screen, and whether a given window has focus or not – all of which can be both read and set from script.

> Note that with Opera browsers, which feature a multiple document interface, the above applies to the active document window and not the application window.

Some additional examples of tasks that can be accomplished using client-side scripting include:

❑ Opening and closing new browser windows, often referred to in this context as "pop-up windows" or simply "pop-ups". The size and position of these can be controlled from script, as can the presence or absence of the pop-up window's toolbars.

❑ Scripting also makes it possible to pass data between different browser windows or between different frames in a frameset, or to control one window or frame from another: for instance, some text entered in a form field in one frame can be used to create custom content in another frame; one of several different pages could be loaded into the original browser window (depending upon the user's choice) from a set of options in a <select> list contained in a pop-up window; and so on.

❑ The URL of the document loaded into a window is also regarded in script as a property of that window, which can be obtained or set using script code, as can the text appearing in the status bar.

❑ The scrolling of a document within a window is also controllable from a script.

Web documents can be customized at load time in a number of ways. For example:

❑ Since scripts can access the current date from the user operating system, we can include this in a web page; that is, we can allow the script to generate the necessary content and HTML at load time, so that if we were to view the source of the document outside the browser environment, we would not find any reference to the actual date, but only some JavaScript (or possibly other script code), which the astute observer might notice contains a reference to something called `Date()` or `newDate()`.

❑ It's also possible to obtain the date and time that an HTML document was last saved – a handy means of letting your visitors know how recent your content is. Other uses for the date might include generating an appropriate greeting based on the time of day, or using a particular set of fonts or colors in the page. The experienced web developer or designer will note that these things can also be accomplished via a CGI, ASP, or other server-side program – the advantages of using a client-side script here are that no trip back to the server is necessary for client-side functionality, and that the document is still dynamic in isolation, that is, even when it's being browsed from the user's local filesystem or from a medium such as a diskette or a CD-ROM.

Of even greater significance are the interactive capabilities that client-side scripting makes possible, where changes to the document's content or presentation can be made in real time in response to user or other events, and the amount of processing that can also be accomplished upon the user's system. In both cases this can be done without making a request to the server and then awaiting a response.

Probably the most ubiquitous example of the former is the "rollover," where one linked image is replaced with another when the user's mouse pointer moves over it. Accomplishing such a task using a server-side script or program would be unworkable – the web server has no way of detecting user events in a document window, and even if it did, the need to fetch an entire document from the server and load it into the browser simply to change a single image would keep such an approach from being timely or bandwidth-effective (we can't download only part of a file and then do anything useful with it).

However, client-side scripting is ideally suited for this sort of task: all the necessary ingredients are already present on the user's computer, and the document display can be updated in a few milliseconds at most. Client-side processing also makes possible such useful tasks as pre-checking forms for erroneous or incomplete input before they're submitted, thus cutting down on round trips to and from the server and saving hits, processing time, and power on a busy web site host. Another example is the calculator application, which can be viewed and used by members of the My Netscape web site – a user can calculate all day without reloading the page or needing to involve the server again in any way, once the page containing it has been loaded.

It is also possible in many cases to use client-side scripting to control multimedia and other assets loaded into a page, such as Java applets, sound files, video and Flash files, etc. Depending upon the media type and the browser plug-in being used to view it, client-side scripting can be used to start and stop the media clip, synchronize it with other media files, and supply text or other data to it from user input or the script itself, in response to user and other events, including events arising within the multimedia files themselves.

What Can't I Do with Client-side Scripts?

Within a web document or browser window, especially with the advent of Dynamic HTML, there's very little that it isn't possible to do with client-side scripting. However, once we attempt to access resources outside this arena, we find ourselves highly restricted. In particular, we can't access either the client or server file system, except to load new files. In general, we can't save data to the client file system either – the lone exception being **cookies**, wherein information totaling 4 kilobytes or less can be saved between sessions. Although cookies are implemented as text files, it should be noted that client-side scripts do not have access to the files themselves, only the data they contain, and even this capability can be easily disabled by the user. Neither can we save files to the server, unless the server has a pre-existing application enabling us to do this.

There is another restriction encountered when we're using a frameset or pop-up window, known as the **same server** or **same domain** rule: even though we can load pages from anywhere on the Web into one of our frames or pop-up windows, we generally can't access that page's internal properties such as we've discussed, or gain any information from it via client-side scripting, unless it comes from the same domain as the frame into which it is loaded. By this we mean very simply that if our frameset is hosted on the server with the `oursite.com` domain name, we can load a page that's hosted at `theirsite.com`, but we can't use any scripting on that page. Neither can we (at least in the case of Netscape versions 4 and above) load local files using the `file://` protocol into web-based windows or framesets that use the `http://` protocol. These are security precautions intended to prevent unscrupulous scripters from reading private or confidential information either from other web sites, or from site visitor's computers. One other security-related constraint that should be mentioned is that the original browser window first opened by the user at the beginning of the current browsing session cannot be closed without getting the permission of the user via an unambiguous modal dialog (a form of what's known in JavaScript as an **alert dialog**) that can't be hidden or dismissed by the programmer.

Client-side scripters also have no access at all to the server operating system, and very little access to the user's Operating System (OS). In the latter case, they can tell what operating system is being used, and that's about it. Again, there are some limited exceptions, depending upon the browser software being used, and the OS it is being run on.

Inappropriate Scripting

Even with all the security and other protections that are provided against misuse of browser scripting, there are always opportunities for the irresponsible or thoughtless site developer to abuse the web site visitor. Possibly the two greatest annoyances reported by site users involve the misapplication of pop-up windows, particularly when there is an overabundance of them, and the use of scripting to "hijack" a user, that is, to redirect the visitor to another, usually unrelated, site with no prior warning. The current writer himself has visited any number of sites where these have been done in concert, locking his browser in an endless loop that could be broken only by forcing the operating system to terminate the browser application.

Hijacking and pop-up window issues aside, it is also best to avoid scripts that endlessly repeat themselves for two reasons: firstly, because of what can possibly best be termed the annoyance factor or distraction factor, and secondly, because endless programming loops can tie up system resources on the visitor's computer, leading to poor performance of the user's system or even to a system crash. This is generally not conducive to leaving a good impression with your site's visitors! A better practice is to limit the number of times an action, such as an animated image or scrolling text message, will repeat itself, or to offer the user an obvious means of turning it off.

It is also inadvisable to use scripting in order to circumvent common user interface conventions and norms. While the reasons for doing so may be readily apparent to us as designers or implementers, it is liable to be opaque to the average user, who rather than finding your new convention (to the effect that the arrow keys tab between form fields and that the tab key submits the form!) to be logical, elegant, and self-explanatory, will be more likely be extremely frustrated by it.

Before we move on to the more technical aspects of including client-side scripts in your HTML pages, we'll offer one final piece of advice: the programmed and interactive features that are offered on a site are as much a reflection of the site's "personality" as the layout, graphics, fonts, and colors used. Employ your scripts for a reason, in a manner consistent with your site's mission, and suited to its target audience.

How Scripts are Deployed

Here we'll discuss the types of scripting that can be included or otherwise made available for use in a web page. We'll also explain the mechanisms that HTML 4.01 provides for doing so via the `<script>` element.

What Kinds of Scripts Can We Use?

Scripts used for client-side processing must consist of valid character data. As we discussed above, scripts are not compiled into or otherwise prepared as binary files, as if for execution as standalone programs, nor processed or rendered by a browser plug-in as are Java applets and multimedia files. Instead, a scripting interpreter built into the web browser interprets them at run time, and their content type will always be some form of text – now we'll discuss just what sort of text, and how that type is determined.

Scripts fall into two broad categories depending on how they are used in a web page: they can either be run once as the page loads, or they can be stored in memory as script **functions** or **procedures** and then executed as needed in response to a specific user-initiated or other event. (A function or procedure is a means of storing a reusable piece of script code so that it may be recalled later by name, rather than having to write the same script multiple times.)

The <script> Element

A script is made available in a web page as the content of either the event handler of an HTML tag, or a `<script>` tag. We'll cover events in more detail below, under "*Events and Intrinsic Events*". For now, the common sense definition of the term "event" as "something interesting happening" will be sufficient. The attributes supported by script are as follows:

```
type        src        charset        defer
```

plus the universal attributes discussed in Chapter 2. Please note that an ending `</script>` tag is always required following the end of any script code that may be present.

Let's go through each of these attributes in turn.

type

This required attribute specifies what scripting language the element's contents are written in, and overrides the default scripting language. The syntax is:

```
type="content_type"
```

where `content_type` is the language identifier (for example, `"text/javascript"`). Note that this attribute supercedes the now deprecated `language` attribute.

src

This attribute is used to specify the location of an external script, if we want to use it in our page. The syntax is:

```
src="url"
```

where `url` denotes the script location.

charset

This attribute specifies the character encoding of the script. The syntax is:

```
charset="charset"
```

where `charset` is the character encoding, for example, `utf-8`.

defer

The defer attribute acts as a hint to the user agent that the script within the tags will not generate any document content, and thus the parser can continue to parse and render away through the rest of the document in which the script is embedded. The syntax is:

```
defer="boolean_value"
```

If it is set to `true`, then the hint is provided.

Script Settings

The HTML specification also recommends that a default scripting language be set for all scripts in a page by including the `<meta>` declaration, for example:

```
<meta http-equiv="Content-Script-Type" type="text/vbscript">
```

This would make VBScript the default scripting language for the whole page. In addition, the specification provides another alternative in lieu of using the `<meta>` tag, which is to set a corresponding HTTP header for processing, using the `http-equiv` attribute (see Chapter 2 for more on this attribute). Note that this is not something done by the page author or scripter but rather by a server-side programmer or server administrator, and we mention it here only for the sake of completeness. The range of values for the `type` attribute in both of these cases is the same as that for the `type` attribute of the `<script>` element. This has been done up until now by use of the `language` attribute, but as we have already discussed, this is now deprecated.

The HTML 4.01 specification does not provide for a default scripting content type or language. The content type must be specified for all scripts. In practice, both Netscape and Microsoft browsers default to `text/javascript` if no type is given; however, the specification explicitly states that a document that does not declare a default script content type and then uses scripted event handlers (see the section on events below) is invalid. User agents should feel free to attempt to interpret these if desired, but browser vendors are under no obligation to ensure that they do so. The content type of a script also determines the language interpreter invoked by the user agent to process the script. The only other common value for the `type` attribute is `text/vbscript`.

Given the set of requirements for the client system, this will be chiefly of interest to developers working on an intranet or other local network, but we should note that a number of examples making use of `type="text/tcl"` are also included in the HTML specification. Until less than a month before this chapter was written, there was no commercially available scripting engine that allowed for the use of Tcl – more usually a systems or server programming language – as a browser scripting language. However, this changed with the March 2001 release of the ActiveTcl interpreter by ActiveState (www.activestate.com); on Windows systems running Personal Web Server, Internet Information Server, or Windows Scripting Host, and with an installation of ActiveTcl, ActivePerl, or ActivePython, it is possible for Internet Explorer to parse scripts written in those languages. The type attributes for the latter two are `text/perlscript` and `text/python`, respectively.

Using Element Identifiers: id and name

It is generally a good idea for authors to assign an identifier to those elements that are likely to be accessed from a script by giving these elements an appropriate name or id attribute. While both JavaScript and VBScript have mechanisms for identifying HTML elements without referring to them by name, authors' jobs will be made much easier, and there will be much less chance for confusion if critical elements are uniquely identified.

Either the name or id attribute, or both, may be used and assigned a value. The HTML 4.01 specification states that name is to be given precedence over id; however, the Document Object Model (DOM) specification, Level 1 (see Chapter 19), prefers the latter, although it still recognizes the former.

In practice, what this means is, that elements in those scripts that are usable by older (version 2 or 3) browsers, such as those involving forms and form elements, images, applets, frames, and multimedia content handled by plug-ins (and included in pages using the <embed> tag) should have names whether or not they are given ids, for reasons of backwards compatibility. This is because older browsers may not recognize the id attribute. Elements that are scriptable only in the newer browsers (version 4 and above) should have an id attribute. Where an element is assigned an id, its value must be unique among all ids in the document. Again, we caution the HTML author that older user agents may not recognize the id attribute. There is additional information concerning the differences between the two in Chapter 21.

Working with Scripts

As we have already mentioned in passing, scripts may be either **inline**, by which we mean that they executed once when the page containing them loads, or **event-driven**, that is, they are held at the ready by the browser's scripting engine until they are executed in response to a user-initiated or other event. The <script> element may be included at any point in the head or body of an HTML document, and any number of scripts or portions of scripts may be placed in your pages. However, there are a couple of generally observed guidelines used by script authors for reasons of good coding practice and organizational logic that are worth following when we place script code that has been supplied by others into our web pages:

1. Code containing event-actuated functions that are to be called repeatedly, and other code that is not included in any particular function but that is necessary for them to be ready for use, should be placed in the head of the document (within <script> tags, of course).

2. Script code that produces new HTML code or other content at a particular point in the page should be placed within a <script> element in the corresponding position in the body of the page. For example, a simple line of JavaScript code for writing the document's last-saved date near the bottom of a page might be included like so:

```
<!DOCTYPE HTML PUBLIC "-//W3C//DTD HTML 4.01//EN
                http://www.w3.org/TR/REC-html401/strict.dtd">
<html>
<head>
    <title>An Embedded Script...</title>
    <meta http-equiv="Script-Content-Type" content="text/vbscript">
</head>
<body>
<h1>Welcome To My Page</h1>
```

```
<p>Hello, I'm awfully glad you've dropped by to see my site...</p>
<p>If you're curious about what I've been up to lately...</p>
<!-- more content goes here... -->
<hr>
<p>
<script type="text/javascript">
    <!--
    document.write("This page was last updated on "+document.lastModified+".");
    //-->
  </script>
</p>
</body>
  </html>
```

We've set the default `Script-Content-Type` of this page to `text/vbscript`, but the script that actually does the work is of type `text/javascript`.

The W3C HTML 4.01 specification sets some guidelines for scripts that modify the contents of a document dynamically as our example does (this is often referred to as "generating HTML on the fly"). All `<script>` elements are processed in the order in which they occur in the page as it is loaded. Any scripts that generate new textual content are evaluated, and this new content takes the place of the `<script>` elements in the page. The new content is expected to consist of valid and well-formed HTML markup that conforms to the document's DTD. For example:

```
<script type="text/javascript">
<!--
document.write("<p>I\'m fine, thanks, and how are <b>you<\/b> today?<\/p>");
//-->
</script>
```

should produce exactly the same effect as if we had simply used:

```
<p>I'm fine, thanks, and how are <b>you</b> today?</p>
```

in the page. Note that special characters (anything except the letters a-z and A-z, the digits 0-9, and the underscore) must be "escaped" using a backslash character when dynamically written to a page in this way.

How Can I Supply Scripts to my Users?

Scripts may be added to web pages in one of two ways. The script code may be placed directly or **embedded** in the page as shown in the example above. It is also possible to use **included** scripts by saving the script into a separate text file and referencing this file in a `<script>` element by using that element's `src` attribute, whose value must be a valid URL pointing to a script file. The reference may be relative or absolute.

This can be helpful to site developers in four ways:

❑ Frequently used scripts don't have to be placed directly into every file in which in they are called; a reference to them can be placed instead. In the case of a large script being used on a site with a great many pages, this could save a significant amount of space on the server.

❑ If this script needs to be changed, only one copy of it has to be updated. This makes the site more easily maintainable.

❑ The script file can be cached on the client, thus saving download time and bandwidth, since it needs only to be called once from the server.

❑ Scripts can be stored on one server and used on others.

Looking again at the above example, we can move the script code into a text file (in this case, the script consists of a single line, so it won't be a very large file). If we save this file with the name `display_saved_date.js` and place it in a "scripts" subdirectory of the site's root directory where we've already located our HTML documents, we can rewrite our "last updated" example as follows:

```
<!DOCTYPE HTML PUBLIC "-//W3C//DTD HTML 4.01//EN"
                "http://www.w3.org/TR/REC-html401/strict.dtd">
<html>
<head>
   <title>An Included Script...</title>
   <meta http-equiv="Script-Content-Type" content="text/vbscript">
</head>
<body>
   <h1>Welcome To My Page</h1>
   <p>Hello, I'm awfully glad you've dropped by to see my site...</p>
   <p>If you're curious about what I've been up to lately...</p>
   <!-- more content goes here... -->
   <hr />
   <p>
   <script type="text/javascript" src="display_saved_date.js">
   </script>
   </p>
</body>
</html>
```

The contents of the `display_saved_date.js` file:

```
document.write("This page was last updated on "+document.lastModified ".");
```

It should be understood that the comment delimiters are not part of the script code and thus aren't to be saved in the script source file – in fact, nothing at all should be placed in a script file other than the text of the scripting code itself. Choosing between embedding a given script in this manner, and including its script code directly in the page is normally an either/or proposition. If the script element has a `src` attribute, user agents are to ignore any content that might be found between the opening `<script>` and closing `</script>` tags – so under most circumstances you shouldn't be tempted to place any there. There is an exception to this – some older user agents don't recognize the `src` attribute, and we can use this behavior to our advantage in dealing with these older browsers, as we'll see later on in this chapter.

What Else Do I Need to Know About <script>?

There are three remaining issues regarding the <script> element that we need to discuss before moving on to talk about other matters:

❏ The first of these hasn't been of great concern to web developers up to this point in time, but is rapidly becoming so – what character set do we choose for our scripts?

❏ The second may become more important as time goes on – use of the defer attribute.

❏ The third will eventually cease to be an issue, but we include it here for the sake of completeness – phasing out the language attribute.

We will look at each of these below:

What Character Set?

As we mentioned above, the content-type of a script is always some type of text – but what character set or sets do we use? In the case of an included inline script, the answer is simple: the script uses the default character encoding of the document in which it occurs. However, an embedded script may use its own encoding, which is set by means of the <script> tag's charset attribute. According to the specification, only those script elements having a src attribute may take a charset; if a script element doesn't have a src, any charset that might be set for it is to be ignored by the user agent. It's a simple enough rule to remember: for a <script> element – no src, no charset. Being able to set a different character encoding for an embedded script is important because it enables us to employ a scripting language such as JavaScript (an ECMAScript-3.0-compliant implementation), which uses only the UTF-16 Latin character set, within a document written with a completely different one, such as, say, Arabic or Chinese or Hindi. This will become increasingly relevant as the World Wide Web becomes more truly international in scope and character, although today's browsers exhibit very limited support for it. For more information regarding internationalization issues, the interested reader is invited to refer to Chapter 18.

Use of the defer Attribute

The HTML 4.01 specification also defines an attribute for the <script> element that may prove of eventual use, although it is not supported as of yet in most user agents: this is the defer attribute, which was introduced in HTML 4.0. This is a Boolean value, which, if set, is intended to inform the browser that the script will not generate any page content, that is, the script contains no JavaScript document.write() statements (or the equivalent in another scripting language). Its purpose is to enable the user agent to continue parsing the HTML past that point in the document without waiting for the browser's scripting engine to create more content. A simple example of its use might be something like this:

```
<!DOCTYPE HTML PUBLIC "-//W3C//DTD HTML 4.01//EN"
                  "http://www.w3.org/TR/REC-html401/strict.dtd">
<html>
<head>
    <title>Using The defer Attribute...</title>
    <meta http-equiv="Script-Content-Type" content="text/tcl">
</head>
<body>
    <h1>Welcome To My Page</h1>
    <p>Hello, I'm awfully glad you've dropped by to see my site...</p>
```

```
   <p>If you're curious about what I've been up to lately...</p>
   <script type="text/vbscript" defer>
     <!--
         MsgBox("See, I can do this while the page continues to render.")
     '-->
   </script>
   <!-- more content goes here... -->
   <hr>
   <p>Well, that's all there is to this page...
but you can see more on the <a href="next.html">next one</a> if you like.</p>
   </body>
</html>
```

Note that this example, since it uses VBScript, will do anything of actual interest only when viewed with Internet Explorer on PC. In any case, the defer attribute has only been implemented on MSIE 5.5 and above.

Use of the language Attribute

As we have seen above, while its use has been deprecated as of HTML 4.0, HTML and other web developers are still liable to encounter the language attribute, which in HTML 3.2 was used to set the scripting language and version to be used in interpreting the script. Its application should be discontinued in favor of the type attribute, but it may be retained where it is known that older user agents are still being employed. Examples of use:

```
<script language="JavaScript">
<script language="JavaScript1.1">
<script language="JScript">
<script language="VBScript">
```

A user agent recognizing the language attribute will generally attempt to employ and make usable in client-side scripts, the features of the highest version available to its script interpreter if only the language is specified and not the language version.

One notable deviation from this rule was Netscape 4, which attempted to implement certain features expected in the then-emerging ECMA-262 scripting language standard, which would have introduced major incompatibilities with previous JavaScript implementations. As a precaution against breaking scripts that were already in use, these anticipated changes were implemented in such a way as to be activated only when the JavaScript language version was explicitly set to "JavaScript1.2". Unfortunately, some scripters adopted the incompatible features in their scripts, so in updating legacy sites containing <script> elements with a language="JavaScript1.2" attribute set, this needs to be left in place if backwards compatibility with Netscape 4 is a concern.

As with newer user agents that recognize the type attribute, older browsers that expect the language attribute will default to the value "JavaScript", should the language attribute not be present.

Which Users Can (or Can't) Make Use of My Scripts?

Without delving too deeply into specifics of scripting languages and language versions, we offer the following as a guide to the HTML elements, document attributes, and browser window features whose attributes can be accessed via scripting in those browsers supporting scripting through version 6 from Microsoft and Netscape.

> *There was in fact a Netscape 5 beta version available in late 1998; however its HTML renderer and script interpreter were very similar to those found in the Netscape 4.X series. The fact that these would have proved extremely difficult to make standards-compliant was a major factor in the decision to scrap that version before final release and to rewrite most of the Netscape codebase from scratch, and helped lead to the creation of the Mozilla project, the development of the Gecko rendering engine and the release of the Netscape 6 and Mozilla browsers.*

We ask the reader to bear in mind that this is only a very rough guide to the scriptable features that are present in the various Microsoft and Netscape browsers. For more exact information, a more comprehensive work such as *JavaScript Programmer's Reference* by Cliff Wootton (ISBN: *1-861004-59-1, Wrox Press, 2001*) should be consulted.

Elements / Scripting Capabilities	Internet Explorer				Netscape		
	IE 3	IE 4	IE 5	IE 6	N 3	N 4	N 6
Forms and Form Controls	✓	✓	✓	✓	✓	✓	✓
Images	-	✓	✓	✓	✓	✓	✓
Links	✓	✓	✓	✓	✓	✓	✓
Applets	-	✓	✓	✓	✓	✓	✓
Layers (`<layer>` / `<ilayer>` tags)	-	-	-	-	-	✓	-
Full range of HTML elements	-	✓	✓	✓	-	-	✓
ActiveX controls	✓	✓	✓	✓	-	-	-
Plug-ins	-	-	-	-	✓	✓	✓
Dialog boxes (`alert`, `confirm`, `prompt`)	✓	✓	✓	✓	✓	✓	✓
Window focus	-	✓	✓	✓	✓	✓	✓
Window status bar text	✓	✓	✓	✓	✓	✓	✓
Frames and framesets	✓	✓	✓	✓	✓	✓	✓
Finding text or HTML in document	-	✓	✓	✓	-	✓	✓

Elements / Scripting Capabilities	Internet Explorer				Netscape		
	IE 3	IE 4	IE 5	IE 6	N 3	N 4	N 6
Window size and positioning	-	✓	✓	✓	-	✓	✓
Window browsing history and navigation	✓	✓	✓	✓	✓	✓	✓
Printing of current document	-	-	✓	✓	-	✓	✓
Window opening and closing	✓	✓	✓	✓	✓	✓	✓

Events and Intrinsic Events

Now it is time for us to take a look at one of the most important concepts involved in scripting – **events**.

What is an Event?

An event is, according to the common sense definition we offered above, something that happens; in more precise terms, it is a change of state in the environment. In the context of the web page, there are two types of events that occur, which we can use to trigger the execution of scripts. **Window events** involve the loading and unloading of documents, focus being given to or taken away from a window or frame, and setting actions to be executed after a specific period of time has elapsed. **User events** occur when the user interacts with elements in the page using the mouse or keyboard or equivalent devices. Intrinsic events span across both of the above types – they are those defined within the HTML 4.01 specification as those events associated with a particular document element or set of elements, and all user agents are expected to support them as such.

How Do We Make Use of Events?

Each intrinsic event supported in HTML 4.01 is scripted using an **event handler**; their general syntax is "on*eventname*", which is used as an HTML attribute of the element with which the event is to be associated. The value of the attribute contains the script code to be executed when the event occurs on that particular element. Here's an example showing the complete syntax:

```
<p id="myPTag" onclick="alert (this.id);">Click Here!</p>
```

In this case, the script code is JavaScript, that is, the default script content type is text/javascript, and should be declared as such using the appropriate <meta> tag in the head of the document, as we saw before. If the user agent supports JavaScript and the HTML 4.01 event handlers, clicking on the paragraph should result in the appearance of the following dialog box:

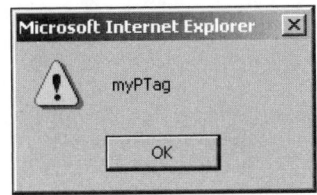

A modal dialog such as the "Alert" pop-up shown here is a message box that halts execution of a program until it's been dismissed by the user. Clicking on the "OK" button usually does this.

Below is the complete set of HTML 4.01 event handlers:

Event Handler	Description – Occurs when...	Applicable Elements
onload	Document has finished loading or all frames within a frameset have finished loading	`<body>,<frameset>`
onunload	Document is removed from a window or frameset	`<body>,<frameset>`
onclick	Mouse button (or equivalent pointing device) is clicked over an element	most elements
ondblclick	Mouse button is double-clicked over an element	most elements
onmousedown	Mouse button is pressed (but not released) over an element	most elements
onmouseup	Mouse button is released over an element	most elements
onmouseover	Mouse is moved onto an element	most elements
onmousemove	Mouse is moved while over an element	most elements
onmouseout	Mouse is moved away from an element	most elements
onfocus	Element receives focus via either the mouse, tabbing, or programming code	`<label>,<input>,<select>,<textarea>,<button>,<a>,<area>`
onblur	Element loses focus via either the mouse or tabbing, or programming code	`<label>,<input>,<select>,<textarea>,<button>,<a>,<area>`
onkeypress	A key is pressed and released over an element	most elements
onkeydown	A key is pressed (and held down) over an element	most elements
onkeyup	A key is released over an element	most elements
onsubmit	A form is submitted	`<form>`
onreset	A form is reset	`<form>`
onselect	User selects some text in a text field	`<input>,<textarea>`
onchange	A control loses input focus and its value has been modified since gaining focus	`<input>,<select>,<textarea>`

There are two things that we need to consider when looking at the preceding table:

❏ The term "most elements" is an abbreviation for "All elements except for `<applet>`, `<base>`, `<basefont>`, `<bdo>`, `<br>`, `<font>`, `<frame>`, `<frameset>`, `<head>`, `<html>`, `<iframe>`, `<isindex>`, `<meta>`, `<param>`, `<script>`, `<style>`, and `<title>`".

❏ Both Microsoft and Netscape browsers support additional event handlers; these include `focus` and `blur` events on windows and frames. The interested reader is encouraged to consult Microsoft's Browser Events page at http://msdn.microsoft.com/workshop/author/dhtml/reference/events.asp. Unfortunately, as of press time, there did not seem to be any central listing of what is supported by Netscape 6/Mozilla; we advise the reader to check Netscape's developer site at http://developer.netscape.com/, the Developer Docs section at Mozilla.org (http://www.mozilla.org/docs/web-developer/), and the relevant newsgroups for up-to-date information on this topic as it becomes available.

Accommodating Script-incapable User Agents

If this were a perfect world, at least from the viewpoint of web developers and designers, everyone's browsing software would follow all the relevant W3C, ECMA, and other specifications as of the moment of their release, and would probably auto-update the moment a new version of one of these standards emerged. Alas, this is not the case. Different user agents support various levels of conformance to different versions of HTML, CSS, and scripting, and it is up to web authors to deal with these differences as well as they possibly can. Previously, we mentioned some of the reasons why the scripts we employ in our pages might or might not function well (or at all) with different browsers, and in this section we'll look at some methods for dealing with these issues.

Hiding Scripting Content from Incompatible Browsers

Some browsers may not recognize the value of the script `type` or `language` attribute, or the scripting code used in a given `<script>` element. Some older user agents may not recognize the `<script>` element at all. In the latter case, the browser is likely to attempt to render any script code within it as text, which is generally not desirable. There are two solutions to this problem: using external scripts, and employing a technique known as "commenting out" the script. We'll look at both of these.

We may choose to employ only scripts that are kept in files separate from the document and referenced via the `src` attribute. This can be desirable for a number of reasons. It avoids the problem altogether of having user agents that don't understand the `<script>` element trying to render the scripting code. It also makes for more modular web application design that's more easily maintained, since the developer can refer to the same script file from any number of pages, and needs only to update that script file instead of all the documents that contain the script. In addition, it reduces the load on the server and the need for the client machine to open a new network connection to reuse the same scripts, since, once downloaded, the script file can be read from the user's cache (presuming, of course, that the user hasn't disabled caching).

Using the `src` attribute also makes it possible to use scripting libraries that are already stored on another server, which can save space on your own. However, some older browsers such as Netscape 2.0 do not recognize the `src` attribute. If this is a concern, it is possible to place script code for these user agents inside the `<script>` element, and only those browsers that do not recognize `src` will attempt to parse the code. Browsers that do understand the `src` attribute will ignore anything inside the `<script>` element and load the external script instead.

This still leaves the problem of what we're to do about browsers that can't run our scripts when the scripts have been embedded directly into the HTML document. Some users may have scripting disabled in their browsers, but this generally isn't a problem, as all of the major and recent browsers that are equipped with a scripting interpreter but have it disabled in the user's preferences will simply ignore anything within the `<script>` element more or less, as though that element had had the CSS property value `display:none` assigned to it. However, older browsers that do not recognize the `<script>` element at all, assuming that they are compliant otherwise with the HTML specification, present the problem mentioned above. They will most likely attempt to render the scripting code contained within that element as page content. These would include Netscape 1.0, older versions of Amaya and Lynx, and IE 1.0 and 2.0 (IE 2.0 is the default browser installed with Windows NT 4.0, and this author has had at least 2 web site design clients in the last two years that use this as their company browser because that's what their operating systems came with – and they refuse to upgrade!).

Fortunately, we can make use of a technique that allows us to wrap the scripting code inside HTML comments; in fact, this is the same technique, which you've seen used in the examples throughout this chapter. This is made possible by the fact that most common browser scripting engines, including the Netscape JavaScript interpreter and Microsoft's interpreters for both JScript and VBScript allow us to use an opening HTML comment (`<!--`) as the first element in a script; these interpreters will ignore this character sequence so long as it is the first non-white space string of characters to occur inside a `<script>` element. Any additional characters will be ignored until the end of the line. At the end of our scripting code, we can then place a closing HTML comment (`-->`). However, this is not a legal sequence of characters in most scripting languages, including JavaScript/JScript and VBScript, and will produce errors when the interpreter encounters it. It would be nice if they understood the closing tag as easily as the opening tag – unfortunately, they don't. In order to get around this problem, we use the scripting language's own comment delimiter to hide the HTML closing comment from the script interpreter.

In JavaScript/JScript, this consists of a double slash character (`//`), in VBScript, we use a single quote mark (`'`), and to declare a single-line comment within a script written in Tcl, Perl, or Python, we use the # character).

In each case, the scripting language's comment delimiter hides any remaining characters on the same line from the script interpreter and keeps the HTML closing comment tag out of harm's way. If this sounds rather complicated, a couple of examples might help make it clearer. First let's look at an example that uses JavaScript:

```
<script type="text/javascript">

  <!-- begin hiding from old browsers

  function cubeIt(value)
  {
      document.write("<p>The original value is: "+value+";<br>");
      document.write("the cube of this value is: " +
      (value*value*value)+".</p>");
  }

  cubeIt(5);

  // end hiding from old browsers -->
</script>
```

Here's the same example rewritten in VBScript:

```
<script type="text/vbscript">
    <!-- begin hiding from old browsers

    Sub CubeIt(value)
        Document.Write "<p>The original value is: "& value &";<br>"
        Document.Write "the cube of this value is: "& (value*value*value) & ".</p>"
    End Sub

    Call CubeIt(5)

    ' finish hiding from old browsers -->
</script>
```

Language Version and Other Scripting Incompatibilities

We've already mentioned the now-deprecated `language` attribute of the `<script>` tag, which was employed not only to declare the scripting language to be used, but also the version of that language as well. (See the *What Else Do I Need to Know About <script>?* section for examples.) We also discussed the fact that different user agents may support different versions of the same language or, may support the core features of the same language version but not manipulation of the same specific document elements. For instance, Netscape 3 and IE 3.0 differ somewhat in the access that JavaScript is granted to HTML page elements via the Document Object Model (DOM). We'll discuss this in much greater detail in Chapter 19. We said earlier in this chapter that one of the elements for which Netscape 3 supports scripting and which MSIE 3 does not is the `<img>` element, known to JavaScript programmers as the **Image object**. Here's a simple example code fragment to demonstrate its use:

```
<!DOCTYPE HTML PUBLIC "-//W3C//DTD HTML 4.01//EN http://www.w3.org/TR/REC-
html1401/strict.dtd">
<html>
<head>
    <meta http-equiv="Content-Type" content="text/html; charset=iso-8859-1">
    <meta http-equiv="Script-Content-Type" content="text/javascript">
    <title>Simple Image Replacement</title>
</head>

<body>
    <a href="http://www.wrox.com/"
        onmouseover="document.myImage.src='logo2.gif';"
        onmouseout="document.myImage.src='logo1.gif';">
        <img name="myImage" width="100" height="100" border="0"
            src="logo1.gif">
    </a>
</body>
</html>
```

In plain English, what this says is, "When the mouse pointer rolls over linked image **logo1.gif**, replace its source file with the image file **logo2.gif**; when the pointer moves away, replace it with **logo1.gif** again." You can see the result here:

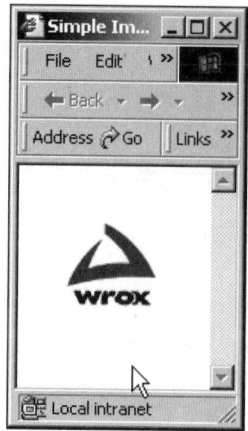 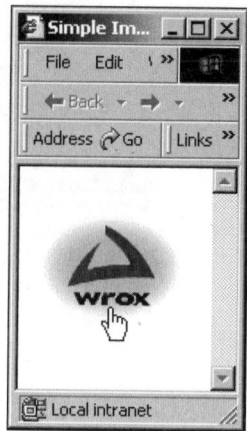

Provided there are image files with these names in the same directory in which the page containing this HTML and script code is located, Netscape versions 3 and above will do precisely that, as will Internet Explorer versions 4 and above. However, Internet Explorer 3 and Netscape Netscape 2 will each give us a script error, reporting that there is no object named myImage that it can recognize. Now let's rewrite this example slightly, employing the technique we spoke of earlier known as **object detection**. The <a> element now looks like this:

```
<a href="http://www.wrox.com/"
   onmouseover="if(document.images)document.myImage.src="logo2.gif";"
   onmouseout="if(document.images)document.myImage.src="logo1.gif";">
   <img name="myImage" width="100" height="100" border="0" src="logo1.gif"></a>
```

What we've done here is to modify the JavaScript code in such a way as to check to ensure that the browser supports the manipulation of images through script. Our code snippet now says to the browser, in effect, "When the linked image named logo.gif is moved over with the mouse pointer – *if you understand what an Image object is* – display the image named logo2.gif in its place". When we try out this altered code in Netscape 2 or IE 3, nothing happens. This may sound rather disappointing, but what it really means is that we've met with success: we've included a nifty interactive feature for our users whose browser software can support it, and we're not interrupting the experience of those using our site whose browsers don't support it with the necessity of dismissing an annoying *"Scripting Error!"* modal dialog.

Let's look at another code sample:

```
<!DOCTYPE HTML PUBLIC "-//W3C//DTD HTML 4.01 Transitional//EN"
                "http://www.w3.org/TR/REC-html401/loose.dtd">
<html>
<head>
   <script type="text/javascript">
   <!--

   function showScreenData()
   {
      var myWidth,myHeight;
      var msg="Your available screen measures\n";
```

```
        myWidth=screen.availWidth;
        myHeight=screen.availHeight;

        msg+=myWidth+" pixels by "+myHeight+" pixels,\n";
        msg+="for an area of "+(myWidth*myHeight)+" pixels square.";

        alert(msg);
    }

    window.onload=showScreenData;

    //-->
    </script>
</head>
<body>

<p>
    When this page has finished loading,<br/>
    you should see a popup dialog containing<br/>
    some information about the screen...
</p>

</body>
</html>
```

When this page is loaded into a browser that provides a scripting interface to the user's screen, the user should see something like this:

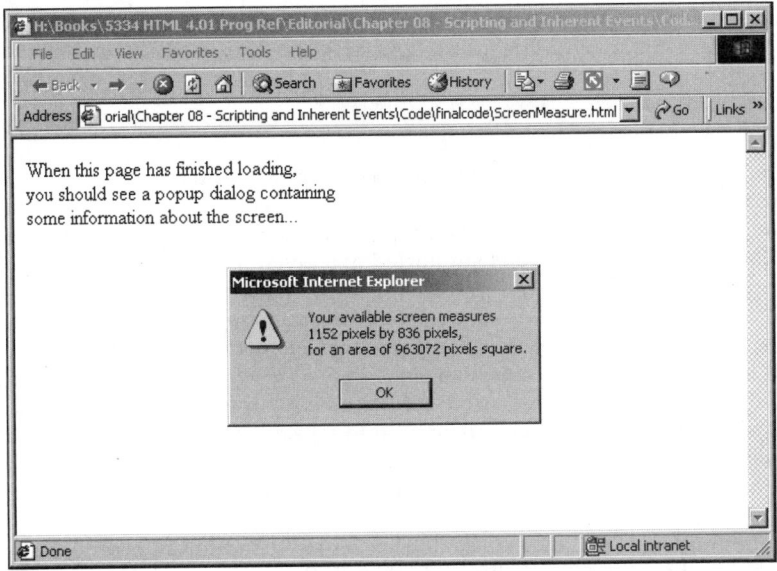

A quick check of any good JavaScript reference will tell you that the `screen` object and its properties are accessible only in browsers that can run scripts in JavaScript 1.2 or higher. In the days of HTML 3.2, the problem of how do deal with browsers that didn't support JavaScript 1.2 or higher would be solved as follows: rewrite the opening `<script>` tag to read:

```
<script language="JavaScript1.2">
```

and browsers that only supported JavaScript 1.0 or 1.1 would not attempt to interpret the script code. Strictly speaking, in HTML 4.0 and above, that's no longer an option, and `language` is deprecated – however, this script function can be rewritten incorporating a little defensive programming:

```
function showScreenData()
{
    if(window.screen)
    {
        var myWidth,myHeight;
        var msg="Your available screen measures\n";

        myWidth=screen.availWidth;
        myHeight=screen.availHeight;

        msg+=myWidth+" pixels by "+myHeight+" pixels,\n";
        msg+="for an area of "+(myWidth*myHeight)+" pixels square.";

        alert(msg);
    }
}
```

As outlined in the W3C standard, the `type` attribute does not explicitly allow for language versioning. This can be detrimental for scripters whose applications employ certain core language features that are independent of any page-related objects that the browser may or may not support. At present, the only manner in which Internet Explorer can cope with such situations is for scripters to use the `language` attribute. However, Netscape 6 and Mozilla both extend the `type` attribute to allow for versioning in the following manner:

```
<script type="text/javascript; version=1.2">
```

which is similar to the syntax to be found in the `<meta http-equiv="..."> `tag. It is not certain whether or not this will be formally adopted by W3C; however, it is apparent that something like this will eventually need to be done, in order to prevent breaking of scripts using version-dependent language features that aren't supported in a given user agent.

Before we leave this topic, we should mention that there is another widely used technique to make scripts "safe" for user agents that don't make given page elements or properties accessible to scripting. This is known as **browser detection**, and (in theory) works just as it sounds like it should: as we remarked earlier in this chapter, every script-capable browser makes available to the scripter certain information about itself, which can be used to take advantage of that browser's feature set, or to bypass calls upon functionality that isn't supported by it. While this is probably as common as object detection, perhaps even more so, it is often not as flexible or as foolproof as object detection.

We'll defer examining the actual mechanics of browser detection to Chapter 16, but what we would need to do with it in this case is to say basically this: "If the browser is a Microsoft or Netscape product *and* it's a version 4 or greater browser, *then* do the routine for getting and displaying the user's screen dimensions and area". There are two potential weaknesses here. The first one is that, quite often, a lot more code is required in order to perform the same test, which we already know can be done with just one line – and we all know that, in general, More Code Is Bad (unless we're lucky enough to be getting paid by the line, of course, which is lamentably not very often).

The second is that we're really not covering all of our bases. There might be other user agents out there now or in the future that aren't from Netscape or Microsoft, or that might not carry a version number of 4 or greater, but that can deal perfectly well with the screen object. There are also browsers – such as Opera and Konqueror – whose user agent, application name and application version strings can be set to whatever the user chooses in their preferences, which means that the browser-detection code could be tricked into evaluating a test condition as "true" and executing a function or other script code block even when it really shouldn't do so.

On the other hand, we don't want to discount browser detection entirely, because there are situations in which scripters do need to know whether a visitor is using a particular browser or browser version, or is on a particular platform or operating system in order to take advantage of browser- or platform-specific features or, conversely, to take precautions against scripting bugs unique to that browser version or OS.

Providing Alternative Content: the <noscript> Element

We've examined in some detail both how to include or embed scripts and some ways to keep those scripts from causing problems for user agents that don't support them. Now we'll consider the question: "Can I provide some alternative content that doesn't require client-side scripting for users whose browsers don't support it, or in which scripting has been disabled?"

The answer is: "Yes" – the <noscript> element is intended for just this purpose.

The <noscript> element supports the universal attributes and core events, all listed for easy reference in Chapter 2.

It may contain any valid HTML content that the page author wants to be seen in browsers that don't support any scripting at all, don't support a particular scripting content-type (that is, a particular scripting language), or have scripting disabled for whatever reason. In order to demarcate the content that is to be shown to non-scripting browsers, it requires both a beginning <noscript> tag and an ending </noscript> tag.

If a browser doesn't support any scripting at all, then it is supposed to render the contents of any and all <noscript> blocks it encounters as they were normal text blocks. (Note that the content model for this element is in fact defined in the HTML 4.01 DTD as block rather than inline.) The same is true for those user agents that do support client-side scripting but have it disabled. Here's a basic example of the <noscript> tag in use:

```
<!DOCTYPE HTML PUBLIC "-//W3C//DTD HTML 4.01 Transitional//EN"
"http://www.w3.org/TR/REC-html401/loose.dtd">
<html>
<head>
<meta http-equiv="Content-Type" content="text/html; charset=iso-8859-1">
<meta http-equiv="Script-Content-Type" content="text/javascript">
<title>NOSCRIPT</title>
</head>
<body>
<script type="text/javascript">
<!--
  document.write("This is some text generated by JavaScript.");
//-->
</script>
<noscript>You should see this text only if JavaScript is not enabled in the
browser.</noscript>
</body>
</html>
```

Note that the `<noscript>` block can contain any valid HTML, including paragraphs, links, images, lists, etc.

This is our sample file, `noscript.htm`, as seen in a web browser. The first shot shows the output in a browser with script enabled:

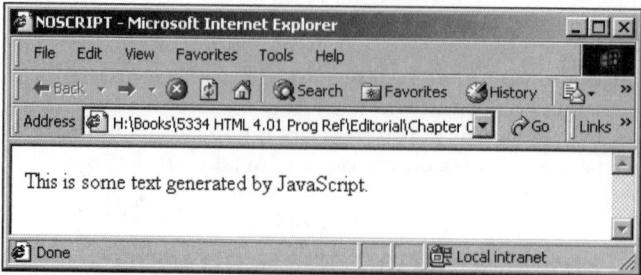

and this second shot shows the output in a browser with script disabled:

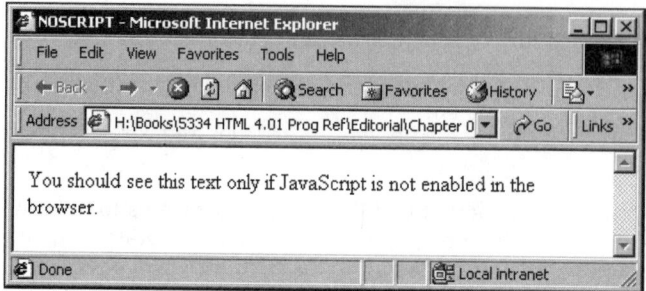

According to the W3C specification, user agents that do support scripting should otherwise render the `<noscript>` element's contents only if the browser isn't equipped to interpret a scripting language called upon at some point in the document preceding that `<noscript>` block. That's what the specification appears to say; in fact, all the major browsers only display `<noscript>` element contents when scripting is disabled in them. It is probably safe to assume that this behavior will continue to be observed for the near future at least. In addition, there is the opposite problem with Netscape 2.0: it displays `<noscript>` content even when scripting is enabled, due to the fact that it was released before the `<noscript>` element was introduced in Netscape 3.0. Fortunately, this browser has almost entirely fallen out of use, but it could possibly be a concern in some situations where users are on older equipment or haven't been able or motivated to upgrade.

Summary

This completes our discussion of the concepts behind client-side scripting, the use of the `<script>` and `<noscript>` elements, and the basics of intrinsic events and event handling as they relate to creating web or other documents with HTML 4.01. For information concerning more advanced topics in web scripting and their relation to HTML and CSS authoring – including a discussion of "Dynamic HTML," browser object models, and the Document Object Model standards issued by the W3C, the interested reader is invited to turn to Chapter 21 of the present work, or to consult a dedicated scripting book, such as *Professional JavaScript* by Nigel McFarlane et al. (ISBN: *1-861002-70-X*).

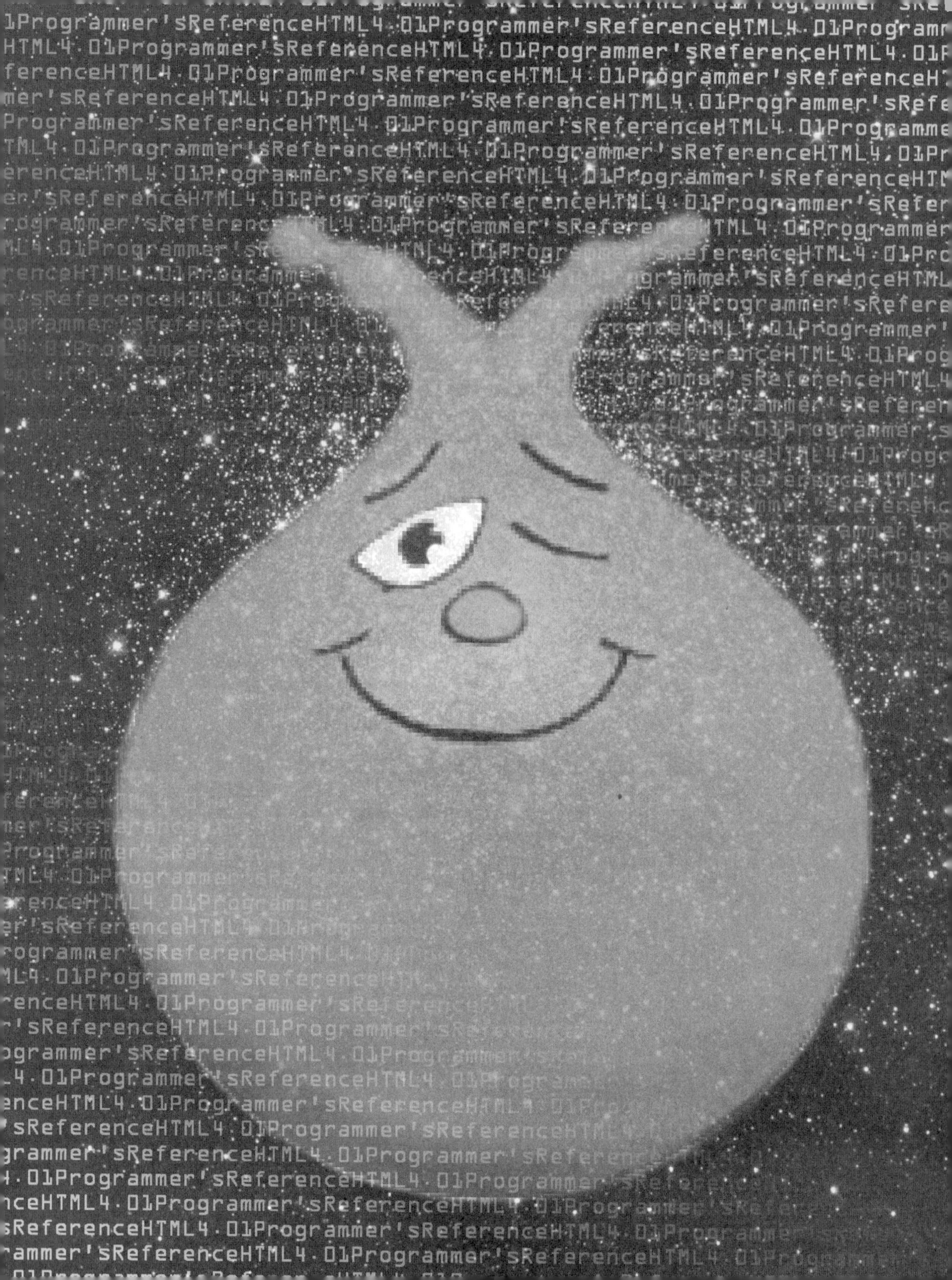

HTML4.01Programmer'sReference

10

Embedding Objects

While what we've looked at in HTML so far, such as links, tables, and forms, offers a lot of important functionality, there are still many things that can't be achieved with just HTML alone. What happens if we want a movie embedded in our web page, or an audio MP3 file? In the first days of the web, we could do little more than browse hyper-linked text pages with the very occasional image if we were lucky. With HTML 2.0, we could only insert images, videos, sounds, and text. This improved further with HTML 3.2, but to add anything more, such as simple animated messages, spreadsheets, word documents, or even full 3D renderings of landscapes, we needed to insert them as objects.

HTML 4.01 allows for this by making the `<object>` element the standard way of doing this. Previously, the placement of objects in web pages was supported in a mish-mash of standard and non-standard ways. Indeed, the `<object>` element supercedes the `<applet>`, `<embed>`, and `<img>` elements, as well as Microsoft's `<bgsound>` element and `dynasrc` attribute. The `<object>` element is mainly used for content types the browser can't handle itself, and therefore an `<object>` element needs to provide both the data to be displayed and the plug-in that handles the display of the data. `<object>`, in theory, provides a single way to embed a whole range of objects into web documents, and offer more universal, cross-platform support for HTML pages.

However, a major source of disappointment is that the <object> element, despite being the standard way of doing this, was until recently, only really available in Internet Explorer. This is because the plug-ins needed to support many objects are not often universally cross-platform compatible. Netscape 6 goes part of the way to rectifying this, by adding support. Despite this, though, in the early versions of Netscape 6 (6.0 and 6.01), support for the <object> element when adding anything other than images, was erratic verging on non-existent at times. However, in the more up-to-date Mozilla milestone builds (0.8 and beyond, which form the basis for future Netscape releases), many of these problems have been resolved, and <object> will therefore work properly in the next major upgrade to Netscape 6 expected in summer 2001. Also, other browsers such as Opera 5, and older browsers like Netscape 4 still have limited support for this element and rely entirely on the old <embed> element to enable components.

In this chapter we will be focusing on the <object> element, as the other elements (except for <img>) have either been deprecated, and are covered in Chapter 15, or in the case of the <embed> and <bgsound> elements, were never part of the standard. Both of these elements are covered in Chapter 16.

The <object> Element – History

Originally, the HTML 2.0 Standard provided only one method for incorporating media into HTML documents: the <img> element. This element has certainly proved worthwhile, but it is, of course, restricted to image media, which means that its usefulness is limited as richer media find their way onto the Web.

For other media though, there was the <embed> element, which was introduced in Netscape 2 and IE 3, and is still in many browsers the only way to insert many types of objects into web pages. With the introduction of Java, the <applet> element was introduced in HTML 3.2, to allow developers to insert Java applets.

The <object> element was originally introduced by Microsoft in Internet Explorer 3 for the inclusion of Microsoft **Component Object Model** or **COM** objects (such as ActiveX Controls and a wide variety of different media types and plug-ins). Internet Explorer introduced this tag with support for ActiveX controls, and Microsoft has continued to develop around it.

> *When Microsoft released its first set of Internet tools in March 1996, it announced **ActiveX** technology – which in all truth was just a new marketing name for its existing **OLE** technology. ActiveX (or 3rd generation OLE technology) was a framework that allowed software components to cooperate even if they had been written by different vendors, at different times using different tools and different languages, and if the objects were located in the same process – same machine or distributed over multiple machines. Some ActiveX controls came with the IE browser.*

The reason the <object> element has proved so popular with the HTML W3C standards body, and was ultimately adopted by it, was that it introduces a uniform way to embed all kinds of object – images, Java applets, movies, etc. We can't use the <embed> tag to place images or Java applets, and we can't use the <img> element for anything other than images, yet the logic behind introducing this content is very similar for each type of object. For each object, regardless of whether it's a graphic, a Java applet, or a RealTime movie, we still need to state the location of the object, the type of object we are including, and a place to download a "helper application" so that the browser can still invoke the object, even if it doesn't have native support for it.

A helper application is one that needs to be downloaded by the browser before it can run a particular object. For instance with some browsers need to download Macromedia's Flash before they can run a Flash animation.

Arguably, the <embed> element handles all of these features as well and could have been adapted to handle images and Java applets; however, the <object> element, together with the param attribute provides a cleaner and more general approach to passing parameters to the component, and that may have been what tipped the scales in its favor.

It's an attractive solution, if a somewhat flawed one in some ways. One problem was that Netscape 4 didn't support the <object> element – Netscape still preferred to use the <embed> element, which was never officially recognized, but as previously mentioned, <object> has been introduced in Netscape 6 and Opera 5, albeit to a limited extent. There is also the problem that several components created by Microsoft only ship with Internet Explorer, and are therefore only available with Internet Explorer, such as the graphic effects filters. In general, it is possible to add a lot of other third-party components with <object> in Netscape 6, such as images and applets, and it is possible to include images in Opera 5. However, at this precise moment in time, the <object> element is not an entirely cross-browser solution.

How the <object> Element Works

Most browsers have built-in native support for common features such as images (GIFs, JPEGs, and PNGs), text, fonts, and colors. When IE 4 was released in 1997, the most common components available on the web were ActiveX controls and Java applets, both of which could be run by the <object> element. However, there has been a considerable shift since then. COM objects have replaced ActiveX controls, and these in turn are in the process of being partially superceded by web services in the .NET framework.

The progress with compression algorithms and higher bandwidth being made available more cheaply means that streaming video, such as MPEGs, AVIs, and Quick time Movies, are now much more commonplace on the web. These require separate applications such as the Windows Media Player, or the Apple Quick Time Movie Player to be available to run them. Secondly, audio has moved beyond large, clunky WAV files. Streaming audio is common in the form of .ra (real audio files), but by far the most common form of audio file is the MP3 format, which has shrunk the size of audio files to a manageable few megabytes, while retaining a sound quality close to that of a CD player. Once again, we need to insert a third party player such as Windows Media Player into our page to be able to play MP3 files.

Technically speaking, most MP3 files are saved at a better sample rate than the average CD player, which saves at 44.1Khz. However, even with files saved at 128KHz, the lossy compression algorithm used in MP3 removes non-audible information to reduce file size. This is still flawed, and you will find CDs audibly superior to MP3 files.

We can use the <object> element to insert these kinds of technologies. However, due to large file sizes, the preferred method for many web users is to download these files separately, and as a result it is becoming less common for web developers to actively embed either video or audio files within a web page. Instead, the most common form of embedded application in a web page is Macromedia's motion web graphics tool – Flash. This allows developers to create animations, interactive graphics, and menus and embed them into web pages. Flash can also handle sound and text, and has become a popular catchall solution for developers. Flash animations are embedded into HTML pages using the <object> element.

To be able to embed an object in a page, the W3C states that we need to specify three types of information:

❑   The implementation of the included object (or the location of the executable code)

❑   The data to be rendered

❑   Additional values required by the object at run time

The first two values are specified within the attributes of the <object> element, while additional values are specified within the <param> element. However, we don't need to specify all three at once. Some objects might not have to be initialized at run time, while others won't have any data to render. When a browser comes across an object it must attempt to render its contents on the web page, otherwise it must attempt to render the contents of the <object> element. For example:

```
<object type="oojit/wotsit">
  If you are reading this text then your browser can't render the object.
</object>
```

Here we have placed some alternative text inside a non-existent object. All browsers will display the alternative text, as they can't render the object.

We can also use the <object> element to embed objects one inside another. The browser will attempt to the render the first <object> – if it can't render that, then it should attempt to render the second <object> element, and so on, until it reaches the innermost <object> element, if it hasn't yet managed to render any objects. If it can't render any objects, then it will render the text contained within. If we wish, we can supply the object as an <embed>, <applet>, or <img> element within the innermost object instead, for those browsers that don't support the <object> element.

It is also possible to insert the <object> element within the document header (within the <head> element), as long as the <object> element isn't intended to render any physical content on the web page. This sounds a little strange, given that the <object> element is primarily intended for embedding multimedia content, but it is a useful technique to consider – for example, we could use an <object> element in the document header to invoke a database, values out of which could then be manipulated by script in the body.

However, looking at the way in which Netscape 6 and Opera 5.x handle the <object> element, it seems we need to ensure ourselves that the element doesn't render, for example by setting it within a style sheet display: none;. IE 5.5 on the other hand automatically won't render any <object> elements appearing in the <head> section.

Now, let's take a look at the <object> element's attributes, and see how we can use an object in our web page.

<object> Attributes

The <object> element supports the following attributes:

archive	border	classid	codebase
codetype	data	declare	height
width	hspace	vspace	name
standby	tabindex	usemap	

plus the usual HTML 4.01 attributes id, class, style, dir, lang, and title, and the common events (see Chapter 2 for more details on these).

archive

This attribute specifies a list of space-separated URLs, which have information relevant to the resource specified in classid and data attributes. The syntax is:

```
archive="urllist"
```

border

This attribute specifies the width of the border to be drawn around the object. The syntax is:

```
border="n"
```

where n is an integer. For border="0", no border is drawn. Like align, this attribute is deprecated in HTML 4.01. Style sheets are the preferred method for adding borders.

classid

This specifies a class identifier for an object (on Windows platforms, this information is stored in the registry on the user's machine, once the object has been installed). The syntax is:

```
classid="class_identifier"
```

The class_identifier is the information used to create an object on our web page. The class identifier (the HTML 4.01 standard specifies that this should be a URL) tells the browser to draw an object of a specified type. However, in Internet Explorer it's treated slightly differently; the classid attribute is the key to the whole element – this is a value that is unique for every instance of the object, and this is how the browser knows which object to load into the page. Here's an example of the classid for the RDS control.

```
<object id="RDS Control" classid="clsid:BD96C556-65A3-11D0-983A-
        00C04FC29E33">
...
```

It is used as an alternative to the data attribute, and is often preferred in Internet Explorer to data, where it doesn't seem to work as well for the <object> element.

codebase

This allows us to specify the URL location and version of the object to be used. The syntax is:

```
codebase="url"
```

However, it's only IE that really implements this attribute, and it implements it in the following way:

```
codebase="url#Version=a,b,c,d"
```

Most components need to be installed on our system before we can use them in our web pages. In IE, the codebase attribute points to a location from where the object can be downloaded and installed on our system for use. It also identifies the version of the file that should be downloaded. If an object isn't available already on our local machine then the system will have to go to the url specified. Of course, if the site specified in the codebase is busy or out of action, then unfortunately our page won't download and insert the requisite object correctly.

As we can see from the syntax, we can optionally append the URL with a version number string. The string has the following format:

❑   **a** – High-order word of the major version of the component available at the specified URL

❑   **b** – Low-order word of the major version of the component available at the specified URL

❑   **c** – High-order word of the minor version of the component available at the specified URL

❑   **d** – Low-order word of the minor version of the component available at the specified URL

If a, b, c and, d are all set to 1 then the component is only downloaded if the release date is later than the installation date on the user's machine.

An example codebase to enable us to run a Macromedia Flash 5 animation looks like this:

```
CODEBASE="http://download.macromedia.com/pub/shockwave/cabs/flash/swflash.ca
          b#version=5,0,0,0"
```

However, this will only work with IE.

codetype

This specifies the Internet Media Type expected by the browser when downloading an object of the type that has been referenced in the classid attribute. It is only relevant if a classid attribute has already been specified. The syntax is as follows:

```
codetype="media_type"
```

Browsers may use the value of the codetype attribute to skip over unsupported media types, without the need to download unnecessary objects. See *"type"* for more details on media types.

declare

This declares the object without instantiating it. The syntax is simply `declare`.

Use this when you are creating cross-references to objects that occur later in the document, or when you are using the object as a parameter within another object.

data

This defines the URL, or the data itself, that is the source for the object. The syntax is:

```
data="source"
```

where `source` can be a URL from which the data can be downloaded, or the data itself as a string of hexadecimal values. We'll look at an example of this later in the chapter.

height and width

These specify the height and width that an object is to be displayed at. The syntax is:

```
width="n"
height="n"
```

where n is the width or height in pixels. This can also be expressed as a percentage value, in which case, the value should be appended with a % symbol.

When using the `<object>` element to display images `width` and `height` are scaleable. That is, we can use them to specify the size of box that we want the image to fit into, and the browser will scale the image to suit, which is exactly the same as how the `<img>` element handles images. However, there is an exception to this rule, in that IE 5.5 puts the image in its original size into a frame, and this frame is scaled to the dimensions specified by the `width`/`height`. We'll see more on this in a minute.

Using `width` and `height` with the `<object>` element helps the page to load faster, because the browser can lay out the rest of the page, as it knows the dimensions of the object before loading it.

hspace and vspace

These attributes are used to control the white space around an object. The syntax is:

```
hspace="n"
vspace="n"
```

where n is a numerical value in pixels. Other elements next to, above, and below the image will be moved away by the specified number of pixels. These attributes are now deprecated with the HTML 4.01 standard.

name

This attribute provides a name to refer to the object by. The syntax is:

```
name="name"
```

where `name` is a unique name within the page. In HTML 4.01, this is equivalent to the `id` attribute, but is only required for form submission.

standby

This attribute specifies a text string that will be used while the object data is loading. The syntax is:

```
standby="text"
```

where `text` is a word, phrase or sentence that describes the object, or provides a meaningful description of the object, when displayed while it loads.

tabindex

This is the tab index for the object within the page. The syntax is:

```
tabindex="n"
```

where n is the position within the tabbing order of the page. By default, all elements in the page that can receive the input focus are part of the tabbing order, in the order they are defined in the HTML source. Each receives the focus in turn as the *Tab* key is pressed. By setting the value of `tabindex` to `-1`, the element is removed from the tabbing order. See Chapter 6, for more on `tabindex` and focus.

usemap

This attribute indicates that the object is an image map containing defined areas that are individual hyperlinks. The `usemap` attribute is used to specify the map file to use with this object. The standard allows for a complete URL to an external map file, but usually a reference `#mapName` to an inline `mapElement` is used. Also, note that this attribute only exists in Internet Explorer 6, and not earlier IE versions. There is more information on image maps in Chapter 5.

Internet Explorer <object> Extensions

Internet Explorer adds other attributes to the `<object>` element:

```
align          accesskey      alt      code
datafld        hidefocus      notab    type
unselectable
```

Note: only the `align` attribute is actually supported in IE 5.5 onwards, the rest are IE 4 only. Now let's look at these in turn:

align

The syntax for the `align` attribute in this context is slightly different from normal:

```
align="top | middle | bottom | left | right | absbottom* | texttop* | absmiddle* |
baseline*"
```

* For explanations of these values, please refer back to Chapter 5, and look at the section on the `<img>` element. This attribute is deprecated in HTML 4.01.

accesskey

This attribute defines the "hot-key" that can be used to activate the element, or switch the input focus to it. This is used where a hyperlink takes the form of an image, rather than a text string. For details of using an image as a hyperlink see Chapter 4. For more about the uses of the `accesskey` attribute, see Chapter 6.

alt

This defines a text alternative to the graphic. See Chapter 5 for more details.

code

This attribute defines the URL to the Java class file implementing the object, if this is the object source instead of an image. Its syntax is:

```
code="url"
```

datafld and datasrc

These attributes are used to connect the `<object>` element to a client-side cached data source in Internet Explorer 4, in a technique called **data binding**. These have since been removed in Internet Explorer 6. For a look at using these attributes, see the "`<frame>`" section of Chapter 8.

hidefocus

This attribute holds a value indicating whether or not the object is indicated visibly when the element is in focus. See Chapter 8 for more information.

notab

This attribute was present very briefly in Internet Explorer 3, but was dropped by the time of version 4. It was used to exclude an element from the tabbing order, but now this can be achieved by setting the `tabindex` attribute to –1.

type

This attribute defines the MIME type for the object, as defined in the registry on a Windows Machine. The syntax is:

```
type="mime-type"
```

where `mime-type` is a unique text string of a standard format, which tells the browser what kind of information the file contains, and which application to use to read or execute it – as appropriate. The MIME-types for popular image formats are "`image/gif`", "`image/jpeg`", and "`image/png`". This is overridden by the `classid` attribute.

unselectable

This attribute specifies that the element cannot be selected. The syntax is:

```
unselectable="on | off"
```

If it is set to `off` (the default), then the element can be selected. Setting it to `on` makes the object unselectable.

Tags <object> Can Enclose

The `<object>` element operates in conjunction with the `<param>` element, which is used to specify the different parameters that each object can take. These parameters are values that the object will require at run time. They must be placed at the beginning of the content of the `<object>` element.

The <param> Element

The `param` element can take the following attributes:

```
name        type        value        valuetype
```

plus the universal attributes and core events discussed in Chapter 2. The majority of these additional elements, which are specific to a particular object, will just use a `name` and a `value`.

name

This attribute specifies the `name` or property of the parameter. This attribute is mandatory for every `<param>` element. The syntax is:

```
name="string"
```

value

This attribute specifies the value to set for the parameter. The syntax is:

```
value="string"
```

type

This attribute has the value of the MIME type that is retrieved if `valuetype` (the data type of the `value` attribute) is set to `ref`. The syntax is:

```
type="string"
```

valuetype

This attribute specifies how the parameter value will be obtained. The syntax is:

```
valuetype="data | ref | object"
```

`ref` is via a URL, while `data` is the default, an implicit value, and `object` is an identifier that refers to the `id` of another `object` defined in the page. IE 6 is the first IE version to support `valuetype` for the `<param>` element.

Using the <object> Element

The `<object>` element is a general-purpose element, designed to insert many different types of content into an HTML document. In order to cope with this diversity, the `type` attribute is used to indicate the type of data the object displays, and the `codetype` attribute indicates the type of application that implements the display of the data. Of interest to us when working with images, is the `type` attribute, which is a string description of the content – such as `"image/gif"` for a GIF image, or perhaps `"video/avi"` for an AVI video clip. In general terms for types other than video, audio, or text, the application that is required to display the data is defined by `"application/<document_type>"`. In the case of the generic image types, like GIF and JPEG, the browser itself handles the display of the image.

In Windows, a list of all the MIME types supported by your machine can be found in registry under: `HKEY_CLASSES_ROOT\MIME\Database\ContentType\`, which can be used by all browsers.

Specifying the Data

The `data` attribute provides the data for the object, either as a URL from where it can be downloaded, or inline as a string of values. As an example, this code will display an AVI file named `MyVideo.avi`. If the browser doesn't support the `<object>` element, it will display the text My Video:

```
<object data="http://mysite.com/video/MyVideo.avi"
        type="video/avi">
  My Video
</object>
```

This is a general example of how we can take advantage of the `<object>` element as a containing element.

The `type` attribute, however, is optional; but if it isn't present, then the only way that the browser can be sure of knowing whether it can handle the object is by downloading it first – not all files can be uniquely identified from, say, a file extension. In addition, not all files necessarily have to have the correct extension anyway, and not all systems even use file extensions. By including the `type` attribute, we can tell the browser exactly what type of file it is. Then, if it can't handle it, it won't waste time and bandwidth downloading it.

259

Fall Back in Browsers That Don't Support an Object

If the browser recognizes the <object> element, then all well and good – the object will be invoked. However, if it doesn't recognize the <object> element, or can't handle the data that forms the source of the object, we can ensure that an alternative will be displayed.

We can include text and other elements that are only visible on a browser that either doesn't recognize the <object> element, or that can't handle the content type of the data it specifies. We do this by placing text or other elements between the opening and closing <object> tags, and outside any parameter tags. Here's an example:

```
<object data="http://mysite.com/video/MyVideo.avi"
        type="application/avi">
   <img src="http://mysite.com/stills/MyPicture.gif"
        alt="This is a picture of my dog">
</object>
```

In this case, browsers that support the <object> element should display a video clip. However, if the browser either doesn't support the <object> element, or can't display AVI files, the viewer will see an ordinary image defined by the <img> element. And if the browser doesn't recognize the <img> element, or can't display the content of it for any reason, the alternative text in the <img> element's alt attribute will be displayed.

Inline Data Definitions for Objects

If the data content of the object is reasonably small, it can be defined by including the data itself in the <object> tag, this is called an **inline definition**:

```
<object data="data:application/x-oleobject;3300,FF00,E3A0, ...etc... ">
</object>
```

This isn't very common as the amount of data needed for inline definition is usually quite impractical.

Inserting Images with an <object> Element

One interesting proposal in HTML 4.01, as we've seen, is the use of the <object> element to embed ordinary graphics files, such as GIF and JPEG files. In its most basic form the use is simple:

```
<object data="wroxLogo.gif">
</object>
```

The data attribute works just like the src attribute in an <img> tag, but can also accept inline data where the image is small. This can speed up the time to view of a page, by reducing the number of server connections required:

```
<object type="image/jpeg"
   data="data:image/jpeg;3300,FF00,2756,E5A0,E3A0,22F6, ...etc... ">
</object>
```

However, unlike the <img> element, which will display a graphic in the browser with this minimal information, this isn't enough for Internet Explorer (versions 4 to 6). It will assume that the height and width settings are set to zero, and we won't see anything, although Netscape 6 and Opera 5.02 will display the graphic quite happily:

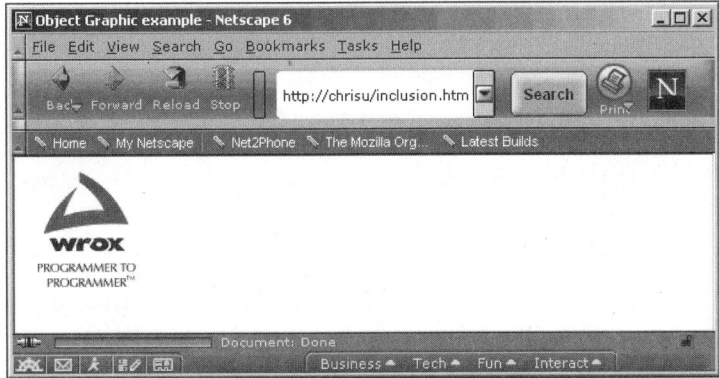

By adding the usual `width` and `height` attributes common to the `<img>` element, and adding the MIME type in the `type` attribute, the image will be displayed in Internet Explorer with the following code:

```
<object type="image/gif" data="wroxLogo.gif"
        width="100" height="100" >
   This is our Wrox Logo
</object>
```

While adding the `height` and `width` now means that we can see the image in Internet Explorer, all is still not well:

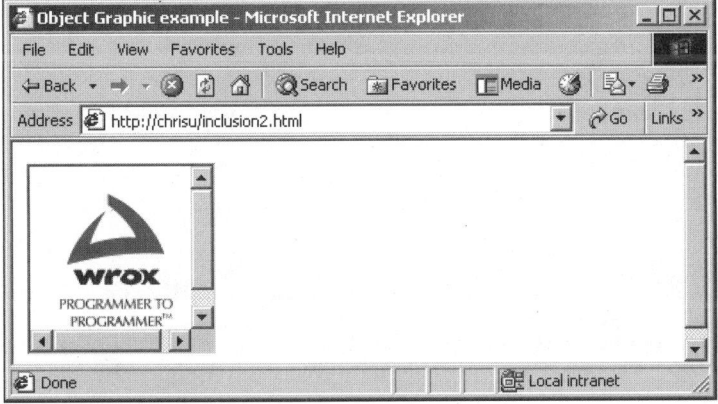

Looking at the result, we can see an example of a **container** with the `<object>` element. Unlike the `<img>` element, in Internet Explorer (versions 4 to 6) the `<object>` element doesn't use the default size of the file to size the container. The `height` and `width` we've specified are used to size a frame, which contains the `<object>` element itself, but not the image. Because it's larger than the available space, the browser automatically adds scroll bars.

Of course, the "proper" way to size an element in HTML 4.01 is to use style sheets to specify the `height` and `width` styles. Below, we've used the `width` attribute in an inline style sheet for brevity. This code produces the same page as above:

```
<object type="image/gif" data="wroxLogo.gif"
        style="width:100px; height:100px">
   This is our Wrox Logo
</object>
```

However, this doesn't solve the problem of the scroll bars. Resizing the image container so that it fits the image also doesn't solve the problem:

```
<object type="image/gif" data="wroxLogo.gif"
        style="width:105px; height:105px">
   This is our Wrox Logo
</object>
```

Now the horizontal scrollbar is removed, but the vertical one remains, although it is now inactive:

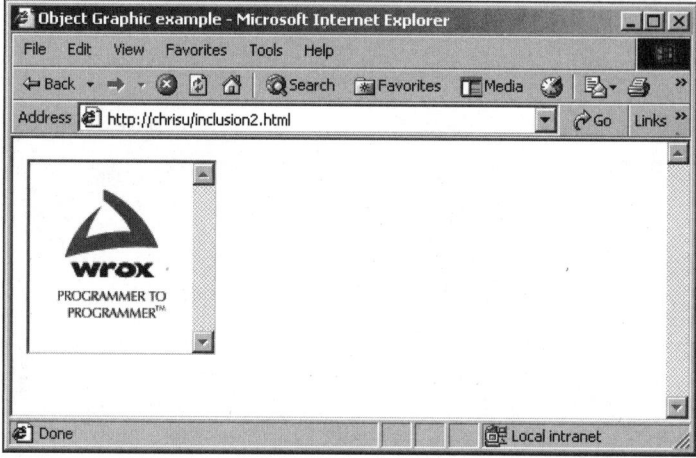

In Internet Explorer therefore, we can't use images inside the `<object>` element without incurring an unsightly scrollbar. This makes it unusable until Microsoft updates this.

Netscape 6 and Mozilla render the image correctly without scrollbars, but there is one anomaly in its representation of images in the `<object>` element. If we resize the image, using a style sheet, Netscape simply sets the image size as the default, ignoring any values set in the style sheet. If we want to stretch the image, as with the `<img>` element, we must use the `height` and `width` attributes:

```
<object type="image/gif" data="wroxLogo.gif"
        height="250" width="100">
   This is our Wrox Logo
</object>
```

This would then stretch the image to fit:

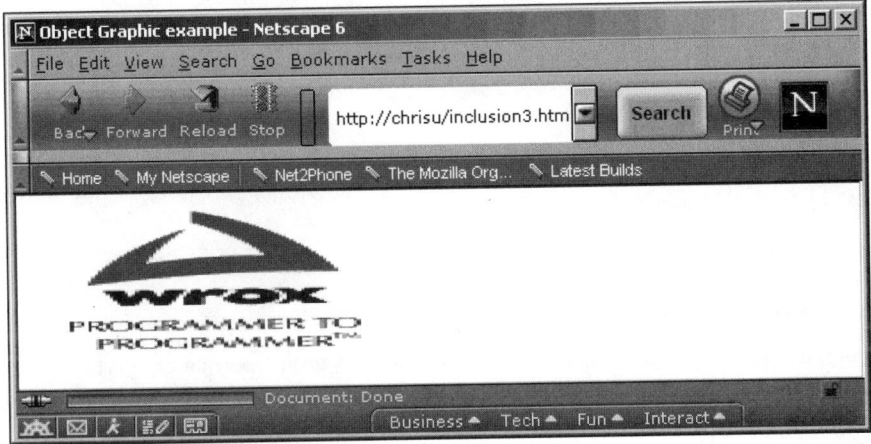

Hidden Image Elements

We can also specify other style properties, for example this code:

```
<object type="image/gif" data="wroxLogo.gif"
        style="visibility:hidden; height:105pt; width:105pt">
   This is our Wrox Logo
</object>
```

loads the image into the `<object>` element on the page, but makes it invisible. While it may seem a little pointless, it is a good way to get the browser to cache images that we want to make available quickly, such as rollovers – like a rotated ad, or a series of frames of animation in an animated-GIF. When the image needs to be displayed, it doesn't need to be downloaded – just lifted from the local system's cache, although it can slow down the loading of the first page, as all the images have to be loaded first.

The Alternative Content

Finally, what happens if the browser doesn't know how to handle the object specified by the `type` and `data` attributes? Here, we've used an unknown value for `type`:

```
<object type="haven't/aclue" data="wroxLogo.gif"
        style="width:100; height:100">
   This is our Wrox Logo
</object>
```

The result is that, after a few moments' indecision, the browser (IE and Netscape 6 only – Opera 5.x displays the image regardless) reports that it can't handle the file and displays the alternative text content of the `<object>` element:

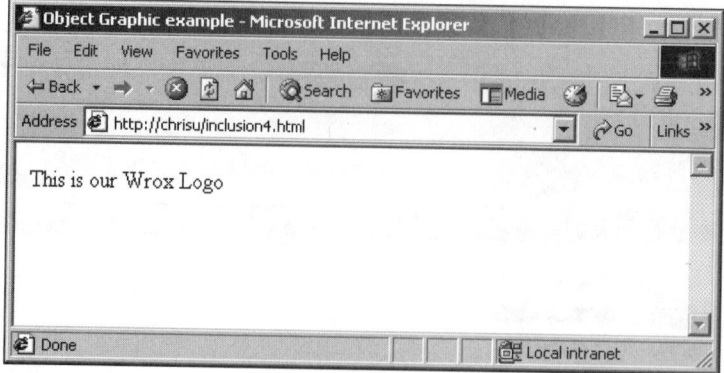

Unfortunately, Internet Explorer's quirky rendering of images with a permanent vertical scrollbar means that adoption of the `<object>` element in preference to the `<img>` element is not likely to happen yet.

Inserting Components into a Web Page

While it isn't possible to look at an example of how to embed every single object or component into web pages, we're going to look at a cross section of components that we can embed into web pages using the `<object>` element.

Showing a Movie

There are several components that are included with each different version of Internet Explorer, which give us the ability to make our web pages come alive by providing special formatting features, animation, video, and much more.

Perhaps the most useful of them is Microsoft's Windows Media Player control, which comes as part of the DirectX SDK and is available in IE 4 and upwards. Windows Media Player allows us to play back popular media formats on the web, including progressive playback of MPEG Audio and Video, AVI files, some types of QuickTime MOVies, MP3, WAV Files, and MIDI. As this component comes with IE, we don't need the `codebase` attribute to locate a version of Windows Media Player.

Here we are going to show how to put in-line video into a web page, by inserting Windows Media Player as an object, like so:

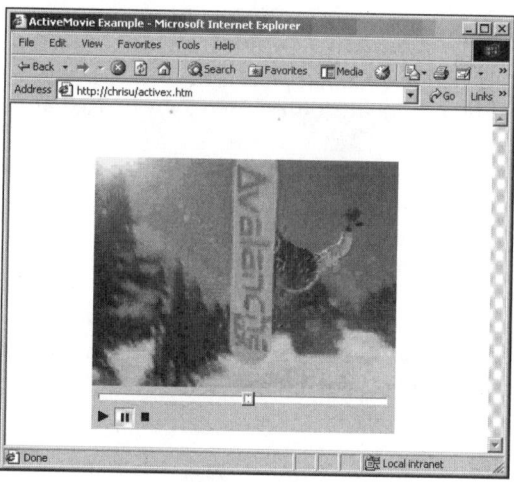

Take a look at the following code:

```html
<html>
  <head>
    <title>ActiveMovie Example</title>
  </head>
  <body>
    <object id="WindowsMediaPlayer" classid="CLSID:05589FA1-C356-11CE-BF01-
        00AA0055595A" style="position:absolute;top:55;left:90">
      <param name="ShowDisplay" value="0">
      <param name="ShowControls" value="1">
      <param name="AutoStart" value="1">
      <param name="AutoRewind" value="-1">
      <param name="Volume" value="-5000">
      <param name="FileName" value="http://webdev.wrox.co.uk/books/0707/
          chapter12/RockClmb.avi">
    </object>
  </body>
</html>
```

The versatility of the Windows Media Player Control is that we can just as easily change the code to play an MP3 sound file, by changing the `FileName` parameter value as follows:

```html
<param name="FileName" value="http://www.beemen.com/NewBeemenPages/
    TheBeemenGoodnightBirmingham.mp3">
```

This will embedded an MP3 file within the web page.

As can be seen, there are a number of `<param>` tags included within the `<object>` element itself: these are all parameters for the Windows Media Player control. If we wanted to embed a different object in our page, the properties for that object would be different, and we would need to enter those different parameters. We are not actually going to spend any time explaining these properties, but further information on Windows Media Player can be found at: http://msdn.microsoft.com/workshop/imedia/directx/docs/wmp/content_authoring_guide.asp.

Inserting a Java Applet with the Object Element

With the `<applet>` element's deprecation in the HTML 4.01 standard, the way to embed Java applets is with the `<object>` element. It isn't quite as straightforward as all that. Java has a somewhat checkered history with web browsers. With its creation by Sun in the mid-1990s, the main browser vendors of the time (Netscape and Microsoft) were quick to realize its potential. They both quickly included versions of the Java Run-Time Environment within their browsers, which could be made use of by the `<applet>` element. However, Sun updated the Java environment on a regular basis, and so the browsers were left supporting out-of-date versions of the software.

While the creation of Opera didn't make much impact on the two main browsers, it did make the browser agent a much smaller entity, and was the first to consider making the Java Virtual Machine an optional add-on to the main browser. This has some ramifications now for putting Java applets in our web pages, because we still can't assume that every browser will automatically have Java installed (and even if we could some people would disable it anyway). Also, even if they did have it installed, it might not be the most up-to-date version, or a version recent enough to run the applet. It also means if we want to run Java applets on a web browser without native Java support, we must install the Java plug-in first via the `codebase` attribute. However, as downloading any component via the `codebase` attribute is a lengthy process, we suggest that if you really intend using Java (even if you're just browsing Java applets) then you should use a browser that contains the Java Virtual Machine.

Ok, we're going to borrow a very simple example Java Clock applet from the Sun Microsystems site, for which Sun holds the copyright, but the license allows it to be freely distributed. This is located at: http://java.sun.com/products/plugin/1.3/demos/applets/Clock/Clock2.java.

This should be saved as `Clock2.java` on your own machine, after which you need to use the JDK 1.3 to compile it as `Clock2.class`.

You can compile it using the command prompt/UNIX command line using the following code:

```
> javac Clock2.class
```

We're not interested in the internal workings of this code, so we're not going to explain how it works. It is enough to know that it will display a vector graphic clock on our web page. What we are interested in doing is embedding this applet in a web page, within the `<object>` element, so that it works in as many browsers as possible.

With Internet Explorer it's enough to supply the details in the `classid` attribute:

```
<object codetype="application/java"
        classid="java:Clock2.class" width="400" height="200">
   Your browser is ignoring the "object" element.
</object>
```

However it is possible to specify the latest version of the JDK as follows:

```
<object codetype="application/java;version=1.3"
        classid="java:Clock2.class" width="400" height="200">
   Your browser is ignoring the "object" element.
</object>
```

In which case we are dependent on having a version of IE with a recent enough JDK. In both cases it should result in something along the lines of:

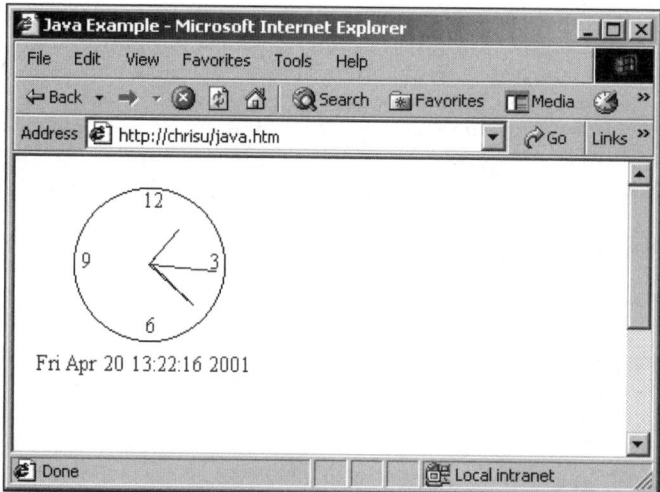

However, for the browsers that don't include native Java support this won't be enough, and we will also need to indicate the location of a Java plug-in to be able to run Java applets. We need to specify the `codebase` as follows – this will be ignored if the browser already has native Java support. In IE versions without the Java SDK the code would be as follows:

```
<object classid="clsid:8AD9C840-044E-11D1-B3E9-00805F499D93" width="300"
        height="200" codebase="http://java.sun.com/products/
        plugin/1.3/jinstall-13-win32.cab#Version=1,2,0,0">
  <param name="code" value="Clock2.class">
  <param name="type" value="application/x-java-applet;version=1.3">
  Your browser is ignoring the "object" element.
</object>
```

However, the `.cab` executable specified is something unique to IE, and to get it work in Netscape 6 we actually need to specify the Sun Java plug-in instead:

```
<object classid="clsid:8AD9C840-044E-11D1-B3E9-00805F499D93" width="300"
        height="200" codebase="http://java.sun.com/products/plugin/
        1.3/plugin-install.html">
  <param name="code" value="Clock2.class">
  <param name="type" value="application/x-java-applet;version=1.3">
  Your browser is ignoring the "object" element.
</object>
```

Here we've used a version of Netscape 6, without the Java SDK included, and the output will look like this:

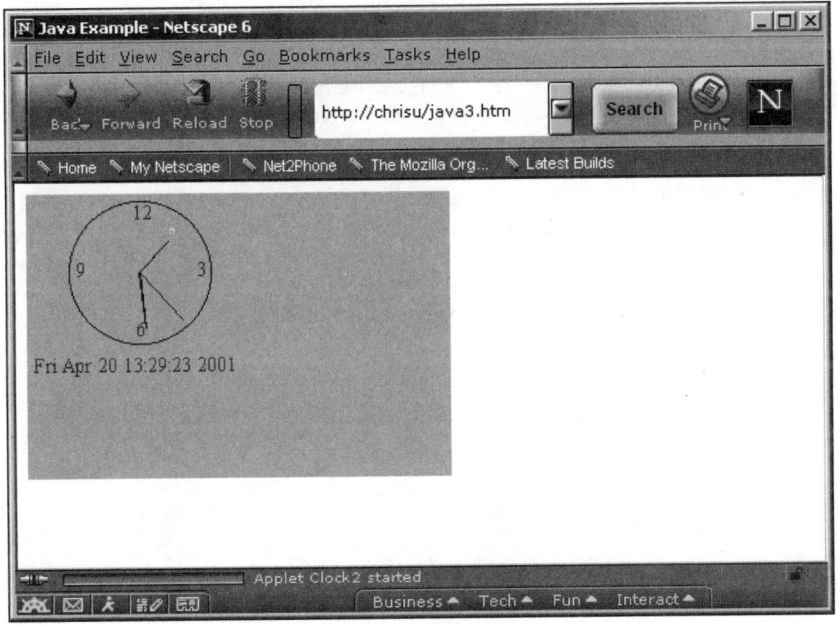

Of course this still leaves the problem of what to do with browsers that don't support the <object> element entirely, such as Netscape 4. In such cases, we can tuck the <applet> tag into the code as follows, making sure to comment it out (for Internet Explorer):

```
<object classid="clsid:8AD9C840-044E-11D1-B3E9-00805F499D93"
        WIDTH=300 height=200 codebase="http://java.sun.com/products/
        plugin/1.3/jinstall-13-win32.cab#Version=1,2,0,0">
  <param name="code" value="Clock2.class">
  <param name="type" value="application/x-java-applet;version=1.3">

    <comment>
      <applet code="Clock2.class" width="170" height="150">
      </applet>
    </comment>

</object>
```

The IE-specific <comment> tag is the only one available, and if it isn't used, then both the <object> and the <applet> elements are interpreted by IE, and the applet will be displayed twice. This is direct contradiction to what we said earlier about objects; the expected behavior should be to ignore the <applet> element. However, with the <applet> element in IE, there seems to be this anomaly, which requires the use of the <comment> tag. There is more on the <applet> element in the Chapter 15.

Inserting a Flash Animation with the Object Element

As mentioned earlier in this chapter, the way to insert a Flash animation into our web page is with the <object> element. Normally with Flash, we'd use the publishing tool (accessed in Flash via the File | Publish menu) to create the HTML for us, and so we wouldn't have to get involved with actual coding, as the publishing tool does this all automatically for us. However there are times when we might want to manually place a Flash animation into our web pages.

It's also worth mentioning that the code created by the publishing tool uses <object> to insert the animation in Internet Explorer, and within the <object> element, there is an <embed> element to insert the animation so that the Netscape 4 and Opera browsers can run it as well. The Netscape 6 browser seems unable to execute it via the <object> element – once again Microsoft .cab files are required to run the Flash tool within <object>, and so Netscape 6 relies on the <embed> element. Now let's look at an example.

We've borrowed a Flash file (savior.swf – see the code download) courtesy of Friends of Ed (http://www.friendsofed.com), which allows us to play a simple arcade game. Once again the code that creates the embedded application is not important, just the method by which we are inserting it. Flash is now commonly included in the latest browsers, but to be on the safe side we've added a codebase attribute to point to the flash download screen.

```
<object classid="clsid:D27CDB6E-AE6D-11cf-96B8-444553540000"
        codebase="http://download.macromedia.com/pub/shockwave/
        cabs/flash/swflash.cab#version=5,0,0,0" width="500"
        height="400">
  <param name="movie" value="savior.swf">
  <param name="quality" value="high">
  <param name="bgcolor" value="#FFFFFF">
  Flash animations not supported with "object"
</object>
```

Assuming the `savior.swf` file is located in the same directory as the web page, which has the above information included, we should see the following in Internet Explorer:

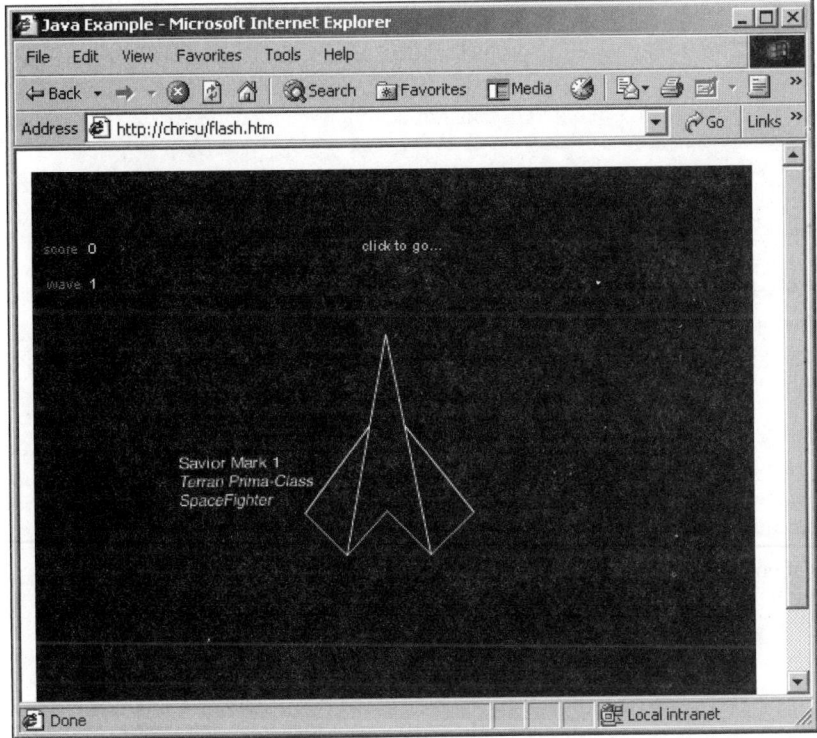

To get this animation to work in Netscape and Opera, we need to enclose the following <embed> element code with the <object> element code:

```
<object classid="clsid:D27CDB6E-AE6D-11cf-96B8-444553540000"
        codebase="http://download.macromedia.com/pub/shockwave/
        cabs/flash/swflash.cab#version=5,0,0,0" width=500
        height=400>
   <param name="movie" value="savior.swf">
   <param name="quality" value="high">
   <param name="bgcolor" value="#000000">
   <embed src="savior.swf" quality="high" bgcolor="#000000" width=550
        height="400" type="application/x-shockwave-flash"
        pluginspace="http://www.macromedia.com/shockwave/download/
        index.cgi?P1_Prod_Version=ShockwaveFlash">
   </embed>
</object>
```

The <embed> element is not even deprecated as it never formed part of any HTML standard, although IE, Netscape, and Opera all support it. The `pluginspace` attribute is equivalent to the IE `codebase` attribute. There is more on the <embed> element in Chapter 16. One last thing to notice is that we don't require the <comment> tag here, as IE will only embed one occurrence of the Flash animation here (as it is meant to), despite the fact that technically there are two specified, because it ignores what is inside an <object> element, as it should if it handles the tag itself.

Inserting an Excel Spreadsheet

It is also possible to insert simple items in Internet Explorer, such as spreadsheets and Word documents. We could use a tool such as FrontPage to do the basic work for us, but all FrontPage is actually doing is creating the requisite `<object>` element and inserting the necessary data as `param` attributes. The following code would insert a blank Excel spreadsheet into our web page.

```
<object classid="CLSID:0002E510-0000-0000-C000-000000000046">
  <param name="DisplayTitleBar" value="false">
</object>
```

This unfortunately won't produce anything on Netscape or Opera, as they don't support COM objects.

Including HTML in Another HTML Document

The HTML 4.01 standard also allows us to use the `<object>` element to "insert HTML documents into our web pages". Inserting web pages into web pages might seem like a pointless pastime, but there are two reasons why it might be very useful:

❑ First, it acts as an alternative to the `<iframe>` element, which is good, given that `<iframe>` isn't officially part of the HTML 4.01 standard. However, there are problems with its use for this purpose. An `<iframe>` element can be targeted by a link or form, and can be focused and printed, while an `<object>` element doesn't support these features.

❑ Secondly, it enables us to easily reuse a single section of code (either HTML or script) many times throughout a site, without having to reproduce the code in its entirety.

We can embed a document using the `data` attribute as follows:

```
<object data="embedded_document.htm">
  Couldn't include document specified.
</object>
```

However, there has been a security hole associated with this ability in IE 5.5. It allows the execution of arbitrary programs using `object type="text/html"` and parsing `index.dat`, by revealing the location of the temporary internet files folder, which could possibly lead to a hacker taking full control over user's computer. There is a patch available to rectify this. Details of this security issue can be found at http://www.microsoft.com/technet/security/bulletin/MS00-055.asp, and details of the patch at http://www.microsoft.com/windows/ie/download/critical/patch11.htm. The patch basically stops this from working. It also doesn't work in Netscape. The only surefire browser to support this is Opera 5.x.

Microsoft also provides the ability to embed script code within HTML documents as **Behaviors**. Behaviors are platform-independent components that can be deployed on the Web. Formerly their predecessor (known as Scriptlets) used the `<object>` element to achieve this. However, this was very much an evolving technology, and it proved to be a flawed way of inserting them, so Behaviors are now embedded using style sheets instead. As a result this is very much a technology beyond the scope of this book and one we won't discuss any further.

Summary

In this chapter, we've introduced and explained how to add objects to our web pages. We gave a brief overview of the `<object>` element. We introduced the different attributes and showed how it could be used to add images to HTML documents, as well as objects such as videos and MP3 files. This is the method that is recommended by the HTML 4.01 standard, and the method that should be used, if possible.

We rounded off the chapter with an overview of how we can embed some of the most popular components within our web pages. However, we suggested that as Internet Explorer doesn't properly support the `<object>` element for images, it is unlikely to displace the `<img>` element in popular usage, but for all other types of media, it is very useful.

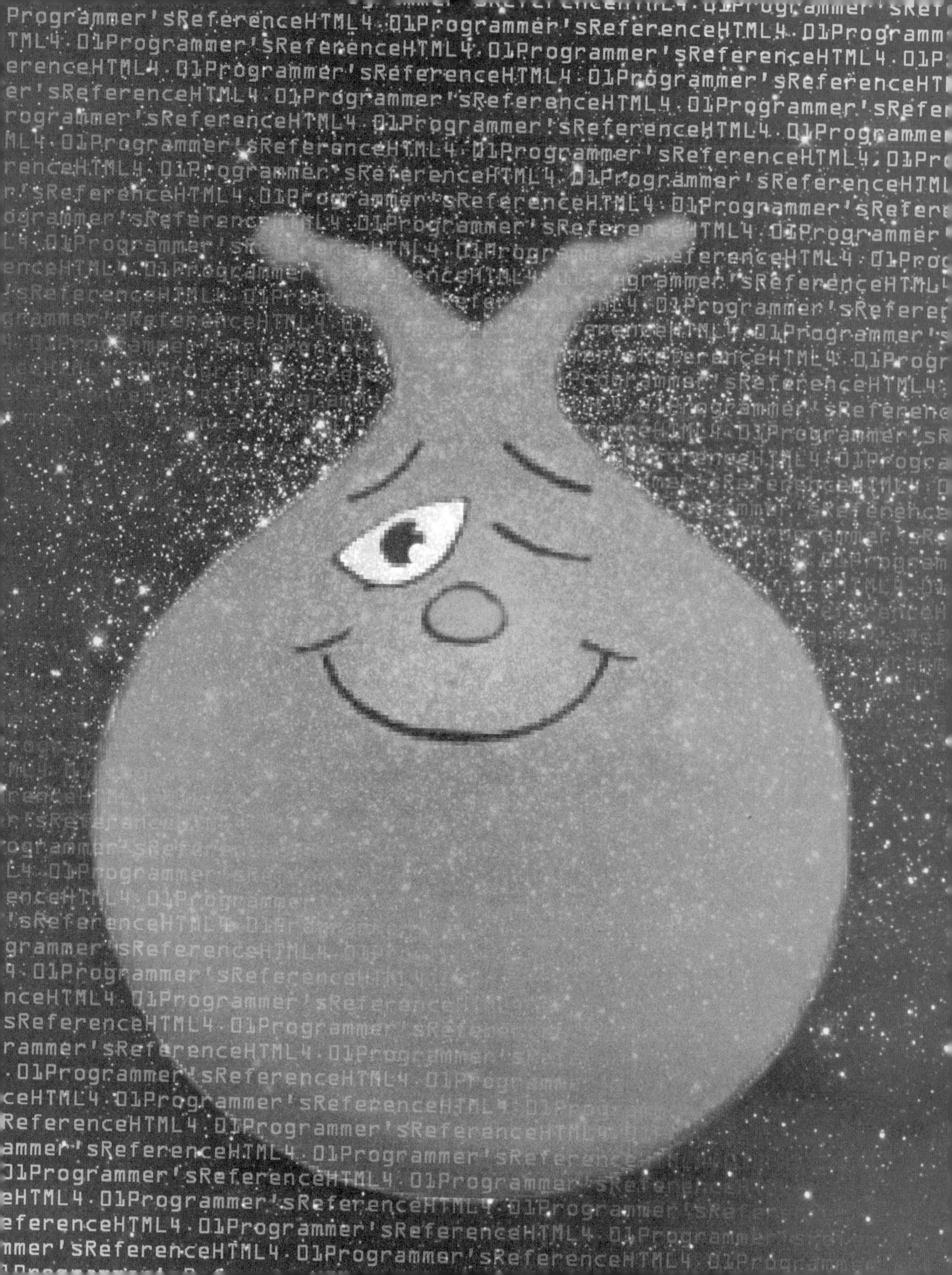
Programmer'sReferenceHTML4.01

11

Style Sheet Fundamentals

As we've already discussed, one of the original aims of the Web was to separate information from presentation. HTML was meant to be a semantic markup language, concerned with the meaning of the content in a document – not its visual representation.

However, as the Web has grown in popularity, the concept of a semantic markup language has been perceived as limiting. Authors wanted higher and higher levels of control over the appearance of their web documents, and weren't content to restrict themselves to basic HTML constructs. This demand was, in many ways, responsible for the messy state of many Web pages today. The response to the growing chaos is a movement back to the basics: the original concept of separating content from presentation. The best way to give authors control over document appearance, while simultaneously keeping the content/presentation separation, is through style sheets.

This and the following three chapters will give a reasonably thorough run through of style sheets. Please be aware that CSS is a big enough subject to have entire books devoted to it, and so in this book we are presenting the most important information.

This chapter gives an overview of style sheets, what they are and the syntax they use; how to attach styles to a document, and how to point to styles kept elsewhere. It goes on to explain CSS concepts such as the cascade, inheritance, and pseudo-classes and pseudo-elements. The chapter finishes up by looking at measurement units and color. The basics in this chapter will be mostly CSS 1 commands that are supported in the latest browsers, along with a few useful CSS 2 commands that are commonly supported. Chapters 12 and 13 will then expand on what we learn here by giving further examples of how to apply and use various style sheet properties.

❑ Chapter 12 goes on to talk about character styling, defining fonts, and so on.

❑ Chapter 13 focuses on the positioning of HTML elements.

❑ Chapter 14 explains how to use aural style sheets so that our pages can be accessible to users with impaired vision.

For the purposes of this and the next two chapters we will focus on layouts for a PC browser. In the back of the book you will find CSS appendices, which list the CSS support provided by the major browsers, and provide summary explanations and information about the commonly supported CSS properties. Let's move on now, to explain what style sheets actually are.

What are Style Sheets?

A style sheet is a set of rules for how the contents of a printed or electronically displayed page should be formatted. When creating web pages, by defining a style sheet we can set up formats for how the elements, tags, and so on of the HTML code behave, and thus structure the way the page is displayed. The use of style sheets originates from the publishing world, where editors decided it would make life a whole lot easier if the text formatting rules for a book were decided on and used before the editing stage. Take this book for example. The authors were given rules on how the content should be formatted. Each chapter's title, and the sub-headings in the chapter are in the same font, as defined in a particular style we predetermined. The same applies for each of the code sections: the author marks the section in a certain style, which is then formatted according to the rules agreed upon. Each paragraph uses consistent fonts and font sizes for each style. If the authors hadn't used these guidelines, the different styles would be very distracting and make the book harder to read and use.

In other words, using the pre-defined styles ensures consistency among many documents. If at a later stage we decide a certain part (for example all chapter headings) should be in a larger font then all we need do is change the style used for marking chapter headings. All sections of the text originally marked with this style will then update to the new style.

The same principle works for web pages as well:

❑ Use of clear and consistent formats makes web pages more readable

❑ To avoid setting the font and size of a heading every time we need it, we use a style sheet

Advantages of Style Sheets

Aside from the fact they have been declared a Recommendation by the W3C, there are three main advantages to using style sheets:

1. Their universality of application. This means that we can develop an external style sheet and then apply it to any document or group of documents, by referencing the style sheet in those documents. We can then change the appearance of any document by simply changing the style sheet it refers to.

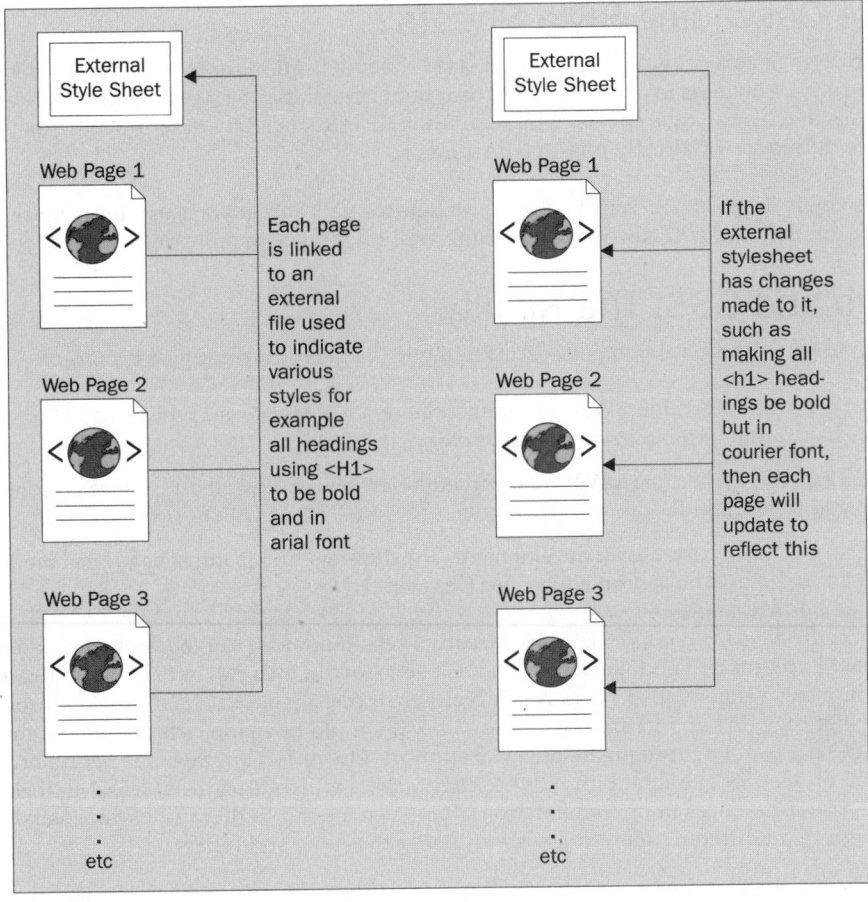

2. Style sheets can convey greater typographic control than is normally possible in HTML, without creating messy code. CSS provides a number of properties that can be used to create effects like drop caps, overlapping text, shadowed text, and so on.

3. Style sheets, unlike HTML element-level formatting, retain the content/presentation split. Style sheet information can be kept totally separate from the actual text information. This can result in smaller file sizes – five 1K documents can reference one 5K style sheet, instead of having five 6K documents, each containing its own style information. This is becoming more important as the world of small devices (mobile phones, Palms, Pocket PCs, and so on) finds greater access to the Web. Furthermore, the split allows the content to be altered without having to reformat the document with the correct HTML tags.

Yes, for the time being we can still use the `<font>` tag to define how an element in HTML looks, but this tag has officially become deprecated (see Chapter 15). It still works in HTML 4.01 but the strict version of XHTML does not support it all.

What are Cascading Style Sheets?

Cascading Style Sheets provide the standard style sheet definition for formatting the display of HTML and XML elements in a web browser or other CSS-compatible user agents. They allow us to define styles in external style sheets, which can then be referenced by other documents. They also allow us to define styles directly within a document.

One of the key features of CSS is its facility to **cascade** formats and make use of **inheritance** from one element by another. We will talk about cascading and inheritance in more detail later in this chapter.

Browsers and CSS: The Reality

There are currently three versions of Cascading Style Sheets for typical web browsers:

- ❏ CSS 1.0 (CSS 1): became a W3C Recommendation in 1996 and was revised in 1999. It defines the mechanics and terminology of the technology.

- ❏ CSS 2.0 (CSS 2): became a W3C Recommendation March 1998. It adds more options and flexibility to CSS 1.0.

- ❏ CSS 3.0 (CSS 3): currently in development. The different CSS features have been modularised and new features have been added. See Chapter 21.

Although the first two versions of CSS are already Web standards, full implementation of even CSS 1 by Internet Explorer (IE) and Netscape (N) has been slow in coming, but is at least functional in the latest browser versions, IE 5.x and N 6.0. Neither IE nor N supports all of the features in CSS 2 and those that they do support are not all the same. It should be made clear, however, that 100% support of CSS 1 is not a prerequisite of CSS 2 support. Opera 5.0, another competing browser, prides itself on its CSS 2 compatibility, but openly admits which features of CSS 1 it does not support. These differences in implementation often even extend to the way various versions of a browser behave on different operating systems using the same style sheet.

All these inconsistencies can be very frustrating, but as the influence of XML in software and programming grows, the general trend is that implementation of the CSS standards will become better and more widespread.

In the meantime, all is not lost. We just need to invest a bit more energy into creating our pages. Since we can use many CSS features but not all of them, we need to do some planning and testing. We need to figure out who our target audience is and become familiar with the types and versions of browsers it uses. If our audience uses primarily IE 3 or N 3, CSS is not the best idea. However if our audience uses IE 4.x and higher or N 4.x or higher or even Opera, we can use at least CSS 1 quite effectively. When using CSS, we should extensively test our pages in our target browsers. If we are not careful, our pages might be unreadable and non-functional, particularly when accessed by a browser that does not support CSS 1 or CSS 2.

One option to get around browsers not supporting our CSS-styled pages is to recommend that users download the latest version of a preferred browser. When this is not possible we can offer an alternative page with inline HTML format settings. The latter suggestion requires additional maintenance, but may be necessary until the majority of users have CSS-compatible browsers.

In the rest of the chapter and in the following chapters, we will let you know if a feature is part of CSS 1 or CSS 2, and if there is a problem in current versions of the major browsers. In Appendix F you will find a listing of each feature for CSS 1 and CSS 2 and whether it is supported in the most common browsers, IE, N, and Opera and their most common versions.

How to Use Styles and Style Sheets

OK, let's get down to business and start learning how to use CSS!

Basic Style Sheet Concepts and Syntax

In general terms of how they have been implemented in browsers, CSS is much stricter than HTML in its dealing with code inaccuracies. For example, with HTML most browsers will 'overlook' instances of invalid tags, invalid attributes, and incorrect nesting. But while CSS (like HTML) will not actually give you any errors, it is not so forgiving, and will produce inconsistencies. Therefore, it is important to get into the habit of using correct syntax; otherwise the styles will not work as intended.

The first thing to know is that a CSS style sheet consists of a sequence of style rules. A **rule** is a statement of which element(s) we want to affect and how they are to be affected.

A CSS rule consists of two main parts: the **selector** and its **declarations**. The format used to define a style rule is as follows:

```
selector {declarations}
```

Selectors

A **selector** defines which element or elements will be affected by the properties and values set in the rule. There are two main types of selectors:

❑ **Type selectors**: These refer to the element that is affected by the properties and values set in the rule. If we want to format paragraphs, the selector for this would be p. This corresponds directly to the <p> tag in HTML. In the code line below, the selector is the <p> tag and we are setting its color value:

```
p { color:blue }
```

Note that either one space or a tab character is usually placed before the { character that starts the declaration.

❑ **Attribute selectors**: The values of the two HTML attributes, class and id, can be used as selectors. The class attribute is very flexible, because we define what the values are and so we can set this class in any HTML element. The value of an id attribute is not so flexible. The latest standards require that the id of an element be unique; that way we can be sure of what we are affecting. Remember also, that the id attribute can be used in scripting, further stressing the importance of the need for unique values for this attribute. To create a class selector we place the value of the class after a period (.). To create an id selector we place the value of the id after a hash mark (#).

The following code illustrates how these can be used. In this example the <style> tag is used within the document to setup the styles. How this tag is used will be explained in subsequent sections. Here two styles have been defined, one called mystyle (which is a class selector) and #a123 (which is an id selector).

Later in the code a <p> tag is using both these styles by referring to the appropriate class and id attributes and an <h1> tag is using the class style only. So the paragraph will be in bold and the font blue. The heading will also be in ~~blue~~. bold.

277

```
<style>
  .mystyle { font-weight:bold }
  #a123 { color:blue }
</style>

  <p id="a123" class= "mystyle"> I am using both styles! </p>
  <h1 class = "mystyle"> Only using one style here </h1>
```

Note: the end tag for the <p> element is used even though it's not required in HTML. It's good practice to always use end tags when applying styles to ensure they function as intended.

Grouping Selectors

We can have more than one selector in a rule, separated by commas. Selectors grouped together for a rule are called a **selector string**. Using selector strings can save us time and code if we want different elements to have the same formatting. The following example declares that the text in <p>, <h1 >, <h2>, <h3>, or <h4> tags will be blue, and that in a <p> or <h3> tag it will be bold as well:

```
p, h1, h2, h3, h4 { color:blue }
p, h3 {font-weight:bold}
```

Declarations: Properties and their Values

The actual styles defined for a selector are called **properties** and their parameters are called **values**. The property comes first, followed by a colon (acting as an equals sign), then the value followed by a semi-colon (used to separate different declarations). Together the property and its value are known as a **declaration**. We can define any number of style declarations, separated by semi-colons. Note that the final declaration doesn't need the semi colon after it. All the declarations for a selector are put in a set of curly brackets. This is called the **declaration block**.

```
selector {
        property1:valueA;
        property2:valueB;
        ...
        }
```

The list of declarations can be given on one line (see below), but the format given above is easier to follow.

```
selector { property1:valueA; property2:valueB; ...}
```

Again using the paragraph selector, the following example shows a declaration block, which defines respectively the font style, font color, background color, and bottom margin values that the <p> tag will use:

```
p {
    font-family:Verdana,Arial,Geneva,sans-serif;
    color:red;
    background-color:white;
    margin-bottom:6px;
    }
```

It does not matter if we have a space between the semicolon and the next property or a space between the colon and the value. It also does not matter if we write all the properties and values on one line or on several as in the example above. Also remember that the final character is optional, and that only one space or tab should be present between the selector and the start of the declaration, before the { symbol.

Attaching Styles to a Document

There are four ways to attach styles to a document using CSS.

- ❏   Linking to external style sheets

- ❏   Embedded style sheets

- ❏   Inline styles

- ❏   Imported style sheets

We will explain how to use each of them and for what situations they are best suited.

Linking to External Style Sheets

Web sites consisting of more than one page are well suited for linked style sheets. Using a linked style sheet guarantees the separation of content from presentation in each page. In many such cases, the person who designs the style sheet has absolutely nothing to do with the content. This style sheet is simply linked to in the head of each document using the `<link>` element.

Any changes or additions made to a linked style sheet results in immediate changes to all refreshed pages that are linked to it. This means that much less work is needed to maintain a site than if all the styles were defined with inline formatting like the `<font>` tag in HTML.

The external file contains all the styles we wish to define and is normally written in a text only program such as notepad and is saved using the `.css` extension. The page document in which these styles are to be used will then use the `<link>` tag to refer to this external style sheet.

Type the following in notepad, or a similar program, saving it as `styles.css`:

```
/* the name of this file is styles.css */
h1 { color:green; font-size:18pt }
p { font-weight:bold; font-size:12pt }
b { font-size: 14pt; }
```

Note that comments in CSS code can be added using the /* and */ markers

Save it in the same folder as the web page document shown below:

```
<html>
  <head>

    <title>CSS example :: external style sheets</title>
    <link rel="stylesheet" type="text/css"
        href="styles.css">

  </head>
```

```
<body>
  <h1>Formatting with CSS!</h1>
  <p>This page is <b>really</b> simple! Just define the
     elements once and off you go!</p>
</body>
</html>
```

The CSS file will be accessed via the `<link>` tag used above. The page will then display the heading in green and using a size of 18 points, the paragraph will be in bold using a size of 12 points except for the bolded part which will be in size 14 points as shown in this screenshot:

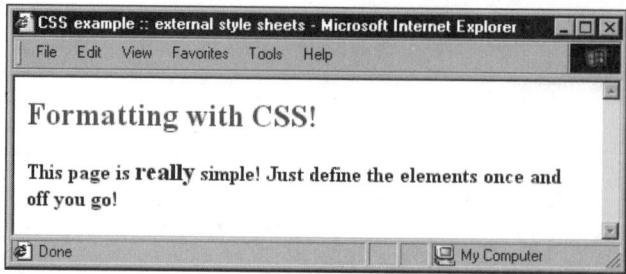

When using the `<link>` tag to refer to an external style sheet, we should include the attributes `rel="stylesheet"` and `type="text/css"`. The attribute `href=` and its value defines the URL of the linked style sheet, telling the server where to find it. If the style sheet is located in another directory or even on another server, we can use relative or absolute addressing to define the location of the style sheet file (see Chapter 4 on Links).

If we now adapt the contents of the `styles.css` file to the following:

```
/* the name of this file is styles.css */
h1 { color:red; font-size:12pt }
p { font-weight:bold; font-size:10pt }
b { font-size: 25pt; }
```

then the page will display differently as the styles have been redefined:

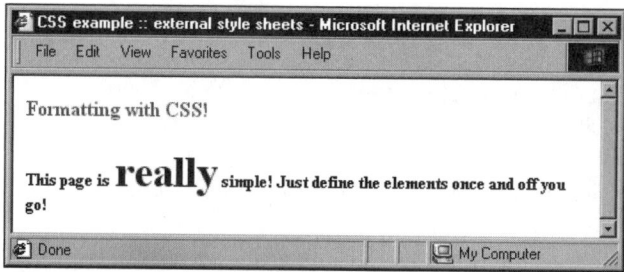

Even though we have linked the page to an external style sheet we can still embed local rules specific to this page by using the `<style>` element. This will be explained in the section on Embedded Style Sheets *later in this chapter.*

This is a CSS 1 command we can count on. Version 3+ of Opera, and all versions of IE 4.x+ and N 4+ should not have a problem with linking style sheets.

Linking Style Sheets for Different Devices

There are several different devices that could potentially display our layout. A bright font on a dark background may look nice on a monitor screen, but if printing the same page on paper, you may not be happy with the results if you don't have a colour printer. On the other hand, when we print, we may need a printing margin of 2 cm, which means giving away precious screen space. And what if a visually impaired user wants to access our site? Our font sizes need to be comparatively larger. Using CSS 2 we can import a different style sheet for each device that might access our page.

When we want to deliver a style sheet for a specific device, we need to add the attribute media= to our HTML page. This attribute tells the device which style sheet has been set up for it and to use it.

```
<html>
  <head>
    <title>CSS example :: different devices</title>
    <link rel="stylesheet" media="screen" href="screen.css">
    <link rel="stylesheet" media="print" href="print.css">
    <link rel="stylesheet" media="aural" href="aural.css">
  </head>
  <body>
  </body>
</html>
```

Here, depending on the device being used, a different style sheet will be linked to and hence a different set of styles appropriate to the device, as defined by the programmer, will be applied. For example if the user was using a printer then the print.css file would be accessed to define the styles to use.

We can also define multiple media to the same set of styles at the same time by providing a comma-separated list of media types in the <link> element in the header.

```
<link rel="stylesheet" media="print, screen" href="mix.css">
<link rel="stylesheet" media="aural" href="aural.css">
```

We can define different style sheets for the following media types:

Media Type	Description
all	for all media types
screen	for computer screen presentations (default)
aural	for voice browsers (see Chapter 14)
braille	for Braille browsers
embossed	for paged Braille printers
handheld	for small display devices, for example, mobile phones or handhelds

Table continued on following page

Media Type	Description
print	for printing
projection	for projectors
tty	for devices with a limited display like a teletype machine
tv	for web-enabled television sets.

If we defined the media type, as "all" this will define all types to the same style. However, we could use a separate link to set another media type, for example "aural", to a different more suitable style sheet.

Embedded Style Sheets

Another way we can use style sheets is to set up an area for our style sheet definitions within our HTML document.

The element `<style> ... </style>` is the container for style rules usually placed in the `<head>` element of the document. The start tag `<style>` must contain the attribute `type="text/css"`. CSS rules are placed between the start tag and the closing tag.

> To prevent browsers that do not support CSS from displaying the CSS commands as text, you should define these CSS commands in comments using `<!--` and `-->` around the style declarations.

The following codewill display exactly the same as the example first given in the section "*Linking to External Style Sheets*", but here the definitions for the style are given within the document instead of being held in an external file:

```
<html>
  <head>
    <title>
      CSS example :: style definitions within a document
    </title>
    <style type="text/css">
      <!--
      /* ..Style Sheet rules.. */
      h1 { color:green; font-size:18pt }
      p { font-weight:bold; font-size:12pt }
      b { font-size: 14pt; }
      -->
    </style>
  </head>
  <body>
    <h1>Formatting with CSS!</h1>
    <p>This page is <b>really</b> simple! Just define the
      elements once and off you go!</p>
  </body>
</html>
```

Comments Within Style Sheets

We can use comments in a linked or embedded style sheet. A CSS comment starts with a slash and an asterisk (/*). To close the comment, use an asterisk and a slash (*/).

```
p { color:blue; } /* changed to blue, Feb. 21, 2001, cj. */
```

Note that CSS comments may not be nested.

Inline Styles

HTML elements within the document body can also be formatted with CSS styles. Using the `style` attribute for an element achieves this. The format defined in the `style` attribute of an element only affects that element and any element it contains. It is more specific and will override any inherited properties, the idea being that it acts as a one-off change to the style of that element. Note that the value given for the `style` attribute is given within double quotes as shown in the code given below:

```
<html>
  <head>
    <title>CSS example :: inline styles</title>
  </head>
  <body>
    <div style="background-color:#FFFFE0">
      <h1 style="color:red; font-size:36pt;">The headline in red</h1>
      <p style="color:green; font-size:24pt;">A green paragraph</p>
      <p style="color:blue; font-size:12pt;">A blue paragraph</p>
    </div>

  </body>
</html>
```

This is how the above code is displayed:

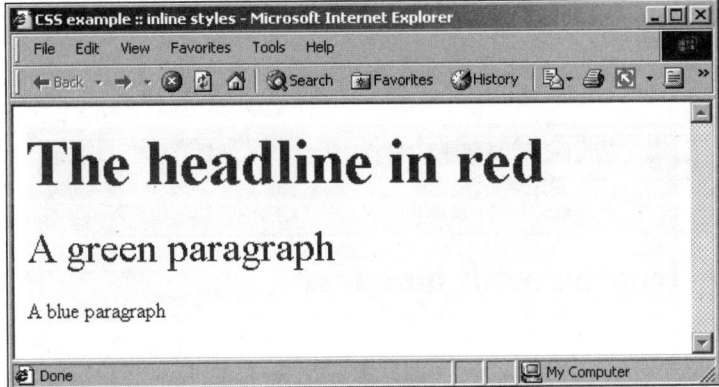

This screenshot was taken with IE 5.5, which applies the `background-color` property to the entire `div` element, thus showing a large colored box. IE 6, N 6 and Opera also treat the property in this way but N 4.X will only apply the background color to the actual text, creating individual colored boxes around each paragraph.

Formatting with <div> and <span>

There are two elements that are very useful in formatting with inline styles: elements <div> and <span>, introduced in HTML 4.0. They define a specific range of space (also known as a **block**) where everything in between the opening and closing tags can inherit the CSS styles you define by using the style attribute for the tag. However some styles are not designed to be inherited, for example, `style = "position:absolute"`. The properties that can't be inherited are listed in Appendix G.

The <div> element is a block-level element and can therefore be used to align other block-level elements like <table>, <p>, <li>, or any combination of elements that are used within the <body> element. It is also important to note that a <div> forces a line break before and after the division. See Chapter 13 for more on block elements and properties.

The <span> element can only be used inline. However, its format can be put directly in its `style` attribute or it can use the `classes` defined in either an external or embedded style sheet. It can replace tags like <font>, <i>, <em>.

The following example shows a <div> element and a <span> element in action:

```
<html>
  <head>
    <title>CSS example :: div and span</title>
  </head>
  <body>
    <h1>
      Headline with <span style="color:blue;">blue text</span>
    </h1>
    <div style="margin-bottom:24px;">
      Text in a division with a bottom margin of 24 pixels in
      relation to the following element.
    </div>
    <p>Paragraph with
      <span style="font-style:italic; color:red;">red italic
          text</span>.
    </p>
  </body>
</html>
```

The above code is displayed like this:

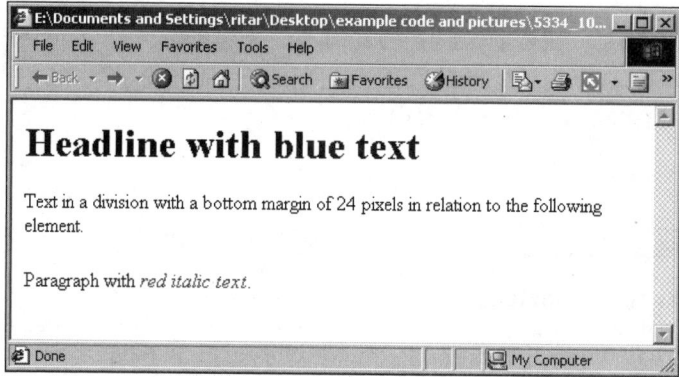

The next example shows a `<span>` element inside a `<div>` element, and how the `<span>` formatting adds to that of the `<div>` formatting for the font style. Note that if both the `<div>` and `<span>` elements defined the same style, then the `<span>` element formatting would override that of the `<div>` element:

```
<html>
  <head>
    <title>CSS example :: span in div</title>
  </head>
  <body>
    <div style="margin-left:24px;font-weight:bold;">
      <p>Paragraph with <span style="font-style:italic;
      font-weight:normal;">normal text in italics</span> but the
      rest is in bold and with a left margin of 24 pixel width.</p>
      <p>Another paragraph with same formats specified in the div tag</p>
    </div>
    <p>Still another paragraph but with default formats.</p>

  </body>
</html>
```

This example is displayed like this:

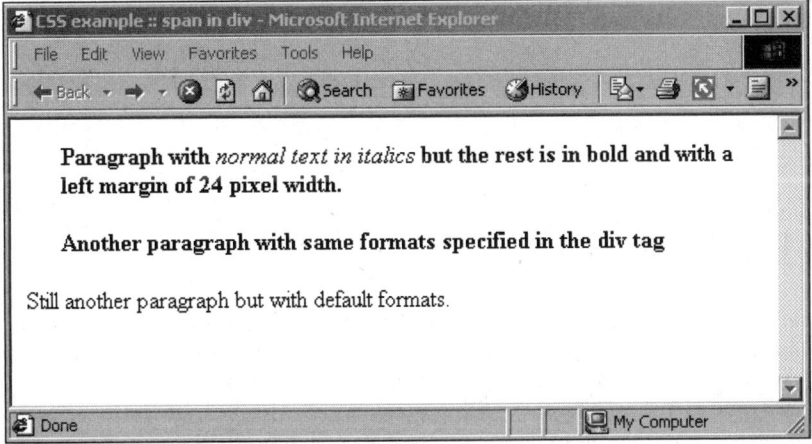

Imported Style Sheets

Importing style sheets is a way of linking an external style sheet from within the `<style>` element in the document head, and is functionally the same as the linked style sheets described previously. It is a part of the CSS 1 Recommendation, but Netscape only supports it properly in version 6.0 and IE on Windows has problems with it in general. Opera and IE 4.x and higher on Macintosh are the only browsers that support it fully. We should avoid using imported style sheets unless we are very sure the browsers of our target audience support it.

The @import url starts the command to add a CSS file to the HTML document. It must appear before all other CSS rules. The CSS file's location is placed inside the brackets. At the end of the string there should be a semicolon:

```
<style type="text/css">
  <!--
    @import url(http://www.domain.com/styles.css);
    /*This URL does not represent an existing style sheet,
    you will need to add your own URL to make this example
    work */
    p { color:blue; background:white; }
  -->
</style>
```

Note: Even if you have linked your page to an external style sheet you can still embed local rules inside the <style> element.

Importing Style Sheets for Different Devices

We can also import style sheets for different devices using @import url. We just need to define the media type after the url declaration:

```
@import url(http://www.somewhere.com/voice.css) aural
```

CSS 2 lets us use @media as a way of importing device-specific styles but there aren't yet many browsers that support it. N 6 and IE 5+ support @media screen and @media print:

```
@media print { }
```

Cascading and Inheritance

The presentation of the elements in a web page is affected by where and how we specify what we require. Two processes are involved in this when we use style sheets, cascading and inheritance. **Cascading** means that a document can reference and be influenced by more than one style sheet from different sources, and also by styles held within the document itself. **Inheritance** refers to the process whereby an element (the child) takes on the properties specified for an element that contains it (the parent), when no more specific properties are specified for it. Take a paragraph <p> element defined with a blue font, as an example. The content of all the elements inside this paragraph element will also be blue unless we define them otherwise. The inheritance of a style saves us the extra work of setting every individual style of every single element we are going to use.

Cascading

Each element in a web page can be influenced by style sheets from a number of sources: the CSS style sheets written by the page designer, the browser's default style settings, and the user's own preferences set up within the browser's program settings. Which will take precedence when the page is actually displayed? Lets briefly discuss each type first.

❑ Browser Default

First there is the style sheet defined in the default browser settings: like the default background color of a page, or the font used for headings and paragraphs. These are the settings that will be used when a page being viewed does not implement CSS, or if the browser does not support CSS.

❑ User-Defined Browser Settings

Secondly, there are the styles set by the user of a browser, which if set up override the browser defaults. If a visitor to a web page does not like, say, small fonts, he or she might use their own settings to override the default browser settings. For example, IE has View | Text Size | medium as the default setting, and so altering this will change all default font sizes by a percentage value. Visually impaired users typically use their own style sheet settings; Chapters 14 and 20 show how to make a page more accessible for these users.

❑ Author Style Sheets

And last but not least, there are the CSS style sheets that we create and attach to our web pages that we have been discussing in this chapter. We must plan our style sheets and the way we link them to our document very carefully, since author style sheets usually override the browser settings set by the user, which in turn override the default browser settings.

The Style Sheet Cascade

The strength of CSS is found in the hierarchical way in which browsers and other user agents interpret them. We can use a combination of linked and embedded style sheets, as well as inline styles, so long as we bear in mind that the browser will rank them in order of importance and behave accordingly when rendering the element (that is, the browser will use a set of rules to determine which of the styles set for a particular element it should use, based on a ranking system). The possible combinations of CSS rules from different sources can either be quite powerful, or a source of chaos! Therefore it is important to understand how styles are implemented depending on where they originate from and in what order they are defined.

The browsers all use the same hierarchy to make these decisions, presented here in the order of precedence they use. Wherever there is a conflict between styles for the same element from different sources, the browser will refer to this hierarchy and override as appropriate.

❑ author: inline – overrides all others

❑ author: embedded – overrides all below

❑ author: linked – overrides all below

❑ user defined browser settings – overrides all below

❑ browser default – doesn't override

Where two different styles are set for the same element within a page, the one that most specifically refers to an instance will take precedence, for example, a style set up for the <p> element in an embedded style sheet will apply to all instances of <p> within the document, except where an inline style has been applied to a specific <p> element.

Sort by Order Specified

If we have defined rules that have the same weight, origin, and specificity, the last rule specified wins. This rule affects style sheets and individual rules. For example, if we use three linked style sheets, the style sheet defined by the third link will be the one that overrides the two before, if they defined formats for the same elements. Similarly, the second will override the first.

Inheritance

The presentation of the elements in a web page can also be affected by inheritance. In general, a nested 'child' element will inherit the properties defined for its parent element. However, not all properties support inheritance (border properties are an example). Take a look at Appendix G for a listing of which properties inherit and which do not. So if we change the style for a particular element (such as <body>) then this will affect the style of any tags held within it:

```html
<html>
  <head>
    <style>
      body {font-family:courier; font-style:italic;}
    </style>
  </head>
  <body>
    <h2> Hello</h2>
    <p> Hello again!</p>
  </body>
</html>
```

The code example above shows how the <h2> and <p> elements both inherit the courier and italic font defined for the <body> element that they are contained within.

There are ways to override this though, should we wish to. Adding the following extra line of code will override the inheritance for the <p> element since we have directly specified how it should be styled:

```html
<style>
  body {font-family:courier; font-style:italic}
  p {font-family:arial; font-style:normal}
</style>
```

The effect can also be achieved by specifying the `<p>` `style` attribute inline:

```
<p style="font-family:arial; font-style:normal"> Hello again!</p>
```

When used properly, cascading and inheritance can help us to set up powerful style sheet rules that apply where we want them to without having to re-specify our styles in every instance. To take the most advantage of this we need to plan our styling carefully, based on the kind of content we have and how much of it there is. Next think about how it could be displayed most effectively and make a list of the different HTML elements we will need to use in our pages. We can then refer to the cascading and inheritance rules above to plan our strategy of where to specify styles for them.

Extending the Rules

Having discussed the simple syntax of CSS rules and the hierarchy that is applied to them, let's now look at a number of methods of extending those rules.

Using the <class> Attribute

We mentioned before that we can use the value of a `class` attribute as a selector. This can also extend to selector strings made up of a `type` selector and a `class` selector. In the example below we have defined different **types** of paragraph classes by putting the p selector together with three different `class` selectors `.normal`, `.large`, and `.small`. They can then be referenced by using the `class` attribute for the `<p>` element, as shown here:

```
<html>
  <head>
    <title>CSS example :: defining classes </title>
    <style type="text/css">
      <!--
        p.normal { font-size:10pt; color:black; }
        p.large { font-size:12pt; color:black; }
        p.small { font-size:8pt; color:red; }
      -->
    </style>
  </head>
  <body>
    <p class="normal">Paragraph with a font size of 10
      points.</p>
    <p class="large">Paragraph with a font size of 12
      points.</p>
    <p class="small">A red paragraph with a font size of 8
      points.</p>
  </body>
</html>
```

This produces the following output:

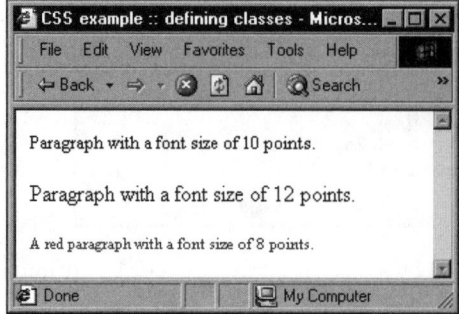

Contextual Selectors

By default, a nested element inherits formatting from the element that contains it. This means if we nest <i> within a <p> element that is using a red, Arial font, the emphasised part will also be in red and Arial.

We can change the default behavior for a nested element by defining the specific context in which the formatting should change. This is done with a **contextual selector** in a CSS rule. To define this, we place the nested selector after the primary selector, the two separated by a space.

For example the following code sets up the style to be used if a <i> element is ever nested within a <p> element. To clarify: it does not define the <p> or <i> styles, but only the <i> style when used within a <p>.

```
p i { color:blue; font-weight:bold; }
```

Similarly, the following defines how the contents of a <p> element is formatted only when it occurs within an <i> element.

```
p i { color:red; font-weight:bold; }
```

The nested elements are influenced in the order they appear in the selector string. In the example below, the italicised section in the paragraph is controlled by the selector string p i. The result is a blue and bold italicised section in the paragraph. The italic section in the headline is by default the same color as the headline.

```
<html>
  <head>
    <title>CSS example :: Descendent Selectors</title>
    <style type="text/css">
      <!--
        h1,p { font-size:10pt; }
        p i { font-size:15pt; font-weight:bold; }
      -->
    </style>
  </head>
  <body>
```

```
    <h1>This italic section <i>is as normally expected</i></h1>
    <p>This italic section uses a <i>special style as it's nested
    </i> within a paragraph tag and we have redefined its
    style.</p>
  </body>
</html>
```

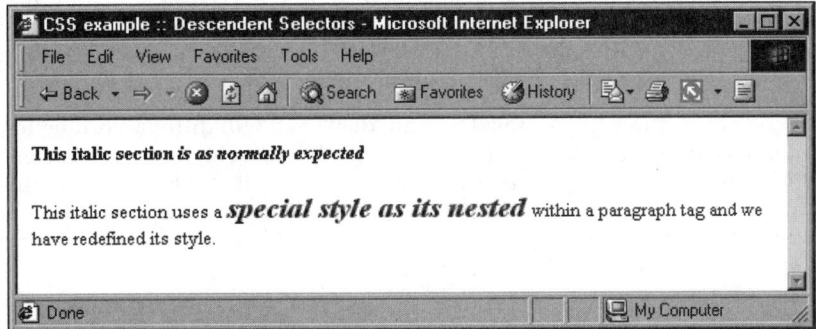

As with normal selectors, we can also group contextual selectors; just use a comma to separate the different definitions. The following defines two contextual styles:

```
.mystyle1 em, p i  { color:green }
```

Pseudo-classes and Pseudo-elements

More happens in an HTML document than is defined by tags alone. For example, there is no element to set the color of visited links on a page, but it can be changed via an attribute: the vlink attribute for the <a> element. CSS allows us to also change the styles of attributes by the use of **pseudo-classes**. Here the selector is formed by the HTML element and a **keyword** designated for the attribute.

CSS also has some keywords in order to create styles for items that don't really exist in HTML either as elements or as an attribute of an element. These are **pseudo-elements**.

Pseudo-classes and pseudo-elements are constructed the same way: the selector string consists of the name of the element, a colon, and then the pseudo-class or pseudo-element keyword. After this, comes the style declaration:

```
a:link {color:green }
```

Pseudo-classes for Links

We can define the layout of links that have not yet been visited, that have been visited, or for the link that is active using the keywords **link**, **visited,** and **active** respectively. For this we use the anchor element as the primary selector.

We can also define the styles for an element or pseudo-class that the mouse pointer is currently hovering over using the keyword **hover**. With respect to links, this is useful as the user can be sure they are over a link (due to its change in style) before clicking onto it.

```
a:link:hover {font-size:1cm}
p:hover {font-size:20pt}
```

In addition, the current element of attention can have its style changed to show it is the one in use. This is done using the **focus** keyword. With respect to links this is useful if the user uses the *Tab* key or similar method to jump through objects on the page. If we change the style for links to reflect this then they will know what link they are on as they jump around the screen without using a mouse.

```
a:focus {outline: solid medium blue}
```

The following code gives three links. How these are displayed will differ according to the situation. At the start all links will be in italic and black font. If the link is being used (clicked on) it will have a font size of 1cm and due to the fact it is the object of attention it will have a solid blue outline around it (although this will depend on the browser used). If the mouse pointer were to hover over the link the color of the font would change to red, but again this will depend on the browser used. Finally if a site as been visited it will have a bold font:

```html
<html>
  <head>
    <title>CSS example :: pseudo classes</title>
    <style type="text/css">
      <!--

          a:link { font-style:italic ; color:black }
          a:visited { font-style:bold }
          a:active { font-size:1cm }
          a:link:hover {font-color:red}
          a:focus {outline: solid medium blue}

      -->
    </style>
  </head>
  <body>
Pick one of the following web sites to go to:
    <p> <a href="www.wrox.com">The main wrox page</a>
    <p> <a href="p2p.wrox.com">The programmer's page</a>
    <p> <a href="www.google.com">A search engine</a>
  </body>
</html>
```

In the example above we see the usual use for these definitions. After the name of the tag there is a colon and at the end there is the definition for the pseudo-class.

Pseudo-elements

Pseudo-elements allow a relatively fine level of control over commonly used typographical formats in block elements. For example, they can be used to set special characteristics for the first letter in a paragraph, for the first line, and so on. They are relatively simple to use. In the following example, we set the first letter of any paragraph to appear in red:

```
p:first-letter { color: red }
```

In CSS 1 there are two pseudo-elements: one that lets us format the first letter of a line of text content, and one that lets us style the first line of text content. These styles let us create a traditional print atmosphere for our page.

> Note: browser support for pseudo-elements is patchy. They were not supported at all up to and including IE 4 and N 4.

:first-letter

We can define the layout for the first letter of the content of a text container:

```
blockquote.one:first-letter { font-size:36pt; color:blue; }
```

:first-line

We can define the layout for the first line of a text container.

```
p:first-line {font-weight:bold; }
h1:first-line {color:#990000; }
```

For example:

```
<html>
<head>
    <title>CSS example :: Units of length and percentage</title>
    <style type="text/css">
      <!--
        p:first-letter { font-size:30pt;}
        p:first-line { font-size:20pt;}
      -->
    </style>
  </head>
  <body>
    <P> NOTICE HOW THE FIRST LETTER AND LINE BEHAVE ACCORDING TO THE STYLE
        WE DEFINED. THIS AN EXAMPLE OF PSEUDO ELEMENTS.
    </p>
  </body>
</html>
```

Gives the following result:

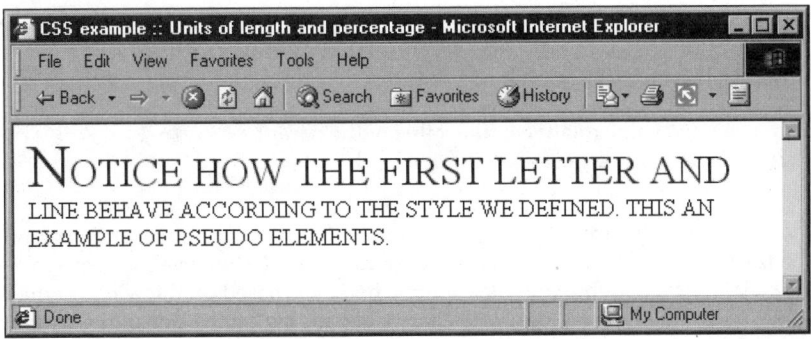

293

:before, :after

CSS 2 introduced two more pseudo-elements: one specifying text to be added before an element, and one to specify text to be added after an element. They only work in the following browsers: N 6.0, IE 5.0 (Mac) and IE 5.5 (Windows):

```
div.note:before { content:"Please note: " }
div.old:after { content:"(Out of Date)" }
```

This CSS rule is useful for marking repeating areas of our HTML document.

For all CSS rules in style sheets and in inline styles, we can define values with the common absolute and relative units of measurement, color values, and background images. The following sections will discuss these.

Measurements

When defining properties that use length, height, and width we will need to specify our properties using units of measurement. The following unit can be used in your definitions:

Units of Length and Percentage

Different CSS commands use different units of measurement for formatting element content. Here is a table of size measurement systems used in CSS, where em, ex, and % are relative measurements; the others are absolute.

Unit	Definition	Example
em	relative to the height of the font used in the element	`h1 {margin:0.5em}`
ex	relative to the height of the character 'x' for the font used by the element	`h2 {margin: 1ex}`
px	size based on the number of screen pixels	`p {font-size:12px}`
in	in for inches (1 in = 2.54 cm)	`p {font-size: 0.5in}`
cm	cm for centimetres	`p {font-size: 0.3cm}`
mm	mm for millimetres	`p {font-size:3mm}`
pt	pt for points (1pt = 1/72 inches)	`p {font-size:12pt}`
pc	pc for picas (1pc= 12 points)	`p {font-size:1pc}`
%	a percentage value relative to the value of the parent element, depending on the properties used	`p {line-height:120%}`

The % option varies in what it bases the % on, for example if we used the line-height property then this is based on the height of the font the element currently uses. If, however, we set a margin property, for example margin-left as defined in the example here, it is based on the width of the window. If we use the code shown here then the margins will change depending on the size of the window used.

```
<html>
  <head>
    <title>CSS example :: Units of length and percentage</title>
    <style type="text/css">
      <!--
        h1 { font-size:14pt; margin-left:10%;}
        h2 { font-size:10pt; margin-left:20%;}
        p  { font-size:1pc; text-indent:5mm; }
      -->
    </style>
  </head>
  <body>
    <h1>Formatting with CSS!</h1>
    <h2>Units of length and percentage</h2>
    <p>This page is <b>really</b> simple! Just define the
       elements once and off you go!</p>
  </body>
</html>
```

With a wide window, the margins look like this:

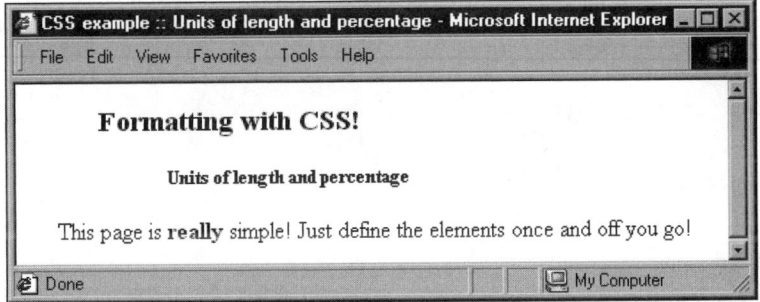

In a narrow window, they look like this:

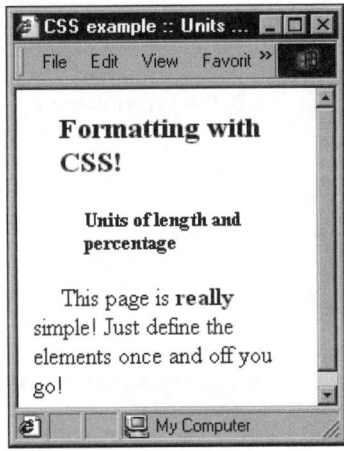

Background Color and Images

The atmosphere of our web page is very important in making it an inviting area to browse in. The easiest way to create an inviting atmosphere is to add background images and color. Unlike in HTML, we can do some fun things with a background in CSS, for example, create a wallpaper effect or include a personal watermark on our page.

Defining a Background Color

This is easy. Just take the `background-color` property and add a color value. We can also make the element background transparent (this is the default value, meaning that the parent element's background color shines through).

There are three ways to define the color of content in CSS: a color name (for example, `white`) hexadecimal code (for example, `#FFFFFF`), or a RGB colour definition (for example, `rgb(255,255,255)`)

Color Names

This is the easiest way to define colors. Just take a color name, for example, `white`, `silver`, `purple`, and so on, as the value of our color. Here is a list of the basic 16 colours defined in HTML 4.01. They work on all browsers. See Appendix D for more information.

aqua	black	blue	fuchsia
gray	green	lime	maroon
navy	olive	purple	red
silver	teal	white	yellow

Hexadecimal

This is the most common way to define colors in HTML. The full value begins with the # symbol followed by two characters to represent the red value, then two characters to represent the green value, and then another two for the blue value.

```
P { color:#CB9923 }
```

This statement is stating the red value is CB, the green value is 99 and the blue value is 23 in hexadecimal notation.

RGB

RGB (Red, Green, Blue) is also known as the 24-bit color scheme. It works the same as the hexadecimal system, just in a different representation (using decimal notation). It can be used in a style sheet or inline style as: `rgb(rrr,ggg,bbb)`. Inside the parentheses there should be nine digits in total, with three digits for each color. `rrr` for red, `ggg` for green, and `bbb` for blue values. Each color is defined either by an absolute number (0-255) or a percentage (0%-100%). The example we gave for the hexadecimal notation would be exactly the same as the following using this notation:

```
P { color: rgb(203,153,035) }
```

The easiest way to determine which number stands for which colour is to use a graphics software package. For example, in Microsoft Paint if we go via the menu Colors | Edit Colors and click the 'Define Custom Colors' button. From there we can select colors and view the corresponding red, green, blue values. There are also many tools for determining color values available on the Web.

Note that different browser interpret the colors defined in the `<div>` element in different ways, some color the whole block, others only the area behind the text. See the screenshots below for an illustration of one of those differences.

The following example uses all three methods of defining color properties:

```html
<html>
  <head>
    <title>CSS example :: Color units</title>
    <style type="text/css">
      <!--
        h1 { color:#FF0000; background-color:yellow }
        body { background-color:rgb(115,155,90); }
        blockquote { background-color:rgb(60%,90%,75%); }
        div { background-color:#FFFFFF; }
      -->
    </style>
  </head>
  <body>
    <h1>Formatting with CSS!</h1>
    <blockquote>Color units</blockquote>
    <div>This page is really simple! Just define the
         elements once and off you go!
    </div>
  </body>
</html>
```

In IE 5.5, this example looks like this:

In Netscape 4.7, it looks like this:

Be sure that there is enough contrast between the background color and the color of the font. Otherwise it may be very hard for users to read. You should also avoid using color as the only distinction between text on your page, as this distinction may not be visible to color blind people viewing your site. See Chapter 20 for more on this.

Adding Background Images

Background images can be used for all sorts of decorative purposes in our web pages. In this section, we'll look at how we can use CSS to do this.

> **It is important to note at this point that background images override background colors.**

Adding a Single Background Image

To specify a background image for a page without positioning, we use the `background-image` property which has the supported value `url (filenamePath)`.

```
body {background-image: url (mybackgoundfile.gif) }
```

This example shows an image only displayed once:

```html
<html>
  <head>
    <style type="text/css">
      body {
            background-image: url(backgroundsmall.gif);
            background-position: center;
            background-repeat: no-repeat;
            }
    </style>
  <body>
    <p>One image is the whole background.</p>
  </body>
</html>
```

Creating Wallpaper – Repeating Images

Remember the wallpaper from your grandma's house? Those cute little flowers repeated all up and down the walls? We can have a wallpaper effect on our web page as well. All we need is one image and then we're set to do all sorts of things with it. By using the property background-repeat, you can set backgrounds for sidebars or for bars across the top of the page, as well as repeat an image in order to cover the whole page.

In this case, we just want one image but we want it to repeat it to create the wallpaper effect. To do this we use the background-repeat property that takes the following supported values:

    repeat   repeat-x   repeat-y   no-repeat

Where repeat (default) causes the image to be repeated endlessly all over the page. repeat-x causes the image to be repeated endlessly horizontally across the page, and with repeat-y the image is repeated endlessly vertically down the page. no-repeat means that the image is only displayed once.

It is a good idea to use subtle, low-key images for wallpaper. Loud images with well-defined figures can be very distracting and even make it difficult to read the text.

As can be seen below, the marble2.gif file shown below is a small image, taking up a small amount of a page. We will use it in the next three examples to show the effect of using background-repeat in various ways.

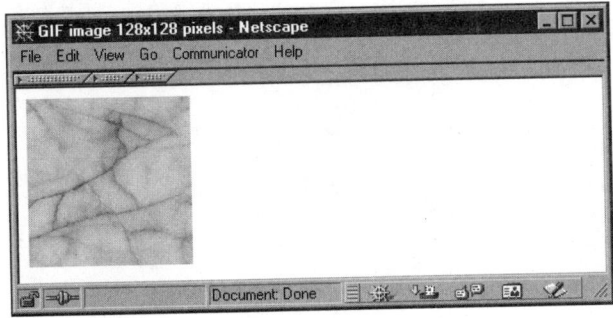

In the following example, we specify that `marble2.gif` should repeat to form wallpaper.

```
<html>
  <head>
    <style type="text/css">
      body {
            background-image: url(marble2.gif);
            background-repeat: repeat;
            }
    </style>
  </head>
  <body>
    <p>One image is repeated over the whole page creating a wallpaper
       effect.</p>
  </body>
</html>
```

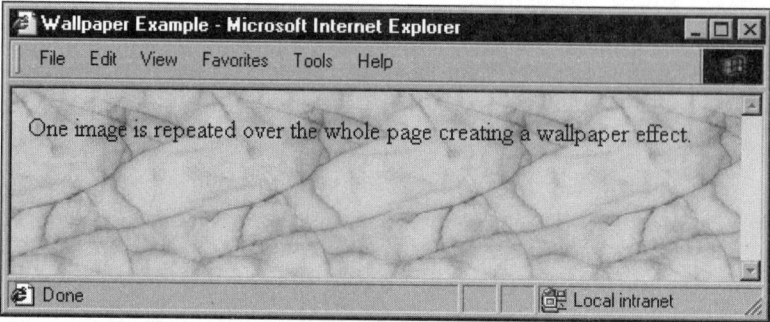

Creating a Sidebar with a Repeating Image

We can use a sidebar to set up a background behind vertical navigational elements. The value for `background-repeat` must be `repeat-y`, that is, along the vertical Y-axis of the page.

A sidebar is defined in the next example, using the file `marble2.gif` as its repeating background:

```
<html>
  <head>
    <style type="text/css">
      body {
            background-image: url(marble2.gif);
            background-repeat: repeat-y;
            }
    </style>
  </head>
  <body>
    <p>This image is fixed and repeated along the left side of the page. We
       can use it as a place to highlight our navigation.</p>
  </body>
</html>
```

This screenshot shows the result:

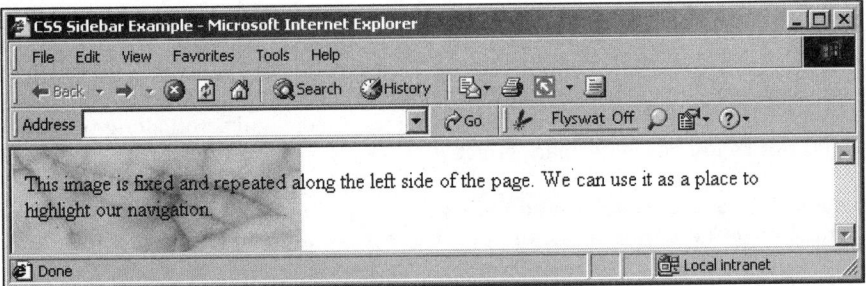

Creating a Crossbar with Repeating Images

We can use a crossbar to set up a background behind horizontal navigation elements. The value for `background-repeat` must be `repeat-x`, that is, along the horizontal X-axis of the page. This can be useful for certain types of messages, such as reminders.

The following example sets up a cross bar:

```
<html>
  <head>
    <style type="text/css">
      body {
            background-image: url(marble2.gif);
            background-repeat: repeat-x;
            background-attachment: fixed;
            }
      </style>
  </head>
  <body>
    <p>This image is fixed and repeated across the top. It's there even if
       you scroll.</p>
  </body>
</html>
```

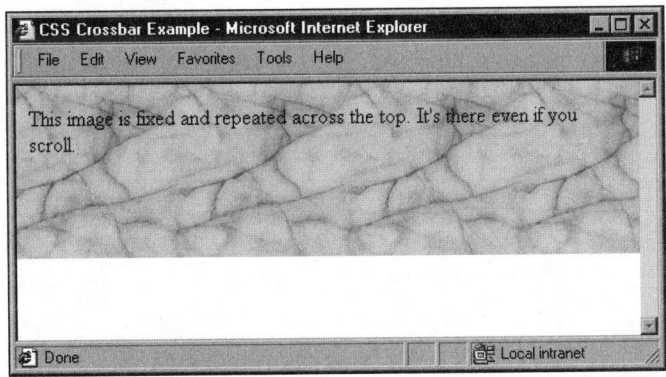

Creating a Watermark

A watermark is an image that stays in the same place even if we scroll up and down the page. Watermarks are useful if we want the whole image to be seen at all times. They are created using the background-attachment property and its fixed value that specifies that the image will stay in the same position in the window regardless of how far we scroll. background-attachment can also take the value scroll, which specifies that the image will scroll along with the window, but this would not create our watermark effect.

This code example shows the specification of a watermark. If you load this up in your browser, notice how the image stays fixed in the upper-left corner of the window:

```
<html>
  <head>
    <style type="text/css">
      body {
            background: url(marble2.gif);
            background-repeat: no-repeat;
            background-attachment: fixed;
            }
    </style>
  </head>
  <body>
    <p>This image is fixed in the upper-left corner. It's there even if you
       scroll.</p>
  </body>
</html>
```

Positioning a Single Background Image

With background-position we define where a background image is positioned on the page. It takes the following supported values:

❑ X%|Y%: These are the percentages along the X (horizontal) and Y (vertical) axis of a page

❑ X|Y: These are the absolute lengths along the X and Y axes of a page

❑ left|center|right: Choose from center, left or right

❑ top|center|bottom: Choose center, top or bottom

These following examples show the specification of positioned background images. Each is followed by a screenshot of the result.

```
<html>
  <head>
    <style type="text/css">
      body {
            background-image:url(marble2.gif);
            background-repeat: no-repeat;
            background-position:1cm 2cm; }
    </style>
  </head>
  <body>
    <p>This image is positioned 1cm from the left and 2cm from the top.</p>
  </body>
</html>
```

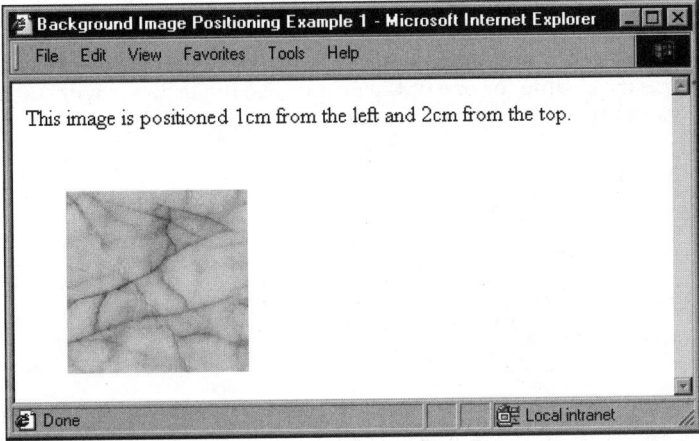

```
<html>
  <head>
    <style type="text/css">
      body {
            background-image:url(marble2.gif);
            background-repeat: no-repeat;
            background-position:top center
            }
    </style>
  </head>
  <body>
    <p>This image is positioned at the top and in the center.</p>
  </body>
</html>
```

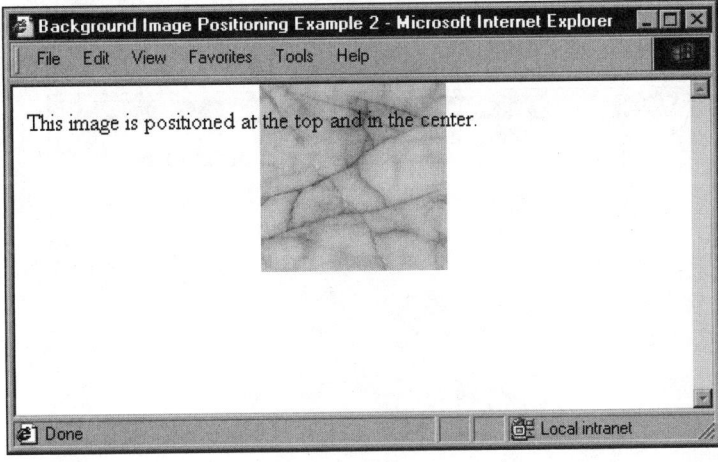

Background Shorthand

The property background is used to define the rule of all five of the background properties at once. If we do not specify a value for one of the properties, the browser will supply a default value. We can define the values in any order for the following supported values:

❑   background-color

❑   background-image

❑   background-repeat

❑   background-attachment

❑   background-position

More browsers support the shorthand background property than the longhand properties, therefore it is a good idea to experiment with it. However, since Netscape defaults to black if you use the background property, you should always specify a background color when you use this property. Opera 3 does not support this because it does not support the background-attachment property.

The next example shows background with all five values specified:

```
<html>
  <head>
    <style type="text/css">
      body { background:url(marble2.gif) #FFFFC0 50% no-repeat fixed }
    </style>
  </head>
  <body>
    <p>This background has a yellow background color with a single fixed
       image in the middle 50% of the screen.</p>
  </body>
</html>
```

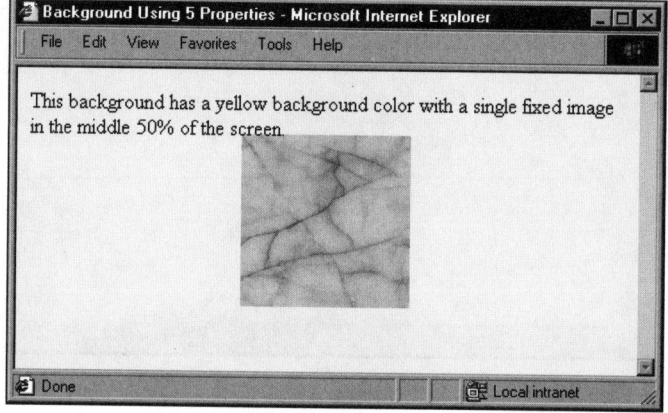

Summary

In this chapter we have introduced the fundamentals of CSS style sheets. You should now have basic knowledge on how to set up CSS rules for elements and a style sheet as well as how to attach your style sheet to a document. You should also have an idea about how styles are cascaded and inherited from one element to another. We have also given you information about measurements, background color, and background images.

Now you are ready for the next chapter where we will focus on specific character styles in CSS, giving you more commands to use in your style sheets!

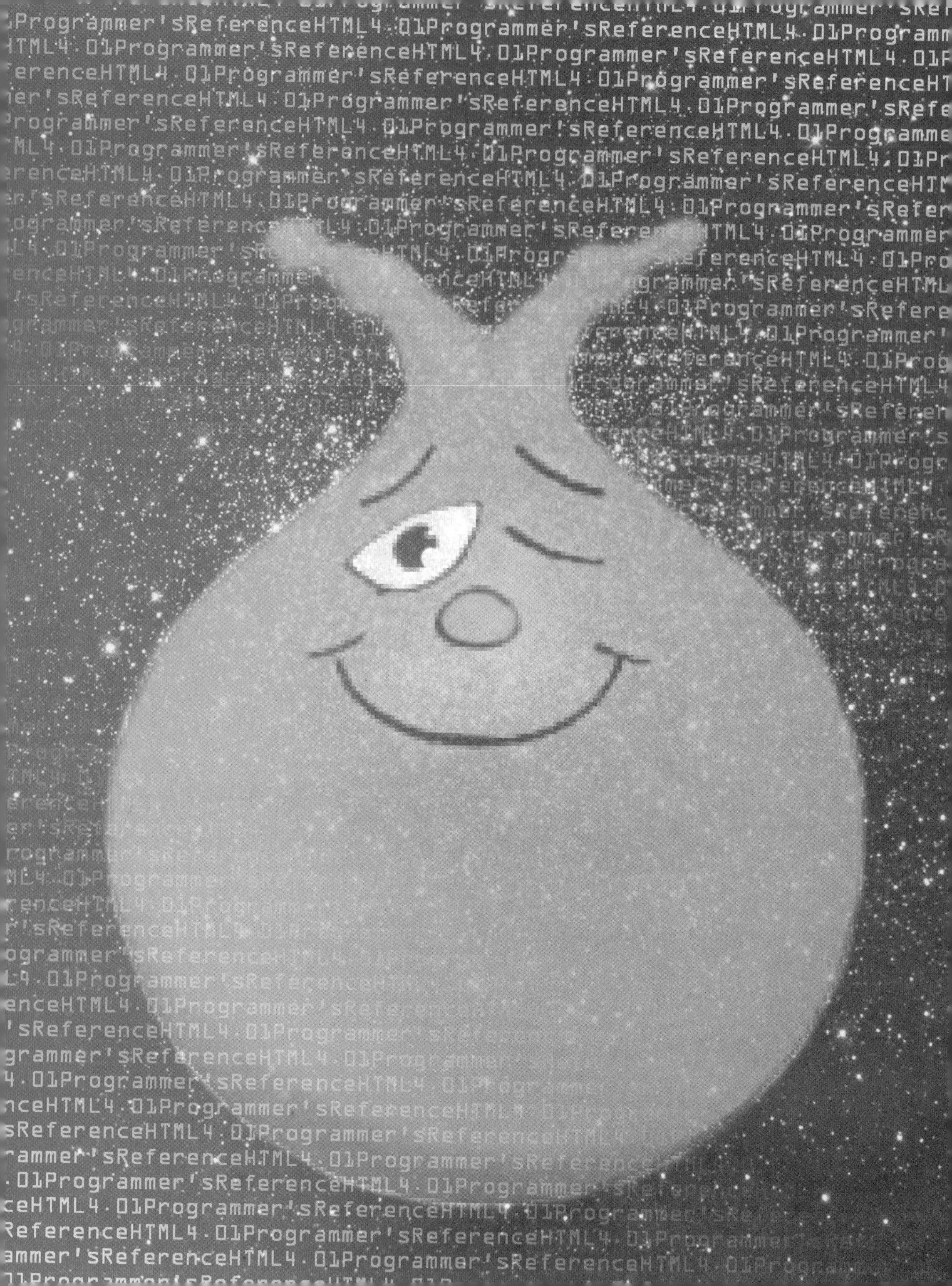
HTML4.01Programmer'sReference

12

Character Styles

This chapter deals with the style sheet rules for formatting characters, words, and sentences. Previously HTML developers have tended to rely heavily on `<font>` and associated styling elements (such as `<i>` and `<b>`) to achieve this formatting, but with such widespread support of style sheets in current versions of the major browsers (IE, Netscape, and Opera), these should really be used wherever possible. As explained in the previous chapter, it is becoming increasingly important to separate your presentation from your content.

In particular we will be focusing on character styles, which are the style sheet rules that define general qualities of the font face. We can define the font, size, weight, and color characteristics for every element found in the `<body>` element, or we could specifically format character styles for text that appears in inline elements such as `<span>`, as well as block elements such as a paragraph or `<div>`, or a table or list. We can even create our own customized classes, which we can then apply where and when we need them, regardless of which element is surrounding the text.

This chapter covers:

❑ Defining fonts

❑ Font sources

❑ Rules for characters and text

The Font Definition

One of the most popular Cascading Style Sheet (CSS) features with web designers is the ability to set font types. Not only do you have control over the way your text-based content is displayed, but you can also make changes to the layout at any time and almost without limitation.

In fact the HTML 4.01 standard actually demands that you use CSS to set font-types via a myriad of properties and has deprecated the HTML <font> element forthwith, to discourage people from this somewhat rigid style element.

The methods we are going to discuss here will give you greater control over how text is displayed on your web pages. You can set up a centralized layout control for every single web page you want by attaching the same style sheet to all pages. This is the way to easily maintain huge sites without touching a single page when styles are changed.

There are two main ways to employ a font. First there is the option of using a small, common subset of fonts, that are installed by default on the majority of operating systems and that are provided as standard with the popular browser types. These fonts can be referenced directly with style sheets, or with the deprecated <font> element. The second method is to define a font by linking to an external font data source. We will be looking at both these methods and discussing their individual pros and cons.

Using Pre-Installed Fonts

Most web sites use a small common subset of fonts from the default fonts available on the major platforms. This allows a web designer to control the layout of a document so most of the users will be able to see pretty much the same results. Most browsers support an even smaller subset of these fonts. The only three fonts that you'll typically be able to guarantee that Netscape, Opera, and IE users all have will be: **Courier New, Arial** and **Times New Roman**.

The Microsoft-introduced Verdana typeface is now very common as well – although it only actually ships with Microsoft products (such as IE, Microsoft Office, and Windows) so users of non-Microsoft platforms are unlikely to have it. In fact, IE 5.5 natively supports ten fonts.

These fonts are Arial, Times New Roman, Courier New, Verdana, Georgia, Trebuchet MS, Comic Sans MS, Arial Black, Impact, and the symbol font set Webdings:

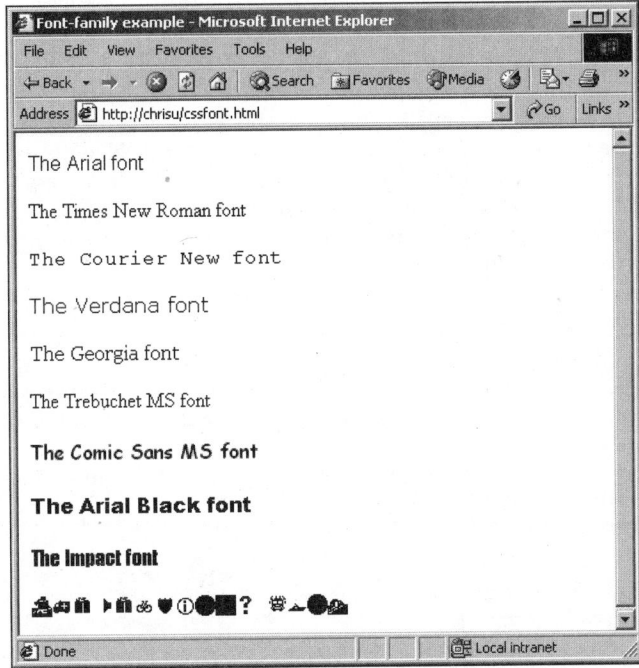

The drawback is, that when we use such a restricted set of fonts, the pre-installed fonts are not always those that correspond to a company's design guidelines. The advantage is that you can guarantee the availability of the three core fonts (and on IE-only intranets, the presence of the ten fonts shown above).

Using a Pre-Installed Font in a Style Sheet (the font-family Property)

The CSS property font-family is used to define one or more fonts for an element, and is the method you should use for specifying pre-installed fonts in your web pages. To define one font for an element using font-family, use the following syntax:

```
h1 {font-family: Arial}
```

To define more than one, you must separate each alternative with a comma:

```
h1 {font-family: Arial, Courier New}
```

The order you list the fonts in the style definition is important: the browser will display the text using the first font it detects as installed on a particular user's OS. It is recommended to enclose all fonts with spaces in the name with quotes, and indeed some browsers require it:

```
h1 {font-family: Arial, "Courier New"}
```

However, most modern browsers, such as IE 5.x, don't require this.

> *Note: If a browser can't find the first font you listed, it will ignore it and use the next available font you define or – if you did not define a font family – revert to the browser default.*

There are five fixed definitions for font families you can use besides or in addition to the font names: `serif`, `sans-serif`, `cursive`, `fantasy`, and `monospace`. In reality, these fixed definitions will just use the Arial, Times New Roman, and Courier New fonts we mentioned earlier. However, what the generic font families are really intended for is not to serve as the single defined font for an element, but to be listed as the last alternative in a `font-family` to ensure there is always a fallback in case the listed fonts are not available. You specify these fixed definitions in the same way you'd specify normal font types:

```
h1 {font-family: monospace}
```

While in most browsers this will mean the <h1> element contents are rendered in Courier New, there might some browsers or language variations that use a different mono-spaced font instead.

Let's look at a quick example now. In this example we just create a simple class, which defines the `font-family` property as a set of two fonts:

```
<html>
<head>
    <title>Font-family example</title>
    <style>
        .font {font-family: "Trebuchet MS", "Courier New"}
    </style>
</head>
<body>
    <p class="font">The quick brown fox jumped over the lazy dog</p>
</body>
</html>
```

If we run this example through IE, we will see the following:

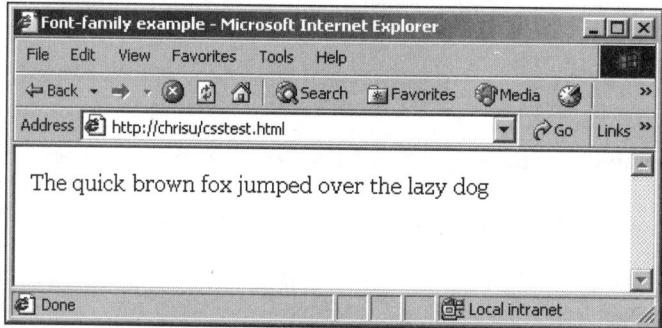

IE comes with Trebuchet installed and is able to display it without any problem. However, Netscape doesn't have this particular Microsoft font. It might be the case that this font is already installed on your operating system (if you have IE 5.x/6 for instance then it will already be available) in which case Netscape and other browsers such as Opera will be able to display it, but if not then you will see the following:

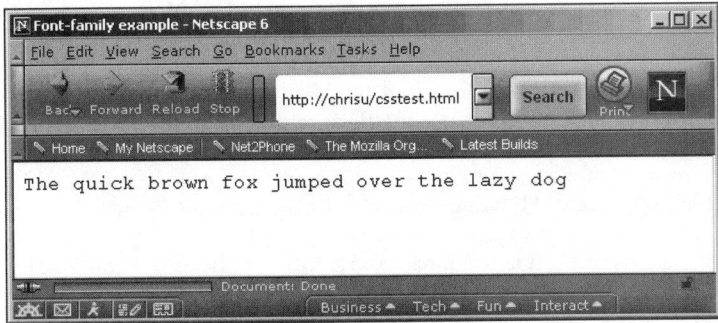

As the browser/operating system hasn't got the Trebuchet font, it defaults to the next choice, which is Courier New.

For those with a good knowledge of fonts, you'll probably have noticed that Trebuchet MS is a sans-serif font, while Courier New is mono-spaced and it's unlikely you'd normally default from one font type to one so different as we have here. This has been done to clearly demonstrate that the browser is actually going to the next font in the list. The default serif font (Times New Roman) is actually the default font the browser would choose if only Trebuchet MS had been specified, and was not available.

Using Font Files and Downloadable Fonts

Downloadable fonts are quite different to pre-installed fonts. They were a feature introduced in the version 4 Microsoft and Netscape browsers. Unlike pre-installed fonts, they are not fully installed on an operating system; instead they are utilized by linking to a web page via a style sheet or property. This allows the browser to view the font, without being able to download the whole font file to the computer. A browser that is able to recognize such fonts loads the respective web-enabled font file to the visitor's computer and places it in the cache.

When you view other pages using the same font file, you won't have to reload the font file, as the browser will be able to recreate the file from the cache to display the text using the intended font.

Copyright Issues

However, there is one large downside with downloadable fonts and that is the overlooked area of copyright. We mentioned that downloaded font files will only be viewable on the browser, and do not become available elsewhere on the computer, and there is a very good reason for this. Fonts are created just like any other software, by third parties, and they are usually sold in the same manner to other software too. While there are plenty of fonts in the public domain (that is, freely available), a large amount of downloadable fonts are copyrighted, and while you are free to view them in web pages, you are not free to use them in your web pages or to distribute them (which you would be doing if someone could download a font by viewing your web page).

Two Solutions

Because the issues of copyright concerning fonts on the Web are quite complex (requiring someone to be able to download a font and view pages with it, but not use it outside that context), there are two solutions to the problem: one developed by Microsoft and the other by Netscape. They are (respectively) .eot files, which are only recognized by IE browsers, version 4.x and above (both on Windows and the Mac), and .pfr files, which are recognized by Netscape version 4.x browsers (and also by IE browsers via an ActiveX plug-in).

Both solutions require special software to set up a font file in the right format for their browser's needs, and both let us also transform font types like Adobe fonts or TrueType into the new file formats. They also require slightly different methods of application within your web pages. To make matters even worse, the Netscape TrueDoc/Bitstream solution was flawed for a long while and couldn't prevent unauthorized web designers from using fonts in their own pages, thus potentially breaching copyright. However, this has recently been rectified.

As a result, the Microsoft solution is the more commonly practiced one, and downloadable fonts, while present in Netscape 4.x, have yet to be implemented in either form in Netscape 6.

The original flaw with .pfr is also probably part of the reason why W3C adopted the @font-face property in the CSS 2 standard, as used by Microsoft, for defining downloadable fonts, rather than the Netscape one. We will look at this solution first, and in greater detail than the less widely used Netscape solution.

Embedding Fonts using @font-face

With an @font-face rule you can specify the definition of a downloadable font file, and with the help of the properties font-family and src you can link a font resource to a style sheet. To link to it correctly, you need to ensure that the font file is located in the same directory as the web page, or that the path to the font file is specified within the src:url definition section of the @font-face rule. For this next example, you need to have created an .eot font file beforehand, using the **Microsoft Web Embedding Fonts Tool (WEFT)**, which we look at shortly, within your domain – this is because web-enabled font files can only work in the domain they were "burned" within, thus preventing free distribution.

However, before you can use Microsoft WEFT, you have to check that your embedded font is actually embeddable. Not all font files can be burned like this, as it is possible for the creator of the file to forbid the embedding of their font file. There is a file you can download from Microsoft that allows you to determine whether or not a particular font is embeddable:

http://www.microsoft.com/typography/downloads/ttfext.exe

If you run it, it will add the standard OpenType font shell-extension properties, so if you right-click on a font file and its properties, a whole new set of tabs and extra details about the font pops up. Among them, the embedded tab informs you whether a particular font file is embeddable or not.

We've downloaded a freely distributable font called "Field Day Filter" from the site http://www.larabiefonts.com, which we're going to embed in a web page in our example. If once you've downloaded it you choose the Field Day Filter font properties, you will see the following:

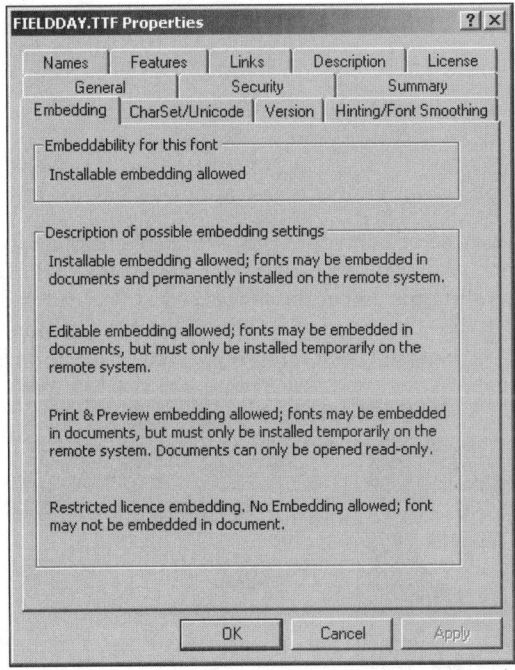

This font can be embedded in the web page, so the next step is to create an `.eot` file with the Microsoft WEFT tool.

> *Note: to be able to embed this font in a web page, and hence to be able to run the following examples, you need to put the font file into the Fonts folder in your Windows directory (called WINNT on Win NT/2000). You should also put the font file in question in the same directory as the web page into which it is to be embedded.*

Microsoft and the Web Embedding Fonts Tool (WEFT)

MSIE has supported downloadable fonts since version 4. The WEFT tool may be used to create downloadable fonts, and it is freely available from the following URL:

http://www.microsoft.com/typography/downloads/weft3/weft3.exe

You can then use this tool to produce downloadable fonts for Microsoft IE.

To be able to use it, you need a web page or web site to be already set up: so you create your project, add the CSS it needs and then launch the WEFT Wizard, which analyzes the required web pages. For this example, we need to create the following page called `field.html`:

```
<html>
<head>
   <title>Downloadable Font Example</title>
   <style type="text/css">
      <!--
      @font-face { font-family:Field Day Filter}
```

```
      -->
    </style>
  </head>
  <body>
    <p style="font-family:Field Day Filter">This is some text in Field Day
Filter</p>
  </body>
  </html>
```

Now you need to put it in a directory on your web server (we used a virtual directory on IIS). Even though this page won't work yet because we haven't installed the Field Day Filter font, it is required by WEFT for generating the embeddable font. Next you can use the wizard in WEFT to define which fonts you want to set up as special "Font Objects", thus making them downloadable fonts. To do this, start weft3.exe and select the **New** option from the **File** menu.

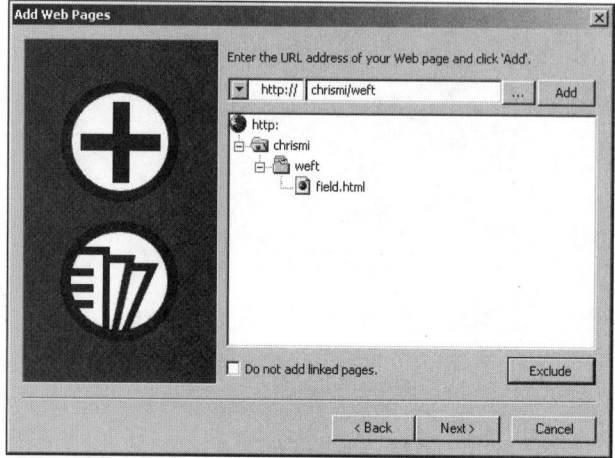

You need to specify the URL and file name of the web page containing the fonts you wish to embed (that is, the full URL of the web page we have just created). Then you can get the WEFT tool to analyze your pages and it will return a list of the fonts it found in that page:

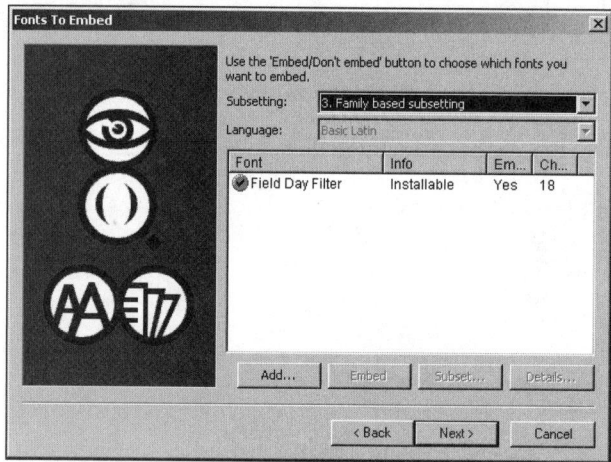

It will confirm that this font is installable, and clicking on Next will take you to the page that lets you create the actual font object, that is the .eot file. Here you need to specify the path to where the .eot file is to be created on your web server, the domain name under which you want to allow the font to be used, and you should also check the tick-box marked Show CSS @font-family declarations, as this supplies you the filename you need to embed in your HTML code – this is useful as the .eot file created normally has a somewhat unintuitive file name.

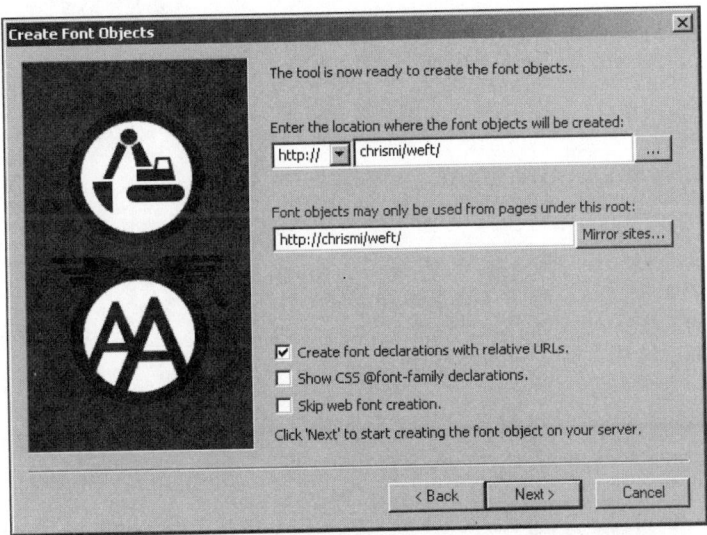

Now, click on the Next> button, and you will be presented with a small box, in which you must insert the actual physical path to where you want the .eot file created, as shown below:

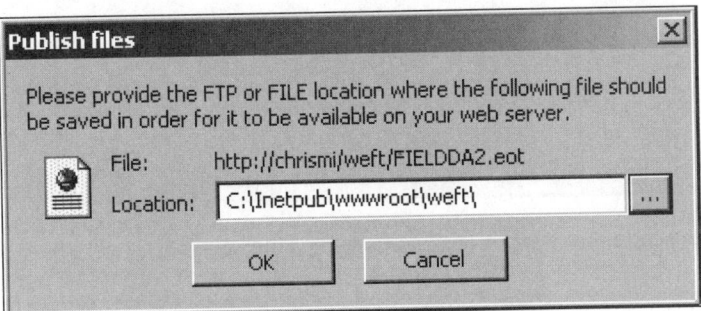

Now all you need to do is click the Next> button on the resulting screen, then click Finish on the final screen. Your field.html code should now look something like this:

```
<html>
<head>
    <title>Downloadable Font Example</title>
    <style type="text/css">
       <!--
       @font-face { font-family:Field Day Filter}
       -->
    </style>
```

```
<style type="text/css">
<!-- /* $WEFT -- Created by: Jon Doe (JonD@anysite.com) on 17/05/2001 -- */
   @font-face {
               font-family: Field Day Filter;
               font-style:  normal;
               font-weight: normal;
               src: url(FIELDDA2.eot);
               }
-->

</style>
</head>
<body>
    <p style="font-family:Field Day Filter">This is some text in Field Day
Filter</p>
</body>
</html>
```

We've placed the `.eot` *file in the root of our web server, which also contains the* `field.html`
file, thus allowing us to dispense with the path information in the URL.

The example is now complete, and we are now able to display an external font as defined in the
style sheet in the document head. It should look like this:

The only part of the code that is of interest to us is the rule:

```
@font-face {
      font-family: Field Day Filter;
      font-style:  normal;
      font-weight: normal;
      src: url(FIELDDA2.eot);
   }
```

The `@font-face` starts the definition for the Field Day Filter font. After that comes the declaration
in curly brackets. The only two properties we need are `font-family` and the web address of the
font data `src:url(file)`.

The font resources shown in the example use the same folder as the HTML document. If you wish,
you can use relative or exact resource locators as appropriate to direct the browser to your
embedded fonts.

Embedding Fonts Using fontdef

The alternative to WEFT and the EOT file format is the PFR (Portable File Resource) technology. This works natively in Netscape 4.x browsers and in IE browsers with the aid of a plug-in (although this is not available on IE for the Mac). Bitstream/TrueDoc created this alternative downloadable font technology used on the Web, although it was originally designed for platform-independent electronic publishing. It aimed to achieve this by inserting fonts within documents rather than depending on ones installed on any given system.

Netscape and Bitstream/TrueDoc

To create a new web-enabled font, or to transform installed fonts to files with the extension .pfr, you need to use the WebFont Wizard, available from the Bitstream web site at:
http://www.bitstream.com/categories/products/index.html.

The WebFont Wizard is available for trial use for a period of 10 days or for the creation of 10 PFR files, beyond this, you are expected to purchase the full WebFont Maker. Unlike the Microsoft WEFT tool, this isn't a full-blown application, just a wizard that only requires 4 steps. In the first step, you must supply it with the name of the font you wish to make into a downloadable form from a list. The Wizard will prevent you from selecting a font that can't be enabled for embedding. Once again, let's choose the Field Day Filter font:

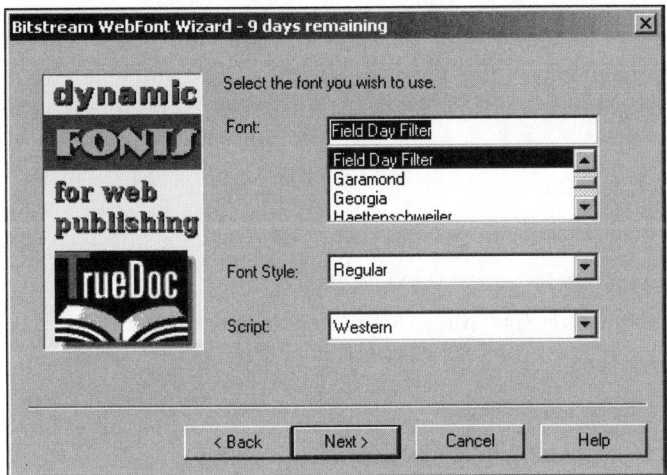

Click on **Next**, and then you get to choose whether you want to select the Standard Character set, a Complete Character set, or a Customized one. We suggest just selecting the Standard one and clicking on **Next** again. Now you need to specify the path names you wish the downloadable font to work on:

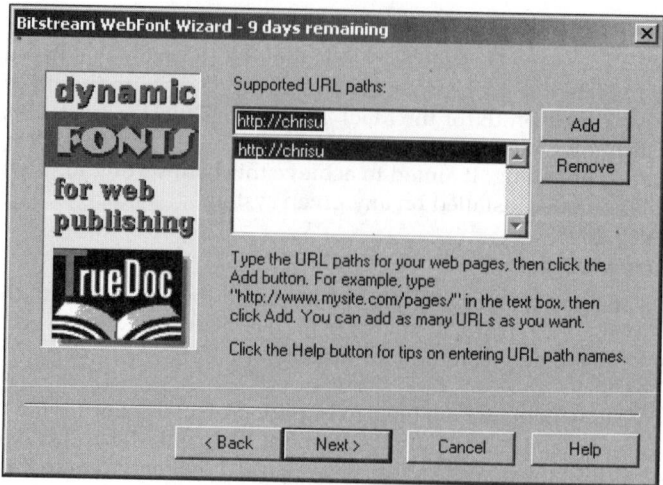

Click on **Next**, then lastly, you have to specify the name of the `.pfr` file and the location it should be created in. Note that if you don't choose a location, the default place that the `.pfr` file will be created is `C:\Program Files\WebFont Wizard` (provided that's where you installed it). Click on **Finish** to create it.

This isn't the end of the fun however; it is more than likely that you will have to enable your web server to be able to recognize the `.pfr` MIME type. In IIS on Windows platforms, the process to do this is as follows:

❑ Open your IIS console (MMC).

❑ Select the server in the right pane.

❑ Right-click to bring up the menu and select **Properties**.

❑ Click on **Edit** (the bottom one!) to bring up the MIME types dialog.

❑ Click on **New Type**.

❑ For associated extension, enter pfr.

❑ For **MIME type**, enter application/font-tdpfr.

❑ Click **OK** and then exit the IIS Server MMC and restart IIS.

Then you're ready to create a file that can view the dynamic font file:

```
<html>
<head>
    <title>Downloadable Font Example</title>
    <link rel="fontdef" src="fd.pfr">
</head>
<body>
    <p style="font-family:Field Day Filter">
        This is some text in Field Day Filter
    </p>
</body>
</html>
```

You can now view this in Netscape 4.x:

You can also enable this within IE by adding the following plug-in to the code:

```
<html>
<head>
    <title>Downloadable Font Example</title>
    <link rel="fontdef" src="fd.pfr">

    <script language="javascript">
    if (navigator.appName == "Microsoft Internet Explorer" &&
    navigator.appVersion.indexOf("Windows", 0) != -1 &&
    navigator.appVersion.substring(0,1) >= 4)
    {
    document.writeln("<OBJECT");
    document.writeln("classid=\"clsid:0246ECA8-996F-11D1-BE2F-
    00A0C9037DFE\"");
document.writeln("codebase=\"http://www.bitstream.com/wfplayer/tdserver.cab#versio
n=1,0,0,10\"");
    document.writeln("id=\"TDS\" width=0 height=0");
    document.writeln(">");
    document.writeln("</OBJECT>");
    }
    </script>
    <link>

</head>
<body>
    <p style="font-family:Field Day Filter">This is some text in
    Field Day Filter</p>
</body>
</html>
```

This script simply writes an `<object>` element in Javascript that enables the Bitstream plug-in, enabling you to use the `.pfr` format in IE.

As we have already intimated, there have been problems with this technology, which meant that at the time of the release of Netscape 4, it was possible to "burn" a `.pfr` file, and then just distribute freely. While the `.pfr` file couldn't be used outside a web page, and it was also not possible to download it and use it freely, it was still possible for the person who burned the file to freely distribute to other people. This problem has been rectified in the most recent versions of the Bitstream/TrueDoc technology. With its cross-browser capabilities it is likely to enjoy use for a while to come.

Embedding Downloadable Fonts

It is also possible to avoid having to create your own embeddable fonts, by referencing fonts that are held on other sites. Once again, the same principle applies, except instead of linking to a file on your hard disk drive, you now to specify the URL of a site that contains files you wish to embed:

```
<html>
<head>
   <link rel=fontdef
          src= "http://www.myserver.com/fonts/chianti.pfr">
   <style type="text/css">
   <!--
   @font-face {font-family:Chianti XBd BT;
               src:url(http://www.myserver.com/fonts/chianti.eot);}
   -->
   </style>
</head>
<body>
   <p style="font-family:Chianti XBd BT">text content</p>
</body>
</html>
```

The browser will ignore the font file it doesn't recognize. Once again, Bitstream/TrueType fonts will be displayed properly only if the remote web server has been correctly configured to accept the respective MIME type (`application/font-tdpfr` for files with the extension `.pfr`), something you have no control over here.

unicode-range

There is also a new facility in the CSS 2 standard that when you define a type via a linked font resource means you can limit the **Unicode** (a unique identification system for a universal character set that supports characters in all the world's languages) and tell the browser which characters are supported by a special font. If you use this feature the browser will transmit the font data to the user only if all characters of a text are within the defined range.

```
<html>
<head>
   <title>Title</title>
   <style type="text/css">
   <!--

   @font-face {font-family:System; src:url(system.eot);
               unicode-range:U+0000-007F;}

   -->
   </style>
</head>
<body>
   <tt style="font-family:System">Text with ß and Ü</tt>
<!--file won't be transmitted -->
</body>
</html>
```

The example above defines the Unicode range U+0000-007F. This is the ASCII character set. If there is a character in an element that that is not supported in this Unicode range (that is, not in the ASCII character set, which in this example are the ß and Ü characters) the font resource will not be downloaded. Currently this doesn't seem to be supported by any browser (up to version 6), although as it uses `@font-face`, it will probably only be supported by IE anyway.

src: local

CSS 2 offers a further property for defining the source of a font, `src: local`. You can use it to check for occurrences of different font types on a user's machine, and if a font isn't available to download it remotely. It can work in either of the following ways:

❏ `src: local("fontname")`
This will reference a particular face of a locally installed font

❏ `src: local("fontname"), url("url") format("font format")`
Here there are two alternatives given, the first is a locally installed font and the second a downloadable font available in specified format.

You can tell a browser to first search the user's computer for a specific font and if it is not there, to download that font instead. In the example below, the rule tells the browser to search for the font "Kino MT" on the user's computer, and tells it where to find the font globally if the search for it has failed locally:

```
@font-face {
    font-family:Kino;
    src:local(Kino MT), url(kino.ttf), format(TrueType);
}
```

Once again, this is not yet supported in any current (version 6) browsers, however it will probably be included in future browsers.

Rules for Characters and Text

There are plenty of rules available in CSS 1/CSS 2 and most current browsers that allow you to alter the style and format of the text displayed. Broadly speaking, these can be broken down into three categories:

❏ The styles that affect a particular font directly

❏ Those that affect the text directly regardless of the font (such as spacing, color, and indentation)

❏ Those that affect aspects that affect the text contained within particular types of element, such as listing text and the visibility of the text

We're going to look at the CSS properties that major browsers currently support, and some new unsupported ones that have been introduced in CSS 2 for each of these categories in the next section. You can find a complete list of style sheet properties in Appendix G.

The Font of an Element

Once you have decided on the fonts you want, and how the user can access them, you can start defining how each element is to be displayed. The rules you can use to define various font properties within CSS 1/CSS 2 and all the main browsers are as follows:

❏ `font-family` (for local fonts, discussed earlier)

❏ `@font-face` (for downloadable fonts, discussed earlier)

❏ `font-style`

❏ `font-variant`

- font-size
- font-weight
- font

In addition, CSS 2 also specifies the font-stretch and font-size-adjust properties, which aren't supported in any major browsers yet.

We will start by considering the rules supported by the browsers, but which haven't been discussed before now, beginning with font-style. You will find that IE 5.x, Netscape 6 and Opera 5 all support the following rules.

font-style

The property font-style defines whether the font appears cursive or not. You can set its values to italic (cursive), oblique (cursive) or normal (default style).

You can set the <h1> element to be italicized as follows:

```
h1 { font-style:italic; }
```

If you want this to affect more than one element, you just separate each element with commas:

```
h1,h2,h3 { font-style:italic; }
```

Here, we've set the <h1>, <h2>, and <h3> elements to be italicized. You can see this demonstrated in the following example:

```
<html>
<head>
    <title>Font style</title>
    <style type="text/css">
        h1,h2,h3 { font-style:italic; }
    </style>
</head>
<body>
    <h1>A level 1 heading</h1>
    <h2>A level 2 heading</h2>
    <h3>A level 3 heading</h3>
    <h4>A level 4 heading</h4>
</body>
</html>
```

In this example we create four levels of heading, and the first three are italicized:

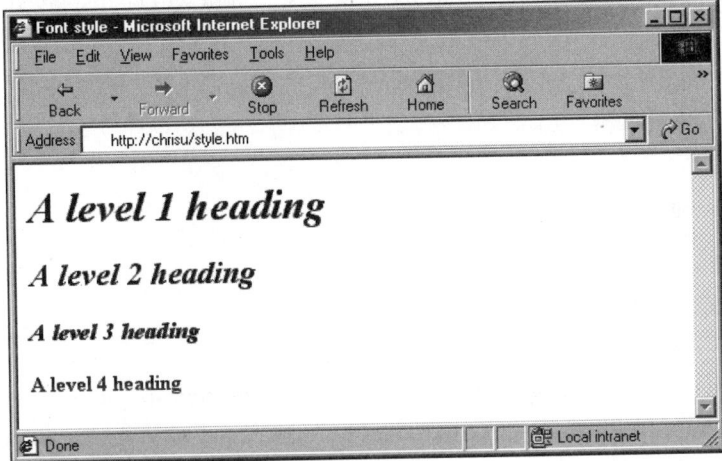

This way of italicizing letters should be preferred to the `<i>` element, despite the fact the `<i>` element has not been deprecated.

font-variant

You can also make a browser display a capitalized font. The values you can set for the property `font-variant` are `small-caps` and `normal`.

```
h1,h2,h3 { font-variant:small-caps; }
```

If you adjust the line in the previous example to read as above and then view it in a browser, you will see the first three headings capitalized, as seen here:

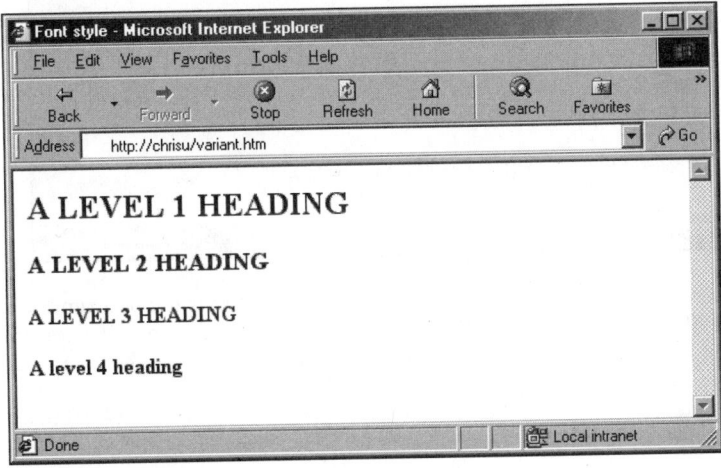

This style has no equivalent HTML element. You'll also find that Netscape 4 doesn't support this rule, though Netscape 6 does.

font-size

The property `font-size` is used to define just how large a font will be displayed. You can use absolute and relative size units for this, and in addition, you can also set the following values:

- `xx-small` = tiny
- `x-small` = very small
- `small` = small
- `medium` = normal
- `large` = large
- `x-large` = very large
- `xx-large` = extra large
- `smaller` = visibly smaller than normal (this is relative to the font size of the parent element)
- `larger` = visibly larger than normal (this is relative to the font size of the parent element)

We can set the font-size rule in the normal ways we just mentioned:

```
h2 { font-size:18pt; }          <!-- Absolute size -->
sup { font-size:80%; }          <!-- Relative size -->
.small { font-size:small; }     <!-- Using values -->
```

Let's take a look at these styles applied to some example text:

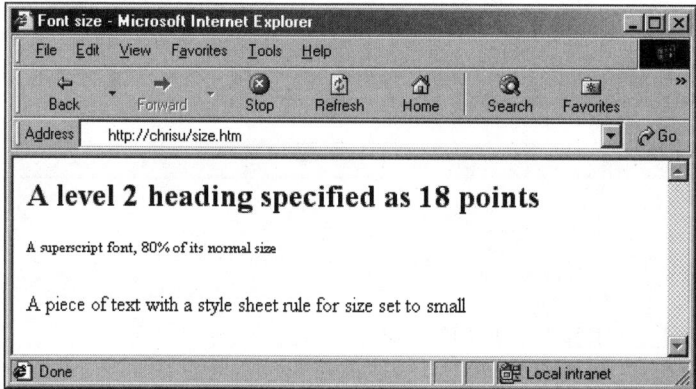

This style also works in Netscape 4, although you might find that the text rendered by the values listed above is smaller than text rendered with the same properties in Netscape 6, IE, and Opera, and in some cases is unreadable. This property is intended to replace the `size` attribute of the deprecated `<font>` element.

font-weight

This attribute is used to define whether a text is bold, normal, or light. For this you can use the values:

```
bold | bolder| lighter |normal (default)
```

Numerically these are represented by 100 being extra light, 400 being normal, 700 being bold, and 900 extra bold (you can use numbers in-between these, but it appears to make very little difference).

Note: Most pre-installed system fonts do not support the numeric units.

If we use weights in an example that emboldens some definition terms and emphasized text:

```
dt { font-weight:bold }
em { font-weight:600 }
```

You can see the effect it has:

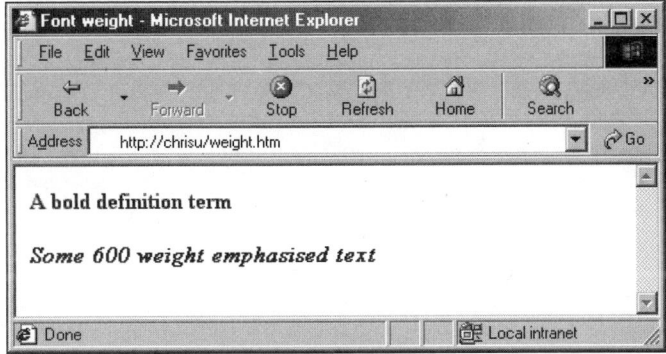

One anomaly worth noting is that Netscape 4 only supports the numerical setting of the rule – setting the property textually, for example as `font-weight:bold` will have no effect. This property is intended to replace the `weight` attribute of the deprecated `<font>` element.

font

The `font` property is used to set up a general CSS rule for a text layout. It is just a shorthand for using any or all of the aforementioned font properties. You can list the values for the font in any combination, such as follows: Use   Style-Size-FAmily

```
p { font:bold italic 12pt Tahoma, serif; }
```

Here we've used it to specify the weighting, style, size, and family on the font. As we've specified two separate fonts, the first, Tahoma, will be used if the browser/operating system has access to it, otherwise the browser will use the default serif type font. Here we've run it on a system that supports Tahoma:

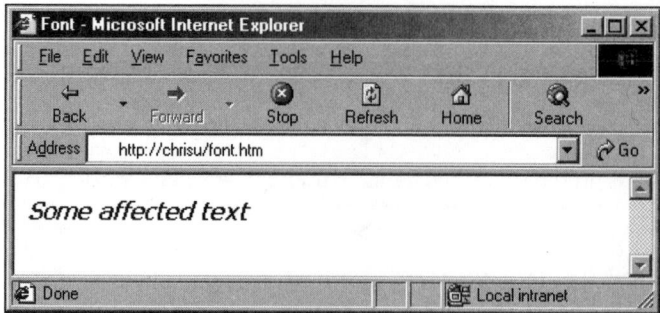

Interestingly enough, Netscape 4.x supports this element and will allow you to set the textual properties font and italic as part of a group, but if you set them individually, it won't recognize them!

CSS 2 only: font-stretch

This property is yet to be implemented on any major browser, however it is outlined in the CSS 2 standard. The font-stretch property is intended to condense or stretch text as necessary – it can take the following values:

```
normal | wider | narrower | ultra-condensed | extra-condensed | condensed | semi-
condensed | semi-expanded | expanded | extra-expanded | ultra-expanded | inherit
```

The order in which these properties condense text is as follows, with the most condensed being first:

- ❏ ultra-condensed
- ❏ extra-condensed
- ❏ condensed
- ❏ semi-condensed
- ❏ normal
- ❏ semi-expanded
- ❏ expanded
- ❏ extra-expanded
- ❏ ultra-expanded

Presumably when this property is supported, to set a rule, you can use it in the following way:

```
h1 {font-stretch: ultra-condensed}
```

CSS 2 only: font-size-adjust

The second property that CSS 2 supports, but hasn't yet been implemented in any major browser is font-size-adjust. This property has been introduced to aid legibility of fonts on some systems. This is because rather than the font-size property (which affects the y-axis) affecting legibility, it is the x-height that affects legibility, or a combination of the font-size and the x-height. These two values can be divided (font size divided by x-height) to produce what is termed an **aspect value** in the CSS 2 standard. The larger the aspect value of a font, the more likely it is to be legible at lower sizes.

For example, the CSS2 standard states that Verdana has an aspect value of 0.58 (when Verdana's font size is 100 units, its x-height is 58 units), while Times New Roman has an aspect value of 0.46, therefore Verdana will be more legible at smaller sizes than Times New Roman.

The `font-size-adjust` property takes the following values:

```
none | aspect value
```

The first property, none, indicates that the font's x-height should not be preserved, while the second refers to the aspect value of the first available font. The bigger the aspect value for a font, the more legible that font will be at small sizes.

Text Properties

We've looked at the CSS properties that can affect a font, but there are also a separate set that can be used to affect the text, regardless of which font is used. These properties are as follows:

- ❏ `word-spacing`
- ❏ `letter-spacing`
- ❏ `text-decoration`
- ❏ `text-transform`
- ❏ `text-indent`
- ❏ `text-align`
- ❏ `color`
- ❏ `line-height`
- ❏ `vertical-align`
- ❏ `justify`
- ❏ `text-shadow` (CSS 2 only)

Not all of these properties are supported correctly even by the version 6 browsers, and considerably less by the earlier browsers. We shall discuss anomalies as they arise. In addition, there are some non-standard properties supported by IE which are:

- ❏ `word-break`
- ❏ `word-wrap`
- ❏ `text-justify`
- ❏ `text-autospace`
- ❏ `text-kashida-space`
- ❏ `text-overflow`
- ❏ `text-underline-position`

We shall mention these properties where relevant.

327

word-spacing

The property word-spacing lets you define how wide the gap between words is. You can use numeric units or a percentage for the value or the value normal. You can actually set the numeric unit value to negative, although you will find this has the effect of making the text disappear in some cases, rather than overlap.

It can be defined as follows:

```
.Text1 { word-spacing: 50px }
```

Here we define a class, which will put 50 pixels between each word. When we put this in an example as follows:

```
<html>
<head>
    <title>Spacing example</title>
    <style type="text/css">
    <!--
        .Text1 { word-spacing: 50px }
        -->
    </style>
</head>
<body>
    <p class="text1">This is some well spaced out text</p>
</body>
</html>
```

It has the following effect on the text:

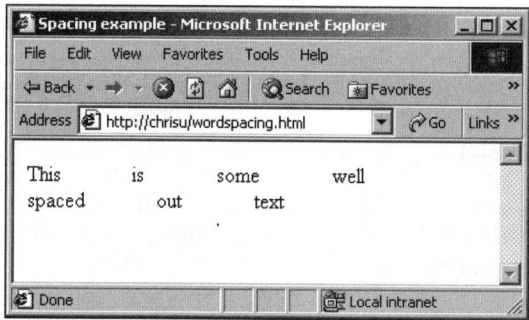

This property is supported in IE 6 and Opera 5. No version of Netscape supports it, and neither does IE 5.x.

There are a couple of IE-only properties that affect word-spacing. The word-break property in IE 5.5+ sets or retrieves line-breaking behavior within words. It can have the values normal, break-all, or keep-all. The break-all value allows arbitrary line breaks in non-Asian text, and is suited for largely Asian texts that also need to contain some non-Asian text. The keep-all value specifies that word breaking is not allowed for Chinese, Korean, and Japanese text, while keeping all other non-Asian languages the same.

The word-wrap property sets or retrieves whether wording should be broken if the text contents of a container overflow out of the container. It can be set to normal, to let it overflow, or break-word to start a new line.

letter-spacing

The property `letter-spacing` lets you define how wide the gap between letters is. Once again you can use numeric units or a percentage for the value.

It can be defined as follows:

```
.Text1 { letter-spacing: 50px }
```

If you change the last example and replace the style rule with the above, you get the following output:

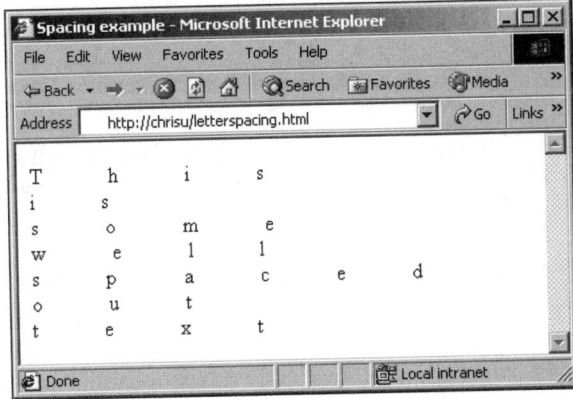

Once again, while this property is supported in IE 6 and Opera 5, no version of Netscape supports it; it is, however, supported in IE 5.5.

text-decoration

This property is used to add certain styles that alter the appearance of the text, such as underlining it or striking through it.

The following example would underline any text defined within the `<strong>` element:

```
strong { text-decoration:underline }
```

If viewed in a browser it would look like this:

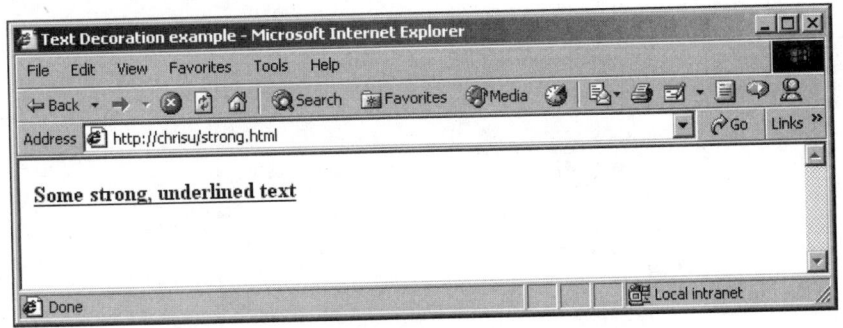

The following values can be used with `text-decoration`:

```
underline | overline | line-through | blink | none
```

The text-decoration property is intended for use in place of the deprecated `<s>` and `<u>` elements, and the totally non-standard `<blink>` element. This property works in all current major browsers and Netscape 4 also.

text-transform

This property makes text appear in either upper-case or lower-case, or it just capitalizes the first letter in each word.

It can take the following values:

```
capitalize | uppercase | lowercase | none
```

It performs a similar function to the `font-variant` property, but it will apply to all text, and not just text created in a particular font. The following example will render everything in the `<h1>` example in upper case:

```
<h1 style="text-transform:uppercase">everything in uppercase</h1>
```

text-indent

With this property you can define whether the first line of a multi-line passage of text is indented. The value for `text-indent` can be defined in numeric units, as a percentage, or as `inherit`.

If you wished to indent the first line of text in the `<span>` element by 7.5 millimeters, then you could do it as follows:

```
<html>
    <title>Indent example</title>
</head>
<body>
    <span style="text-indent:7.5mm">First line of text,</span>
    Second line of text.
    <br/>
    Third line of text.
</body>
</html>
```

This would be displayed as follows:

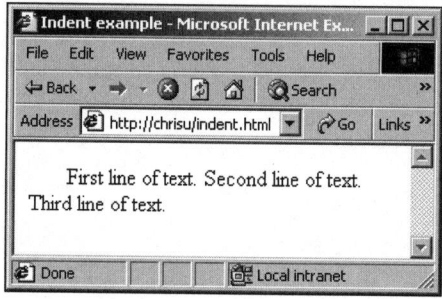

This property will work in all major browsers, Netscape 4 included.

Centering and Justifying Text

These properties are used to center and justify elements, or to align them on the right-hand or left-hand side.

❑ `text-align`

❑ `text-justify`: non-standard, supported only in IE

`text-align` was introduced in CSS 1, and should work for Netscape and IE. It can take the following values:

```
left | right | center | justify
```

The only value that requires any extra explanation is the `justify` value, which justifies (alters the spacing to stretch or squeeze the text into one line) the text.

If you wanted to justify the contents of the `<p>` and `<blockquote>` elements, you could set the `text-align` property as follows:

```
p,blockquote { text-align:right }
```

The `text-justify` property is proposed in IE and will only work if `text-align` is set to `justify`. It defines a further set of values that give the browser extra criteria when justifying the text. The possible values are:

```
auto | distribute | distribute-all-lines | distribute-center-last | inter-cluster
| inter-ideograph | interword | kashida | newspaper
```

Check the MSDN site at http://msdn.microsoft.com/workshop under the HTML/CSS reference for further details of these values.

color

This property will define the color of the text contained within an element. There are three ways to define the color of content in CSS: a color name (such as `white`), hexadecimal code (for example, `#FFFFFF`), or a RGB color definition (like `rgb 255,255,255`). We have discussed this in depth in the "*Colors*" section of Chapter 3, and refer the reader back there for further explanation.

You could specify that everything inside the `<b>` and `<i>` elements is to appear in red as follows, using this property:

```
b,i { color:red }
```

line-height

For elements with a lot of text, you can define the vertical height of a line of text with the `line-height` property. It can be set to a numerical unit, a percentage, or the values `normal` and `inherit`, both of which we have looked at earlier and work in the usual way.

This is quite a useful property when used in combination with `font-size`, and indeed it functions in much the same way.

If we wish to specify two pseudo-classes for the `<p>` element, one for large text, and one for small text, we could do it in the following way:

```
p.large { font-size:14pt; line-height:16pt; }
p.small { font-size:8pt; line-height:8pt; }
```

vertical-align

This only applies to inline elements or table cell elements. You can align neighboring elements with the property `vertical-align`. This is useful when you have, for example, an element with different font sizes, and you want them to line up at the same point. The values you can use for this property are:

```
top | middle | bottom | baseline | sub | super | text-top | text-bottom
```

The `baseline` value indicates that the text should be aligned with the bottom of the parent element's box, while the `text-bottom` indicates that text should be aligned to the bottom of the parent element's font and `text-top` indicates that the text should be aligned to the top of the parent element's font. The `sub` and `super` values are there to ensure that text is aligned with subscript or superscript. The other values should be self-explanatory.

This property comes in particularly useful when aligning elements within a table, as we are doing in the next example:

```
<html>
<head>
    <title>Vertical Align example</title>
</head>
<body>
<table border=1>
    <tr height="100">
        <td style="vertical-align:top">Table Cell top text</td>
        <td style="vertical-align:middle">Table Cell middle text</td>
        <td style="vertical-align:bottom">Table Cell bottom text</td>
    </tr>
</table>
</body>
</html>
```

Note that we've used the deprecated attribute `height` in the `<tr>` element, mainly because we haven't discussed yet how to achieve this with style sheets; we do so in the next chapter.

This will show up in the browser as follows:

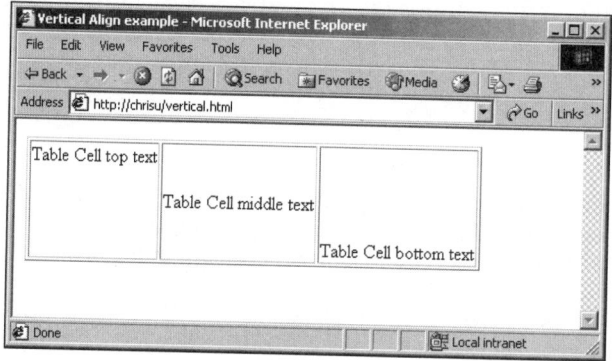

This property is supported in all of the major browsers.

CSS 2 only: text-shadow

The `text-shadow` property accepts a comma-delimited list of possible shadow effects, which can be applied to the text.

The accepted values in CSS 2 are:

```
none | inherit | color | length
```

Each shadow must specify a shadow offset, and optionally, a blur radius and color.
The way that the offset works is that you can specify two values, the first being the horizontal distance from the text for the length of the shadow, and the second value being the vertical distance from the text, again for the length of the shadow. After the offset values, you can also optionally add a blur radius to the series of values and also a color as well.

To specify one shadow with just an offset for the `<h1>` element, you could put it as follows:

```
h1 { text-shadow: 0.8em, 0.8em }
```

To specify a shadow with an offset and with a blur radius and a shadow color as well for the `<h1>` element, you could do the following:

```
h1 { text-shadow: 4px 4px 8px blue }
```

Note that this property is new to CSS 2 and isn't supported in any browser yet.

auto-space, kashida-space, text-overflow, and underline-position

The `text-autospace` (sets or retrieves the auto-spacing of text), `text-kashida-space` (sets or retrieves the kashida or whitespace expansion when performing justification), `text-overflow` (indicates whether ellipses are displayed when text overflows), and `text-underline-position` (sets or retrieves the underline position of the text) are all new and proposed introductions to the IE 6 browser. As they are not supported outside IE 6, and certainly do not form part of the CSS 2 standards, we won't be discussing them further. You can find more details of them at the MSDN site at:

http://msdn.microsoft.com/workshop/c-frame.htm?/workshop/author/default.asp.

Go to CSS, then the CSS Attribute reference, using the Table of Contents.

Classification Properties

HTML has different **display types** for elements. In the first version of the Cascading Style Sheets standards (CSS 1), the main types were **inline, block,** and **list** item elements (as discussed in Chapters 2 and 3). By default, each element was meant to be one of these types. For example, a paragraph (`<p>`) is a block element, while a link (`<a>`) is an inline element. This display type would provide implicit information to the browser on how to display a particular element, such as with a line break or without. However, in practice, these three definitions didn't prove wide enough, and so in CSS 2, further definitions were introduced, such as the following, for tables: **table, inline table, table-row, table-row-group, table-header-group, table-footer-group, table-column, table-column-group, table-cell,** and **table-caption**. We look at all of these in the next chapter.

Also, CSS 2 introduced the types **compact, run-in**, and **marker** as well. Defining elements as either compact or run-in can lead to a rather complex set of considerations being taken into account when elements are rendered by the browser, because basically they let an element be defined as either being inline or block, depending upon the context it is used within. For example, you might have a run-in element before or after a pseudo-element; in which case, the size of the compact or run-in element will be taken into account when the browser calculates the size of the pseudo-element. In practice, these rather complex properties aren't yet supported by any current browsers. The last element, marker, defines content generated before or after a box as being an inline element. Once again, it isn't supported in any browsers yet, so we won't be considering this any further either.

With CSS though, your style sheet can redefine the display types of an element and make it act like a different type of element. For example, you could make a paragraph into an inline element (regardless of whether you would ever need to).

There is a set of properties that are supported in current browsers that take advantage of the characteristics of an element type – they are as follows:

- ❏ display
- ❏ white-space
- ❏ visibility
- ❏ clip (see Chapter 13)
- ❏ overflow (see Chapter 13)
- ❏ list-style-type (see Chapter 13)
- ❏ list-style-image (see Chapter 13)
- ❏ list-style-position (see Chapter 13)
- ❏ list-style (see Chapter 13)
- ❏ position (see Chapter 13)
- ❏ float (see Chapter 13)
- ❏ clear (see Chapter 13)

display

The display property determines the display type of an element. CSS 1 defines the following four values for display:

- ❏ block: Shows the element as a block level element, with a line break following it.
- ❏ inline: Shows the element inside text; will not result in a line break.
- ❏ list-item: Like a block element but displayed with a bullet.
- ❏ none: The element is not displayed, and no space is reserved on the page.

While the theoretical default value of display is block, browsers essentially treat an element as having the recommended display type if no display type is specified. Also, slightly unusually, an element won't inherit the display value of its parent. You will find that some browsers are permitted to ignore the display property altogether, the major ones being Netscape 6 and Opera 4. Also, the IE 6 public preview had problems rendering occasional elements with this property set.

CSS 2 introduced several new `display` values for tables, which are listed above. In CSS 2, any element (say a paragraph) can be a table, or part of a table. This isn't so useful for the average web designer, since HTML already has enough table elements, but will be very useful for other languages like XML, which do not have set elements. In those languages, CSS tables are an absolute necessity for displaying table data.

CSS 2 also introduced the new element types, `run-in` and `compact`. They are called **dual-mode** elements because the elements are either inline or block, depending on the content they contain. This will then enable particular properties to be used, properties that can only be used with the block-level elements for example. They have associated display types that we discussed earlier. However, once again, none of the major browsers support these properly, so we won't be looking at them in any more detail here.

Instead, we'll look at a quick example that utilizes some of the CSS 1 display properties. You can do a neat hiding trick with the `none` value – a displayed element with the value of `none` takes up no space on a page, as opposed to the `visibility` property, which does. This will be of use when we come to use scripting, and can dynamically reveal elements in response to mouse events – useful in examples such as a dynamic pop-up menu. We discuss scripting further in Chapters 9 and 19.

In the following example, you don't see the word content, but you do see the headline as an inline element to the right of the word text:

```
<html>
<head>
    <title>Display</title>
</head>
<body>
    <p id="Dynamicparagraph" style="display:none">content</p>
    text
    <h1 style="display:inline">Headline</h1>
    text
</body>
</html>
```

When viewed in a browser it looks like this:

The text "content" has the `display` property set to `none`, and so is completely invisible here.

visibility

visibility lets you create elements and hide them on the web page. The usefulness is of this feature again is only realized in combination with scripting. However, the difference between visibility and the display properties (as we also discussed above) is that the hidden element will still take up space on a page even when it is not displayed if you use the visibility property. This functionality is still useful, as you can use it to define text, elements, objects, or blocks that will show up after you click a button, without displacing other text, such as in a quiz with hidden answers.

The values you can use are as follows:

- ❑ hidden: the content of an element is hidden

- ❑ visible: the content of an element is visible

- ❑ inherit: the visibility setting is inherited from the element's parent (this is the default)

- ❑ collapse: this only applies when used in table rows, and can be used to collapse items within the table, to hide them. Otherwise, when used elsewhere it will have the same effect as hidden.

In the following example, you can see text 1 but not the other two:

```
<html>
<head>
    <title>Visibility example</title>
    <style type="text/css">
    <!--
        .Text1 { position:absolute; top:100px; left:50px; width:200px;
visibility:visible; }
        .Text2 { position:absolute; top:150px; left:50px; width:200px;
visibility:hidden; }
        .Text3 { position:absolute; top:200px; left:50px; width:200px;
visibility:hidden; }
    -->
    </style>
</head>
<body>
    <div class="Text1">This is text 1</div>
    <div class="Text2"> This is text 2</div>
    <div class="Text3"> This is text 3</div>
</body>
</html>
```

If you view this in a browser you will see only the following:

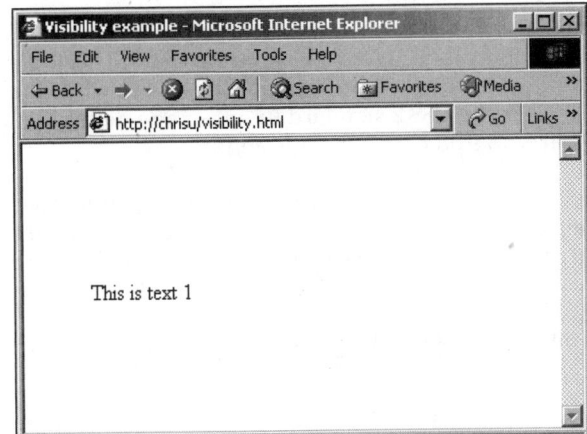

Note that while this example will work in all current browsers, and also in Netscape 4, there is a slight anomaly being exploited here. While with current browsers, you don't have to explicitly position an element to be able to use the visibility property, you will find that this **is** the case within Netscape 4. This is a good point to bear in mind if you want your page to work correctly in all browsers that support style sheets.

white-space

The white-space property indicates how whitespace should be handled within an element (we looked at the concept of whitespace in detail in Chapter 3). The white-space property applies only to block elements, and specifies what should be done with extraneous whitespace by the browser (such as tabs, returns, extra spaces, and so on).

The underlying consideration is that whitespace should not affect the appearance of a web page; rather, browsers should ignore returns and tabs, and collapse more than one space to a single space for display purposes. With the white-space property, you can specify exactly how the browser in fact handles the whitespace.

The allowed values for white-space in CSS 2 are:

```
normal | pre | nowrap | inherit
```

A value of normal means that whitespace will be handled in the traditional manner. Any tabs, returns and extraneous spacing will be ignored.

A value of pre keeps all whitespace as it appears in the element. This is the equivalent to the HTML tag <pre>. Essentially, the element is treated as being preformatted.

A value of nowrap means that the contents of the element will only wrap (break to a new line) when an explicit line break (<br />) is in the contents. The content of the element will not wrap to a new line simply because the line does not fit in the page horizontally.

If no white-space value is specified, the whitespace of an element is normal. An element **does** inherit the white-space value of its parent element, so by default the setting is inherit. This property is supported in all current major browsers.

Summary

This chapter has been font heavy! We have learned not only how to define fonts but how to tell your page where to find the fonts it needs for a page using a style sheet. We tackled the two competing definitions for downloadable fonts and concluded that while the `.eot` format is the only one that can be used with the CSS 2 standard `@font-face` definition, the `.pfr` format is currently the only one that works on both Netscape and IE.

We have has also covered all sorts of text properties that take using the font several steps further, from formatting for manipulating characters themselves, to how a line of text should look. We also looked at some of the classification properties that handle how the display type of different elements is handled with style sheets, and we looked at how the visibility of different elements can be set.

In the next chapter, we will look at how elements are positioned and packaged when using style sheets.

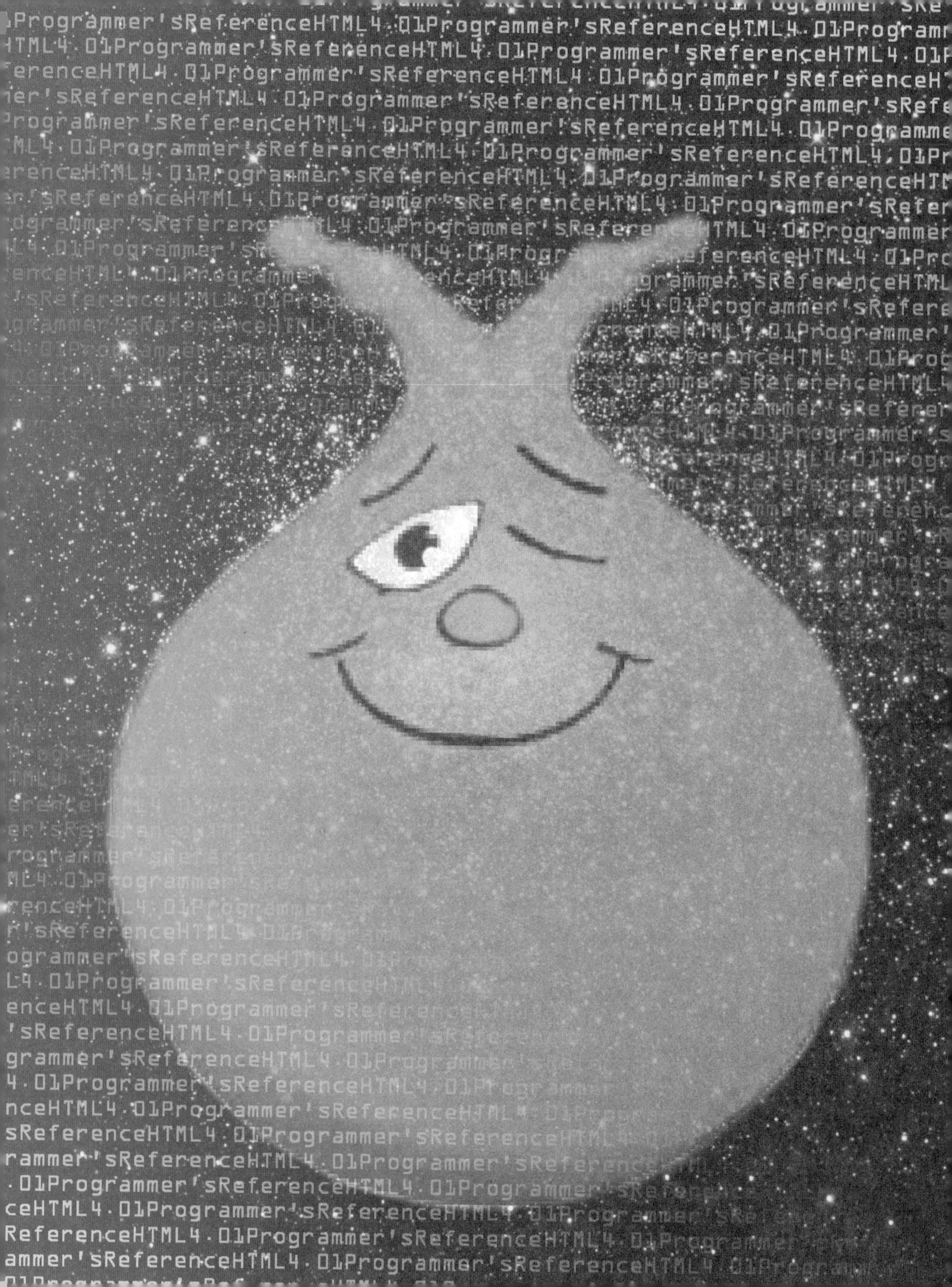
Programmer'sReferenceHTML4.01

13

CSS Positioning and Packaging

This chapter discusses the CSS properties we can use to style both inline and block elements in HTML. These styles include padding, borders, and margins as well as positioning of the element on a web page.

As a reminder, block elements are elements that cause a line break before their opening tag and after their closing tag, that is; a new block element will start on a new line. Inline elements do not cause such a break before their closing and opening tags and more than one can appear on a single line.

The topics this chapter covers can be broken down into the following:

❑ The Box Model

❑ Padding

❑ Borders

❑ Margins

❑ Positioning of elements

❑ Width and height of elements

❑ Styling lists

❑ Styling tables

This chapter will show some useful functions that all have one drawback: In the real world, not every browser supports every property for every element and if a browser does support a particular property, it may support it differently from another browser.

This chapter will focus on examples using the browsers: Internet Explorer 5.0 (IE 5), Netscape 6.01 (N 6), and Opera 5.11 (Opera 5), as used on Windows 98 (or Macintosh 9.1 where noted). We won't go into major detail about every browser available as it's beyond the scope of this chapter (it would be a whole book in itself!). Likewise, we will not review browsers that have not yet been officially released such as the Preview Edition of Internet Explorer 6.0. Although we can expect such browsers to be capable of at least what their predecessors were, there is no guarantee.

Be sure to check Appendix F, which summarizes property support in the most commonly used browsers.

> **Remember: The only way to be certain is to test your code in the browsers your target audience uses!**

Now that we have the disclaimers out of the way, let's start with some basic ideas!

The Box Model

As we've discussed in earlier chapters, HTML 4.01 has two main types of elements:

❑ **Block** elements: These include <p>, <div>, the headings <h1>...<h6>, <blockquote>, <pre>, <table>, and of course, the ubiquitous <body>

❑ **Inline** elements: These include <span>, <em>, <a>, etc.

There are also elements that do not clearly fall into either category. They cannot appear by themselves but must be used with their designated parent elements (which are themselves block elements).

❑ **Other** elements: These include <li>, <caption>, <th>, <tr>, and <td>

We can use CSS properties to set margins and borders and padding in any of these types of elements. To understand the principle behind how these formats work, we need to introduce what is known as the Box Model. To better understand this model, visualize a large box with smaller boxes that fit inside it. The center-most box is where the content is.

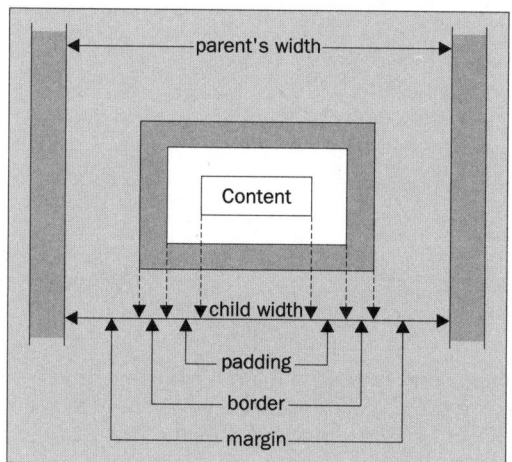

Each aspect of the space around the content (text for example) can be visualized as a box nested inside another box. The space between the boxes and the thickness of the boxes themselves can be set with certain properties. The properties we will discuss in this chapter include `padding`, `border`, and `margin`. There are also other properties that we can use to position the content in the box, as well as to position the box on the browser page.

To begin with, let's take the example of a `<p>` element. The text contained in `<p></p>` tags takes up a certain amount of space in the **content** box. The edges of this box are the exact edges of the highest and lowest characters as well as the edges of the leftmost and rightmost characters in the text; a tight-fitting box.

The content box is inside the **padding**. Padding is just what it sounds like. It is the cushioning space between the content and any borders we may have around that content. If the padding is set to '0', then there is no padding and the content box fits exactly inside the **border** box.

We can do a number of things to improve the border box; use different line styles for example, which we'll discuss later in the chapter, as well as using different widths and colors. If the border width is set to '0', then it collapses into the padding area and takes up no space.

Outside the border box is the **margin** box. The margin is the distance between the outer edge of the border of the element, and the inside edge of its parent element, even if the parent element is the `<body>` element.

Also, we are not restricted to having only one box in another at a time. We can have a list, which consists of several smaller boxes side-by-side, or a table with different sized boxes arranged inside the larger table box.

Packaging Our Content

So now what we have are all these boxes, which are plain and boring, and with sizes that could fit a bit better. Let's alter them to be appropriate to the contents contained, by making sure the boxes are not packed too tightly in each other (by ensuring that there is enough 'packing material'), and that the box decoration is suitable. This will make it much easier for the browser to convey our content to the user. This diagram shows how the padding, border, and margin fit around the content

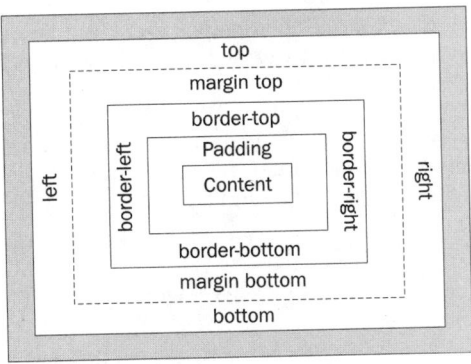

Let's start by making sure our content is packed properly inside the innermost box. First we need to figure out how much to pad our goods.

Padding: The Packing Material

Our first box can contain different types of content. The content can be contained in any type of element, whether block or inline, regardless of whether it is text or an image. Images will take up as much space as we let them. Text, as we discussed in the previous chapter, takes up a certain amount of space, depending on a number of characteristics such as: font family, size, weight, height, and decoration. In order for the text to be legible on a visual browser, there needs to be clear space around the words. Otherwise it can be difficult for users to read. Padding solves this problem.

Padding is therefore, the gap between the border of an element and the outer edge of the content. It is the stuffing that keeps the content from being squashed by the border box. We control how much padding is placed next to each side of the content.

Padding properties

Below are the four explicit padding properties, and the shorthand property:

❑ `padding-top`

❑ `padding-right`

❑ `padding-bottom`

❑ `padding-left`

❑ `padding` (the shorthand property)

> *The values for shorthand properties always start at the top and work clockwise to the right, then bottom, and then to the left. If we specify four values this will set all four sides individually. If we specify three values, then the top will be set with the first value, left and right with second value, and finally bottom with third value. If we specify two values, the first will set the top and bottom, and the second will set the right and left. If we only specify one value, all four sides will be the same. This shorthand pattern is reused in the other shorthand properties.*

The supported values are:

```
length       percentage       inherit
```

Where `length` is measured in pixels (px), points (pt), picas (pc), millimeters (mm), inches (in), etc. (See Chapter 11). The percentage is determined by the relationship to parent element.

The default for padding is '0', that is: *no* padding. We cannot use negative values, as our content can't be packed in anything less than nothing! Padding can be used on both inline and block-level elements, but elements do not inherit padding from their parent elements. For example, this code snippet gives some content 5mm of padding, (and a border to show where the padding ends):

```
<p style="border:thin solid; padding:5mm;">
   This a paragraph element with 5mm of padding inside a border box.
</p>
```

Here is how the code above looks in IE 5, N 6, and Opera 5.11 on Windows:

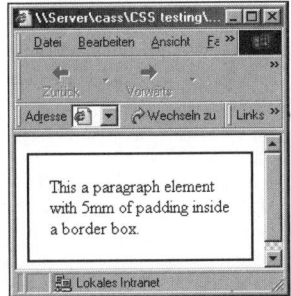 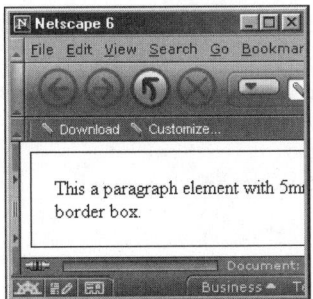 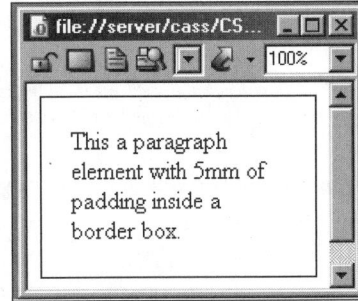

There are browser differences that we need to take into account. The previous screenshots demonstrate this. If the user resizes a window, IE 5 realigns the text and border while keeping the padding. N 6 realigns the text only to a certain point, after which, making the window smaller will only cut the box off. Opera 5.11 acts more or less like IE 5.

The same code in Opera 5 on a Macintosh results in a box that will only let you resize the window to a certain point before cutting the text off.

Borders: The First Box

Finally, we get to the box, which holds the content. There are all sorts of ways we can define how this box should look. We want it to be nicely designed to enhance our content. These designs are created with border properties.

To make these border properties work, we need to take into account the following aspects of design: the width of the border, the style of the border, and the color of the border. A characteristic of all border properties is that we can use them on inline, block, and the other elements mentioned at the beginning of the chapter. None of the properties are inherited by their child elements.

Border Width

The thickness of the wall of a box gives it its stability. We can define the width of a border for all four sides together, or for each side separately.

As with all other border properties, we can set `border-width` on both inline and block level elements. This property isn't inherited by child elements either, and has a default of '0'.

Properties

❑ `border-top-width`

❑ `border-right-width`

❑ `border-bottom-width`

❑ `border-left-width`

❑ `border-width` (The 'shorthand' property, this follows the same pattern as for the `padding` property.)

The supported values are:

```
thin        medium        thick        length
```

Some browsers have problems if we try to set a style for a single side of a box. Setting the `border-width` *shorthand property value for the whole box and then setting the property value for a single side helps.*

Here is a code example showing how borders are displayed:

```html
<html>
  <head>
    <style type="text/css">
    h1,h2,h3 { border:hidden; border-top-width:thin;
             border-top-style:solid; }
    body     { border:solid 2mm; border-top-width:5mm;
             border-top-style:groove; }
    </style>
  </head>
  <body>
    <br />
    <h1>Setting Borders</h1>
    <p>The body has a solid 2mm border on three sides. The top is
    grooved and 5mm thick. The heading also has a thin border but
    only visible on top.</p>
  </body>
</html>
```

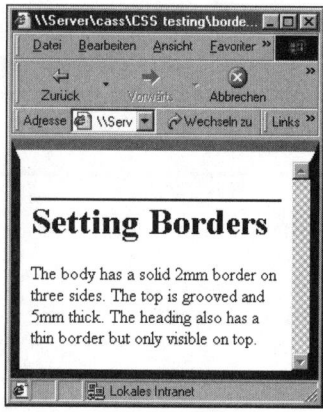 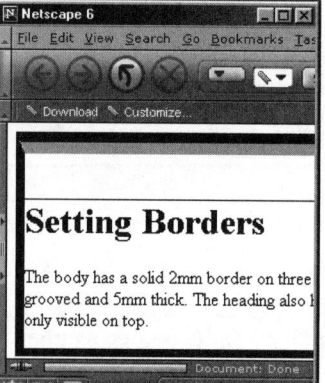 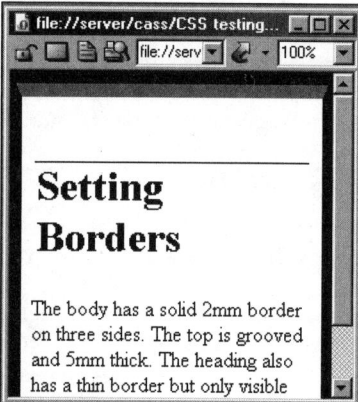

The above screenshots are quite interesting. IE 5 on the left does not show the upper border in the same way as the other two browsers because it has problem with the `groove` value for `border-top-style` (this is the same in all versions of IE 4.0 and above). In addition, it has given the screen a scrollbar, not on the outside of the body border but on the inside. No padding has been set in the code, yet IE 5 and Opera 5 both have space between the heading and text parts and the body border. N 6 does not put this padding in.

Border Color

We can define the color of the border if we use the property border-color. As with all border properties, we can use border-color on both inline and block-level elements. The default is the color value of the element itself (which will normally be black). This property is also not inherited by the child elements.We can even give each side of the border box a different color using the following properties:

Properties

- border-top-color
- border-right-color
- border-bottom-color
- border-left-color
- border-color (The shorthand property. This uses the same pattern as the padding shorthand.)

Supported values:

> color (See Chapter 11 and Appendix D)

This is an example code segment, which sets the border box to a very thick light blue:

```
<div style="border-width:1cm; border-style:solid;
       border- color:#99CCFF;">text</div>
```

Border Style

How fancy do we want our box to be? With the property border-style, we can define a plain box or one with a bit of flair. There are different styles we can choose from, and we can also set each side of the box separately.

As with all border properties, we can use border-style on both inline and block-level elements. This property is also not inherited by the child elements. The default value is 'none'.

Properties

- border-top-style
- border-right-style
- border-bottom-style
- border-left-style
- border-style (The shorthand property. This follows the same pattern as the padding shorthand property.)

The supported values are:

```
hidden     dotted     dashed      solid
groove     ridge      inset       outset
double     none (No style or invisible border - default.)
```

Internet Explorer has problems with, `groove`, `ridge`, `inset`, and `outset` and does not support `hidden` at all. As of IE 5.5, this property applies to inline elements. With older versions of IE, inline elements must have an absolute `position` or layout to use this property. Element layout is set, by providing a value for the `height` property, or the `width` property.

This code segment produces examples of all the different borders:

```
<p>
  <span style="border:hidden 5px;padding: 3px;">hidden</span>
  <span style="border:dotted 5px;padding: 3px;">dotted</span>
  <span style="border:dashed 5px;padding: 3px;">dashed</span>
  <span style="border:solid 5px;padding: 3px;">solid</span>
  <span style="border:groove 5px;padding: 3px;">groove</span>
  <span style="border:ridge 5px;padding: 3px;">ridge</span>
  <span style="border:inset 5px;padding: 3px;">inset</span>
  <span style="border:outset 5px;padding: 3px;">outset</span>
  <span style="border:double 5px;padding: 3px;">double</span>
</p>
```

This is the result shown in Netscape 6:

Border Shorthand

The `border` property lets us defines all three basic 'border' properties at the same time. The `border` property takes a space-separated list of three values that denote the `border-width`, `border-style`, and `border-color`. These apply to all four sides of the border.

Properties

❑ `border-top`

❑ `border-right`

❑ `border-left`

❑ `border-bottom`

❑ `border`

Here is a code segment using the `border` property:

```
<p style="border:thick inset rgb(192,192,255);">text</p>
```

Margins: More Packing Material

Margins are very much like padding, they just happen to be outside of the box in the gap between the inner box and the next box if there is one. If there are no margins then boxes next to each other will touch (with some browser-specific exceptions). If we are only dealing with a single box, the margin is the space between the box and the next element.

Margins

Margin properties cannot be inherited from parent elements, and their default values are '0'.

Properties

❑ `margin-top`

❑ `margin-right`

❑ `margin-right`

❑ `margin-bottom`

❑ `margin` (The shorthand property. This follows the same pattern as for the padding shorthand property.)

Supported Values:

    auto   length   percentage

Where `auto` depends on the values of other properties, and `percentage` is relative to the total width of the contained element and inside width of the containing element.

> Margins do support negative values, which can allow overlapping of elements, but due to inconsistent browser support, this needs to be tested thoroughly.
>
> Margins don't work for internal table elements except: table captions and the table element itself. Therefore this property set is not in the later tables section.

Here is the code example from the earlier section on border width, with a specific margin added to the `<h1>` element:

```
<html>
  <head>
    <style type="text/css">
      h1,h2,h3 { border:hidden; border-top-width:thin;
               border-top-style:solid; margin: 40px; }
      body     { border:solid 2mm; border-top-width:5mm;
               border-top-style:groove; }
    </style>
  </head>
  <body>
    <br>
    <h1>Setting Margins</h1>
    <p>This is the same code as we saw in a border example,
       except the &lt;h1&gt; has a margin of 40px giving it
       space between it and the body element.
    </p>
  </body>
</html>
```

349

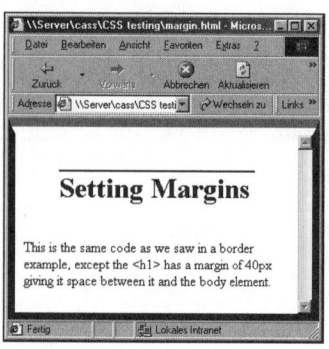 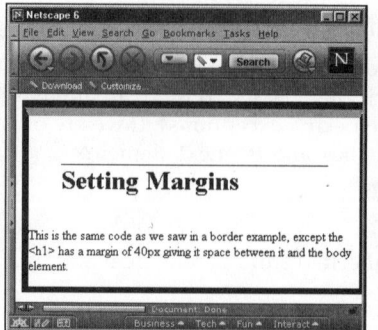 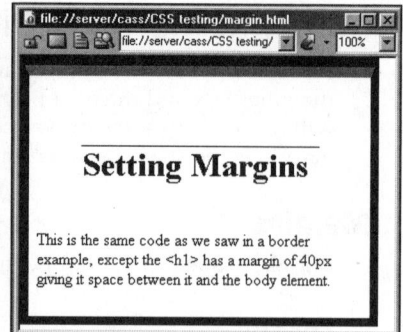

In the above screenshots we see the same behavior as in the border width example, but with a margin around the header.

Margin Collapse

What if we have two elements with margins defined, but both are contained in the same parent element and touch margins? In general, if these elements are stacked vertically, for example in a list, the bottom margin of the upper element and the top margin of the bottom element collapse. The margin, in this case, would be the larger value of the two. This collapse does not occur if the elements are placed horizontally next to each other.

Margins between floated or positioned elements and any other element do not collapse.

Width and Height of Elements

Sometimes it is not so obvious what size of box and how much packing material the content actually occupies. We can calculate this by adding up how much space all the individual properties take up.

Positioning Elements

When we continue with the packing box analogy, we now get to the point where we want to place our decorated boxes full of content in just the right position in the display case. Web designers pride themselves in creating pages, with all the elements positioned and styled in such a way that the content is not only accessible but also aesthetically pleasing. Using HTML exclusively to do this is possible, but needs lots of little tricks, often including use of the famous transparent GIF and liberal use of non-reusable <div> elements and tables. These tricks make it hard for non-visual browsers, which have to wade through all sorts of unnecessary tables and unidentifiable images. Giving us alternatives to the tricks is one important goal of CSS.

In CSS 2, there are properties that allow the exact positioning of an element in a browser window (as long as the browser supports them). These properties include those for absolute and relative positioning, the amount of space the content of an of element takes, text flow around elements, the overlapping of elements, and more.

One property, z-index, takes advantage of the *idea* of layers (not to be confused with Netscape's <layer> element or IE's <iframe> element).

Positioning is not inherited in general, though the children of containing elements, such as <div> default to what their parent does.

We can define an element position in three ways (other than using HTML). Using the property, `position`, we can give an element either a relative, absolute, or fixed position. Adding the properties: `top`, `right`, `bottom`, and `left` or a combination thereof, lets us further define the exact relationship that one element has to its containing element.

Properties

❑ `position`

The supported values are:

```
static      relative      absolute      fixed
```

Where `static` (Default) makes the element a normal box that simply goes along with the flow of the document. Properties such as `top` and `bottom`, `right` and `left` have no effect here. `relative` causes the position of a box to be first determined by the normal flow of the page. Then the box is shifted relative to the size of the screen. When a box is positioned relatively, the position of the following box moves into the space normally taken by the relatively positioned box, even if the view of the next element may be obstructed. `absolute` positioned boxes are taken out of the normal flow of the page. This means they have no affect on the layout of elements that come later. In addition, their margins don't collapse with any other margins. With `fixed`, the position of the box is calculated the same way as with the `absolute` value, but so that the box is fixed with respect to one or more sides of the screen and will not move even when the screen is scrolled.

An element is considered *positioned* if its `position` property has a value other than `static`. Of course, a static element has a 'position' but it is determined by the flow of the other elements around it on the page, rather than by direct manipulation.

Positioned elements generate positioned boxes, laid out on a web page according to a possible combination of four properties: `top`, `right`, `bottom`, and `left`. It is like being able to determine exactly where the boxes should be placed on a display table relative to other boxes also on display. These placement properties can be used with all elements (except elements that receive their content dynamically, from databases for example), but are not inherited.

Properties

❑ `top`: This specifies how far the top edge of a box is positioned in relation to the top edge of the box's parent element. We can use negative values, thereby placing a box above the top edge of the parent element – this principle goes for the other three properties as well.

❑ `right`: This specifies how far the right edge of a box is positioned to the left of the right edge of the box's parent element.

❑ `bottom`: This specifies how far the bottom edge of a box is positioned above the bottom of the box's parent element.

❑ `left`: This specifies how far the left edge of a box is positioned to the right of the left edge of the box's parent element.

There is no shorthand property for this.

The supported values are:

```
length          percentage          auto
```

Where percentage is relative to the width of the containing element, even if it is only the <body> element. The value of auto depends on which related properties also have the value auto.

This code snippet shows how to position a <div> relatively.

```
<div style="position:relative; top:100px;">
  <img src="smiley1.gif" />
</div>
```

Layering Elements (z-index)

The layers that make up our document do not have to be lined up one after the other. We can place elements on top of each other in a particular order. This can result in interesting effects, which otherwise would need to be done with graphics. For this we use the z-index property. Using numbers, either positive or negative, we determine how the elements are stacked on top of each other. The lowest number indicates which layer is on the bottom of the stack, that is, furthest back into the background of the page.

We can use z-index with both inline and block elements, but must take care that using it to style inline elements makes sense.

The following code segment defines the styles and the stacking order of three classes used in <div> elements in the body:

```
<head>
  <style type="text/css">
        body { background-color:#663366 }
        .layer1 { font-family:monospace; font-size:190pt;
                  font-weight:900; color:#AA0000; z-index:1;
                  position:absolute; left:-100px; top:-120px }
        .layer2 { font-family:monospace; font-size:24pt;
                  font-weight:500; color:#999999; z-index:3;
                  position:absolute; left:40px; top:80px }
        .layer3 { font-family:monospace; font-size:100pt;
                  font-weight:300; color:#BB0000; z-index:2;
                  position:absolute; left:-20px; top:0px }
  </style>
</head>
<body>
  <div class="layer1">Position</div>
  <div class="layer3">Position</div>
  <div class="layer2">
    <ul>
      <li>Projects:</li>
      <li>Keywords:</li>
      <li>Link Lists:</li>
    </ul>
  </div>
</body>
</html>
```

This is how the code above looks in IE 5 for Macintosh:

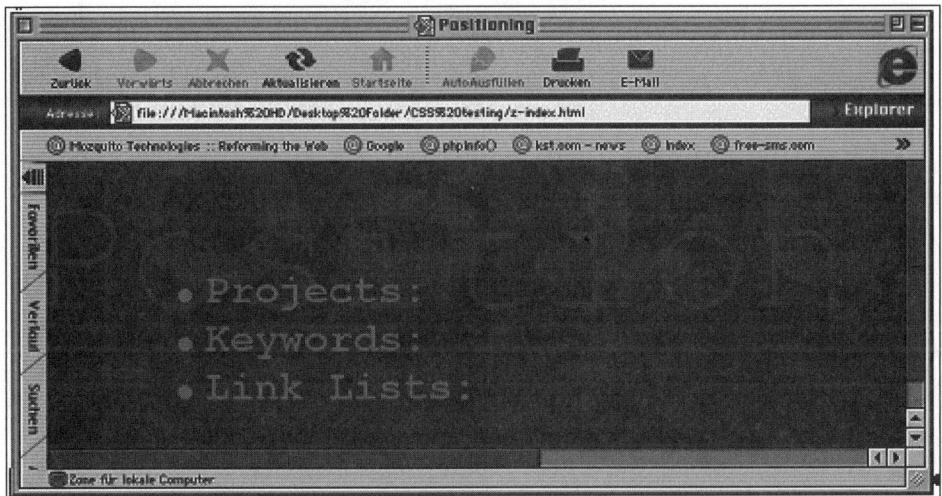

clip

Now that we've positioned the display of an element where we want, we can determine whether our user gets to see the whole thing or just a part. It's like having our box partially closed. With the CSS 2 property `clip`, we can specify the part of an element that should be visible, and the rest of this element is clipped to this rectangle. It is like Netscape's proprietary `clip` attribute.

This property is not inherited and applies to block elements. It is currently supported in IE 4 and higher for Windows and IE 5 for Macintosh, as well as N 4 and higher.

The supported values are:

```
rect()        auto
```

`rect()` takes the four edge values of the rectangle inside the parentheses ('top', 'right', 'bottom', and 'left'). These values refer to how far away they are from the inside edge of the element box, that is, these are all box internal references. The values set with `length`. `auto` let the browser display the entire contents of the element.

Do not use incorrect/illogical values for rect(), for example, a top value of 60px and a bottom value of 60px when the image is only 100px high. This would give a negative value of –20 for the height of the image. This will confuse the browser and will most likely cause everything but the background of the page to disappear, especially in N 6. In addition, instead of a value of 0px, the value should be set to auto. (This tip targets IE because auto is not supported in N 4.)

```
<html>
  <head>
    <style type="text/css">
          .cliptext { position:absolute; top:150px; left:150px;
                      width:150px; height:150px;
                      color:yellow; background-color:blue;
                      clip:rect(25px 125px 125px 25px); }
```

```
                  .clipimage { position:absolute; top:165px; left:15px;
                              clip:rect(10px 60px auto 10px); }
         </style>
    </head>
    <body>
      <div>
        This is the original image, which is sized at 100px/100px.
      </div>
      <div>
        <img src="smiley1.gif" height="100" width="100">
      </div>
      <div>The clipped image below has lost 10px off the top,
           60px off the right side, none off the bottom and 10 off
           the left side.
      </div>
      <div class="clipimage">
          <img src="smiley1.gif" height="100" width="100">
      </div>
      <div class="cliptext">
        This text is yellow on a blue square, but it's getting cut
        off by clipping.
      </div>
    </body>
  </html>
```

These are the results viewed in IE 5 and Netscape 6:

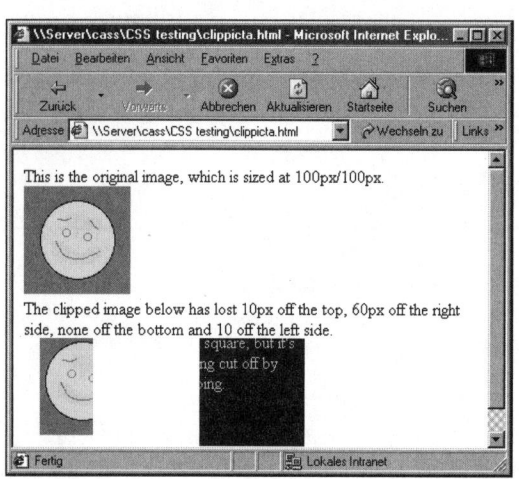
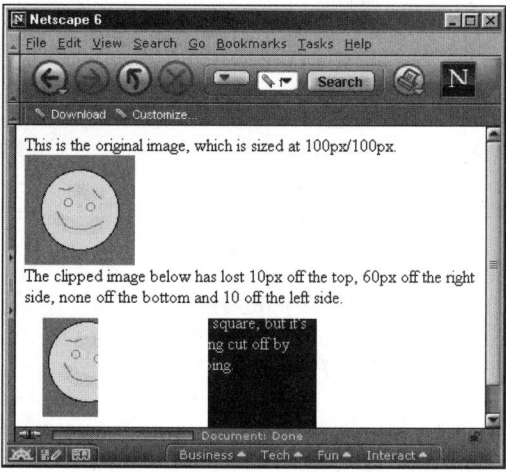

width and height

The width and height of certain elements can be manipulated with the width and height properties. These properties are not to be confused width and height values calculated by adding up the space different styles on an element take up. These properties do not apply to inline elements (whose width is the physical width of their content), but they do apply to block properties and to what are called replaced elements.

Replaced elements, are elements for which a browser knows only intrinsic dimensions. These replaced elements include `<img>`, `<input>`, `<textarea>`, `<select>`, and `<object>`. Basically, the browser sees replaced elements as containers for external files that need a certain amount of screen space. The space can be set with width and height.

`width` and `height` cannot use negative numbers and are not inherited.

The supported values are:

```
length       percentage      auto
```

`length` takes a positive number for a fixed absolute dimension. The value of `percentage` is a positive number relative to the parent element. `auto` (the default), is an element's intrinsic width or height, that is, the width or height of the element itself, for example the width and height of an image.

This code example exemplifies setting the dimensions of both an image as well as a block of box:

```
<html>
  <head>
  </head>
  <body>
    <div style="position:absolute; top:10%; left:10%;">
      <img src="smiley1.gif" style="height:150px; width:75px" />
    </div>
    <div style="position:absolute; top:10%; left:40%;">
      <img src="smiley1.gif" style="height:75px; width:150px" />
    </div>
    <div style="position:absolute; top:20px; left: 100px;
        width: 150px; height: 150px;">
      You can pretend to be serious, but you can't pretend to
      be witty. - Sacha Guitry (1885-1946)
    </div>
  </body>
</html>
```

Here is what it looks like in IE 5, N 6, and Opera 5 for Windows:

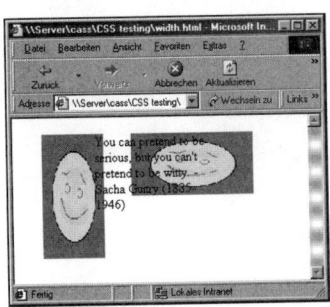 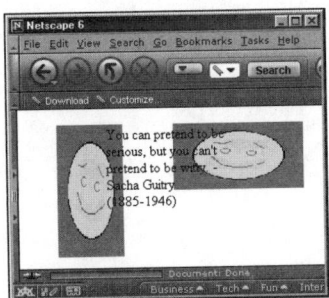 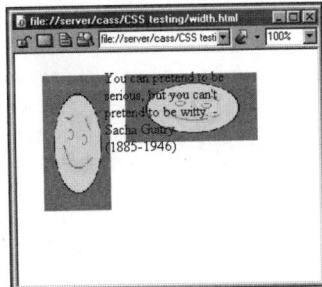

To expand on this topic, CSS 2 also has the properties: `min-width`, `max-width`, `min-height`, and `max-height`, which allow us to set the minimum and/or maximum element dimensions with numeric values and percentages. N 6 and Opera 5 support these properties, but IE does not.

float

float lets us wrap text around an element similarly to HTMLs's `align="left"` and `align="right"`, except we can float any element. It's a bit like using Styrofoam peanuts in a packing box. Certain objects float to the top. In this case, elements float to the side of the box. Floating objects is basically putting them in the margin of the following element.

float works with all elements (unless they are positioned or generated content).

The supported values are:

    left   right   none   inherit

Where `left` puts the element into the left margin of the following element, and `right` puts the element into the right margin of the following element. When `none` is used the elements behave as usual, following each other linearly.

This is a code example using `float`, followed by screenshots of `float` in action in IE 5, N 6, and Opera 5:

```
<html>
  <head>
  </head>
  <body>
    <div style="float:left; width:100px;">
      <img src="smiley1.gif"/>
    </div>
    <p>Even if you are on the right track, you will get run
       over if your just sit there. - Will Rogers</p>
    <br />
    <div style="float:right; width:100px;">
      <img src="smiley1.gif" />
    </div>
    <p>He was the world's only armless sculptor. He put
       the chisel in his mouth and his wife hit him on the back
       of the head with a mallet. - Fred Allen</p>
    <br />
    <div style="float:none; width:100px;">
      <img src="smiley1.gif" />
    </div>
    <p>It's a rare person who wants to hear what he doesn't
       want to here. - Dick Cavett</p>
  </body>
</html>
```

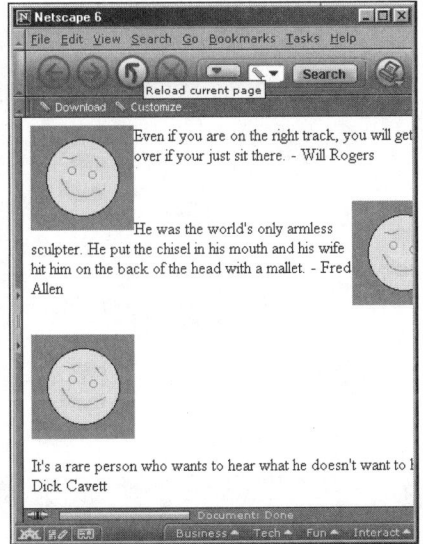

In the screenshots above, IE 5 and N 6 don't quite manage to make use of the `<br>` tag.

clear

The property `clear` is used to prevent the floating action we discussed in the previous section. `clear` applies to the "following" object. The previous object is still marked as `float` but the current element doesn't float around it. `clear` only works with block level elements and is not inherited.

The supported values are:

```
left        right        both        none
```

If `float:left` is defined on an element earlier in the source, the clear element content is displayed after the floating element. If `float:right` is defined on an element earlier in the source, the clear element content is displayed after the floating element. With `both`, the content of the cleared element is displayed after the floating element regardless of which side the float is. The value of `none` allows floating on either side.

This code example is very similar to the one in the `float` section. `clear` has been added to the `<p>` elements.

```
<html>
  <head>
  </head>
  <body>
    <div style="float:left; width:100px;">
      <img src="smiley1.gif"/>
    </div>
    <p style="clear:left">Even if you are on the right track,
                          you will get run over if your just sit
                          there. - Will Rogers</p>
    <br />
```

```
        <div style="float:right; width:100px;">
          <img src="smiley1.gif" />
        </div>
        <p style="clear:right">He was the world's only armless
                            sculpter. He put the chisel in his mouth
                            and his wife hit him on the back of the
                            head with a mallet. - Fred Allen</p>
        <br />
        <div style="float:none; width:100px;">
          <img src="smiley1.gif" />
        </div>
        <p style="clear:right">It's a rare person who wants to
                            hear what he doesn't want to here. -
                            Dick Cavett</p>
      </body>
    </html>
```

This is how the example is shown in IE 5, Netscape 6, and Opera 5:

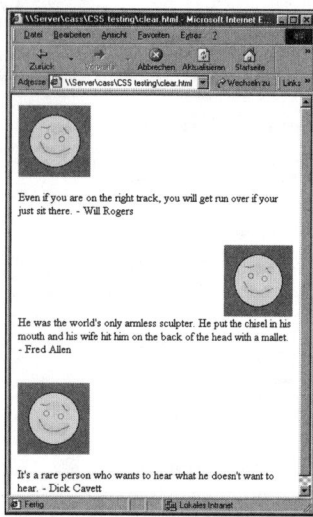

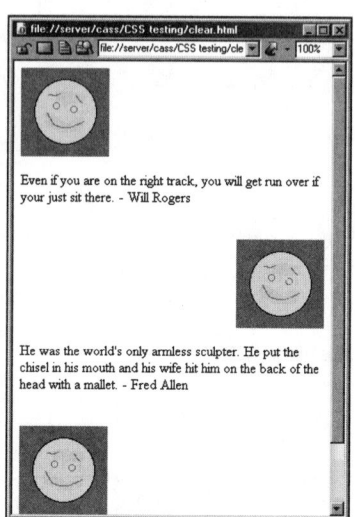

In these screenshots using `float` and `clear`, Opera 5 adds extra space after the elements that are being cleared.

overflow

Normally a browser has no problem displaying content of an element in the area it has been assigned to. Sometimes, however the content of an element exceeds the borders of the element. This is normally not desired behavior. Here are some of the possible scenarios where the content can exceed its display borders:

❏ If the line cannot be broken (for example, content in a `<pre>` element)

❏ The element is contained in another element and the contained element has a `width` and/or `height` value higher than that of the containing element

❏ The element has an absolute position

❏ The element has a margin with a negative value

The property `overflow` tells a browser how to react, when the nested element needs more room to be displayed than the surrounding element offers. There are four values for the property `overflow` for dealing with the problem:

The supported values are:

```
visible      hidden      scroll      auto
```

`visible` (the default) lets the content simply "overflow" the borders of its containing element. With `hidden` the content of the nested element is simply cut off by the borders of the surrounding area. When the value `scroll` is used the area surrounding the nested element is not adjusted but a scrollbar is created, which lets the user scroll to see the content of nested element. `auto` is basically the same as scroll but only if a scrollbar is necessary. This is good if we don't know in advance what content will be inserted into the area. The elements themselves are not adjusted.

Browser support for this property is not consistent over operating systems. IE 4 and up, N 6, and Opera 5 on Windows support this, but on Macintosh, IE 5 does, but Opera 5 and N 6 do not.

Tables often have problems with CSS, so this style probably needs to be set directly in the element contained in the table row.

The following code segment utilizes the same image, one that is larger than the area set in its parent `<div>` element. It is also in a table so everything is side by side.

```
<html>
  <head>
  </head>
  <body>
    <div style="top:5px; left:20px; width:200px;
        overflow:hidden; position:absolute;">
      <img src="marble2.gif" width="450" height="250"/>
    </div>
    <div style="top:5px; left:270px; width:200px;
        overflow:scroll; position:absolute;">
      <img src="marble2.gif" width="450" height="250"/>
    </div>
    <div style="top:5px; left:520px; width:200px;
        overflow:visible; position:absolute;">
      <img src="marble2.gif" width="450" height="250"/>
    </div>
  </body>
</html>
```

Setting the value of overflow to hidden, scroll, and visible can be seen below:

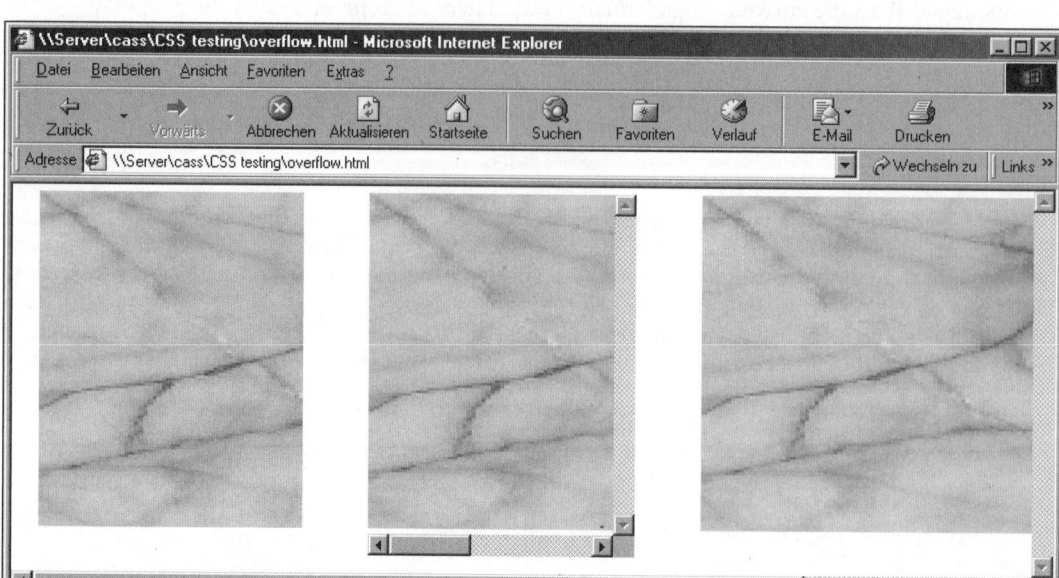

This screenshot is in IE 5. N 6 does pretty much the same thing, as do these browsers on Macintosh. Opera 5 does not support the overflow property.

Styling Lists

Lists are a common and useful way of presenting information. They are easy to set up as well, using <li> elements in the <ul> element for an unordered list, or <ol> element for an ordered list. However, styling a list in HTML with anything but plain bullets or numbers requires a lot of code tweaking and patience, but CSS makes it much easier.

The properties discussed in this section are CSS 1, and for the most part, should not be a problem for IE 4.x and higher, for N 6 or for Opera 3 and up, except where stated.

In the first part of this section, we will talk about setting styles for list markers. Then we will discuss setting other styles for the list.

List Markers

Lists very often have some sort of marker to set off each item on the list. In standard HTML, our only choices are a simple disc bullet, a hollow circle, and a square for unordered lists. For ordered lists, we have numbers, uppercase and lower case letters, as well as small and capital Roman numerals. CSS 1 provides these standard marker options and CSS 2 adds a few more specialized ones.

Here are the properties that set the marker styles:

❑ list-style-type: This sets what shape or style the marker should be. The standard styles for unordered lists are none, disc (default), circle, and square. For ordered lists decimal, decimal-leading-zero (CSS 2), lower-alpha, upper-alpha, lower-roman, and upper-roman. CSS 2 also gives us: lower-greek, lower-latin, upper-latin, and foreign language markers depending on the fonts installed on the system (for example: hebrew and hirigana).

❑ list-style-position: This specifies whether the marker (for example: bullet) stands inside or outside of the list item box. Using this value also causes the text, which wraps to the left margin of the list item, appear underneath the marker.

❑ list-style-image: This lets us use a URL to specify our own marker.

❑ list-style: This is the shorthand property with which we can set all of the above properties at one time.

list-style-type

We can define the specific type of marker for any element, which has its display set to list-item. If it is an ordered list, the appearance of the numbers can be specifically formatted as well. A list item inherits the list-style-type value of its parent.

> *N 6 is the only browser that supports both CSS 1 and CSS 2 markers.*

If no list-style-type value is specified, the default is disc, that is, a normal bullet.

list-style-position

The values inside or outside for the property list-style-position add an indent to a list item. The property list-style-position:outside (default) puts the marker (for example: bullet) in a box floating to the left of the list item box. list-style-position:inside puts the marker inline of the normal flow of the list item box.

When the text is longer than the line, the text wraps to the next line. If list-style-position:inside is used, then the wrapped text will be seen directly underneath the marker.

> *IE doesn't seem to favorably support inside. The markers tend to merge with the text.*

Check out the screenshot in the next section to see what the markers look like.

list-style-image

We can use our own bullet in lists! Using list-style-image:url(), we tell the list where to find the image for the bullet. For example:

```
ul { list-style-image:url(point.gif) }
```

A list-style-image can be specified as either a URL, or by the keyword none. If no list-style-image value is set, the default is none. An element *does* inherit the list-style-image of its parent. To stop an element from inheriting the list-style-image of its parent, we can set its list-style-image to none (this does not work in Opera).

This is a code segment of a list, using the various list marker styles available:

```
<ol>
   <li style="list-style: none">No marker</li>
   <li style="list-style: disc">Normal bullet</li>
   <li style="list-style: circle">Empty circle</li>
   <li style="list-style: square">Square bullet</li>
   <li style="list-style: decimal">Number</li>
   <li style="list-style: decimal-leading-zero">
      0 before the number - Only in NN 6 </li>
   <li style="list-style: lower-roman">Lower Roman</li>
   <li style="list-style: upper-roman">Upper Roman</li>
   <li style="list-style: lower-alpha">Lower alpha</li>
   <li style="list-style: upper-alpha">Upper alpha</li>
   <li style="list-style: lower-latin">
      Lower Latin - Only in NN 6</li>
   <li style="list-style: upper-latin">
      Upper Latin - Only in NN 6</li>
   <li style="list-style: lower-greek">
      Lower Greek - Only in NN 6</li>
   <li style="list-style: hiragana">
      Hiragana - Only in NN 6</li>
   <li style="list-style: upper-roman outside">
      To the left of the indent point</li>
   <li style="list-style: upper-roman inside">
      To the right of the indent point</li>
   <li style="list-style-image: url(Redcheck.gif)">
      Bullet image</li>
</ol>
```

Here is a screenshot in N 6, which supports the most marker types. IE and Opera support the other markers as well. For the foreign language markers, the appropriate fonts must be installed on the system:

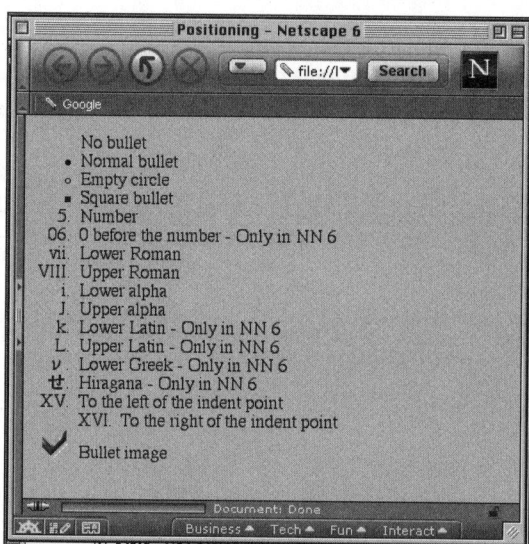

Margins, Borders, and Backgrounds for Lists

In addition to setting which style of list marker we want, we can also set the dimensions and styles of the margins, borders, and backgrounds, using the properties discussed earlier.

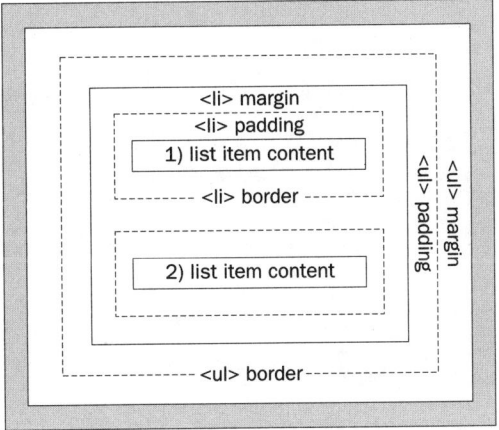

Background style settings vary between browsers. IE 5 and Opera 5 do not include the markers when displaying the background of a list, even when it is set in the parent `<ol>` or `<ul>` elements unless the `list-style-position` is set to `inside`. However, Netscape does.

Padding style settings vary between browsers, as well. If we have the `list-style-position` set to `inside`, and then set the padding for a list item, N 6 and IE 5 place the padding to the left of the marker. Opera 5 does not. What Opera 5 does is put the padding between the content and the marker.

More interesting browser behavior: To resize the window displaying a list, IE 5 and Opera 5 will break the text so all of the text fits between the right and left window margins up to the point where the outside margins are threatened, and then the text is covered. N 6 for Macintosh will not break the text in order to display all of it in a smaller window. It adds a scrollbar at the bottom instead.

Here is some code that sets the style of each individual list item. Below it are screenshots of Macintosh showing the different behaviors. Notice the gap between the list items in Opera. This gap is not there in the other two browsers.

```
<html>
  <head>
    <style type="text/css">
      body { background-color:#FFFFFF }
/* These styles effect the list items individually */
      li { list-style: url("redcheck.gif") inside;
           background: url("marble2.gif");
           margin-left: 10px;
           border: red groove;
           padding: 5px }
    </style>
  </head>
  <body>
```

```
    <ol>
      <li>Making a list</li>
      <li>Checking it twice</li>
      <li>Gonna find out who's naughty or nice...</li>
    </ol>
  </body>
</html>
```

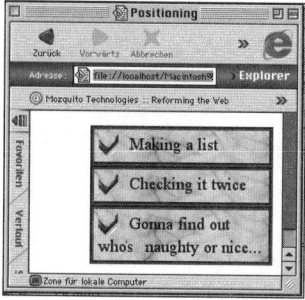 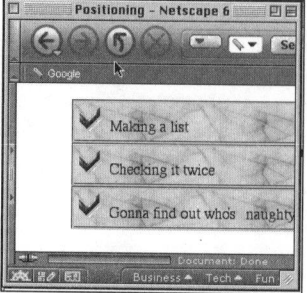 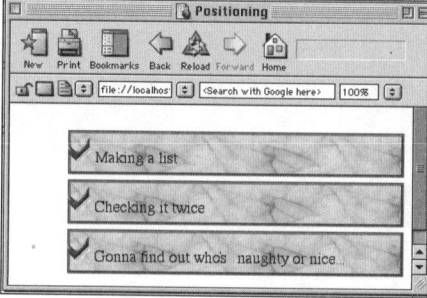

Here is the same code segment again. The only difference is that now the styles are set in the <ol> element and affect the list as a whole:

```
<html>
  <head>
    <style type="text/css">
      body { background-color:#FFFFFF }
/* These styles effect the list as a whole */
      ol    { list-style: decimal inside;
              background: url("marble2.gif");
              margin-left: 10px;
              border: red groove;
              padding: 5px }
    </style>
  </head>
  <body>
    <ol>
      <li>Making a list</li>
      <li>Checking it twice</li>
       <li>Gonna find out who's naughty or nice...</li>
    </ol>
  </body>
</html>
```

Here are the screenshots from IE 5, Netscape 6, and Opera 5 on Macintosh:

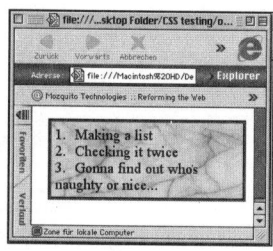  

Styling Tables

A table is another example of one or more boxes of content nested in a bigger box. A table lets us use a set of boxes that are not only arranged one after another, as in a list, but also side-by-side in rows. We can also set up different size boxes that extend over one table cell. Unfortunately, styling HTML tables with CSS is a delicate operation. On the flip side, once our external CSS styles are set up the way we want, they are reusable and easily adjustable without having to alter individual table-related elements.

So we are back to use our old standby elements, `<table>`, `<tr>`, and `<td>` along with some back up from `<th>`.

Before we get too far, we must stress that all `<table>` elements absolutely need to be closed. Not only is this good coding practice, it is the first requirement for a table to display properly over *all* browsers, let alone to get the styles to work. Some browsers can tolerate non-closed `<tr>` elements, but not all of them. A broken table may not only smash our content, but it could also crash the user's browser. In addition, as we move forwards towards greater support for XHTML, future browsers will enforce stricter attention to well-formedness.

We cannot assign most styles to the `<table>` or `<tr>` elements, and must use the `<td>` element instead. Exceptions are `background-image` and `color` on the `<table>` tag. For other styles, results may vary significantly depending on not only the browser but the complexity of the table as well, so their use is not recommended.

Table layout

Different browsers have different approaches to calculating how they should build the layout of a table on a web page. CSS 2 has given web designers a bit of control in deciding which approach the browser should use. This decision is made using the property `table-layout` within the `<table>` element.

The supported values are:

    fixed   auto   inherit

With `inherit` we can set whether the table should inherit `table-layout` settings from its parent element when it otherwise wouldn't, when using nested tables for example.

There are two possible ways a browser can calculate the layout of a table:

- `fixed`: The first algorithm ignores the content, and simply uses the first `width` specified for a column other than `auto`. This is not a good value to use if the widths of the columns become wider after the first width setting.

- `auto`: (The default): The second algorithm, which is much slower, first looks at each cell before making a decision, then it calculates the rows and columns based on all the settings. This is the safest route but takes significantly more time to display the table.

> *Having explained all that, here's the bad news: although different browsers claim to support different aspects of this property, no browser does it well enough for this to be as useable as it is meant to be. So in the meantime browsers will use* auto *as the default.*

Table Column Width and Row Height

When we ship a box full of little boxes, we need to make sure all the little boxes fit inside the bigger box. In CSS, we can define the width and height of our columns and rows, using the properties `width` and `height` in the `<table>` element.

Below is some example code for a table:

```
<html>
  <head>
    <style type="text/css">
      table { table-layout:fixed width:200px; height:100px;
            border:solid 1px}
      td { text-align:center; border: solid 1px;  }
      td.first { vertical-align:top; }
      td.second {vertical-align:bottom;}
      caption { caption-side:top; border:double 3 px;}
    </style>
  </head>
  <body>
    <table>
      <caption>
        Table Width and Height
      </caption>
      <tr>
        <td class="first">row 1 column 1</td>
        <td class="second">row 1 column 2</td>
      </tr>
      <tr>
        <td class="first">row 2 column 1</td>
        <td class="second">row 2 column 2</td>
      </tr>
    </table>
  </body>
</html>
```

Here is how the table is displayed in IE 5, Netscape 6, and Opera 5:

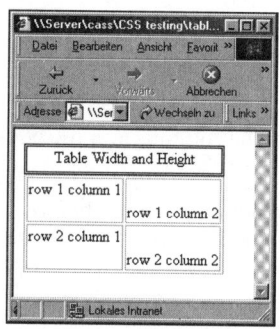 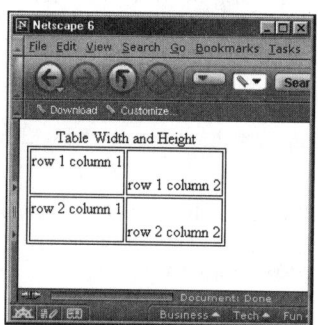 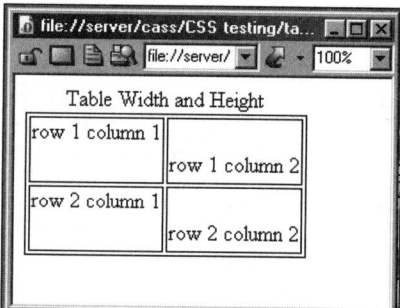

Notice in these screenshots that the tables in N 6 and Opera5 did not properly interpret the caption styles.

Table Overflow

Sometimes a cell simply has more content than will fit in a predetermined cell size. This is one place where the overflow property we talked about before can come in handy. Since the default value for table overflow is visible, the content spills over into the next column or even outside of the table. This is not really desirable since it is not only messy looking, but it may disturb other parts of the page layout.

If we set overflow to hidden, then the extra content is simply clipped to the size of the cell. Use of the scroll value gives oversized content a scrollbar, and the user doesn't have to miss out on any of it.

Table Captions

When we ship a box, it is nice when there is some sort of label giving a general description of what is inside. HTML tables have the <caption> element to give a general description of what the table contains. CSS 2 gives the option of setting the caption with the style property caption-side. This style gives the caption more options for placement. Instead of only being at the top, a caption can be placed on any side of the table.

Unfortunately, caption-side is only supported in N 6 and then only the top and bottom values. It will display the right side value, but works best if we have set the width and height of the caption space. Opera 5.11 attempts to display it, but has problems with anything but top (which is the default anyway).

The supported values are:

| top | right | bottom | left |

Where top is the default.

The example table code in the previous section describing column width and row height, uses the property caption-side:top.

Empty Cells in Tables

Empty cells are not especially pretty in normal HTML tables. The CSS 2 property, empty-cells is an answer to this, and is starting to be supported. This property lets us either show a formatted but empty cell, or hide it. If a whole row is empty, then we can have the whole row disappear without taking up any screen space.

So far, this property is still buggy and only Opera, and N 6 have started implementing it. With empty-cell:show, Opera shows the cells with only the padding, and N 6 just shows very thin cells (see the next screenshot). With empty-cell:hide, N 6 removes all visibility, but in Opera the background color is still there.

The supported values are:

| show | hide | inherit |

`show` causes empty cells to be shown with the same formatting as full cells. `hide`, hides the formatting of an empty cell. If a whole row is empty, no screen space is set aside for it. `inherit` takes the value from the parent element.

Here is our sample table with the `empty-cell` property included:

```
<html>
  <head>
    <style type="text/css">
      table { table-layout:fixed width:200px; height:100px;
             border:solid 1px}
      td { text-align:center; border: solid 1px;  }
      td.first { vertical-align:top; empty-cell:show;}
      td.second {vertical-align:bottom; empty-cell:hide;}
      caption { caption-side:top; border:double 3 px;}
    </style>
  </head>
  <body>
    <table>
      <caption>
        Table Width and Height
      </caption>
      <tr>
        <td class="first"> </td>
        <td class="second">row 1 column 2</td>
      </tr>
      <tr>
        <td class="first">row 2 column 1</td>
        <td class="second"></td>
      </tr>
    </table>
  </body>
</html>
```

Here are some screenshots of how IE 5 and N 6 act with `empty-cell:show`, and `empty-cell:hide`. Opera 5 acts exactly the same as N 6:

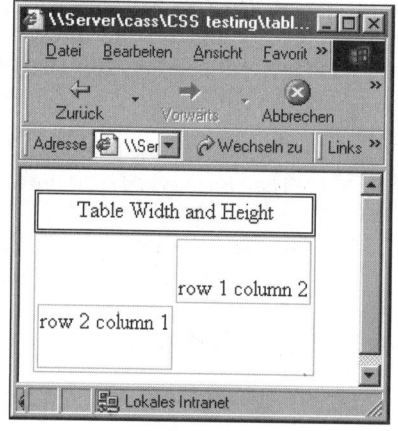
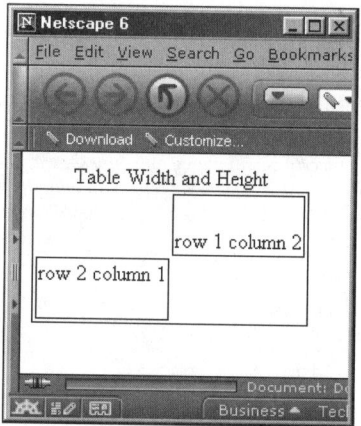

About Table Display Properties

CSS 2 presented us with an expanded list of values for the `display` property we discussed in the previous chapter. These values now include several table-specific value keywords. These are supposed to let us set the `display` value of any element in order to construct a table environment. Although, some people might think it an interesting idea to define the display of a `<p>` element as a table cell, these properties are meant more for XML-based markup languages, some of which may not include elements such as `<table>`, `<td>`, or `<tr>`.

In addition to the fact that we already have perfectly useable table elements, the implementation of these table display properties is only in its infancy. IE 5 and up supports a couple, and N 6 claims to support them all, but the support is imperfect at best.

Due to the lack of proper browser support, we won't say much about these `display` properties, but they are useful to be aware of them for future reference.

Netscape 6 claims to support (the equivalent HTML elements are in parentheses): `table` (`<table>`), `inline-table`, `table-row-group` (`<tbody>`), `table-column-group` (`<colgroup>`), `table-column` (`<col>`), `table-row` (`<tr>`), `table-cell` (`<td>`), and `table-caption` (`<caption>`).

IE 5 and higher support the following two display values: `table-header-group` (`<thead>`) and `table-footer-group` (`<tfoot>`).

Summary

In this chapter, we have covered quite a lot. We have introduced the Box Model and shown how elements work when they are inside another element, for example, how block elements are treated like boxes in boxes. We have learned how to position and define the dimensions of elements as well as how to style lists and tables using CSS 2 and the principles of the Box Model.

In the next chapter, we will go further with CSS 2 and learn how to use it for creating style sheets that allow the visually impaired to access the Web.

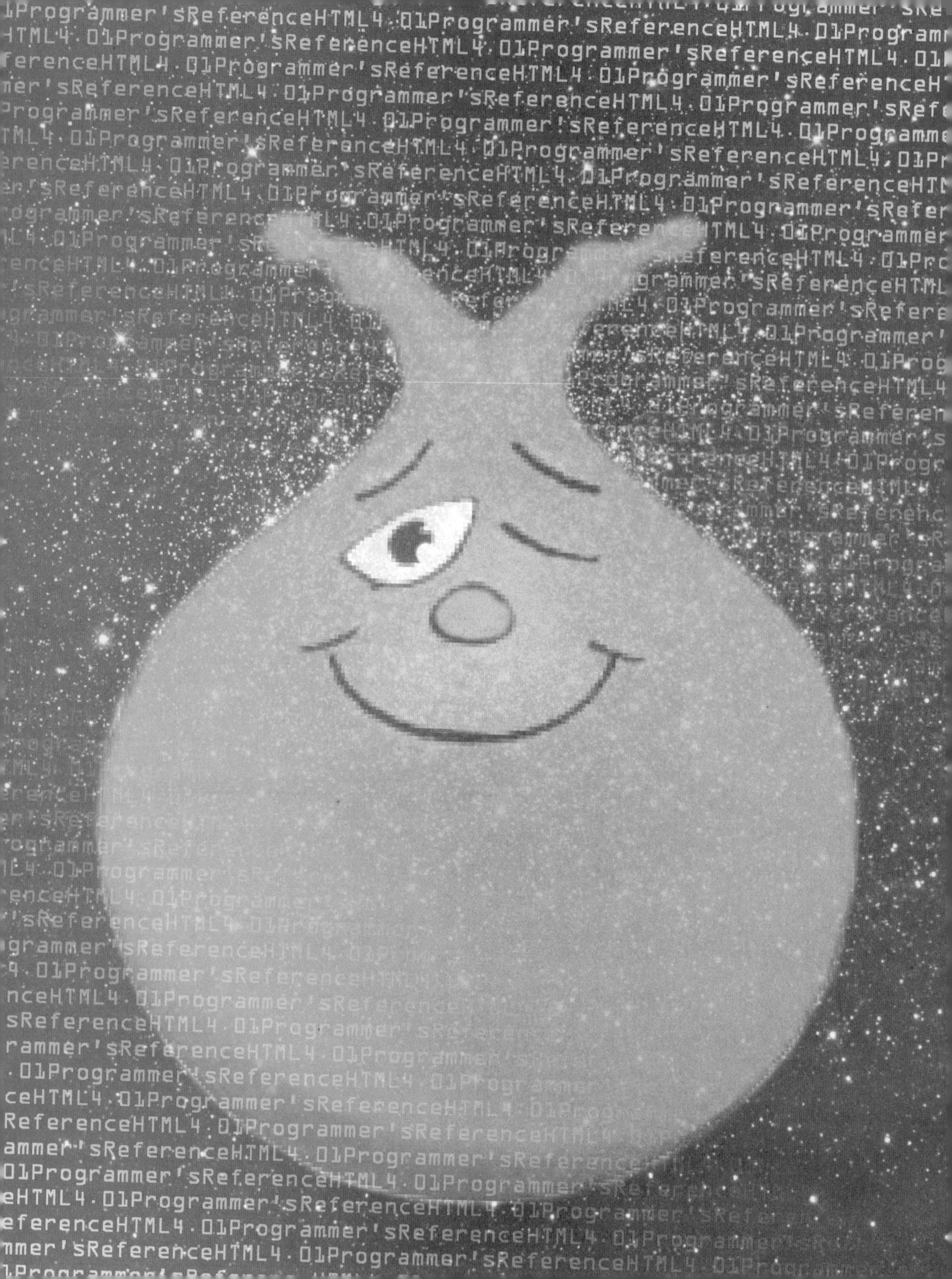
Programmer'sReferenceHTML4.01

Aural Style Sheets

The CSS-2 standard includes support for aural style sheets, which provide control over several aspects of including sound in the web experience. Although not widely supported yet, the specification holds the promise of improving web accessibility for visually impaired users, as well as providing telephone-based web access and improving native browser support for relatively low bandwidth multimedia web applications.

In this chapter we will cover:

❑   Uses for Aural Style Sheets

❑   Media Types

❑   The Aural Style Sheet Specification Overview

❑   Related Web Accessibility Issues

Uses for Aural Style Sheets

Currently there are four potential markets proposed for aural style sheets:

- Users requiring enhanced accessibility
- Web-based multimedia developers
- Developers of non-visual web content
- Telephone-based web access

Although there is no client-side support and very little server-side support (the Microsoft Web Telephony Engine is the only implementation at press time) for the standard at present, support for the visual components of CSS 2 although sparse, is improving. Aural style sheet support will improve, as new tools are developed to take advantage of the specification.

Web Accessibility Initiative

An obvious potential use for aural style sheets is to provide control over the audible presentation of page content for visually impaired users. There are a few text-reader browsers, plug-ins, and standalone applications that use a synthesized voice to read textual content on web pages (for example, Simply Web 2000, pwWebSpeak, and JAWS for Windows), but they do not provide any of the contextual inflections of daily speech. They also lack any facility for providing auditory users with additional information about the page content through the use of gender or positioning of the speaker, mixing of environmental sounds with text to provide context for the page, and other audible cues. A fully compliant browser would be able to immerse the user in a 3-dimensional auditory field that could provide a far richer browsing experience than current browsers afford. See Chapter 20 for more on accessibility and operability.

Multimedia

Aural style sheet support could also leverage existing hardware and software support to provide true multimedia experiences for users without requiring the installation of plug-ins or Java applets, although there is no client that does this presently. As bandwidth increases, the market for more interactive web pages will also increase. Aural style sheets can provide multimedia designers with a powerful tool for product recognition development by allowing them to develop style sheets providing look, sound, and feel in a single document. They also have the potential to be very competitive with existing technologies that require plug-ins because there are many business clients who do not allow plug-in installation on their machines or block certain network ports, which rules out things like Flash, RealAudio, and other streaming media technologies. Style sheets work over the usual ports and an HTTP connection

Alternative Delivery Media

As more and more devices connect to the web, it is inevitable that some of them will have limited visual capabilities coupled with extensive auditory capabilities (web-enabled phones come immediately to mind). It is probable that these will have an on-board voice synthesizer and server-side engines will be able to provide support without requiring a "talking engine" on the client. Aural style sheets can provide platform-optimized content delivery for these devices through the use of CSS 2 media types.

Telephone-Based Access

Microsoft has issued a prototype Web Telephony Engine (WTE) specification including server software, and developer's kits to promote telephone-based web access using services provided under Windows 2000 Server. It leverages existing Microsoft technologies like the MS Speech API, Text-To-Speech Engine (TTS), Telephone API (TAPI), and the Voice Over IP standard (H.323) to deliver web content over a telephone handset. WTE uses a subset of the CSS 2 aural style sheet markup to direct the server in delivering the aural content. For more information, see the Microsoft web site at http://www.Microsoft.com/.

Media Types

The introduction of media types in CSS 2 allows designers and programmers to optimize content for various platforms from printing devices (printers and computer screens) to aural devices (speech synthesizers) to tactile devices (Braille devices). Some style sheet properties are platform-specific (font-family is useless on a speech synthesizer and pause-before is useless on a Braille device) and different media types may require different values for shared properties. CSS 2 provides two ways to address these issues: @media or the media attribute of the HTML <link> element.

Specifying Media Dependency

@media acts a container to allow developers to specify multiple target media types for multiple sets of rules in a single style sheet. Each rule set is enclosed in curly braces. Multiple media types can be specified for a single rule set using a comma-delimited list:

```
@media print, screen {
                    body { font-family: Arial, Helvetica, sans-serif }
                    }
@media aural {
              body {voice-family: Sharon, female }
              }
```

<link media="mediaType"> is an alternative method of specifying media types that is supported in more browsers than the @media method. The <link> tag is placed in the <head> of the page and target media are denoted by a comma-delimited list enclosed in double quotation marks:

```
<head>
  <title>Targeted Media</title>
  <link rel="stylesheet" type="text/css" media="print, screen, _
        projection" href="media.css">
  <link rel="stylesheet" type="text/css" media="aural" href="aural.css">
</head>
```

Recognized Media

The recognized media types in the CSS 2 specification are named according to the rule sets' target devices. Device names are not case-sensitive (TV = tv = tV = Tv) and the current list is expected to grow as technologies and rendering devices are developed. The current list is available in Chapter 11.

Media Groups

CSS 2 property definitions usually apply to several devices at the same time. Rather than specify each device individually in the property definitions, the W3C groups the devices together according to various shared characteristics. A property applies to all media within its listed media group(s). A single medium may belong to more than one media group. If a property is appropriate to all media groups, it is classified as "all". The media groups are:

```
continuous/paged
visual/aural/tactile
grid/bitmap
interactive/static
all
```

The following table from the CSS 2 specification shows the relationship between the media types and media groups:

Media Types	Media Groups			
	continuous/paged	visual/aural/tactile	grid/bitmap	interactive/static
aural	continuous	aural	N/A	both
braille	continuous	tactile	grid	both
embossed	paged	tactile	grid	both
handheld	both	visual	both	both
print	paged	visual	bitmap	static
projection	paged	visual	bitmap	static
screen	continuous	visual	bitmap	both
tty	continuous	visual	grid	both
tv	both	aural, visual	bitmap	both

Now let's look at one specific media type – aural, and the style sheet specification relating to it.

Aural Style Sheet Specification Overview

In this section, we will look at the various sections of the CSS 2 Aural Style Sheet specification. Each aural style sheet property will be examined and an example based on the W3C specification will be provided. Because of the relative newness of the specification, this will essentially be a technology preview, although you can try your hand at Aural Style Sheets if you have access to a Windows 2000 Server with the WTE services installed and open an account in the voice application developer's community at voxeo.com (http://community.voxeo.com/).

Aural Style Sheet properties are used in the same way that other CSS properties are and can be integrated into existing style sheets or placed in separate style sheets for ease of maintenance, then included in documents as required (see Chapters 11-13 on CSS for examples of assigning style properties to HTML elements and classes).

Properties

The CSS 2 aural style sheet specification provides designers and programmers with extensive control over the perceived auditory physical space (sound location), temporal space (sound timing), and sound quality (voice type, inflection, pitch, etc.). The controls are referred to as **properties** and are grouped according to their functions.

Note: An understanding of cascading and inheritance is important in grasping how the aural style sheet properties will behave in relation to each other. See Chapter 11 for an explanation of these concepts.

Basic

volume

The volume property controls the dynamic range of a sound. It is intended to be modifiable on the client side for user comfort (for example, by using the volume knob on a playback device to set its volume level relative to noise levels in the user's vicinity) The user may set the maximum and minimum volume levels (fairly high in a noisy environment like a car or low in a quiet environment like inside a library), with the author's settings specifying the dynamic range of an element within the user's settings. volume can take the following values:

number	percentage	silent	x-soft
soft	medium	loud	x-loud
inherit			

number is any number between 0 and 100, with 0 being the minimum audible sound level and 100 the maximum comfortable sound level as set by the user.

```
h1 { volume: 75 }
h2 { volume: 60 }
```

percentage is calculated relative to the inherited sound level value, then clipped to the range 0 – 100 as above. In the example below, the page's volume has been set to 80% of the user's volume setting (the same as volume:80) and text enclosed by <h1></h1> is played at 75% of the page's volume, or 60% of the user's volume setting (0.80 x 0.75 = 0.60, the same as volume:60).

```
body { volume: 80% }
h1 { volume: 75% }
```

silent means no sound at all; this is not the same as the value 0, which means the lowest audible sound. Using silent does not mean that the sound will not be played, only that no sound will be output. It is analogous to using the mute button on a CD player – it takes the same amount of time to get to the next song, you just don't hear anything.

```
A.broken { volume: silent }
```

x-soft is the same as number = 0. The following are equivalent:

```
h6 { volume: 0 }
h6 { volume: x-soft }
```

soft is the same as number = 25. The following are equivalent:

```
h6 { volume: 25 }
h6 { volume: soft }
```

medium is the same as number = 50. It is the default value used when a volume value is not specified. The following are equivalent:

```
h6 { volume: 50 }
h6 { volume: medium }
```

loud is the same as number = 75. The following are equivalent:

```
h6 { volume: 75 }
h6 { volume: loud }
```

x-loud is the same as number = 100. The following are equivalent:

```
h6 { volume: 100 }
h6 { volume: x-loud }
```

speak

The speak property determines if and how an element will be played, and can take these values:

```
normal        none        spell-out        inherit
```

normal renders an element and its children using language-dependent pronunciation rules that are provided by the rendering agent (server or client depending upon the application). It is the default value.

```
body { speak: normal }
```

none does not audibly render an element. Unlike volume:silent, speak:none skips the element (like pressing skip on a CD player). However, children of the element can override this setting and be spoken. In the example below, ordered lists of the class "oldInfo" (<ol class="oldInfo">) are skipped, but list items of the class "newInfo" (<li class="newInfo">) would still be spoken, even if they were contained in an <ol class="oldInfo"></ol> object.

```
OL.oldInfo { speak: none }
LI.newInfo { speak: normal }
```

spell-out audibly renders the text one letter at a time instead of reading the text as a word. This allows an abbreviation or acronym to be spelled out ("ASP" can be recognized as an acronym and not a poisonous snake).

```
span.acronym { speak: spell-out }
```

pause

pause has three properties: `pause-before`, `pause-after`, and `pause` (which is a short-hand method for setting the first two properties).

pause-before

This property sets the amount of time that will elapse between the end of the previous element and the begining of the current element being spoken.

pause-after

This property sets the amount of time to elapse after the current element has been spoken and before the next element can begin being spoken.

These two properties take the following values:

```
time        percentage       inherit
```

`time` represents the pause length in absolute terms in units of seconds (s) or milliseconds (ms).

```
h1 { pause-before: 20ms }
h1 { pause-after: 30ms }
```

`percentage` represents the pause length as a percentage of the inverse of the `speech-rate` property covered below. When calculating time for a `pause`, find the average time for a word [60 secs / Words Per Minute], and then set the `pause`. For example, if we set `speech-rate: 120`, then the average time for a word is **60/120 wpm = 0.5sec/word (or 500ms/word)**. Now we can set a natural sounding pause based on how long it takes to say a word. So for `speech-rate:120` (120 words per minute or 500ms per word), `pause-before:80%` means a pause of 400ms (500ms x 0.80) before the element is spoken. This is the preferred method of specifying pauses since it is anticipated that users will be able to change the `speech-rate` property and absolute pause lengths may cause users problems in understanding the content.

Note: speech-rate is covered fully in the later section on voice characteristics.

```
h1 { pause-before: 10% }
h1 { pause-after: 15% }
```

pause

The `pause` property combines the settings for the previous two properties into one setting. It requires values for both `pause-before` and `pause-after`. `pause-before` is the first value and `pause-after` is the second value. If a value is omitted, `pause` sets both of the other properties to the value it does have (for example, `pause:30ms` sets both `pause-before` *and* `pause-after` to 30ms). The same values as the previous two pause properties can be used with `pause`. These examples are equivalent to the examples given above:

```
h1 { pause: 20ms 30ms }
h1 { pause: 10% 15% }
```

377

cue

Just as there are three 'pause' properties, there are also three 'cue' properties: cue-before, cue-after, and cue. The cue properties are used to provide 'auditory icons' (identifying sounds played before and/or after a particular element to identify it aurally, somewhat like using bullets in front of list items) for users. If pause properties are also specified, the order of playback is:

```
cue-before, pause-before, <element>, pause-after, cue-after
```

cue-before

This property plays a specified sound file before the element is aurally rendered.

cue-after

This properties plays a specified sound file after the element is rendered.

The cue properties take the following values:

```
uri        none        inherit
```

uri must point to an audio file. If uri is not an audio file, it is ignored and treated as though the relevant cue property had been set to none.

```
h1 { cue-before: uri("audio/ding.wav") }
h1 { cue-after: uri("audio/dong.wav") }
```

none indicates that no sound is to be played.

```
h1.stealth { cue-before: none }
h1.stealth { cue-after: none }
```

cue

cue combines cue-before and cue-after settings into one setting. It requires values for both properties. cue-before is the first value and cue-after is the second value. If only one setting is supplied, cue applies it to both cue-before and cue-after (cue:none sets cue-before:none *and* cue-after:none). The following are equivalent to the examples for the other cue properties:

```
h1 { cue: uri("audio/ding.wav") uri("audio/dong.wav") }
h1.stealth { cue: none }
```

Mixing

The mixing properties allow the style sheet creator to specify how different sounds can be made to interact with each other, by playing some music at the same time as the content of an element is spoken for example, and specifying that the music should repeat until the speech has finished.

play-during

This allows a sound file to be played in the background while an element is spoken. The value of play-during is not inherited from a parent element. It takes the following values:

```
uri       mix       repeat       auto       none
```

uri is required, and is the location of the sound file that is to be played while the element is spoken.

```
h1 { play-during: uri("happyFeet.aiff") }
```

mix causes the sound inherited from the parent element's play-during property to continue playing and mixes the sound from uri with it. If mix is not present in the current element's play-during property, then only the sound file in the current element's uri value will be played. In the example below, h1 is a child of body, so "You Are My Sunshine" (URMySunshine.mp3) will play over "1812 Overture" (overture1812.mp3) – surprisingly, this actually works musically.

```
body { play-during: url("overture1812.mp3") }
h1 { play-during: url("URMySunshine.mp3") mix }
```

repeat causes the sound to repeat if its playing time is shorter than the element's content. It also causes the sound to be clipped upon completion of the element if its playing time is too long. If repeat is not present, the sound file plays once and stops.

```
h1 { play-during: url("CarolOfTheBells.au") repeat}
```

auto causes the parent element's sound to continue playing while the current element is spoken. In the example, "Happy Feet" (happyFeet.aiff) continues playing while the content of h1 is spoken.

```
body { play-during: url("happyFeet.aiff") }
h1 { play-during: auto }
```

none causes silence during the current element's aural rendering. The sound of any parent element is also silenced during the aural rendering of the current element and continues when the current element is completed.

```
h1 { play-during: url("raucousNoise.wav") }
span.quiet { play-during: none }
```

Spatial

Spatial audio information can be important in telling multiple speakers apart. It can also be used to convey other information when needed. Stereo reproduction equipment can provide side-to-side placement of speakers and sounds. Stereo headphones, and multi-channel systems can generate full three-dimensional sound environments. The spatial properties are azimuth and elevation.

azimuth

`azimuth` controls the left-to-right placement of the element's content. Locations are measured in degrees (deg) and range from –360 degrees to 360 degrees with 0 degrees, 360 degrees, and -360 degrees all located directly in front of the user. `azimuth` takes the following values:

```
angle          left-side      far-left        left
center-left    center         center-right    right
far-right      right-side     leftwards       rightwards
inherit
```

`angle` is the number of degrees that an element is to either side of 0 degrees (straight ahead) from the front of the user. Clockwise movement is positive and counter-clockwise is negative, so the user's right is 90 degrees clockwise (or –270 degrees counter-clockwise), behind is 180 degrees clockwise (or –180 degrees counter-clockwise), and left is 270 degrees clockwise (or –90 degrees counter-clockwise). The following examples are equivalent:

```
h1 { azimuth: 110deg }
h1 { azimuth: -250deg }
```

The modifier `behind` may be used to flip the named positions so that they represent placement with respect to 180 degrees behind the user.

Here follows a table showing the degrees either side of 0 for the named values of `azimuth`.

Allowed Values	Degrees Either Side of 0
left-side	270 degrees or –90 degrees
left-side behind	270 degrees or –90 degrees
far-left	300 degrees or –60 degrees
far-left behind	240 degrees or –120 degrees
left	320 degrees or –40 degrees
left behind	220 degrees or –140 degrees
center-left	340 degrees or –20 degrees
center-left behind	200 degrees or –160 degrees
center	0 degrees
center behind	180 degrees or –180 degrees
center-right	20 degrees or –340 degrees
center-right behind	160 degrees or –200 degrees
right	40 degrees or –320 degrees

Allowed Values	Degrees Either Side of 0
`right behind`	140 degrees or –220 degrees
`far-right`	60 degrees or –300 degrees
`far-right behind`	120 degrees or –240 degrees
`right-side`	90 degrees or –270 degrees
`right side behind`	90 degrees or –270 degrees

These values have the following syntax:

```
h1 { azimuth: left-side }
h2 { azimuth: right behind }
```

`leftwards` moves the sound counter-clockwise 20 degrees from the current angle (this always subtracts 20 degrees, even if the source is already behind the user). In the example below, the value of `h1.lefter` is the same as (`azimuth: 80 deg`).

```
h1 { azimuth: 100deg }
h1.lefter { azimuth: leftwards }
```

`rightwards` moves the sound clockwise 20 degrees from the current angle (this always adds 20 degrees, even if the source is already behind the user).

elevation

`elevation` defines the up-and-down location of the sound over a range of 90 degrees (directly overhead) to –90 degrees (directly below). 0 degrees is the forward horizon. Elevation values are inherited. Elevation takes the following values:

```
angle      below      level      above
higher     lower      inherit
```

`angle` is the number of degrees that an element is above or below 0 degrees (straight ahead, level) in front of the user. Upward movement is positive and downward movement is negative.

```
h1 { elevation: 45deg }
```

`below` is –90 degrees (directly below), `level` is 0 degrees, and `above` is 90 degrees (directly above)

```
h1{ elevation: above }
```

`higher` adds 10 degrees to the current elevation (to a maximum of 90 degrees), while `lower` subtracts 10 degrees from the current elevation (to a minimum of -90 degrees).

```
h1 { elevation: 50deg }
h1.upto60 { elevation: higher }
```

Voice Characteristics

Voice characteristic properties allow designers to create different speakers that can provide contextual information to aural page users. They give aural designers control over the aural presentation of spoken content in much the same way that font characteristics give visual designers control over the visual presentation of textual content.

speech-rate

This determines how quickly text will be spoken. It is a loose measurement of how quickly text will be spoken since the same absolute speech rate can sound different in different languages (somewhat like the differences in font size across computing platforms). Speech rate takes the following values:

```
number      x-slow      slow        medium
fast        x-fast      slower      faster
inherit
```

number is the rate at which words are spoken, as an average number of "words per minute" (wpm).

```
h1 { speech-rate: 120 }
```

The following are the explicit values of speech-rate:

x-slow is 80wpm

slow is 120wpm

medium is 180-200wpm (medium accepts a range to account for different language speeds)

fast is 300wpm

x-fast is 500wpm

The speech-rate in the following examples is equivalent:

```
h1 { speech-rate: slow }
h1 { speech-rate: 120 }
```

faster adds 40wpm to the speech-rate inherited from the parent element, while slower subtracts 40wpm from the speech-rate inherited from the parent element.

```
body { speech-rate: slow }
h1.goto160 { speech-rate: faster }
```

voice-family

This is the aural analog of the visual font-family property. It contains a comma-delimited prioritized list of voice family names to be used in rendering the element. It can take the following values:

```
generic-voice       specific-voice        inherit
```

generic-voice is the name of a generalized voice family and can be male, female, or child.

```
h { voice-family: female }
p.sibling { voice-family: child }
```

specific-voice is the name of a specific voice instance (for example: announcer, Paul, Martha, Vulcan, dog). In the example, the user agent will attempt to use the specific-voice 'George' and will use the generic-voice 'male' if George is not available:

```
h1 { voice-family: George, male }
```

Note: There is no list of specific voices available as yet.

pitch

This is the average frequency of the speaking voice in Hertz (Hz) (or cycles per second – cps). The greater the frequency number, the higher the pitch of the voice. Default pitch values are dependent on the voice-family, with voice-family:male equivalent to pitch:120 and voice-family:female equivalent to pitch:210. pitch can take the following values:

```
frequency      x-low       low        medium
high           x-high      inherit
```

frequency is the average frequency (in Hertz [Hz]) of the speaking voice.

```
h1 { pitch: 200 }
```

x-low, low, medium, high, and x-high do not map to any specific frequency, but are dependent on the element's voice-family setting. The only requirement is that the frequency progression from lowest to highest must map to the terms (that is, x-low has a lower frequency than low, etc.).

pitch-range

This is the frequency range over which a voice is allowed to vary to convey inflection and has the following values:

```
number         inherit
```

pitch specifies the base frequency for the voice and pitch-range constrains how far the voice will be allowed to vary from this base frequency, determining how animated the voice will sound. The value for number is in the range 0 to 100. This indicates how much the voice's pitch may vary. 0 is monotonic, 50 is normal speech and is the default value. Anything over 50 will sound animated or excited.

```
h1 { pitch:130; pitch-range: 70 }
```

stress

This determines how high local inflection peaks in an element's voice will be. In stressed languages (for example, English), different sentence parts may be assigned different levels of stress markers. `stress` is used with `pitch-range` to constrain the magnitude of the stress markers and takes the following values:

```
number        inherit
```

`number` is a value between 0 and 100 that represent each language's total stress range. Although the default value is 50 the actual range of variation that 50 represents is language-dependent and will be different for each language.

```
h1 { pitch:120; pitch-range: 60; stress: 75 }
```

richness

This determines how bright a voice will be (its level of overtones), and takes the following values:

```
number        inherit
```

`number` is a single numerical value from 0 to 100 with the default value being 50. The higher the value for `richness`, the more the voice will carry in a large room. Lower `richness` values produce a "smooth" voice with few overtones that will not carry well in a large room.

```
body { richness:65 }
```

Speech Properties

The aural style sheet speech properties allow designers and users to specify how table headers, punctuation, and numerals are to be rendered.

speak-header

The `speak-header` property applies only to tables with defined headers. It determines how often table headers are repeated when reading tabular data. It takes three values:

```
once        always        inherit
```

The following table is used to illustrate the examples for this property's values:

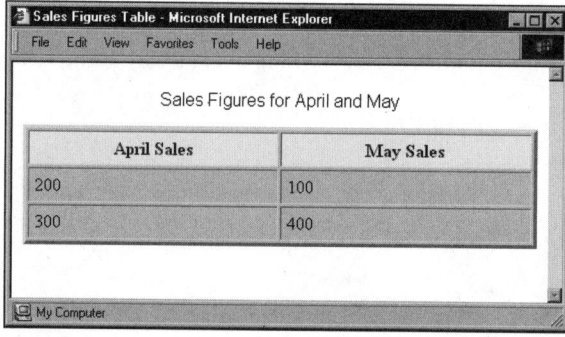

once is the default value for speak-header. It causes the table header to be spoken one time at the beginning of each series of cells (for example, "April sales, two hundred, three hundred").

```
th {speak-header: once }
```

always causes the table header to be read before each cell in the header's data grouping (for example, "April sales, two hundred, April sales, three hundred").

```
th.detailed { speak-header: always }
```

speak-punctuation

This property determines whether the aural user agent will render punctuation as appropriate pauses in the spoken text or call the punctuation marks by name as the text is rendered. It takes three values:

```
code        none        inherit
```

code will cause punctuation such as commas, periods, etc. to be named as the text is read. For example, if speak-punctuation:code is present, the phrase "stop now," will be read as "stop now comma" by the user agent.

```
p.punctual { speak-punctuation: code }
```

none causes punctuation to be rendered as appropriate pauses in the reading of the text when it is present. It is the default setting for speak-punctuation.

```
p.natural { speak-punctuation: none }
```

speak-numeral

This property determines whether numerals are spoken as full numbers or individual digits. It is language-dependent, that is, the numeral "2" would render "two" in English and "tsvy" (zwei) in German. It takes the following values:

```
digits        continuous        inherit
```

digits causes numbers to be spoken as individual digits when it is present. speak-numeric:digits will cause "2001" to be rendered as "two zero zero one" in English.

```
span:listDigits { speak-numeral: digits }
```

continuous causes numbers to be spoken as full numbers when it is present. speak-numeric:continuous will cause "2001" to be rendered as "two thousand one" in English. It is the default value for speak-numeric.

```
span.sayNumber { speak-numeric: continuous }
```

Related Web Accessibility Issues

The accessibility issues listed here are those most pertinent to the production of web documents that are intended to be used by non-visual devices but are only a brief overview. Further accessibility issues and methods to address them are discussed in Chapter 20.

Avoid Frames

It is very difficult to maintain the contextual relationship between frames on non-visual devices. If we expect our site to be accessed by people using non-visual devices, we should avoid the use of frames whenever possible or provide alternative content using the <noframes> tag.

Don't Use Tables for Layout

Using tables solely for visual layout control is also very accessibility-limiting. Complex graphic layouts make no sense when an aural or Braille browser attempts to interpret the contents of the table's cells. Try to keep the use of tables to a minimum and think about the content of the tables you do use. Does the layout of the table make sense? Is the data grouped logically? Data grouped in rows is generally easier for an aural browser to interpret than data grouped in columns.

Use the Alt Attribute in <img> and <area> Tags

When designing for web accessibility, it is important to always place descriptive, meaningful text in the alt attribute of every <img> and <area> tag. Phrases like "a man walking on a beach at sunset" are better for alt attributes than "images/mnbch.jpg 13.7k" because they provide useful information to vision-impaired users (and users with image auto-loading turned off). When we have multiple long descriptions, it is easiest to assign them to variables using a server-side technology like Active Server Pages (ASP), and then write the variables into the page as needed. This method is safer than using a client-side scripting language for this purpose as we do not have to worry about user agent support.

Abstract vs. Literal Markup

Literal markup tags (for example, <b>, <i>) may be shorter to write than their abstract equivalents (for example; <strong>, <em>) but the abstract equivalents are much more useful because they provide interpretable instructions across multiple platforms and user agents. We all know what italic text *looks* like, but what does it *sound* like? Literal tags have no meaning outside of the medium they were designed for. Therefore, abstract tags are needed to provide a method for indicating special treatment of content while allowing the user agent interpret the instructions in a medium-appropriate manner.

Summary

In this chapter we discussed the potential uses for the aural style sheet properties specified in CSS 2. We then went on to look at the different media types available to us in our style sheets and then looked more specifically at the aural style sheet properties and values in terms of their intended purpose and how to use them. Finally we briefly overviewed some of the accessibility issues we should consider when creating pages that may be accessed by non-visual devices.

Throughout the chapter, we have noted that browser and other device support for aural style sheets is lacking at present. As the CSS 2 specification as a whole becomes more widely supported, we can reasonably expect that at least some software and hardware developers will incorporate the technology required to support its aural features in their products. When this happens we will be able to take advantage of the extra functionality and accessibility offered by this new presentational tool.

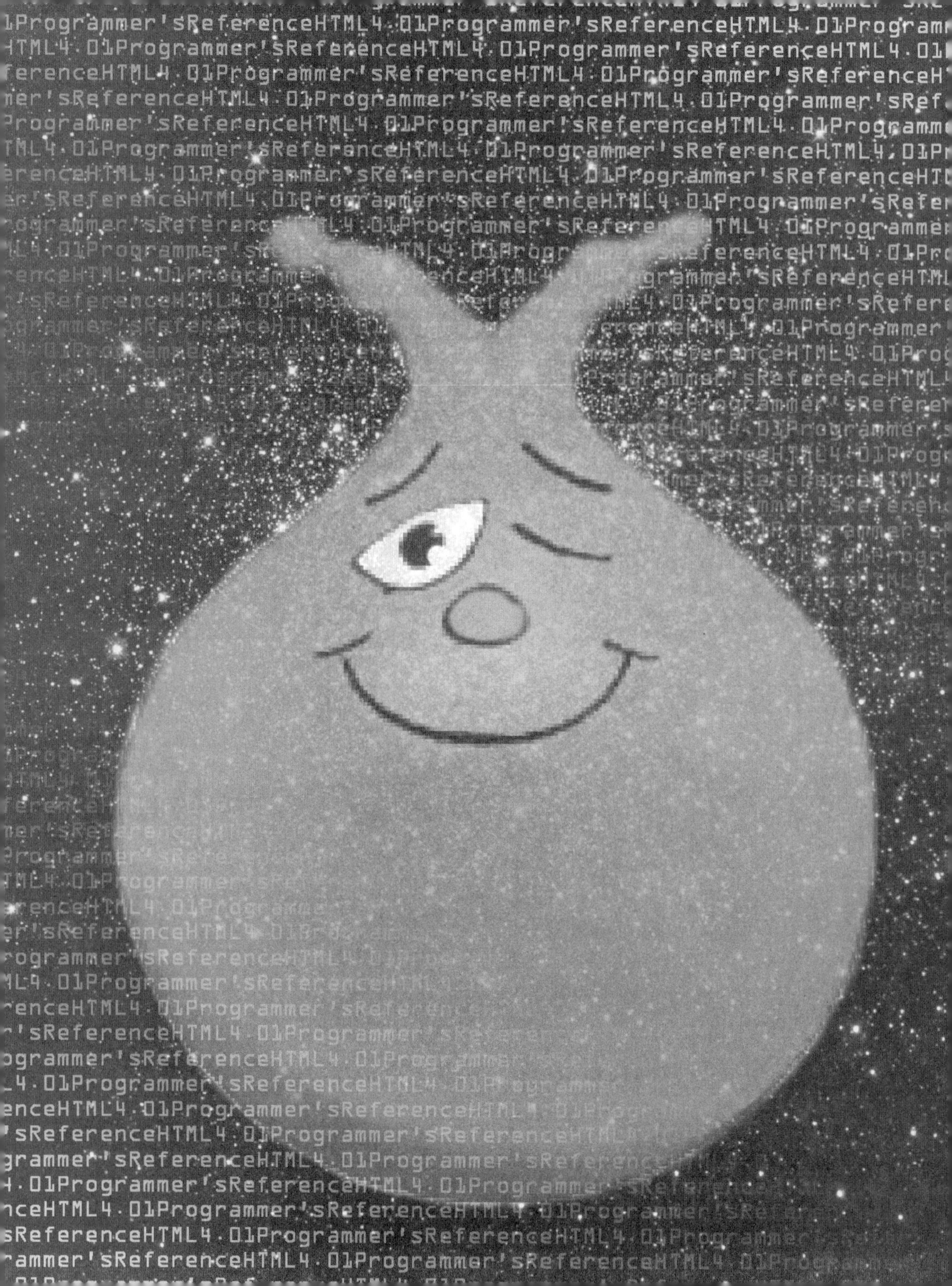
HTML4.01Programmer'sReference

15

Deprecated Elements and Attributes

As the HTML language changes and evolves over time, certain new elements are added to the specification. As new elements are added or other means of marking up or displaying content become standard (CSS, for example), certain existing HTML elements become redundant, or are no longer as useful as they once were. These existing elements are then said to be **deprecated** in favor of the new elements or methods used to display content. A deprecated HTML element (or attribute) is one that may become **obsolete** in future versions of the HTML specification, although software manufacturers generally continue to support deprecated elements in order to ensure backward compatibility. In this chapter, we will look at:

❏   Why standards change

❏   The role the W3C plays in the addition and removal of elements from the HTML standard

❏   The focus of deprecation in the HTML 4.01 specification

In addition, we will also briefly discuss each deprecated or obsolete HTML element and attribute and how they are being replaced (if at all), with element, attribute, or CSS property equivalents. See Chapters 11-13 for more on CSS.

Note: all of the full code examples shown in this chapter are available in the code download, available from http://www.wrox.com/.

Working with Changing Standards

As we discussed above, the HTML specification is evolving all the time. Literally millions of HTML authors apply the W3C's HTML specifications to each of the HTML documents they author. Some of these authors provide feedback to the W3C's various working groups, who recommend changes, additions, or deletions to the specification. Since the HTML specification is already in a very refined state, many of the recommendations or changes do not get implemented in successive versions of the specification, but some do. These new recommendations generally serve to fine-tune the existing HTML language (by consolidating or removing elements) or implement support for additional technologies, such as CSS or XML. New revisions of specifications are designed to build upon existing specifications, while attempting to enable support for future specifications.

It is important for HTML authors to adhere to recognized specifications. The main reason for standards compliance is to ensure that the widest range of user agents (browsers and other software) understand and support your HTML documents. Pages that are built to particular HTML specifications are less likely to break. While it is true that web browser software manufacturers generally continue to support deprecated and even obsolete elements in many successive software versions, using only HTML elements specified in the most current revision of the HTML specification helps HTML authors to build good coding habits by generating documents that are compatible with the widest range of user agents or web browsers. This reduces or eliminates the need to create multiple versions of HTML documents to support multiple user agents (browsers).

W3C Versioning and Deprecation

Given the mission of the W3C is to promote interoperability and encourage an open forum to discuss ideas, issues, and technologies related to the World Wide Web, the W3C periodically releases new versions of specifications that incorporate any changes to the previous specification. Changes to a specification can vary from minor typographical changes to adding, deprecating, or obsolescing of elements.

Versioning and DTDs

Versioning of HTML specifications is centered on the concept of Document Type Definitions (DTDs). A DTD is an SGML (Standard Generalized Markup Language) document that defines the elements of a specific SGML application, HTML for example. The DTD defines relationships between elements, and which attributes and values these specific elements may take. The DTD also defines how specified tags are to be interpreted by the application presenting the document. Basically, the HTML DTD defines how web browsers and other software applications should interpret HTML elements and attributes, but in no way affects the presentation of the HTML. In addition, if the HTML author uses elements not specified in the DTD, the browser will display those elements without error. A DTD simply sets the parameters of a valid HTML document.

As we have already seen in Chapter 1 (see the "*<!DOCTYPE> Declaration*" section), there are three different DTDs you can use in HTML 4.01, which we will now review briefly:

❑ The Strict DTD (which is also the default, if none is specified) includes only HTML elements and attributes that are not deprecated, and also does not include support for frames. To specify the Strict DTD, use the following declaration:

```
<!DOCTYPE HTML PUBLIC "-//W3C//DTD HTML 4.01//EN"
            "http://www.w3.org/TR/html4/strict.dtd">
```

❑ The loose (or transitional) DTD includes all HTML elements supported by the Strict DTD, but also includes support for deprecated elements and attributes. The transitional DTD also includes support for the `<iframe>` element. To specify the Transitional DTD, use the following declaration:

```
<!DOCTYPE HTML PUBLIC "-//W3C//DTD HTML 4.01 Transitional//EN"
                      "http://www.w3.org/TR/html4/loose.dtd">
```

❑ The Frameset DTD includes all HTML elements supported by the Strict and Transitional DTDs, but also includes support for frames. To specify the Frameset DTD, use the following declaration:

```
<!DOCTYPE HTML PUBLIC "-//W3C//DTD HTML 4.01 Frameset//EN"
                      "http://www.w3.org/TR/html4/frameset.dtd">
```

The Frameset DTD is the one to use to ensure the greatest scope of user agent and backward compatibility. In looking toward the future, however, the HTML author must be prepared to update documents to conform with the new DTDs as support for deprecated and obsolete elements is removed.

HTML Deprecation

The deprecation in the different HTML specifications has served to condense and streamline the language by condensing similar elements or by looking to other technologies' specifications for definitions of functionality. SGML, for example, provides most of the base DTD for HTML.

HTML version 2.0 was essentially the first version of HTML developed by the **Internet Engineering Task Force (IETF)** HTML Working Group. HTML 2.0 set the standard for the core features of the HTML language and was simply a culmination of practices current for 1994.

HTML version 3.2, released in 1996, built upon the previous HTML 2.0 version by adding some formatting elements: tables, text wrapping around images, sub- and superscript text, etc. HTML 3.2 also introduced the Java Applet `<applet>` element that provided the first glimpse of today's current rich HTML user interface design capabilities. The elements deprecated in the 3.2 version of HTML were the `<xmp>`, `<plaintext>`, and `<listing>` text formatting elements.

HTML version 4.0, released in December 1997, then again (with minor editorial corrections) in April 1998, built heavily on the previous versions of HTML. This version included increased support for multimedia, and introduced support for scripting languages, style sheets, accessibility for users with disabilities, and internationalization (or i18n, see Chapter 18 for more on this). The elements deprecated in the 4.0 version of HTML were mainly elements focused on presentation of text and other objects in an HTML document. The `<applet>` element was also deprecated in favor of the much more versatile `<object>` element.

HTML version 4.01, released in December 1999, was essentially just an editorial revision of the HTML 4.0 specification, with the majority of the changes being to explanations and wording. To support greater backward-compatibility, version 4.01 restored some of the element attributes removed in the version 4.0 specification. HTML versions 4.0 and 4.01 are basically focused on separating document structure and data from the markup and presentation of that data. The deprecation of many of the HTML formatting elements and attributes are a move in that direction.

Deprecated Elements

In this section we will discuss the various deprecated HTML elements included in the HTML 4.01 specification. We will discuss each deprecated HTML tag and its possible attributes in turn. Additional attributes that are deprecated are being discussed separately because many attributes, a good example being bgcolor, can apply to more than one HTML tag. Also, in some cases, an attribute is only deprecated for some tags, and not others – the align attribute for example is deprecated for all tags except the <col>, <colgroup>, <tbody>, <td>, <tfoot>, <th>, <thead>, and <tr> elements.

Deprecated HTML Tags

The following tags are deprecated in the HTML 4.01 specification mainly due to redundancy either in the form of other HTML tags or CSS properties.

Tag	HTML Spec. Introduced	Recommended HTML 4.01 Alternative
<applet>	3.2	<object>
<basefont>	3.2	CSS, see below
<center>	3.2	CSS, see below
<dir>	2.0	<ul>
<font>	3.2	CSS, see below
<isindex>	2.0	<input type="text">
<menu>	2.0	<ul>
<s>	3.2	CSS, see below
<strike>	3.2	CSS, see below
<u>	3.2	CSS, see below

<applet>

This tag was introduced in the HTML 3.2 specification and is used to embed a Java applet in an HTML page. The tag and all intrinsic attributes are deprecated in the HTML 4.01 specification. The <applet> tag is being replaced with the more generic <object> tag (see Chapter 10 for more information on this).

Attributes

The following table lists the attributes that can be used with this tag. Confusingly, some attributes that apply to deprecated tags are not deprecated when used with other tags.

Attribute name	Optional or required?	Applies only to this tag?	Explanation to be found:
codebase	optional	no	See Chapter 10; the "*<object> attributes*" section
code	required	yes	See deprecated attributes below...
object	optional	yes	See deprecated attributes below...
name	optional	no	See Chapter 4; the "*Destination Anchors – the name and id Attributes*" section
archive	optional	no	See deprecated attributes below...
width	required	no	See Chapter 5; the "*<img> element*" section
height	required	no	See Chapter 5; the "*<img> element*" section

Examples

The following example demonstrates how to embed an applet (with only the required attributes set) in an HTML document using the deprecated `<applet>` tag.

```
<applet code="myApplet.class" width="400" height="200">
My java applet
</applet>
```

As you can see, the opening `<applet>` tag requires a corresponding closing `</applet>` tag. Browsers that do not support Java applets ignore the applet and instead render any text inserted between the opening and closing applet tags.

The following example demonstrates how to embed an applet in an HTML document using the `<object>` tag according to the HTML 4.01 specification.

```
<object codetype="application/java" classid="java:myApplet.class"
        width="400" height="200">
My java applet
</object>
```

As you can see, embedding an applet using the `<object></object>` tags requires an additional attribute (`codetype`) that specifies the type of object to be embedded since the `<object>` tag is used to embed more than one type of object.

\<basefont\>

This tag was introduced in the HTML 3.2 specification and is used to specify the size, face, and color of the base font for text in the HTML document. The tag can be used as many times as necessary to format sections of text within an HTML document. The basefont tag is an inline element and, therefore requires no closing \</basefont\> tag, but because of this, the attributes of multiple \<basefont\> tags do not cascade. If attributes set in preceding \<basefont\> tags are not set in subsequent \<basefont\> tags, the attribute that is not set reverts to the default setting. If the \<basefont\> tag is not used in an HTML document, the text defaults to the settings in the browser's user preferences. The \<basefont\> tag is not being replaced by another HTML tag, but rather by styles applied to the \<body\> and other HTML tags.

Attributes

The following table lists the attributes that can be used with this tag:

Attribute name	Optional or required?	Applies only to this tag?	Explanation to be found:
size	required	no	See Chapter 3; the "\<basefont\> element" section
color	optional	no	See Chapter 3; the "\<basefont\> element" section
face	optional	no	See Chapter 3; the "\<basefont\> element" section

Examples

The following example demonstrates how to implement the \<basefont\> tag in an HTML document:

```
<html>
   <head>
      <title>Exploring &lt;basefont&gt;</title>
   </head>
   <body>
      This is the default browser font setting.<br>

      <basefont size="1" color="#ff0000"
               face="arial,verdana,sans-serif">
         The font is now arial, red, size one <br>

      <basefont size="2" color="purple" face="serif">
         The font is now serif, purple, size two <br>

      <basefont size="3" color="gray" face="courier">
         The font is now courier, gray, size three <br>

      <basefont size="4" color="#00ff00" face="verdana">
         The font is now verdana, green, size four <br>
```

```
        <basefont size="5" color="orange" face="palatino">
            The font is now palatino, orange, size five <br>

        <basefont size="6" color="#0000ff" face="tahoma">
            The font is now tahoma, blue, size six <br>

        <basefont size="7" color="brown" face="georgia">
            The font is now georgia, brown, size seven <br>

        <basefont>
            Notice how by not setting any of the attributes in the
            &lt;basefont&gt; tag, none of the previous font settings
            cascade or persist, but are returned to the default values.
    </body>
</html>
```

The preceding example demonstrates how the `<basefont>` tag sets the size, color, and face properties of all subsequent text until either the document ends or another `<basefont>` tag is encountered. The example also illustrates the absence of the cascading effect that the style elements provide.

The following example demonstrates how to replicate the example above using the HTML `<style>` element.

```
<html>
<head>
    <title>Exploring &lt;Style&gt;</title>
    <style type="text/css">
        P.par1 {font-size:"xx-small"; color:"#ff0000"; font-family:"arial";}
        P.par2 {font-size:"x-small"; color:"purple"; font-family:"serif";}
        P.par3 {font-size:"small"; color:"gray"; font-family:"courier";}
        P.par4 {font-size:"medium"; color:"#00ff00"; font-family:"verdana";}
        P.par5 {font-size:"large"; color:"orange"; font-family:"palatino";}
        P.par6 {font-size:"x-large"; color:"#0000ff"; font-family:"tahoma";}
        P.par7 {font-size:"xx-large"; color:"brown"; font-family:"georgia";}
    </style>
</head>
<body>
    <p>This is the default browser setting</p>
    <p class="par1">The font is now arial, red, size xx-small</p>
    <p class="par2">The font is now serif, purple, size x-small</p>
    <p class="par3">The font is now courier, gray, size small</p>
    <p class="par4">The font is now verdana, green, size medium</p>
    <p class="par5">The font is now palatino, orange, size large</p>
    <p class="par6">The font is now tahoma, blue, size x-large</p>
    <p class="par7">The font is now georgia, brown, size xx-large</p>
</body>
</html>
```

Although not true in the preceding examples, the `<style>` element method of applying font formatting requires less code in cases where the document is extremely long or there are many changes, as CSS styles allow the reuse of the class as many times as necessary, and also allow the HTML coder to separate the data from the formatting.

<center>

Netscape introduced the <center> tag before it was able to add support for the HTML <div> element. Although the <center> element is exactly equivalent to <div align="center">, the <center> element's wide deployment allowed it to be included in the HTML 3.2 specification. The element is used to align the elements it contains with the center of the next outermost container element, the <body> element, for example. The <center> tag is being replaced by style sheet properties, such as text-align:center.

Examples

The following example demonstrates how to implement the <center> tag in an HTML document:

```
<html>
    <head>
        <title>Exploring &lt;center&gt;</title>
    </head>
    <body>
        <p>Here is some normal text.</p>

        <center>
            <p>Here is some centered text.</p>
        </center>

        <p>Here is some more normal text.</p>
    </body>
</html>
```

The preceding example demonstrates how the <center> tag aligns the text with the center of the body of the HTML document.

The following example demonstrates how to replicate the example above using the HTML <style> element:

```
<html>
<head>
    <title>Exploring &lt;Style&gt;</title>
    <style type="text/css">
        p.par1 {text-align:center}
    </style>
</head>
<body>
    <p>Here is some normal text</p>

    <p class="par1">
        Here is text centered with the &lt;style&gt; element
    </p>

    <p>Here is some more normal text.</p>
</body>
</html>
```

The <dir> and <menu> Elements

These tags were introduced in the HTML 2.0 specification and are used to create unordered, (usually) bulleted, single- or multi-columned lists (achieved by nesting) in the HTML document. The <dir> and <menu> elements are exactly equivalent to the <ul> element in nearly every browser implementation.

Attributes

The following table lists the attributes that can be used with this tag.

Attribute name	Optional or required?	Applies only to this tag?	Explanation to be found:
compact	optional	no	See Chapter 3; the "Lists" section

Examples

The following example demonstrates how to implement the <dir> and <menu> tags in an HTML document.

```
<html>
<head>
    <title>Exploring &lt;dir&gt; and &lt;menu&gt;</title>
</head> .
<body>
    <p>
    Following is a list created with the &lt;dir&gt; element.
        <dir compact>
            <li>Item 1</li>
            <li>Item 2</li>
            <li>Item 3</li>
        <dir>
            <li>Item 3.1</li>
            <li>Item 3.2</li>
            <li>Item 3.3</li>
        </dir>
        </dir>
    </p>
    <p>
        Following is a list created with the &lt;menu&gt; element.
        <menu>
            <li>Item 1</li>
            <li>Item 2</li>
        <menu compact>
            <li>Item 2.1</li>
            <li>Item 2.2</li>
            <li>Item 2.3</li>
        </menu>
            <li>Item 3</li>
        </menu>
    </p>
</body>
</html>
```

The next example demonstrates how to replicate the example above using the HTML `<ul>` element:

```
<html>
<head>
   <title>Exploring &lt;ul&gt;</title>
</head>
<body>
   <p>
   Following is a list created with the &lt;ul&gt; element.
      <ul>
         <li>Item 1 </li>
      <ul>
         <li>Item 1.1</li>
         <li>Item 1.2</li>
         <li>Item 1.3</li>
      </ul>
         <li>Item 2</li>
         <li>Item 3</li>
      </ul>
   </p>
</body>
</html>
```

`<font>`

This tag was introduced in the HTML 3.2 specification and is used to specify the size, face, and color of the font for text between its opening and closing tags (`<font>...</font>`) in the HTML document. The attributes of multiple `<font>` tags do not cascade, and if attributes set in preceding `<font>` tags are not set in subsequent `<font>` tags, the attribute that is not set reverts to the default setting. If the `<font>` tag is not used in an HTML document, the text defaults to the settings in the browser's user preferences. The `<font>` tag is not being replaced by another HTML tag, but rather by styles applied to the `<body>` and other HTML tags.

Attributes

The following table lists the attributes that can be used with this tag:

Attribute name	Optional or required?	Applies only to this tag?	Explanation to be found:
size	optional	no	See Chapter 3; the "*<basefont> element*" section
color	optional	no	See Chapter 3; the "*<basefont> element*" section
face	optional	no	See Chapter 3; the "*<basefont> element*" section

Examples

The following example demonstrates how to implement the `<font>` tag in an HTML document:

```
<html>
<head>
    <title>Exploring &lt;font&gt;</title>
</head>
<body>
    <p>This is the default browser font setting.<br></p>

    <p>
        <font size="1" color="#ff0000" face="arial">
            The font is now arial, red, size one <br>
        </font>
    </p>

    <p>
        <font size="2" color="purple" face="serif">
            The font is now serif, purple, size two <br>
        </font>
    </p>

    <p>
        <font size="3" color="gray" face="courier">
            The font is now courier, gray, size three <br>
        </font>
    </p>

    <p>
        <font size="4" color="#00ff00" face="verdana">
            The font is now verdana, green, size four <br>
        </font>
    </p>

    <p>
        <font size="5" color="orange" face="palatino">
            The font is now palatino, orange, size five <br>
        </font>
    </p>

    <p>
        <font size="6" color="#0000ff" face="tahoma">
            The font is now tahoma, blue, size six <br>
        </font>
    </p>

    <p>
        <font size="7" color="brown" face="georgia">
            The font is now georgia, brown, size seven <br>
            <font size="4">
                The font is now georgia, brown, size four - notice how
                attributes cascade for nested &lt;font&gt; tags <br>
            </font>
        </font>
```

```
    <font>
       Notice how by not setting any of the attributes in the
       &lt;font&gt; tag, the font settings are returned to
       the default values
    </font>
  </p>
 </body>
</html>
```

The above example demonstrates how the `<font>` element sets the size, color, and face properties of the text it contains. The example also illustrates the cascading effect that nested font tags produce. This cascading effect is the basis for the CSS syntax that the `<style>` elements provide.

The following example demonstrates how to replicate the example above using the HTML `<style>` element.

```
<html>
<head>
   <title>Exploring &lt;Style&gt;</title>
   <style type="text/css">
      p.par1 {font-size:xx-small; color:#ff0000; font-family:arial;}
      p.par2 {font-size:x-small; color:purple; font-family:serif;}
      p.par3 {font-size:small; color:gray; font-family:courier;}
      p.par4 {font-size:medium; color:#00ff00; font-family:verdana;}
      p.par5 {font-size:large; color:orange; font-family:palatino;}
      p.par6 {font-size:x-large; color:#0000ff; font-family:tahoma;}
      p.par7 {font-size:large;}
      div {font-size:xx-large; color:brown; font-family:georgia;}
   </style>
</head>
<body>
   <p>This is the default browser setting</p>
   <p class="par1">The font is now arial, red, size xx-small</p>
   <p class="par2">The font is now serif, purple, size x-small</p>
   <p class="par3">The font is now courier, gray, size small</p>
   <p class="par4">The font is now verdana, green, size medium</p>
   <p class="par5">The font is now palatino, orange, size large</p>
   <p class="par6">The font is now tahoma, blue, size x-large</p>
   <div class="div">
      The font is now georgia, brown, size xx-large
      <p class="par7">
         The font is now georgia, brown, size large - notice how
         attributes cascade for nested style classes
      </p>
   </div>
 </body>
</html>
```

The `<style>` element method of applying font formatting requires less code, and also allows the HTML coder to separate the data from the formatting. CSS style rules can also be reused for several HTML documents by storing them in an external file or stylesheet.

\<isindex\>

This tag was introduced in the HTML 2.0 specification and is used to create a single-line text field (for entering a query string) that is outside of any form element and separated by horizontal rules above and below in the HTML document. The number of characters that can be entered into this field is unrestricted. Space characters are replaced with the "+" character. When the user presses the *"Enter"* or *"Return"* key, the contents of the text field are submitted to the server in the query string. A program running on the server must be able to interpret the query string to return the requested HTML. Multiple \<isindex\> tags may be used within the same HTML document, either in the head or the body; however, only the last field created with the \<isindex\> tag containing a value will be submitted. The \<isindex\> tag is deprecated in favor of the \<input type="text"\> HTML \<form\> element.

Attributes

The following table lists the attributes that can be used with this tag:

Attribute name	Optional or required?	Applies only to this tag?	Explanation to be found:
prompt	optional	yes	See deprecated attributes below…

Examples

The following example demonstrates how to implement the \<isindex\> tag in an HTML document.

```
<html>
<head>
    <title>Exploring &lt;isindex&gt;</title>
    <isindex>
</head>
<body>
    <isindex prompt="Search for:">
</body>
</html>
```

The preceding example demonstrates using the \<isindex\> tag to create a simple single line text input field that is submitted to the base URL of the HTML document when the *"Enter"* or *"Return"* key is pressed.

The following example demonstrates how to replicate the example above using the HTML \<hr\>, \<form\>, and \<input\> elements.

```
<html>
<head>
    <title>Exploring &lt;form&gt; and &lt;input&gt;</TITLE>
</head>
<body>
    <hr>
    <form>
        Search for:
        <input type="text">
    </form>
    <hr>
</body>
</html>
```

As you can see, you can use the HTML <form> and <input> elements to produce the same results as the <isindex> element produces. The difference is that when using the HTML <form> element, the input field must have the focus to automatically submit the form when the *"Enter"* or *"Return"* key is pressed. With the <isindex> element, any time the *"Enter"* or *"Return"* key is pressed, the contents of the input field are submitted anyway, without need for this focus to be specified (for information about focus, see Chapter 6, *"Forms"*).

The <s> and <strike> Elements

These elements were introduced in the HTML 3.2 specification, and are used to render their respective contents as strikethrough text in the HTML document. The <s> and <strike> elements are deprecated in favor of CSS styles.

Examples

The following example demonstrates how to implement the <s> and <strike> tags in an HTML document:

```
<html>
<head>
   <title>Exploring &lt;s&gt; and &lt;strike&gt;</title>
</head>
<body>
<p>
   This is normal text.<br>
   <s>
      This is text formatted with the &lt;s&gt; tag. <br>
   </s>
   <strike>
      This is text formatted with the &lt;strike&gt; tag. <br>
   </strike>
</p>
</body>
</html>
```

The next example demonstrates how to replicate the example above using the HTML <style> element:

```
<html>
<head>
   <title>Exploring &lt;style&gt;</title>
      <style>
         span.strike {text-decoration:line-through;}
      </style>
</head>
<body>
   This is normal text.<br>
   <span class="strike">
      This is text formatted with the &lt;style&gt; line-through property.
   </span>
</body>
</html>
```

<u>

This tag was introduced in the HTML 3.2 specification and is used to render its contents as underlined text in the HTML document. The <u> element is deprecated in favor of CSS styles.

Examples

The following example demonstrates how to implement the <u> tag in an HTML document to create underlined text.

```
<html>
<head>
    <title>Exploring &lt;u&gt;</title>
</head>
<body>
    This is normal text. <br>
    <u>
        This is text formatted with the &lt;u&gt; tag. <br>
    </u>
</body>
</html>
```

The following example demonstrates how to replicate the example above using the HTML <style> element.

```
<html>
<head>
    <title>Exploring &lt;style&gt;</title>
    <style>
        span.underline {text-decoration:underline;}
    </style>
</head>
<body>
    This is normal text. <br>
    <span class="underline">
        This is text formatted with the &lt;style&gt; underline property.
    </span>
</body>
</html>
```

Deprecated HTML Attributes

The following table lists all attributes that are in any way deprecated, and also any tags for which the attribute remains current.

Attribute	Related Tag(s) for which it is deprecated (HTML 4.01)	Related Tag(s) for which it is current (HTML 4.01)	Recommended HTML 4.01 alternative
align	<caption> <applet> <iframe> <img> <input> <object> <legend> <table> <hr> <div> <h1> <h2> <h3> <h4> <h5> <h6> <p>	<col> <colgroup> <tbody> <td> <tfoot> <th> <thead> <tr>	CSS syntax:text-align:position

Table continued on following page

Attribute	Related Tag(s) for which it is deprecated (HTML 4.01)	Related Tag(s) for which it is current (HTML 4.01)	Recommended HTML 4.01 alternative
alink	`<body>`		CSS syntax: A:active{color:color}
alt	`<applet>`	`<area> <img> <input>`	N/A
archive	`<applet>`	`<object>`	N/A
background	`<body>`		CSS syntax: background:color or background:URL (image.gif)
bgcolor	`<table> <tr> <th> <td>`		CSS syntax: Background-color:color
border	`<applet> <img> <object>`	`<table>`	CSS syntax: Border-width:#px
clear	` `		CSS syntax: clear:position
code	`<applet>`		N/A
codebase	`<applet>`	`<object>`	N/A
color	`<basefont> <font>`		CSS syntax: color:color
compact	`<dir> <dl> <menu> <ol> <ul>`		N/A
face	`<basefont> <font>`		CSS syntax: font-family:fontname
height	`<applet> <th> <td>`	`<iframe> <img> <object>`	CSS syntax: height:#px
hspace	`<applet> <img> <object>`		CSS syntax: padding-left:#px padding-right:#px
language	`<script>`		type= "text/languagename"
link	`<body>`		CSS syntax: A:link{color:color;}
name	`<applet>`	`<a> <button> <form> <frame> <iframe> <img> <input> <map> <meta> <object> <param> <select> <textarea>`	N/A
noshade	`<hr>`		CSS syntax: border-style:solid

Attribute	Related Tag(s) for which it is deprecated (HTML 4.01)	Related Tag(s) for which it is current (HTML 4.01)	Recommended HTML 4.01 alternative
nowrap	`<td> <th>`		CSS syntax: white-space:nowrap
object	`<applet>`		N/A
prompt	`<isindex>`		N/A
size	`<hr>`	`<input>` `<select>`	CSS syntax: height:#px
size	`<font> <basefont>`	`<input>` `<select>`	CSS syntax: Font-size:#pt, or px, named size, or em
start	`<ol>`		CSS2 syntax: Counter-reset: countername countervalue
text	`<body>`		CSS syntax: color:color

type	`<li> <ol> <ul>`	`<a> <button>`
		`<input> <link>`
		`<object>`
		`<param>`
		`<script>`
		`<style>`
			CSS syntax: list-style-type:stylename;

value	`<li>`	`<button>`
		`<input>`
		`<option>`
		`<param>`
			CSS2 syntax:Counter-reset: countername countervalue;

version	`<html>`		Document type declaration, see earlier in chapter.
vlink	`<body>`		CSS syntax:A:visited{color :colorValue;
vspace	`<applet> <img>` `<object>`		CSS syntax: padding-bottom:#px padding-top:#px

width	`<pre> <td> <th>`
	`<hr>`
		`<col>`
		`<colgroup>`
		`<iframe> <img>`
		`<object>`
		`<table>`
			CSS syntax: width:#px

width	`<applet>`	`<col>`
		`<colgroup>`
		`<iframe> <img>`
		`<object>`
		`<table>`
			N/A

align

This attribute specifies the alignment of the individual HTML element. The values that can be assigned to align attributes are: top, middle, bottom, left, center, right, and justify. The align attribute is being replaced by various CSS elements. The syntax for the align attribute is:

```
align="position"
```

alink

This attribute specifies the color of selected hyperlinks in an HTML document. The value of the alink attribute can either be an acceptable color name (see Appendix D for a list of accepted colors) or the corresponding hexadecimal RGB value. The alink attribute is deprecated in favor of the CSS A:active{color:colorValue;} property. The syntax for the alink attribute is:

```
alink="colorname | hexadecimal value"
```

alt

This attribute specifies alternative text in the case that the browser is unable to render an element. The alt attribute is especially important for browsers that cannot render certain elements, as it provides a textual alternative to the object that it failed to render. The title attribute is the acceptable alternative to the alt attribute when using the <object> element. The syntax for the alt attribute is:

```
alt="text"
```

archive

This attribute specifies a space-delimited list of URLs that contain multiple java classes or other additional resources that will be loaded in the browser all at once in order to improve applet performance. The archive attribute is only deprecated for the <applet> element. The URLs specified by the archive attribute are relative to the codebase of the applet. No absolute path, such as http://www.yoursite.com/applet/MyAppletArchive.zip may be used. The syntax for the archive attribute is:

```
archive="filename"
```

background

This attribute specifies the URL of a selected image to use as the backdrop of an HTML document. The background attribute is deprecated in favor of the CSS background-color:URL or color property. The syntax for the background attribute is:

```
background="url"
```

bgcolor

This attribute specifies the color of the backdrop of an HTML document. The value of the bgcolor attribute can either be an acceptable color name (see Appendix D for a list of accepted colors) or the corresponding hexadecimal RGB value. The bgcolor attribute is deprecated in favor of the CSS background:URL or color property. The syntax for the bgcolor attribute is:

```
bgcolor="colorname | hexadecimal value"
```

border

This attribute specifies the thickness of the border around an HTML element in pixels. The border attribute is deprecated for all HTML elements except <table>. The border attribute is deprecated in favor of the CSS border-width:#px property. The syntax for the border attribute is:

```
border="#px"
```

clear

This attribute specifies how the browser should handle the next line after a line break caused by a <br /> element. The value of the clear attribute can either be all, left, right, or none. For example, if the value of the clear attribute is "left", the next line will begin only when there is nothing positioned in the left margin of the containing HTML element. The clear attribute is essentially telling the browser to wait until the left margin clears before beginning the next line. The clear attribute is deprecated in favor of the CSS clear:position property.

For more of an explanation of the clear attribute, including an example, check out Chapter 3, "Text Formatting"; the "
 (Line Break) Element" section. The syntax for the clear attribute is:

```
clear="position"
```

code

This attribute specifies the file name of the Java applet's compiled code. The path to the applet file specified by the code attribute is relative (for example, /code/myApplet.class) only to the codebase of the applet. No absolute paths, such as http://www.yoursite.com/applet/MyApplet.class may be used. The syntax for the code attribute is:

```
code="filename"
```

codebase

This attribute specifies the directory for the Java Applet code. If the codebase attribute is not specified, the applet files are assumed to be in the same directory as the HTML file calling the applet. The syntax for the codebase attribute is:

```
codebase="url"
```

color

This attribute specifies the font color of the text in an HTML document. The value of the `color` attribute can either be an acceptable color name (for a list of acceptable colors, see Appendix D) or the corresponding hexadecimal RGB value. The default setting of the `color` attribute is `"black"` or `"#000000"`, which is the value used if the `color` attribute is not specified. The `color` attribute is deprecated in favor of the CSS `color:colorname` or `hexadecimal` RGB value property. The syntax for the `color` attribute is:

```
color="colorname | hexadecimal value"
```

compact

This is a (Boolean) attribute that tells the browser to render less space between lines. Including the `compact` attribute in the element sets the value to `true`. The default value of this attribute is `false`. In most current browsers this attribute is ignored. The `compact` attribute is deprecated in favor of the CSS `letter-spacing` or `word-spacing` properties The syntax for the `compact` attribute is simply `compact`.

face

This attribute specifies a comma-separated list of font faces for text in an HTML document. The value of the `face` attribute must match a named system font on the client. The default setting of the `face` attribute is whatever font is set as default in the browser's user preferences. If more than one font is listed, the browser tries each font in order. If the browser cannot match a font in the list then the browser's default font is chosen. The `face` attribute is deprecated in favor of the CSS `font-family:fontname` property. The syntax for the face attribute is:

```
face="fontname1, fontname2, fontname3"
```

height

This attribute sets the pixel height of an HTML element's display area. The `height` attribute is deprecated for the `<td>`, `<th>`, and `<applet>` elements in favor of the CSS `height:pixelcount` property. The syntax for the `height` attribute is:

```
height="pixelcount"
```

hspace

This attribute sets the amount of white space or padding (in pixels) on the left and right of the HTML element's display area. The `hspace` attribute is deprecated in favor of the CSS `padding-left:pixelcount` and `padding-right:pixelcount` properties. The syntax for the `hspace` attribute is:

```
hspace="pixelcount"
```

language

This attribute specifies the name of the scripting language of the HTML element. The `language` attribute has been deprecated in favor of the `type=text/languagename` attribute. The syntax for the language attribute is:

```
language="languageName"
```

link

This attribute specifies the color of hyperlinks that have not been visited in an HTML document. The value of the `link` attribute can either be an acceptable color name (see Appendix D for a list of accepted colors) or the corresponding hexadecimal RGB value. The `link` attribute is deprecated in favor of the CSS `A:link{color:colorValue;}` property. The syntax for the link attribute is:

```
link="colorname | hexadecimal value"
```

name

This attribute specifies a name for the HTML element. The `name` attribute allows scripts and elements within the same HTML document to communicate with or manipulate the element, and it is only deprecated for the `<applet>` element. The syntax for the `name` attribute is:

```
name="name"
```

noshade

This is an optional Boolean attribute that instructs the browser to render an `<hr />` element as a single, one color, solid line. The `noshade` attribute is replaced with CSS border property syntax. For example, the following statement:

```
<hr style="border:thin gray solid;width:50px" />
```

This produces identical results to:

```
<hr noshade width="50" height="1" />
```

The syntax for the `noshade` attribute is simply `noshade`. For more information on using `<hr />`, see Chapter 3; *"The <hr /> (Horizontal Rule) Element"* section.

nowrap

This is an optional Boolean attribute that instructs the browser to disable automatic text wrapping for the specified `<th>` or `<td>` cell. The `nowrap` attribute is replaced with CSS syntax: `white-space:nowrap`. The syntax for the `nowrap` attribute is simply `nowrap`.

object

This attribute specifies the file name of the Java applet's compiled code that stores a serialized representation of an applet's state. The path to the applet file specified by the object attribute is relative (for example, /code/myApplet.class) only to the codebase of the applet. No absolute path, such as http://www.yoursite.com/applet/MyApplet.class may be used. The syntax for the object attribute is:

```
object="filename"
```

prompt

This attribute specifies a prompt or label for the text field created by the <isindex> element. If no prompt is specified, the browser will display its own custom prompt message. The prompt attribute only applies to the <isindex> element, which is also deprecated – therefore there is no replacement. The syntax for the prompt attribute is:

```
prompt="promptMessage"
```

size

This attribute specifies the font size of text in an HTML element, the pixel height of an <hr /> element, or the character width of an <input> element. For the <font> element, the value of the size attribute can be any positive integer between 1 and 7, or any signed integer between –6 and +6. The default setting of the size attribute is 3, which is the value used if the size attribute is not specified. If a signed integer is specified, the value is added to the font size set by the <basefont> tag. If the sum of the signed integer size attribute is greater than or equal to 7, the size is set to seven. If the sum of the signed integer size attribute is less than or equal to 1, the size is set to one. The size attribute can also be a named size, which is then mapped to one of the seven numbered sizes as follows:

Named Font Size	Numbered Font Size Equivalent
xx-small	1
x-small	2
small	3
medium	4
large	5
x-large	6
xx-large	7

The value of the size attribute for the <hr /> element can be any positive integer, and defaults to 2. The value of the size attribute for the <input> element can be any positive integer, and defaults to 20. The size attribute is deprecated for all HTML elements except <input>. For font size, the replacement is the CSS syntax: font-size: named or numbered size. For the <hr /> element, the replacement is the CSS syntax: height: number of pixels. The syntax of the size attribute is:

```
size="namedFontSize | numericalFontSize"
```

start

This attribute specifies where the browser should start numbering for list (`<li>`) items in an ordered list (`<ol>`). The default setting for the `start` attribute is 1, which is the value used if the `start` attribute is not specified. The `start` attribute is replaced with CSS2 syntax: `counter-reset: countername countervalue`. The syntax of the `start` attribute is:

```
start="startNumber"
```

text

This attribute specifies the foreground color of text in an HTML document. The value of the `text` attribute can either be an acceptable color name (see Appendix D for a list of accepted colors) or the corresponding hexadecimal RGB value. The `text` attribute is deprecated in favor of the CSS `color: color name` and `hex RGB value` properties. The syntax for the `text` attribute is:

```
text="colorname" or text="#hexdecimal value"
```

type

This attribute specifies the style of a list item (`<li>`, `<ol>`, or `<ul>`) in an HTML document. The value of the `type` attribute can either be `"disc"`, `"square"`, `"circle"`, `"1"`, `"a"`, `"A"`, `"i"`, or `"I"`. For example, `<li type="disc">`. The `type` attribute is only deprecated for the `<ol>`, `<ul>`, and `<li>` elements in favor of the CSS `list-style-type:stylename` property. The syntax for the `type` attribute is:

```
type="stylename"
```

value

This attribute specifies how the browser should number a list (`<li>`) item in an ordered list (`<ol>`). There is no replacement for this attribute, and it's syntax is:

```
value="integer"
```

version

This attribute specifies which HTML DTD (Document Type Declaration) version the current HTML document supports. The `version` attribute has been deprecated because it simply restates the version information specified in the DTD. The syntax for the `version` attribute is

```
version="version"
```

vlink

This attribute specifies the color of visited hyperlinks in an HTML document. The value of the `vlink` attribute can either be an acceptable color name (see Appendix D for a list of acceptable colors) or the corresponding hexadecimal RGB value. The `vlink` attribute is deprecated in favor of the CSS `a:visited{color:color name | hex RGB value}` property. The syntax for the `vlink` attribute is:

```
vlink="colorName | hexadecimalValue"
```

411

vspace

This attribute sets the amount of white space or padding (in pixels) above and below the HTML element's display area. The vspace attribute is deprecated in favor of the CSS padding-top:pixelcount and padding-bottom:pixelcount properties. The syntax for the vspace attribute is:

```
vspace="pixelCount"
```

width

This attribute sets the pixel width of an HTML element's display area. The width attribute is deprecated for the <pre>, <td>, <th>, <hr>, and <applet> elements in favor of the CSS width:pixelcount property. The syntax for the height attribute is:

```
width="pixelCount"
```

Obsolete Elements

In this section we will discuss the various obsolete HTML elements included in the HTML 4.01 specification. The obsolete HTML elements in this specification all perform essentially the same function as the <pre> and <samp> elements. Remember that because these elements are declared obsolete by the W3C in the HTML specification, it is likely that future browsers will no longer support them whereas most browser manufacturers continue to build support into their browsers for deprecated elements.

The following tags are obsolete in the HTML 4.01 specification due to redundancy in the form of other HTML elements, specifically <pre> and <samp>.

Tag	HTML Spec. Introduced	Replaced With
<listing>	2.0	<pre> or <samp>
<plaintext>	2.0	<pre> or <samp>
<xmp>	2.0	<pre> or <samp>

<listing>

The <listing> tag was introduced in the HTML 2.0 specification and is used to render its contents in mono-spaced HTML font. The <listing> element is obsolete – use the <pre> element in its place.

The following example demonstrates how to implement the <listing> tag in an HTML document:

```
<html>
<head>
   <title>Exploring &lt;listing&gt;</title>
</head>
<body>
   <p>
```

412

```
        This is normal text. <br>
           <lisitng>
              This is text formatted with the &lt;listing&gt; tag.
           </listing>
        </p>
     </body>
     </html>
```

The next example demonstrates how to replicate the example above using the HTML `<pre>` and `<samp>` elements instead:

```
<html>
<head>
   <title>Exploring &lt;pre&gt; and &lt;samp&gt;</title>
</head>
<body>
   <p>
   This is normal text. <br>
      <pre style="font-size:xx-small;">
         This is text formatted with the &lt;pre&gt; tag.
      </pre>
      <samp style="font-size:xx-small;">
         This is text formatted with the &lt;samp&gt; tag.
      </samp>
   </p>
</body>
</html>
```

`<plaintext>`

The `<plaintext>` element was introduced in the HTML 2.0 specification and is used to render all text (including HTML tags) occurring after it as mono-spaced HTML font.

The following example demonstrates how to implement the `<plaintext>` tag in an HTML document:

```
<html>
<head>
   <title>Exploring &lt;plaintext&gt;</title>
</head>
<body>
   <p>
   This is normal text. <br>
      <plaintext>
         This is text formatted with the &lt;plaintext&gt; tag.
      </plaintext>
   </p>
</body>
</html>
```

<xmp>

The <xmp> tag was introduced in the HTML 2.0 specification and is used to render its contents in mono-spaced HTML font. The <xmp> element is obsolete, use the <pre> or <samp> elements in its place.

The following example demonstrates how to implement the <xmp> tag in an HTML document:

```
<html>
<head>
        <title>Exploring &lt;xmp&gt;</title>
</head>
<body>
    This is normal text. <br>
    <xmp>
        <p> This is text formatted with the <xmp> tag.</p>
    </xmp>
</body>
</html>
```

Summary

In this chapter, we discussed:

❑ What the W3C's HTML specifications are, why they change, and the importance of adhering to recognized standards

❑ How the W3C's various working groups review suggestions, errata, and recommendations and then make decisions resulting in a new specification versioning

❑ DTDs and how they specify rules for a valid HTML document and guide document conformance to certain specifications, and that a DTD does not actually specify how an HTML document is displayed in the browser

We also took a detailed look at each individual deprecated and obsolete HTML element, and how each element could either be replaced with another element, with a CSS property, or not at all.

It is important to understand why the changes discussed here come about and how, and how to deal with them in your code – otherwise, there may come a time when your code will cease to work properly on newer browsers, as older elements and attributes become obsolete.

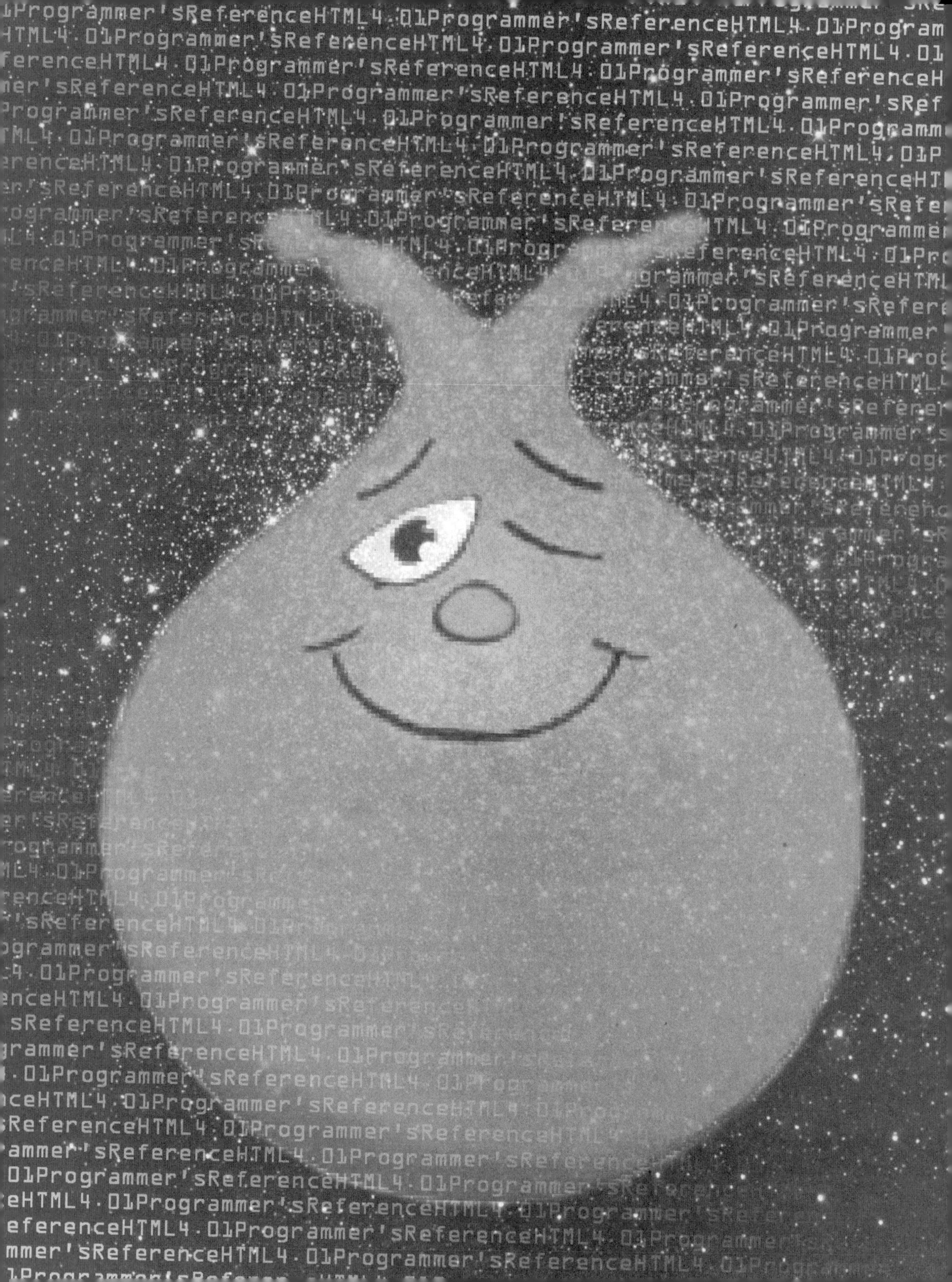
HTML4.01Programmer'sReference

16

IE- and Netscape-Specific Tags and Styles

Throughout the progression of versions, browser manufacturers have seen fit to include proprietary tags in order to enrich the user's experience, to gain additional marketing clout, and to garner developer mind-share by creating dependencies on their own proprietary technology. These proprietary tags are rarely supported by the other major browsers, and sometimes never make it into a formal specification. In this chapter, we will discuss the cross-browser controversy, and then briefly discuss each proprietary tag supported by Microsoft's Internet Explorer (IE) and Netscape (N).

Cross-Browser Controversy

The cross-browser controversy stems from the fact that throughout each of the major versions or releases of the Netscape and IE Web browsers, each browser's support of the W3C HTML, DOM, and CSS specifications has been at best variable. While both major browsers have to hold some things in common, specification support is still largely open to interpretation. Also, each of these companies is trying to get its technology recognized or approved as the standard, thus deprecating and eliminating the need for the other company's solutions to similar problems. These different interpretations of specifications, coupled with the addition of proprietary elements designed to support their own proprietary components and/or plugin models – to try to "lock-in" users – has created possibly the biggest headache HTML authors of today have to face: cross-browser support.

Version 1 Browsers

Fueled by the popularity of Mosaic, an early web browser, Marc Andreessen's Netscape crashed onto the web browser scene in 1994 with its beta version 1 browser that supported all the major elements included in the HTML 2.0 specification. Proprietary tags (those supported only by the browser manufacturer and not the W3C) first made their appearance in the 1.1 beta version of Netscape. Also included in this version was limited support for some HTML 3 elements, even though HTML 3 did not become a specification for another year. The first version of Internet Explorer (IE) was slower to market than Netscape, finally appearing in August of 1995. This version of IE supported all the major HTML 2 Elements, but not much else. At this point Netscape was far and away the more popular of the two browsers, and many of the idiosyncrasies of the implementation have become *de facto* standards that gained official recognition in future releases of the HTML specification.

Version 2 Browsers

Microsoft was quick to release its beta version 2 browser in October of 1995. The IE 2.0 beta added support for HTML tables and several of the new HTML version 3.0 elements. Netscape also released a beta version 2 browser in October 1995. This version of Netscape also added support for some of the new HTML elements. In addition, Netscape version 2, beta, now supported frames and Java. With another beta release in December of 1995, Netscape added support for JavaScript.

Version 3 Browsers

Netscape issued its first version 3 browser beta release in April of 1996. This release signaled the beginning of the modern era of web design with increased formatting, layout, and interactivity support. Subsequent "point" releases of N 3 added no new HTML support, but focused on fixes to security holes and JavaScript functionality. IE version 3 was really the catch-up version. In this version, Microsoft brought its support for HTML tables up to specifications. This version also added support for frames and scripting, both VBScript and JavaScript. It also added support for Cascading Style Sheets and Java applets. Even with all the added features in IE, Netscape was able to rely on its hard-won proponents allowing it to prevail as the most popular browser.

Version 4, 5, and 6 Browsers

Between 1997 and 2000, IE versions 4 and 5 really revolutionized the browser market. Microsoft won the hearts of HTML authors and web developers everywhere by adding 'anytime, anywhere' control over the DOM. Nearly every element, property, attribute, or value could now be modified dynamically through scripting. Netscape also enabled a great deal of control over certain presentational attributes. IE also offers native XML support (via an optional component: `msxml.dll`), something not offered by N 4.x. The version 4 and 5 browsers also began the trend of further separation of form from content; with the increased support for style sheets/CSS 2 recommendations. Netscape never really released a version 5 browser, instead choosing to issue several versions of N 4, abandoning plans for a version 5 in favor of the all-new version 6 browser recently released. N 6 shows some promise with its strict support of the XML, HTML, DOM, and CSS 1 (and some but not all of CSS 2) specifications. Due to some initial bugs, instability, and being extremely resource-intensive on some platforms, N 6 has not as yet rallied a particularly strong following; in fact its version 4.7 has higher usage statistics. With a few point releases, it is conceivable Netscape could once again climb to the top of the browser pile (version 6.01 is already significantly improved), but currently Internet Explorer has a commanding grip on that much-coveted position.

It is unfortunate that, in the past, competition drove these two corporations to undermine efforts that would allow HTML authors to truly code according to the HTML specification, and thus make rich content enjoyable by all, regardless of browser. In the coming months and years, we are going to see standards compliance become even more of a major selling point in new versions of browser software. In sharp contrast to the past, the major browser manufacturers will have to concentrate on supporting a solid standard rather than trying to manipulate it to their own respective ends.

IE-Specific HTML Tags

The following tags never quite made it into a formal HTML specification, and are proprietary to IE.

Tag	IE Versions	NN Equivalent	HTML 4.01 Equivalent
`<bgsound>`	2, 3, 4, 5	`<embed>`	`<object>`
`<marquee>`	2, 3, 4, 5	N/A	N/A
`<rt>`	5	N/A	N/A
`<ruby>`	5	N/A	N/A
`<xml>`	5	N/A	N/A

<bgsound>

The `<bgsound>` tag was introduced in IE version 2.0 and is used to specify a sound file to play in the background of an HTML page. The `<bgsound>` tag must be enclosed within the `<head></head>` tags and does not require a closing `</bgsound>` tag. To ensure current and future specification compliance, use the `<object>` tag instead.

Attributes

Attribute name	IE Versions	Optional or required?	Explanation to be found:
`balance`	4, 5	optional	See below
`id`	4, 5	optional	See Chapter 2
`lang`	4	optional	See Chapter 2
`loop`	2, 3, 4, 5	optional	See below
`src`	2, 3, 4, 5	required	See Chapter 5
`volume`	4, 5	optional	See below

balance

An attribute that controls the left/right division of sound to the speakers. The default value of the balance attribute is "0", or centered. The possible values can range from -10000 to +10000, with negative integers boosting the left channel and positive integers boosting the right channel. The syntax for the balance attribute is:

```
balance="number"
```

loop

An attribute that specifies the number of times the sound clip should play when activated. The possible values can range from -1 to any positive number. The default value of the loop attribute is "-1" which causes the clip to repeat an infinite number of times. If no value for the loop attribute is specified, the clip will play once. A value of 0 or 1 also causes the clip to play once. Any other positive integer as a value causes the clip to be played that number of times. The syntax for the loop attribute is:

```
loop="number"
```

volume

This specifies the volume setting for the specified clip. The possible values for the volume attribute can range from -10000 to 0. The default value for the volume attribute is "0", which is the full volume of the wave output volume setting on the client computer. Any value less than zero attenuates the volume of the clip in direct proportion to its distance from 0. The syntax for the volume attribute is:

```
volume="number"
```

Examples

The following example demonstrates how to implement <bgsound> in an HTML document.

```
<html>
  <head>
    <bgsound src="ringin.wav" balance="-1000" loop="3"
             volume="-500">
  </head>
</html>
```

The preceding example embeds a background sound in an HTML document to play three times, predominantly in the left speaker(s), and at a volume slightly less than standard. As can be seen, the <bgsound> tag requires no closing tag because its settings are all controlled by its attributes.

The following example demonstrates how to embed a background sound in an HTML document using the <object> tag according to the HTML 4.01 specification. This example will only work on IE running on a Windows platform with Windows Media Player installed, and only serves to demonstrate the HTML 4.01-compliant usage of the <object> element.

```
<html>
  <head>
    <object id="MediaPlayer"
            classid="CLSID:22D6F312-B0F6-11D0-94AB-0080C74C7E95"
            width="150" height="200">

      <param name="FileName" value="ringin.wav">
      <param name="AutoStart" value="1">
      <param name="AutoRewind" value="1">
      <param name="PlayCount" value="3">
    </object>
  </head>
</html>
```

As can be seen, embedding a background sound using the <object> and <param> tags achieves similar results to the <bgsound> element while complying with HTML 4.01 specifications.

<marquee>

The <marquee> tag was introduced in IE version 2.0 and is used to specify HTML content that is to be rendered in a scrolling fashion. The <marquee> element is a block element, which means it requires opening and closing. There is no direct equivalent to the <marquee> tag in the HTML 4.01 specification, but similar effects can be achieved with DHTML.

Attributes

Attribute name	IE Versions	Optional or required?	Explanation to be found:
event-name	4, 5	optional	See Chapter 2
accesskey	5	optional	See Chapter 2
align	2, 3	optional	See Chapter 2
behavior	2, 3, 4, 5	optional	See below
bgcolor	2, 3, 4, 5	optional	See Chapter 2
class	4, 5	optional	See Chapter 2
datafld	4, 5	optional	See Chapter 2
dataformatas	4, 5	optional	See Chapter 2
datasrc	4, 5	optional	See Chapter 2
dir	5	optional	See Chapter 2
direction	2, 3, 4, 5	optional	See below
height	2, 3, 4, 5	optional	See Chapter 5
hspace	2, 3, 4, 5	optional	See Chapter 5

Table continued on following page

Attribute name	IE Versions	Optional or required?	Explanation to be found:
id	4, 5	optional	See Chapter 2
lang	4, 5	optional	See Chapter 2
loop	4, 5	optional	See below
scrollamount	2, 3, 4, 5	optional	See below
scrolldelay	2, 3, 4, 5	optional	See below
style	4, 5	optional	See Chapter 2
tabindex	5	optional	See Chapter 2
title	4, 5	optional	See Chapter 2
truespeed	4, 5	optional	See below
vspace	2, 3, 4, 5	optional	See Chapter 5
width	2, 3, 4, 5	optional	See Chapter 5

behavior

An attribute that specifies how HTML elements are scrolled within a <marquee>. The possible values for the behavior attribute are "scroll", "alternate", and "slide". The default value of the behavior attribute is "scroll", which causes the text to move in the direction specified by the direction attribute (see below). A value of "alternate" will cause the text to reverse position when the content reaches the edge of the <marquee> container, specified by the width attribute (see below). A value of "slide" will cause the text to scroll to the edge of the <marquee> container, specified by the width attribute, then stop. The syntax for the behavior attribute is:

```
behavior="namedBehavior"
```

direction

An attribute that specifies the direction in which the HTML elements contained within a <marquee> should scroll. The possible values of the direction attribute are "left", "right", "down", and "up". The default value of the direction attribute is "left", which causes the content to scroll from the right to the left of the container. The other possible values cause the HTML content to scroll in their respective directions. The syntax for the direction attribute is:

```
direction="direction"
```

loop

An attribute that specifies the number of times the content should scroll. The possible values can range from −1 to any positive number. The default value of the loop attribute is "-1" or infinite. A value of "0" also causes the content to loop an infinite number of times. If no value for the loop attribute is specified, the clip will play once. A value of "1" also causes the content to scroll once. Any other positive integer as a value causes the content to be scrolled that number of times. The syntax for the loop attribute is:

```
loop="number"
```

422

scrollamount

An attribute that specifies the number of pixels the text scrolls between each subsequent drawing of the `<marquee>`. The value of the `scrollamount` attribute can be any positive integer (within reason, remember 1024 x 768 is the high-average screen size setting). The syntax for the `scrollamount` attribute is:

```
scrollamount="numberpixels"
```

scrolldelay

This attribute specifies the time between each drawing of the `<marquee>`, in milliseconds. The value of the `scrolldelay` attribute can be any positive integer. The syntax for the `scrolldelay` attribute is:

```
scrolldelay="milliseconds"
```

truespeed

A Boolean attribute that indicates if the exact scroll delay value should be used. The default value of the `truespeed` attribute is `false`, which indicates that the marquee advance its contents in 60 millisecond intervals. If the `truespeed` attribute is set to `true`, the marquee advances by the pixel value assigned to the `scrollamount` attribute at a frequency, in milliseconds, specified by the value assigned to the `scrolldelay` attribute. Note that any value under `60` assigned to the `scrolldelay` attribute is ignored, and the marquee advances by the value assigned to the `scrollamount` attribute each 60 milliseconds. The syntax for the `truespeed` attribute is:

```
truespeed="boolean"
```

Examples

The following example demonstrates how to implement the `<MARQUEE>` tag in an HTML document.

```
<marquee behavior="alternate" loop="4" direction="down" scrolldelay="100">
  Scroll this!
</marquee>
```

The preceding example implements a simple marquee containing scrolling text in an HTML document that scrolls up, then down four times at 100 millisecond intervals before stopping.

To replicate the functionality of the `<marquee>` element in other browsers requires use of client-side JavaScript, VBScript, or alternatively DHTML, which are outside the scope of this book.

`<ruby>` and `<rt>`

The `<ruby>` and `<rt>` tags were introduced in IE version 5.0. The `<ruby>` and `<rt>` tag combination serves to provide pronunciation support by annotating specified base text (`<ruby>`) with pronunciation help (`<rt>`). The `<ruby>` tag is used to specify base HTML text for which the pronunciation support is provided. The `<rt>` element renders an annotation above (and in a smaller print) the associated "ruby" text. There is no direct equivalent to the `<ruby>` and `<rt>` tags in the HTML 4.01 specification, but similar effects can be achieved using style sheets.

Attributes

Attribute name	IE Versions	Optional or required?	Explanation to be found:
accesskey	5	optional	See Chapter 2
class	5	optional	See Chapter 2
dir	5	optional	See Chapter 2
id	5	optional	See Chapter 2
lang	5	optional	See Chapter 2
language	5	optional	See Chapter 2
name	5	optional	See Chapter 2
style	5	optional	See Chapter 2
tabindex	5	optional	See Chapter 2
Title	5	optional	See Chapter 2

Examples

The following example demonstrates how to implement the <ruby> and <rt> tags in an HTML document. The font size in the example is set to large because the annotation is two font sizes smaller.

```
<ruby style="font-size: large">
  Annotate this text!
  <rt>Here is the annotation</rt>
</ruby>
```

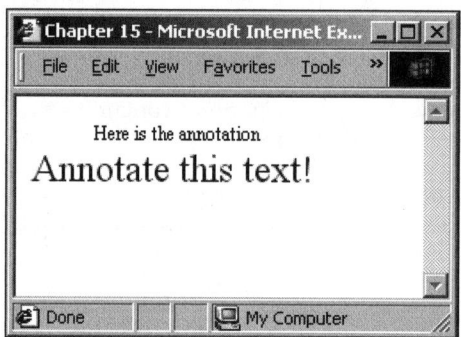

The following sample demonstrates how to annotate text in an HTML document using CSS syntax. The rt text in this example is positioned relatively to the ruby text and set with a font size two steps smaller than the ruby text. The only drawback to this method is that we cannot have the ruby text at the top of the page, as the annotation will not be visible (hence the

).

```
<html>
  <head>
    <style>
      .rt{
          font-size:small;
          position:relative;
          top:-45px;
          }
      .ruby{
          font-size:large;
          }
    </style>
  </head>
  <body>
    <br><br><!--Added for spacing-->
    <span class="ruby">
      <div>Annotate this text!</div>
      <span class="rt">
        Here is the annotation
      </span>
    </span>
  </body>
</html>
```

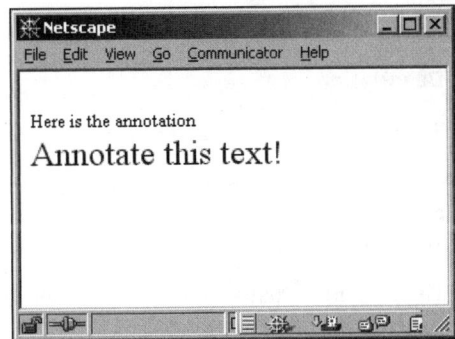

As can be seen, using CSS styles, we can achieve similar results to those accomplished using the
`<ruby>` and `<rt>` elements.

`<xml>`

The `<xml>` tag was introduced in IE version 5.0 and is used to specify XML content that serves as an
XML data island or XML data that is embedded directly in the HTML document. The XML content of
the data island can be accessed and manipulated using the XML DOM and client-side scripting
functionality. There is no direct equivalent to the `<xml>` tag in the HTML 4.01 specification, but
similar effects can be achieved by client or server-side scripting and/or the XML DOM.

Attributes

Attribute name	IE Versions	Optional or required?	Explanation to be found:
id	5	optional	See Chapter 2
src	5	optional	See Chapter 5

Examples

The following example demonstrates how to implement the `<xml>` tag in an HTML document:

```
<xml id="myXML">
  <contacts>
    <name>John Doe</name>
    <address>123 AnyStreet</address>
    <city>AnyTown</city>
    <state>AnyState</state>
  </contacts>
</xml>
```

To replicate the functionality of the `<xml>` element requires client-side JavaScript or VBScript and knowledge of the XML Document Object Model (XML DOM).

IE-Specific Styles

The following table lists the proprietary styles that IE supports, and although many of these styles have been proposed to the W3C for inclusion in a future CSS recommendation, they are not supported outside IE at this time.

Attribute	Description	IE Versions
behavior	The way the text in a `<marquee>` element scrolls	5
ime-mode	The state of an Input Method Editor (IME); an IME allows authors to input and edit Chinese, Japanese, and Korean characters	5
layout-grid	The properties that specify the layout of characters	5
layout-grid-char	The size of the character grid used for rendering the text content of an element	5
layout-grid-line	The gridline value used for rendering the text content of an element	5
layout-grid-mode	A string specifying whether the text layout grid uses two dimensions	5
layout-grid-type	The type of grid used for rendering the text content of an element	5
line-break	Line-breaking rules for Japanese text	5
ruby-align	The position of the ruby text specified by the `<rt>` object	5
ruby-overhang	The position of the ruby text specified by the `<rt>` object	5

Attribute	Description	IE Versions
ruby-position	The position of the ruby text specified by the `<rt>` object	5
text-autospace	The autospacing and narrow space width adjustment of text	5
text-justify	The type of alignment used to justify text in the object	5
text-kashida-space	The ratio of kashida expansion to white space expansion when justifying lines of text in the object	5.5
text-underline-position	The position of the underline decoration that is set through the `textDecoration` property of the object	5.5
word-break	The line-breaking behavior within words, particularly where multiple languages appear in the object	5
word-wrap	The breaking of words when the content exceeds the boundaries of its container.	5.5
writing-mode	The direction and flow of the content in the object	5.5
scrollbar-3dlight-color	The color of the top and left edges of the scroll box and scroll arrows of a scroll bar	5.5
scrollbar-arrow-color	The color of the arrow elements of a scroll arrow	5.5
scrollbar-base-color	The color of the main elements of a scroll bar, which include the scroll box, track, and scroll arrows	5.5
scrollbar-darkshadow-color	The color of the gutter of a scroll bar	5.5
scrollbar-face-color	The color of the scroll box and scroll arrows of a scroll bar	5.5
scrollbar-highlight-color	The color of the top and left edges of the scroll box and scroll arrows of a scroll bar	5.5
scrollbar-shadow-color	The color of the bottom and right edges of the scroll box and scroll arrows of a scroll bar	5.5
zoom	The magnification scale of the object	5.5

IE-Specific HTML Attributes

The following table lists the proprietary attributes that IE supports, but are not supported by the W3C or any other browser at this time.

Attribute	Description
balance	See above
behavior	See above
bgproperties	See Chapter 2
bordercolordark	See Chapter 7
bordercolorlight	See Chapter 7
bottommargin	See Chapter 2
dataformatas	See Chapter 2
datafld	See Chapter 2
datapagesize	See Chapter 2
datasrc	See Chapter 2
direction	See above
dynsrc	See Chapter 5
framespacing	See Chapter 8
leftmargin	See Chapter 2
loop	See above
rightmargin	See Chapter 2
scroll	See above
scrollamount	See above
scrolldelay	See above
topmargin	See Chapter 2
truespeed	See above
volume	See above

Netscape-Specific HTML Tags

The following tags never quite made it into a formal HTML specification, and are proprietary to Netscape.

Tag	N Versions	IE Equivalent	HTML 4.01 Equivalent
`<blink>`	2,3,4,6	N/A	N/A
`<ilayer>`	4	N/A	N/A
`<keygen>`	2,3,4,6	N/A	N/A
`<layer>`	4	`<div>`	`<div>`
`<multicol>`	2,3,4,	N/A	N/A
`<noembed>`	2,3,4,6	N/A	N/A
`<nolayer>`	4	N/A	N/A
`<spacer>`	3,4	N/A	N/A

<blink>

The `<blink>` tag was introduced in Netscape version 2.0 and is used to cause text to blink on and off in an HTML document. There is no direct equivalent to the `<blink>` tag in the HTML 4.01 specification, but similar effects can be achieved using DHTML or the CSS 2 `text-decoration:blink` property.

Attributes

Attribute name	N Versions	Optional or required?	Explanation to be found:
`class`	4	optional	See Chapter 2
`id`	4	optional	See Chapter 2
`style`	4	optional	See Chapter 2

Examples

The following example demonstrates how to implement the `<blink>` element in an HTML document:

```
<blink>
    This is my blinking text
</blink>
```

The preceding example causes the specified text to blink when the HTML document is loaded. Browsers that do not support the `<blink>` element ignore the tags and render any text between the opening and closing tags as simple text.

To replicate the functionality of the `<blink>` element in IE requires some client-side JavaScript, VBScript, or DHTML. To replicate in N 6 or Opera 5, the CSS 2 property `text-decoration:blink` can be used.

<ilayer>

The <ilayer> tag was introduced in Netscape version 4.0 and is used to create an inline layer that can contain a different HTML page in a separate section of the current HTML document. The <iframe> tag in the HTML 4.01 specification can achieve similar effects.

Attributes

Attribute name	N Versions	Optional or required?	Explanation to be found:
event-name	4	optional	See Chapter 2
above	4	optional	See below
background	4	optional	See Chapter 2
below	4	optional	See below
bgcolor	4	optional	See Chapter 2
class	4	optional	See Chapter 2
clip	4	optional	See below
height	4	optional	See Chapter 5
id	4	optional	See Chapter 2
left	4	optional	See below
name	4	optional	See Chapter 2
pagex	4	optional	See below
pagey	4	optional	See below
src	4	required	See Chapter 5
style	4	optional	See Chapter 2
top	4	optional	See below
visibility	4	optional	See below
width	4	optional	See Chapter 5
z-index	4	optional	See below

above

The above attribute is an optional attribute that indicates that the specified element should be rendered above (in the z-order of the document) the element specified by the value. The z-order of a document is the positioning of elements from front to back, just as "x" represents horizontal position and "y" represents vertical position. The above attribute can also be used to return the HTML element above the specified element in the z-order of the document. The syntax for the above attribute is:

```
above="objectID"
```

below

The below attribute is an optional attribute that indicates that the specified element should be rendered below (according to the document's z-order) the element specified by the value. The below attribute can also be used to return the HTML element below the specified element in the z-order of the document. The syntax for the below attribute is:

```
below="objectID"
```

clip

The clip attribute is an optional attribute that specifies, in pixels, the clipping area of the containing element. Only content that renders within the clipping rectangle is displayed, as opposed to having the containing element expand to fit the content. The clip attribute accepts up to four comma-separated values corresponding to the top left corner and the bottom right corner of the rectangle. If only two values are supplied, the browser assumes that the left and top values are both zero, and the bottom and right values are taken from the supplied values. The syntax for the clip attribute is:

```
clip="pixelcount, pixelcount, pixelcount, pixelcount"
```

left

The left attribute is an optional attribute that specifies the rendered horizontal offset of the parent element within the HTML document. The value of the left attribute can be any positive integer (within reason, remember that 1024 x 768 is the average screen size setting). The syntax for the left attribute is:

```
left="pixelcount"
```

pagex

The pagex attribute is an optional attribute that specifies a point of reference for the rendered horizontal offset of the containing element, specified by the left attribute (see above) within the HTML document. The value of the pagex attribute can be any positive integer (within reason, remember 1024 x 768 is the average screen size setting). The syntax for the pagex attribute is:

```
pagex="pixelcount"
```

pagey

The pagey attribute is an optional attribute that specifies a point of reference for the rendered vertical offset of the parent element, specified by the top attribute (see below) within the HTML document. The value of the pagey attribute can be any positive integer (within reason, remember 1024 x 768 is the average screen size setting). The syntax for the pagey attribute is:

```
pagey="pixelcount"
```

top

The top attribute is an optional attribute that specifies the rendered vertical offset of the parent element within the HTML document. The value of the top attribute can be any positive integer (within reason, remember 1024 x 768 is the high-average screen size setting). The syntax for the top attribute is:

```
top="pixelcount"
```

visibility

The `visibility` attribute is an optional attribute that specifies whether the parent element is visible. The default of the visibility attribute is to inherit the visibility of the parent layer. The possible values for the `visibility` attribute are "hidden", "inherit", and "show". The syntax for the `visibility` attribute is:

```
visibility="namedConstant"
```

z-index

The `z-index` attribute is an optional attribute that specifies the z-order of the parent element. To "stack" elements within an HTML document, we simply assign a higher number to the `z-index` attribute of elements we wish to render closer to the front of the document. The value of the `z-index` attribute can be any integer. The default value is "0" The syntax for the `z-index` attribute is:

```
z-index="number"
```

Examples

The following example demonstrates how to implement the `<ilayer>` element in an HTML document:

```
<ilayer width="200" height="50" left="10" top="10" bgcolor="green"
        z-index="0">
   I'm an iLayer
</ilayer>
<ilayer width="200" height="25" left="15" top="0" bgcolor="yellow"
        z-index="2">
   I'm on top of the green layer,<br> but under the web page layer.
</ilayer>
<ilayer left="23" top="-30" clip="400,200" src="http://www.wrox.com">
</ilayer>
```

The above example results in this display in Netscape 4:

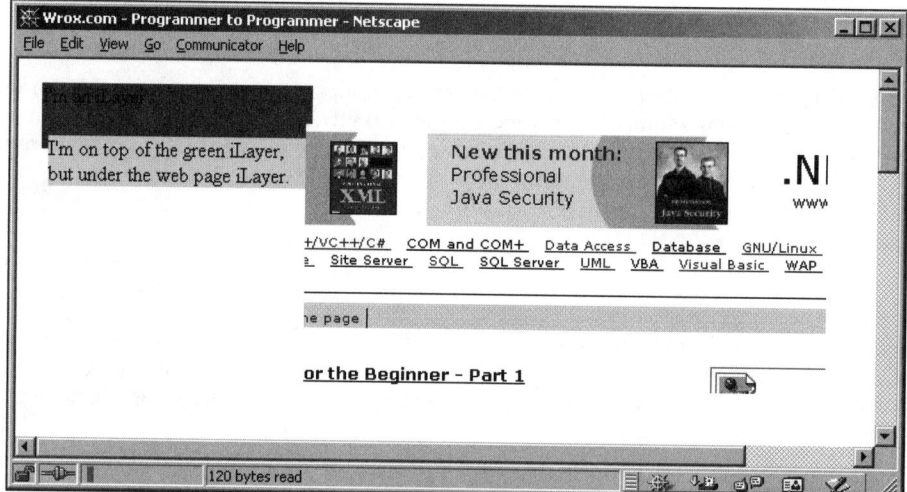

The preceding example creates three inline layer elements in the HTML document. The three inline layers are stacked on top of each other using the z-index attribute and are relatively positioned using the left and top attributes. Browsers that do not support the <ilayer> element ignore the tags and render any text between the opening and closing tags as simple text.

The following example demonstrates how to insert an inline frame in an HTML document using the <iframe> tag according to the HTML 4.01 specification:

```
<html>
  <head>
    <style>
      .Level1 {width:200px;
               height:150px;
               position:absolute;
               left:150px;
               top:100px;
               z-index:2
              }
      .iFrame2 {width:200px;
               height:70px;
               position:absolute;
               left:100px;
               top:70px;
               z-index:3
              }
      .iFrame3 {width:200px;
               height:60px;
               position:absolute;
               left:50px;
               top:40px;
               z-index:1
              }
    </style>
  </head>
  <body>
    <iframe class="Level1" src="http://www.wrox.com">
    </iframe>

    <iframe class="iFrame2" src="yellow.html">

    </iframe>

    <iframe class="iFrame3" src="green.html">
    </iframe>
  </body>
</html>
```

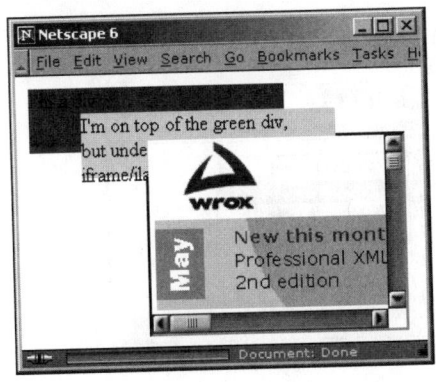
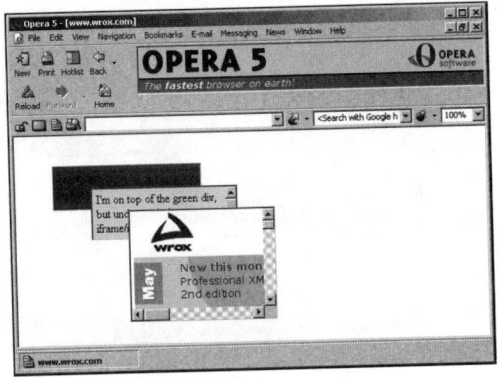

As can be seen, we can achieve similar layering results to those the `<ilayer>` tag produces by using the `<iframe>` tag (which N 6 also supports). The difference is that for all browsers (excluding IE 5.5), the `.Level1` frame is always at the top of the z-order, meaning another layer cannot hide it.

`<keygen>`

The `<keygen>` tag was introduced in Netscape 2.0 and is used to generate encryption key information for forms submitted from an HTML document. The `<keygen>` element must be located within a `<form>` element, and causes the browser to render a select list of available encryption key sizes within the form. When the form is submitted, the user may see a security confirmation dialog. To use the `<keygen>` element each client browser must have a digital certificate installed, as it builds upon intrinsic Netscape public-key encryption schemes. There is no direct equivalent to the `<keygen>` tag in the HTML 4.01 specification.

Attributes

Attribute name	NN Versions	Optional or required?	Explanation to be found:
challenge	2	optional	See below
class	4	optional	See Chapter 2
id	4	optional	See Chapter 2
name	4	optional	See Chapter 2

See error

challenge

An attribute that specifies the string value that the encrypted key value is packed into. The syntax for the challenge attribute is:

```
challenge="string"
```

Examples

The following example demonstrates how to implement the `<keygen>` element in an HTML document:

```
<form>
  <keygen challenge="123456789000000">
</form>
```

These are the results in Netscape 6 and 4 respectively:

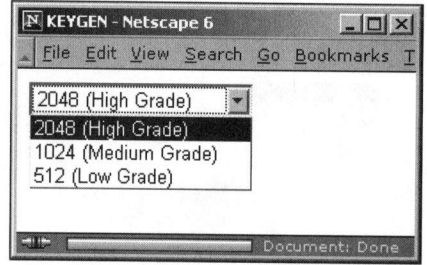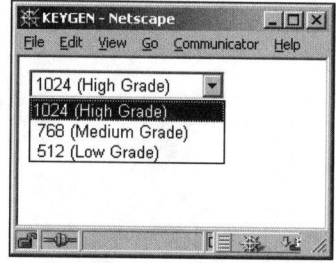

The preceding example implements a <keygen> element in an HTML document and specifies the "public key" for verification with the challenge attribute. Browsers that do not support the <keygen> element simply ignore the tag. Browsers that support this tag generate a select list of available encryption key sizes within the form, depending on the browser version.

To replicate the functionality of the <keygen> element requires some knowledge of SSL, client and server certificates, and browser configuration, which are beyond the scope of this book.

<layer>

The <layer> tag was introduced in Netscape version 4.0 and is used to create a layer that can contain a different HTML page in a separate section of the current HTML document. The difference between the <ilayer> and <layer> tags is that a <layer> is absolutely positioned, whereas an <ilayer> is relatively positioned. The <div> tag in the HTML 4.01 specification can achieve similar effects to those of the <layer> as it can serve as a container for content, which can have aspects of its presentation altered, or imported from an external HTML document. It is worthy to note that N 4.x also supports a non-standard src attribute for <div>, which functions much the same as for a <layer> tag.

Attributes

Attribute name	N Versions	Optional or required?	Explanation to be found:
event-name	4	optional	See Chapter 2
above	4	optional	See above
background	4	optional	See Chapter 2
below	4	optional	See above
bgcolor	4	optional	See Chapter 2
class	4	optional	See Chapter 2
clip	4	optional	See above
height	4	optional	See Chapter 5
id	4	optional	See Chapter 2
left	4	optional	See above
name	4	optional	See Chapter 5
pagex	4	optional	See above
pagey	4	optional	See above
src	4	required	See Chapter 5
style	4	optional	See Chapter 2
top	4	optional	See above
visibility	4	optional	See above
width	4	optional	See Chapter 5
z-index	4	optional	See above

Examples

The following code sample demonstrates how to implement the `<layer>` element in an HTML document:

```
<layer width="200" height="200" left="10" top="10" bgcolor="red">
  I'm a layer
</layer>
<layer width="200" left="60" top="90" bgcolor="green" z-index="2">
  I'm on top!
</layer>
<layer width="200" left="50" top="50" bgcolor="yellow" clip="53,53"
      z-index="0">
  I'm a layer<br>Clipped!
</layer>
```

Below is a screenshot of the result of the above in Netscape 4:

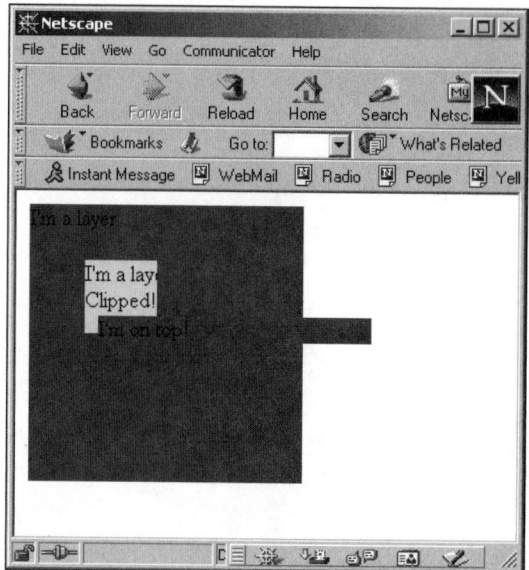

The preceding example creates three `layer` elements in the HTML document. The three layers are stacked on top of each other using the `z-index` attribute and are absolutely positioned using the `left` and `top` attributes. Browsers that do not support the `<layer>` element ignore the tags and render any text between the opening and closing tags as simple text.

The following example demonstrates how to create a `<div>` element in an HTML document according to the HTML 4.01 specification:

```
<html>
  <head>
    <style>
      .div1 {width:200px;
             height:200px;
             position:absolute;
```

```
                    left:10px;
                    top:10px;
                    background-color:red;
                    layer-background-color: red;
                    clip: rect(0px 200px 200px 0px);
                    }
            .div2 {width:200px;
                    height:50px;
                    position:absolute;
                    left:80px;
                    top:20px;
                    background-color:green;
                    layer-background-color: green;
                    clip: rect(0px 200px 50px 0px);
                    z-index:2;
                    }
            .div3 {width:200px;
                    position:absolute;
                    left:50px;
                    top:50px;
                    background-color:yellow;
                    layer-background-color: yellow;
                    z-index:0;
                    clip:rect(0,50,100,0);
                    }
        </style>
    </head>
    <body>
        <div class="div1">
            I'm a div.
        </div >
        <div class="div2">
            I'm on top!
        </div >
        <div class="div3">
            I'm a div that has been<br>clipped!
        </div >
    </body>
</html>
```

Here are the results in IE 4, Netscape 4, and Netscape 6:

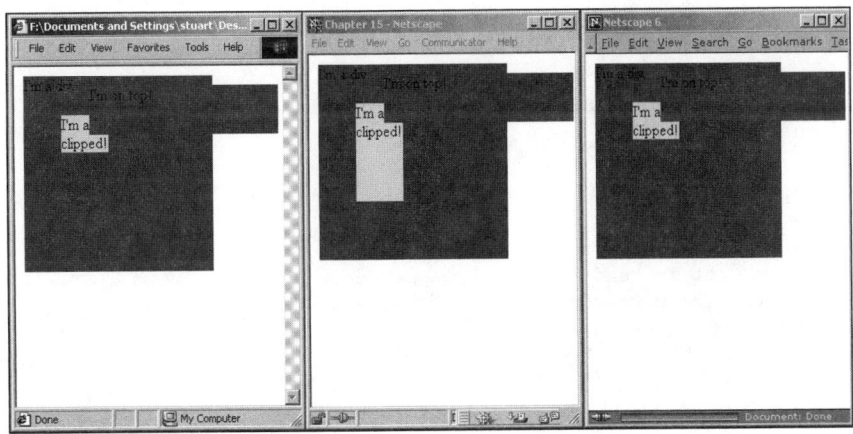

As can be seen, the `<div>` element achieves similar results to the `<layer>` element.

437

<multicol>

The <multicol> tag was introduced in Netscape version 3.0 and is used to define multiple column formatting in an HTML document. The effect is to render long sections of HTML content into newspaper-style columns. There is no direct equivalent to the <multicol> tag in the HTML 4.01 specification, but similar effects can be achieved by using style sheets.

Attributes

Attribute name	N Versions	Optional or required?	Explanation to be found:
class	4	optional	See Chapter 2
cols	3, 4	required	See below
gutter	3, 4	optional	See below
id	4	optional	See Chapter 2
style	4	optional	See Chapter 2
width	3, 4	optional	See Chapter 5

cols

This attribute specifies the number of (relatively) equal columns to split the HTML content into. The syntax for the cols attribute is:

```
cols="number"
```

gutter

This attribute specifies the number of pixels to be placed between each column. The syntax for the gutter attribute is:

```
gutter="pixelCount"
```

Examples

The following example demonstrates how to implement the <multicol> element in an HTML document:

```
<html>
  <body>
    <multicol cols="3" gutter="10" width="400">
      This content is rendered as three newspaper-style columns in the HTML
      document. The more content, the more useful this element is.
    </multicol>
  </body>
</html>
```

Below is a screenshot of the result of this code in Netscape 4:

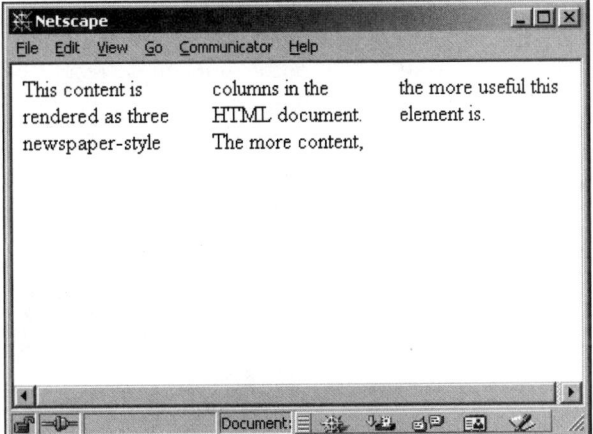

The preceding example causes the specified text to be divided into three equal columns when the HTML document is loaded. Netscape 6 does not support the <multicol> element. Browsers that do not support the <multicol> element ignore the tags and render any text between the opening and closing tags as simple text.

To replicate something similar to the functionality of the <multicol> element, we can use the HTML 4.01 <table> element and distribute the contents manually: see Chapter 7.

<noembed>

The <noembed> tag was introduced in Netscape version 2.0 and is used to render HTML text in the case of browsers being unable to render content specified by the <embed> tag. There is no direct equivalent to the <noembed> tag in the HTML 4.01 specification.

Examples

The following example demonstrates how to implement the <noembed> element in an HTML document:

```
<html>
  <body>
    <embed src="ringin.wav"></embed>
    <noembed>
      To enjoy the multimedia on this page, you must
      upgrade your browser or install a multimedia plugin.
    </noembed>
  </body>
</html>
```

The preceding example causes browsers that cannot render the multimedia specified by the embed tag to display the text contained in the <noembed> element. Browsers that do not support the <noembed> element ignore the tags and render any text between the opening and closing tags as simple text, which is how it works.

To replicate the functionality of the <noembed> element we can use the HTML 4.01 "alt" attribute: see Chapter 10.

<nolayer>

The <nolayer> tag was introduced in Netscape version 4.0 and is used to render HTML text when browsers are unable to render content specified by the <layer> tag. There is no direct equivalent to the <nolayer> tag in the HTML 4.01 specification, but similar results can be achieved with client-side script.

Examples

The following example demonstrates how to implement the <nolayer> element in an HTML document:

```
<html>
  <head>
  </head>
  <body>
    <layer>
      <nolayer>
        <div>
      </nolayer>
      Please enjoy the content.
      <nolayer>
        </div>
      </nolayer>
    </layer>
  </body>
</html>
```

The preceding example causes browsers that cannot render the content specified by the layer tag to display the <div> tags contained in the <nolayer> elements. Browsers that do not support the <nolayer> element ignore the tags and render any text between the opening and closing tags as simple text.

To replicate the functionality of the <nolayer> element use the HTML 4.01 "alt" attribute: see Chapter 10.

<spacer>

The <spacer> tag was introduced in Netscape version 3.0 and is used to render whitespace in an HTML document. There is no direct equivalent to the <spacer> tag in the HTML 4.01 specification, but similar effects can be achieved by using CSS properties, like width, letter-spacing, and word-spacing.

Attributes

Attribute name	N Versions	Optional or required?	Explanation to be found:
align	3, 4	optional	See Chapter 2
class	4	optional	See Chapter 2
height	3, 4	optional	See Chapter 5

Attribute name	N Versions	Optional or required?	Explanation to be found:
id	4	optional	See Chapter 2
size	3, 4	optional	size = number, where number is the number of pixels
style	4	optional	See Chapter 2
type	3, 4	optional	See below
width	3, 4	optional	See Chapter 5

type

The type attribute is an optional attribute that specifies the appearance of the specified element. The possible values for the type attribute are "block", "horizontal", or "vertical". A value of block defines equal horizontal and vertical dimensions to be added within and between lines of HTML content. A value of horizontal adds space within the same line of content. A value of vertical adds space between lines of content. To specify the horizontal and vertical values, the size attribute must be set. The syntax for the type attribute is:

```
type="namedConstant"
```

Examples

The following example (using Netscape 4.7) demonstrates how to implement the <spacer> element in an HTML document:

```
<html>
  <head>
  </head>
  <body>
    This is some HTML content.
    <spacer type="horizontal" size="100">
      This is some HTML content on the same line.<br>
    <spacer type="vertical" size="100">
      This is some HTML content on the next line.
  </body>
</html>
```

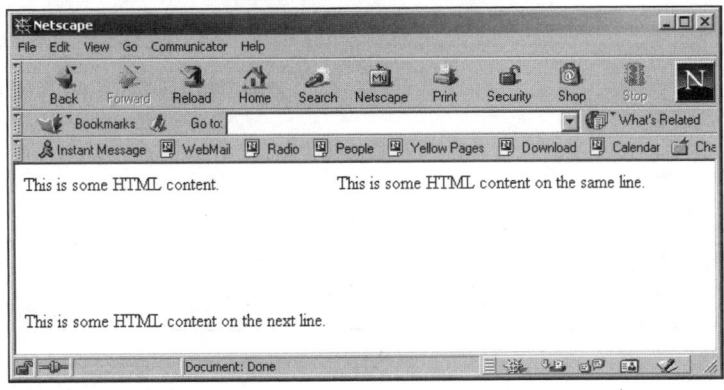

The preceding example causes the browser to render whitespace between the specified HTML content when the document is loaded. Browsers that do not support the `<spacer>` element ignore the tags and render any text between the opening and closing tags as simple text.

The following example demonstrates how to render whitespace between HTML content using the `<span>` tag and CSS styles according to the HTML 4.01 specification:

```
<html>
  <head>
  </head>
  <body>
    This is some HTML content.
    <span style="position:absolute;padding-left:200">
      This is some HTML Content on the same line.
    </span>
    <BR>
    <span style="position:absolute;padding-top:100">
      This is some HTML content on the next line.
    </span>
  </body>
</html>
```

This is how it appears in Netscape 4 and IE 5:

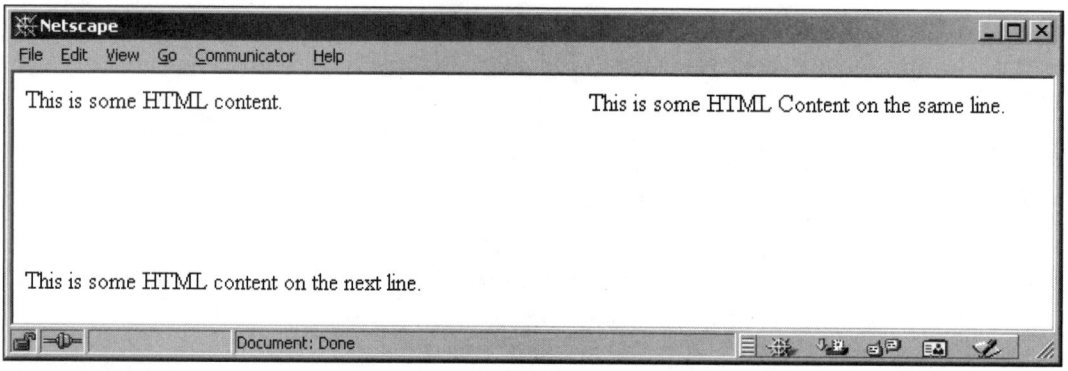

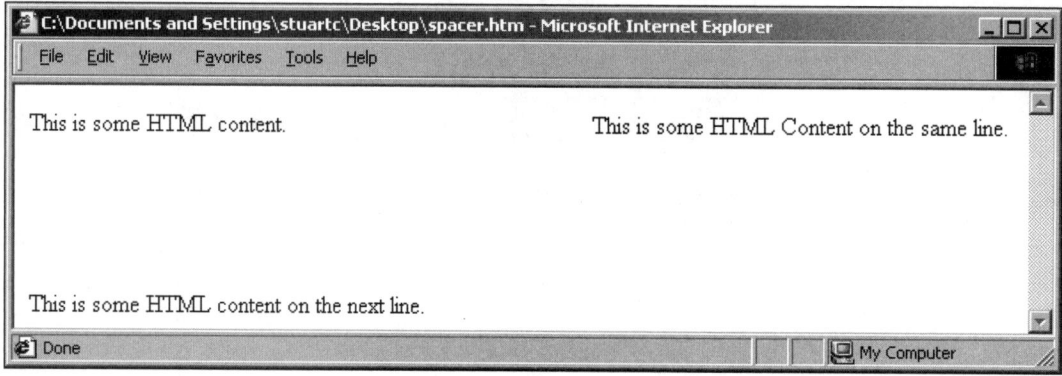

As can be seen, using an absolutely positioned `<span>` element and setting its padding can achieve the same results as the `<spacer>` element.

Netscape-Specific Styles

The following table lists the proprietary `white-space` style that only Netscape supports, and is not supported by the W3C or other browsers at this time.

Attribute	Description	N Versions
white-space	The way the browser renders whitespace around HTML elements	4

Netscape-Specific HTML Attributes

The following table lists the proprietary attributes that Netscape supports, but are not supported by the W3C or any other browser at this time.

Attribute	Description
above	See above
below	See above
challenge	See above
clip	See above
gutter	See above
hidden	See below
left	See above
mayscript	See below
pagex	See above
pagey	See above
pluginspage	See below
point-size	See Chapter 3
top	See above
weight	See Chapter 3
z-index	See above

The following attributes have not been explained elsewhere:

hidden

An attribute of <embed>, hidden renders an object invisible to the viewer of a page and causes text to flow as if it were not there. This is useful for embedding sound files in a page where you would want them to play, but not visibly show their presence to the user.

mayscript

This attribute of the deprecated applet element allows the page creator to specify whether or not a Java applet will be able to access JavaScript features. It can be set to yes or no. It must be set to yes to avoid crashing the browser when a Java applet designed to access JavaScript is used.

pluginspage

This attribute of <embed> specifies the URL of a web page that acts as the access point for a plug-in the user will require to run the embedded object. The plug-in can usually be downloaded from this page.

Summary

In this chapter, we briefly discussed the cross-browser controversy and the major differences between the various versions of Netscape and Microsoft Internet Explorer. Then we took a detailed look at each individual proprietary tag supported by either IE or Netscape and how most of the elements could either be replaced by other HTML 4.01 elements or client-side script with CSS properties in order to create cross-browser compatible pages.

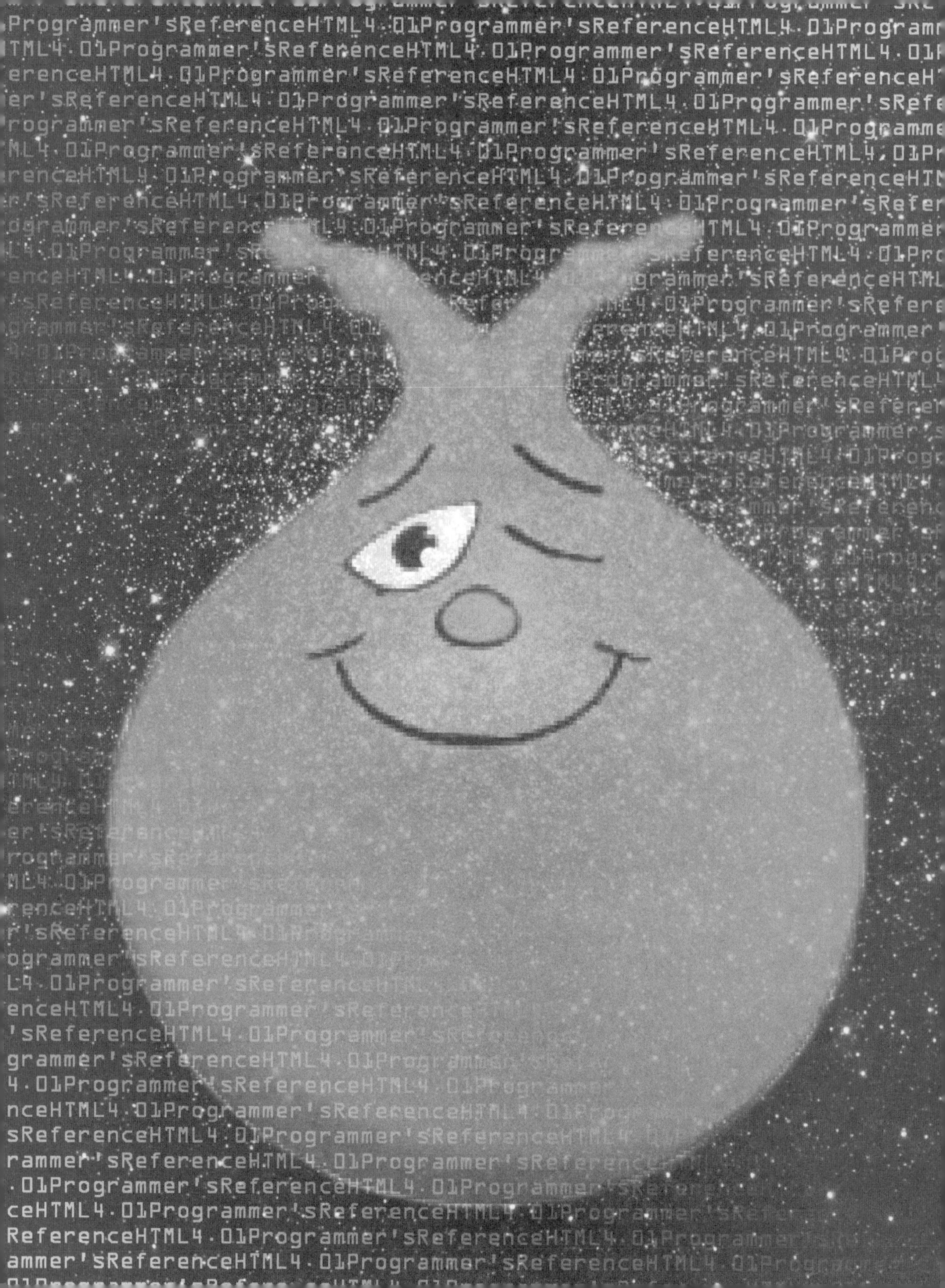
Programmer'sReferenceHTML4.01

Cross-Browser and Cross-OS Coding

As the Internet and World Wide Web grew, they moved from free and open networks and services to corporate profit centers. Server developers raced to develop graphical browsers that would take advantage of the proprietary features of their products, then gave the browsers away free so that they could rapidly develop large installed user bases for their products. Development was occurring at a rapid pace and browser developers were submitting proposals for extensions to the HTML standard faster than the W3C could review them.

In this environment, Netscape and Microsoft emerged as the two major forces in browser development with their respective Netscape (N) and Internet Explorer (IE) products. The problem was that, as the two companies jockeyed for market share, they introduced multitudes of proprietary HTML tags, properties, and methods that performed similar functions in ways that were incompatible with each other. Sometimes, the browsers weren't even compatible with their own previous versions! Thus, the need for cross-browser and cross-OS coding skills emerged.

In this chapter we will look at some of the considerations and techniques that must be employed to deal with the idiosyncrasies of the current three major browsers (Internet Explorer, Netscape, and Opera). We will also look at some basic techniques to use when support for legacy (as in "not standards-compliant") browsers must be provided for a web site or application. While it is always preferable to write standards-compliant code that separates form from content, there will be times when this cannot be done because the target user base relies on an operating system (OS) or browser feature that does not support the W3C HTML 4.01 standard. At those times, it may be necessary to fall back to an earlier HTML standard or proprietary method to implement the web design or application. However, adhering to the standards and separating the form of your pages from their content whenever possible will make your code maintenance much easier over time.

Cross-browser and cross-OS issues that are covered in this chapter include:

❑ Determining Which Browsers to Support

Here we look at defining our user groups and supported feature sets – determining whom the site is for, so that only appropriate technologies are used. We then offer a quick review of the major client operating systems, followed by a look at the common clients currently used online.

❑ Browser and OS Detection Methods

Here we look at four different types of detection that you can perform. Firstly we look at OS Detection – determining what operating system your client is using. Next, DOM Detection, which involves determining how the client's Document Object Model is structured so that we can properly access objects on the web page. Next, we look at Object Detection, involving determining what objects the client supports, so that we don't try to manipulate non-existent objects. Finally, we discuss Browser Detection (Sniffing), where we find out exactly which browser our client is using, so that we can tailor our pages to take advantage of proprietary features or work around known bugs/problems.

❑ Scripting Support Across Browsers

Here we take a look at how scripting support differs across browsers, focusing mainly on the different flavors of JavaScript (ECMAScript, JScript, and JavaScript), and also taking a quick look at VBScript, and when to use it.

❑ The Document Object Model (DOM)

This section looks at simplifying coding across the DOMs – what to look for in the different DOMs, and a technique for writing single functions that work across multiple DOMs.

❑ Cross-Browser Style Sheets

In this part we look at two ways in which you can customize your style sheets to further advance your cross browser coding: firstly, how to develop a single style sheet to work across multiple browsers, then looking at a method of dynamically delivering the correct customized style sheet for multiple browsers.

❑ Solutions to Specific Problems

In this final section we look at some commonly encountered cross browser/OS coding problems:

❑ Display Resolution Differences – why pages look different across platforms

❑ Rendering Images in Tables – how to ensure images and text line up in tables if you must ensure backward-compatibility

❑ Element Positioning – dealing with the different default offsets used by various browsers

❑ Consistent Font Rendering – how to ensure your fonts render consistently across platforms/browsers

Determining Which Browsers to Support

It is impossible to provide the same user experience to all who use your web site. Users may be accessing the site with everything from text-only browsers like Lynx, to 3D VRML-enabled browsers or specialty browsers for the visually impaired that read the site contents out to users or deliver them as Braille. So, before sitting down to write the first line of code, it is important to define your target user group(s) in terms of OS, browser, and plug-in choices. This definition should include the version numbers of these items since different versions support different features (see Appendix A for a list of elements and their attributes, and which browsers support them).

Defining User Groups and Supported Feature Sets

The target audience for the web site you're coding is one of the most important pieces of information you can have. It will help you determine the browsers you must support, the features you can realistically implement in light of this, and the methods you can use to carry out this implementation. Sites designed for corporate users must be careful about the use of plug-ins and Java applets since many corporations do not allow the downloading and installation of any software on corporate machines, including applets. Because of the training costs associated with new software, many corporate users are also one or two generations behind the current browser releases, so you may not be able to take advantage of the latest techniques.

Many individuals are also using browsers that are not current releases or are not comfortable letting unfamiliar programs like plug-ins or Java applets run on their machines. In these cases, relying on plug-ins like Flash, or code in Java applets, or insisting on upgrades to current browsers to provide essential functionality for your site will ensure that the site is unusable by the people for whom it was designed. That is why it is important for you to know who the intended audience is. Whenever you are programming or designing a site, it is helpful to ask yourself these questions:

❑ Who are the target users (age, technical expertise, familiarity with computers)?

❑ What operating systems will they probably be using?

❑ What browser versions will they probably be using?

❑ What screen resolution will they probably be using?

❑ Will they all be willing and able to use plug-ins (access, permission, and ability to install), and if not, how will equivalent services be provided?

❑ Will all users be willing and able to use Java applets (access, permission, and ability to install); if not, how will equivalent services be provided?

❑ Will all users be able to upgrade to a newer browser version if needed? If not, what services does the most restrictive browser provide? If some can't upgrade, will you provide enhanced services to those who can upgrade?

❑ Do you have the ability to test each of the OS/browser configurations you intend to support? If not, how will you verify that the site works correctly on configurations you can't test?

Once you have the answers to these questions, you're ready to determine which of the following methods are appropriate for your project.

The OS Spectrum

There are dozens of computer OSes available that have had web browser applications written for them. Most of them are highly specialized and will not often be encountered. Three OSes are frequently encountered though: the various flavors of Windows, MacOS, and UNIX/Linux.

Windows

There are several versions of Windows currently in use and more are on the way. Windows 3.0+ (Win16) is rarely encountered any more, having been replaced several years ago by Windows 95 (Win32). Windows 95, 98, and ME are the primary "consumer-level" Microsoft OSes. Windows NT 4.0 and Windows 2000 (Win32) are the "professional-level" Microsoft OSes. They come in various versions from desktop workstation to specialized enterprise servers. The consumer-level and professional-level Windows versions are due to be replaced between late 2001 and early 2002 by variations on the Windows XP OS.

MacOS

Apple released OSX (OS 10) in March 2001. The first major revision of the MacOS in almost a decade, it is essentially an Apple shell for UNIX. It has had some teething problems, but its use should become more common since it will be the default system loaded on new Macs starting sometime in Q2/Q3 2001. MacOS 9.X is the currently shipping version at the time of this writing (March 2001) and is expected to be supported through to at least 2004. Most Mac browsers require OS 8.X for multimedia support, and preclude the use of older Motorola 68XXX version Macs.

Unix/Linux

There are hundreds of versions of Unix available today. Although many of the Unix versions make popular server platforms (particularly Linux running Apache server), Unix/Linux has not gained much popularity as a personal computer OS – this kind of use is more common within universities and small businesses that wish to save money. Their popularity for personal computers may change if web appliances and low-cost computers gain market share, but at the time of this writing, Unix/Linux are primarily the platforms of users who enjoy dealing with the intricacies of the operating system. There are several browsers designed for Unix/Linux, including offerings from Netscape, Microsoft, and Opera.

The Browser Spectrum

There are a large number of browsers available. The major browsers are reviewed below, but you should be aware that there are also many specialty browsers for specific applications (for example, Braille and/or screen-reading browsers for visually-impaired users and virtual 3D browsers for rendering spatially-oriented content). It is a good idea to ensure that you know the specialty browsers' capabilities if you anticipate their use by your planned user base.

Netscape Navigator/Communicator/Gecko (NS)

Despite the fact that we are referring to Netscape browsers as merely "Netscape" throughout this book, Netscape's browser products actually come in three levels, for multiple OSes:

❑ Netscape Navigator – a standalone browser that may include an e-mail client and limited HTML authoring support.

❑ Netscape Communicator – an (apparently discontinued) Internet Suite consisting of a browser bundled with e-mail, scheduling, net meeting, and authoring software.

❑ Netscape Gecko – a set of browser core rendering routines that can be incorporated into a variety of packages to provide web services without having to write a browser from scratch.

> *Note*: *We felt that the differences in HTML handling between these 3 "levels" of product were not significant enough for us to go into in other chapters, as they are very subtle, and their mass inclusion would unnecessarily complicate matters. For more information, go to* http://developer.netscape.com.

Netscape appears to have dropped the Communicator package with the release of its Netscape 6.0 browser although updated versions of many of the Communicator components can be installed with the browser. The SSL certificates for the Netscape 3.0 series browsers expired at the end of 1999, so they can no longer be used for secure transactions and constitute about 0.25% of the browsers currently used. The Netscape 6.0 series browsers, including v.6.01, have had problems with bugs. So, although they are currently considered among the most standards-compliant browsers available, they only constitute about 0.3% of the current browser market.

The standards compliance of the Netscape 6 and Gecko 5 browsers also means that they may not be able to run sites designed for use with Netscape 4 (N 4) or Internet Explorer 4/5 browsers, due to changes in the way that page elements are addressed. The most popular of the Netscape line of browser products, the N 4 series browsers and compatibles, making up about 11% of the browser market, roughly the same as the IE 4 market share.

N 4 provides moderate support for CSS 1 and HTML 4.0/4.01, and minimal access to page objects compared to its rivals IE 4 and Opera 4. Many DHTML effects require the use of proprietary tags and JavaScript extensions.

Microsoft Internet Explorer (IE)

IE is available for the Windows and Macintosh PPC platforms, as well as various flavors of UNIX (see http://www.microsoft.com/unix/ie/default.asp). After a slow start, IE has become the primary browser used on the Web today, with about 87% of all users. The most recent Windows release, IE 5.5, includes varying degrees of support for the CSS 1 and CSS 2 standards, ECMAScript edition 3, VBScript 5.0 (windows only), XML, HTML 4.01, and several proprietary technologies (for example scriptlets, data-binding, and behaviors – see *IE5 Dynamic HTML Programmer's Reference* by Brian Francis et al. (*ISBN: 1-861001-74-6*), published by Wrox Press).

IE 5 for the Macintosh provides better support for these technologies than the Windows implementation. IE 6 is expected to provide full CSS 1 support and substantial CSS 2 support. All versions from 4.0 onward provide usable support for HTML 4.01 and CSS 1.

Opera

Until recently, Opera users had to pay for their browser, unlike IE and N users. This caused a depression in Opera's acceptance, and it currently has less than 1% market share in total. Earlier versions had limited support for technologies other than HTML 3.2. However, with the release of versions 4 and 5, Opera has added substantial Java, JavaScript, and CSS 1/CSS 2 support. Opera 5 also includes substantial support for XML and WML. Specific information regarding standards support for a particular version of Opera is available at http://www.opera.com/operaX/specs.html (substitute the X for the major version number you are interested in, for example, 4 or 5), and information on Opera 5.X (Windows) HTML support is included in Appendix A.

Opera does have some interesting features that can make sites behave differently than designed, such as the ability to open more than one window at a time within a single browser instance. Opera 5 was released as "adware" (a series of ads show in the browser unless the user pays a fee for the key to turn them off) and this may help Opera penetrate the browser market more deeply. Opera 5 currently has about 0.25% of the market share.

America Online (AOL)

At the time of this writing (March 2001) AOL uses branded versions of IE as its bundled browser, even though it owns Netscape. According to the "Webmaster Info" section of its web site (http://webmaster.info.aol.com/), about 80% of AOL members are using IE 5.0 or better as their browser. AOL claims over 28 million members, and the needs of such a sizable chunk of the market should be factored into the development of any public web sites. AOL adds many proprietary components to its bundled browsers that often work in tandem with its servers. For example, most images are automatically recompressed using AOL's proprietary algorithms and can frequently cause pages that rendered perfectly on non-AOL browsers to break or look shabby when displayed in an AOL browser. Fortunately, AOL's Webmaster Info section details many of the problems and idiosyncrasies of the AOL browsers. The section is frequently updated – you can find the latest AOL users statistics and browser version information there.

Browser and OS Detection Methods

Before an HTML page can be customized to provide equivalent presentation across multiple browsers and OSes, we have to determine what we are dealing with on the client machine. This is done either on the server (using technologies like Active Server Pages or CGI scripts) or on the client (using some sort of client-side scripting technique such as client-side JavaScript – one of the most common forms of scripting language – see Chapter 9 for more details). Since we are only guaranteed access to the client, we will develop some client-based methods to determine the browsing environment. We have tried to use names that make the code as self-explanatory as possible, but you can use any names that you want for your own code.

There are four main methods for determining the browsing environment on a client machine. In order of increasing specificity they are **OS detection**, **Document Object Model (DOM) detection**, **object detection**, and **browser detection**. Each method has strengths, weaknesses, and specific techniques, which we will look at now.

OS Detection

OS detection is sometimes needed to ensure that clients using different operating systems receive equivalent functionality from a web site. OS detection is the least difficult checking method to use, but it also provides the least information about the client. It is most useful for ensuring that objects and methods that differ across platforms are properly employed. It is also useful for setting CSS attributes appropriate to a particular platform, since as we will see later, some browsers are sufficiently different across platforms that even though the versions may have the same revision number, their behaviors may be very different. IE 5.0 for the Macintosh and Windows are a current example of this. CSS 1 support in MacIE 5.0 is much broader than it is in WinIE 5, so it is important to know which OS is being used to ensure proper formatting of your pages if you are using CSS. The following script determines the client browser's operating system and displays it in the HTML page. It could just as easily be used to select appropriate style sheets or access OS-specific functions in a browser.

```
<!doctype html public "-//W3C//DTD HTML 4.01//EN"
   "http://www.w3.org/TR/html4/strict.dtd">
<html>
  <head>
    <title>OS Detection</title>
    <script type="text/javascript">
      <!--
        function My()
        {
          this.os = navigator.platform;
        }
        var my = new My()
      -->
    </script>
  </head>
  <body>
    <script type="text/javascript">
      <!--
        document.write("<p>This browser is running on the " + my.os
                       + " operating system.<\/p>");
      -->
    </script>
  </body>
</html>
```

Here's what the output looks like in a browser (in this case Netscape 6):

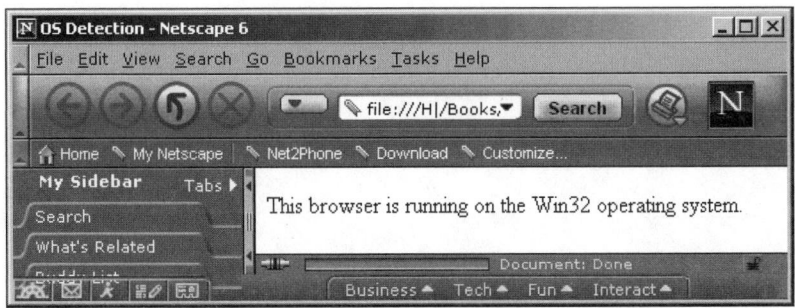

We use the JavaScript object constructor function `My()` to inspect the `platform` property of the `navigator` object in the JavaScript DOM (see Chapter 19 for more information on the DOM) to determine the browser's operating system and assign it to the `os` property of the calling object `var my = new My()`:

```
function My()
    {
        this.os = navigator.platform;
    }
var my = new My()
```

In this trivial example, we place a little more JavaScript in the `<body>` of the page, using `my.os` to let the user know what OS is being used. We could just as easily use `my.os` in logic functions to customize content, presentation options, or any other use that requires knowledge of the OS:

```
<script type="text/javascript">
    <!--
        document.write("<p>This browser is running on the " + my.os _
        + " operating system.</p>");
    -->
</script>
```

DOM Detection

DOM detection is most effective for determining whether or not a client browser is standards-compliant. Although several methods or objects could be used to check for DOM level 1 compliance, the `document.getElementById` method is frequently used since recently released compliant browsers support it for accessing page objects while earlier browsers do not. A test for `document.getElementByID` allows us to quickly determine whether or not a browser is reasonably compliant with the W3C DOM level 1. Additional checks can also be added to check for specific DOM objects and should be used if they are required to implement the site's design.

Support for the various W3C DOM levels is an important step towards the Holy Grail of write once, run anywhere code for web clients. To the extent that WinIE 5.5, MacIE 5, Opera 5, and N 6 support the DOM, we can write cross-browser code by simply writing valid, well formed HTML and JavaScript without having to worry about proprietary methods and objects. We'll see this in a later example that uses a single code section to manipulate a `<div>` object in N 6.0, IE 5.0, and Opera 5.0, something that was largely impossible prior to the release of compliant browsers. Here's a simple script to check for DOM compliance:

```
<!doctype html public "-//W3C//DTD HTML 4.01//EN" _
    "http://www.w3.org/TR/html4/strict.dtd">
<html>
<head>
    <title>DOM Detection</title>
    <script type="text/javascript">
        <!--
            function Is()
            {
                this.compliant = document.getElementById;
            }
            var is = new Is()
        //-->
    </script>
```

```
    </head>
    <body>
        <script type="text/javascript">
        <!--
        if(is.compliant)
            {
                document.write("<p>This browser acceptably complies
                with W3C standards. </p>");
            }
        else
            {
                document.write("<p>This browser is non-compliant.</p>");
            }
        //-->
        </script>
    </body>
</html>
```

> In this code example, and the ones that follow, some of the **document.write** lines
> are deliberately broken with a carriage return and extra white space for presentation
> purposes (such as the one above containing the text "This browser acceptably...").
> When copying these examples to try them out yourself, make sure you get rid of this
> excess white space, as it might cause the code to break.

Here we see the JavaScript object constructor function Is() checking for the getElementById
method of the browser's document object before setting our user-defined compliant property of
the calling object var is() = new Is():

```
<script type="text/javascript">
    <!--
    function Is()

    {
        this.compliant = document.getElementById;
    }
    var is = new Is()

    // -->
</script>
```

Since is.compliant will be undefined if it is not supported by the browser, we can use a
JavaScript if() statement to check for its definition and branch to the appropriate
document.write() statement to tell the user whether or not the browser is W3C DOM Level 1
compliant. When is.compliant is defined, if(is.compliant) will evaluate to true.
Otherwise, it will evaluate to false.

```
<script type="text/javascript">
    <!--
        if(is.compliant)
        {
            document.write("<p>This browser complies with W3C
            standards.</p>");
        }
        else
```

```
        {
            document.write("<p>This browser is non-compliant.</p>");
        }
    // -->
</script>
```

Non-compliant browsers may support proprietary DOMs that can also be detected to provide the advantages of object detection without the need to test for multiple objects. For example, IE 4.X and 5.X use the `document.all` collection in their DOMs. By checking for `document.all`, we can fairly safely assume that we are working with IE 4.X or 5.X and take advantage of proprietary services in these browsers (and work around their bugs), without specifically checking for each service using object detection. We simply assign the results of a check for `document.all` to `this.ieDOM` as shown below, then use `if(is.ieDOM)` as we used `if(is.compliant)`.

Note: If you are designing for IE or Netscape and are concerned that some of your users may use Opera in alias mode, you should specifically check for it as outlined in the Special Cases, Traps, and Pitfalls *section of this chapter).*

With the check for `document.all` added to our object constructor, it looks like:

```
function Is()
{
    this.compliant = document.getElementById;
    this.ieDOM = document.all;
}
```

Object Detection

By checking for objects such as images or layers, it is possible to provide more generalized support for HTML, and script-based features, without having to determine the exact browser type or version on the client machine. The idea is that if a particular object is accessible on the client, then it can be manipulated without regard to the browser type or version containing the object. While this is generally true, it is a good idea to verify that the code works across all of a project's targeted browsers. The two main advantages here are that we can avoid error messages when an object is not supported and we don't have to update our browser detection script each time a new browser is released or updated. If the object is supported in the new/updated browser, it will automatically be provided to the browser. Sometimes, we can also make some assumptions about the client based on whether or not proprietary objects are present, just as we did with the DOM. This example checks for the `image` and `document.layers` objects and makes assumptions about the client based on its findings:

```
<!doctype html public "-//W3C//DTD HTML 4.01//EN" _
    "http://www.w3.org/TR/html4/strict.dtd">
<html>
<head>
    <title>DOM Detection</title>
    <script type="text/javascript">
        <!--
        function Has()
        {
            this.images = document.images;
            this.layers = document.layers;
        }
```

```
            var has = new Has();
            var strLayers = "This is a version of Netscape 4";
            var strNoLayers = "This is <strong>not</strong> a version
                            of Netscape 4";
     // -->
   </script>
</head>
<body>
<script type="text/javascript">
   <!--
      if(has.images)
      {
          document.write('<img src="images/test.gif" width="10"
          height="10" alt="test image">');
      }
      else
      {
          document.write("<p>If your browser supported images, a
                          picture would be here.</p>");
      }
          if(has.layers)
      {
          document.write(strLayers);
      }
      else
      {
          document.write(strNoLayers);
      }
   // -->
 </script>
 </body>
 </html>
```

First, we use the JavaScript object constructor function Has() to check for various objects in the browser's document object. Then we set various properties for the calling object var has = new Has(), depending on the objects that are supported by the browser:

```
<script type="text/javascript">
   <!--
      function Has()
      {
         this.images = document.images;
         this.layers = document.layers;
      }

      var has = new Has();
```

We also define some string variables (strLayers and strNoLayers) for use later on. In a production page, these could be functions or code segments that should run conditionally based on the client's determined capabilities.

```
      var strLayers = "This is a version of Netscape 4";
      var strNoLayers = "This is <strong>not</strong> a
                         version of Netscape 4";
   //   -->
   </script>
```

457

Next, in the page's body we use two JavaScript `if..else()` statements to provide different content depending on the objects supported by the user's browser. In the first instance, we either display an image or inform the user that an image is available to browsers that support images. This can be useful if we are using multiple images to support rollover buttons on a page. By checking for `document.images`, we can determine whether or not the client can manipulate the `document.images` object and set up a conditional section in our code to keep us from wasting time and bandwidth trying to download images that can't be used if support is not available.

```
<script type="text/javascript">
  <!--
    if(has.images)
    {
        document.write('<img src="images/test.gif" width="10"
        height="10" alt="test image">');
    }
    else
    {
        document.write("<p>If your browser supported images,
                        a picture would be here.</p>");
    }
```

In the second instance, we select a predefined variable and write it to the browser depending on whether or not `layers` are supported.

```
    if(has.layers)
    {
        document.write(strLayers);
    }
    else
    {
        document.write(strNoLayers);
    }
  // -->
</script>
```

Browser Detection

Browser detection (or "sniffing") is the most specific method for determining the capabilities of client browsers. It is also the most involved and high maintenance method. The JavaScript `navigator` object has been around since JavaScript 1.0 and can be queried to determine the client's browser name and its major and minor version numbers. The advantage to browser detection is that very specific code can be written to customize page content and formatting to take advantage of the capabilities and avoid the bugs of particular browsers. The disadvantages are that the code can quickly become extremely cumbersome and difficult to maintain and, unless very carefully written, the code must be updated each time a new browser release occurs. The latter problem is not quite as critical now as in the early days of browser development when significant browser revisions might occur 2-3 times each year. The following code checks for the major Netscape, IE, and Opera browser versions and reports back on what it finds. It's quite a sizeable chunk of code, and we will break it down over the following few pages:

```
<!doctype html public "-//W3C//DTD HTML 4.01//EN"
"http://www.w3.org/TR/html4/transitional.dtd">

<head>
<title>Browser Detection</title>
<script language="javascript" type="text/javascript">
<!--
function Is()
{
   var browserID = navigator.userAgent.toLowerCase();
   var browserVer = navigator.appVersion.toLowerCase();
   var browserName = navigator.appName.toLowerCase();
   var locMSIE;   //location of "msie" in browserID
   var locNS6;            //location of "netscape6" in browserID
   var locOpera; //location of "opera" in browserID

   this.Rev = parseFloat(browserVer);
   this.majorRev = parseInt(browserVer,10);
   locMSIE = browserID.indexOf("msie");
   locNS6 = browserID.indexOf("netscape6");
   locOpera = browserID.indexOf("opera");

   this.other = true
   this.ns = ((browserName == "netscape") &&
       (browserID.indexOf("spoofer")==-1) &&
       (browserID.indexOf("compatible")==-1) && (locOpera==-1));

   if(locNS6!=-1)
   {
      this.majorRev = 6
   }
   this.ns4 = this.ns && (this.majorRev==4);
   this.ns6 = this.ns && (this.majorRev==6);
   this.ns6up = this.ns && (this.majorRev>6);

   this.ie = ((locMSIE!=-1) &&
       (browserID.indexOf("spoofer")==-1) && (locOpera==-1));
   if(locMSIE!=-1)
   {
      this.Rev = parseFloat(browserID.substring(locMSIE+5))
      this.majorRev = parseInt(this.Rev)
   }
   this.ie4 = this.ie && (this.majorRev==4);
   this.ie5 = this.ie && (this.majorRev==5);
   this.ie5up = this.ie && (this.majorRev>5);

   this.opera = (locOpera!=-1);
   if(this.opera && (locMSIE!=-1 || browserName=="netscape"))
   {
      this.Rev = parseFloat(browserID.substring(locOpera + 6))
      this.majorRev = parseInt(this.Rev)
   }
   this.opera4 = this.opera && (this.majorRev==4);
   this.opera5 = this.opera && (this.majorRev==5);
   this.opera5up = this.opera && (this.majorRev>5);
```

459

```
        if(this.ns || this.ie || this.opera)
        {
            this.other = false
        }
    }

    var is = new Is()
    // -->
    </script>
    </head>

    <body>
    <script language="javascript" type="text/javascript">
    <!--
    if(is.other)
    {
        document.write("<p>You are using a browser that is not
                        produced by Netscape, Microsoft, or
                        Opera.</p>")
    }
    else
    {
        if(is.ns)
        {
            document.write("<p>This browser is Netscape");
            if(is.ns4){document.write(" version 4</p>")};
            if(is.ns6){document.write(" version 6</p>")};
            if(is.ns6up){document.write(", version is greater than 6</p>")};
        }
        else if(is.ie)
        {
            document.write("<p>This browser is Internet Explorer");
            if(is.ie4){document.write(" version 4</p>")};
            if(is.ie5){document.write(" version 5</p>")};
            if(is.ie5up){document.write(", version is greater than 5</p>")};
        }
        else if(is.opera)
        {
            document.write("<p>This browser is Opera");
            if(is.opera4){document.write(" version 4</p>")};
            if(is.opera5){document.write(" version 5</p>")};
            if(is.opera5up){document.write(", version is greater than 5</p>")};
        }
    }
    // -->
    </script>
    </body>
    </html>
```

Once again, we use the object constructor function `Is()` to inspect various properties of the JavaScript `navigator` object, then assign values to properties of the calling `var is = new Is()` object. This time, however, the constructor is pretty complicated since we are looking for a number of specific things. First, we declare some variables we will need later on: `browserID`, `browserVer`, `browserName`, `locMSIE`, `locNS6`, and `locOpera`. Note that the strings returned by inspecting the `navigator` object's `userAgent`, `appVersion`, and `appName` properties are converted to lower case before they are stored in the `browserID`, `browserVer` and `browserName` variables to make matching search strings easier.

```
<script language="javascript" type="text/javascript">
<!--
function Is()
{
    var browserID = navigator.userAgent.toLowerCase();
    var browserVer = navigator.appVersion.toLowerCase();
    var browserName = navigator.appName.toLowerCase();
    var locMSIE;      //location of "msie" in browserID
    var locNS6;       //location of "netscape6" in browserID
    var locOpera;     //location of "opera" in browserID
```

The first properties we assign are the browser revision numbers `Rev`, `majorRev`, and `minorRev`. Usually, we can parse the floating-point version of the revision (for example, 4.02) from `browserVer` and assign it to `Rev` to get the browser version, then parse the integer version of the revision (for example, 4) from `browserVer` and assign it to `majorRev` for the major revision number, so we'll do that here. However, some browser versions report the Netscape version they claim compatibility with instead of their own version number. We will deal with each of those instances in the section for that browser. If we need the minor revision number, we can subtract `this.majorRev` from `this.Rev` (for example, for Netscape 4.76, the minor rev is .76 since 4.76 – 4 = .76).

```
    this.Rev = parseFloat(browserVer);
    this.majorRev = parseInt(browserVer,10);
```

Next, we check to see if we are working with IE, Netscape 6, or Opera by looking in the `browserID` string for the identifying text `"msie"` or `"netscape6"` or `"opera"`, then assigning their locations to `locMSIE` and `locNS6`. If the texts aren't found, `locMSIE`, `locNS6`, and `locOpera` will be set to –1.

```
    locMSIE = browserVer.indexOf("msie");
    locNS6 = browserVer.indexOf("netscape6");
    locOpera = browserID.indexOf("opera");
```

Now we start the actual "sniffing". First, we set a "catch-all" property for browsers other than what we are looking for:

```
    this.other = true
```

Next, we start checking for the browsers we are interested in. If the browser is Netscape, then `navigator.appName` will return `"Netscape"`. Next, we look for the strings `"spoofer"`, `"compatible"`, and `"opera"` to make sure they are **not** present. Since all of these conditions must be `true` for the browser to be NS, we check for all of them and use the logical AND (`&&`) to require all of the checks to be `true`:

```
    this.ns = ((browserName == "netscape") &&
        (browserID.indexOf("spoofer")==-1) &&
        (browserID.indexOf("compatible")===-1) && (locOpera==-1));
```

Of course, nothing is ever as easy as it should be. Netscape 6 is really Gecko 5 in fancy clothing, so it reports that it is Netscape 5, which is incorrect. Even worse, Netscape does not report version numbers consistently in version 6! So for now, if we're using Netscape 6, we'll set the correct values manually. We'll do a similar thing again later for IE because it reports the NS version it claims compatibility with, not its true version number.

```
if(locNS6!=-1)
{
    this.majorRev = 6
}
```

Now that we're certain of the versions, we'll set the properties for the various Netscape versions. To ensure that our code doesn't break when Netscape 7 is released, we'll include a catch-all ns6up property that should work for all Netscape versions from 6 onwards:

```
this.ns4 = this.ns && (this.majorRev==4);
this.ns6 = this.ns && (this.majorRev==6);
this.ns6up = this.ns && (this.majorRev>6);
```

Next, we go through the similar checks for IE. When we check for version numbers this time, we'll parse the browserID string to extract the correct version number since browserVer will only tell us what version of Netscape IE says it is compatible with. Since the version number comes right after the string "msie" we'll find that and get the number that immediately follows it using parseFloat():

```
this.ie = (locMSIE!=-1) &&
    (browserID.indexOf("spoofer")==-1) && (locOpera==-1));
if(locMSIE!=-1)
{
    this.Rev = parseFloat(browserID.substring(locMSIE+5));
    this.majorRev = parseInt(this.Rev);
}
this.ie4 = this.ie && (this.majorRev==4);
this.ie5 = this.ie && (this.majorRev==5);
this.ie5up = this.ie && (this.majorRev>5);
```

The checks for Opera should be a bit easier since, so far, no one mimics or spoofs Opera and, by default, it reports its proper version number when asked. However, users can set an alias (see below, in the "Special Cases, Traps, and Pitfalls" section), so we have to check for the alias setting to ensure the correct version number is reported. We will do this by checking for the presence of the string "opera" with either "msie" or "netscape" using the logical AND (&&) and OR (||), then rechecking the version numbers if that is true:

```
this.opera = (locOpera!=-1);
if(this.Opera && (locMSIE!=-1 || browserName=="netscape"))
{
    this.Rev = parseFloat(browserID.substring(locOpera + 6))
    this.majorRev = parseInt(thisRev)
}
this.opera4 = this.opera && (this.majorRev==4);
this.opera5 = this.opera && (this.majorRev==5);
this.opera5up = this.opera && (this.majorRev>5);
```

Finally, we update our `this.other` property using the logical OR ($||$) if we've found a browser of interest:

```
if(this.ns || this.ie || this.opera)
    {
        this.other = false
    }
}

var is = new Is()
// -->
</script>
```

Now, we use `if()..else if()` to let the user know what we've found:

```
<script language="javascript" type="text/javascript">
<!--
if(is.ns)
{
    document.write("<p>This browser is Netscape");
    if(is.ns4){document.write(" version 4</p>")};
    if(is.ns6){document.write(" version 6</p>")};
    if(is.ns6up){document.write(", version is greater than 6</p>")};
}
else if(is.ie)
{
    document.write("<p>This browser is Internet Explorer");
    if(is.ie4){document.write(" version 4</p>")};
    if(is.ie5){document.write(" version 5</p>")};
    if(is.ie5up){document.write(", version is greater than 5</p>")};
}
else if(is.opera)
{
    document.write("<p>This browser is Opera");
    if(is.opera3){document.write(" version 3</p>")};
    if(is.opera4){document.write(" version 4</p>")};
    if(is.opera5){document.write(" version 5</p>")};
    if(is.opera5up){document.write(", version is greater _
than 5</p>")};
}
// -->
</script>
```

You can find a much more elaborate browser sniffer that combines all of the techniques used here to provide a detailed report of a user's browser configuration at http://www.webreference.com/tools/browser/javascript.html. It reports on the user's OS, browser type, available objects, installed JavaScript version, and screen properties, among other things.

Special Cases, Traps, and Pitfalls

In general, when checking for browser versions, always set a catch-all property for versions beyond the current highest version of each browser you are checking for and unknown browsers that you may encounter. This will keep your code from halting when the next version of a particular vendor's browser is released, unless there are major changes between versions, for example, changes between Netscape 4 and Netscape 6. Also, trap for "spoofer" and "compatible" versions of the major browsers or you may end up with user complaints when the "compatible" browser doesn't support a particular feature (Opera can identify itself as Netscape or IE even though it doesn't support Netscape or Microsoft's proprietary features).

America Online (AOL)

America Online users can usually be detected by looking for the string "AOL" in `navigator.userAgent`. However, it is important to also check the major version of the browser because AOL uses everything from IE 3.02 to IE 5.5 in all of its packaged releases, so AOL 6 may really be anything from IE 3.02 to IE5.5. There is also a known bug in AOL 4 that may cause the first window opened in the browser to return `false` when checking for AOL This can also happen in *any* window of the AOL 4 IE 3.02 edition.

Opera in Alias Mode

Opera allows the user to set aliases for the browser so that it will report itself to be IE 5 or Netscape 3, 4, or 5 instead of Opera so that sites that restrict access to a particular browser type and version will allow access to Opera. The `navigator.userAgent` property will report as the aliased browser, but will also have `Opera` in the string.

Unfortunately, the fact that it calls itself Netscape or IE doesn't mean that it is truly compatible with these browsers, so if you really need to restrict access or rely on specific features of these browsers, you can check for Opera as outlined in the *"Browser Detection"* section above or you can check for the `window.opera` object. In our browser sniffing script, we could replace

```
this.opera = (locOpera!=-1);
```

with:

```
is.opera = window.opera;
```

and get the same result. If you need to get accurate version information, and so are using the `navigator` object, you **must** use `navigator.userAgent` to get the correct info.

Gecko vs. Netscape 6

Netscape 6 is really Mozilla 5/Gecko in a shell. If you use the `navigator.appVersion` property to check the version number of N 6, it returns "5" because that's the version of Mozilla that is being used. You must check for the string `"netscape6"` to positively identify Netscape 6.

Internet Explorer 5

If you use the `navigator.appVersion` property to check the version number of IE 5, it returns "4" because that's the version of Netscape that it is supposed to be compatible with. You must check for the string `"msie"` and then the version number that follows it to find IE 5.0, since IE 5.0 reports the same version number as IE 4.0.

Scripting Support Across Browsers

Proprietary objects and methods aren't the only browser-specific things you will run into as you develop cross-browser pages and applications – you will also have to contend with variations in scripting languages. JavaScript is the most common client-side scripting language currently in use on the Web. It comes in many forms, with many proprietary variations (Microsoft actually uses "JScript" which is **not** identical to Netscape's JavaScript), and is even supported by text-only browsers like Lynx. VBScript was Microsoft's attempt to upstage Netscape's JavaScript initiative, but since it is only supported in IE on the Windows and Mac platforms, it is not widely used outside of IE-centric intranets. There are also server-side scripting languages like Perl, HTMLScript, and PHP, but they are beyond the scope of this book.

JavaScript, JScript, and ECMAScript

JavaScript was introduced by Netscape in Navigator 2.0. Microsoft introduced its own answer to JavaScript for Internet Explorer (JScript – a slightly different version) shortly thereafter. In a bid to establish its own product as the standard web scripting language, Netscape then submitted its JavaScript 1.1 release to the **European Computer Manufacturer's Association (ECMA)** for ratification. This became the basis for the ECMAScript standard that defines JavaScript's core functionality. Netscape and Microsoft have continued to add client- and server-side extensions to the ECMAScript cores of their scripting languages, so while core functions and objects work reliably across browsers that support the ECMAScript standard, advanced capabilities like regular expression support and DHTML object manipulation cannot be counted on to work the same way across browsers. In fact, any serious scripting will probably have to be done at least twice to support the major browsers, although there are some programming methods that we'll look at in the DOM section that can reduce the need for multiple code versions.The following table provides a quick reference for the JavaScript versions supported by various browsers at the time of this printing. For a more detailed browser compatibility chart see http://www.webreview.com/browsers/browsers.shtml.

Browser	JavaScript Version	JScript Version	ECMA-262 (ECMAScript)*
NS 2.x (Win/Mac)	1.0		
NS 3.X (Win/Mac)	1.1		
NS 4.0 – 4.05 (Win/Mac)	1.2		
NS 4.06 – 4.08 (Win/Mac)	1.3		
NS 4.5 – 4.X (Win/Mac)	1.3		yes
NS 6.0 (Win/Mac)	1.5		yes
NS 2.0 (Unix)	1.0		
NS 3.0 (Unix)	1.1		

Table continued on following page

Browser	JavaScript Version	JScript Version	ECMA-262 (ECMAScript)*
NS 4.06 (Unix)	1.1		
IE 3.X (Win)	1.0	1.0	
IE 4.X (Win)	1.2	3.0	yes
IE 5.0 (Win)	1.3	5.0	yes
IE 5.5X (Win)	1.5	5.5	yes
IE 6.0beta (Win)	1.5	6.0	yes
IE 3.0 (Mac)	1.0	1.0	
IE 4.0 (Mac)	1.2	3.0	yes
IE 5.X (Mac)	1.3	5.0	yes
Opera 4.X	1.3		yes
Opera 5.X	1.3		yes

*The only real recognised version of ECMAScript

You can exploit the capabilities of later browser versions by using the transitional HTML 4.01 DTD, writing multiple versions of your scripts, and identifying the required JavaScript version in the `<script>` tag. Earlier browser versions will use the highest version numbered script they support and ignore anything they don't support. If the functions in each script set use the same names, they will be redefined each time a script set is read until they are the most recent version that the browser supports. However, Netscape 3.X has a bug that allows it to try running JavaScript 1.2 scripts, which it doesn't support, so you will have to check for it in JavaScript 1.2 code and exclude it if you are concerned about Netscape 3.X browsers. Here is a simple example:

```
<!doctype html public "-//W3C//DTD HTML 4.01//EN" _
"http://www.w3.org/TR/html4/transitional.dtd">

<html>
<head>
   <title>Script Test</title>
<script "language="javascript"><!--
   function doSomething()
   {
       document.write("JavaScript1.0 and below.")
   }
// -->
</script>
<script language="javascript1.1">
<!--
```

```
      function doSomething()
      {
          document.write("JavaScript1.1 and below.")
      }
// -->
</script>
<script language="javascript1.2">
    <!--
    function doSomething()
    {
        document.write("JavaScript1.2 and below.")
    }
// -->
</script>
<script language="javascript1.3">
<!--
    function doSomething()
    {
        document.write("JavaScript1.3 and below.")
    }
// -->
</script>
<script language="javascript1.5">
<!--
    function doSomething()
    {
        document.write("JavaScript1.5 and below.")
    }
// -->
</script>
</head>
<body>
<script language="javascript">
    doSomething();
</script>
</body>
</html>
```

Since we use the same name each time we declare the function, it is re-defined until the browser finds a version of JavaScript it does not support. We can then call doSomething() in the body of the page and the browser will report the highest version of JavaScript that it supports (or at least the highest that we are asking it to support). Further discussion regarding the subtle differences between the various versions of the Javascript, ECMAscript, and JScript languages is beyond the scope of this chapter – interested readers should refer to *Professional JavaScript* by Nigel McFarlane et al. (ISBN: *1-861002-70-X*).

VBScript

Although VBScript is very easy to learn and use for anyone with experience programming in Basic or Visual Basic, it is natively supported only in IE on the Windows platform and IE 5.0+ on the Mac platform. Netscape support on the Win32 platform was provided through a plug-in, but it was expensive and rarely used, so it is no longer available. Unless you are coding for IE that will be used on an intranet, it is generally best to avoid VBScript on the client for cross-browser pages.

The Document Object Model (DOM)

Until the release of the W3C's **Document Object Model (DOM)** recommendation, accessing a web page's structure was a largely proprietary matter. Starting with Netscape 2.0, a limited number of document and form elements could be accessed by JavaScript. Eventually, the image object was added, then Microsoft opened the entire page to access in IE 4.0 through the document.all collection that includes all elements on a web page. With the publishing of the W3C's DOM level 1 specification, browser designers now have a set of core objects and referencing methods available that should simplify coding. Netscape 6.0 and IE 5.0 already provide simplified cross-browser support through their implementations of the W3C standard-compliant document.getElementById method for accessing document objects.

Simplifying Coding Across DOMs

The primary method for writing readable cross-browser compatible code manipulates browser objects using user-defined JavaScript objects based on DOM or browser sniffing. The user-defined objects allow us to write one set of code that works across multiple browsers. Here we use the technique to move text around on a page:

```
<!doctype html public "-//W3C//DTD HTML 4.01//EN" _
    "http://www.w3.org/TR/html4/strict.dtd">
<html>
<head>
<title>Cross-DOM Coding Example</title>
<script type="text/javascript">
<!--
// perform DOM/object check
function Is()
{
   this.other = true
   this.compliant = document.getElementById;
   this.ie4 = document.all;
   this.ns4 = document.layers;
   this.opera = document.opera;
   if(this.compliant || this.ie4 || this.ns4 || this.opera)
   {
      this.other=false
   }
}
var is = new Is();

// do something with the information
var doc;
var styl;
var lyr;
var uTop;   //units for location cords (px, pt, etc)
var uLeft; //units for location cords (px, pt, etc)

// set DOM characteristics
if(!is.other)
{
   if(is.compliant && !is.opera)
   {
```

```
         doc = 'document.getElementById("';
         styl = '").style';
         lyr = "";
         uTop = "px";
         uLeft = "px";
      }
      else if(is.ie4 && !is.opera)
      {
         doc = "document.all.";
         styl = ".style";
         lyr = "";
         uTop = "px";
         uLeft = "px";
      }
      else if(is.ns4 && !is.opera)
      {
         doc = "document.";
         styl = "";
         lyr = "layers.";
         uTop = "";
         uLeft = "";
      }
      else if(is.opera)
      {
         doc = 'document.getElementById("';
         styl = '").style';
         lyr = "";
         uTop = "";
         uLeft = "";
      }
//    add other special cases here as required
}

function moveDiv(currDiv, newTop, newLeft)
{
   var thisDiv = new Object();
   var thisTop = newTop + uTop;
   var thisLeft = newLeft + uLeft;
   if(is.other)
   {
      alert("I'm sorry, your browser does not support moving the
      object on the page.");
   }
   else
   {
      thisDiv = eval(doc + currDiv + styl);
      thisDiv.top = thisTop;
       thisDiv.left = thisLeft;
   }
}

function hideSpan(spanID)
{
   if(is.other)
   {
```

```
            alert("I'm sorry, your browser does not support hiding the
            link on the page.");
      }
      else
      {
         var thisSpan = new Object();
         thisSpan = eval(doc + lyr + spanID + styl);
         thisSpan.visibility = "hidden";
      }
   }
   // -->
   </script>
   <style type="text/css">
   <!--
   DIV {
      position:           absolute;
      top:                40px;
      left:               40px;
      color:              red;
      font-weight:        bold;
   }
   SPAN {
      visibility:         visible;
   }
   -->
   </style>
   </head>
   <body>
   <layer name="moveLink">
   <span id="moveLink">
   <a href="javascript:moveDiv('example',100,100);
   hideSpan('moveLink')">Click here to move Div</a></span>
   </layer>
   <div id="example">
      <p>This is the example div.</p>
   </div>
   </body>
   </html>
```

After we determine the browser using our DOM/object sniffing routine, we set variables to hold the browser-specific parts of the object we will create – doc, styl, lyr, uTop, and uLeft. We will use doc to hold the method for the identified DOM to address the page element we want to manipulate, styl for the DOM's method for addressing the element's style attributes, lyr to hold Netscape 4's method for addressing layers, and uTop and uLeft to hold the CSS units for how far we are moving the object:

```
var doc;
var styl;
var lyr;
var uTop;
var uLeft;
```

Next we assign DOM-specific values for the variables. This will allow us to add new browsers by declaring a new set of variable values without having to rewrite all of our functions to account for the new DOM/browser quirks. Here is how the browsers we are looking at address an object on a page:

Browser Type	How page element addressed:	How style is addressed:
compliant	`document.getElementById(elementId)`	`.style.propertyName`
IE 4	`document.all.elementID`	`.style.propertyName`
Netscape 4	`document.elementID`	`.propertyName`

In this example, since Opera is a little quirky and doesn't allow us to use units for moving our object to its new location – we'll have to give it its own set of values for the variables and exclude it from any other DOM it claims compatibility with or our script won't work:

```
//set DOM characteristics
if(!is.other)
{
    if(is.compliant && !is.opera)
    {
        doc = 'document.getElementById("';
        styl = '").style';
        lyr = "";
        uTop = "px";
        uLeft = "px";
    }
    else if(is.ie4 && !is.opera)
    {
        doc = "document.all.";
        styl = ".style";
        lyr = "";
        uTop = "px";
        uLeft = "px";
    }
    else if(is.ns4 && !is.opera)
    {
        doc = "document.";
        styl = "";
        lyr = "layers.";
        uTop = "";
        uLeft = "";
    }
    else if(is.opera)
    {
        doc = 'document.getElementById("';
        styl = '").style';
        lyr = "";
        uTop = "";
        uLeft = "";
    }
//      add other special cases here as required
}
```

Next, we write a function `moveDiv()` to construct our generic object `thisDiv`, and assign our location variables `thisTop` and `thisLeft`. `moveDiv()` will use them to move a `<div>` on the page when the user clicks the "Move Div" link in the page body:

```
function moveDiv(currDiv, newTop, newLeft)
{
    var thisDiv = new Object();
    var thisTop = newTop + uTop;
    var thisLeft = newLeft + uLeft;
    if(is.other)
    {
        alert("I'm sorry, your browser does not support moving the _
        object on the page.");
    }
    else
    {
        thisDiv = eval(doc + currDiv + styl);
        thisDiv.top = thisTop;
        thisDiv.left = thisLeft;
    }
}
```

Since the link only moves the <div> once, we will also include a function to hide it once the <div> is moved:

```
function hideSpan(spanID)
{
    if(is.other)
    {
        alert("I'm sorry, your browser does not support hiding the _
        link on the page.");
    }
    else
    {
        var thisSpan = new Object();
        thisSpan = eval(doc + lyr + spanID + styl);
        thisSpan.visibility = "hidden";
    }
}
```

N 4 has very limited support for the <span> tag, so we will wrap the <span> containing the link in a <layer> tag with the same name as the <span>'s id attribute. Now, N 4 will work with the <layer> while all other browsers will work with the <span> since they will ignore the <layer> tag. We included the lyr object we had defined earlier in the hideSpan() function just so that we could deal with this situation:

```
<layer name="moveLink">
<span id="moveLink"><a href="javascript:moveDiv('example',100,100);_
hideSpan('moveLink')">Click here to move Div</a></span>
</layer>
```

The main advantage of this method is that we can easily add support for new browsers by modifying our sniffer code and adding another if..else if statement to support the new browser without having to revise our debugged moveDiv() and hideSpan() functions.

Cross-Browser Style Sheets

Until the release of Netscape 6, WinIE 5.5, MacIE 5, and Opera 4.02, there was very little consistent support for non-proprietary style sheets. WinIE 3.X had some basic CSS 1 support, but it was very spotty and sometimes incorrect. WinIE 4.X was better, but it was not until the release of WinIE 5.5/MacIE 5 that Microsoft's support for CSS 1 became really useful; IE 6 promises to have full CSS 1 support and substantial CSS 2 support. Netscape 4.X had very little CSS 1 support, which was was very buggy, relying instead on Netscape's proprietary JavaScript style sheets (JSSS) that were dropped with the release of Netscape 6.0. For these reasons, the style attributes that can be reliably set across all browsers are very limited. For maximum control over the display of a standards-compliant page, it is necessary to develop a set of style sheets that deal with each supported browser's quirks, then use the method outlined in the next section to link to the required style sheet when the page is loaded.

Single Cross-Browser Style Sheet

Many browsers claiming style sheet support do not properly implement the CSS 1 or CSS 2 standards. Inheritance of font attributes is particularly troublesome and must be addressed by redundantly specifying font attributes for each page element. So, even though you may specify `body{font-family:Arial;}`, you will still need to specify `table{font-family:Arial;}` if you want the contents of your tables to be rendered correctly. Generally, you should declare font parameters for all of the block elements that you will be using on your site. If in doubt, declare them for **all** of the block elements. It is easier to do this at the start than to go back and add them later. It is also helpful to organize your style sheet in alphabetical order, dividing it into sections for elements, classes, and `id`s. Using these suggestions, a minimal cross-browser style sheet might look like:

```
address, blockquote, body, caption, center, dd, dir, div, dl, dt, form, h1, h2,
h3, h4, h5, h6, menu, ol, p, td, th, ul
{
font-family:    Arial, Helvetica, sans-serif;
font-size:      1em;
margin-left:    0px;
margin-top:     0px;
}
```

This will set the font to `Arial` on machines that support it, degrading to `Helvetica`, then the user's generic sans-serif font if `Arial` and `Helvetica` are not available. The font-size is set to the user's default font size by specifying 1em. A specific font-size could just as easily be specified using 12px or 12pt to set the font size to 12 pixels in height or the browser's interpretation of 12pt (Netscape 4.X renders fonts about 1pt smaller on screen than IE and Opera do, defeating the purpose of the single style sheet). See Appendix F for a current chart detailing each major browser's support of each CSS 1 property or value. Only properties or values that are labeled as "Y" in all the browsers that you are supporting should be used in the single cross-browser style sheet.

This style sheet can be included in each page or saved as a file (such as `general.css`) and linked to each page using:

```
<link rel="stylesheet" href="general.css" type="text/css">
```

in the `<head>` section of each page. Do not import a general use style sheet using `@import url(/style/general.css)` unless `@import` is supported in all the browsers you have identified for your target audience.

Customizing Style Sheets to Browsers

If you want to use custom style sheets for each browser, name the style sheets by browser name and version with a `.css` extension (for example, `ie4.css`, `ns6.css`, `opera5.css`), then use browser sniffing as set up in the "*Browser Detection*" section to link to an appropriate style sheet using JavaScript. Be sure that a generic stylesheet is included between `<noscript></noscript>` tags so that core style attributes are included even if the user has disabled JavaScript:

```
<script language="javascript">
var strStartCSSLink = '<link rel="stylesheet" type="text/css" href="';
var strEndCSSLink = '.css">';
var strCSSLink;
if(is.ie4){strCSSLink = strStartCSSLink + "ie4" + strEndCssLink};
if(is.ie5){strCSSLink = strStartCSSLink + "ie5" + strEndCssLink};
if(is.ns4){strCSSLink = strStartCSSLink + "ns4" + strEndCssLink};
if(is.ns6){strCSSLink = strStartCSSLink + "ns6" + strEndCssLink};
if(is.opera4){strCSSLink = strStartCSSLink + "op4" + strEndCssLink};
if(is.opera5){strCSSLink = strStartCSSLink + "op5" + strEndCssLink};

document.write(strCSSLink + "\r\n")
</script>
<noscript>
   <link href="generic.css" rel="stylesheet" type="text/css">
</noscript>
```

Since only the 4.0 and up versions of the major browsers have usable CSS support, it isn't necessary to set up style sheets for any earlier browsers. You can add support for additional browsers by sniffing for them, then adding additional if-statements to the list.

Solutions to Specific Problems

There are many cross-browser problems that don't really fall into any particular category. Basic solutions to some of the more common problems are covered here. You may need answers to problems that are not covered here. If so, you will find many online resources such as www.webReference.com, www.webReview.com, or www.DevX.com may deal with your problem in much greater depth.

Browser Window Offset Differences

Different browsers assume different default values for the number of pixels that window content is offset from the window's edges. This number of pixels varies between both browser versions and OSes:

Browser	Horizontal Offset	Vertical Offset
WinNetscape 4.X	8	8
WinNetscape 6.X	8	8
MacNetscape 4.X	8	8
MacNetscape 6.X	8	8

Browser	Horizontal Offset	Vertical Offset
WinIE 4.X	10	15
WinIE 5.X	10	15
WinIE 6.0 beta	10	15
MacIE 4.X	8	8
MacIE 5.X	8	8
Opera 4.X	8	8
Opera 5.X	8	8

To work around this problem when you need to position content in a particular location on screen, you can set margin attributes for the body tag in the 4.0+ version browsers to override the defaults. In standards-compliant browsers, this can be done in the page's style sheet:

```
body {margin-left: 0px; margin-top: 0px}
```

For most legacy browsers (such as Netscape 4.X, Opera 3.X, IE 3.X, etc.) that do not have CSS-support, the margins must also be set in the body tag itself even though this produces invalid HTML 4.01 code:

```
<body leftmargin="0" topmargin="0" marginwidth="0" marginheight="0">
```

You can, of course, set the margins to any value that you need. The point here is that specifying the margins overcomes the problem with the different default values assumed by the browsers. There is a caveat here: this does not work in Netscape versions prior to 4.0, IE versions prior to 3.02, or Opera versions prior to 3.0, so you will be stuck with the default values for those browsers.

Display Resolution Differences

Different OSes assume different screen resolutions (the number of dots per inch [dpi] on the screen) and different screen dimensions (the number of horizontal and vertical dots on the screen). For example, until MacOS 9.X, the Macintosh default screen resolution was 72 dpi, while the Windows default was 96 dpi, so images and text appeared larger but less crisp on the Mac when compared to Windows. If you expect part of your audience to be using lower-end equipment, the usable screen area of Mac-Win cross-compatible pages is about 580 x 350 pixels out of 640 x 480 supposedly available pixels (to account for the pixels taken up by the browser's controls, etc.). As long as your content remains within these parameters, your clients should not have to scroll your pages. If you must make them scroll, it is better to require them to scroll up and down (vertically) and not side-to-side (horizontally). If you are not intending to support older low-resolution monitors, then you can design with 720 x 460 pixels size in mind (based on the default 800 x 600 Mac screen).

Although MacOS 9.X now defaults to the Windows standard 96 dpi and 800 x 600 resolution, the default setting for MacIE 5.0 automatically scales font sizes specified in point (pt) sizes (1pt = 1/72 inch) to present them on screen at actual size. The only way to reliably retain the relationship between image and font sizes is to specify font sizes in pixels. This is counter to the recommended practice of specifying font sizes in relative terms (for example, 10 em), but is the only effective method to retain page layout across browsers and platforms. Remember that font sizes less than 10pt (or 10px) will not be legible on Macs running anything earlier than MacOS 9.X because there will not be enough pixels available to display the font legibly. Examples of how four of the most common fonts display across Windows and Mac platforms are available online at http://developer.apple.com/internet/fonts/fonts_gallery.html

Rendering Images in Tables

A common HTML 3.2 trick for positioning images and text on a page was to cut the images up into pieces and reassemble them in tables on the page. This ensured the relative positions of the page elements, and also increased the perceived loading speed of the page (the page seems to load faster if you can see pieces coming up on screen instead of having to wait until the whole screen has loaded). This resulted in some rather elaborate nested table schemes that were prone to breakage across browsers. With the adoption of HTML 4.0+, images and text can be positioned using overlapping <div>s and the table layouts are not so critical. However, if you must maintain backwards compatibility, here are some things to remember when rendering images in tables:

❑   Do not leave any space between the table data (<td>) tag and the image tag:

```
<td><img src="pic.gif"></td> //this displays correctly

<td>
   <img src="pic.gif"> //breaks (leaves gaps between images)
</td>
```

❑   Specify the table width as the width of the assembled image.

❑   Specify the table's cellpadding, cellspacing, and border attributes as "0".

❑   Specify each cell's height and width to be the same as the height and width of the image fragment it contains.

❑   The size of the contents of spanned columns and rows must equal the sum of the individual rows and columns that are spanned.

❑   All images in cells in a table column must be the same width.

❑   All images in cells in a table row must be the same height.

❑   Avoid placing cells containing text near cells containing images unless you know that the text will render in an area smaller than the image it is placed near. Otherwise, the table may expand to fit the text and destroy the alignment of your images. For example, if the image above the text cell is 100px wide and the adjacent image cell is 20px high, the text content must render within a 100 x 20 pixel space or images following the text in the table will not line up properly.

Example of correct coding methods:

```
<table cellpadding="0" cellspacing="0" border="0" width="400">
<tr>
<td height="10" width="250"><img src="p1.gif" width="250" _ height="10"
alt="fragment1"></td>
<td height="10" width="150"><img src="p2.gif" width="150" _ height="10"
alt="fragment2"></td>
</tr>
<tr>
<td height="30" width="250"><img src="p3.gif" width="250" _ height="30"
alt="fragment3"></td>
<td height="30" width="150"><img src="p4.gif" width="150" _ height="30"
alt="fragment4"></td>
</tr>
<tr>
<td colspan="2" height="20" width="400"><img src="p5.gif" _ width="400"
height="20" alt="fragment5"></td>
</tr>
</table>
```

This code gives the following output in a browser:

Consistent Font Rendering

Font rendering varies across platforms and browsers on the same platform. WinNetscape 4.0 displays fonts about 1pt smaller than the same font will display on WinIE 4/5. All Mac browsers on MacOS 8.X assume 72 dpi screen resolution, so fonts smaller than 10 pt are unreadable on them. One method for dealing with these problems is to develop custom style sheets for each of the problem browsers, then link to the appropriate style sheet using browser sniffing when the page loads as outlined in the "*Customizing Style Sheets to Browsers*" section of this chapter. If the page absolutely must look the same across browsers and platforms, specifying font sizes in pixels is the only current option that works reliably. It is important to remember, though, that hard-coding font sizes can cause problems for users who need alternative font sizes for usability reasons, so specific pixel or point sizes should be used sparingly. The 10px font that looked great on the 800 x 600 monitor at work may be nearly invisible on the 1600 x 1200 monitor at home.

Summary

Historically, developing cross-browser code has been a long and painful process fraught with dangerous pitfalls and intricacies that were almost impossible to adequately address. And although that is still largely true, the advent of largely standards-compliant browsers promises to make cross-browser coding easier, faster, and cheaper, though perhaps not yet painless. As time passes, use of the the older, non-compliant browsers will decline to the point that they will no longer need to be considered on production web sites and, hopefully, the time and effort now spent ensuring backwards-compatibility will be devoted to improving the web's accessibility for all people. Until then, there are two keys to developing cross-browser code.

The first key is to know who your target audience are so that you can select the right tools and features to support their experience of your pages. If your target audience will be using IE 3.02 or Netscape 2.2, there is no use developing in HTML 4.01 – you should be using HTML 3.2 and forgetting about CSS and dynamic HTML. However, if your target audience may be using a broad range of browsers, determine what functionality is essential across all platforms/browsers and develop the cross-browser code to deliver those services. Then, as time and funding permit, build on your cross-browser code to provide browser-specific enhancements, starting with the most popular recent browser releases since they are probably going to remain in service the longest.

The second key is to write valid, well-formed, compliant code. Since support for the various standards is increasing, writing valid, well-formed, compliant code whenever possible will provide a maintainable site that will provide the greatest functionality with the least investment of time, effort, and money.

This chapter has primarily focused on techniques and issues applicable to browsers that support HTML 4.01, CSS 1, and the W3C DOM level 1. It has also covered some techniques for working with older browsers, although not in the same depth. Further information on writing cross-browser code is available at the Wrox site as well as the web sites provided in the chapter.

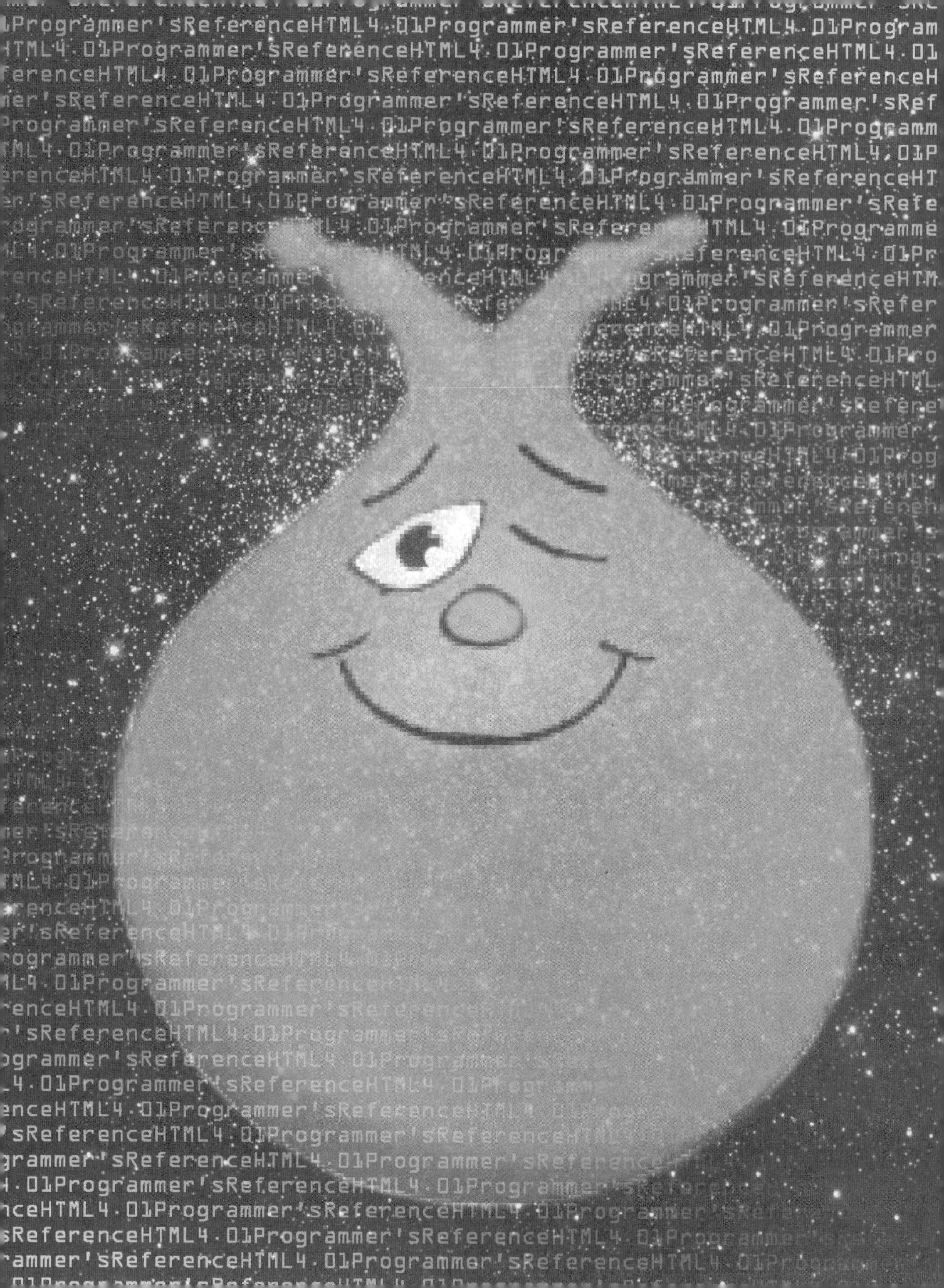
HTML4.01Programmer'sReference

18

Internationalization

Up until very recently, the Web has not been very World Wide. In fact, support for languages other than English is still extremely scarce. HTML documents and the URLs used to locate them are limited to languages that conform to the ISO Latin-1 character set, which is not very many. In this chapter, we will discuss the languages of the World Wide Web, including character set encoding, and language locales. We will also discuss:

❑   The internationalization of HTML and URLs

❑   Bi-directional text

❑   Browser support for internationalization standards

World Wide Web?

Until recently, the phrase "World Wide Web" has been somewhat of an inaccuracy. **Internationalization** support for meaningful and understandable HTML, URLs, and HTTP headers has been limited to languages that conform to the ISO Latin-1 character set, which is a superset of the ASCII character set. The ISO Latin-1 character set basically provides support for most of the western European languages, and also Afrikaans and Swahili. This limited character set leaves a lot of the world left to support. In the past, in order to display languages that did not conform to the ISO Latin-1 specification, HTML authors had to devise clever ways to display unsupported languages in the browser. However, recently there has been a move in the standards community to adopt a new character set that could ideally support all languages and combinations of languages – this new character set is Unicode. The W3C's Internationalization Working Group is currently working on a solution to the problem. This new draft is called the **HTML i18n Internet Draft**.

Note: The *i18n* portion is just shorthand for "*internationalization*" – "i" + "18" (for the number of characters in: "nternationalizatio")+ "n."

Character Encoding

Character encoding is the process of taking a fixed group of characters and mapping them to a range of numbers or numeric codes that the hardware or software understands. The number of characters that can be displayed is limited to the range of the specified codes.

ISO Latin-1

The current specification, ISO Latin-1, is capable of displaying 256 distinct characters, each represented by an eight-bit hexadecimal number (octet) in the range of "00" to "FF." The hexadecimal values "00" – "1F"are reserved for control characters such as tab, backspace, linefeed, esc and others. The values "7F" – "A0" are not used in the ISO Latin-1 specification. This brings the grand total of actual characters supported to a mere 190 characters, a far cry from the support required to display the characters of all the world's languages.

Unicode

Unicode is the character encoding that the HTML i18n Internet Draft proposes to use as the new standard for HTML character encoding. Unicode is 16-bit encoded, which means that there is possible support for 65,536 distinct characters. Each character is represented by two octets giving the range of "0000" to "FFFF." Unicode is also backward compatible to a certain degree, or at least mnemonically intuitive. For example, the ISO Latin-1 character set defines the hexadecimal value for "Z" as "5A." The hexadecimal value for "Z" in Unicode is "005A." In fact, the first 256 character codes in Unicode are identical to those in the ISO Latin-1 specification.

The Future of Encoding

Some languages are not based on a set grouping of characters that, when combined, form the sounds that make up words. Instead, some languages such as Japanese and Chinese denote a specific character or combination of existing characters for each concept or sound that makes up a word. As new words are added to such languages, eventually even 16-bit Unicode will not be enough to handle the influx of new characters. Eventually, 32-or 64-bit versions of character encoding will have to be implemented.

Specifying Language Locales

The HTML 4.01 specification supports some HTML tags and attributes that enable the specification of a language locale for certain elements. The specification of a language locale for an element does not mean that the browser translates the element's text. According to the W3C HTML 4.01 specification, these language codes can potentially be useful in assisting search engines or speech synthesizers, helping a browser (or other software) make decisions about sets of quotation marks, hyphenation, ligatures, and spacing, and assisting spelling and grammar checkers. Each language locale is represented by a two-character code. The syntax for specifying the language locale for an element's text is as follows:

```
<element lang="languageCode">
```

For example, <p lang="fr"> specifies that the language of the paragraph text is French. The browser should display the contents of the paragraph element according to the acceptable cultural practice for the French language (for example, including the correct quotation marks, hyphenation, spacing, etc.)

The list of supported language locale codes is maintained by ISO 639, and can be found in Appendix C – *"HTML Locales and Character Sets"*.

As you will see from the appendix, this list is quite extensive. Just because a language is in the list does not mean that the software (web browser) will support it, although measures are being taken to move in that direction. In the next section, we will discuss how to use these language codes to specify a language for HTML elements.

Internationalization of HTML

The HTML 4.01 specification includes support for internationalization efforts in the form of a new element and new attribute:

The <bdo> Element and the dir attribute

Element or Attribute	IE versions supported	Netscape versions supported
<bdo>	IE 5+	N/A
dir	IE 5+	NN 6

The <bdo> element was added in the HTML 4.0 specification, and serves to override the i18n Bi-Directional (BiDi) rendering of enclosed text. This is accomplished by applying the Unicode bi-directional algorithm, which automatically reverses the sequence of characters in a specified portion of text. This is a move toward the internationalization of the World Wide Web, as some languages read right-to-left. The <bdo> element requires the dir attribute to set the direction of the text it contains.

The dir attribute was added to the HTML 4.01 specification in order to allow control over the direction of text in HTML elements. The dir attribute also affects the directionality of tables. The dir attribute accepts "ltr" and "rtl" as possible values. A value of "ltr" indicates to the browser that the specified text is to be rendered left-to-right (as the text in this book is). A value of "rtl" indicates to the user agent that the specified text is to be rendered right-to-left (for languages like Hebrew, Arabic, or Aramaic). The dir attribute is supported by most HTML elements: the ones that don't are <applet>*, <base>, <basefont>*, <br>, <frame>, <frameset>, <iframe>, <param>, and <script>.

Note: The elements with asterisks after them are deprecated.

The following example demonstrates how to apply the <bdo> element and the dir attribute to different HTML elements:

```
<html dir="rtl">
  <head>
    <title>The "bdo" element and "dir" attribute</title>
  </head>
  <body>
    This is the main body text.

    <p dir="ltr">
      This is "ltr" paragraph text.
    </p>
```

```
    <p>
        This is "rtl" paragraph text, inherited from
        the "DIR" attribute in the &lt;HTML&gt; tag.
    </p>

    <p>
        <bdo dir="rtl">
            This is "rtl" paragraph text, text reversed.<br>
            .desrever txet ,txet hpargarap "ltr" si sihT -- !!eeS
        </bdo>
    </p>
    </body>
</html>
```

The browser will, however, attempt to align the specified text according to that direction. The screenshot below shows how the above example is rendered in IE 5.5:

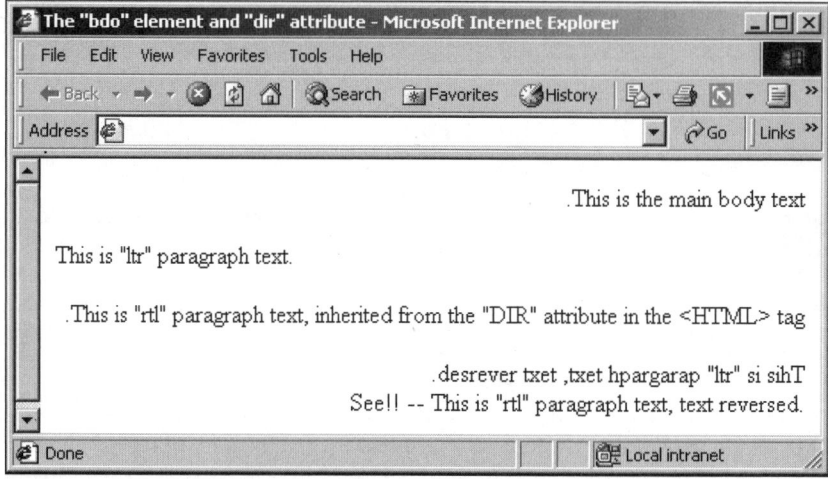

Notice how the IE 5.5 browser renders elements with the `dir` attribute set to "rtl" as aligned right. The preceding example will not render the characters in the specified direction unless you override the bi-directional algorithm.

accept-charset

Attribute	IE versions supported	Netscape versions supported
accept-charset	IE 5+	Netscape 6

The `accept-charset` attribute was added to the HTML 4.01 specification in order to allow form elements to list accepted character sets (see Appendix C) accepted by the web server processing the form. This list of character sets can be comma and/or space separated. The `accept-charset` attribute applies only to the `<form>` element, and has no affect on the way text is rendered by the browser. The following example demonstrates how to implement the `accept-charset` attribute:

```
<html>
  <head>
    <title>accept-charset Element</title>
  </head>
  <body>
    <form method="post" accept-charset="iso-8859-5">
      Form Field
      <input type="text">
    </form>
  </body>
</html>
```

lang

Attribute	IE versions supported	Netscape versions supported
lang	IE 5+	Netscape 6

This attribute was added to the HTML 4.01 specification in order to specify the language of HTML elements. The `lang` attribute accepts a two-character language code (from the language table above) as possible values. The value of the language code is not case sensitive. The language code may be supplemented by a dialect code. For example, `language="en-us"` specifies United States English (characters and pronunciations) for the contents of the HTML elements. White space between the language code and language sub-code is not allowed. The `lang` attribute is supported by most HTML elements, but those that don't support it are as follows: <applet>*, <base>, <basefont>*, <br>, <frame>, <frameset>, <iframe>, <param>, and <script>.

Note: The elements with asterisks after them are deprecated.

The following example demonstrates how to apply the `lang` attribute to an HTML element:

```
<html lang="en-us" dir="ltr">
  <head>
    <title>The "lang" attribute</title>
  </head>
  <body>
    This is the main body text, in English.

    <p lang="fr">
      This is french paragraph text.
    </p>

    <p lang="de">
      This is German paragraph text.
    </p>
  </body>
</html>
```

The preceding example instructs the user agent that the main body text is set to be United States English. The text of the first paragraph is set to be French, meaning that all accepted cultural practices of the French language with regards to quotations, hyphenation, etc. should be followed when marking up that text. Finally, the text of the third paragraph is set to be German – the browser should mark up that text according to German cultural practices.

Internationalization of URLs

Another main focus of the i18n Internet draft is the internationalization of URLs. The current URL character set is the same ISO Latin-1 character set as used in HTML – by utilizing the Unicode character set for URLs instead, we can expand the number of domain names that are available for use. Up until now the same characters in English, Chinese, and Aramaic represent http://www.wrox.com. In Unicode, the characters in each individual language each have their own values, so, in essence, the URL http://www.wrox.com could exist in as many languages as Unicode supports (see Appendix C) because the character values that make up the URL in English would be different from the character values that make up the URL in another language, for example, Finnish. Using Unicode also allows languages other than English to provide meaningful, mnemonic names to their domains, thus bringing the Web ever closer to its World Wide aspirations.

Summary

In this chapter, we looked at how Internationalization is being implemented on the Web. We discussed:

❑ The languages of the World Wide Web

❑ Character set encoding

❑ Language codes

We also looked at the internationalization of HTML and URLs, bi-directional text, and finally, browser support for internationalization element standards. Hopefully, as these standards become more widely used, the World Wide Web will eventually become truly "World Wide"!

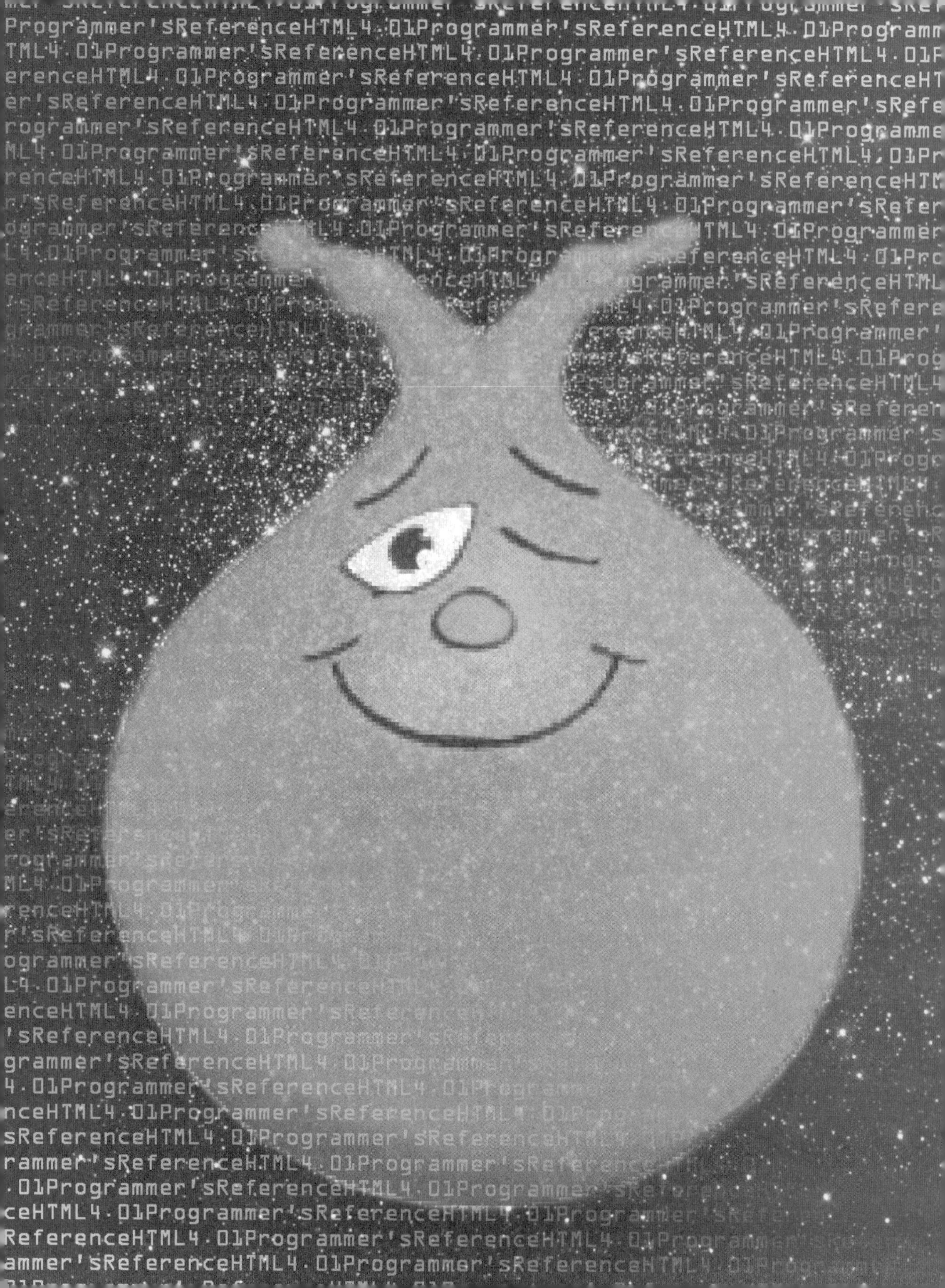

19

Dynamic Pages:
DHTML and the Document Object
Model

Introduction

As in our earlier discussion of general scripting-related issues (see Chapter 9), this chapter is not intended to be a scripting tutorial as such. Rather, we will try to show web page authors and designers using HTML and CSS how their work impacts upon and relates to that of the client-side applications developer.

We'll start out by taking a look at what is commonly known as "Dynamic HTML", offering a definition of it, and explaining how it came about through the evolution of browser object models in the 2nd- and 3rd-generation user agents.

Next, we will:

❑ Examine the standard Document Object Model (DOM), Level 1 and Level 2, recommended by the W3C, which serves as a formalization of the concepts behind Dynamic HTML.

❑ Explain how the DOM conceptualizes and models the structure of documents and the relationships between the elements that make up those documents.

❑ Discuss the "mapping" that takes place between HTML elements with their attributes on the one hand and scripting objects with their properties on the other. It should be beneficial even for non-programmers involved in HTML authoring to have an idea of what some of the interfaces defined in DOM Level 1 and refined in the DOM Level 2 can provide to scripters for identifying and manipulating both individual document elements and collections of them.

❑ Look at how the DOM Level 2 Specification for Styles impacts client side scripting, and hence, the HTML/CSS developer.

❑ Provide a detailed overview of the improved event handling available through the implementation of DOM Level 2.

In addition, we'll offer an admonition: the "good old days" when any web page that "looked passable", regardless of how badly-formed the HTML in that page might be, are over. The concept of "valid" markup is central to an understanding of Dynamic HTML in web-based applications; good web design now demands that web documents be accurately marked up and styled, especially with the advent of XML and XHTML.

What is "Dynamic HTML"?

The phrase "Dynamic HTML" has never had a rigorous definition in the sense that most other terms relating to web design and development have had or acquired, and has come to mean somewhat different things to different people. For instance, we all know what "HTML" or "markup" or "content" mean – we can look these terms up in a dictionary, RFC document, in the relevant standard from W3C, and arrive at a fairly unambiguous understanding of them. "Dynamic HTML" began life largely as a marketing term used by various browser vendors to promote technologies that became available in the 4th-generation versions of their products, and didn't mean exactly the same thing, depending upon whose client software you were using at the time.

It's probably safe to say that what most developers are referring to when speaking of Dynamic HTML involves dynamism on the *client*, that is, the ability to make changes in real time to a web document after it has been downloaded by the user, without requiring additional trips back to the server.

Dynamic HTML, often contracted to "DHTML", can be regarded as a natural extension of document scripting such as we discussed earlier in Chapter 9, in which the document becomes, in a limited fashion, a framework to support client-side applications. However, where we could change only specific attributes of a relatively small range of page elements in the earlier browsers, DHTML can be regarded as the ability to update the content and presentation of most if not all the elements in an HTML document.

> *A complete DHTML framework would include the ability to manipulate text and other page elements along with their presentational styles, and to delete and even create new page elements "on the fly", in response to user input, preprogrammed, or other events.*

There are a number of versions of DHTML, as found in the most recent browsers that are commercially available today. The levels of support can be summarized as follows:

❏ **Netscape 2/3 and MSIE 3**: Access to certain classes or collections of web page elements through the use of the JavaScript scripting language (and in the case of MSIE, VBScript as well). Following the usage suggested in the W3C DOM specifications, we refer to this as "DOM-0" (see the "*Browser Support for the DOM-0*" section for more on this).

❏ **Netscape 4**: Limited access to element positioning and content via a new and special element and corresponding object (the `Layer` object) developed just for this purpose. This browser also had improved event-handling capabilities (event capturing) that were not dependent upon handlers embedded in HTML markup. Since this implementation is largely dependent on the wrapping of elements in this "container" tag and does not support the real-time updating of CSS styles, we deem that it only gets about half the job done, and call it "DOM-½" (see the "*The 4th Generation:"" DOM-½ and DOM-¾*" section for more details of this)

❏ **MSIE 4**: Ability to access and change nearly all attributes of all elements programmatically, including CSS styles and textual content. However this is accomplished through the use of a proprietary object model (the `document.all` collection). This browser also introduced improved event handling through a mechanism known as event bubbling, which we'll discuss later in this chapter. We refer to this as "DOM-¾" to signify that it's a little closer to the object model eventually adopted by W3C than what Netscape implemented in its version 4 browser.

❏ **MSIE 5**: Adoption of the DOM-standard methods for accessing elements without the need to refer to the `document.all` collection, although this collection was retained for backwards compatibility. Event capturing remains unimplemented.

❏ **MSIE 6** (in beta as of this writing): It appears that the IE object models for HTML elements and styles will implement the DOM Level-2 specifications quite closely, with one or two relatively minor exceptions. However, it also seems that the DOM-2 event model will remain incompletely reflected in this browser's event handling scheme, as it promises only to support event bubbling.

❏ **Netscape 6/Mozilla**: These user agents appear to support nearly all the features required of a DOM-2 compliant application with regard to HTML elements and CSS styles. The event model supported also reflects that of DOM Level 2 quite closely, including event capturing and bubbling, as well as a complete implementation of its `Event` object and its properties and methods.

While these implementations are widely divergent, they share a number of essential features or ingredients in common, which can be categorized as:

❏ Text and possibly other content, contained within a logical structure created through the use of markup. Usually by "markup", we mean HTML. There are other markup languages, such as XML, SVG, and XSL, which also lend themselves to DOM scripting, but fall outside the scope of this book.

❏ A method of specifying how content is to be presented. Most often we are speaking in terms of visual presentation using Cascading Style Sheets. In Netscape 4, some of this is accomplished by the use of the `<layer>`, `<ilayer>`, `<div>`, and `<span>` elements.

❏ The means to access, read, and make changes to attributes or properties of the content, structure, and presentation of a document programmatically, in real time. This is accomplished through the use of a scripting or programming language, most often JavaScript, which is used to manipulate the corresponding objects, which we'll be discussing throughout most of the rest of this chapter.

Working together in concert, these components of DHTML can be used to create web pages that are no longer merely "documents" in the sense of printed pages that act only as containers for static information – they can begin to serve as a platform for applications.

The Evolution of Scripting

In the beginning there was static content. Then came Netscape 2.0. This browser introduced something new to the web: a scripting language named LiveScript, which quickly became known as "JavaScript". Up until this time, surfing the web had consisted of the user (a) clicking on a link or button, (b) waiting for a new document to load up in their browser, and (c) reading the text and/or viewing the images that appeared on their computer screen. When finished, they clicked on the next bit of linked text or the next linked image that caught their interest, and repeated the process. Even though in retrospect, Netscape 2 provided only a very limited amount of functionality, it was still real-time programmability of features in web browsers and the pages viewed through them.

It was not just JavaScript alone that made this possible, however. A programming language at its core doesn't really do anything more than perform calculations. While this certainly has its uses, it becomes much more interesting when we can write programs that can take advantage of a user's environment, or, more specifically, of a graphical user interface. What Netscape 2.0 introduced to authors of web pages was not just another computer language, but a means for programs written in this language to access features both of web documents and of the browsers that render them, that is, it made **object models** available to programmers. But before we talk about object models themselves, we ought to first explain a little bit about objects.

Objects

If you've already done some programming in an object-oriented language such as C++, Java, Smalltalk, or JavaScript, you'll probably want to skip the next few paragraphs and move straight on to our account of the iterations of object models offered in succeeding browsers. Otherwise, bear with us we while digress for a bit into just what objects are and what they can do for us in terms of programming.

An Object, in programming terms, is a way of depicting or modeling a real-life object. The classic example is that of a car. A real automobile has certain attributes, such as *color, size, make, model*, and so on, and can perform certain actions that we can also readily identify – for instance, it can accelerate, decelerate, and turn.

As it is with cars, so it is in this respect with programming objects. In fact, in an object-oriented language, we could create a `Car` object that represents a real-life automobile and give it the attributes we discussed above – known in programming parlance as **properties**, and make it capable of performing said actions, usually termed **methods**.

To prove it, here's an example written in JavaScript, which defines an object called `Car`, and its properties, `size`, `color`, `make`, `model`, and `year`:

```
function Car(size,color,make,model,year)
{
    this.size=size;
    this.color=color;
    this.make=make;
    this.model=model;
    this.year=year;
    this.speed=0;
}
```

Currently, Car has a speed of zero, so let's give our car an accelerate() method, so that it can move (that is, have a non-zero speed):

```
function accelerate(changeInSpeed)
{
  return this.speed+=changeInSpeed;
}
```

In ordinary language, this means, "Change the speed by the amount changeInSpeed".

```
Car.prototype.accelerate=accelerate;
```

The statement containing the word prototype is the way that we tell JavaScript that a method belongs to a particular object. Here we're saying: "Acceleration is an action that can be performed by any Car." The Car that we've created is a generic object known as a **class object**; now let's create a specific instance of a Car, which we'll call myVan:

```
var myVan=new Car("midsize", "burgundy", "Mazda", "MVP van", 1990);
```

What we've done here is to name an instance of the Car class and assign values to its properties. Now let's make it do something interesting:

```
myVan.accelerate(50);
```

In object-oriented terms, we've called the accelerate() method of myVan; that is, we've called a class method of Car – since accelerate() is a method of the class or prototypical Car, it's also a method of any instance of Car.

To recap: an object is a model of something in real life – a generalized and idealized one – whose qualities are described by properties, and whose actions by methods.

If an object can be considered a noun, then its properties are adjectives and its methods are verbs. In most programming languages, we create the most general class or prototype object that we can, then derive instances of that class for particular examples of it that we want to work with. It's also important to realize that objects can contain other objects, either singly or in collections.

For example, since a real-life automobile has four tires, our Car object could also be expected to have a set of four Tire objects, each of which might have properties like diameter, pressure, amountOfWear, and perhaps even a method such as roll() (it might also have a goFlat() method, which we'd hope not to see invoked very often!).

For more on JavaScript objects and their use, consult *Beginning JavaScript* by Paul Wilton (ISBN: *1-861004-06-0*), published by Wrox Press, or some of the other appropriate references in the bibliography section at the end of the chapter.

What are Object Models?

Now we have set the scene, let's get back on track, and talk about object models. An **object model** is a set of objects used to describe all the parts or features of a device or an application. Just as we used objects to help us describe some of the features of an automobile and its parts, so we can use them to describe the parts of a software application, which can be likened to a machine of sorts. Whereas a car is a machine that provides transportation from Point A to Point B, a software program is a sort of machine that provides transportation of data from A to B, performing tasks such as preparing a payroll, keeping track of the addresses in our address book, or converting HTML markup into something that looks like a document that can be viewed on a computer monitor – which is what a web browser does. A **Browser Object Model**, then, is a way of using objects to describe web browsers and the information that they process and display.

The object models employed in browsers have changed over time – in successive iterations of browser software, there have been and still are differences in the object models employed by user agents from different vendors, but there are certain major features that haven't changed much, and which we can reasonably expect to remain consistent in the foreseeable future. The top-level object containing all other objects is known as **window**, and corresponds to an instance of a browser window. This serves as the **global** object in browser scripting (a global object is a sort of universal or application-wide object with which all other objects in our object model are associated). In Chapter 9, we discussed some of the properties and methods of the `window` object and of some of the objects that it contains as members, including the `navigator` object, whose member properties and methods contain information about the browser software and its behavior. The objects corresponding to core language features (such as `Date` and `Math`) can also be considered to belong to `window`, but as they don't pertain directly to the content or formatting of HTML documents, we won't be discussing them any further here.

The Document Object Model

The remainder of this chapter will center on the other object of major importance to descend from `window`: the **document** object. As you might have already guessed, this object corresponds to an HTML document: in fact, it corresponds in some ways with the `<html>` element, and the `document` object's properties and methods describe the attributes and behavior of a web document. Just as `<html>` contains all the other HTML tags to be found in a web page, so `document` contains other objects that correspond to them. However, in the early browsers that supported scripting, not all elements had corresponding objects:

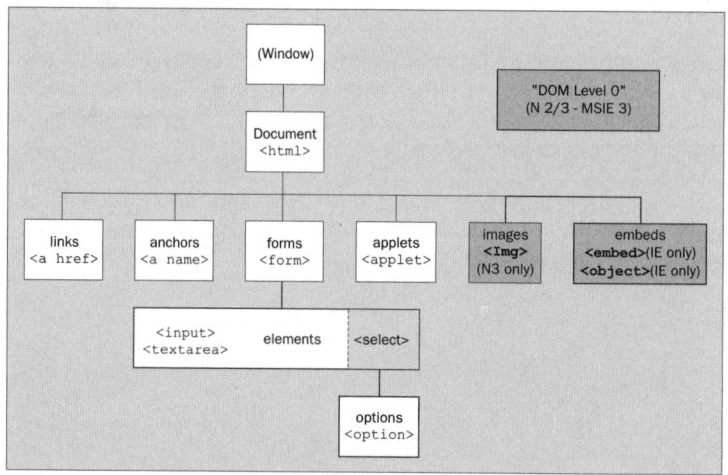

The figure shows which elements were reflected as scriptable objects in Netscape versions 2 and 3 as well as Microsoft IE 3. You may notice that all of the names of the objects are plural rather than singular. This is because each of these actually represents a **collection** of all the like tags in the page. For instance, **links** (customarily written in JavaScript as `document.links` and in VBScript as `Document.Links`) stands for the set of all hyperlinks (`<a href="">` tags) found within the HTML document, **forms** (`document.forms`) stands for the set of all `<form>` tags, **images** (or `document.images`) stands for the set of all `<img>` elements, and so on.

Each `Form` object contains another object collection, the **elements** collection, which contains all the `<input>`, `<textarea>`, and `<select>` elements in the form, and any `<select>` elements in the form each contain an **options** collection of all its `<option>` elements.

The object model above is often referred to as "DOM-0" (short for "Document Object Model, Level 0"). It is still supported in the 5th- and 6th-generation browsers largely for reasons of backwards compatibility. Although this support may eventually be phased out, there are still a great many scripts that employ it, and there is no reason not to continue to do so for the time being, especially for client-side form processing.

Browser Support for DOM-0

There are a couple of differences in DOM support worthy of note here. While Netscape 3 added support for the images collection (and thus spawned the now-ubiquitous image rollover) IE 3 supported it originally for the Macintosh platform only. Microsoft later made available an updated scripting engine for MSIE 3.02/Windows, but by this time most users simply waited until IE 4.0 was released before upgrading. There were great differences in the manner in which the two vendors decided to implement support for multimedia and related content. Netscape offered developers a new and strictly proprietary `<embed>` tag, while Microsoft used the now-standard `<object>` element to permit inclusion of Windows-only ActiveX controls in web pages intended for its browsers in order to play multimedia clips, interact with the user's operating system, and provide other applet-like and plug-in-like functions.

Netscape also supported much of its plug-in functionality by means of a `navigator.plugins` object collection (which represents any browser plug-ins native to the browser), and, to add to the confusion, also offered `document.plugins`, which are synonymous with `document.embeds` (these represent any multimedia embedded in a document via use of `<embed>` elements that require plug-ins). It should be emphasized that `navigator.plugins` and `document.plugins` are completely separate collections of dissimilar objects, even though both are specific to Netscape browsers – there are some situations where you might want to use both, such as when you have embedded media that the browser has no plug-in for, but it is generally recommended that the use of `document.plugins` be avoided, as it will just cause confusion, and you can generally acquire such plug-ins, making the above case a non-issue.

Both browsers also support a `document.forms` collection, which includes all the `<form>` elements in a web page. In turn, each individual form object contains a set of `element` objects corresponding to the set of HTML `<input>`, `<textarea>`, and `<select>` elements within the `<form>` tag so referenced.

There were several problems with this early object model. Not all page elements were accessible to scripting: for instance, there was no way to change the properties of an HTML table, nor of its rows or cells, once it had been rendered in the page. Furthermore, no purely textual elements such as `<p>` or `<blockquote>` or their contents were accessible at all. Web designers and scripters who wanted to create effects with dynamic text had three options, although none of them were truly satisfactory:

❏ They could dynamically update the text in the browser status bar using the `window.status` property.

❏ The text contained in form elements could be changed via their value attributes; however, this required the use of `<input>` elements (often when no input was being asked for), which was not very pleasing to designers because it interfered with the formatting and layout of their pages, and these elements and their content could not be counted on to display uniformly across browsers and platforms. Another drawback to consider was that the presentational attributes such as fonts, size, or color of the text couldn't be set by the page author using this method (or the previous one in fact).

❏ Finally, the designer could use text images, which could be made to appear in a consistent manner across browsers and platforms. Unfortunately, this meant that changes in page content had to be implemented using graphics editing software, and the required load time was increased. This also supposed that the user's software supported dynamic images, which left out most IE 3 users. (It should be noted that they were a minority – between 20 and 30 percent during the heyday of Netscape 3.)

In all three of these cases there was a further disadvantage: the text most likely couldn't be indexed by search engines.

Another shortcoming of "DOM-0" was that not all properties of those objects that were exposed to scripting were changeable. For example, while you could programmatically change the source file of an image that had already been loaded into a page via its `Image.src` property, you couldn't alter its width or height. This meant that you couldn't replace an image with a differently-sized one, or the new image would be distorted by being forced to fit the dimensions of the old one.

The means by which page elements could be accessed from scripts were nearly identical between different object collections. Both of the browsers we've concentrated on implemented all of the element collections as arrays, so that a scripter could refer to them by index numbers, in the order in which they occurred in the page (counting them left to right, in rows running from top to bottom). Since arrays have a built-in `length` property, programmers could often write scripts without having to know ahead of time how many of a given type of element there were in a page; that number could be determined at run time. Since having to count a large number of elements can be quite tedious in a large document or set of documents, many of the elements collections were also implemented as **hashes**. A hash is essentially a type of array in which each element has a string identifier – in other words, a name. This property corresponds exactly to the name attribute of the HTML tags `<a>`, `<applet>`, `<embed>`, `<img>`, `<object>`, `<form>`, `<input>`, `<select>`, and `<option>`. So, someone writing or implementing a script could refer to the HTML element `<img src="images/my_image.gif" name="myImg">` as `document.images["myImg"]` or `document.images.myImg`. In the case of the `<a>` element, things worked a little differently. There were two distinct object collections reflecting the two distinct purposes to which it's employed: the `links` collection (`<a href>`) could only be accessed by index, while the elements of `document.anchors` (`<a name>`) could only be referred to by name.

By now you should have a good idea of what elements were able to be programmed in the first scripting-capable web browsers from Netscape and Microsoft, how they mapped onto programming objects, and how they could be accessed. Indexing of page elements is done automatically by the browser's scripting parser, but it will still make everyone's life easier if you remember to give tags that are important to your site – such as images being used as navigation elements – a unique name attribute. If you're already using `id` in order to follow the HTML 4 standard, there's nothing wrong with using the same value for name as well.

The 4th Generation: "DOM-½" and "DOM-¾"

The object models in the 4th-generation browsers from Netscape and Microsoft both added new object collections, offering a number of new capabilities, including:

❏ Real-time positioning of elements on a page

❏ Inline documents

❏ Dynamic updating of content

These new features were added for a number of reasons, chief of which was a desire to offer site builders greater inducements to develop sites tailored to the companies' browsers.

Netscape 4 Layers

The ways in which these were implemented in each browser were very different. With Netscape 4, Netscape proposed and implemented the idea of positionable container elements known as **layers**, which represented the standard <div> and <span>, as well as the nonstandard <layer> and <ilayer> tags. These four tags all belong to the layers collection. We've set out their properties and methods (applicable to all four) in the tables below:

Properties	Description
name	name attribute of the layer
id	id attribute
document	Document element from which any elements within the layer descend
window	Window containing the layer; note that the document containing the layer is layer.window.document
parentLayer	Layer containing the present one
siblingAbove, siblingBelow	Layers above and below the current layer in the stacking order, sharing the same parent layer
src	Source HTML file of layer (attribute of <layer> or <div>)
left, top (x, y)	Position relative to the containing element
pageX, pageY	Position relative to the page
zIndex	Layer's place in the stacking order
width, height	Dimensions of the layer
bgcolor	Layer's background color
clip	Clipping

Table continued on following page

Properties	Description
above, below	Respectively, get:above returns the layer above the present one (z-order), and get:below returns the layer below the current one (z-order)
background	URL of an image to be displayed behind the content in the layer; not settable
visibility	Takes one of four values: visible and show (which are synonymous) make the layer visible, while hidden and hide (also synonymous) cause the layer to be hidden from view – visibility is both gettable and settable. Note that hide and show are Netscape only.

Methods	Description
load()	Load a new document into a layer
moveAbove(), moveBelow()	Move to above or below the layer in the stacking order
moveTo(), moveBy(), moveToAbsolute()	Move layer to an position relative to the containing element, by a specified amount, or to a given point relative to the page
resizeTo(), resizeBy()	Resize the layer to a specified size or by a specified amount

The italicized properties listed above are read/write; the others are write only.

Under the Netscape 4.x DOM, which we refer to as "DOM-½", the layers collection contains the elements listed above. We should note that all <layer> and <ilayer> elements are included, but only those <div>s and <span>s that have been absolutely or relatively positioned using CSS make it in. The members of this collection are accessible by index, name, and id. New Layer objects can be created using the new Layer() constructor function and then manipulated programmatically, which means that the corresponding tags don't have to be present in the HTML source for those user agents that don't support them (namely, anything else other than Netscape 4.x). While it's not quite a frame, the Layer object contains its own Document, like a frame, and it supports the same properties and methods that any other "DOM-0" Document could be expected to. In practice, this made scripting for the Layer itself very easy in some respects, but scripting for elements contained within layers potentially very complicated. A good example of what happens can be seen in the case of the humble image rollover, which since Netscape 4 first hit the market has tripped up a lot of scripters, who used absolute positioning to make their navigation bars stay where they wanted them, and plopped their images into them:

```
<div id="myDiv" style="position:absolute; left:100px; top:50px">
  <img name="myImage" src="my_img.gif" width="50" height="40">
</div>
```

They were then dismayed to find that their image replacement scripts didn't function when the pages containing these scripts were viewed in Netscape 4. To replace the source of the image in any browser supporting the image object, we expect to write something like this:

```
document.images.myImage.src="my_other_img.gif"
```

except that Netscape 4's JavaScript interpreter promptly chokes up on this and reports that: "document.images.myImg is not an object". As Netscape 4 considers *any* absolutely-positioned `<div>` or `<span>` to be a layer, we've got to deal with that layer's intervening document object whether we really want to or not. For example:

```
window.document.layers.myDiv.document.images.myImage.src="my_other_img.gif";
```

which seems like a lot of extra work, doesn't it? Nested layers can be downright nightmarish: the child layer is considered an element of the parent layer's layers collection, so in a case like this;

```
<style>#parentLayer, #childLayer { position: relative; }</style>

<div id="parentLayer">
  <div id="childLayer"><img name="myImage"></div>
</div>
```

it's quite conceivable to wind up with something like this:

```
document.layers.parentLayer.document.layers.childLayer.document.images.myImage.src
="my_other_img.gif"
```

As with the `forms` and `images` collections, there is a shortcut whereby we can abbreviate the above, like this:

```
document.parentLayer.document.childLayer.document.myImage.src="my_other_image.gif"
;
```

However, we still can't escape the necessity of tracking each Layer's document object and attendant object collections. This is one of the things that make cross-browser DHTML a major headache when Netscape 4 must be accommodated.

A Layer's content can be updated in real time by one of three methods:

❑ Setting its `src` property to point to a new URL

❑ Using its `load()` method to load a new document into the layer

❑ Rewriting its interior content on the fly by making use of the `open()`, `write()`, and `close()` methods of its `document` object property.

Note that `src` is a property of the `Layer` object itself, and not of its contained Document. Its positioning properties `left`, `top`, and `zIndex` are also directly descended from `Layer`, and not from a `style` object, as you may have noted from the previous chapter. In fact, Netscape 4 doesn't provide for any scripting of styles in real time, instead offering something called JavaScript Style Sheets (JSSS), which is really nothing other than a more unwieldy alternative to CSS syntax. At any rate, what Netscape did in its first DHTML implementation was to provide a new, "special" element – represented in script by the `Layer` object – created just for the purpose of being able to move it and change its content.

However, it really has nothing to do with the structure or logic of an HTML document, and tends to mess up the object model of any document in which it's used rather badly – a small sample of which we've just seen above. So while Netscape seemed to deliver on its promises to web developers and designers in its initial DHTML implementation, it really only took them about halfway to where they wanted to be – real-time control over content and presentation in web documents – and in doing so it largely put the cart before the horse. Hence, "DOM-½".

Internet Explorer Fights Back

Microsoft's Internet Explorer, after lagging seriously behind Netscape in its first three versions, leaped ahead with the release of its 4th-generation browser. Microsoft conceived of a much different sort of object model from Netscape's: instead of implementing a special element just to provide DHTML effects and functionality, it took the view that **all** web page elements ought to be accessible as programming objects.

Microsoft, like Netscape, implemented a new object collection for scripters wanting to use its browser as a platform. Unlike Netscape's, this collection, known as `document.all`, did not introduce any new HTML tags; instead, it included all of those that already existed in a page. This object model did everything that Netscape 4's did, and then some. Where Netscape 4 required an author to wrap dynamic content in a new and special container element, all one needed to do for any element in IE 4 in order to access its attributes programmatically was to refer to it as `document.all.myElement`. One distinct advantage in this approach was that all elements could be referred to directly, rather than requiring programmers to go through intermediary `document` objects – one very happy side effect of which was that it didn't break existing scripts as Netscape often did.

The `<img>` element in the above HTML sample could still be addressed as `document.images.myImage`, or it could be accessed as `document.all.myImage` in order to make use of the new properties and methods of the members of the `all` collection (that is, of each HTML element object), which are outlined in the tables below:

Properties	Description
id	`id` attribute
name	`name` attribute
sourceIndex	Order of placement in the `all` collection
style	Inline styles applying to an element
className	Name of the style class applying to the document
tagName	Element's tag name

Properties	Description
all	Collection of all elements contained within this one (including Document)
parentElement	Element containing the present one
children	Collection of all elements contained directly within the current one
innerHTML, outerHTML	HTML within an element, excluding/including the tag itself
innerText, outerText	Text within an element, excluding/including the tag itself
offsetLeft, offsetTop	Gettable positioning attributes
offsetWidth, offsetHeight	Gettable size attributes

Methods	Description
contains()	Returns true if an element contains the given element
getAttribute()	Gets a tag attribute
removeAttribute()	Removes a tag attribute
setAttribute	Sets a tag attribute
insertAdjacentHTML()	Inserts markup following an element
insertAdjacentText()	Inserts text following an element
item() *	Returns an element of the given name or id, returns a collection, if more than one element shares the same name attribute
tags() *	Returns a collection of elements with the given tag name

The asterisks in the table above indicate a method of the all collection.

Another advantage of the IE 4 DOM, which we've nicknamed "DOM-¾" (since it came much closer to what was eventually adopted by W3C in the Document Object Model Level 1 and Level 2 Specifications), was that it permitted direct access to CSS inline styles in real time via an element object's **style** collection. This allowed web programmers to change an element's positioning, size, color, background color, font properties, etc.

All in all, the IE 4 object model provided developers with much more power and flexibility than its Netscape 4 counterpart. As we've seen, the Netscape 4 object model, while it did provide for updating, positioning, and content of elements, allowed little if any access to any other aspects of element presentation via script. The implementation of positioned content as Layers, each containing its own document, proved particularly frustrating and unwieldy to scripters who had to put up with telescoping object references when dealing with nested elements. Internet Explorer 4, however, provided much more direct access to elements, didn't introduce any new proprietary HTML tags, and allowed dynamic access to element styles. It is not surprising that what was eventually adopted by the W3C bore much more resemblance to the IE4 object model, and that Netscape's Layers were rejected almost out of hand when that standards body's DOM specifications were developed. Let's turn our attention now to what was adopted in the late 1990s as the new recommended standard.

The Document Object Model Today

The DOM standard as set down by the W3C is a set of documents that define an object model that is both vendor- and language-independent, which both Netscape and Microsoft have pledged to support. It includes provisions for formalizing the object models much as implemented in the 2nd- and 3rd-generation browsers, referring to these object collections as "DOM Level 0," and recommends that vendors continue to support these for reasons of backwards compatibility. It also provides a set of standard interfaces for accessing all elements in marked-up (such as XML and HTML) documents. Of course, like all web standards, the DOM standard is something of a shifting target. As of this writing, all of the following – with one exception, the Level 2 HTML DOM – had achieved status of formal recommendations:

- **DOM Level 1 Core** – Basic interfaces for accessing markup elements, their attributes, and their content in general terms.including creating, updating, and removing them from documents
- **DOM Level 1 (HTML)** – Additional interfaces specific to HTML elements; in particular it defines the `HTMLElement` object
- **DOM Level 2 Core** – Builds on Level 1 Core, providing additional interfaces for XML and HTML documents
- **DOM Level 2 (HTML)**– Builds on Level 1 HTML, providing object definitions corresponding to specific HTML tags
- **DOM level 2 (Views)** – Provides a definition for a "view" of a document necessary to the Styles and Events documents
- **DOM Level 2 (Styles)** – Provides interfaces for accessing style sheets, style rules, and inline styles applying to a document and its elements
- **DOM Level 2 (Events)** – Describes event types, handlers for events, and event propagation in HTML documents
- **DOM Level 2 (Traversal and Range)** – Provides additional interfaces to aid programmers in navigating and manipulating the structure of a document

As this book went to press, DOM Level 3 had just been released as Working Draft. DOM-3 is expected to include specifications for content models, for the loading and saving of documents, and to address the unfinished work begun in the Level 2 Event Model recommendations – in particular, to provide a more detailed object model for keyboard events as well as a means of grouping event listeners. We'll discuss the Level 2 Event Model later in this chapter, but let's start at the beginning, with the Document Object Model Core.

Core and HTML DOM, Levels 1 and 2

DOM Core Levels 1 and 2 represent an XML or HTML document as a set of **nodes** arranged in a containment hierarchy. A node may be thought of as being the most generic possible sort of "piece" of a document. Depending upon its type, a node may contain other nodes, sometimes known as "children". We won't try to cover all of the interfaces the DOM exposes in this chapter, but we will discuss those that allow us to identify elements and their attributes, get and set attribute values, determine element content, and modify or delete or even create new elements in an HTML document.

Let's look at an example of this containment hierarchy, which reflects the series of parent-child relationships between elements containing one another, or nested within one another. Suppose we have a simple web page containing a table created using the following HTML:

```html
<html>
  <head>
  </head>
  <body>
    <table id="myTable">
      <tbody id="myTBody">
        <tr>
          <td>This is the first cell in the table.</td>
          <td></td>
        </tr>
        <tr>
          <td></td>
          <td></td>
        </tr>
        <tr id="myTRow">
          <td></td>
          <td id="myTData"></td>
        </tr>
        <tr id="anotherTRow">
          <td></td>
          <td>This cell's roughly in the middle.</td>
        </tr>
        <tr>
          <td id="anotherTData"></td>
          <td>This cell's the last one in this table.</td>
        </tr>
      </tbody>
    </table>
  </body>
</html>
```

Perhaps the best way to think of how the DOM represents this is as a tree-like structure, where the various nodes having children can be thought of as "branches" and those that have none as "leaves":

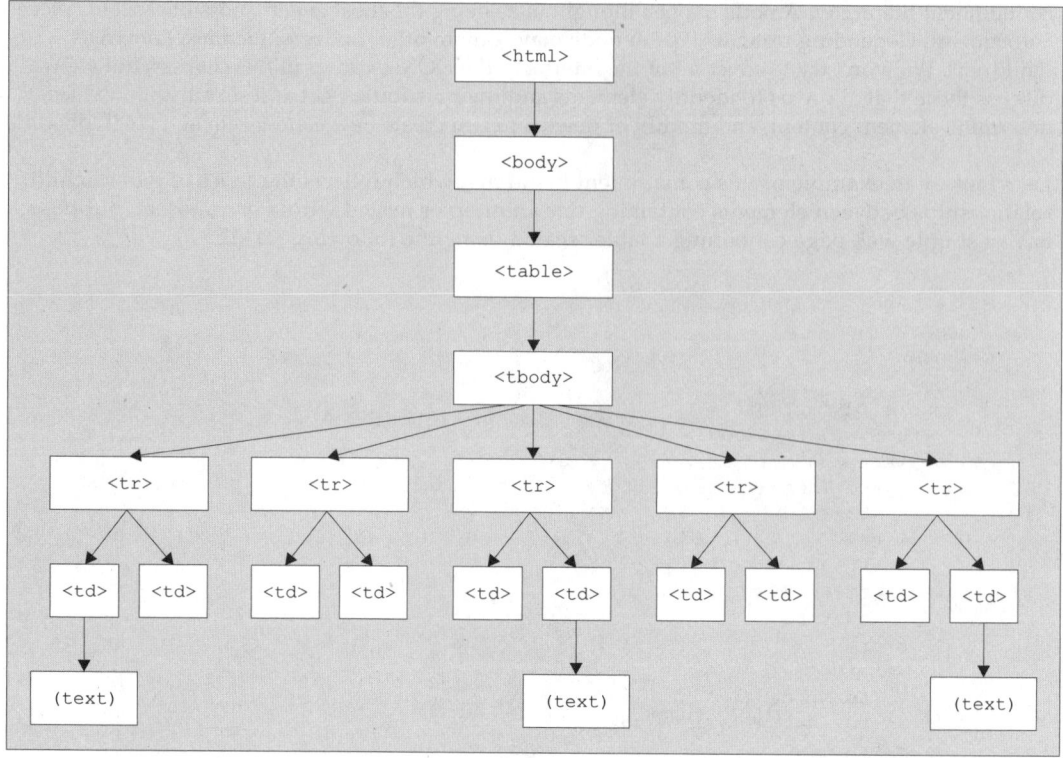

Nodes may be of one of twelve different types; here we'll be most concerned with those corresponding to HTML tags, tag attributes, content (text), and the document itself. The others are probably more of interest to XML authors or scripters working with XML documents, corresponding to document fragments, comments, entities, entity references, processing instructions, CDATA sections, and notations. The twelve types are detailed in the following table:

NodeType	Integer Value	Permitted Child Node Types
ELEMENT_NODE	1	Element, Text, Comment, ProcessingInstruction, CDATASection, EntityReference
ATTRIBUTE_NODE	2	Text, EntityReference
TEXT_NODE	3	[none]
CDATA_SECTION_NODE*	4	[none]

NodeType	Integer Value	Permitted Child Node Types
ENTITY_ REFERENCE_NODE*	5	Element, ProcessingInstruction, Comment, Text, CDATASection, EntityReference
ENTITY_NODE*	6	Element, ProcessingInstruction, Comment, Text, CDATASection, EntityReference
PROCESSING_ INSTRUCTION_NODE*	7	[none]
COMMENT_NODE	8	[none]
DOCUMENT_NODE	9	Element (maximum of 1), ProcessingInstruction, Comment, DocumentType
DOCUMENT_TYPE_NODE*	10	[none]
DOCUMENT_ FRAGMENT_NODE	11	Element, ProcessingInstruction, Comment, Text, CDATASection, EntityReference
NOTATION_NODE*	12	[none]

* XML-DOM only; included for completeness.

> **Note: whereas the preferred usage for tag names in HTML 4.01 (and mandatory under the XHTML 1.0 standard) is lowercase, when using these as arguments to this function, they should be written in all-uppercase characters.**

This knowledge enables a scripter to write code that can ascertain what sort of node or element it is being called upon to work on without knowing what type it is in advance.

The HTML DOM defines a generic HTMLElement object from which element-specific objects corresponding to actual HTML tags are derived. HTMLElement objects share the following properties: tagName (inherited from the Node interface), id, style, className, lang, dir, and title, which correspond, in order, to the tag name of the element and its id, style, class, lang, dir, and title attributes.

DOM 1 and 2 define a number of methods and properties by which relationships between elements can be described; these provide the means for determining if an element has any child elements or nodes (including attributes), what those child elements are, the parent element of the element, and the sibling elements (if any exist) of the element. Perhaps the method of this type that lends itself most easily to basic DHTML scripting is getElementsByTagName(). This method takes the name of an HTML tag as an argument, and returns an array of all elements of that name contained by the element of which it is called as a method. For example, in the above sample page, the <table> element could be identified as:

```
document.getElementsByTagName("TABLE").item(0);
```

Note that this collection, like all object collections, is indexed beginning with the number 0. Now if we write:

```
var myTable=document.getElementsByTagName("TABLE").item(0);
```

we can then identify the `<tbody>` element as:

```
var myTBody=myTable.getElementsByTagName("TBODY").item(0);
```

and we can define the rows with:

```
var myTRow = new Array();
for(var count=0;count<myTBody.getElementsByTagName("TR").length;count++)
   myTRow.item(count)=myTBody.getElementsByTagName("TR").item(count);
```

and so on. We should note that the ability to refer an element collection as an array is really just a convenience and that, strictly speaking, DOM guarantees only that a collection has an `item()` method that can be used to count through the collection's elements, for example:

```
for(var count=0;count<myTBody.getElementsByTagName("TR").length;count++)
   myTRow.item(count) = myTBody.getElementsByTagName("TR").item(count);
```

The DOM also gives us means to identify an element directly, by way of its `name` or `id` attribute. Unlike `getElementsByTagName()`, which may be applied by any element, these are methods of `document` only: `document.getElementById("myElId")` returns the element whose `id` attribute is `myElId`. For instance, returning again to the above table example, the table cell indicated by `<td id="myTData"></td>` can be uniquely identified in script as `document.getElementById("myTData")`. The HTML DOM `getElementsByName()` method works in a similar fashion, except that it first looks for matching `name` and then, if it finds none, matching `id` attributes. In the case where more than one tag in a page bears the same `name` attribute, this method returns an array containing all tags with that name. However, since each `id` attribute value within a page must be unique, `getElementById()` is the preferred method, and the other is included mostly for the sake of backwards compatibility.

Attributes of tags are represented in the DOM standard by object properties, as they were in DOM-0 and the object models of the 4th-generation browsers. Generally speaking, the names of these will be the same as for the tag attributes to which they correspond. However, as we shall see shortly when we discuss style scripting, there is one major exception to this rule.

For instance, let's say we needed to see what all the `title` attributes were for the cells in the second row of our table above. (Of course, we haven't listed any, but we could do so easily enough.) We could write a bit of JavaScript code to accomplish this, like so:

```
var importantTRow=document.getElementById("myTBody")
         .getElementsByTagName("TR").item(1);
var importantTData=importantTRow.getElementsByTagName("TD");
var output="";
for(var j=0;j<importantTData.length;j++)
   output+="Cell "+(j+1)+" title: "+importantTData.item(j).title+"\n";
   alert(output);
```

We can set many tag attributes following much the same procedure.

DOM provides another set of methods for getting, setting, and removing attributes that are not so easy to use, but which are much more powerful. For instance, we could rewrite the critical expression above as `importantTData[j].getAttribute("title")`, and if we needed to set each title attribute to a new value, we could write:

```
importantTData.item(j).setAttribute("title","This is cell number "+(j+1))
```

As time goes on, these are likely to become the preferred methods for getting and setting element properties. They have already been implemented in IE 5 and Netscape 6. DOM also gives us a means of "zeroing out" element properties that we no longer need, which is much more satisfactory then traditional methods such as setting a property to zero, null, or the empty string.

This means takes the form of the `removeAttribute()` and `removeAttributeNode()` methods. The former simply nullifies the attribute whose name is passed as its argument; the latter returns the removed attribute so that its value can be used before it is tossed out forever.

There are many additional "generic" features for accessing the elements of HTML (and XML) documents to be found in the DOM core, which are listed in the "*Core DOM Features*" table, found in Appendix.

HTML DOM Levels 1 and 2 give us a framework of objects corresponding directly to HTML tags, each of these embodying tag-specific properties and methods. For example, they provide an `HTMLFormElement` object that has features recognizable to any experienced HTML author or client-side JavaScript programmer: in this case, these are the `elements`, `length`, `name`, `acceptCharset`, `action`, `enctype`, `method`, and `target` properties, and the `submit()` and `reset()` methods. You might notice the exact correspondence between these properties and the attributes of the `<form>` tag, with the exception of the `accept-charset` attribute, which is missing a hyphen. This is standard practice in converting attribute names, which may contain hyphens, to DOM property names, which may not. We'll see quite a bit more of this when we discuss DOM style scripting shortly.

In general, we can extrapolate these objects, properties, and methods from a listing of HTML 4.01 tags, attributes, and intrinsic event handlers (see Chapter 9 for more on this). For the time being at least, we can continue to access these objects by employing either the DOM-0 object references (for example, `document.forms.item(0)` or `document.forms.namedItem("myForm")`) or those allowable by DOM Levels 1 and 2:

❑ `document.getElementsByTagName("FORM")[0]`

❑ `document.getElementsByName("myForm")[0]`

❑ `document.getElementById("myForm")`

Of course, where backwards compatibility is a concern, the DOM-0 references can still be safely used without breaking scripts in newer W3C-DOM compliant user agents.

DOM Level 2 – CSS-DOM

The DOM Level 2 CSS Specification provides the client-side scripter with a number of interfaces for accessing and making programmatic changes in HTML document styles and style sheets. As the HTML DOM interfaces correspond to HTML elements such as tags and attributes, so these correspond to the constructs familiar to the document author using Cascading Style Sheets. The fundamental interfaces are as follows:

❑ CSSStyleSheet – a CSS style sheet of type "text/css"

❑ CSSRuleList – an ordered collection of CSS rules

❑ CSSRule – an abstracted CSS style rule or @-rule of any of the following types:

    ❑ CSSStyleRule – an individual style rule

    ❑ CSSMediaRule – represents a CSS @media rule

    ❑ CSSFontFaceRule – a CSS @font-face rule

    ❑ CSSPageRule – a CSS @page rule

    ❑ CSSImportRule – a CSS @import rule

    ❑ CSSCharsetRule – a CSS @charset rule

    ❑ CSSUnknownRule – represents an @-rule not supported by the user agent

❑ CSSStyleDeclaration – represents a CSS statement block

❑ CSSValue – a CSS value, either simple or complex

❑ CSSPrimitiveValue – a single CSS value

❑ CSSValueList – an ordered collection of CSS values

❑ RGBColor – corresponds to a CSS RGB color value

❑ Rect – corresponds to a CSS rect value (such as found with clipping and other box properties that are determined in terms of top-right-bottom-left)

❑ Counter – the value of a counter or counters function

The following interfaces are also defined:

❑ ViewCSS – a CSS view

❑ DocumentCSS – a document with a CSS view

❑ DOMImplementationCSS – permits the programmer to create a new CSS style sheet outside the context of any document; however, DOM Level 2 does not allow for any method to associate this style sheet with an document

❑ ElementCSSInlineStyle – represents style information attached to an element by means of its style attribute

❑ CSS2Properties – allows for an alternative mechanism to access the properties found in the CSSStyleDeclaration object (support for this interface is optional)

The objects most likely to be of interest to web scripters are `ElementCSSInlineStyle`, `CSSStyleRule`, `CSSRuleList`, and `CSSStyleSheet`. The first of these corresponds to an HTML tag's `style` attribute, and is implemented in both Netscape 6/Mozilla and IE 4 and above as an element's `style` property.

Note: IE 4 does not *actually* support `ElementCSSInlineStyle` as such, but does support a functionally equivalent analogue of the form:

```
document.all[elementID].style.styleProperty=value;
```

We have two ways of setting a page element's inline style. First, we can set it in the static document using, for example:

```
<p id="myP" style="font-family:Arial,sans-serif">some content</p>
```

We can accomplish exactly the same thing with this JavaScript statement:

```
document.getElementById("myP").style.fontFamily="Arial,sans-serif";
```

The first portion of this statement should be familiar from a few paragraphs back – we've identified the page element with the `id` attribute `myP`. Also, as we've already shown, nearly any tag attribute can be accessed as an object property simply by appending it to the element reference using "dot" notation, as we've done with the inline `style` attribute. The declaration contained within this attribute translates into object notation as follows: the property name gets appended to `style`, and the value moves to the right-hand side of the JavaScript statement.

There are two additional details we need to take note of here: First, as we intimated above, anytime we have a markup attribute or property containing a hyphen and we need to translate it into object notation, we have to lose the hyphen. The rule for accomplishing this is straightforward – we just drop the hyphen, and run the two words together using intercap notation. Some other examples:

❑ `background-color` (CSS) becomes `backgroundColor` (script)

❑ `text-decoration` (CSS) becomes `textDecoration` (script)

❑ `font-weight` (CSS) becomes `fontWeight` (script)

Single-word CSS properties, of course, don't require any conversion: They just get tacked onto `style` as-is. So you shouldn't have much trouble with figuring out what `document.getElementById("myP").style.left="35px";` will do to an absolutely-positioned element. Secondly, notice that the quoted attribute value remains quoted even in script. It begins life in markup as a string value, and stays that way when translated through CSS-DOM. The only other conversion we need worry about is remembering to change the CSS colon (`:`) to an equals sign (`=`).

Even more powerful is the ability to change style classes on the fly, which is accomplished by means of an element object's `className` property. For example, suppose we have the following style classes defined in an HTML document:

```
.firstClass {font:normal normal 13px Courier,monospace;
             text-decoration:underline;}
.secondClass {font:italic normal 14px Times,serif; text-decoration:none;
              color:#FFFF00;}
```

and we have our HTML paragraph as:

```
<p id="myP" class="firstClass">Some text here.</p>
```

We can change the appearance of our paragraph quite dramatically with a single line of code:

```
document.getElementById("myP").className="secondClass";
```

Properly speaking, this isn't really part of CSS-DOM, as the `className` property is covered in HTML DOM Level 1, but it seems appropriate to discuss it here along with the other aspects of CSS scripting.

CSS-DOM provides interfaces for changing the style rule for a given selector, so that it's possible, for instance, to change all the `<h1>` elements in a page from blue to red in one line of script. One way this can be accomplished is by rewriting the text of a rule using its `cssText` property. It is also possible using script to change the style sheet for an entire page on the fly. To explain these in detail would fall outside the scope and size of this chapter: the interested reader is encouraged to consult one or more of the appropriate resources cited in the bibliography for additional information.

DOM Level 2 – Events

The W3C's Events Specification in DOM Level 2 was designed with two goals in mind. It was planned to provide a generic framework for events to be propagated and routed through a document's tree-like structure, and for information about them to be made available to programmers via the properties of the `Event` object. The specification also allows for what is known as event capturing, which enables us to control event propagation and to perform actions in response to events.

It was also intended, like the other sections of the DOM standards recommendations, to provide backwards compatibility with what had already been implemented by browser vendors, by supporting as much of those previous event systems as was possible within the context of the new model. It attempts to accomplish this through supporting the intrinsic events associated with certain page elements as given in the HTML 4.01 standard, and by allowing for a model in which events can be associated with any element regardless of element or event type.

There are three broad types of events with which we can work: UI events, UI logical events, and mutation events. Let's define each of these before we proceed:

❑ **UI events** (User Interface events) happen when a user interacts with a document through an external device such as the mouse or keyboard. Typical of this class of events would be those that take place when a user rolls the mouse pointer over an element, clicks on an element, or strikes a key on the keyboard.

❑ **UI logical events** occur when focus changes on an element, or an element is otherwise "triggered" in a device-independent fashion. For instance, tabbing between form elements and clicking on a different form element from the one currently having focus would both engender this type of event.

❑ **Mutation events** take place when the structure of a document is modified any way.

Events can be associated with page elements in one of several ways, one of those being the HTML event handler attributes that we discussed in connection with intrinsic events in Chapter 9. By way of refreshing your memory, here's a sample:

```
<p style="background-color:#FFFF00">
  Here is some text in a paragraph.<br>
  <span onmouseover="this.style.backgroundColor='#CCCCFF';"
        onmouseout="this.style.backgroundColor='#FFFF00';">
    Here is some text in a nested span element.
  </span>
  <br />Here is some more text outside the span.
</p>
```

As also mentioned in Chapter 9, the JavaScript keyword this refers to the current element or object: in this case, the <span>. What we've done here is to tell the browser, "When the mouse pointer passes over the <span>, change its background color to light purple; when the pointer moves away again, change it to back light yellow." – we've assigned a script directly to each of its mouseover and mouseout event handlers. If we want to assign a complex bit of script to an event handler, particularly one we might want to call from several points within a document, we can also place the script inside a function and call the function from the event handler, like so:

```
<!DOCTYPE HTML PUBLIC "-//W3C//DTD HTML 4.01//EN" "http://www.w3.org/TR/REC-
        html401/strict.dtd">
<html>
  <head>
    <meta http-equiv="Content-Type" content="text/html; charset=iso-8859-1">
    <meta http-equiv="Script-Content-Type" content="text/javascript">
    <title><span> Color Change</title>
<script type="text/javascript">
<!--
    function changeBgToPurple()
    {
       document.getElementById("mySpan").style.backgroundColor="#CCCCFF";
    }
    function changeBgToYellow()
    {
       document.getElementById("mySpan").style.backgroundColor="#FFFF00";
    }
//-->
</script>
  </head>
  <body>
    <p style="background-color:#FFFF00">
      Here is some text in a paragraph.<br />
      <span id="mySpan" onmouseover="changeBgToPurple();"
            onmouseout="changeBgToYellow();">
        Here is some text in a nested span element.
      </span>
      <br /> Here is some more text outside the span.
    </p>
  </body>
</html>
```

There is a third method of accomplishing this task, which involves assigning the events to page elements through script only:

```
<body>
  <p>Here is some text in a paragraph.<br />
    <span id="mySpan" style="background-color:#FFFF00">
      Here is some text in a    nested span element.
    </span>
    <br />Here is some more text outside the SPAN.
  </p>
<script type="text/javascript">
<!--
    function changeBgToPurple(event)
    {
      this.style.backgroundColor="#CCCCFF";
    }
    function changeBgToYellow(event)
    {
      this.style.backgroundColor="#FFFF00";
    }
    document.getElementById("mySpan").onmouseover = changeBgToPurple;
    document.getElementById("mySpan").onmouseout = changeBgToYellow;
//-->
</script>
</body>
```

There are some things that we ought to take note in this example. First of all, we've placed the `<script>` section following the HTML elements it affects. This is because we can't define event handlers in script for elements that haven't been parsed yet. We can sidestep this restriction by defining a function that's not called until the page has been loaded and placing our event handler assignments within it, like so:

```
function assignEventHandlers()
{
  document.getElementById("mySpan").onmouseover = changeBgToPurple;
  document.getElementById("mySpan").onmouseout = changeBgToYellow;
}
window.onload=assignEventHandlers;
```

in which case we could move the script block into the head of the page (or anywhere else within it, or even into a separate .js file) with no ill effects. If it appears that we're treating event handlers as if they were any other HTML tag attributes, this is almost correct, with one important difference: rather than calling the function, we assign it as a JavaScript Function object to the event property of the HTML element object for which we wish to set the event handler. That's why we don't use parentheses with the function name here, as we did when we assigned the function inside the HTML tag's event handler.

You may have noticed that the handler functions as rewritten for the third example are passed a parameter called event, which stands for and gives us access to the event itself (as represented by an Event object, about which we'll have more to say presently). Following the DOM specification here, Netscape requires that this object be passed explicitly to an event handler function when it's used in this fashion; Internet Explorer does not – in MSIE, an event handler function assumes that information about the event will be found as window.event, that is, as an event property of the global Window object.

512

Finally, DOM Level 2 includes a new, fourth method of associating events with HTML elements by allowing DOM objects to be registered as **event listeners**. This extends programmers' abilities by allowing them to associate more than one handler with a given event. While it is certainly possible to re-write event handler functions or to write "wrapper" code to combine functions to the same end, this new approach, which includes the ability to "unregister" or remove event listeners, is much more flexible. It also allows us to intercept events during either of the two phases of event flow:

❑ The **capture phase**, during which the event propagates "downward" through the element containment hierarchy to the event with which it's associated (also known as the event's **target**).

❑ The **bubble phase,** in which it does just the opposite.

We'll discuss these two phases in greater detail shortly, but for now let's examine the basic mechanics of event listeners, which rests in two methods of the Node object:

```
Node.addEventListener(eventType,function,capture);

Node.removeEventListener(eventType,function,capture);
```

eventType is one of the event names we've already discussed, which are the same as the event handler names with the omission of the on prefix, such as mouseover, mouseout, or click. function stands for the name of the function we wish to assign to the event. The third parameter passed to these methods we denote by capture; this is a Boolean value, which determines whether we call the handler function during the capture phase (value set to true) or the bubble phase (false). Note that the value for this parameter as called by removeEventListener() must be the same as for the addEventListener() method by which we assigned the event listener. This is because it's entirely possible to assign two completely different actions to be performed in response to the two different phases of the same event on the same element! Recalling that HTMLElement objects inherit these methods just as they do all the other methods of Node, let's rewrite our last example making use of event listeners (the addEventListener() method was only introduced as part of DOM 2, and is supported by Netscape 6/Mozilla, but not IE – see below). Using exactly the same changeBgToPurple() and changeBgToYellow() functions as we last defined them, we can write:

```
var theSpan=document.getElementById("mySpan");

theSpan.addEventListener("mouseover",changeBgToPurple,false);
theSpan.addEventListener("mouseout",changeBgToYellow,false);
```

If we decide that we've become tired of the purple rollover background color, we can easily change it programmatically, and while we're at it, we'll change the text color (and change it back with a mouseout event) as well by removing one of the original event listeners and adding some new ones:

```
function changeBgToGreen()
{
   this.style.backgroundColor="#CCFFCC";
}

function changeTextToRed()
{
   this.style.fontColor="#FF0033";
}
```

```
function changeTextToBlack()
{
   this.style.fontColor="#000000";
}

function giveMeGreen()
{
   theSpan.removeEventListener("mouseover",changeBgToPurple,false);
   theSpan.addEventListener("mouseover",changeBgToGreen,false);
   theSpan.addEventListener("mouseover",changeTextToRed,false);
   theSpan.addEventListener("mouseout",changeTextToBlack,false);
}
```

We've supplied an input button that does this in the accompanying example file span_mouseover4.html (see the code download, available from **www.wrox.com**). You can examine the code for yourself, and observe it in action using Netscape 6 or a recent Mozilla release. First roll the mouse over the text in the span, then, when you're ready to see the new behavior, click the form button, and then try the rollover again.

The above code was tested using Netscape 6.01 and Mozilla 0.8.1, but it will not function as written in any version of Internet Explorer available as of this writing. However, the MSIE 6 beta now supports two new methods, attachEvent() and detachEvent(), that allow us to add multiple handlers for a given event. The relevant portions of an IE 6- compatible version of the above would look like this:

```
var theSpan=document.getElementById("mySpan");

theSpan.attachEvent("onmouseover",changeBgToPurple);
theSpan.attachEvent("onmouseout",changeBgToYellow);

function giveMeGreen()
{
   theSpan.detachEvent("onmouseover",changeBgToPurple);
   theSpan.attachEvent("onmouseover",changeBgToGreen);
   theSpan.attachEvent("onmouseover",changeTextToRed);
   theSpan.attachEvent("onmouseout",changeTextToBlack);
}
```

An IE 6-compatible version of the previous example may also be found in the download; see span_mouseover5.html.

Other differences worth noting between the IE-specific methods and those found in the DOM events specification are as follows:

❑ Internet Explorer doesn't allow for distinguishing between the event capture and bubble phases within the same methods. We must employ separate setCapture() and releaseCapture() methods to intercept events during their capture phase.

❑ The methods used in MSIE take the name of the event handler rather than the name of the event as the first argument ("onmouseover" as opposed to "mouseover").

❑ In Microsoft's implementation, those methods providing for interception of events are methods of HTMLElement rather than of Node, so they can't be used on text nodes, unlike the DOM methods, which can. This means, that in order to employ IE's analogues to event listeners, the content upon which they're to be used must be wrapped in an HTML tag.

Let's discuss in a little more depth the propagation and flow of events through the document hierarchy or "tree", according to the DOM event model. As we said earlier, events travel in two directions in relation to their target element through this hierarchy: "down" the document tree from the document root to the target (capture phase), and then back "up" (bubble phase). What the DOM 2 event model does for us is to allow us to assign an event handler at any point along the event's path. Referring back to our table example, let's suppose that the user clicks inside one of its cells; not only can we assign an `onclick` handler to the table cell in order to intercept that click, but we can also assign one to the row that contains that cell, and (for example) the `<tbody>` element containing that row, and to the table that contains that `<tbody>` element, and so on. Not all events bubble, but most of them do so. We'll show you how to find out shortly.

Of course, some elements have default actions assigned to them in association with certain events. For instance, a form input button will attempt to submit the form when clicked – a link, when clicked on, will cause the browser to load the URL pointed to by that link. In either instance, the `click` event bubbles up through the containment hierarchy until it reaches the end – the document object, where the default action takes place. That is, unless something is done to intervene, and cancel the event. This can be done at any point during the event's bubble phase.

So, supposing we had a link within our table cell, we could set `onclick` event handlers for the link, the containing cell, and the containing row to perform various tasks, then set an additional one on the `<tbody>` or `<table>` element to cancel the event so that our tasks are completed, and should their result meet a certain condition or set of conditions that we've determined, we can cancel the loading of the new document at that point, before the event can reach the top of the document tree.

Of course, we can also write our event handlers so that, if those conditions are not met, the event flow is allowed to continue unimpeded and the new document permitted to load. We can also cancel events during the capture phase, before they reach their intended target. We can also make sure that we capture an event that bubbles up from an element within a page simply by attaching an event handler for that event to the `document` object.

In order to see how event cancellation is accomplished, we need to examine the `Event` object. Just as the objects we've already discussed are used to model elements in an HTML document, so the `Event` object models an event; and just like those element objects, it possesses properties that describe the event and methods that can be used to stop an event's default action or cancel it out altogether. The `event` parameter we saw above, being passed to event handler functions in Netscape 6/Mozilla, is in fact an `Event` object. The DOM-2 `Event` object's methods and properties are shown in the following tables:

Property	Description
bubbles	Boolean value – if `true`, the event bubbles
cancelable	Boolean value – if `true`, the event can be canceled
currentTarget	The Node to which the current event handler is assigned
eventPhase	Indicates the phase in which the event is being processed; takes one of three constant values: CAPTURING_PHASE, AT_TARGET, or BUBBLING_PHASE
target	The Node from which the event originated

Table continued on following page

Property	Description
timeStamp	The time at which the event occurred
type	Indicates the type of a event as a string value, for example "click", "focus", "mouseout", and so on

Method	Description
preventDefault()	Cancels an event (if its cancelable property is true), that is, it keeps the event's default action from occurring. However, it does not stop event propagation
stopPropagation()	Stops the propagation of the event in either direction (during the event's capture phase or its bubble phase)

Please note that the methods of the Event object are only effective upon the current or active event.

DOM Level 2 also provides some additional properties for mouse-related events such as click, mouseover, mouseout, mousedown, mouseup, and mousemove. These are shown below in the following table:

Property	Description
altKey ctrlKey metaKey shiftKey	Each of these is a Boolean value that, if true, indicates that the related key was pressed when the event took place
button	Indicates which mouse button was pressed or released; the values returned and what they correspond to are as follows: 1: left button; 2: right button; 3: middle button
clientX clientY	Left and top coordinates of the mouse pointer at the time the event took place; these are the horizontal and vertical distances in pixels, respectively, from the left-top corner of the browser window
relatedTarget	For mouseover events, this property indicates the node that the pointer has just left; for mouseout events, it identifies the node, that the mouse pointer has just entered
screenX screenY	The coordinates, in pixels, of the mouse pointer from the left-top corner of the user's screen

As we've mentioned before, Internet Explorer right through to version 6 beta does not completely support the W3C DOM Level 2 event model, but does offer a fairly close approximation in many if not all ways. However, the differences are not superficial. First and foremost, MSIE does not recognize an abstract Event object or class as such, as Netscape 6 and Mozilla do; instead, it regards each instance of an event as the current value of a window.event property. Nor does it provide for event capturing and bubbling as discrete processes; therefore, there is no equivalent in Internet Explorer to the W3C eventPhase property. Nor is there a currentTarget property as such; instead, programmers use the this keyword to indicate the element to which an event handler is assigned. The timeStamp property is nonexistent and has no analogue whatsoever in the IE event model. Finally, in place of the two event cancellation methods specified in DOM-2, MSIE provides two properties, which can be set to cancel default events and event bubbling. These are, respectively, returnValue and cancelBubble, each of which can be set to a Boolean true in order to accomplish what Netscape 6 does by implementing the DOM-2 Event methods.

With regard to mouse events, Internet Explorer also differs quite a bit from the standard. Its button property may take on one of no fewer than eight different integer values, rather than the three given in the W3C specification:

❑ 0: none

❑ 1: left button

❑ 2: right button

❑ 3: left and right buttons

❑ 4: middle button

❑ 5: left and middle buttons

❑ 6: middle and right buttons

❑ 7: all three mouse buttons depressed at one time

In place of the relatedElement property, MSIE provides two properties, fromElement and toElement, which indicate the elements the mouse pointer is leaving or entering, in the case of mouseover and mouseout events.

DOM Level 2 does not define an event model for keyboard events, deferring this to a future version of the standard; however, HTML 4.01 does define three keyboard-related events:

❑ keydown – a key is depressed

❑ keyup – a key that has been pressed is released

❑ keypress – a key is pressed, then released

These are analogous to the mousedown, mouseup, and click events. Both Internet Explorer and Netscape provide ways to obtain information about the keys involved. In MSIE, the key's Unicode value is given by the key event's keyCode property; in Netscape, keydown and keyup store the key's ASCII value in a keyCode property, and keypress events have a charCode property that yields the same information. Both browsers provide ways to determine if a modifier key (*shift*, *Alt*, *Ctrl*) was also pressed. For reasons of space, we won't cover the details here, but encourage the reader who wishes to know more about them to consult some of the resources we've listed in the end of the chapter, including the relevant documentation from Microsoft, Netscape, and other browser vendors.

DOM-2 also provides a model for **mutation** events, which we mentioned earlier. These are intended to allow for notification of changes in a document. We won't go into a great deal of detail, but we will list some basic information about mutation events and the mutation event model here:

❑ The model is meant to allow notification of any changes that might take place in the structure of a document

❑ These changes include alterations in the document's element hierarchy, specifically, the alteration, addition, or removal of elements

❑ Changes in the attributes of elements are also included in this model, as are changes in the text that may be contained by DOM elements

❑ Mutation events are not cancelable as of DOM Level 2. However, this is subject to change in future additions to the standard

❑ A single change in a document or its structure can engender multiple mutation events. The DOM Level 2 recommendation does not specify any order in which these are to be fired or processed, leaving this to browser and other software implementations.

❑ The mutation event model also specifies a set of HTML events, which includes those events corresponding to the intrinsic events we discussed in Chapter 9. In addition, it also defines `resize` and `scroll` events which take place, respectively, when the document window is resized or scrolled by the user.

Neither Netscape nor Microsoft appears to have made any serious attempts at implementation of mutation events in the latest versions of their web browsers.

This completes our overview of the Document Object Model. We hope we've neither overwhelmed the HTML author who doesn't have an extensive background in programming or web scripting; nor annoyed our more experienced readers with any omissions we've made in the interest of brevity.

We've tried to provide a broad overview of the specifications and their implementation (or lack thereof). We've also given those of you with an interest or need to know about these issues, the basics of what is possible by way of building dynamic, interactive, web-based client applications, and pointed you in the direction of more complete and useful information to take this further.

What does DOM Mean for HTML Authors?

The statement that "The DOM does not have any ramifications for the way you write XML and HTML documents…" is somewhat misleading in isolation; it really needs be taken in context. The astute reader of the DOM specification will note that what its authors are really saying is that "The DOM does not have any ramifications for the way you write XML and HTML documents provided the HTML author is following the established rules for HTML 4.01/XHTML 1.0 as laid down in the appropriate specification(s)". In this case, the context is one in which authors and authoring software have historically produced ill-formed documents, and of this practice. This is no longer the case user agents have been entirely too forgiving.

Historically speaking, the World Wide Web has been a place where authors and designers have done whatever they could get away with, in terms of how well structured their documents were. With the advent of the DOM Levels 1 and 2, and the implementation of these W3C recommendations in the 5th and subsequent generations of web browsers, these "bad old days" are rapidly coming to an end. Formerly, browsers were very forgiving of poor markup and a lack of real structure in web documents, and in most cases they could afford to be – after all, the main objective was to have something that could be read by viewers. Those developers and designers who strove for control over the details of how their creations were to be viewed had to battle with different implementations, including different interpretations of attributes, the attributes themselves differing between browsers, and sometimes even with competing tag sets.

Now that static pages (static as defined by the viewer) are graduating into something more, the picture of web-based applications in which the client plays an active part is beginning to change. No longer are web pages merely collections of text and images. Now they are becoming software platforms, whose structure is every bit as relevant as the information they contain. Web development is finally beginning to catch up with the rest of the software development world, which has known for years about the importance of separating one's content, structure, and presentation in the interest of efficiency and interoperability.

Among other concepts that we've discussed in this chapter, as well as previous ones, is the concept of a **one-to-one mapping** between tags or document elements and programming or scripting objects. This is central to the DOM. It is the reason why, for instance, the `<font>` tag has been deprecated and been replaced by Cascading Style Sheets – because it corresponds neither to an actual page element, nor to an easily mappable display attribute of an element. It is the reason why HTML documents must be valid and well-formed.

Recalling again our document "tree" diagram from earlier in this chapter, it is fairly easy to see how we may deduce such a tree-like structure from a set of elements, that are well-formed, in which all elements (tags) are clearly defined, and where there exists a well-defined containment hierarchy.

Let us consider this example of an ill-formed HTML fragment:

```
<p>Here is a paragraph with some <b>bold <em>and</b> emphasized</em> text,<font
color="green"><p>followed another fairly short paragraph containing some text
which is green</font> and some more text which isn't.
```

A web browser might be able to guess, for example, that the appearance of the 7th through 9th words was intended to be something like this:

bold *and* *emphasized*

When a definite static display was all that was expected of a document, that would have sufficed quite well, however now that documents are no longer just electronic versions of typewritten ones, this won't do at all. If a web document is to be a structured repository of information, how are we to structure something like this? To which element and corresponding object does the word "*and*" belong? Is it part of a bold element or of an emphasized one? How are we supposed to construct a set of programming objects for something like this? And, once we've done so, how are we supposed to deal with all the other myriad possibilities that arise from having allowed for this case? The short answer is that we can't – from now on, we're simply going to have to follow the rules, and this requires the creation of valid and well-formed documents that the DOM can successfully represent.

Summary

In this chapter, we've:

- ❏ tried to cover the basics of object models, including a thumbnail history of browser object models in general and a survey of the W3C Document Object Model Levels 1 and 2 in particular.

- ❏ seen how an HTML document, which consists of a set of tags written under well-defined rules, along with their attributes and content, maps onto a set of programming objects and properties in a one-to-one correspondence.

- ❏ shown how these objects are organized into collections and how they may be accessed and manipulated using a scripting language such as JavaScript.

- ❏ examined these objects and their features in some detail, and tried to show the HTML author how their documents (and their structures) impact on the work of web scripters and developers of web-based applications.

- ❏ looked at the DOM model for reflecting CSS styles into programmable objects and how this enables us to create and change the appearance and even layout of our documents in real time by manipulating the objects through script.

- ❏ presented an overview of events in web pages and the different means by which script functionality can be connected to web page elements, including the new (as of DOM Level 2) eventListener interface, and given a basic example of how events themselves can be modeled and programmed as objects.

Finally, we've tried to offer some advice and insight into what all this dynamic DOM stuff really means for web page authors, and how their work effects those who are providing the programming that will power the next generation of applications based on HTML (and XML) documents within web browsers and similar types of client software. We hope you have found this chapter interesting, informative and useful!

Bibliography: Recommended Reading

Beginning JavaScript by Paul Wilton (ISBN: *1-861004-06-0*), Wrox Press

JavaScript Bible by Danny Goodman (ISBN: *0764533-42-8*), IDG Books

JavaScript: The Definitive Reference by David Flanagan (ISBN: *1565923-92-8*), O'Reilly & Associates

Professional JavaScript by Nigel McFarlane et al (ISBN: 1861002-70-X), Wrox Press

W3C, Document Object Model Level 1 (Second Edition):
http://www.w3.org/TR/2000/WD-DOM-Level-1-20000929/

W3C, Document Object Model Level 2 Core (W3C Recommendation):
http://www.w3.org/TR/2000/REC-DOM-Level-2-Core-20001113/

Other DOM-related documentation available at:
http://www.w3.org/DOM/

A very good DOM viewer utility is available at:
http://www.brainjar.com/dhtml/domviewer/ – works in MSIE 5.5 and Netscape 6.0/Mozilla

Mozilla/Netscape 6 Support Documents:
http://www.mozilla.org/docs/web-developer/

For support of the MSIE object model and Internet Explorer DOM Levels 1 and 2, see:
http://msdn.microsoft.com/workshop/Author/om/doc_object.asp

Peter-Paul Koch's JavaScript/DOM Pages:
http://www.xs4all.nl/~ppk/js/index.html?version5.html

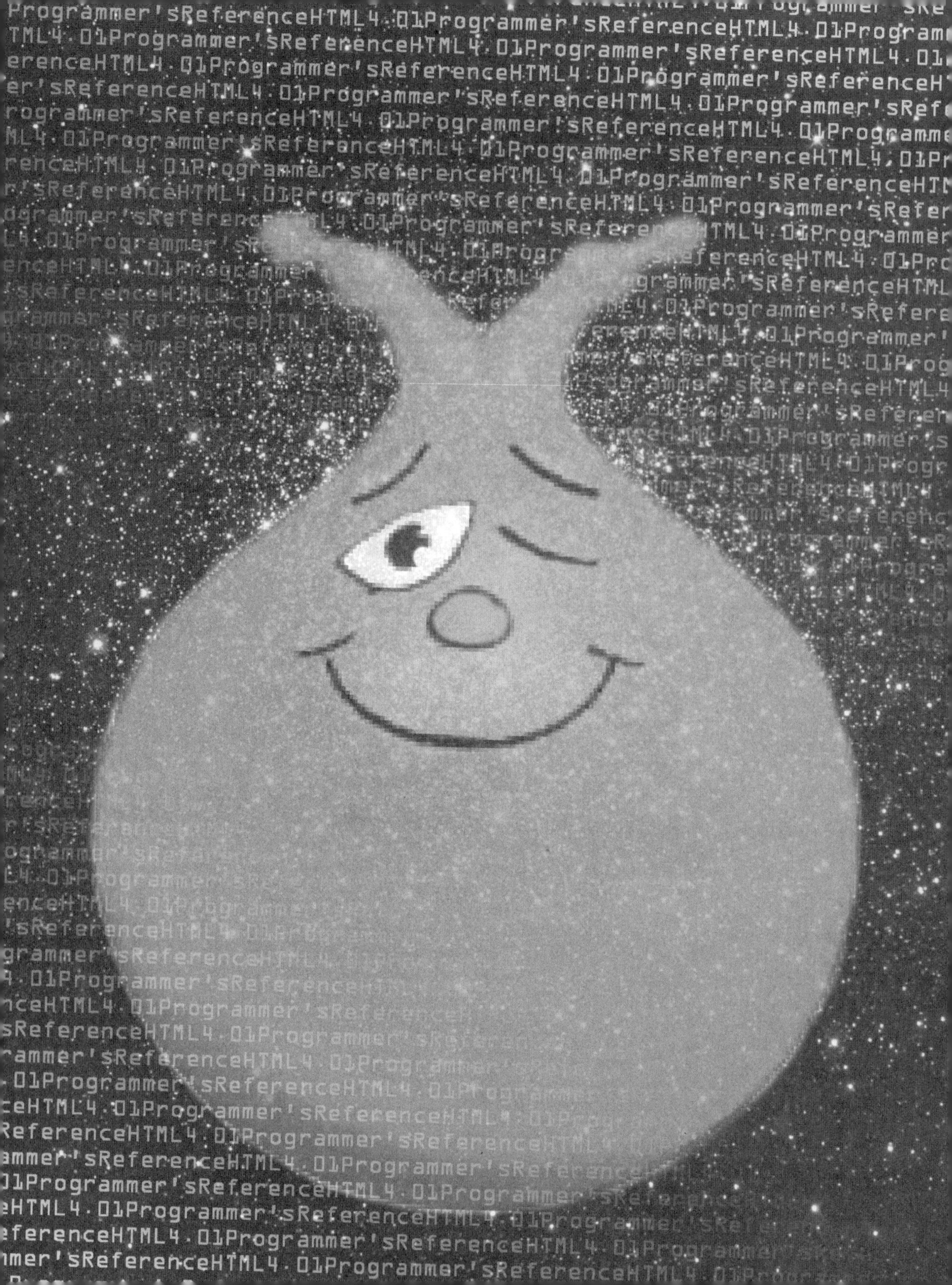
HTML4.01Programmer'sReference

20

Accessibility and Interoperability

Accessibility is an often-misunderstood term where web technologies are concerned, but the practice of making languages accessible and inherently interoperable is something that should be learned by anyone who has to write even the smallest fragment of HTML.

Accessibility and **interoperability** basically refer to the practices of ensuring that your HTML (and other integrated protocols and formats, for example Cascading Style Sheets) are able to be used properly by all people connected to the Web, regardless of physical/cognitive ability, platform, software, or any other limitation within their environment. This is not only a moral requirement; it also makes good business and developmental sense, and furthermore is covered by law in some countries.

What we will cover in this chapter:

❑ Why accessibility?

❑ The Web Accessibility Initiative, its working groups and its relationship to HTML

❑ The essentials for creating accessible HTML documents

❑ Some hints and tips for accessible HTML

❑ Why most pages are not already accessible

❑ Future directions

Why Accessibility?

So, let's explore the reasons for making your Web content (more) **accessible**:

1. To expand the available audience. By making sure that as many people as possible can view and interact with your material, you are expanding the available audience. For example, if your pages were only usable by people with the latest browser, and only 1% of your visitors have that browser, then you have already alienated 99% of your site's visitors before they even get to your content! Clearly it makes sense to ensure that your pages are not device specific, and instead are available to people using as wide a range of devices as possible. This may still apply, to a lesser extent, to corporate intranets where everyone is likely to be using the same technology – who is to say that you will still be using the same software in a year, or that you won't take on board a worker with a disability who needs special software?

2. There is also a certain amount of moral obligation. For example, what would happen if a blind user accessed your page, and your content was available entirely as images with no text-only alternatives for use with their screen reader? In fact, for this reason, some countries such as USA, Canada, and those that make up the European Union, have laws asserting that government sites must be accessible to people with disabilities, providing no huge obstacles that prevent people from using their pages. For examples of these policies, see http://www.w3.org/WAI/Policy/.

3. It can help to ease the development process, for example, future-proofing. Just because a certain piece of software is widely used now, that won't necessarily be the case in 5, 2, or even 1 year's time. When content is device independent, you also have a greater possibility that it will need to be updated less frequently. This requires some forethought and planning, but clearly you will benefit in the long run.

The World Wide Web (WWW), as originally conceived, was an information space where anyone could share their ideas and publish and download information. However, practice rarely follows theory, and proprietary and inaccessible formats were introduced, along with a flurry of bad practices. From the very start, there were problems in that the WWW was so inclusive in what information it could contain, that people became lax and started to develop content for their particular platform. They started to ignore the needs of others and something clearly needed to be done.

Introducing the Web Accessibility Initiative

That something proved to be the setting up of the Web Accessibility Initiative (WAI) with a remit to ensure that the evolution of the Web takes into account accessibility issues. It aims towards a time when all people can access the Web, and not only the ones with special software applications, or those with physical or cognitive abilities that others do not possess (such as sight).

The WAI is a particular domain of the World Wide Web Consortium (http://www.w3.org/). It is split into several working groups covering various aspects of the initiative, including content accessibility guidelines, protocols and formats, education and outreach, and user agent accessibility. These groups regularly produce helpful guidelines, which can be accessed from the WAI web site, http://www.w3.org/WAI/.

Web Content Accessibility Guidelines (WCAG)

These guidelines are a product of the WAI's Web Content Accessibility Guidelines Working Group, which is mainly concerned with the production and promotion of a set of guidelines that developers can follow easily and intuitively to make their Web content accessible. WCAG is a list of 14 **guidelines** (generic rules for creating accessible content) each of which has **checkpoints** (lists of guideline related points that a developer or designer can go through to gauge how well their content fares compared to the particular guideline being addressed). WCAG 1.0 is highly HTML oriented, and work has been underway for quite some time now on WCAG 2.0, which will concentrate on much more generic Web accessibility principles.

The Guidelines

The WCAG 1.0 guidelines are a generic list of rules that set out the main pieces of advice for creating accessible web content. They are abstract in nature, and come with a piece of explanatory text as to the background philosophy. We will not repeat them here, as the latest version is always readily available from the WAI web site, specifically http://www.w3.org/TR/WAI-WEBCONTENT/.

A particular strand throughout the guidelines is the concept of **graceful transformation** (this basically means that the content is available to everyone regardless of environmental, physical, software, or other constraint(s)), however, the final three guidelines, 12 to 14, cover different aspects of accessibility, namely navigation and clarity of language. The final guideline serves to demonstrate that the WCAG were designed with the real world in mind by stressing that the clear and simple language it recommends us to use should be appropriate for the content of the site and its audience. Following this recommendation would not force us, for example, to produce a technical documentation site written in language that children between the ages of 5-7 can understand! The Guidelines aim to help us to use our common sense in these matters, rather than imposing rules on us arbitrarily.

The Checkpoints

Each guideline comes with a list of generic and technology-specific "checkpoints". These can be gone though one-by-one by content providers to see how their particular application fares. To facilitate this, the checkpoints are ranked, from Priority 1 (P1) through Priority 2 (P2) to Priority 3 (P3), with P1 being the most urgent, and P3 being the least urgent. These three ranks correspond to the keywords "MUST", "SHOULD", and "MAY", that is, you MUST follow P1 checkpoints, SHOULD follow P2, and MAY follow P3 if you want to conform.

If a particular piece of web content complies with every single checkpoint of a certain priority, then we say it conforms to a certain "level" of WCAG compliance. For example, if your document complies with every P1 checkpoint, then it is WCAG Level-A compliant, and you get to display that fact on your page. To be Level-AA (Double A) compliant, it must follow all P1 and P2 checkpoints, and for Level-AAA (Triple A) compliancy, it must follow all of the checkpoints, that is, P1, P2, and P3. There is no way of ensuring that people comply to this rating system, and the ratings themselves are often very subjective, but finely grained techniques for evaluating accessibility are being developed, which will help to make this a more precise and accountable process in the future.

The WAI & HTML

During the design and development stage of the HTML 4.01 specification, the WAI worked closely with the W3C HTML Working Group to ensure that accessibility features were built in, and that HTML 4.01 did not present any major accessibility problems. In particular, the WAI Protocols and Formats Working Group are chartered to perform this job.

Generally speaking, the group had to ensure that HTML itself follows the WCAG guidelines, and also allows people to create WCAG-compliant web content. This constant liaison between the WAI and HTML Working Group resulted in the following new accessibility features in HTML 4.01:

❑ Alternative textual representations are now required to accompany images represented by the <img> element and image maps represented with <area>.

❑ A much stricter distinction between semantics and presentation with full integration of Cascading Style Sheets (CSS).

❑ Better form structures, including the addition of the accesskey attribute, the ability to group form controls semantically, the ability to group select options semantically, and active labels.

❑ The ability to markup a text description of an included object (within the <object> element) for the benefit of those who cannot use that included object but can access the content of text.

❑ To facilitate longer and more in depth descriptions of certain elements, the addition of the longdesc attribute to <img>, <frame>, and <iframe>, and the summary attribute to <table>.

❑ The addition of the title and lang attributes to most elements.

❑ Additions to the range of target media (tty, braille, and so on) for use with style sheets.

❑ The addition of more structural and semantic elements to <table>, including <caption> and <colgroup>.

❑ The addition of a new client-side image map mechanism (the <map> element) that allows authors to integrate image and text links. Previous versions of HTML did not allow for text based links within the <map> element, and so it was impossible to semantically group a set of related links as, for example, a navigation bar.

❑ Additional elements for inline phrasing have been added; namely the <abbr> and <acronym> elements.

The HTML 4.01 specification has been designed to ensure that it is both accessible and interoperable, but WCAG 1.0 was required in order to address how to use HTML where this information could not be included in the specification. For example, although the HTML 4.01 specification tells you that you must include an alt attribute for your images, it does not state that this should be a meaningful non-empty value. WCAG 1.0 (which is a W3C Recommendation and therefore shares exactly the same status as the HTML 4.01 specification) points out how best practices such as this can lead to greater accessibility.

In addition to the specification and WCAG, the WAI Content Accessibility Guidelines Working Group also issued a list of HTML Accessibility Techniques as a note, shortly after WCAG 1.0 was published, in order to help us as developers and designers because the techniques for creating accessible HTML are not as clear-cut as we may think. Indeed it could be said that "validation is a science, interoperability is a skill, and accessibility is an art form." An example of this lack of clarity is that many people would argue over what constitutes a perfect `alt` attribute in the `<img>` element – some people prefer a description of the image, and others may prefer a replacement for the purpose of the image. Imagine a botanical web site that had a picture of a sunflower as a welcoming image. Those people who would prefer a description of the image itself may use something like:

```
<img src="sunflower.gif" alt="[Picture of a sunflower]">
```

Whereas others may prefer the purpose of the image, which may be represented as:

```
<img src="sunflower.gif" alt="Welcome to this site">
```

Usually there is no "right" or "wrong" answer, only endless debates over which method is better! Some examples do make it obvious what would be preferable to use though:

```
<img src="page_heading.gif" alt="[Banner heading]">
```

```
<img src="page_heading.gif" alt="H.J.S. And Son, Est. 1990">
```

Clearly, the emphasis here is on making sure that the meaning of each particular piece of code that relates to the user is duplicated as accurately as possible in the alternative text (that is, it is at least adequate to allow the page to meet its intended function).

Note: a good technique for ensuring you write good alternative texts is to try to imagine what the page would be like if the text were to be substituted for your graphic. Would the page still make sense – would it convey similar information? A simple method of doing this is to view your page through a text only browser such as LYNX, which will allow you to see how this will look automatically (LYNX can be downloaded from http://lynx.browser.org/).

Notwithstanding all of this, if we want to make our pages accessible, then we would do well to read through the WCAG techniques, available from http://www.w3.org/TR/WCAG10-TECHS/. Doing so will enable us to get a better grasp of the theoretical and hence practical aspects of accessibility. Although it is tempting to just learn these techniques rather than the reasons behind them, it also makes good sense to learn the reasons, in case we come across a situation that is not addressed here.

Thankfully, for the most part, accessibility is just common sense.

The Essentials for Making HTML Accessible

The two main rules for making HTML accessible are:

❏ Provide textual equivalents

❏ Separate content from presentation

Provide Textual Equivalents

This rule ensures that if something is portrayed in non-textual content (such as an image) and someone for some reason can't see that image, for example, if they are blind and using a screen reader to speak the text to them or if they are using LYNX, it can be interpreted easily by any browser.

> Note: a screen reader is a piece of software that allows visually impaired people to have web content read out to them, as long as it is in a text-based format, or can be converted to a text based format. This is why it is critical to always provide a textual alternative for non-textual-based content, such as multimedia).

For example, if you were using the words "My Site Title" in a large image at the top of your page, anyone who couldn't see that image would miss out on the heading. However, if you set the `alt` (alternative) attribute to "*My Site Title*", like this

```
<img src="title.gif" alt="My Site Title">
```

then it becomes possible for this textual alternative to be accessed. It is a requirement in HTML 4.01 that the `alt` attribute be present. Some HTML authoring tools such as the W3C's Amaya (http://www.w3.org/Amaya/), for example, don't let you add an image into the document unless you set an `alt` attribute as well, thus enforcing the standard.

Alternative representations should be provided for any sort of non-textual media wherever possible, not only for images. When using streaming media, make sure that these alternatives are properly synchronized with the media presentation in question. The rule also applies, for example, to ASCII art: large diagrams need some form of alternative representation. You could provide a title and a hypertext link to a long description, and/or another alternative.

The `<object>` element can also be used, as it can embed certain forms of multimedia in the page and allows for complex content within it while providing useful alternatives to other user agents. That is, it allows you to associate complex text (with phrasing such as `<em>` and including hyperlinks) to complex media objects. For example:

```
<object data="mypresentation.mp3" type="audio/mpeg">
<p>
<a href="mypresentation.mp3">My presentation</a>:
<a href="transcript.html">transcript</a>
</p>
</object>
```

For more on the use of the object element in embedding images, see Chapter 10, the "*Fallback in Browsers That Don't Support Objects*" section.

Separate Content from Presentation

The separation of content from presentation is a very important concept indeed, and should be forefront in the mind of any person writing HTML. By separating content from presentation, you are making your content repurposable, and hence interoperable. As a general rule, content should be portrayed with HTML, and presentation with CSS, which is explained fully in Chapters 11-13 of this book.

That's quite a few buzzwords for one sentence, so let's take a look at exactly what they mean:

Content

The content (or basic material) of your page is composed of structure and semantics. For example, the headings in an HTML document are a part of the structure, and the text is a part of its semantics. "Semantic" is basically a synonym for "meaning". Semantic parts of your document are those bits which are there to convey your information/meaning to the reader.

Presentation

This is anything that affects the look or feel of your document, for example, the color, size, and weight of your fonts, the background images that you use, and even the width of the margins. This should all be controlled with CSS. Style sheets have the advantage that they are reusable, and (best of all from an accessibility point of view) can be overridden by the user. Also, specialized style sheets can be provided for different devices that may access the document. See Chapter 11 for a fuller explanation of this.

Many people are still using elements such as <font> in their markup, which is now considered by the W3C to be harmful, and has indeed been deprecated in HTML 4.01. If we hardcode a color or style in the document, it makes it very difficult to present it to a user in a way that is accessible to them, because hard-coded markup is difficult to repurpose. For more information on deprecation, see Chapter 15.

Repurposability

Repurposability means that your content can be reused in different contexts. For example, we might wish to make use of the headings, <h1> through <h6>, to provide an overview of our document. If we are use "bold" text (<b>) or similar presentational effects for our headings, then people cannot easily perform this extraction. Repurposability is very important indeed.

Now that we have explained these terms and why they are important, let's have a look at some of the methods we can use to separate our content from its presentation.

Methods

From the very earliest days of HTML, the people responsible for its development were careful to ensure that the elements and attributes were for structure and semantics only, but due to the fact that an efficient style sheet language was not created for quite some time, some features slipped through the net. These features (for example, the presentational elements such as <b>, <font>, and so on) are being gradually deprecated from HTML. Hence it is advisable for content developers to avoid deprecated features of W3C technologies.

An example of why you should use the right markup for the right content is using `<pre>` for layout. `<pre>` is used here as it will keep the spacing within it conserved. If you had the following:

```
<pre>
Main story:
My butler today decided that          Sidenote:
he would like to take the day         My cousin came to visit me,
off work.                             sampling the new teas that I had got
</pre>                                from her on holiday.
```

This makes sense in a browser, for example, in IE 5.5:

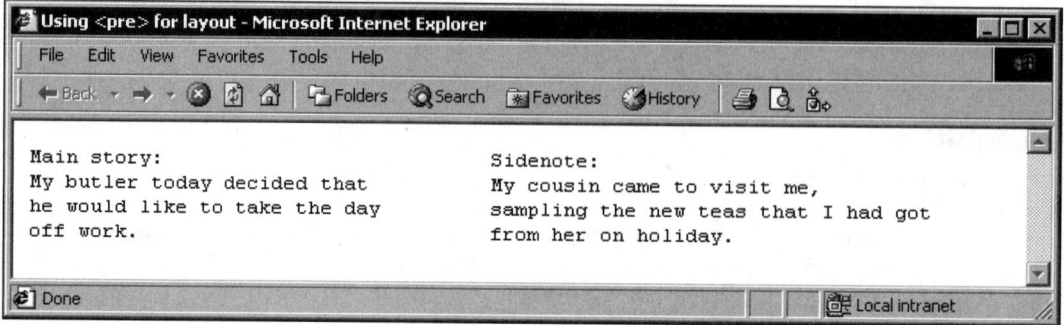

but a screen reader might read it out as "Main story: Sidenote: My butler today decided that My cousin came to visit me, he would like to take the day sampling the new teas that I had got off work. from her on holiday."

It would be better to use markup for the structure, and layout for the presentation:

```
<div class="main">
  <h2 id="main">Main story</h2>
  <p>My butler today decided that he would like to take
     the day off of work.</p>
</div>
<div class="sidenote">
  <h2 id="side">Sidenote</h2>
  <p>My cousin came to visit me, sampling the new teas that
     I had got from on holiday.</p>
</div>
```

We can then use a style sheet to add the formatting (which is additionally useful since you can then style your information very precisely, which you can't do if the information is presented within a `<pre>` section):

```
div.main { float: left; }
div.sidenote { float: right; }
```

Many people would in fact think of using tables for this, but this would not be good practice. This is because many tables simply do not make sense when **linearized** (linearizing is the process of removing all the table-associated markup from a page so that the content is presented in a linear fashion). In other words, screen readers treat the table elements as if they weren't there, but occasionally they are used to separate the blocks of content into distinctly separate sections.

Another benefit of separating content from presentation is that it becomes easier to form logical structures in the document to facilitate navigation. For example, you can separate your content into block structures and headings, and label them, which enables the user to get an easy overview of the document. If you are simply using the "bold" element (<b>) to demarcate your headings, then there is no way in which this can be done. Labeling can be done with the id attributes (well, it can also be done using the name attribute, but this has been deprecated in HTML, notwithstanding the fact that it had a greater range of implementation in current tools than id).

Hints and Tips for Accessible HTML

Here are 17 useful tips for accessible HTML, which will help you to make your pages accessible and to be successful in ticking off the WCAG checkpoints. The W3C has issued a note about WCAG 1.0 Accessibility Techniques for HTML available from http://www.w3.org/TR/WCAG10-HTML-TECHS/, which contains many further examples, and is fairly exhaustive on the subject (although just wait for the techniques for WCAG 2.0!).

> Note: The two most difficult structures to make accessible in HTML are tables and frames (addressed here by hints 11 and 13), due to the complexity of the mechanisms, and the fact that the rendering of them in different user agents often varies widely. HTML does contain certain elements and attributes that help content developers create accessible tables and frames, but it is important that these are understood, and that they are used properly. We should avoid using tables and frames for layout and presentation where possible, but occasionally, they are necessary and it is sometimes a lot easier to simply make a frameset more accessible by adding the necessary code than it is to completely re-write an entire site.

1. Textual Alternatives

Always provide textual alternatives. This has been mentioned before, but it is certainly worth repeating as a core concept of accessibility. For example, include alt attributes in images, and client-side image maps. Also, the <object> element allows complex content within it, which is to be used as an alternative for people who cannot access the multimedia content pointed at by the object element in question (for more on this see Chapter 10). This has been included as a WCAG Level A priority because its use overcomes so many of the hurdles web users may face.

2. Presentational Markup

Avoid presentational markup. Use <em> and <strong>, or their CSS equivalents, rather than <i> and <b>, and use blockquote for quotes, rather than indenting text. The full list of presentational markup in HTML 4.01 that should be avoided is as follows:

b	basefont	big	center	font
frameset	i	s	small	strike
tt	u			

Many of these elements are defined in the "transitional" document type. As a general rule, try to create documents that use the HTML 4.01 Strict Document Type Definition (DTD). For more about document types, see Chapter 1.

Note that CSS can also be used to repair certain rendering problems in browsers, for example, some user agents don't display <pre> as having preserved white space unless it is set, as follows:

```
pre { white-space: pre; }
```

3. Title Links

Title your links. By titling links that do not have an adequate description, you are letting your page users know where they are going. For example:

```
<p>Go to my <a href="mypage.html">page</a> on the subject for more
   information.</p>
```

Would be better as:

```
<p>Go to my <a href="mypage.html" title="Johns page on how to configure
   widgets for springtime">page</a> on the subject for more information.</p>
```

This method can also be used to guide users when providing alternative format files as the destination of hyperlinks:

```
<p>
See the
<a href="mypage.txt" title="this page in plain text Format">Text</a>,
and
<a href="mypage.wml" title="wireless markup language(WAP) version">WML</a>
versions of this page.
</p>
```

The preferred way to point to alternative versions of a page is to use the link element, thereby specifying to the browser, rather than the user, that there are alternative versions of a page available for use with any profile in place, for example:

```
<link rel="alternate" type="text/plain" href="mypage.txt"
      title="A plain text equivalent of this page">
```

Note that this method is not supported by a great number of user agents currently, so if it is possible that equivalents are necessary for your document, it might be worth considering linking to them from the document itself as well as linking them from its header.

4. Provide Illustrations

Provide illustrations where possible to accentuate and enhance the meaning of the textual content. For example, provide icons and diagrams where these are required. Sometimes, people with cognitive impairments may find it easier to work through a site that is clearly signposted. Indeed, almost anyone prefers a site with good graphics that accentuate the meaning of the text.

Note: Please remember our rule about providing textual alternatives though, that states you should never rely upon multimedia alone to get the message across. Text is repurposable; images aren't.

5. Link Mechanisms

Never show link mechanisms, for example, links such as "click here". Instead, utilize sensible link texts, for example replacing "click here" with a short title of the content being linked to. Why is the "click here" link text such a bad practice? Firstly, this does not make a great deal of sense when using a device that does not have a selection mechanism that "clicks", and secondly, when overviews of your page are created, the link text may be used out of context. If a page contains descriptive links, it will be easier for someone looking at it to gauge what it is about.

6. Spelled Out URLs

Avoid in-your-face URLs. An in-your-face URL is a link that is spelled out rather than linked to. For example:

Bad practice:

```
<p>For more details, try <a title="the World Wide Web Consortium"
    href="http://www.w3.org/">http://www.w3.org/</a>.</p>
```

Good practice:

```
<p>For more details, try the <a title="World Wide Web Consortium"
    href="http://www.w3.org/">the W3C</a>.</p>
```

This is how these examples look when viewed in a browser:

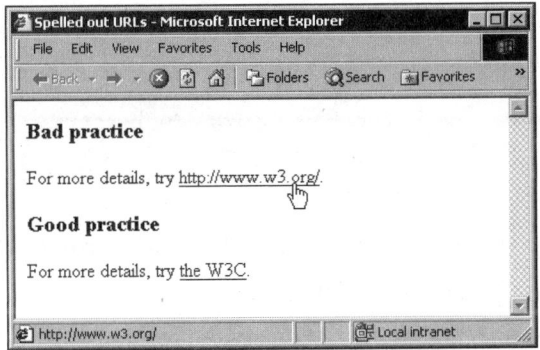

The exception to this rule is where a document must be printable. You could use the following piece of CSS when it becomes more widely supported:

```
@media print { a:after { content: " (" attr(href) ")"; } }
```

This takes the content of the `href` attribute in the link, and displays it after the link text in brackets when, and only when, it is being printed out.

7. Doctypes and Validation

Always include a DTD – validate your code. It is very important that you validate your code to make sure that there are no parsing errors, or odd coding in there. It is also very beneficial to check your code to see just how good a job you have done in writing your page!

This method of creating a page that conforms to published grammars may well seem counter-intuitive. In other words, people tend to simply write pages using the tags as they need them, rather than thinking "well, I can't use that tag because I am using HTML 4.01 Strict". This is a very difficult problem to address, but when using HTML 4.01 the best advice is simply to know the specification well, hence writing markup naturally. As long as we remember to avoid presentational markup, it should be fairly easy to write in HTML 4.01 Strict. Indeed, HTML 4.01 Strict is occasionally not strict enough (still allowing certain forms of presentational markup).

Remember, write your documents in HTML 4.01 Strict, but accept Transitional in tools. There is no lack of decent validators around, for example http://validator.w3.org/, so really there is no excuse for not validating your code.

8. Metadata

Use metadata. Metadata (data that describes data) is a very good way of letting people know about your page – for example, by making your pages easier for search engines to index. HTML 4.01 has the `<meta>` element with which to add metadata (see Chapter 2 for more on this), but people will probably want to use more effective metadata formats in the future, such as the W3C's Resource Description Framework (RDF), which can be very expressive. For example, you can make very finely grained accessibility assertions about your page, and create detailed navigation and relationship mechanisms.

HTML 4.01 itself doesn't contain any way of embedding RDF metadata in the pages, so you have to create your own by using a metadata profile, and associate it using the profile attribute in the `<head>` element, before you can use the `<link>` element to link to your RDF file.

For example:

```
<head profile="http://example.org/">
  <link rel="metadata" type="application/rdf+xml"href="myrdf.rdf"
       title="RDF metadata about this document">
[...]
```

> Note: `application/rdf+xml` is an as yet (May 2001) unregistered MIME type for XML RDF applications.

Machine-readable information (and the "Semantic Web") is something that developers should be tracking very keenly in the future, as it will have many potential accessibility applications, for example, the automatic evaluation and repair of HTML using EARL – the Evaluation And Report Language (http://www.w3.org/2001/03/earl/). EARL is an RDF-based framework for making evaluations about certain parts of a document. For example, it would be possible to use EARL to say whether or not a page passes a certain WCAG checkpoint, or whether or not it passes the W3C's validator, and then use that information to repair the problems, if necessary.

9. Language Markup

Reflect language changes in your document by using markup. You can do this by using the `lang` attribute that is allowed by most elements. If you want to set the language of a whole document, you can put it in the `<html>` tag, or you can use it inline for specifying language definitions for partial areas of the document. For more on the `lang` attribute, see the universal attributes in Chapter 2, and also Chapter 18.

When marked up with the correct language, screen readers and other alternative output devices (for example, Braille machines) can adjust their settings accordingly. At present there are very few devices that actually do anything with this information, but that does not stop future tools implementing it. For example, speech tones on voice readers would be different for a document written in Italian (which has the general rule of stressing the penultimate syllable) than English (which has stress all over the place).

10. Spacer Images

Don't use images for spacers if you can help it. This is more of an interoperability point – not all browsers can display images, and not all browsers display text wrapped around images in the same way. Also, pragmatically speaking, having 100 spacer images to indent text on a page means that the page download time is increased. Instead use CSS by setting the margin, indent, or padding properties. For example, some people like to indent the first line of a paragraph by using a spacer image:

```
<p>
   <img src="blank.gif" width="20" height="20"
        alt=" ">Once upon a time [...]
</p>
```

Instead, you should set a text-indent property in CSS:

```
p { text-indent: 1em; }
```

Also to be avoided are images for layout; we should use positioning in CSS instead.

11. Accessible Tables

Make tables accessible. The basic thing to concentrate on when using tables is the purpose of the table: what am I using this table for – need I be using one at all? It is important to capture the meaning of the table so that this information can be conveyed to the user, hence providing summaries and captions is very important. If using a table for layout, you should either use summary="Layout table", or a description of what you are laying out as appropriate. Note that browsers often don't have a default rendering for the <caption> element, so it is best to provide one when using it.

Also, use the <tr>, <th>, <td>, <col>, <colgroup>, <thead>, <tbody>, and <tfoot> elements properly. Information on how to do this is available in Chapter 7. Provide navigation mechanisms where appropriate (such as the id attribute), and group respective data with the scope, axis, and header attributes.

Here is a good example of an accessible table:

```
<table summary="This is a table charting the average sales of
        sprockets during the summer holiday period"
        id="sprockets">
<caption>Sprocket Sales - Summer Period</caption>
<thead>
<tr>
   <th id="type" scope="col" abbr="Type">Sprocket Type</th>
   <th id="manu" scope="col">Manufacturer</th>
   <th id="sales" scope="col">Sales</th>
</tr>
</thead>
<tbody>
<tr>
   <th id="ms" scope="row">MegaSprocket</th>
   <td>H. J. Sprocket</td>
   <td>23,738</td>
```

```
    </tr>
    <tr>
       <th id="us" scope="row">UltraSprocket</th>
       <td>Sprocket and Son</td>
       <td>20,352</td>
    </tr>
    <tr>
       <th id="ss" scope="row">SuperSprocket</th>
       <td>Sprockets and Deeleys 'r' us</td>
       <td>21,282</td>
    </tr>
    </tbody>
    </table>
```

This can be used with a style sheet such as the one that follows:

```
table#sprockets caption {
    font-weight: bold;
    color: #a00000;
}
table#sprockets {
    border: 2px solid #d0e0e0;
    padding: 0.2em;          ,
    background-color: #f0f7ff;
    color: #000000;
}
table#sprockets th {
    border: 1px solid #c0c0c0;
}
table#sprockets td {
    border: 1px solid #e0e0e0;
}
@media aural {
    table#sprockets:before { content: attr(summary); }
}
```

Using these two documents together gives us the following output on IE 5.5:

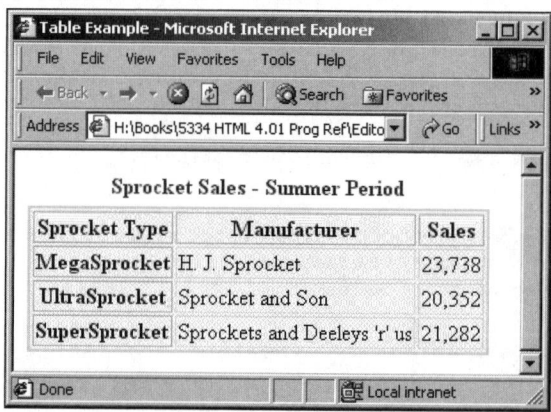

Here, the semantics of the table are very clear indeed, as summaries and captions are given. The scope of each table heading is clearly identified, and all table headers have been given IDs so that you can point to them.

Another very important guideline that we should follow is to avoid using tables for layout, and if they must be used, make sure that the content still makes sense when the tables are removed (that is, make sure it makes sense when separated into lines without a grid). Note that it is difficult for some user agents to interpret what is going on inside a table. The best way to check if your tables make sense is to remove the table markup and see if it still reads correctly.

For example:

```
<table summary="Layout table">
  <tr>
    <td>Welcome To: </td>
    <td><img src="title.gif" alt="My Site"></td></tr>
  <tr>
    <td>Table of contents: </td>
    <td>[<a href="home.html">My Homepage</a>]
        [<a href="jokes.html">My Jokes</a>]</td>
  </tr>
</table>
```

which linearizes as:

```
<p>Welcome To: </p>
<p><img src="title.gif" alt="My Site"></p>
<p>Table of contents: </p>
<p>[<a href="home.html">My Homepage</a>]
    [<a href="jokes.html">My Jokes</a>]</p>
```

This should still make sense to a reader when viewed on screen. In fact, as the layout is not vital to the meaning of the content here, it would be a much better approach to use CSS positioning to lay out the relevant elements. Tables were added to HTML to enable people to display tabular data, not to lay out elements, but unfortunately the late implementation of CSS meant that people resorted to bad habits, and it is difficult to get people to stop doing something once they have learned it.

12. Non Link Printable Characters (NLPCs)

Where you have directly adjacent links, provide NLPCs around or between them. NLPCs are characters used to separate a list of links.

For example:

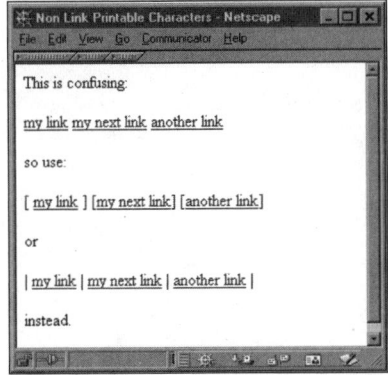

This is because some user agents do not render directly adjacent links separately, confusing the user as to whether something is a list of links or just one large link. Setting a background-color on hover and focus properties in CSS can also help:

```
a:hover, a:focus { background-color: #fff0e0; }
```

Note that I set both the hover and focus selectors for device interoperability: most users will likely be using a mouse (and hence a:hover), but for those that aren't, and are instead utilizing keyboards, the a:focus selector should cover it. See Chapter 11, the "Pseudo Elements" section, for a fuller description of these selectors.

13. Accessible Frames

The usual accessibility concepts carry through to the implementation of frames: make them semantic, and provide equivalents. Avoid frames if they will only be used for cosmetic reasons. If you're only using frames for decoration, try to use other methods. If there is some frames functionality that you definitely require then use frames, but be fully aware of the consequences. For more information on frames, go to Chapter 8.

In order to minimize difficulties for your users, you can include the following features in your frame documents:

❑ The first thing that you should ensure is that each frame has a title attribute set, so that it can be used, for example, as a link title if frames are not supported by a particular user agent.

❑ Make sure that you provide adequate non-frame equivalents. People are getting increasingly infuriated with frames, due to the fact that it is difficult to refer to content, and difficult to save it. Also, people with browsers that cannot display frames are usually left with no way to access the content of frame-based pages. Always provide title and longdesc (where appropriate) attributes for your frames, and make sure that there are alternative navigation methods available. For example, you could use the <noframes> element to provide a table of links to the pages you have used within your frameset.

❑ The content frames link to should always be able to include some kind of generic alternatives mechanism, and thus should always be HTML. In other words, HTML should always be used because it allows you to associate textual alternatives to multimedia embedded objects. For example, you can then use the alt attribute on your elements to denote the text-only representation, and if the frame refreshes, so will the alternative!

❑ Another point to note is that frame sizes should be in percentages for device independence.

Here is a good example of a (fairly) accessible frameset:

```
<!DOCTYPE html PUBLIC "-//W3C//DTD HTML 4.01 Frameset//EN"
SYSTEM "http://www.w3.org/TR/html401/DTD/frameset.dtd">
<html lang="en">
  <head>
    <title>Sprockets Weekly</title>
  </head>
```

```
    <frameset cols="20%, 80%" title="Our big document">
      <frame src="toc.html" name="toc" title="Table of Contents">
      <frame src="main.html" name="main" title="Main Content">
      <noframes>
        <h1>Sprockets Weekly</h1>
        <p><a href="toc.html">Table of Contents</a>.</p>
      </noframes>
    </frameset>
  </html>
```

Remember that frames are rarely ever fully accessible (some user agent is bound to mess up): consider why you are using frames and whether a non-frames version, or an alternative (using `<object>` and CSS) would be acceptable.

14. Long Descriptions and Description Links

Use the `longdesc` attribute rather than (invisible) **D-Links (Description Links)**. A D-Link is simply a small link that is provided after some content, to a fuller explanation. For example, this acts a bit like an `alt` tag, except that it could reference an entire page about the image – especially useful when describing something very complex. `longdesc` is a highly useful attribute that enables you to give a link to a long description of your image that is more accessible to devices such as screen text readers. For example:

```
<img src="MonaLisa.gif" alt="Leonardo Da Vinci's Mona Lisa"
     longdesc="monalisa.html">
```

The `longdesc` should be an HTML file containing information about your picture, and could possibly contain links to alternative representations of the content.

15. Animations

Animations should be used sparingly in your pages, and try not to use ones that flicker at all. User agents are becoming better at allowing the users to stop animations (for example, IE5.5 allows you to hit the stop (or keyboard: *Escape* in some earlier versions of IE) button once a page has been fully loaded, freezing the images). Nevertheless many people still find animations distracting, and for some people it is difficult or impossible to read moving text.

Flickering should be especially avoided in pages, due to the risk of epileptic seizures for some of your visitors. The last thing that you want to do to your site viewers is physically harm them.

16. Abbreviations and Acronyms

Mark up abbreviations and acronyms with their respective elements, and provide expansions in the way of titles. For example:

```
<abbr title="World Wide Web Consortium">W3C</abbr>
```

You need only do this for the first instance of each particular acronym or abbreviation.

Note: browser support for these elements is limited. Netscape 6 and Opera 5.x display the expansion in the status bar, while older browsers do nothing.

17. Color

Don't rely on color alone. Some people cannot tell the difference between certain colors (for example, red-green color blindness, which is very common), so you should not use color alone to denote changes in content. Instead, use correct markup for emphasis (for example, the <em> element), and use style sheets to provide the presentational aspect. Users with particular needs can then override the style sheet you have implemented with their own, incorporating their own special styling designed to meet their particular needs.

You should also make sure that your color combinations and schemes contrast and display properly, for example, don't use yellow text on a yellow background! Light on dark or dark on light is preferred (usually the latter).

Why Most Pages Are Not Accessible

You may have noticed while surfing the Web that the majority of sites do not reach even the minimum level of accessibility, WCAG Level A compliancy. There are many reasons for this, but the biggest one is simply the fact that very few people understand just how difficult it is for some people to use the Web. HTML pages may consist of very rich media and scripting: JavaScript, Java Applets, Flash, and all sorts of embedded multimedia, and these technologies are very difficult to implement in an accessible manner. The two most common reasons given for not making embedded scripting/multimedia accessible are:

❑ It works for me!

❑ I have deadlines to conform to, and my boss told me to make a "flashy" page.

The first point is common-sense ridiculous: just because a page works for the author doesn't mean that it will work for everyone. Of course, it would also be ridiculous to suggest that a page can be "fully" accessible to all as well – but it's certainly easy enough to follow a few simple tips and at least make sure that your page has no significant accessibility barriers. The best thing to do is to test it on as many browsers and screen readers as you can possibly get your hands on. It can be quite humbling to view a page that you have used IE 5.5 to view in development with Lynx. We should also note that some browsers are very buggy, and some do not implement accessibility features very well. You don't have to provide hacks for every single browser deficiency out there, but you should at least be aware of them.

The second is a much larger problem to dispel. Web design is big business nowadays, and people expect their pages to look professional. Many designers work to deadlines, and many bosses don't understand the business advantages that accessibility can bring. Also, in training, many web site designers learn very bad practices that are difficult, but not impossible, to break out of later on. Many people do not actually realize just how quick and easy it is to add accessible alternatives.

A strategy that you can try if constrained by management, is to emphasize how standards compliant your pages are. The online development community is becoming increasingly aware of standards compliance. For example, Netscape 6 is portrayed as being a highly standards-compliant browser, and the IE 6 Preview Version has an excellent "standards compliance" mode that is switched on when a document has a recognized DTD set. Standards-compliance mode means that some CSS features (and others) are utilized that are not utilized in "normal mode". If you maintain pages that conform to certain W3C standards or utilize certain W3C products, such as HTML, XHTML, CSS, WCAG, Amaya, and so on, then you may find that there will be a logo that you can display on your pages to reinforce their accessibility to users and management. For example, the code for the WCAG Level A compliance logo is:

```
<a href ="http://www.w3.org/WAI/WCAG1A-Conformance"
          title="Explanation of Level A Conformance">
  <img height="32" width="88"
    src="http://www.w3.org/WAI/wcag1A"
    alt="Level A conformance icon,
        W3C-WAI Web Content Accessibility Guidelines 1.0"></a>
```

Note that paradoxically and ironically, if you use the WCAG-AA or WCAG-AAA conformance icons, you are actually breaking a P2 checkpoint, which states that you shouldn't use text in images (which the logos do). The reason for this checkpoint is that it is difficult for people to magnify text in bitmapped images. The alternatives are an HTML + CSS version, or preferably, an SVG version (see below).

Future Directions

So, where is accessibility going next? What new features should we be looking out for? People are gradually beginning to learn that accessible content means more business, and a better Web overall, and there is plenty of activity taking place to deal with accessibility problems. This includes a number of directions being considered by the WAI. Let's take a brief look at future paths for accessibility:

Accessible Multimedia

The W3C is working on ways to make multimedia inherently accessible. For example, they have pioneered the XML languages Scalable Vector Graphics (SVG) and Synchronized Multimedia Integration Language (SMIL). These languages are rich with accessible features, and it is easy to associate alternatives with any media created. Implementations are slow as ever, but more companies and individuals are picking them up. For more on both SVG and SMIL, see Chapter 21, *"New and Upcoming Standards"*.

Adaptive Content

One great future direction is adaptive content. This is the process of ensuring that the right content goes to the right person. For example, if a user states in some "profile" that they have stored on their computer that they are not color blind in any way, then that profile could be sent to the server on a page request and the appropriate HTML page and CSS style sheet be sent back. If someone indicates that their browser cannot use CSS, but can use proprietary `<font>` markup, then that can be delivered too. See Chapter 21, the *"Telling the Processor What to Output"* section for more on this.

Summary

We have looked at why accessibility is a problem in the WWW, and why fixing it is something that anyone can easily do, benefiting both themselves and others. We have seen what the WAI is, and how it was set up to help people understand what accessibility is, and how it releases material that can be used by others to create accessible web sites. In particular, we looked at the Web Content Accessibility Guidelines, and how they apply to HTML. We then looked at certain hints and tips to help make your HTML more accessible, and rounded it off with a discussion about the future of web accessibility.

We have seen that writing accessible and interoperable content can be a tremendous benefit for both the author and the user, but that it also takes a certain amount of training and a keen eye. However, the benefits are the same as those for any new skill learned: once you know how to write accessible content, you can keep on doing it.

Overall then:

❏ Think carefully about what your content means, and how best to represent it

❏ Become familiar with the HTML specification, and the WCAG guidelines and checkpoints, but more importantly, concentrate on the philosophy behind it

❏ Separate your content from presentation, and provide alternatives

❏ Emphasize how accessible your content is!

❏ Keep a lookout for new and more accessible technologies being developed by the W3C

Programmer'sReferenceHTML4.01Programmer'sReferenceHTML4.01Programmer'sReferenceHTML4.01

21

New and Upcoming Standards

This reference book has been primarily written to help you with HTML 4.01, but this is not enough to make your web pages last well into the future, or to let your pages be accessed by unlimited devices. This chapter will talk about why we need standards, how they help the Web develop, what the latest standards are, and what standards we can look forward to in the future.

Developing Trends

The Web has started to mature, slowly moving away from an anything-goes environment towards **media convergence** and **device independence**. Media convergence occurs when the different types of media are better integrated with each other and into the Web – integrating text, sound, color, and pictures is becoming easier and more effective. Device independence means that new and future technologies will allow data from a single source to be displayed appropriately on different platforms, regardless of whether the devices are PCs or mobile phones, or any other device. This co-operation to enable the distribution of data to different platforms is called **interoperability**. The only way true interoperability can be achieved is through a common recognized set of standards.

Why should you as a web designer care about standards? Your site works the way you want it to, but can you see it on a mobile phone? If you are like most people, you want your work to be as accessible as possible, to as many people as possible, for as long as possible, and all this with as little work as possible. This is why the Web became so popular so quickly – it was easy to publish anything for the entire world to see immediately. But over the very few years since its birth, the Web has become a world of bells, whistles, and non-standard coding (see Chapter 16 for examples of IE- and Netscape-specific coding). Not only do these things limit viewers from the real content of many sites; they require huge resources to create, maintain, and display – Can we say "browser bloat"? However, times and attitudes are changing.

People are realizing that it is a real hassle to make sure their site looks the same on 3 different versions of IE and 4 different versions of Netscape, not to mention on Windows, Mac, and Linux, among others. Then there are the mobile devices: cell phones, Palms, etc. (including those not yet invented, or course!). And what if you want to print the information that is displayed on those devices? Let us add to the list the new laws requiring accessibility for the disabled, applicable especially to public and government sites. On top of that, there's the database question: How should the content be organized and accessed?

The answer to dealing with all of this is to the ability to **define once, display everywhere**. This is a rather simple sounding idea that might seem impossible when you think of all the various devices, their capacities, limitations, and purposes. The only way this can happen is if all platforms and devices can work together, speaking the same scalable language. This is where standards step in.

Who Develops Web "Standards"?

Before we discuss what the standards are, let's review who develops the standards.

The W3C

As mentioned earlier in this book, the **World Wide Web Consortium (W3C)** is an organization that develops and introduces new technologies to the Web. It consists of representatives from many different companies working together to develop solutions for technical problems. They are responsible for all the official versions of HTML, as well as many other Internet technologies, and are continually updating and improving their work. The W3C is not an official standards organization *per se*, but does release **Recommendations** of how the group as a whole thinks a technology should be implemented. Because of the position the W3C has in relation to the World Wide Web its recommendations are often considered *de facto* standards. There is more information about the W3C at its web site at http://www.w3c.org.

The WAP Forum

Another group that works closely with the W3C is the **WAP Forum**, an organization currently developing better technologies for accessing the Web via wireless devices. Forum membership represents over 90% of the global handset market, as well as leading infrastructure providers, software developers, and other organizations. There is more information about the WAP Forum at its web site at http://www.wapforum.org.

In addition to the larger groups above there are numerous other organizations such as OASIS, which participate in developing various Internet and web technologies.

Consumers vs. Companies

In the end however, it comes down to the relationship between consumers and the companies who implement the "standards" or their own technologies. It is often said, that if the consumers aren't interested in something, the companies will not implement it. If it has been implemented already, and the customers don't like the technology, the company will drop it. On the other hand, if the companies never implement a technology, the consumers can't try it out. Here is an actual interchange overheard at the 8th International World Wide Web Conference held in Toronto, Canada, May 1999:

Question posed by Håkon Lie (formerly of the W3C, now with Opera):

"Why is there no full support for CSS1?"

Answer given by an immensely large software company, which shall remain unnamed:

(We are) "giving priority to user requests."

When different companies implement the same standards, but to different levels, or with proprietary additions, consumers must still switch between different types of software or hardware to access the different bells and whistles that make each company competitive. Chaos ensues.

Companies should work in conjunction with organizations like the W3C and the WAP Forum. Technology developed as a group effort tends to increase a market more effectively than battles between different technologies. When a party (a company for example) develops a technology by itself, it may potentially miss aspects that another party might see. Developing a technology as a group does not need to stifle competition or innovation, because the competition comes in the different ways a technology is implemented. Indeed, a commonly agreed upon set of rules looks limiting to begin with, but actually can open up more windows of opportunity for everyone, than a closely kept company secret. In the end we want a win-win situation for everyone: customers and companies alike.

The times are changing, and the standards recommended by the W3C are promoting interoperability as a group effort. But how can we learn to "interoperate"?

Modularization

The W3C has learned that the development of any type of new technology needs a clear conceptual standard guiding its future development. Many current technologies cannot be easily changed or added to without being redesigned in some fundamental way. Such self-containment invites proprietary additions and therefore compatibility conflicts. It also limits the development of the ideas that went into the technology to begin with. In the end, it is the users who can't see that web site because they don't have all the latest plug-ins.

Modularization provides the mechanism for giving a technology a guiding light into the future. When a technology is organized as modules defined by a set of general rules, it is much easier to create interfaces and specifications that allow communication with other technologies as well as additional modules. Applications implementing a modularized technology need contain only relevant components, and are therefore easier to test and maintain. Bugs are more easily localized and modules more easily updated or replaced. Modules can also be reused in different environments so the wheel is not constantly being reinvented.

Rather than leading to mutations (just think of all the browser-specific tags), modularization allows everyone to use the same rules to enhance the interoperability of a technology as a whole, while still allowing creativity and innovation.

Hot Technologies You Should be Familiar With

In this section, we'll take a very brief look at new technologies that have already been labeled as "standard" or are on their way to becoming "standard", but haven't already been discussed in detail in previous chapters:

❑ XML

❑ XHTML 1.0

❑ XHTML 1.1 Modularized

❑ XHTML Basic

❑ SMIL 1.0

❑ MathML

The red threads running though these and future standards are the concepts of **modularization** and **interoperability**.

XML: Describing Data

XML (eXtensible Markup Language) has been quite the buzzword for the past few years, but still very few people understand what it is or what it can and cannot do. As an ever-increasing number of web sites are becoming database-driven, and the choice of data format is often XML, it is important to understand its capabilities. In this section, we'll explain what XML really is, a few terms you might come across, and what this all means for modularization and your work.

The Purpose of XML

First of all, don't let the Markup part of the name mislead you. Both XML and HTML have their roots in SGML and use angle brackets, but this is where the similarities end. HTML is a static set of markup elements that is designed only for structuring a text-based document so it can be displayed in a web browser on a desktop computer. XML is a grammar for creating new markup, which can be specifically tailored to describe and structure data. XML has nothing to say about how the data should actually be displayed on a browser. There are other technologies for that.

Tim Berners-Lee, the inventor of HTML, envisions XML as a component of what he calls the **Semantic Web**, "a web of data that can be processed directly or indirectly by machines", which can be searched as though it were one giant database, rather than one giant book" (http://www.w3.org/2001/sw). For example, right now, when you search for something on the Web, a search engine can only look for documents containing a word you specify. This is like skimming a book for a keyword regardless of the different contexts or meanings the word can have. In a database, a piece of information can be uniquely defined. The vision of the Semantic Web is to be able to search for a piece of data on the Web and only get back results that are applicable to what you are looking for. One of the main tools to achieve this goal is data defined with XML.

What XML Does and Does Not Do

When we say that XML is used to describe the content of data, this does not mean there is an XML tag for every single type of content. On the contrary, XML just provides the angle brackets and the rules to define your own tags and structure, so you can tailor them to your data.

The following example is a To Do list marked up as XML data:

```
<list type="todo">
  <heading>My ToDo List</heading>
  <action priority="1" status="complete">get toilet
        paper</action>
  <action priority="2" status="open">finish chapter</action>
  <action priority="3" status="complete">clean room</action>
</list>
```

The tags in this code snippet are very clear about what kind of information they contain. It is a list of type "todo". It has a heading and the actions needing to be done, including their priority and status. But still, this XML snippet cannot DO anything by itself. We cannot stick this as-is in IE and expect the browser to know what to do with it, other than just displaying the code. It is just pure information wrapped in XML tags. We need intermediary software to send it, receive it, display it, or otherwise process it, such as Database Servers with XML compatibility (for example, SQL Server 2000).

Another point of interest is that the tags and attributes in the example above (`<action>` and `priority="1"`) are not defined in any XML standard. These tags and attributes were created by the author. However, what is set in the XML standards is the rules for creating these tags.

OK this is nice, but really, why would anyone want to use XML? Well, there are several reasons:

First, there is the whole question of data exchange. Following XML rules makes it easy to handle and exchange data, a vital element in, for example, the business world, either B2B or internally in a company. There are now many tools available to help you create, store, and transfer your XML data.

When you create your own markup in XML, you are not dependent on product vendors with proprietary data organization and management. XML is a standard and can be made to work with any application following the same standard. Of course, there will always be different implementations of the standards and vendors will still come up with proprietary formats, but XML has been designed to be flexible enough to hopefully reduce the temptation to stray from the path.

The markup you define using XML can make your data as self-describing as you want. This makes it more palatable for human consumption, as well as self-documenting.

XML lets you define not only the description of the data, but also the structure of the data and how each element interacts with the others. This lets you build rules against which your data documents can be checked for well-formedness and validity, to make sure everything is structured correctly. This can save you headaches in the future especially when transferred data needs to be converted into another XML format on a different system.

Defining the Structure of an XML Document Type

In order for XML data to be useful, its structure must be defined, that is, all the elements and attributes used in a particular type of XML document must be officially set up. Otherwise the devices accessing the information won't know how to interpret those elements. The two best-known ways of defining the structure of a document are with Document Type Definitions and XML Schemas.

Document Type Definitions (DTD) are an application of an SGML validation system. DTDs have been around a while, and there is a separate one for each version of HTML, as we saw in Chapter 1. Originally the intention was that DTDs were to be referenced directly by a browser, as machine-readable documents. However, so far none of the browser manufacturers have taken this route. Instead, the information on how to interpret each element defined in any HTML DTD has been hard coded directly into the browsers. This is why very old browsers have a hard time with more recent versions of HTML. They don't have the newer tags hardcoded into the program, or any way of referencing the actual DTD. The same goes for browser-specific elements.

Some of the limitations of DTDs are that they are very complicated to write and each element has certain dependencies. For example, how elements function is dependent on the order in which they appear in the DTD. DTDs are useful for validating names of elements and attributes, and for controlling multiplicity (the number of times a certain element can occur). However, DTDs cannot be used to carry out advanced validation such as range or type checking, and there is of course no support for **namespaces**, an integral part of XML-based languages.

The other "well-known" way of defining the structure of an XML document is by using an **XML Schema,** a type of document description analogous to a DTD. Schemas have several advantages over DTDs. Schemas are XML documents themselves and therefore share many of the same features as the XML languages they define. A Schema has different constraints and controls for setting up a new XML-based language than a DTD does. For example, the order in which an element or attribute is defined in a Schema is not as restrictive as it is in a DTD. There is also a greater number of datatypes available to Schemas. And of course, Schema technology is also extensible – the major theme in XML-based markup.

Originally, the language of Schemas, which became a W3C Recommendation in May 2001, was intended to be simple enough for a web designer to use but, alas, this is not how things have developed. A simplified version of Schemas has been proposed, but since the companies involved have not been able to reach a consensus of what should be included and what should be left out, an official simple Schema syntax has yet to appear. As a result, DTDs, which are supposed to be phased out eventually, will be with us for a while longer than expected. In the meantime, it looks as if the W3C is depending on third parties to create user-friendly Schema development tools to compensate for the high learning curve for Schema technology itself.

DTDs and XML Schemas are not the only options for defining an XML markup language. Here are several others, which give various levels of structure in your data.

XDR is Microsoft's version of XML Schema. Microsoft decided to not wait until XML Schema reached Recommendation level before releasing its own implementation, which is basically DTDs defined in XML. XDR is a major component in Microsoft's Biztalk business solutions (look at http://www.biztalk.org, or get hold of *Professional Biztalk* By Stephen Mohr et al. (ISBN: *1-861003-29-3*), published by Wrox Press). More information about XDR itself can be found at http://msdn.microsoft.com/library/psdk/xmlsdk/xmlp7k6d.htm.

The complexity of XML Schemas has inspired other parties to create their own versions of a simple Schema syntax. Among these are:

- **Tree Regular Expressions for XML (TREX)** by W3C invited expert James Clark

- **Regular Language Description for XML (RELAX)** developed by Murata Makoto under the auspices of the Japanese Standards Association

- **Schematron** by Rick Jelliffe

TREX is essentially the most relevant aspects of XML Schema with the assumption that these are the features that will be needed and used most. The features that are left out are those that are most complicated and not needed very often. TREX is limited to the validation of elements and their attributes and does not include features that would allow changes to the data or its structure. It supports namespaces and XML datatypes, as well. Further information about TREX can be found at http://www.oasis-open.org/committees/trex/index.shtml.

RELAX takes the features of DTDs and adds the expanded range of Schema datatypes, as well as XML-instance syntax and namespace support. The RELAX core has been submitted to the International Standards Organization as a technical report. You can find links to the latest information in English about RELAX at http://www.xml.gr.jp/relax/.

Schematron has very different approach to structuring XML documents from DTDs and Schemas. It relies more heavily on finding tree patterns in XML data than on comparing them to a set grammar, for example, defined by a DTD or Schema. Schematron schemas work very well with XPath and XSLT technologies, which we will discuss in the next section.

As an interesting side note, in an interview for *XMLHack*, Rick Jelliffe himself described XML Schemas as DTDs on steroids and Schematron schemas as DTDs on acid! You can find this interview at http://www.xmlhack.com/read.php?item=121. You can find more information about Schematron at http://www.ascc.net/xml/resource/schematron/schematron.html.

Transforming Raw XML Data into a Usable Form

So let's say you have chosen or created an XML-based language and marked up your data with the appropriate tags. This is great, but there is still the question of how any particular device or application can display this data. Most desktop browsers can only display content marked up in HTML, and in the newer browsers, CSS. HTML plus CSS is not an option for most other devices. This is where the **eXtensible Stylesheet Language (XSL)** comes in. XSL can be used to transform raw XML data into whatever form is needed, whether it is HTML styled with CSS, or XHTML Basic for cell phones, or some other XML markup language. What we provide here is only a brief overview, as XSL is such a deep and detailed subject – for more information on XSL, check out *Professional XSL* by Andrew Watt et al. (ISBN: *1-861003-57-9*), published by Wrox Press.

The XSL system is made up of three languages, each with a specific task:

- **XSLT (XSL Transformations)** describes a template-based language allowing one document structure to be mapped into another, for example, raw XML data into a different XML dialect, PDF, or HTML document, etc. XSLT 1.0 has been a W3C Recommendation since November 1999 and has already been implemented by several fully compliant XSLT processors.

❑ **XPath (XML Path Language)** is a very powerful XSL navigational and filtering tool. It defines specific parts or patterns of an XML document to be used in the selection of specific data. XPath defines an XML document as a tree of nodes. It uses syntax similar to filesystem addressing, basically setting a hierarchal path to each specific element (and attribute, processing instruction, etc.) in a document so it can be accessed and manipulated whenever needed.

❑ **XSL-FO (XSL Formatting Objects)** defines the display format of an XML document using a box model also used with CSS. It purposely has many similarities with HTML and CSS to facilitate learning it. The XSLT transformation can include XSL-FO to make the document display user-device-specific. If the document is to be viewed on a normal PC browser, the display format generated can be HTML/XHTML. You could even define a document to be viewed on a PDF viewer. If the presentation is to be on a voice-enabled browser then the content can be marked up with aural style sheet elements. See Chapter 14 for more information on aural style sheets.

Telling the Processor What to Output

In order to reach the goal of describe once – display anywhere, the software that transforms XML data into something a web-enabled device can understand needs a way of getting information about that device.

At the moment, there is no sure-fire way of getting very detailed information from a browser, but the W3C is developing a technology framework for this called **CC/PP (Composite Capabilities/Preferences Profiles.)** In this framework, when a device requests a web page, a server-side implementation of CC/PP would send back a request for the device's capability profile. If the device supports CC/PP, it would be able to send back a detailed profile that would let the server send a page transformed and especially formatted for that device. If the device does not have a CC/PP profile to send back, the server can create one by asking the device questions. CC/PP is better than current methods, which basically just guess what a browser can do, by finding out software and hardware versions, as well as a few other pieces of information, which may not be enough information. CC/PP can ask for actual properties describing the browser and its current capabilities. This allows for sophisticated content negotiation techniques between web servers and clients, to produce XML-based markup, appropriate for that specific client and its current settings.

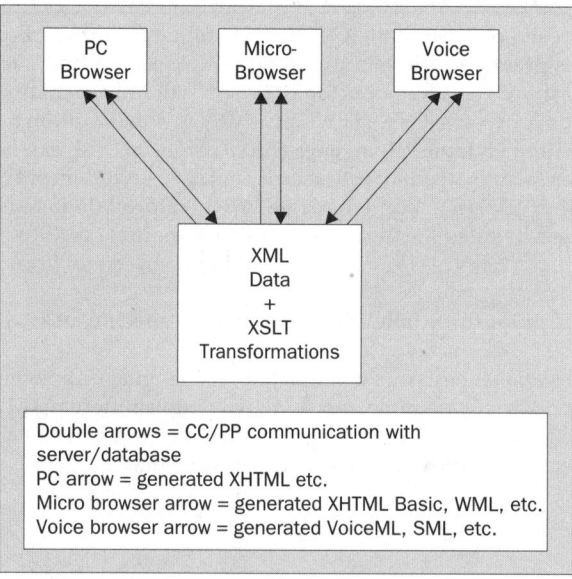

Double arrows = CC/PP communication with server/database
PC arrow = generated XHTML etc.
Micro browser arrow = generated XHTML Basic, WML, etc.
Voice browser arrow = generated VoiceML, SML, etc.

CC/PP is being designed to work with any web-enabled device that follows W3C Recommendations, from PDAs to desktop machines, to laptops, to WAP phones, to phone browsers, to web television units, and to specialized browsers for users with disabilities. Even those web devices that aren't able to send CC/PP profiles can still be asked more detailed questions than current questioning software does. Proxies may also be used to provide markup transformation, transmission, or caching services for CC/PP-enabled clients and servers. For more information about CC/PP, visit: http://www.w3.org/Mobile/CCPP/.

Currently there are no publicly announced implementations of CC/PP, but Apache's Cocoon, a web publishing system that implements XML and XSL, does something similar to what is envisioned for CC/PP. Cocoon allows browser-specific document publishing using the media attribute in XSL. For example, if `media="wap"` is used, then only a page that a WAP-enable phone can display is sent. More information about Cocoon can be found at http://xml.apache.org/cocoon/guide.html.

Now that we've taken a look at the core technologies that are the future of the web, let's get more practical. One way of preparing XML data is to create other more purpose-specific markup languages. That is the **X** in eXtensible.

XHTML 1.0

HTML continues to evolve. As we first discussed in Chapter 1, the latest step in its evolution is the leap to **XHTML**, the **eXtensible Hypertext Markup Language**. XHTML 1.0 has been a W3C Recommendation since January 2001. The next version XHTML 1.1 is a Proposed Recommendation. We'll look at XHTML 1.0 in this section first, before going on to XHTML 1.1 later.

"Oh, no! Not another version of HTML!" you might say – "the last version is giving me enough headaches". But wait! The differences between HTML 4.01 and XHTML 1.0 are not earth shattering. XHTML is simply HTML 4.01 defined in XML. Those who venture into the world of XML/XHTML will be confronted with the basic XML concepts of **well-formedness** and **validity**. Well-formedness means that all the elements in the code are correctly formed and placed in relationship to the other elements. Valid means that only correct elements and attributes are used.

What sort of changes will you need to make? Here is the short list of things that XHTML code needs to work now and in the future. Each point will be explained in the following sections:

❑ The DOCTYPE, root element, and namespace need to be declared in the header

❑ The code needs to well-formed

❑ The code needs to be valid

❑ CSS and scripting data must not interfere with the XML parser

In addition to changes in how you write your code, you also need to be aware that not all the changes needed to transform an HTML document into an XHTML document are accepted in every browser.

DOCTYPES, Root Elements, and Namespaces

Using the XHTML standard means your documents can be formally read by an XML parser (if your browser has one). To make this happen you need an **XML Declaration** and a **DOCTYPE** in the header of your document.

The XML declaration is not required, but if you don't use it, the XML parser will not be activated and the browser will default to its hard coded version of HTML 4.0 for displaying the document. In the examples below you will also notice that the XML Declaration includes an `encoding` attribute. This is required if you want a character encoding other than the browser default (usually `UTF-8` or `UTF-16`). If you do use the XML Declaration, be aware that only the latest browsers have XML parsers – older browsers may simply display the code as text.

Note: The first version released of IE 5.0 for Mac has a bug in its XML parser, which sometimes chokes on the `<?xml 1.0?>` declaration. This has since been fixed but there are people still using this version.

The `DOCTYPE` references the **DTD (Document Type Definition)** in the header of the document. This tells the world as well as the XML parser which W3C standard the document should conform to. Like HTML 4.01, XHTML 1.0 has three `DOCTYPES`:

❑ XHTML 1.0 Strict: This `DOCTYPE` is not backwards compatible, and disallows use of deprecated tags. CSS or other XML-compatible styles are required for formatting that goes beyond the browser default settings:

```
<?xml version="1.0" encoding="iso-8859-1"?>
<!DOCTYPE html PUBLIC "-//W3C//DTD XHTML 1.0 Strict//EN"
          "http://www.w3.org/TR/xhtml1/DTD/xhtml1-strict.dtd">
```

❑ XHTML 1.0 Transitional: This `DOCTYPE` is backwards compatible, and lets you use deprecated tags. This is what you should use if your users have older browsers:

```
<?xml version="1.0" encoding="iso-8859-1"?>
<!DOCTYPE html PUBLIC "-//W3C//DTD XHTML 1.0 Transitional//EN"
          "http://www.w3.org/TR/xhtml1/DTD/xhtml1-transitional.dtd">
```

❑ XHTML 1.0 Frameset: This is required when using frame sets. Frames fans should not get too excited however. Frames have been officially deprecated, so one day you will have to replace your frame sets with something else, for example, CSS2 (when it has better browser support):

```
<?xml version="1.0" encoding="iso-8859-1"?>
<!DOCTYPE html PUBLIC "-//W3C//DTD XHTML 1.0 Frameset//EN"
          "http://www.w3.org/TR/xhtml1/DTD/xhtml1-frameset.dtd">
```

Root Elements and Namespaces

Next you need to include the **root element** and **namespace**. After the `DOCTYPE` declaration, every document must start with an `<html>` tag, and end with a closing `</html>` tag. This is the root, or all-encompassing element of any XHTML document. The "root" element is the main node of the XML tree structure of a XHTML document. There can be only one root element in a document. All the other elements contained in the HTML root are subordinate to, that is, children of that root node.

The opening <html> tag needs to include the XML namespace attribute xmlns for XHTML. An XML namespace is the collection of the names of the elements and attributes used in a specific XML-based markup language. Ideally, a browser should be able to use this information to avoid ambiguity when two different namespaces or tag sets are used in the same document, especially when both may contain tags that look the same but have different attributes. The elements in each tag set would use a specific prefix before each element name. It's a bit like a train chugging down a track and coming to a track switch. Ideally, when the browser comes to a tag in a different namespace it should switch to another track.

Currently, browsers can't do anything with the namespace attribute. The HTML tag set they use is hard coded into the program and they have no way of processing anything else, but hopefully we'll have namespace-aware browsers in the future. This will become more necessary as people start creating their own sets of markup elements and using them publicly.

```
<html xmlns="http://www.w3.org/1999/xhtml">
  <body>
    ...body content...
  </body>
</html>
```

Well-formed Documents

The concept of a well-formed document seems like common sense, but no one has ever forced us to write well-formed HTML, not even the browsers. This is actually one of the main reasons browsers have become so large. Today's browsers have been designed to try to outguess even the most-badly written HTML document. But this takes a lot of resources and has resulted in browser bloat.

So one of the most important things you need to get used to is that XHTML documents must be well-formed if they are to be parsed correctly. When a browser has an XML parser built in, there is no need for it to guess what kind of document it is looking at if the document can simply be parsed. If a document is not well-formed, it simply won't be displayed. You might think, "Oh what a hassle" or "I don't need to worry about that yet". But hey, if the document is well-formed from the beginning, there is no tweaking necessary in the future.

Elements Must Be Correctly Nested

It has always been sloppy to let your tags overlap, not least because different browsers are likely to display the overlap differently. For example, when the HTML processor in IE looks at a page, it starts from the beginning of the code, while Netscape's HTML processor starts from the bottom. In addition, this again requires the browser to do a lot of resource-hogging guesswork.

In XHTML, all tags must be correctly nested, even if this means repeating tags:

This code snippet is well-formed:

```
<p><b>Captain <i>Scarlett</i> and the </b>Mysterons</p>
```

This code snippet, however, is not well-formed:

```
<p><b>Captain <i>Scarlett</b> and the </i>Mysterons</p>
```

Elements Have to Be Closed

At this point all browsers and all versions of HTML up to version 4.0 allow "incomplete" tags and tag sets. For example, the two best known, most commonly used incomplete tag sets in HTML are probably <p> and <br>. With <p>, not only is it possible to open two paragraphs in succession, without closing the first, but you don't even need to open a paragraph at the point where the paragraph starts. So, both of the next two examples will be accepted by all current browsers:

```
<p>Text to make up the first paragraph
<p>And more text to make up the second paragraph
```

```
<p>Text to make up the first paragraph<p>
And more text to make up the second paragraph
```

In XHTML, this is no longer allowed because these code fragments are not well-formed. If either of these fragments were in an otherwise valid XHTML document, which was then put through a validator, the validator would spit out at least four errors. So, now when you use "paired" tags you must include both opening and closing tags, as in this fragment:

```
<p>Text to make up the first paragraph</p>
<p>And more text to make up the second paragraph</p>
```

There are some HTML elements, which have no content and are therefore "empty", for example,
 (line break), <img > (image) and <hr> (horizontal line). Because these "empty" elements don't have standard closing tags, in XHTML they must be closed by adding a backslash before the closing bracket, or be rejected by validators:

❑
 becomes

❑ <img src="any.gif"> becomes <img src="any.gif"/>

❑ <hr> becomes <hr/>

Note: Including a single space before the backslash in a "empty" tag works more reliably in browsers generally, that is, <br /> rather than <br/>, although both are valid.

Tag Names and Attributes Must Be in Lowercase

Writing tag names, attributes, and attribute values in upper case has become the *de facto* web page standard even though in HTML it technically doesn't matter. However if you want to use XHTML, this is no longer the case. XHTML, like XML, has been defined as case sensitive, and the decision was made to user lower case for all tag names, attributes, and attribute values. So from now on, when writing in XHTML, all tag names and attributes must be written in lower case:

No longer acceptable:

```
<LINK REL="STYLESHEET" HREF="style/default.css" TYPE="text/css">
```

Well-formed:

```
<link rel="stylesheet" href="style/default.css" type="text/css" />
```

Attributes Must Have Values

In HTML, it is legal to shorten certain attributes and rely on default values for those attributes. Using XHTML requires that this guesswork be removed. This reduces the resources the browser needs, as well as making the code cleaner. So, all the information for an attribute needs to be supplied, including the =" " and its value:

In the following example `checked` and `disabled` are minimized:

```
<input type="checkbox" checked>
<button value="Press Here" disabled>
```

Below is the well-formed way of writing this line:

```
<input type="checkbox" checked="checked"/>
<button value="Press Here" disabled="disabled" />
```

Attribute Values Must Be in Quotes

In HTML, you didn't need quote marks around attribute values, but when using XHTML you do. It is still up to you, however, whether to use single quotes or double quotes (but each pair must be of the same kind):

In the following examples the quotes are either missing or inconsistent:

```
<input id=text>
<input id='text">
```

The example below, however, is well formed:

```
<input id="text" />
```

This is an example of how you could use both single and double quotes in an attribute. This only works for attributes that allow character data:

```
<input id="input" value="Enter a 'value' here!" />
```

Valid Documents

A valid document is one that contains only the elements and attributes contained in the namespace declared in the HTML root element. Right now browsers cannot check namespaces but hopefully the future will bring browsers that can. This will become more important as developing XML-based technologies will use more than one namespace in a document. For the moment, we have to rely on external validators to help us make sure we use the right elements and attributes in our documents.

Changing Names to ids

HTML 4.0 introduced the `id` attribute, which replaces the deprecated `name` attribute. XHTML, true to its XML roots, takes the `id` one step further and requires that if the (optional) `id` is used, it must be unique. The purpose of both the "name" and "id" attributes is to provide an identifier for an element. The main difference between the two attributes is that if you do use an `id`, its value must be unique, while the value of a `name` need not. This means that two different elements in an XHTML document cannot have the same `id` value.

There are several very good reasons for using unique ids regardless of whether you are using XHTML or not:

❑ Data submission: ids are often used in forms. The value of an id is what identifies a piece of information submitted to a database. Depending the database system, a unique id tells the database, for example, that one person is different than another even, if they are both named John. Imagine the chaos if you had three form controls, a name input, an address input, and a city input which each of these had an id="input"; a relational database would complain and only record one of the values. An XML database would say "You're kidding, right?" and reject the whole submission because it is invalid.

❑ Error prompting: Using a scripting language such as JavaScript, you can have an alert box pop up if someone doesn't fill out an input field in a form before submitting. That alert box usually refers to the id of the field that was not filled out. If more than one field has the same id how would the user know which field the alert box refers to?

❑ Manipulating objects: Many Web designers use JavaScript to manipulate objects on a page, for example, images used as navigational elements. You can reference objects by their order in directory rather than with an id. The first object is object "0", the second is "1", etc. But if you need to change the order by adding a new object, then you need to change all of these numbers. This is a pain. Using unique id's lets you reference these objects in an orderly fashion independent of directory order. There is also no ambiguity which object a script is referencing.

❑ Manageable code: It is just common sense to give each element a unique id. Not only do that, but give an id value that makes sense, so that if others need to look at your code it more understandable.

❑ Future tags for XHTML: The next step after XHTML 1.0 is XHTML 1.1, which allows Modularization. Many designers look forward to the time when they will be able to use modules with new specialized tag sets, yet to be developed. These new tags will of course follow the strict rules required by XML and future browsers will parse pages using these rules.

Note: There is a bug in the XHTML 1.0 strict DTD. The deprecated name attribute was not excluded from the <a></a> anchor tag, so an anchor tag with a name attribute will validate under XHTML 1.0 strict even though it shouldn't.

Validation and Conversion Aids

Most of the changes you need to make to convert your existing HTML code into XHTML are relatively minor, but actually making the changes by hand can be a huge amount of work. There are several tools available that help you not only convert your old files to XHTML, but help you make them well-formed and valid as well. The W3C provides an online validation service at http://validator.w3.org/.

You can also check you pages locally on your own hard drive by downloading and installing Dave Raggett's **HTML Tidy** found at (http://www.w3.org/People/Raggett/tidy/). On this page there is a list of versions for just about any operating system. HTML Tidy can be configured to "tidy" up your documents by checking for and fixing problems with well-formedness and validity.

Mozquito Technologies also has a software package that not only lets you check documents using one of the three XHTML 1.0 DOCTYPES for well-formedness and validity, it also includes a new namespace, XHTML-FML 1.0. This is a tag set for the Mozquito version of the HTML 4.0 Forms elements. You can download a 30-day trial version of the Mozquito Factory at http://www.mozquito.com.

Once your pages are valid, you can proudly display the logo below (found at http://www.w3.org).

Scripts and Styles in a Document

A browser has several mechanisms for processing the code in a document. If a browser has an XML parser, it is used to process XHTML. Unfortunately, CSS styles and JavaScript are not understood by this parser, and cause it to choke. If you embed styles or scripting data in your XHTML document, you need to put them inside **character data (CDATA)** tags so that the XML parser knows to skip those parts:

```
<style>
<![CDATA[
        body {background-color:#FFFFFF;
              background-image:url(img.gif);
              background-repeat:no-repeat;
              background-attachment:fixed;
              }
        ]]>
</style>
```

```
<script type="text/javascript">
  <![CDATA[
    document.write("<b>This is great!<\/b>");
  ]]>
</script>
```

I'm sure you're asking, "Does this work on my browser?" The answer to this is yes *but* only if your browser has an XML parser. This means IE 5.0 and higher, Netscape 6.0 and higher, and Opera 5.0 and higher. Unfortunately, this is an aspect of XHTML that fails in the area of backwards compatibility. Older browsers can access the style and scripting information but only if the style and scripting code is in comments, but then the newer browsers have problems. The best solution at the moment is to reference external style sheets and scripts, bypassing the CDATA question entirely.

Beyond XHTML 1.0

Now that we've gone and shown how simple changing to XHTML 1.0 can be, and that people have even started to use it – let's junk it. Well, this may sound rather harsh, but that is what will happen eventually. XHTML 1.0, despite its roots, is not modular. There are the three DOCTYPES we mentioned and that's it. But that's OK. It was only ever meant as a bridge to help us from HTML to XHTML 1.1 and its modules.

XHTML 1.1

When we talk about XHTML and modularity, we are talking about XHTML 1.1. This is the point where we finally get off the fence and look towards the future of designing web pages. As of May 2001, XHTML 1.1 was still on the W3C's Proposed Recommendation list but it shouldn't be long before it reaches final Recommendation stage.

XHTML 1.1 has the same requirements as XHTML 1.0 when it comes to how the document set up:

❑ The DOCTYPE, root element and namespace need to be declared in the header.

❑ The code needs to be well-formed.

❑ The code needs to be valid.

❑ CSS and scripting data must not interfere with the XML parser.

Here is a sample XHTML 1.1 document with the DOCTYPE declaration in the header:

```
<?xml version="1.0"?>
<!DOCTYPE html PUBLIC "-//W3C//DTD XHTML 1.1//EN"
          "http://www.w3.org/TR/xhtml11/DTD/xhtml11.dtd">
<html xmlns="http://www.w3.org/1999/xhtml" xml:lang="en">
  <head>
    <title>XHTML 1.1</title>
  </head>
  <body>
    ...body content...
  </body>
</html>
```

The small differences between XHTML 1.0 Strict and XHTML 1.1 are:

❑ The lang attribute has been removed in favor of the xml:lang attribute.

❑ The name attribute in the <a> and <map> elements has been totally replaced by the id attribute.

Some of the not-so-small differences are:

❑ <ruby> elements have been added. Ruby is the term used for a run of text used for notation or pronunciation in the vicinity of another run of text known as the "base". Ruby is often used when working with Asian fonts.

❑ All deprecated functions and elements found in XHTML 1.0 and HTML 4.0 have been removed. This means that styles such as CSS are absolutely necessary if you want any sort of style layout other than the browser default settings.

❑ All XHTML elements and attributes have been organized into modules. This brings us to the next section.

XHTML Modularization

The big difference between XHTML 1.0 and XHTML 1.1 is **modularization**. Modularization is one step in enabling you to extend XHTML's reach on emerging platforms. The W3C has worked out a system in the Recommendation titled the Modularization of XHTML (April, 2001), which not only lets you reuse tools created by the W3C, but also lets you add your own. In this Recommendation, you will find all the requirements for setting up your own XHTML dialect using DTDs. You can mix and match DTD modules, like playing with Lego blocks, creating tailor-made DTDs for hybrid document types. The following sections are only a brief overview of what the Modularization of XHTML entails. Please visit http://www.w3.org/TR/xhtml-modularization/ for the complete details.

XHTML Abstract Modules

Document Type Definitions can be a bit intimidating at first glance. To make it easier for humans to actually understand what a DTD is supposed to do, it is divided into smaller modules called **Abstract Modules**. These modules are structured with normal text in addition to a few simple conventions, so that you should be able to understand which elements and attributes a DTD defines without too many problems.

XHTML Abstract Modules define the XHTML elements, their attributes, and the rules defining what kind of data a specific element can contain and how these elements can be nested (the content models). Here are the modules already available to you for creating a new document type.

The Core Modules

These modules are required in all XHTML dialects:

❑ **The Structure Module:** This delivers the structure for the XHTML document and, together with the DOCTYPE declaration and the XML declaration, builds its framework. The elements included in this module are `<html>`, `<head>`, `<title>`, and `<body>`.

❑ **The Text Module:** This defines the text container elements, and their attributes and content modules. The elements are: `<abbr>`, `<acronym>`, `<address>`, `<blockquote>`, `<br/>`, `<cite>`, `<code>`, `<dfn>`, `<div>`, `<em>`, `<h1>`, `<h2>`, `<h3>`, `<h4>`, `<h5>`, `<h6>`, `<kbd>`, `<p>`, `<pre>`, `<q>`, `<samp>`, `<span>`, `<strong>`, and `<var>`.

❑ **The Hypertext Module:** This consists of the `<a>` element, which defines hypertext links to other resources.

❑ **The List Module:** This provides elements for unordered lists, ordered lists, and definition lists. The elements are `<ul>`, `<ol>`, `<li>`, `<dl>`, `<dt>`, and `<dd>`.

❑ **The Object Module:** This module delivers the `<object>` element if an external application is called. The following modules are not required in all XHTML dialects, and serve as extensions to the core, when more specialized functions are required.

The Presentational Text Modules

❑ **The Presentation Module:** This provides elements, their attributes, and a minimal content model for simple presentation-related markup. The elements are `<b>`, `<big>`, `<hr/>`, `<i>`, `<small>`, `<sub>`, `<sup>`, and `<tt>`.

❑ **The Edit Module**: This module defines elements and attributes for use in editing-related markup; `<del>`, `<ins>`. These elements are new and are used to indicate inserted and deleted content in edited pages. Web-based information citations can be given with the attribute `cite="(URI)"`, and the attribute `datetime` can put the date and time of a change on the edited material.

❑ **The Bidirectional Text Module:** This is a result of the move towards internationalization. The `<bdo>` element, along with the `dir` attribute can be used with the inline Text Module elements to declare the direction of text.

The Forms Modules

❑ **The Basic Forms Module:** This module provides the basic form elements found in HTML 3.2. It includes `<form>`, `<label>`, `<input>`, `<select>`, `<option>`, and `<textarea>`.

❑ **The Forms Module:** This provides all of the forms features found in HTML 4.0. It includes `<form>`, `<input>`, `<select>`, `<option>`, `<textarea>`, `<button>`, `<fieldset>`, `<label>`, and `<optgroup>`. As you see, this module also contains all the content sets and their elements as seen above in the Basic Forms Module. It is a superset of the Basic Forms Module, and therefore, these modules may not be used together in a single document type.

The Tables Modules

❑ **The Basic Tables Module:** This provides basic table-related elements. The elements are `<caption>`, `<table>`, `<td>`, `<th>`, and `<tr>`.

❑ **The Tables Module:** This provides all of the table-related elements: `<caption>`, `<table>`, `<td>`, `<th>`, `<tr>`, `<col>`, `<colgroup>`, `<tbody>`, `<thead>`, and `<tfoot>`. The elements `<tbody>` and `<thead>` are especially useful for indicating where you are in a table when using a non-visual browser. You cannot have both the Basic Tables Module and the Tables Module together in one document type since the Basic Tables Module is a subset of the Tables Module.

The Image Modules

❑ **The Image Module:** This provides basic image embedding with `<img>`, and may be used in some implementations independently of client-side image maps.

❑ **The Client-side Image Map Module:** This provides the elements `<area>` and `<map>` for client-side image maps. It requires that the Image Module (or another module that supports the `<img>` element) be included.

❑ **The Server-side Image Map Module:** This provides support for image-selection and transmission of selection coordinates with the `ismap` for `<img>`. It requires that the Image Module (or another module that supports the `<img>` element) be included.

The Frames Modules

In XHTML 1.0, frames were deprecated and the current Proposed Recommendation for XHTML 1.1 does not include the frame modules. However, the Modularization of XHTML Recommendation does include the following frames modules for the purposes of backwards-compatibility and individual need.

❑ **The Frames Module:** This provides the frame-related elements `<frameset>`, `<frame>`, and `<noframes>`.

❑ **The Target Module:** The content of a frame can specify destination targets for a selection. This module adds the `target` attribute to the following elements so they can be the targets of a frameset. This module includes `<a>`, `<area>`, `<link>`, `<form>`, and `<base>`.

❑ **The Iframe Module:** This module contains one element, `<iframe>`, which defines inline frames.

Other Modules

- **The Intrinsic Events Module:** This module adds the attributes `onblur`, `onfocus`, `onreset`, `onsubmit`, `onload`, `onunload`, `onchange`, `onselect` to the following elements: `<a>`, `<area>`, `<form>`, `<body>`, `<frameset>`, `<label>`, `<input>`, `<select>`, `<textarea>`, `<button>`, and `<frame>`.

- **The Meta-information Module:** This defines the `<meta>` element that describes information within the XHTML document `<head>` element.

- **The Scripting Module:** This defines the elements `<script>` and `<noscript>` that are used to contain information pertaining to executable scripts or the lack of support for executable scripts.

- **The Style Sheet Module:** This enables the processing of style sheets, and is used to define the layout of an XHTML document and the appearance of its elements.

- **The Style Attribute Module:** According to the Proposed Recommendation of XHTML 1.1, the `<style>` attribute has been deprecated. However, the Modularization of XHTML Recommendation includes it, meaning that DTD builders can still include inline CSS style support for their XHTML languages.

- **The Link Module:** This defines a `<link>` element that can be used to define links to external resources. These resources often enhance the user agent's ability to process the associated XHTML document.

- **The Base Module:** This defines the `<base>` element that can be used to define a base URL against which relative URIs in the document will be resolved.

- **The Ruby Annotation Module:** This is used to define Ruby text, for example, when including Asian fonts. The elements are `<ruby>`, `<rbc>`, `<rtc>`, `<rb>`, `<rt>`, and `<rb>`. Note that this module is included in XHTML 1.1, but so far not in the Modularization of XHTML Recommendation. However, you can still use the module in putting together your own XHTML DTD. Look at the Ruby Annotation Proposed Recommendation (April 2001) at http://www.w3.org/TR/ruby/ for more information on the Ruby DTD Module.

- **The Name Identification Module:** This module defines the deprecated attribute `name` for the other deprecated elements. This is for the purposes of backwards-compatibility. If you do use this, be aware that you still have to use the `id` attribute, and the values for both need to be the same. In addition, the `name` attribute cannot be used as an XML fragment identifier.

- **The Legacy Module:** This defines elements and attributes that have been deprecated by the W3C in previous versions of HTML and XHTML. While the use of these elements and attributes is no longer encouraged, they facilitate the step from backwards-compatibility to current standards. Please note that in the Recommendation for XHTML Modularization the frames modules are not listed under the Legacy Module but are in the Legacy Module DTD.

XHTML DTD Modules

As we've mentioned before, XHTML uses a Document Type Definition (DTD) to define what the elements and attributes are, and how they should interact. This DTD is a separate machine-readable document that defines the rules and functionality of the markup language. It is a kind of "user's guide" for applications to check the well-formedness and validity of an XHTML document. Even if a browser cannot handle a DTD, they are useful to look at if you ever have questions of which elements and attributes are being used in a markup language.

It's not hard to look for basic information. Here is an example of what a DTD module looks like. As whole DTDs and even some DTD modules are relatively long, we have chosen the Inline Structural Module for the `<br />` and `<span>` elements, a short module where you can see some basic features of a DTD.

```
<!-- ............................................................ -->
<!-- XHTML Inline Structural Module ............................. -->
<!-- file: xhtml-inlstruct-1.mod

        This is XHTML, a reformulation of HTML as a modular XML application.
        Copyright 1998-2001 W3C (MIT, INRIA, Keio), All Rights Reserved.
        Revision: $Id: xhtml-inlstruct-1.mod,v 4.0 2001/04/02 22:42:49 altheim
        Exp $ SMI

        This DTD module is identified by the PUBLIC and SYSTEM identifiers:

            PUBLIC "-//W3C//ELEMENTS XHTML Inline Structural 1.0//EN"
            SYSTEM "http://www.w3.org/TR/xhtml-modularization/DTD/xhtml-
            inlstruct-1.mod"

        Revisions:
        (none)
..................................................................... -->

<!-- Inline Structural

        br, span

        This module declares the elements and their attributes
        used to support inline-level structural markup.
-->

<!-- br: forced line break ............................ -->

<!ENTITY % br.element  "INCLUDE" >
<![%br.element;[

<!ENTITY % br.content  "EMPTY" >
<!ENTITY % br.qname  "br" >
<!ELEMENT %br.qname;  %br.content; >

<!-- end of br.element -->]]>

<!ENTITY % br.attlist  "INCLUDE" >
<![%br.attlist;[
<!ATTLIST %br.qname;
        %Core.attrib;
>
<!-- end of br.attlist -->]]>

<!-- span: generic inline container .................... -->

<!ENTITY % span.element  "INCLUDE" >
<![%span.element;[
<!ENTITY % span.content
```

```
        "( #PCDATA | %Inline.mix; )*"
   >
   <!ENTITY % span.qname  "span" >
   <!ELEMENT %span.qname;  %span.content; >
   <!-- end of span.element -->]]>

   <!ENTITY % span.attlist  "INCLUDE" >
   <![%span.attlist;[
   <!ATTLIST %span.qname;
         %Common.attrib;
   >
   <!-- end of span.attlist -->]]>

   <!-- end of xhtml-inlstruct-1.mod -->
```

Inside each set of comments, a particular part of the module is explained, starting out with the module title and then the file type and whether any revisions have been made to the original module. After this comes a section stating which elements the module defines, in this case <br /> and <span>. The next section actually defines the <br /> element, and is not as easy to read as the previous sections.

```
   <!ENTITY % br.element  "INCLUDE" >
```

The above code is a command to include the <br /> element as an entity in the DTD.

```
   <![%br.element;[

   <!ENTITY % br.content  "EMPTY" >
   <!ENTITY % br.qname  "br" >
   <!ELEMENT %br.qname;  %br.content; >

   <!-- end of br.element -->]]>
```

The section sets what kind of content the <br /> tag can have (none, in this case) and its name.

```
   <!ENTITY % br.attlist  "INCLUDE" >
```

The next command above is to set up the list of attributes available to the <br /> element.

```
   <![%br.attlist;[
   <!ATTLIST %br.qname;
         %Core.attrib;
   >
   <!-- end of br.attlist -->]]>
```

This section above sets which attributes <br /> can have, in this case, the universal attributes found in the Common Attributes Definitions module and include id, class, and title. The section for the <span> element is structured the same way with just a few differences, that is, it can have text content and more attributes.

Here is a link to a tutorial included in the Modularization of XHTML for putting together your own simple DTD, as well as working with XHTML modules for your own XHTML DTD:

http://www.w3.org/TR/xhtml-modularization/dtd_developing.html#sec_E.4

As the XHTML DTD is a seperate document too, and because it describes the rules and the functions of a modular markup language, the XHTML DTD is also based on a series of modules:

❏ **XHTML Character Entities Module:** This defines a collection of named character entities made available by the respective XHTML DTD.

❏ **XHTML Modular Framework Module:** This consists of a set of support modules, which define tools to simplify the definition of XHTML DTD content models.

❏ **XHTML Module Implementations Module:** This contains the formal definition of each of the XHTML Abstract Modules as a DTD module and therefore is a type of "template" describing how to write a Document Type Definition.

❏ **XHTML DTD Support Modules:** These are elements of the XHTML DTD that are hidden from regular users but need to be understood when creating other XHTML family members.

If you are interested in creating your own XHTML family member, you can get all the details on how to do this at http://www.w3.org/TR/xhtml-building.

Extensibility: The "X" Within XHTML

The whole XHTML world has turned towards **extensibility** – the "X" in XHTML. Extending XHTML will be the ultimate challenge for client manufacturers, document authors, and content providers when they realize they need to provide more than just presentational markup for their customers. Anyone can use the extensible architecture of XHTML to set up document types that meet their needs. Of course, if you want to do this, then you will have to follow the rules of XHTML Modularization in order to be integrated within the growing number of XHTML family members.

To become an XHTML family member, a new module has to follow certain rules:

❏ Standards: Modules must implement methods defined by the W3C.

❏ Unique Identifiers: Modules must use unique identifiers to tell the client agent (that is, a browser) that it should use this different module found in a certain DTD or Schema instead of the original module.

❏ Required Modules: XHTML languages will need to include a minimum set of modules: the Basic Structure Module, the Hypertext Module, the Text Module, and the List Module within the respective DTD or Schema.

❏ Namespaces: Additional sets of elements and attributes have to be defined in their own unique XML namespaces, to avoid conflicts with other languages that contain identically-named elements.

❏ Validation: Documents written with this new XHTML language must validate against the DTD or Schema for that language.

One example of an extended version of XHTML is **XHTML-FML**, the Forms Markup Language from Mozquito Technologies, a member of the W3C. FML is an XHTML dialect with its own DTD and namespace. The DTD includes the same elements and attributes as XHTML 1.0, as well as additional DTD modules that replace the XHTML Forms module. Since current browsers do not recognize the new FML namespace, Mozquito technology inserts the element functionality directly into the XHTML document, getting around the browser's hard coded tag base. For more information about XHTML-FML, Mozquito Technologies support of XHTML and its work with the W3C, please visit http://www.mozquito.com.

XHTML Basic

Basic is a good name for this dialect of XHTML, because it is designed for devices that can only handle the basics, for example, mobile phones, palm organizers, car navigation systems, TVs, smart watches, pagers, etc. Other devices that are not necessarily small but have limited RAM and CPU power include printers, vending machines, digital book readers, and kitchen appliances. The capabilities of small devices are growing by leaps and bounds, but they will not be able to process XHTML even to the level of today's normal PCs for a long time yet. However, these devices have already started to make inroads into the Internet.

Creating a mini-version of an HTML-type language is not a new idea. **Compact HTML (cHTML)** has been in limited use for a few years and the Japanese have been quite successful with **iMode**, a type of mobile content delivery platform that uses cHTML as it's base language. The WAP Forum's **Wireless Markup Language (WML)** also belongs to the list of markup languages for mobile phones. All of these languages are proprietary though, device-specific, and are not mutually compatible, so the W3C developed XHTML Basic, which will replace them in future.

XHTML Basic is one of the first implementations of XHTML Modularization to have become a W3C Recommendation, doing so in December 2000. XHTML Basic includes the minimum number of XHTML modules to be an XHTML language. It can be used as it is, but it is meant to be a **host language**. A host language is a base to which you can add other XHTML modules or your own.

Creating an XHTML Basic document requires putting thought into scale and organization. Many normal XHTML tags cannot be used because they are simply impractical or impossible to use in a small environment. Sticking to Accessibility Guidelines will get you far. Here are the types of tags that just don't work:

❑ **Inline Styles**: The document should link to an external style sheet instead. If a device cannot use a style sheet, it should not forced to download unusable data.

❑ **Scripting languages and Objects:** These are power-hungry, device-dependent applications that small devices choke on. The developing XHTML Events module has a limited solution for small devices, but in the meantime forget mouseovers (especially if the device has no mouse!), applets and Flash films.

❑ **Text extensions**: Most simple web clients can display only mono-space fonts. Bi-directional text, bolded text, etc. are not supported. Again, take advantage of style sheets and don't let your content be dependent on your layout.

❑ **Frames**: These were meant for browsers that actually have enough screen space to play with.

❑ **Image maps**: These were designed for visual pointing devices like the mouse; something a mobile phone does not have.

We are all used to the bells and whistles on our browsers, so being "limited" by the above modules might seem like giving up a lot. But remember, a small device such as a pager doesn't give you much to begin with – these "limitations" are actually opportunities to separate your content from your layout – helping you towards the goal of defining once and displaying everywhere!

Well, so what can you do with XHTML Basic? Here are its modules and their elements:

❑ **The Structure Module**: `<body>`, `<head>`, `<html>`, `<title>`

❑ **The Text Module**: `<abbr>`, `<acronym>`, `<address>`, `<blockquote>`, `<br>`, `<cite>`, `<code>`, `<dfn>`, `<div>`, `<em>`, `<h1>`, `<h2>`, `<h3>`, `<h4>`, `<h5>`, `<h6>`, `<kbd>`, `<p>`, `<pre>`, `<q>`, `<samp>`, `<span>`, `<strong>`, and `<var>`. You can link your XHTML Basic documents to a style sheet that is appropriate to the device you are targeting.

❑ **The Hypertext Module**: `<a>`

❑ **The Link Module**: `<link>`. The media attribute is especially important for linking device-specific style sheets.

❑ **The List Module**: `<dl>`, `<dt>`, `<dd>`, `<ol>`, `<ul>`, `<li>`

❑ **The Basic Forms Module**: The basic `forms` module, which has elements similar to the ones in HTML 3.2: `<form>`, `<label>`, `<input>`, `<select>`, `<option>`, and `<textarea>`.

❑ **The Basic Tables Module**: This includes `<caption>`, `<table>`, `<td>`, `<th>`, and `<tr>`. There is no nesting of tables allowed.

❑ **The Image Module**: You can use the `<img>` element, but keep the number and size of your images to the absolute minimum, for example, 20x20 pixels for a mobile phone screen.

❑ **The Object Module**: `<object>` and `<param>`. If the device can support it, you can use this for including device appropriate objects.

❑ **The Meta-information Module**: The `<meta>` element is helpful for document identification, character set encoding, and search engine keywords.

❑ **The Base Module**: `<base>`. This adds the `<base>` element to the content of the `<head>` element for setting a URL as the base for all the relative URLs in the document.

The Basic Document Type

An XHTML Basic document has to follow the same rules as any other XHTML document:

❑ The document header must include the XHTML Basic DOCTYPE declaration:

```
<!DOCTYPE html PUBLIC "-//W3C//DTD XHTML Basic 1.0//EN"
    "http://www.w3.org/TR/xhtml-basic/xhtml-basic10.dtd">
```

❑ The document must be valid according to the DTD

❑ The document must be well-formed

❑ The body of the document must be contained in its root `<html>` element along with the appropriate namespace declaration

Although XHTML Basic can be used, as it is – a simple XHTML language with text, links, and images – it is actually meant to be a host language. A host language can contain a mix of other markup languages integrated into one document type. So in true XHTML tradition, device-specific modules can be developed to enhance the Basic vocabulary. There is no reason not to develop an Events extension for palm devices just because a pager won't support it. With the help of XML and CC/PP, the right elements for the target device can be sent on demand. Just remember to keep your content separate from your layout!

SMIL 1.0

The **Synchronized Multimedia Integration Language (SMIL)** is another W3C project that is bringing us closer to greater media convergence, interoperability, and the grand goal of separating presentation from content.

Currently, streaming text, images, and sound seamlessly requires specialized software and extreme bandwidth. Such presentations are also very device dependent. SMIL is a standard XML-based markup language that lets web developers synchronize text, graphics, and sound using simple HTML-like tags that can be supported on an ever-increasing number of platforms and devices.

When different media components are separated into individual files, devices of various levels of capacity can choose which components they can handle. Either that, or users can decide whether they want the whole presentation or just the content, an issue important for Accessibility Guidelines. When a medium is specifically defined as such, it can be translated into a different form. Visual data beyond text can be converted into sound data for the visually impaired. This is also important for technologies currently in development, for example, **haptic** displays, which translate digital images into touchable 3D information for the visually impaired (http://haptic.mech.northwestern.edu/links/).

The SMIL Document Type

The **Document Head** includes the `<head>`, `<meta>`, and `<layout>` elements. The `<layout>` element lets you use SMIL Basic Layout Language, which is very similar to and shares many properties with CSS2.

The `<body>` element can include:

❑ **Synchronization Elements:** These are the `<par>` (parallel) and `<seq>` (sequential) elements. Timing is what is important here. The `<par>` lets components, which should be shown over time, overlap or run parallel to each other. The `<seq>` element lets you set up files to run sequentially.

❑ The **Media Object Elements**: This includes the `<ref>`, `<animation>`, `<audio>`, `<img>`, `<video>`, `<text>`, and `<textstream>` elements. To increase the readability of a SMIL document, you should make sure the media object type (`animation`, `audio`, `img`, `video`, `text`, or `textstream`) is reflected in the element name.

❑ The **SMIL Time Model**: This is for setting synchronization with Time Model Values.

❑ The **Switch Element**: This is a nifty element, which lets you display an alternative file if for some reason the browser cannot display the first file reference.

❑ **Test Attributes**: These let you use Boolean-like test attributes that can be added to any synchronization element, and that test system capabilities and settings.

❑ **Hyperlinking Elements**: These let you set up navigational links between objects.

Here is an example of a very simple SMIL file called `smiley.smil` (which can be found in the code download available from `Wrox.com`):

```
<smil>
  <head>
    <meta name="smilExample" content="Just a picture" />
    <layout>
      <root-layout width="119" height="119" background-color="white" />
      <region id="smiley.gif" left="0" top="0" width="119" height="119"/>
    </layout>
  </head>
  <body>
    <img src="smiley.gif" alt="goofy smiley face" region="smiley.gif" />
  </body>
</smil>
```

The file extension needs to be `.smil`. As you can see the markup looks very similar to HTML. There is the root `<smil>` element, which contains the whole document. The `<head>` element contains the `<layout>` element, the `<root-layout>` element sets the background, and the `<region>` indicates where the image is to be positioned. Finally, the `<body>` element contains an `<img>` element that references the image file that the layout is to be applied to, and some `alt` text, if the image cannot be displayed for whatever reason.

Here is what it looks like in Real Player 8:

Several mainstream applications support SMIL to some extent. These include Microsoft's Internet Explorer 5.5, Apple's Quicktime 4.1, and RealNetwork's RealPlayer 8.0. There are also quite a few applications available for creating SMIL documents. For the latest on SMIL implementations, check out http://www.w3.org/AudioVideo/.

The Future of SMIL

The standard is not at a standstill by any means. A modularized **SMIL 2.0** is currently in Working Draft form at the W3C. SMIL's functionality has been partitioned into nine new modules, all reusable extensions written in XML, each with an associated DOM. Highlights include being able to better describe how a multimedia presentation behaves over time, associate hyperlinks with media objects, and describe the layout of the presentation on a screen. In addition, it will be possible to mix SMIL syntax and semantics with other XML-based languages, in particular those that need to represent timing and synchronization. For example, SMIL 2.0 components can be used for integrating timing into XHTML and into Scalable Vector Graphics (SVG), which is described in the "*SVG*" section, later in this chapter.

MathML

The **Mathematical Markup Language** (**MathML**) is an XML-based language for displaying mathematical notation and content on the Web. It first became a W3C Recommendation in April 1998 and MathML 2.0 became a Recommendation in February 2001.

As with XML, MathML tries to address some of the limitations of HTML. Even though the Web was initially conceived and implemented by scientists for scientists, the capability to include mathematics in HTML has been restricted to using graphics. This is a rather primitive way of doing things, not only because of the increased download time, but also because there is no separation between presentation and content. Search engines have no way of knowing what kind of information is in a graphic. The information is also not available to other applications, which might want to use the information for indexing or for further calculations.

MathML lets you separate presentation from content by providing two tag sets, one for setting up the mathematical meaning of the notation and the other for the presentation of the notation.

While it is possible to hand-code simple MathML, it is rather complex and anyone who wants to generate larger scale MathML documents should use a special editor to make life easier. There are several available, for example MathType can even take a Word document and convert it into MathML notation – Check out http://www.mathtype.com/. Then there is the popular Mathematica, which gives very powerful cross platform math tools including MathML. Mathematica is at http://www.wolfram.com/.

Emerging Standards

In this section, we'll take a very brief look at current technologies that have not yet been labeled as "standards", but are close to it:

❑ SVG

❑ WML

❑ XForms

SVG

Scalable Vector Graphics (SVG) is a language to describe the way graphics are to be displayed on the Web. SVG is an XML-based markup language to incorporate high-resolution graphics using three types of graphic objects: vector graphic shapes (for example, paths consisting of straight lines and curves), images, and text.

SVG has many advantages over other image formats, and particularly over JPEG and GIF, the most common graphic formats. Here is a list of properties in which SVG is better than other formats:

❑ **Plain text:** SVG files can be read and modified by a range of tools, and are usually much smaller and more compressible than comparable JPEG or GIF images.

❑ **Scalable:** Unlike bitmapped GIF and JPEG formats, SVG is a vector format, which lets images be printed with high quality at any resolution, without the pixelized look.

❑ **Zoomable:** You can zoom in on any portion of an SVG image and not see any degradation.

❑ **Searchable and selectable text:** Unlike normal images, you can make the text in a SVG image searchable, like city names in a map.

❑ **Scripting and animation:** SVG enables dynamic and interactive graphics.

❑ **XML:** SVG is an XML grammar and therefore has the advantages of interoperability, internationalization, and event manipulation with DOM and JavaScript as well as transformation with XSL.

SVG is currently a Candidate Recommendation and the W3C is encouraging implementations to help it develop, and get rid of the bugs. SVG has already been implemented in a very limited fashion in the Mozilla project and is a part of Netscape 6, although this support needs much improvement before it is satisfactory. The Adobe SVG Viewer 2.0 for both IE and Netscape is quite nice. You can download the plug-in for all platforms at http://www.adobe.com/svg/viewer/install/main.html.

The W3C also has a page listing many of the current implementations of SVG at: http://www.w3c.org/Graphics/SVG/SVG-Implementations.html.

SVG is dependent on SMIL Animation and it looks like the two will be developed side-by-side.

WML

The **Wireless Markup Language (WML)** is an XML-based markup language developed by the WAP Forum, the leader in the mobile phone industry. It is not an official W3C Recommendation but nevertheless has become a *de facto* standard in the Western world.

WML is a reduced markup language not meant for normal browsers but for the **micro browsers** used by WAP-enabled mobile phones. It is designed to function with minimal hardware, memory, and CPU resources. There are WML micro browser emulators available on line so you can check how your WML documents look on different phone models without having to actually view them on a mobile phone.

Micro browsers can also interpret a very basic scripting language called **WMLScript**, which is based on ECMAScript, but such scripts cannot be embedded in the WML document to run directly on the client. WML documents refer to the WMLScripts, which need to be compiled first on the server.

Eventually, the plan is to phase WML out, and let XHTML Basic take over. As described earlier in this chapter, XHTML Basic is modularized in order to enable XHTML to be compatible with a wider range of devices than WML.

XForms

HTML forms are an essential for web users to interact with web applications. However, the Form capabilities of HTML are severely outdated and limited, so the W3C is working hard on the next generation – to be called **XForms**. It should become a Recommendation around the beginning of 2002, although we are already seeing implementations of the user interface.

Here are a few things we can expect from XForms:

❑ Easier user interaction with the Web page

❑ Integration with XHTML

❑ Platform and device independence

❑ Separation of user interface from data and logic

❑ A data model with defined data types and data logic

❑ XML and Unicode used to exchange data

A new and expanded set of elements and attributes above and beyond HTML will include the following features:

❑ Fields as data types with field groups as typed records

❑ Constraints – on or between fields and groups – covering input validation, calculated fields, and data dependencies

❑ Regional data input formats for currency values, phone numbers, dates, and postal addresses

❑ Templates for defining reusable field groups

❑ Shared information for multi-page forms, including multiple pages per HTML document, and suspend/resume modes

❑ New kinds of input protocols, for example microphones, cameras, scanners, and pen-based input for signatures and Signed forms

XForms will be a bonus to anyone who ever felt the need to curse while trying to get JavaScript to work in an HTML form, and then found out that the scripting will only function in one browser.

Since XForms are based on XML and designed to be device independent, it will be possible to add other XML applications like VoiceXML (sound markup as described in the upcoming "*VoiceXML*" section) and WML to XForms, to increase device independence and accessibility.

It shouldn't take too long before browsers will support XForms, if only due to pressure from a growing e-commerce market. Before this happens, however, there will be independent implementations by companies with vested interests in web forms.

Implementations of XForms

Mikko Honkala at the University of Helsinki has already implemented parts of the XForms user interface in the open source browser, X-Smiles. This browser lets you embed an XForm in XSL-FO (mentioned earlier in the section on XSL), SMIL, and SVG documents. You can find out more about X-Smiles at http://www.xsmiles.org/.

Mozquito Technologies, driving force behind X-Forms in the W3C and developer of XHTML-FML, an XForms prototype, is currently working on an early implementation XForms adapted to current browser capabilities. Check http://www.mozquito.com/ for more information about Mozquito XForms.

Other Technologies in the Works

In this section, we'll take a very brief look at new technologies that will most likely become standards in the future but are not yet mature enough for widespread implementation:

❑   XHTML Events

❑   DOM Level 3

❑   CSS3

❑   CSS Mobile

❑   VoiceXML

XHTML Events

The **XHTML Events** module defines markup for declaring events and handlers in XML-based languages by taking advantage of Document Object Model (DOM) Level 2 event interfaces.

The DOM specifies an event model that provides the following features:

❑   A generic event system

❑   Registering event handlers

❑   Tying and routing events together with a tree structure

❑   Context information for each event

❑   An event flow architecture describing how events are captured, bubbled, and canceled

The XHTML Events module has two levels: an XHTML Basic Events Module, and an XHTML Events Module. The XHTML Basic Events Module provides simple DOM2 event model support for simple applications and simple devices, such as WAP-enabled phones. The XHTML Events Module provides full DOM Level 2 event model support.

DOM Level 3

The W3C is currently developing **DOM Level 3**. Level 3 will extend Level 2 by finishing the support for XML 1.0 with namespaces, and will extend the user interface events (keyboard and device-independent events). It will also add abstract content model support for DTDs, XML Schema, etc., the abilities of loading and saving documents or content models, and explore further mixed markup vocabularies and the implications on the DOM API, and will support XPath.

Other W3C Working Groups are also working independently to extend the DOM platform to integrate SVG, SMIL, and MathML.

You can expect DOM Level 3 to become a W3C Recommendation around the beginning of 2002.

CSS 3

Although even CSS1 is not yet supported 100% by any browser, and the changes introduced by CSS2 have been partially implemented in the latest generation 5 and 6 browsers, the CSS Working Group still has big plans for the future. It has restructured CSS into modules. CSS was actually the first W3C project to be thrown onto the modularization bandwagon.

At first glance, CSS3 looks really exciting, especially the SVG module and the planned compatibility of some modules with XHTML Basic, but alas, the development of CSS3 as a whole is not progressing very quickly. Don't plan on being able to use any CSS3 module soon.

Here is a preview of the core modules (the first three on the list) and the modules most likely to survive. A quick peek at http://www.w3.org/TR/css3-roadmap/ will give you the latest status on each module as well as indications of which ones will most likely be dropped:

- **Selectors**: Describes the selectors of CSS3; selectors are used to select elements in an HTML or XML document, in order to attach (style) properties to them
- **Values and units**: What values and units are to be used and how
- **Value assignment/cascade/inheritance**: How properties interact, and the core of how CSS operates.
- **Box model/vertical**: The basics of text flow, including how to "float" blocks of text (including vertical writing modes) or images, but excluding columns, tables, and other advanced layouts
- **Positioning**: The process of placing an element somewhere other than where it would normally be in the normal flow of the document
- **Color/gamma/color profiles**: Basic color descriptions and color handling in multiple environments. It should eliminate cross-platform image display problems
- **Colors and Backgrounds**: How element foregrounds and backgrounds are formatted
- **Line box model**: Inline elements, and the inline content of block elements
- **Text/bidi/vertical alignment**: The handling of text in user agents
- **Fonts**: The handling of fonts in user agents
- **Ruby**: New style properties for complex fonts, for example, Asian or Arabic fonts, being developed in co-operation with the Internationalization Working Group

- ❑ **Generated content/markers**: How content is generated and how markers such as lists are displayed
- ❑ **Replaced content**: How replaced content is handled and what qualifies as replaced content
- ❑ **Paged media**: New properties for controlling aspects like running headers and footers, page numbers, and print-style cross-references
- ❑ **User interface**: Features for styling some interactive, dynamic aspects of web pages: the look of form elements in their various states, cursors and colors to describe GUIs (graphical user interfaces) that blend well with the user's desktop environment, and a proposal for "kiosk" mode
- ❑ **WebFonts**: For making fonts more web-friendly
- ❑ **Tables**: For making working with tables even better
- ❑ **Columns**: New properties for more flexible column layout
- ❑ **SVG**: For expressing SVG using a CSS style sheet

So why has CSS been split up into a long list of small modules? Rather than attempting to integrate numerous updates into a single and large specification, it will be much easier and more efficient to be able to update individual pieces of the specification. Only having to update modules means the whole specification is easier to maintain.

Aside from technical maintenance, it may be impractical and unnecessary for an alternative device to support all of CSS. For example, an aural browser may be concerned only with aural styles, whereas a visual browser may care nothing for aural styles. In a case like this, the user agent may only need to implement a subset of CSS.

CSS Mobile

CSS Mobile is a subset of CSS2, and looks very much like CSS1 on a reduced scale. It provides a minimum set of properties, values, selectors, and cascading rules, tailored to the needs and constraints of mobile devices, similar to the relationship of XHTML to XHTML Basic. It also specifies how developers can create style sheets for presenting documents across multiple devices and media types.

An important issue related to CSS Mobile as well as XHTML Basic is that devices are designed to support at least the minimum set of features in these mobile technologies. You need to be aware of the constraints of each device so that you don't have to create style sheets for each version of each device. When everyone agrees on the base features, we will be closer to the goal of interoperability.

CSS Mobile will also take a while to become a Recommendation, however it is much further along in general than CSS3.

VoiceXML

VoiceXML is an XML grammar for representing human-computer audio dialogs on the Web. It was first developed by the VoiceXML forum, an organization founded by AT&T, IBM, Lucent, and Motorola and now made up of several hundred corporate members. In the meantime, VoiceXML has been submitted to the W3C where work on the technology is continuing.

The main goal of VoiceXML is to bring the advantages of web-based development and content delivery to interactive voice-response applications, such as voice browsers with audio output (computer-synthesized and/or recorded) and audio input (voice and/or keypad tones). In the future, voice-activated mobile phones and other voice-capable devices and appliances will support it, if not be inspired by it.

VoiceXML, in the XML tradition, promotes the separation of content and presentation. The content it describes is human-machine interaction provided by voice response systems, which includes:

❑ Output of synthesized speech (text-to-speech)

❑ Output of audio files

❑ Recognition of spoken input

❑ Recognition of DTMF input (the tones used in telephones for tone dialing)

❑ Recording of spoken input

❑ Telephony features such as call transfer and disconnect

Until now telephony solutions required specially trained technicians to install, configure, and maintain them. As VoiceXML was developed in XML, developers can integrate this new language with existing XML-based tools. This brings telephony integration within reach of many web developers. VoiceXML markup is easy enough for defining simple interactions yet provides language features to support complex dialogs. It simplifies creation and delivery of web-based, personalized interactive voice-response services and enables phone and voice access to integrated call center databases, information and services on web sites, and company intranets.

You can find more information about VoiceXML at:http://www.w3.org/TR/voicexml/ and http://www.voicexml.org/.

A current implementation of VoiceXML1.0 is the US English version of the IBM WebSphere Voice Server SDK. Webreference.com also has a VoiceXML channel available at http://www.webreference.com/news/.

Summary

So there you go, a survey of technologies that are being used to shape the future of the World Wide Web. We've talked about:

❑ Modularization

❑ What XML does and doesn't do

❑ New hot technologies (XML, XHTML 1.0, XHTML 1.1 Modularized, XHTML Basic, SMIL 1.0, and MathML)

❑ Technologies of the future (XHTML Events, DOM Level 3, CSS3, CSS Mobile, and VoiceXML)

What does all this mean to you as a web designer? The answer is that these new technologies, for the most part, will not only offer you further advancements in display capabilities for your web pages, but will also help make it possible for you to define your web pages once, but still be able to display them on devices of all levels of capabilities.

For more information on XSL, SVG, SMIL, VoiceXML, and many other of the technologies touched upon in this chapter, please refer to *Professional XML 2nd Edition*, by Nik Ozu et al. (ISBN: *1-861005-05-9*), published by Wrox Press.

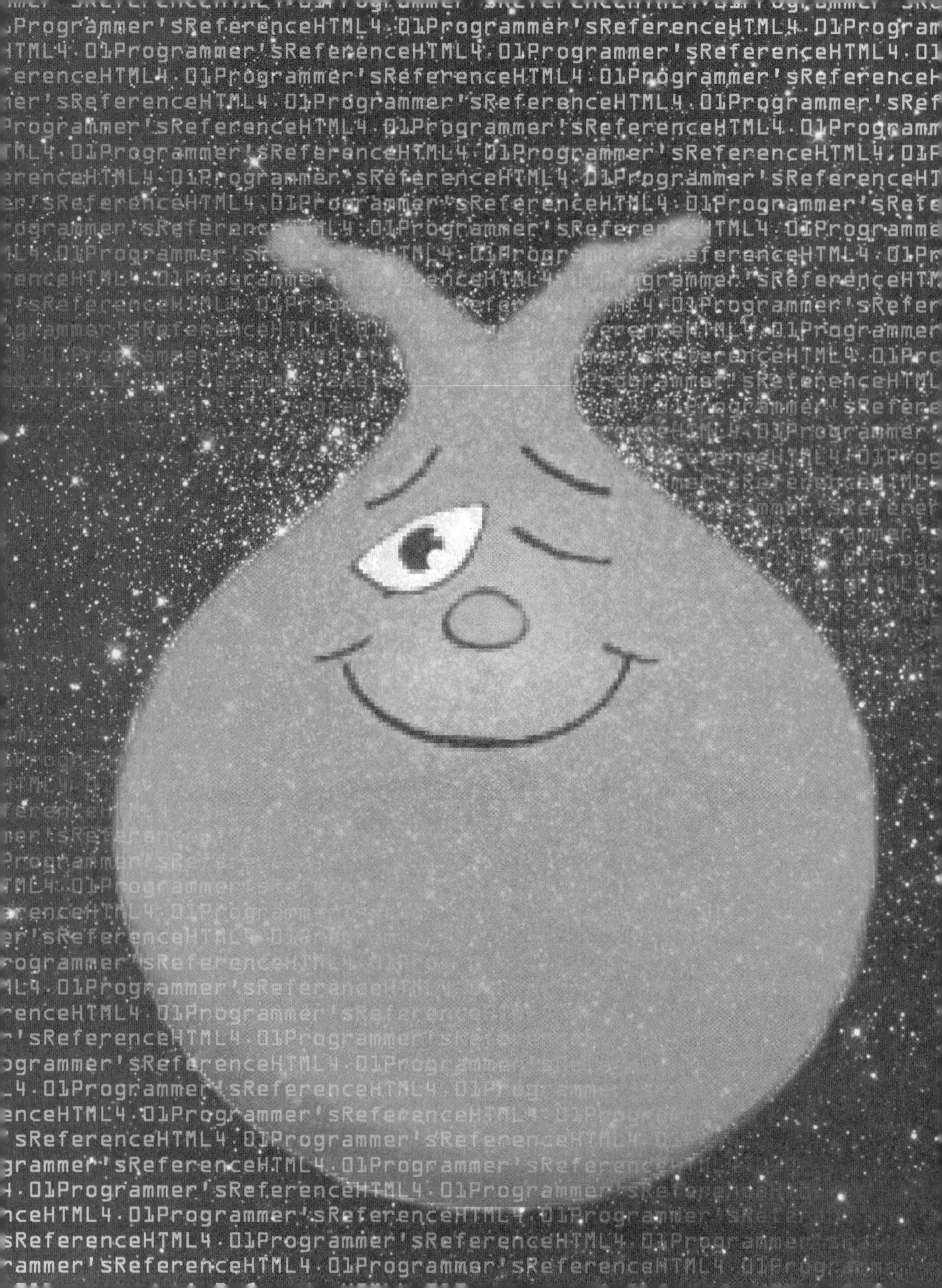
HTML4.01Programmer'sReference

The Wrox Ultimate HTML Database

This section comprises an alphabetical listing of every single HTML element tag, with a brief description followed in bold text by the HTML and browser versions that support that element. Each element also has a table that lists all the attributes applicable to it (if any), and we show the HTML specifications and browsers that support each attribute. Where element attributes are deprecated in a later specification, this is indicated in the table by a capital letter 'D'. However, as there are so few differences between HTML 4.01 and its predecessor HTML 4.0, only HTML 4.01 is shown in the following tables; where any differences do occur, they are indicated with an asterisk and an explanatory footnote under the table concerned.

Note: all browsers listed are the Windows versions.

! –

Denotes a comment that is ignored by the HTML parser.
ALL

!Doctype

Declares the type and content format of the document.
ALL

a

Defines a hypertext link. The `href` or the `name` attribute must be specified. **ALL**

Attributes	2.0	3.2	4.01	N3	N4	N6	IE3	IE4	IE5	IE 5.5	IE6	O5.x
`<event_name>=` `script_code`	✗	✗	✓	✗	✓	✓	✓	✓	✓	✓	✓	✓
`accesskey=` `key_character`	✗	✗	✓	✗	✗	✓	✗	✓	✓	✓	✓	✗
`charset=string`	✗	✗	✓	✗	✗	✓	✗	✗	✗	✗	✗	✗
`class=classname`	✗	✗	✓	✗	✓	✓	✓	✓	✓	✓	✓	✓
`coords=string`	✗	✗	✓	✗	✓	✓	✗	✗	✗	✗	✓	✗
`datafld=column_name`	✗	✗	✗	✗	✗	✗	✗	✓	✓	✓	✓	✗
`datasrc=id`	✗	✗	✗	✗	✗	✗	✗	✓	✓	✓	✓	✗
`dir=ltr|rtl`	✗	✗	✓	✗	✗	✓	✗	✗	✓	✓	✓	✗
`href=url`	✓	✓	✓	✓	✓	✓	✓	✓	✓	✓	✓	✓
`hreflang=langcode`	✗	✗	✓	✗	✗	✓	✗	✗	✗	✗	✗	✗
`id=string`	✗	✗	✓	✗	✓	✓	✓	✓	✓	✓	✓	✓
`lang=language_type`	✗	✗	✓	✗	✗	✓	✗	✓	✓	✓	✓	✗
`language=` `javascript|vbscript`	✗	✗	✗	✗	✗	✗	✗	✓	✓	✓	✓	✗
`methods=string`	✓	✗	✗	✗	✗	✗	✗	✓	✓	✓	✓	✗
`name=string`	✓	✓	✓	✓	✓	✓	✓	✓	✓	✓	✓	✓
`rel=same|next|parent|` `previous|string`	✓	✓	✓	✗	✗	✓	✓	✓	✓	✓	✓	✓
`rev=string`	✓	✓	✓	✗	✗	✓	✓	✓	✓	✓	✓	✓
`shape=circ|circle|` `poly|polygon|` `rect|rectangle`	✗	✗	✓	✗	✗	✓	✗	✗	✗	✗	✓	✗
`style=string`	✗	✗	✓	✗	✓	✓	✓	✓	✓	✓	✓	✓
`tabindex=number`	✗	✗	✓	✗	✗	✓	✗	✓	✓	✓	✓	✗

Attributes	2.0	3.2	4.01	N3	N4	N6	IE3	IE4	IE5	IE 5.5	IE6	O5.x
target=<window_name>|_parent|_blank|_top|_self	✗	✗	✓	✓	✓	✓	✓	✓	✓	✓	✓	✓
title=string	✓	✓	✓	✗	✗	✓	✓	✓	✓	✓	✓	✓
type=button|reset|submit	✗	✗	✓	✗	✗	✓	✗	✗	✗	✗	✗	✗
urn=string	✓	✗	✗	✗	✗	✗	✗	✓	✓	✓	✓	✗

abbr

Indicates a set of characters that denote an abbreviation (for example, "abbrev."). **HTML 4.01, N6, IE4+, Opera 5.x**

Attributes	2.0	3.2	4.01	N3	N4	N6	IE3	IE4	IE5	IE 5.5	IE6	O5.x
<event_name>=script_code	✗	✗	✓	✗	✗	✓	✗	✗	✗	✗	✗	✓
class=classname	✗	✗	✓	✗	✗	✓	✗	✗	✗	✗	✗	✓
dir=ltr|rtl	✗	✗	✓	✗	✗	✓	✗	✗	✗	✗	✗	✗
id=string	✗	✗	✓	✗	✗	✓	✗	✗	✗	✗	✗	✓
lang=language_type	✗	✗	✗	✗	✗	✗	✗	✗	✗	✗	✗	✗
style=string	✗	✗	✓	✗	✗	✓	✗	✗	✗	✗	✗	✓
title=string	✗	✗	✓	✗	✗	✓	✗	✗	✗	✗	✗	✓

acronym

Indicates a sequence of characters that compose an acronym (for example, "TLA"). **HTML 4.01, N6, IE4+, Opera 5.x**

Attributes	2.0	3.2	4.01	N3	N4	N6	IE3	IE4	IE5	IE 5.5	IE6	O5.x
<event_name>=script_code	✗	✗	✓	✗	✗	✓	✗	✓	✓	✓	✓	✓

Table continued on following page

Attributes	2.0	3.2	4.01	N3	N4	N6	IE3	IE4	IE5	IE 5.5	IE6	O5.x
accesskey= key_character	✗	✗	✗	✗	✗	✗	✗	✗	✓	✓	✓	✗
class=classname	✗	✗	✓	✗	✗	✓	✗	✓	✓	✓	✓	✓
dir=ltr|rtl	✗	✗	✓	✗	✗	✓	✗	✗	✓	✓	✓	✗
id=string	✗	✗	✓	✗	✗	✓	✗	✓	✓	✓	✓	✓
lang=language_type	✗	✗	✓	✗	✗	✗	✗	✓	✓	✓	✓	✗
language=javascript| vbscript	✗	✗	✗	✗	✗	✗	✗	✓	✓	✓	✓	✗
style=string	✗	✗	✓	✗	✗	✓	✗	✓	✓	✓	✓	✓
tabindex=number	✗	✗	✗	✗	✗	✗	✗	✗	✓	✓	✓	✗
title=string	✗	✗	✓	✗	✗	✓	✗	✓	✓	✓	✓	✓

address

Specifies information such as address, signature and authorship. **ALL**

Attributes	2.0	3.2	4.01	N3	N4	N6	IE3	IE4	IE5	IE 5.5	IE6	O5.x
<event_name>= script_code	✗	✗	✓	✗	✗	✓	✗	✓	✓	✓	✓	✓
accesskey=key_ character	✗	✗	✗	✗	✗	✗	✗	✗	✓	✓	✓	✗
class=classname	✗	✗	✓	✗	✓	✓	✗	✓	✓	✓	✓	✓
dir=ltr|rtl	✗	✗	✓	✗	✗	✓	✗	✗	✓	✓	✓	✗
id=string	✗	✗	✓	✗	✓	✓	✗	✓	✓	✓	✓	✓
lang=language_type	✗	✗	✓	✗	✗	✗	✗	✓	✓	✓	✓	✗
language=javascript| vbscript	✗	✗	✗	✗	✗	✗	✗	✓	✓	✓	✓	✗
style=string	✗	✗	✓	✗	✓	✓	✗	✓	✓	✓	✓	✓
tabindex=number	✗	✗	✗	✗	✗	✗	✗	✗	✓	✓	✓	✗
title=string	✗	✗	✓	✗	✗	✓	✗	✓	✓	✓	✓	✓

applet

Places a Java Applet or other executable content in the page. **HTML 3.2, deprecated in HTML 4.01, N3+, IE3+, O5.x**

Attributes	2.0	3.2	4.01	N3	N4	N6	IE3	IE4	IE 5	IE 5.5	IE6	O5.x
`<event_name>=` `script_code`	✗	✗	D	✗	✗	✓	✗	✗	✗	✗	✗	✓
`accesskey=key_` `character`	✗	✗	✗	✗	✗	✗	✗	✗	✓	✓	✓	✗
`align=top|middle|` `bottom|left|right|` `absmiddle|baseline|` `absbottom|texttop`	✗	✓	D	✓	✓	✓	✓	✓	✓	✓	✓	✗
`alt=text`	✗	✓	D	✓	✓	✓	✓	✗	✗	✗	✗	✓
`archive=url`	✗	✗	D	✓	✓	✓	✗	✗	✗	✗	✗	✓
`border=number`	✗	✗	D	✗	✗	✗	✗	✗	✗	✗	✗	✓
`class=classname`	✗	✗	D	✗	✓	✓	✗	✓	✓	✓	✓	✓
`code=filename`	✗	✓	D	✓	✓	✓	✓	✓	✓	✓	✓	✓
`codebase=path|url`	✗	✓	D	✓	✓	✓	✓	✓	✓	✓	✓	✓
`datafld=column_name`	✗	✗	✗	✗	✗	✗	✗	✓	✓	✓	✓	✗
`datasrc=id`	✗	✗	✗	✗	✗	✗	✗	✓	✓	✓	✓	✗
`disabled`	✗	✗	✗	✗	✗	✗	✗	✗	✗	✗	✗	✗
`download=number`	✗	✗	✗	✗	✗	✗	✗	✓	✗	✗	✗	✗
`height=number`	✗	✓	D	✓	✓	✓	✓	✓	✓	✓	✓	✓
`hspace=number`	✗	✓	D	✗	✓	✓	✓	✓	✓	✓	✓	✓
`id=string`	✗	✗	D	✗	✓	✓	✗	✓	✓	✓	✓	✓
`lang=language_type`	✗	✗	✗	✗	✗	✓	✗	✗	✓	✓	✓	✗
`language=javascript|` `vbscript`	✗	✗	✗	✗	✗	✗	✗	✓	✓	✓	✓	✗
`mayscript=yes|no`	✗	✗	✗	✗	✓	✗	✗	✗	✗	✗	✗	✗
`name=string`	✗	✓	D	✗	✗	✓	✗	✓	✓	✓	✓	✓
`object=string`	✗	✗	D	✗	✗	✓	✗	✓	✓	✓	✗	✓
`src=url`	✗	✗	✗	✗	✗	✗	✗	✓	✓	✓	✓	✗

Table continued on following page

Attributes	2.0	3.2	4.01	N3	N4	N6	IE3	IE4	IE 5	IE 5.5	IE6	O5.x
style=string	✗	✗	D	✗	✓	✓	✗	✓	✓	✓	✓	✓
tabindex=number	✗	✗	✗	✗	✗	✗	✗	✗	✓	✓	✓	✗
title=string	✗	✗	D	✗	✗	✓	✗	✓	✓	✓	✓	✓
vspace=number	✗	✓	D	✗	✓	✓	✓	✓	✓	✓	✓	✓
width=number	✗	✓	D	✓	✓	✓	✓	✓	✗	✗	✗	✓

area

Specifies the shape of a "hot spot" in a client-side image map. **ALL except HTML 2.0**

Attributes	2.0	3.2	4.01	N3	N4	N6	IE3	IE4	IE 5	IE 5.5	IE6	O5.x
<event_name>=script_code	✗	✗	✓	✗	✓	✓	✗	✓	✓	✓	✓	✓
accesskey=key_character	✗	✗	✓	✗	✗	✓	✗	✗	✓	✓	✓	✗
alt=text	✗	✓	✓	✓	✓	✓	✓	✓	✓	✓	✓	✓
class=classname	✗	✗	✓	✗	✓	✓	✓	✓	✓	✓	✓	✓
coords=string	✗	✓	✓	✓	✓	✓	✓	✓	✓	✓	✓	✓
dir=ltr|rtl	✗	✗	✓	✗	✗	✓	✗	✗	✓	✓	✓	✗
href=url	✗	✓	✓	✓	✓	✓	✓	✓	✓	✓	✓	✓
id=string	✗	✗	✓	✗	✓	✓	✓	✓	✓	✓	✓	✓
lang=language_type	✗	✗	✓	✗	✗	✓	✗	✓	✓	✓	✓	✗
language=javascript|vbscript	✗	✗	✗	✗	✗	✗	✗	✓	✓	✓	✓	✗
name=string	✗	✗	✗	✗	✓	✗	✗	✗	✗	✗	✗	✗
nohref	✗	✓	✓	✓	✓	✓	✓	✓	✓	✓	✓	✓
notab	✗	✗	✗	✗	✗	✗	✓	✗	✗	✗	✗	✗
shape=circ|circle|poly|polygon|rect|rectangle	✗	✓	✓	✓	✓	✓	✓	✓	✓	✓	✓	✓
style=string	✗	✗	✓	✗	✓	✓	✓	✓	✓	✓	✓	✓

Attributes	2.0	3.2	4.01	N3	N4	N6	IE3	IE4	IE 5	IE 5.5	IE6	O5.x
tabindex=number	✗	✗	✓	✗	✗	✓	✓	✓	✓	✓	✓	✗
target=<window_name>|_parent|_blank|_top|_self	✗	✗	✓	✓	✓	✓	✓	✓	✓	✓	✓	✓
title=string	✗	✗	✓	✗	✗	✓	✓	✓	✓	✓	✓	✓

b

Renders text in boldface where available. **ALL**

Attributes	2.0	3.2	4.01	N3	N4	N6	IE3	IE4	IE 5	IE 5.5	IE6	O5.x
<event_name>=script_code	✗	✗	✓	✗	✗	✓	✗	✓	✓	✓	✓	✓
accesskey=key_character	✗	✗	✗	✗	✗	✗	✗	✗	✓	✓	✓	✗
class=classname	✗	✗	✓	✗	✓	✓	✗	✓	✓	✓	✓	✓
dir=ltr|rtl	✗	✗	✓	✗	✗	✓	✗	✗	✓	✓	✓	✗
id=string	✗	✗	✓	✗	✓	✓	✗	✓	✓	✓	✓	✗
lang=language_type	✗	✗	✓	✗	✗	✓	✗	✓	✓	✓	✓	✗
language=javascript|vbscript	✗	✗	✗	✗	✗	✗	✗	✓	✓	✓	✓	✗
style=string	✗	✗	✓	✗	✓	✓	✗	✓	✓	✓	✓	✓
tabindex=number	✗	✗	✗	✗	✗	✗	✗	✗	✓	✓	✓	✗
title=string	✗	✗	✓	✗	✗	✓	✗	✓	✓	✓	✓	✓

base

Specifies the document's base URL. **ALL**

Attributes	2.0	3.2	4.01	N3	N4	N6	IE3	IE4	IE 5	IE 5.5	IE6	O5.x
href=url	✓	✓	✓	✓	✓	✓	✓	✓	✓	✓	✓	✓
id=string	✗	✗	✗	✗	✗	✓	✗	✗	✓	✓	✓	✗
target=<window_name>| _parent|_blank| _top|_self	✗	✗	✓	✓	✓	✓	✓	✓	✓	✓	✓	✓

basefont

Sets the base font values to be used as the default font when rendering text. **HTML 3.2, deprecated in HTML 4.01, N3+, IE 3+, O5.x**

Attributes	2.0	3.2	4.01	N3	N4	N6	IE3	IE4	IE 5	IE 5.5	IE6	O5.x
class=classname	✗	✗	✗	✗	✓	✓	✗	✓	✗	✗	✗	✗
color=color	✗	✗	✗	✗	✗	✓	✓	✓	✓	✓	✓	✗
face=font_family_name	✗	✗	✗	✗	✗	✓	✓	✓	✓	✓	✓	✗
id=string	✗	✗	D	✗	✓	✓	✗	✓	✓	✓	✓	✗
size=1|2|3|4|5|6|7	✗	✓	D	✓	✓	✓	✓	✓	✓	✓	✓	✗

bdo

Turns off the bi-directional rendering algorithm for selected fragments of text. **HTML 4.01, N6, IE 5+, O5.x**

Attributes	2.0	3.2	4.01	N3	N4	N6	IE3	IE4	IE 5	IE 5.5	IE6	O5.x
accesskey= key_character	✗	✗	✗	✗	✗	✗	✗	✗	✓	✓	✓	✗
class=classname	✗	✗	✓	✗	✗	✓	✗	✗	✓	✓	✓	✗
dir=ltr|rtl	✗	✗	✓	✗	✗	✓	✗	✗	✓	✓	✓	✗

Attributes	2.0	3.2	4.01	N3	N4	N6	IE3	IE4	IE 5	IE 5.5	IE6	O5.x
id=string	✗	✗	✓	✗	✗	✓	✗	✗	✓	✓	✓	✗
lang=language_type	✗	✗	✓	✗	✗	✓	✗	✗	✓	✓	✓	✗
language=javascript|vbscript	✗	✗	✗	✗	✗	✗	✗	✗	✓	✓	✓	✗
style=string	✗	✗	✓	✗	✗	✓	✗	✗	✗	✗	✗	✗
tabindex=number	✗	✗	✗	✗	✗	✗	✗	✗	✓	✓	✓	✗
title=string	✗	✗	✓	✗	✗	✓	✗	✗	✓	✓	✓	✗

bgsound

Specifies a background sound to be played while the page is loaded. **IE3+**

Attributes	2.0	3.2	4.01	N3	N4	N6	IE3	IE4	IE 5	IE 5.5	IE6	O5.x
balance	✗	✗	✗	✗	✗	✗	✗	✓	✓	✓	✓	✗
id=string	✗	✗	✗	✗	✗	✗	✗	✓	✓	✓	✓	✗
lang=language_type	✗	✗	✗	✗	✗	✗	✗	✗	✗	✗	✗	✗
loop=number	✗	✗	✗	✗	✗	✗	✓	✓	✓	✓	✓	✗
src=url	✗	✗	✗	✗	✗	✗	✓	✓	✓	✓	✓	✗
volume=number	✗	✗	✗	✗	✗	✗	✗	✗	✗	✗	✗	✗

big

Renders text in a font larger relative to the current font. **HTML 3.2+, N4+, IE4+, O5.x**

Attributes	2.0	3.2	4.01	N3	N4	N6	IE3	IE4	IE 5	IE 5.5	IE6	O5.x
<event_name>=script_code	✗	✗	✓	✗	✗	✓	✗	✓	✓	✓	✓	✓
accesskey=key_character	✗	✗	✗	✗	✗	✗	✗	✗	✓	✓	✓	✗
class=classname	✗	✗	✓	✗	✓	✓	✗	✓	✓	✓	✓	✓

Table continued on following page

587

Attributes	2.0	3.2	4.01	N3	N4	N6	IE3	IE4	IE5	IE 5.5	IE6	O5.x
dir=ltr|rtl	x	x	✓	x	x	✓	x	x	✓	✓	✓	x
id=string	x	x	✓	x	✓	✓	x	✓	✓	✓	✓	✓
lang=language_type	x	x	✓	x	x	✓	x	✓	✓	✓	✓	x
language=javascript|vbscript	x	x	x	x	x	x	x	x	✓	✓	✓	x
style=string	x	x	✓	x	✓	✓	x	✓	✓	✓	✓	✓
tabindex=number	x	x	x	x	x	x	x	x	✓	✓	✓	x
title=string	x	x	✓	x	x	✓	x	✓	✓	✓	✓	✓

blink

Causes the text to flash on and off within the page. **N3+**

Attributes	2.0	3.2	4.01	N3	N4	N6	IE3	IE4	IE5	IE 5.5	IE6	O5.x
class=classname	x	x	x	x	✓	x	x	x	x	x	x	x
id=string	x	x	x	x	✓	x	x	x	x	x	x	x
style=string	x	x	x	x	✓	x	x	x	x	x	x	x

blockquote

Denotes a quotation in text, usually a paragraph or more. **ALL**

Attributes	2.0	3.2	4.01	N3	N4	N6	IE3	IE4	IE5	IE 5.5	IE6	O5.x
<event_name>=script_code	x	x	✓	x	x	✓	x	✓	✓	✓	✓	✓
accesskey=key_character	x	x	x	x	x	x	x	x	✓	✓	✓	x
cite=url	x	x	✓	x	x	✓	x	x	x	x	✓	✓
class=classname	x	x	✓	x	✓	✓	x	✓	✓	✓	✓	✓
dir=ltr|rtl	x	x	✓	x	x	✓	x	✓	✓	✓	✓	x
id=string	x	x	✓	x	✓	✓	x	✓	✓	✓	✓	✓

Attributes	2.0	3.2	4.01	N3	N4	N6	IE3	IE4	IE5	IE 5.5	IE6	O5.x
lang=language_type	x	x	✓	x	x	✓	x	✓	✓	✓	✓	x
language=javascript|vbscript	x	x	x	x	x	x	x	✓	✓	✓	✓	x
style=string	x	x	✓	x	✓	✓	✓	✓	✓	✓	✓	✓
tabindex=number	x	x	x	x	x	x	x	x	✓	✓	✓	x
title=string	x	x	✓	x	x	x	✓	✓	✓	✓	✓	✓

body

Defines the beginning and end of the body section of the page. **ALL**

Attributes	2.0	3.2	4.01	N3	N4	N6	IE3	IE4	IE5	IE 5.5	IE6	O5.x
<event_name>=script_code	x	x	✓	x	✓	✓	x	✓	✓	✓	✓	✓
accesskey=key_character	x	x	x	x	x	x	x	x	✓	✓	✓	x
alink=color	x	✓	D	✓	✓	✓	✓	✓	✓	✓	✓	✓
background=string	x	✓	D	✓	✓	✓	✓	✓	✓	✓	✓	✓
bgcolor=color	x	✓	D	✓	✓	✓	✓	✓	✓	✓	✓	✓
bgproperties=fixed	x	x	x	x	x	x	x	x	✓	✓	✓	x
bottommargin=number	x	x	x	x	x	x	x	✓	✓	✓	✓	x
class=classname	x	x	✓	x	✓	✓	✓	✓	✓	✓	✓	✓
datafld=column_name	x	x	x	x	x	x	x	x	x	x	x	x
dataformatas	x	x	x	x	x	x	x	x	x	x	x	x
datasrc=id	x	x	x	x	x	x	x	x	x	x	x	x
dir=ltr|rtl	x	x	✓	x	x	✓	x	x	✓	✓	✓	x
id=string	x	x	✓	x	✓	✓	✓	✓	✓	✓	✓	x
lang=language_type	x	x	✓	x	x	✓	x	✓	✓	✓	✓	x
language=javascript|vbscript	x	x	x	x	x	x	x	✓	✓	✓	✓	x
leftmargin=number	x	x	x	x	x	x	✓	✓	✓	✓	✓	x

Table continued on following page

Attributes	2.0	3.2	4.01	N3	N4	N6	IE3	IE4	IE 5	IE 5.5	IE6	O5.x
link=color	x	✓	D	✓	✓	✓	✓	✓	✓	✓	✓	✓
nowrap	x	x	x	x	x	x	x	x	✓	✓	✓	x
rightmargin=number	x	x	x	x	x	x	x	✓	✓	✓	✓	x
scroll=yes|no	x	x	x	x	x	x	x	✓	✓	✓	✓	x
style=string	x	x	✓	x	✓	✓	✓	✓	✓	✓	✓	✓
tabindex=number	x	x	x	x	x	x	x	x	✓	✓	✓	x
text=color	x	✓	D	✓	✓	✓	✓	✓	✓	✓	✓	✓
title=string	x	x	✓	x	x	✓	x	✓	✓	✓	✓	✓
topmargin	x	x	x	x	x	x	x	✓	✓	✓	✓	x
vlink=color	x	✓	D	✓	✓	✓	✓	✓	✓	✓	✓	✓

br

Inserts a line break. **ALL**

Attributes	2.0	3.2	4.01	N3	N4	N6	IE3	IE4	IE 5	IE 5.5	IE6	O5.x
class=classname	x	x	✓	x	✓	✓	✓	✓	✓	✓	✓	✓
clear=all|left|right|none	x	✓	D	✓	✓	✓	✓	✓	✓	✓	✓	✓
id=string	x	x	✓	x	✓	✓	x	✓	✓	✓	✓	✓
style=string	x	x	✓	x	✓	✓	x	✓	✓	✓	✓	✓
title=string	x	x	✓	x	x	✓	x	✓	x	x	x	✓

button

Renders an HTML button such that enclosed text is used as the button's caption. **HTML 4.01+, N3+, IE4+, O5.x**

Attributes	2.0	3.2	4.01	N3	N4	N6	IE3	IE4	IE 5	IE 5.5	IE6	O5.x
<event_name>=script_code	x	x	✓	x	x	✓	x	✓	✓	✓	✓	x

Attributes	2.0	3.2	4.01	N3	N4	N6	IE3	IE4	IE 5	IE 5.5	IE6	O5.x
accesskey= key_character	✗	✗	✓	✗	✗	✓	✗	✓	✓	✓	✓	✗
class=classname	✗	✗	✓	✗	✗	✓	✗	✓	✓	✓	✓	✗
datafld=column_name	✗	✗	✗	✗	✗	✗	✗	✗	✓	✓	✓	✗
dataformatas=html|text	✗	✗	✗	✗	✗	✗	✗	✗	✓	✓	✓	✗
datasrc=id	✗	✗	✗	✗	✗	✗	✗	✓	✓	✓	✓	✗
dir=ltr|rtl	✗	✗	✓	✗	✗	✓	✗	✗	✓	✓	✓	✗
disabled	✗	✗	✓	✗	✗	✓	✗	✓	✓	✓	✓	✗
id=string	✗	✗	✓	✗	✗	✓	✗	✓	✓	✓	✓	✗
lang=language_type	✗	✗	✓	✗	✗	✓	✗	✓	✓	✓	✓	✗
language=javascript| vbscript	✗	✗	✗	✗	✗	✗	✗	✓	✓	✓	✓	✗
name=string	✗	✗	✓	✗	✗	✓	✗	✗	✓	✓	✓	✗
style=string	✗	✗	✓	✗	✗	✓	✗	✓	✓	✓	✓	✗
tabindex=number	✗	✗	✓	✗	✗	✓	✗	✓	✗	✓	✓	✗
title=string	✗	✗	✓	✗	✗	✓	✗	✓	✓	✓	✓	✗
type=button| reset|submit	✗	✗	✓	✗	✗	✓	✗	✓	✓	✓	✓	✗
value=string	✗	✗	✓	✗	✗	✓	✗	✗	✓	✓	✓	✗

caption

Specifies a caption to be placed next to a table. **ALL except HTML 2.0**

Attributes	2.0	3.2	4.01	N3	N4	N6	IE3	IE4	IE 5	IE 5.5	IE6	O5.x
<event_name>= script_code	✗	✗	✓	✗	✗	✓	✗	✓	✓	✓	✓	✓
accesskey= key_character	✗	✗	✗	✗	✗	✗	✗	✗	✓	✓	✓	✗
align=top|bottom| left|right	✗	✓	D	✓	✓	✓	✓	✓	✓	✓	✓	✓

Table continued on following page

Attributes	2.0	3.2	4.01	N3	N4	N6	IE3	IE4	IE5	IE 5.5	IE6	O5.x
class=classname	x	x	✓	x	✓	✓	x	✓	✓	✓	✓	✓
dir=ltr|rtl	x	x	✓	x	x	✓	x	x	✓	✓	✓	x
id=string	x	x	✓	x	✓	✓	x	✓	✓	✓	✓	✓
lang=language_type	x	x	✓	x	x	✓	x	✓	✓	✓	✓	x
language=javascript|vbscript	x	x	x	x	x	x	x	✓	✓	✓	✓	x
style=string	x	x	✓	x	✓	✓	x	✓	✓	✓	✓	✓
tabindex=number	x	x	x	x	x	x	x	x	✓	✓	✓	x
title=string	x	x	✓	x	x	✓	x	✓	✓	✓	✓	✓
valign=bottom|top	x	x	x	x	✓	x	✓	✓	✓	✓	✓	x

center

Causes enclosed text and other elements to be centered on the page. **HTML 3.2, deprecated in HTML 4.01, N2+, IE2+, O5.x**

Attributes	2.0	3.2	4.01	N3	N4	N6	IE3	IE4	IE5	IE 5.5	IE6	O5.x
<event_name>=script_code	x	x	x	x	x	x	x	✓	✓	✓	✓	x
accesskey=key_character	x	x	x	x	x	x	x	x	✓	✓	✓	x
class=classname	x	x	x	x	✓	✓	x	✓	✓	✓	✓	x
dir=ltr|rtl	x	x	x	x	x	✓	x	x	✓	✓	✓	x
id=string	x	x	x	x	✓	✓	x	✓	✓	✓	✓	x
lang=language_type	x	x	x	x	x	x	x	✓	✓	✓	✓	x
language=javascript|vbscript	x	x	x	x	x	x	x	✓	✓	✓	✓	x
style=string	x	x	x	x	✓	✓	x	✓	✓	✓	✓	x
tabindex=number	x	x	x	x	x	x	x	x	✓	✓	✓	x
title=string	x	x	x	x	x	✓	x	✓	x	x	x	x

cite

Renders text in italics. **ALL**

Attributes	2.0	3.2	4.01	N3	N4	N6	IE3	IE4	IE5	IE 5.5	IE6	O5.x
`<event_name>=` `script_code`	✗	✗	✓	✗	✗	✓	✗	✓	✓	✓	✓	✓
`accesskey=` `key_character`	✗	✗	✗	✗	✗	✗	✗	✗	✓	✓	✓	✗
`class=classname`	✗	✗	✓	✗	✓	✓	✗	✓	✓	✓	✓	✓
`dir=ltr|rtl`	✗	✗	✓	✗	✗	✓	✗	✓	✓	✓	✓	✗
`id=string`	✗	✗	✓	✗	✓	✓	✗	✓	✓	✓	✓	✓
`lang=language_type`	✗	✗	✓	✗	✗	✓	✗	✓	✓	✓	✓	✗
`language=javascript|` `vbscript`	✗	✗	✗	✗	✗	✗	✗	✗	✓	✓	✓	✗
`style=string`	✗	✗	✓	✗	✓	✓	✗	✓	✓	✓	✓	✓
`tabindex=number`	✗	✗	✗	✗	✗	✗	✗	✗	✗	✓	✓	✗
`title=string`	✗	✗	✓	✗	✗	✓	✗	✓	✓	✓	✓	✓

code

Renders text as a code sample in a fixed width font. **ALL**

Attributes	2.0	3.2	4.01	N3	N4	N6	IE3	IE4	IE5	IE 5.5	IE6	O5.x
`<event_name>=` `script_code`	✗	✗	✓	✗	✗	✓	✗	✓	✓	✓	✓	✓
`class=classname`	✗	✗	✓	✗	✓	✓	✗	✓	✓	✓	✓	✓
`dir=ltr|rtl`	✗	✗	✓	✗	✗	✓	✗	✗	✓	✓	✓	✗
`id=string`	✗	✗	✓	✗	✓	✓	✗	✓	✓	✓	✓	✓
`lang=language_type`	✗	✗	✓	✗	✗	✓	✗	✓	✓	✓	✓	✗
`language=javascript|` `vbscript`	✗	✗	✗	✗	✗	✗	✗	✓	✓	✓	✓	✗
`style=string`	✗	✗	✓	✗	✓	✓	✗	✓	✓	✓	✓	✓
`title=string`	✗	✗	✓	✗	✗	✓	✗	✓	✓	✓	✓	✓

col

Used to specify column based defaults for a table. **HTML 4.01, N4+, IE3+**

Attributes	2.0	3.2	4.01	N3	N4	N6	IE3	IE4	IE 5	IE 5.5	IE6	O5.x
`<event_name>= script_code`	x	x	✓	x	✓	✓	x	x	x	x	✓	x
`align=center|left| right|justify|char`	x	x	✓	x	x	✓	✓	✓	✓	✓	✓	x
`bgcolor=color`	x	x	x	x	x	x	x	x	✓	✓	✓	x
`char=string`	x	x	✓	x	x	✓	x	x	x	x	✓	x
`charoff=string`	x	x	✓	x	x	✓	x	x	x	x	✓	x
`class=classname`	x	x	✓	x	x	✓	x	✓	✓	✓	✓	x
`dir=ltr|rtl`	x	x	✓	x	x	✓	x	✓	✓	✓	✓	x
`id=string`	x	x	✓	x	x	✓	x	✓	✓	✓	✓	x
`lang=language_type`	x	x	x	x	x	✓	x	x	✓	✓	✓	x
`span=number`	x	x	✓	x	x	✓	✓	✓	✓	✓	✓	x
`style=string`	x	x	✓	x	x	✓	x	✓	✓	✓	✓	x
`title=string`	x	x	✓	x	x	✓	x	✓	x	x	x	x
`valign=bottom|middle| top|baseline`	x	x	✓	x	x	✓	x	✓	✓	✓	✓	x
`width=number`	x	x	✓	x	x	✓	x	✓	✓	✓	✓	x

colgroup

Used as a container for a group of columns. **HTML 4.01, N4+, IE3+**

Attributes	2.0	3.2	4.01	N3	N4	N6	IE3	IE4	IE 5	IE 5.5	IE6	O5.x
`<event_name>= script_code`	x	x	✓	x	✓	✓	x	x	x	✓	✓	x
`align=center|left| right|justify|char`	x	x	✓	x	x	✓	✓	✓	✓	✓	✓	x
`bgcolor=color`	x	x	x	x	x	x	x	x	✓	✓	✓	x
`char=string`	x	x	✓	x	x	✓	x	x	x	x	x	x

Attributes	2.0	3.2	4.01	N3	N4	N6	IE3	IE4	IE 5	IE 5.5	IE6	O5.x
charoff=string	x	x	✓	x	x	✓	x	x	x	x	x	x
class=classname	x	x	✓	x	x	✓	x	✓	✓	✓	✓	x
dir=ltr|rtl	x	x	✓	x	x	✓	x	✓	✓	✓	✓	x
id=string	x	x	✓	x	x	✓	x	✓	✓	✓	✓	x
lang=language_type	x	x	x	x	x	✓	x	✓	✓	✓	✓	x
span=number	x	x	✓	x	x	✓	x	x	x	✓	x	x
style=string	x	x	✓	x	x	✓	x	✓	✓	✓	✓	x
title=string	x	x	✓	x	x	✓	x	✓	x	x	x	x
valign=bottom|middle|top|baseline	x	x	✓	x	x	✓	x	✓	✓	✓	✓	x
width=number	x	x	✓	x	x	✓	x	✓	✓	✓	✓	x

comment

Denotes a comment that will not be displayed. **IE4+**

Attributes	2.0	3.2	4.01	N3	N4	N6	IE3	IE4	IE 5	IE 5.5	IE6	O5.x
id=string	x	x	x	x	x	x	x	✓	✓	✓	✓	x
lang=language_type	x	x	x	x	x	x	x	✓	✓	✓	✓	x

dd

The definition of an item in a definition list, usually indented from other text. **ALL**

Attributes	2.0	3.2	4.01	N3	N4	N6	IE3	IE4	IE 5	IE 5.5	IE6	O5.x
<event_name>=script_code	x	x	✓	x	x	✓	x	✓	✓	✓	✓	✓
accesskey=key_character	x	x	x	x	x	x	x	x	✓	✓	✓	x
class=classname	x	x	✓	x	x	✓	✓	✓	✓	✓	✓	✓

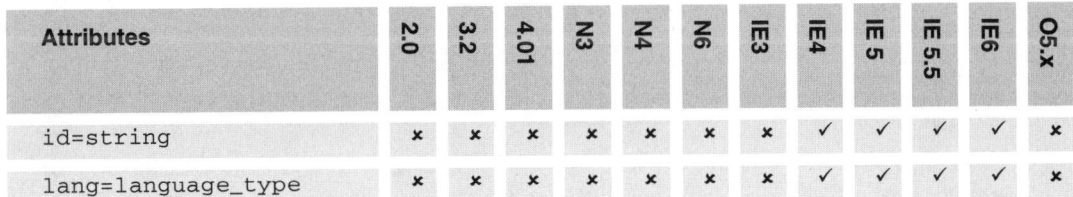

Table continued on following page

Attributes	2.0	3.2	4.01	N3	N4	N6	IE3	IE4	IE5	IE 5.5	IE6	O5.x
dir=ltr|rtl	x	x	✓	x	x	✓	x	x	✓	✓	✓	x
id=string	x	x	✓	x	✓	✓	✓	✓	✓	✓	✓	✓
lang=language_type	x	x	✓	x	x	✓	x	✓	✓	✓	✓	x
language=javascript|vbscript	x	x	x	x	x	x	x	✓	✓	✓	✓	x
nowrap	x	x	x	x	x	x	x	x	✓	✓	✓	x
style=string	x	x	✓	x	✓	✓	✓	✓	✓	✓	✓	✓
tabindex=number	x	x	x	x	x	x	x	x	✓	✓	✓	x
title=string	x	x	✓	x	x	✓	x	✓	✓	✓	✓	✓

del

Indicates a section of the document that has been deleted since a previous version. **HTML 4.01, N6, IE4+, O5.x**

Attributes	2.0	3.2	4.01	N3	N4	N6	IE3	IE4	IE5	IE 5.5	IE6	O5.x
<event_name>=script_code	x	x	✓	x	x	✓	x	✓	✓	✓	✓	✓
accesskey=key_character	x	x	x	x	x	x	x	x	✓	✓	✓	x
cite=url	x	x	✓	x	x	✓	x	x	x	x	✓	✓
class=classname	x	x	✓	x	x	✓	x	✓	✓	✓	✓	✓
datetime=date	x	x	✓	x	x	✓	x	x	x	x	✓	✓
dir=ltr|rtl	x	x	✓	x	x	✓	x	x	✓	✓	✓	x
id=string	x	x	✓	x	x	✓	x	✓	✓	✓	✓	✓
lang=language_type	x	x	✓	x	x	✓	x	✓	✓	✓	✓	x
language=javascript|vbscript	x	x	x	x	x	x	x	✓	✓	✓	✓	x
style=string	x	x	✓	x	x	✓	x	✓	✓	✓	✓	✓
tabindex=number	x	x	x	x	x	x	x	x	✓	✓	✓	x
title=string	x	x	✓	x	x	✓	x	✓	✓	✓	✓	✓

dfn

The defining instance of a term. **ALL except HTML 2.0**

Attributes	2.0	3.2	4.01	N3	N4	N6	IE3	IE4	IE5	IE 5.5	IE6	O5.x
`<event_name>= script_code`	✗	✗	✓	✗	✗	✓	✗	✓	✓	✓	✓	✓
`accesskey= key_character`	✗	✗	✗	✗	✗	✗	✗	✗	✓	✓	✓	✗
`class=classname`	✗	✗	✓	✗	✓	✓	✗	✓	✓	✓	✓	✓
`dir=ltr|rtl`	✗	✗	✓	✗	✗	✓	✗	✗	✗	✓	✓	✗
`id=string`	✗	✗	✓	✗	✓	✓	✓	✓	✓	✓	✓	✓
`lang=language_type`	✗	✗	✓	✗	✗	✓	✗	✓	✓	✓	✓	✗
`language=javascript| vbscript`	✗	✗	✗	✗	✗	✗	✗	✓	✓	✓	✓	✗
`style=string`	✗	✗	✗	✗	✓	✓	✗	✓	✓	✓	✓	✓
`tabindex=number`	✗	✗	✗	✗	✗	✗	✗	✗	✓	✓	✓	✗
`title=string`	✗	✗	✓	✗	✗	✓	✗	✓	✓	✓	✓	✓

dir

Renders text so that it appears like a directory-style file listing. **ALL, but deprecated in HTML 4.01**

Attributes	2.0	3.2	4.01	N3	N4	N6	IE3	IE4	IE5	IE 5.5	IE6	O5.x
`<event_name>= script_code`	✗	✗	D	✗	✗	✗	✗	✓	✓	✓	✓	✓
`accesskey= key_character`	✗	✗	✗	✗	✗	✗	✗	✗	✓	✓	✓	✗
`class=classname`	✗	✗	D	✗	✓	✓	✗	✓	✓	✓	✓	✓
`compact`	✓	✓	D	✗	✓	✓	✓	✗	✓	✓	✓	✗
`dir=ltr|rtl`	✗	✗	D	✗	✗	✓	✗	✗	✓	✓	✓	✗
`id=string`	✗	✗	D	✗	✓	✓	✗	✓	✓	✓	✓	✓
`lang=language_type`	✗	✗	D	✗	✗	✓	✗	✓	✓	✓	✓	✗

Table continued on following page

Attributes	2.0	3.2	4.01	N3	N4	N6	IE3	IE4	IE 5	IE 5.5	IE6	O5.x
language=javascript|vbscript	x	x	x	x	x	x	x	✓	✓	✓	✓	x
style=string	x	x	D	x	✓	✓	x	✓	✓	✓	✓	✓
tabindex=number	x	x	x	x	x	x	x	x	✓	✓	✓	x
title=string	x	x	D	x	x	✓	x	✓	✓	✓	✓	✓
type=button|reset|submit	x	x	x	x	✓	x	x	x	x	x	x	x

div

Defines a container section within the page, and can hold other elements. **ALL except HTML 2.0**

Attributes	2.0	3.2	4.01	N3	N4	N6	IE3	IE4	IE 5	IE 5.5	IE6	O5.x
<event_name>=script_code	x	x	✓	x	x	✓	x	✓	✓	✓	✓	✓
accesskey=key_character	x	x	x	x	x	x	x	x	✓	✓	✓	x
align=center|left|right	x	✓	D	✓	✓	✓	✓	✓	✓	✓	✓	✓
class=classname	x	x	✓	x	✓	✓	✓	✓	✓	✓	✓	✓
datafld=column_name	x	x	x	x	x	x	x	✓	✓	✓	✓	x
dataformatas=html|text	x	x	x	x	x	x	x	✓	✓	✓	✓	x
datasrc=id	x	x	x	x	x	x	x	✓	✓	✓	✓	x
dir=ltr|rtl	x	x	✓	x	x	✓	x	x	✓	✓	✓	x
id=string	x	x	✓	x	✓	✓	✓	✓	✓	✓	✓	✓
lang=language_type	x	x	✓	x	x	✓	✓	✓	✓	✓	✓	x
language=javascript|vbscript	x	x	x	x	x	x	x	✓	✓	✓	✓	x
nowrap	x	x	x	x	✓	x	✓	x	✓	✓	✓	x
style=string	x	x	✓	x	✓	✓	x	✓	✓	✓	✓	✓
tabindex=number	x	x	x	x	x	x	x	x	✓	✓	✓	x
title=string	x	x	✓	x	x	✓	x	✓	✓	✓	✓	✓

dl

Denotes a definition list. **ALL**

Attributes	2.0	3.2	4.01	N3	N4	N6	IE3	IE4	IE 5	IE 5.5	IE6	O5.x
<event_name>= script_code	x	x	✓	x	x	✓	x	✓	✓	✓	✓	✓
accesskey= key_character	x	x	x	x	x	x	x	x	✓	✓	✓	x
class=classname	x	x	✓	x	✓	✓	✓	✓	✓	✓	✓	✓
compact	✓	✓	D	x	✓	✓	✓	✓	✓	✓	✓	x
dir=ltr|rtl	x	x	✓	x	x	✓	x	✓	✓	✓	✓	x
id=string	x	x	✓	x	✓	✓	✓	✓	✓	✓	✓	✓
lang=language_type	x	x	✓	x	x	✓	x	✓	✓	✓	✓	x
language=javascript| vbscript	x	x	x	x	x	x	x	✓	✓	✓	✓	x
style=string	x	x	✓	x	✓	✓	x	✓	✓	✓	✓	✓
tabindex=number	x	x	x	x	x	x	x	x	✓	✓	✓	x
title=string	x	x	✓	x	x	✓	x	✓	✓	✓	✓	✓

dt

Denotes a definition term within a definition list. **ALL**

Attributes	2.0	3.2	4.01	N3	N4	N6	IE3	IE4	IE 5	IE 5.5	IE6	O5.x
<event_name>= script_code	x	x	✓	x	x	✓	x	✓	✓	✓	✓	✓
accesskey= key_character	x	x	x	x	x	x	x	x	✓	✓	✓	x
class=classname	x	x	✓	x	✓	✓	x	✓	✓	✓	✓	✓
dir=ltr|rtl	x	x	✓	x	x	✓	x	✓	✓	✓	✓	x
id=string	x	x	✓	x	✓	✓	x	✓	✓	✓	✓	✓
lang=language_type	x	x	✓	x	x	✓	x	✓	✓	✓	✓	x

Table continued on following page

Attributes	2.0	3.2	4.01	N3	N4	N6	IE3	IE4	IE 5	IE 5.5	IE6	O5.x
language=javascript|vbscript	x	x	x	x	x	x	x	✓	✓	✓	✓	x
nowrap	x	x	x	x	x	x	x	x	✓	✓	✓	x
style=string	x	x	✓	x	✓	✓	x	✓	✓	✓	✓	✓
tabindex=number	x	x	x	x	x	x	x	x	✓	✓	✓	✓
title=string	x	x	✓	x	x	✓	x	✓	✓	✓	✓	✓

em

Renders text as emphasized, usually in italics. **ALL**

Attributes	2.0	3.2	4.01	N3	N4	N6	IE3	IE4	IE 5	IE 5.5	IE6	O5.x
<event_name>=script_code	x	x	✓	x	x	✓	x	✓	✓	✓	✓	✓
accesskey=key_character	x	x	x	x	x	x	x	x	✓	✓	✓	x
class=classname	x	x	✓	x	✓	✓	x	✓	✓	✓	✓	✓
dir=ltr|rtl	x	x	✓	x	x	✓	x	x	✓	✓	✓	x
id=string	x	x	✓	x	✓	✓	x	✓	✓	✓	✓	✓
lang=language_type	x	x	✓	x	x	✓	x	✓	✓	✓	✓	x
language=javascript|vbscript	x	x	x	x	x	x	x	✓	✓	✓	✓	x
style=string	x	x	✓	x	✓	✓	x	✓	✓	✓	✓	✓
tabindex=number	x	x	x	x	x	x	x	x	✓	✓	✓	x
title=string	x	x	✓	x	x	✓	x	✓	✓	✓	✓	✓

embed

Embeds documents of any type in the page, to be viewed in another suitable application. **N3+, IE3+, O5**.x

Attributes	2.0	3.2	4.01	N3	N4	N6	IE3	IE4	IE5	IE 5.5	IE6	O5.x
accesskey= key_character	x	x	x	x	x	x	x	x	✓	✓	✓	x
align=absbottom| absmiddle|baseline| bottom|left|middle| right|texttop|top	x	x	x	x	✓	x	x	✓	✓	✓	✓	x
alt=text	x	x	x	x	x	x	x	✓	x	x	x	x
border=number	x	x	x	x	✓	x	x	x	x	x	x	x
class=classname	x	x	x	x	✓	x	x	✓	✓	✓	✓	x
code=filename	x	x	x	x	x	x	x	✓	x	x	x	x
codebase=path|url	x	x	x	x	x	x	x	✓	x	x	x	x
height=number	x	x	x	✓	✓	x	✓	✓	✓	✓	✓	x
hidden=string	x	x	x	x	✓	x	x	x	x	x	x	x
hspace=number	x	x	x	x	✓	x	x	✓	x	x	x	x
id=string	x	x	x	x	✓	x	x	✓	✓	✓	✓	x
lang=language_type	x	x	x	x	x	x	x	x	✓	✓	✓	x
language=javascript| vbscript	x	x	x	x	x	x	x	x	✓	✓	✓	x
name=string	x	x	x	✓	✓	x	✓	✓	✓	✓	✓	x
palette=foreground| background	x	x	x	x	✓	x	✓	x	x	x	x	x
pluginspage=string	x	x	x	x	✓	x	x	x	✓	✓	✓	x
pluginurl	x	x	x	x	✓	x	x	x	x	x	x	x
src=url	x	x	x	✓	✓	x	✓	✓	✓	✓	✓	x
style=string	x	x	x	x	✓	x	x	✓	✓	✓	✓	x
title=string	x	x	x	x	x	x	x	✓	✓	✓	✓	x
type=button|reset| submit	x	x	x	x	✓	x	x	x	x	x	x	x
units=en|ems|pixels	x	x	x	x	✓	x	✓	✓	✓	✓	✓	x
vspace=number	x	x	x	x	✓	x	x	✓	x	x	x	x
width=number	x	x	x	✓	✓	x	✓	✓	✓	✓	✓	x

fieldset

Draws a box around the contained elements to indicate related items. **HTML 4.01, N6, IE4+, O5.x**

Attributes	2.0	3.2	4.01	N3	N4	N6	IE3	IE4	IE 5	IE 5.5	IE6	O5.x
`<event_name>=` `script_code`	✗	✗	✓	✗	✗	✓	✗	✓	✓	✓	✓	✓
`accesskey=` `key_character`	✗	✗	✗	✗	✗	✗	✗	✗	✓	✓	✓	✗
`align=center|left|` `right`	✗	✗	✗	✗	✗	✗	✗	✓	✓	✓	✓	✗
`class=classname`	✗	✗	✓	✗	✗	✓	✗	✓	✓	✓	✓	✓
`dir=ltr|rtl`	✗	✗	✓	✗	✗	✓	✗	✗	✓	✓	✓	✗
`id=string`	✗	✗	✓	✗	✗	✓	✗	✓	✓	✓	✓	✓
`lang=language_type`	✗	✗	✓	✗	✗	✓	✗	✓	✓	✓	✓	✗
`language=javascript|` `vbscript`	✗	✗	✗	✗	✗	✗	✗	✓	✓	✓	✓	✗
`style=string`	✗	✗	✓	✗	✗	✓	✗	✓	✓	✓	✓	✓
`tabindex=number`	✗	✗	✗	✗	✗	✗	✗	✗	✓	✓	✓	✗
`title=string`	✗	✗	✓	✗	✗	✓	✗	✓	✓	✓	✓	✗

font

Specifies the font face, size, and color for rendering the text. **HTML 3.2, deprecated in HTML 4.01, N3+, IE3+, O5.x**

Attributes	2.0	3.2	4.01	N3	N4	N6	IE3	IE4	IE 5	IE 5.5	IE6	O5.x
`<event_name>=` `script_code`	✗	✗	✗	✗	✗	✗	✗	✓	✓	✓	✓	✗
`accesskey=` `key_character`	✗	✗	✗	✗	✗	✗	✗	✗	✓	✓	✓	✗
`class=classname`	✗	✗	D	✗	✓	✓	✗	✓	✓	✓	✓	✓
`color=color`	✗	✓	D	✓	✓	✓	✓	✓	✓	✓	✓	✓
`dir=ltr|rtl`	✗	✗	D	✗	✗	✓	✗	✗	✓	✓	✓	✗

Attributes	2.0	3.2	4.01	N3	N4	N6	IE3	IE4	IE5	IE 5.5	IE6	O5.x
face=font_family_name	x	x	D	✓	✓	✓	✓	✓	✓	✓	✓	✓
id=string	x	x	D	x	✓	✓	x	✓	✓	✓	✓	✓
lang=language_type	x	x	D	x	x	✓	x	✓	✓	✓	✓	x
language=javascript|vbscript	x	x	x	x	x	x	x	✓	✓	✓	✓	x
point-size=string|number	x	x	x	x	✓	x	x	x	x	x	x	x
size=number	x	✓	D	✓	✓	✓	✓	✓	✓	✓	✓	✓
style=string	x	x	D	x	✓	✓	x	✓	✓	✓	✓	✓
tabindex=number	x	x	x	x	x	x	x	x	✓	✓	✓	x
title=string	x	x	D	x	x	✓	x	✓	✓	✓	x	x
weight	x	x	x	x	✓	x	x	x	x	x	x	x

form

Denotes a form containing controls and elements, whose values are sent to a server. **ALL**

Attributes	2.0	3.2	4.01	N3	N4	N6	IE3	IE4	IE5	IE 5.5	IE6	O5.x
<event_name>=script_code	x	x	✓	x	✓	✓	✓	✓	✓	✓	✓	✓
accept-charset=string	x	x	✓	x	x	✓	x	x	✓	✓	✓	x
action=string	✓	✓	✓	✓	✓	✓	✓	✓	✓	✓	✓	✓
autocomplete	x	x	x	x	x	x	x	x	✓	✓	✓	x
class=classname	x	x	✓	x	✓	✓	x	✓	✓	✓	✓	✓
dir=ltr|rtl	x	x	✓	x	x	✓	x	x	✓	✓	✓	✓
enctype=string	✓	✓	✓	✓	✓	✓	x	✓	✓	✓	✓	✓
id=string	x	x	✓	x	✓	✓	x	✓	✓	✓	✓	✓
lang=language_type	x	x	✓	x	x	✓	x	✓	✓	✓	✓	x
language=javascript|vbscript	x	x	x	x	x	x	x	✓	✓	✓	✓	x

Table continued on following page

Attributes	2.0	3.2	4.01	N3	N4	N6	IE3	IE4	IE5	IE 5.5	IE6	O5.x
method=get|post	✓	✓	✓	✓	✓	✓	✓	✓	✓	✓	✓	✓
name=string	✗	✗	✓	✗	✓	✓	✗	✓	✓	✓	✓	✓
style=string	✗	✗	✓	✗	✓	✓	✗	✓	✓	✓	✓	✓
target=<window_name>|_parent|_blank|_top|_self	✗	✗	✓	✓	✓	✓	✓	✓	✓	✓	✓	✓
title=string	✗	✗	✓	✗	✗	✓	✗	✓	✓	✓	✓	✗

*included for backwards compatibility; use the id attribute to identify elements

frame

Specifies an individual frame within a frameset. **HTML 4.01, N3+, IE3+, O5.x**

Attributes	2.0	3.2	4.01	N3	N4	N6	IE3	IE4	IE5	IE 5.5	IE6	O5.x
<event_name>=script_code	✗	✗	✗	✗	✓	✓	✗	✓	✓	✓	✓	✗
align=center|left|right	✗	✗	✗	✗	✓	✗	✓	✗	✗	✗	✗	✗
application	✗	✗	✗	✗	✗	✗	✗	✗	✓	✓	✓	✗
bordercolor=color	✗	✗	✗	✓	✓	✓	✗	✓	✓	✓	✓	✗
class=classname	✗	✗	✓	✗	✓	✓	✗	✓	✓	✓	✓	✓
datafld=column_name	✗	✗	✗	✗	✗	✗	✗	✓	✓	✓	✓	✗
datasrc=id	✗	✗	✗	✗	✗	✗	✗	✓	✓	✓	✓	✗
frameborder=no|yes|0|1	✗	✗	✓	✓	✓	✓	✓	✓	✓	✓	✓	✓
height=number	✗	✗	✗	✗	✗	✗	✗	✗	✓	✓	✓	✗
id=string	✗	✗	✓	✗	✓	✓	✗	✓	✓	✓	✓	✓
lang=language_type	✗	✗	✗	✗	✗	✓	✗	✓	✓	✓	✓	✗
language=javascript|vbscript	✗	✗	✗	✗	✗	✗	✗	✓	✓	✓	✓	✗
longdesc=url	✗	✗	✓	✗	✗	✓	✗	✗	✗	✗	✗	✓
marginheight=number	✗	✗	✓	✓	✓	✓	✓	✓	✓	✓	✓	✓

Attributes	2.0	3.2	4.01	N3	N4	N6	IE3	IE4	IE 5	IE 5.5	IE6	O5.x
marginwidth=number	x	x	✓	✓	✓	✓	✓	✓	✓	✓	✓	✓
name=string	x	x	✓	✓	✓	✓	✓	✓	✓	✓	✓	✓
noresize=noresize|resize	x	x	✓	✓	✓	✓	✓	✓	✓	✓	✓	✓
scrolling=auto|yes|no	x	x	✓	✓	✓	✓	✓	✓	✓	✓	✓	✓
src=url	x	x	✓	✓	✓	✓	✓	✓	✓	✓	✓	✓
style=string	x	x	✓	x	x	✓	x	✓	x	x	x	x
tabindex=number	x	x	x	x	x	x	x	x	✓	✓	✓	x
title=string	x	x	x	x	✓	✓	✓	✓	✓	✓	✓	x
width=number	x	x	x	x	x	x	x	x	✓	✓	✓	x

frameset

Specifies a frameset containing multiple frames and other nested framesets.
HTML 4.01, N3+, IE3+, O5.x

Attributes	2.0	3.2	4.01	N3	N4	N6	IE3	IE4	IE 5	IE 5.5	IE6	O5.x
<event_name>=script_code	x	x	✓	x	x	x	x	x	x	x	x	✓
border=number	x	x	x	✓	✓	✓	x	✓	✓	✓	✓	x
bordercolor=color	x	x	x	✓	✓	x	x	✓	✓	✓	✓	x
class=classname	x	x	✓	x	✓	✓	x	✓	✓	✓	✓	✓
cols=number	x	x	✓	✓	✓	✓	✓	✓	✓	✓	✓	✓
dir=ltr|rtl	x	x	x	x	x	✓	x	x	x	x	x	x
frameborder=no|yes|0|1	x	x	x	✓	✓	x	✓	✓	✓	✓	✓	x
framespacing=number	x	x	x	x	x	x	✓	✓	✓	✓	✓	x
id=string	x	x	✓	x	✓	✓	x	✓	✓	✓	✓	✓
lang=language_type	x	x	x	x	x	✓	x	✓	✓	✓	✓	x
language=javascript|vbscript	x	x	x	x	x	x	x	✓	✓	✓	✓	x

Table continued on following page

Attributes	2.0	3.2	4.01	N3	N4	N6	IE3	IE4	IE 5	IE 5.5	IE6	O5.x
rows=number	✗	✗	✓	✓	✓	✓	✓	✓	✓	✓	✓	✓
style=string	✗	✗	✓	✗	✗	✓	✗	✗	✗	✗	✗	✓
title=string	✗	✗	✓	✗	✗	✓	✗	✓	✓	✓	✓	✓

head

Contains tags holding information about the document that won't be displayed. **ALL**

Attributes	2.0	3.2	4.01	N3	N4	N6	IE3	IE4	IE 5	IE 5.5	IE6	O5.x
class=classname	✗	✗	✗	✗	✓	✓	✗	✓	✓	✓	✓	✗
dir=ltr|rtl	✗	✗	✓	✗	✗	✓	✗	✗	✗	✗	✗	✗
id=string	✗	✗	✗	✗	✓	✓	✗	✓	✓	✓	✓	✗
lang=language_type	✗	✗	✓	✗	✗	✓	✗	✗	✓	✓	✓	✗
profile=url	✗	✗	✓	✗	✗	✓	✗	✗	✓	✓	✓	✗

h(n)

The six elements (h1 through h6) render text as a range of heading styles. **ALL**

Attributes	2.0	3.2	4.01	N3	N4	N6	IE3	IE4	IE 5	IE 5.5	IE6	O5.x
<event_name>= script_code	✗	✗	✓	✗	✗	✓	✗	✓	✓	✓	✓	✓
accesskey= key_character	✗	✗	✗	✗	✗	✗	✗	✗	✓	✓	✓	✗
align=center| left|right	✗	✓	D	✓	✗	✓	✓	✓	✓	✓	✓	✓
class=classname	✗	✗	✓	✗	✓	✓	✗	✓	✓	✓	✓	✓
dir=ltr|rtl	✗	✗	✓	✗	✗	✓	✗	✗	✓	✓	✓	✗
id=string	✗	✗	✓	✗	✓	✓	✗	✓	✓	✓	✓	✓
lang=language_type	✗	✗	✓	✗	✗	✓	✗	✓	✓	✓	✓	✗

Attributes	2.0	3.2	4.01	N3	N4	N6	IE3	IE4	IE5	IE 5.5	IE6	O5.x
language=javascript|vbscript	x	x	x	x	x	x	x	✓	✓	✓	✓	x
style=string	x	x	✓	x	✓	✓	x	✓	✓	✓	✓	✓
tabindex=number	x	x	x	x	x	x	x	x	x	x	x	x
title=string	x	x	✓	x	x	✓	x	✓	✓	✓	✓	✓

hr

Places a horizontal rule in the page. **ALL**

Attributes	2.0	3.2	4.01	N3	N4	N6	IE3	IE4	IE5	IE 5.5	IE6	O5.x
<event_name>=script_code	x	x	✓	x	x	✓	x	✓	✓	✓	✓	✓
align=center|left|right	x	✓	D	✓	✓	✓	✓	✓	✓	✓	✓	✓
class=classname	x	x	✓	x	x	✓	x	✓	✓	✓	✓	✓
color=color	x	x	x	x	x	x	✓	✓	✓	✓	✓	x
dir=ltr|rtl	x	x	✓	x	x	✓	x	x	x	x	x	x
id=string	x	x	✓	x	✓	✓	✓	✓	✓	✓	✓	✓
lang=language_type	x	x	✓	x	x	✓	x	✓	x	x	x	x
language=javascript|vbscript	x	x	x	x	x	x	x	✓	✓	✓	✓	x
noshade	x	✓	D	✓	✓	✓	✓	✓	✓	✓	✓	x
size=number	x	✓	D	✓	✓	✓	✓	✓	✓	✓	✓	✓
src=url	x	x	x	x	x	x	x	✓	x	x	x	x
style=string	x	x	✓	x	✓	✓	✓	✓	✓	✓	✓	✓
tabindex=number	x	x	x	x	x	x	x	x	✓	✓	✓	✓
title=string	x	x	✓	x	x	✓	x	✓	✓	✓	✓	✓
width=number	x	✓	D	✓	✓	✓	✓	✓	✓	x	x	✓

html

The outermost tag for the page, identifying the document as containing HTML elements. **ALL**

Attributes	2.0	3.2	4.01	N3	N4	N6	IE3	IE4	IE 5	IE 5.5	IE6	O5.x
class=classname	✗	✗	✗	✗	✗	✓	✗	✗	✓	✓	✓	✗
dir=ltr|rtl	✗	✗	✓	✗	✗	✓	✗	✗	✓	✓	✓	✗
id=string	✗	✗	✗	✗	✗	✓	✗	✗	✓	✓	✓	✗
lang=language_type	✗	✗	✓	✗	✗	✓	✗	✗	✗	✗	✗	✗
version=url	✗	✗	D	✗	✗	✓	✗	✗	✗	✗	✓	✓
xmlns=url	✗	✗	✗	✗	✗	✗	✗	✗	✓	✓	✓	✗

i

Renders text in an italic font where available. **ALL**

Attributes	2.0	3.2	4.01	N3	N4	N6	IE3	IE4	IE 5	IE 5.5	IE6	O5.x
<event_name>= script_code	✗	✗	✓	✗	✗	✓	✗	✓	✓	✓	✓	✓
accesskey= key_character	✗	✗	✗	✗	✗	✗	✗	✗	✓	✓	✓	✗
class=classname	✗	✗	✓	✗	✓	✓	✗	✓	✓	✓	✓	✓
dir=ltr|rtl	✗	✗	✓	✗	✗	✓	✗	✗	✗	✓	✓	✗
id=string	✗	✗	✓	✗	✓	✓	✗	✓	✓	✓	✓	✓
lang=language_type	✗	✗	✓	✗	✗	✓	✗	✓	✓	✓	✓	✗
language=javascript| vbscript	✗	✗	✗	✗	✗	✗	✗	✓	✓	✓	✓	✗
style=string	✗	✗	✓	✗	✓	✓	✗	✓	✓	✓	✓	✓
tabindex=number	✗	✗	✗	✗	✗	✗	✗	✗	✓	✓	✓	✗
title=string	✗	✗	✓	✗	✗	✓	✗	✓	✓	✓	✓	✓

iframe

Used to create inline floating frames within the page. **HTML 4.01, N6, IE3+, O5**.x

Attributes	2.0	3.2	4.01	N3	N4	N6	IE3	IE4	IE 5	IE 5.5	IE6	O5.x
align=absbottom| absmiddle|baseline| bottom|left|middle| right|texttop|top	✗	✗	D	✗	✗	✓	✗	✓	✓	✓	✓	✓
application	✗	✗	✗	✗	✗	✗	✗	✗	✓	✓	✓	✗
border=number	✗	✗	✗	✗	✗	✗	✗	✓	✗	✓	✓	✗
bordercolor=color	✗	✗	✗	✗	✗	✗	✗	✓	✓	✓	✓	✓
class=classname	✗	✗	✓	✗	✗	✓	✗	✓	✓	✓	✓	✓
datafld=column_name	✗	✗	✗	✗	✗	✗	✗	✓	✓	✓	✓	✗
datasrc=id	✗	✗	✗	✗	✗	✗	✗	✓	✓	✓	✓	✗
frameborder= no|yes|0|1	✗	✗	✓	✗	✗	✓	✗	✓	✓	✓	✓	✓
framespacing=number	✗	✗	✗	✗	✗	✗	✗	✓	✗	✗	✗	✗
height=number	✗	✗	✓	✗	✗	✓	✗	✓	✓	✓	✓	✓
hspace=number	✗	✗	✗	✗	✗	✗	✗	✓	✓	✓	✓	✗
id=string	✗	✗	✓	✗	✗	✓	✗	✓	✓	✓	✓	✓
lang=language_type	✗	✗	✗	✗	✗	✓	✗	✓	✓	✓	✓	✗
language=javascript| vbscript	✗	✗	✗	✗	✗	✗	✗	✓	✓	✓	✓	✗
longdesc=url	✗	✗	✓	✗	✗	✓	✗	✗	✗	✗	✗	✓
marginheight=number	✗	✗	✓	✗	✗	✓	✗	✓	✓	✓	✓	✓
marginwidth=number	✗	✗	✓	✗	✗	✓	✗	✓	✓	✓	✓	✓
name=string	✗	✗	✓	✗	✗	✓	✗	✓	✓	✓	✓	✓
noresize=noresize| resize	✗	✗	✗	✗	✗	✗	✗	✓	✗	✗	✗	✗
scrollingauto|yes|no	✗	✗	✓	✗	✗	✓	✗	✓	✓	✓	✓	✓
src=url	✗	✗	✓	✗	✗	✓	✗	✓	✓	✓	✓	✓
style=string	✗	✗	✓	✗	✗	✓	✗	✓	✓	✓	✓	✓
tabindex=number	✗	✗	✗	✗	✗	✗	✗	✗	✓	✓	✓	✗
title=string	✗	✗	✓	✗	✗	✓	✗	✓	✓	✓	✓	✓
vspace=number	✗	✗	✗	✗	✗	✗	✗	✓	✓	✓	✓	✗
width=number	✗	✗	✓	✗	✗	✓	✗	✓	✓	✓	✓	✓

ilayer

Defines a separate area of the page as an inline layer that can hold a different page. **N4**

Attributes	2.0	3.2	4.01	N3	N4	N6	IE3	IE4	IE5	IE 5.5	IE6	O5.x
`<event_name>=` `script_code`	✗	✗	✗	✗	✓	✗	✗	✗	✗	✗	✗	✗
`above=object_id`	✗	✗	✗	✗	✓	✗	✗	✗	✗	✗	✗	✗
`background=string`	✗	✗	✗	✗	✓	✗	✗	✗	✗	✗	✗	✗
`below=object_id`	✗	✗	✗	✗	✓	✗	✗	✗	✗	✗	✗	✗
`bgcolor=color`	✗	✗	✗	✗	✓	✗	✗	✗	✗	✗	✗	✗
`class=classname`	✗	✗	✗	✗	✓	✗	✗	✗	✗	✗	✗	✗
`clip=number[,number,` `number,number]`	✗	✗	✗	✗	✓	✗	✗	✗	✗	✗	✗	✗
`id=string`	✗	✗	✗	✗	✓	✗	✗	✗	✗	✗	✗	✗
`left=number`	✗	✗	✗	✗	✓	✗	✗	✗	✗	✗	✗	✗
`name=string`	✗	✗	✗	✗	✓	✗	✗	✗	✗	✗	✗	✗
`pagex=number`	✗	✗	✗	✗	✓	✗	✗	✗	✗	✗	✗	✗
`pagey=number`	✗	✗	✗	✗	✓	✗	✗	✗	✗	✗	✗	✗
`src=url`	✗	✗	✗	✗	✓	✗	✗	✗	✗	✗	✗	✗
`style=string`	✗	✗	✗	✗	✓	✗	✗	✗	✗	✗	✗	✗
`top=number`	✗	✗	✗	✗	✓	✗	✗	✗	✗	✗	✗	✗
`visibility=` `show|hide|inherit`	✗	✗	✗	✗	✓	✗	✗	✗	✗	✗	✗	✗
`width=number`	✗	✗	✗	✗	✓	✗	✗	✗	✗	✗	✗	✗
`z-index=number`	✗	✗	✗	✗	✓	✗	✗	✗	✗	✗	✗	✗

img

Embeds an image or a video clip in the document. **ALL**

Attributes	2.0	3.2	4.01	N3	N4	N6	IE3	IE4	IE 5	IE 5.5	IE6	O5.x
`<event_name>=` `script_code`	✗	✗	✓	✗	✓	✓	✗	✓	✓	✓	✓	✓
`accesskey=` `key_character`	✗	✗	✗	✗	✗	✗	✗	✗	✓	✓	✓	✗
`align=absbottom|` `absmiddle|baseline|` `bottom|left|middle|` `right|texttop|top`	✓	✓	D	✓	✓	✓	✓	✓	✓	✓	✓	✓
`alt=text`	✓	✓	✓	✓	✓	✓	✓	✓	✓	✓	✓	✓
`border=number`	✗	✓	D	✓	✓	✓	✓	✓	✓	✓	✓	✓
`class=classname`	✗	✗	✓	✗	✓	✓	✓	✓	✓	✓	✓	✓
`controls`	✗	✗	✗	✗	✗	✗	✓	✗	✗	✗	✗	✗
`datafld=column_name`	✗	✗	✗	✗	✗	✗	✗	✓	✓	✓	✓	✗
`datasrc=id`	✗	✗	✗	✗	✗	✗	✗	✓	✓	✓	✓	✗
`dir=ltr|rtl`	✗	✗	✓	✗	✗	✓	✗	✗	✓	✓	✓	✗
`dynsrc=string`	✗	✗	✗	✗	✗	✗	✓	✓	✓	✓	✓	✗
`height=number`	✗	✓	✓	✓	✓	✓	✓	✓	✓	✓	✓	✓
`hspace=number`	✗	✓	D	✓	✓	✓	✓	✓	✓	✓	✓	✓
`id=string`	✗	✗	✓	✗	✓	✓	✓	✓	✓	✓	✓	✓
`ismap`	✓	✓	✓	✓	✓	✓	✓	✓	✓	✓	✓	✓
`lang=language_type`	✗	✗	✓	✗	✗	✓	✗	✓	✓	✓	✓	✗
`language=javascript|` `vbscript`	✗	✗	✗	✗	✗	✗	✗	✓	✓	✓	✓	✗
`longdesc=url`	✗	✗	✓	✗	✗	✓	✗	✗	✗	✗	✗	✓
`loop=number`	✗	✗	✗	✗	✗	✗	✓	✓	✓	✓	✓	✗
`lowsrc=url`	✗	✗	✗	✓	✓	✓	✗	✓	✓	✓	✓	✗
`name=string`	✗	✗	✓	✗	✓	✓	✗	✓	✓	✓	✓	✓
`src=url`	✓	✓	✓	✓	✓	✓	✓	✓	✓	✓	✓	✓

Table continued on following page

Attributes	2.0	3.2	4.01	N3	N4	N6	IE3	IE4	IE 5	IE 5.5	IE6	O5.x
start=number|string	✗	✗	✗	✗	✗	✗	✓	✗	✓	✓	✓	✗
style=string	✗	✗	✓	✗	✓	✓	✓	✓	✓	✓	✓	✓
tabindex=number	✗	✗	✗	✗	✗	✗	✗	✗	✓	✓	✓	✗
title=string	✗	✗	✓	✗	✗	✓	✓	✓	✓	✓	✓	✓
usemap=url	✗	✓	✓	✓	✓	✓	✓	✓	✓	✓	✓	✓
vspace=number	✗	✓	D	✓	✓	✓	✓	✓	✓	✓	✓	✓
width=number	✗	✓	✓	✓	✓	✓	✓	✓	✓	✓	✓	✓

*included for backwards compatibility; use the id attribute to identify elements

input

Specifies a form input control, such as a button, text or check box. **ALL**

Attributes	2.0	3.2	4.01	N3	N4	N6	IE3	IE4	IE 5	IE 5.5	IE6	O5.x
<event_name>=script_code	✗	✗	✓	✗	✓	✓	✓	✓	✓	✓	✓	✓
accept-charset	✗	✗	✓	✗	✗	✓	✗	✗	✗	✓	✓	✗
accesskey=key_character	✗	✗	✓	✗	✗	✓	✗	✓	✓	✓	✓	✗
align=center|left|right	✓	✓	D	✓	✓	✓	✓	✓	✓	✓	✓	✓
alt=text	✗	✗	✓	✗	✗	✓	✗	✗	✗	✓	✓	✓
autocomplete	✗	✗	✗	✗	✗	✗	✗	✗	✓	✓	✓	✗
checked	✓	✓	✓	✓	✓	✓	✓	✓	✓	✓	✓	✓
class=classname	✗	✗	✓	✗	✓	✓	✓	✓	✓	✓	✓	✓
datafld=column_name	✗	✗	✗	✗	✗	✗	✗	✓	✓	✓	✓	✗
dataformatas	✗	✗	✗	✗	✗	✗	✗	✓	✓	✓	✓	✗
datasrc=id	✗	✗	✗	✗	✗	✗	✗	✓	✓	✓	✓	✗
dir=ltr|rtl	✗	✗	✓	✗	✗	✓	✗	✗	✓	✓	✓	✗
disabled	✗	✗	✓	✗	✗	✓	✗	✓	✓	✓	✓	✓
id=string	✗	✗	✓	✗	✓	✓	✓	✓	✓	✓	✓	✓

Attributes	2.0	3.2	4.01	N3	N4	N6	IE3	IE4	IE5	IE 5.5	IE6	O5.x
lang=language_type	✗	✗	✓	✗	✗	✓	✗	✓	✓	✓	✓	✗
language=javascript|vbscript	✗	✗	✗	✗	✗	✗	✗	✓	✓	✓	✓	✗
maxlength=number	✓	✓	✓	✓	✓	✓	✓	✓	✓	✓	✓	✓
name=string	✓	✓	✓	✓	✓	✓	✓	✓	✓	✓	✓	✓
notab	✗	✗	✗	✗	✗	✗	✓	✗	✗	✗	✗	✗
readonly	✗	✗	✓	✗	✗	✓	✗	✓	✓	✓	✓	✓
size=number	✓	✓	✓	✓	✓	✓	✓	✓	✓	✓	✓	✓
src=url	✓	✓	✓	✓	✓	✗	✓	✓	✓	✓	✓	✓
style=string	✗	✗	✓	✗	✓	✓	✓	✓	✓	✓	✓	✓
tabindex=number	✗	✗	✓	✗	✗	✓	✓	✓	✓	✓	✓	✗
title=string	✗	✗	✓	✗	✗	✓	✓	✓	✓	✓	✓	✓
type=button|reset|submit	✓	✓	✓	✓	✓	✓	✓	✓	✓	✓	✓	✓
usemap=url	✗	✗	✗	✗	✗	✓	✗	✗	✗	✗	✗	✓
value=string	✓	✓	✓	✓	✓	✓	✓	✓	✓	✓	✓	✓
vcard_name=filename	✗	✗	✗	✗	✗	✗	✗	✗	✓	✓	✓	✗

ins

Indicates a section of the document that has been inserted since a previous version. **HTML 4.01, N6, IE4+, O5.x**

Attributes	2.0	3.2	4.01	N3	N4	N6	IE3	IE4	IE5	IE 5.5	IE6	O5.x
<event_name>=script_code	✗	✗	✓	✗	✗	✓	✗	✓	✓	✓	✓	✓
accesskey=key_character	✗	✗	✗	✗	✗	✗	✗	✗	✓	✓	✓	✗
cite=url	✗	✗	✓	✗	✗	✓	✗	✗	✗	✗	✓	✓
class=classname	✗	✗	✓	✗	✗	✓	✗	✓	✓	✓	✓	✓
datetime=date	✗	✗	✓	✗	✗	✓	✗	✗	✗	✗	✓	✓

Table continued on following page

Attributes	2.0	3.2	4.01	N3	N4	N6	IE3	IE4	IE5	IE 5.5	IE6	O5.x
dir=ltr|rtl	x	x	✓	x	x	✓	x	x	✓	✓	✓	x
id=string	x	x	✓	x	x	✓	x	✓	✓	✓	✓	✓
lang=language_type	x	x	✓	x	x	✓	x	✓	✓	✓	✓	x
language=javascript|vbscript	x	x	x	x	x	x	x	✓	✓	✓	✓	x
style=string	x	x	✓	x	x	✓	x	✓	✓	✓	✓	✓
tabindex=number	x	x	x	x	x	x	x	x	✓	✓	✓	x
title=string	x	x	✓	x	x	✓	x	✓	✓	✓	✓	✓

isindex

Indicates the presence of a searchable index. **ALL, but deprecated in HTML 4.01**

Attributes	2.0	3.2	4.01	N3	N4	N6	IE3	IE4	IE5	IE 5.5	IE6	O5.x
accesskey=key_character	x	x	x	x	x	x	x	x	✓	✓	✓	x
action=string	x	x	x	✓	✓	x	✓	x	✓	✓	✓	x
class=classname	x	x	D	x	✓	✓	x	✓	✓	✓	✓	✓
dir=ltr|rtl	x	x	D	x	x	✓	x	x	x	x	x	x
id=string	x	x	D	x	✓	✓	x	✓	✓	✓	✓	x
lang=language_type	x	x	D	x	x	✓	x	✓	✓	✓	✓	x
language=javascript|vbscript	x	x	x	x	x	x	x	✓	✓	✓	✓	x
prompt=string	x	✓	D	✓	✓	✓	✓	✓	✓	x	x	✓
style=string	x	x	D	x	✓	✓	x	✓	✓	✓	✓	✓
tabindex=number	x	x	x	x	x	x	x	x	✓	✓	✓	x
title=string	x	x	D	x	x	✓	x	x	x	x	x	✓

kbd

Renders text in a fixed-width font, as though entered on a keyboard. **ALL**

Attributes	2.0	3.2	4.01	N3	N4	N6	IE3	IE4	IE 5	IE 5.5	IE6	O5.x
`<event_name>=` `script_code`	x	x	✓	x	x	✓	x	✓	✓	✓	✓	✓
`accesskey=` `key_character`	x	x	x	x	x	x	x	x	✓	✓	✓	x
`class=classname`	x	x	✓	x	✓	✓	x	✓	✓	✓	✓	✓
`dir=ltr|rtl`	x	x	✓	x	x	✓	x	x	✓	✓	✓	x
`id=string`	x	x	✓	x	✓	✓	x	✓	✓	✓	✓	✓
`lang=language_type`	x	x	✓	x	x	✓	x	✓	✓	✓	✓	x
`language=javascript|` `vbscript`	x	x	x	x	x	x	x	✓	✓	✓	✓	x
`style=string`	x	x	✓	x	✓	✓	x	✓	✓	✓	✓	✓
`tabindex=number`	x	x	x	x	x	x	x	x	✓	✓	✓	x
`title=string`	x	x	✓	x	x	✓	x	✓	✓	✓	✓	✓

keygen

Used to generate key material in the page. **N3+**

Attributes	2.0	3.2	4.01	N3	N4	N6	IE3	IE4	IE 5	IE 5.5	IE6	O5.x
`challenge=string`	x	x	x	x	✓	x	x	x	x	x	x	x
`class=classname`	x	x	x	x	✓	x	x	x	x	x	x	x
`id=string`	x	x	x	x	✓	x	x	x	x	x	x	x
`name=string`	x	x	x	x	✓	x	x	x	x	x	x	x

label

Defines the text of a label for a control-like element. **HTML 4.01, N6, IE4+**

Attributes	2.0	3.2	4.01	N3	N4	N6	IE3	IE4	IE 5	IE 5.5	IE6	O5.x
`<event_name>= script_code`	x	x	✓	x	x	✓	x	✓	✓	✓	✓	x
`accesskey= key_character`	x	x	✓	x	x	✓	x	✓	✓	✓	✓	x
`class=classname`	x	x	✓	x	x	✓	x	✓	✓	✓	✓	x
`datafld=column_name`	x	x	x	x	x	x	x	✓	✓	✓	✓	x
`dataformatas= html|text`	x	x	x	x	x	x	x	✓	✓	✓	✓	x
`datasrc=id`	x	x	x	x	x	x	x	✓	✓	✓	✓	x
`dir=ltr|rtl`	x	x	✓	x	x	✓	x	x	✓	✓	✓	x
`disabled`	x	x	x	x	x	x	x	x	x	✓	✓	x
`for=element_name`	x	x	✓	x	x	x	x	✓	✓	✓	✓	x
`id=string`	x	x	✓	x	x	✓	x	✓	✓	✓	✓	x
`lang=language_type`	x	x	✓	x	x	✓	x	✓	✓	✓	✓	x
`language=javascript| vbscript`	x	x	x	x	x	x	x	✓	✓	✓	✓	x
`style=string`	x	x	✓	x	x	✓	x	✓	✓	✓	✓	x
`tabindex=number`	x	x	x	x	x	x	x	x	✓	✓	✓	x
`title=string`	x	x	✓	x	x	✓	x	✓	✓	✓	✓	x

layer

Defines a separate area of the page as a layer that can hold a different page. **N4**

Attributes	2.0	3.2	4.01	N3	N4	N6	IE3	IE4	IE 5	IE 5.5	IE6	O5.x
`<event_name>= script_code`	x	x	x	x	✓	x	x	x	x	x	x	x
`above=object_id`	x	x	x	x	✓	x	x	x	x	x	x	x
`background=string`	x	x	x	x	✓	x	x	x	x	x	x	x

Attributes	2.0	3.2	4.01	N3	N4	N6	IE3	IE4	IE 5	IE 5.5	IE6	O5.x
below=object_id	✗	✗	✗	✗	✓	✗	✗	✗	✗	✗	✗	✗
bgcolor=color	✗	✗	✗	✗	✓	✗	✗	✗	✗	✗	✗	✗
class=classname	✗	✗	✗	✗	✓	✗	✗	✗	✗	✗	✗	✗
clip=number[,number, number,number]	✗	✗	✗	✗	✓	✗	✗	✗	✗	✗	✗	✗
id=string	✗	✗	✗	✗	✓	✗	✗	✗	✗	✗	✗	✗
left=number	✗	✗	✗	✗	✓	✗	✗	✗	✗	✗	✗	✗
name=string	✗	✗	✗	✗	✓	✗	✗	✗	✗	✗	✗	✗
pagex=number	✗	✗	✗	✗	✓	✗	✗	✗	✗	✗	✗	✗
pagey=number	✗	✗	✗	✗	✓	✗	✗	✗	✗	✗	✗	✗
src=url	✗	✗	✗	✗	✓	✗	✗	✗	✗	✗	✗	✗
style=string	✗	✗	✗	✗	✓	✗	✗	✗	✗	✗	✗	✗
top=number	✗	✗	✗	✗	✓	✗	✗	✗	✗	✗	✗	✗
visibility=show|hide|inherit	✗	✗	✗	✗	✓	✗	✗	✗	✗	✗	✗	✗
width=number	✗	✗	✗	✗	✓	✗	✗	✗	✗	✗	✗	✗
z-index=number	✗	✗	✗	✗	✓	✗	✗	✗	✗	✗	✗	✗

legend

Defines the title text to place in the 'box' created by a `fieldset` tag. **HTML 4.01, N6, IE4+**

Attributes	2.0	3.2	4.01	N3	N4	N6	IE3	IE4	IE 5	IE 5.5	IE6	O5.x
<event_name>= script_code	✗	✗	✓	✗	✗	✓	✗	✓	✓	✓	✓	✗
accesskey= key_character	✗	✗	✓	✗	✗	✓	✗	✗	✓	✓	✓	✗
align=bottom|center| left|right|top	✗	✗	D	✗	✗	✓	✗	✓	✓	✓	✓	✓
class=classname	✗	✗	✓	✗	✗	✓	✗	✓	✓	✓	✓	✗
dir=ltr|rtl	✗	✗	✓	✗	✗	✓	✗	✗	✓	✓	✓	✓

Table continued on following page

Attributes	2.0	3.2	4.01	N3	N4	N6	IE3	IE4	IE5	IE 5.5	IE6	O5.x
id=string	✗	✗	✓	✗	✗	✓	✗	✓	✓	✓	✓	✗
lang=language_type	✗	✗	✓	✗	✗	✓	✗	✓	✓	✓	✓	✗
language=javascript|vbscript	✗	✗	✗	✗	✗	✗	✗	✓	✓	✓	✓	✗
style=string	✗	✗	✓	✗	✗	✓	✗	✓	✓	✓	✓	✗
tabindex=number	✗	✗	✗	✗	✗	✗	✗	✗	✓	✓	✓	✗
title=string	✗	✗	✓	✗	✗	✓	✗	✓	✓	✓	✓	✗
valign=bottom|top	✗	✗	✗	✗	✗	✗	✗	✓	✗	✗	✗	✗

li

Denotes one item within an ordered or unordered list. **ALL**

Attributes	2.0	3.2	4.01	N3	N4	N6	IE3	IE4	IE5	IE 5.5	IE6	O5.x
<event_name>= script_code	✗	✗	✓	✗	✗	✓	✗	✓	✓	✓	✓	✓
accesskey= key_character	✗	✗	✗	✗	✗	✗	✗	✗	✓	✓	✓	✗
class=classname	✗	✗	✓	✗	✓	✓	✓	✓	✓	✓	✓	✓
dir=ltr|rtl	✗	✗	✓	✗	✗	✓	✗	✓	✓	✓	✓	✗
id=string	✗	✗	✓	✗	✓	✓	✓	✓	✓	✓	✓	✓
lang=language_type	✗	✗	✓	✗	✗	✓	✗	✓	✓	✓	✓	✗
language=javascript|vbscript	✗	✗	✗	✗	✗	✗	✗	✓	✓	✓	✓	✗
style=string	✗	✗	✓	✗	✓	✓	✓	✓	✓	✓	✓	✓
tabindex=number	✗	✗	✗	✗	✗	✗	✗	✗	✓	✓	✓	✗
title=string	✗	✗	✓	✗	✗	✓	✗	✓	✓	✓	✓	✓
type=button|reset| submit	✗	✓	D	✓	✓	✓	✓	✓	✓	✓	✓	✓
value=string	✗	✓	D	✓	✓	✓	✓	✓	✓	✓	✓	✓

link

Defines a hyperlink between the document and some other resource. **ALL**

Attributes	2.0	3.2	4.01	N3	N4	N6	IE3	IE4	IE5	IE 5.5	IE6	O5.x
<event_name>= script_code	x	x	✓	x	x	✓	x	x	x	✓	✓	x
charset=string	x	x	✓	x	x	✓	x	x	x	x	x	x
class=classname	x	x	✓	x	x	✓	x	x	x	x	x	x
dir=ltr|rtl	x	x	✓	x	x	✓	x	x	x	x	x	x
disabled	x	x	x	x	x	✓	x	✓	x	x	x	x
href=url	✓	✓	✓	✓	✓	✓	✓	✓	✓	✓	✓	x
hreflang=langcode	x	x	✓	x	x	✓	x	x	x	x	✓	x
id=string	x	x	✓	x	✓	✓	x	✓	✓	✓	✓	x
lang=language_type	x	x	✓	x	x	✓	x	✓	x	x	x	x
media	x	x	✓	x	x	✓	x	x	x	x	x	x
methods=string	✓	x	x	x	x	x	x	x	x	x	x	x
name=string	x	x	x	x	x	x	x	x	✓	✓	✓	x
rel=same|next|parent| previous|string	✓	✓	✓	✓	✓	✓	✓	✓	✓	✓	✓	x
rev=string	✓	✓	✓	✓	✓	✓	✓	x	✓	✓	✓	x
style=string	x	x	✓	x	✓	✓	x	x	x	x	x	x
target=<window_name>| _parent|_blank| _top|_self	x	x	✓	x	x	✓	x	x	✓	✓	✓	x
title=string	✓	✓	✓	✓	✓	✓	✓	✓	x	x	x	x
type=button|reset| submit	x	x	✓	x	✓	✓	✓	✓	✓	✓	✓	x
urn=string	✓	x	x	x	x	x	x	x	x	x	x	x

listing

Renders text in fixed-width type. Use `pre` instead. **HTML 2.0, deprecated in HTML 3.2, IE3+**

Attributes	2.0	3.2	4.01	N3	N4	N6	IE3	IE4	IE 5	IE 5.5	IE6	O5.x
`<event_name>=` `script_code`	✗	✗	✗	✗	✗	✗	✗	✓	✓	✓	✓	✗
`accesskey=` `key_character`	✗	✗	✗	✗	✗	✗	✗	✗	✓	✓	✓	✗
`class=classname`	✗	✗	✗	✗	✗	✗	✗	✓	✓	✓	✓	✗
`dir=ltr|rtl`	✗	✗	✗	✗	✗	✗	✗	✗	✓	✓	✓	✗
`id=string`	✗	✗	✗	✗	✗	✗	✗	✓	✓	✓	✓	✗
`lang=language_type`	✗	✗	✗	✗	✗	✗	✗	✓	✓	✓	✓	✗
`language=javascript|` `vbscript`	✗	✗	✗	✗	✗	✗	✗	✓	✓	✓	✓	✗
`style=string`	✗	✗	✗	✗	✗	✗	✗	✓	✓	✓	✓	✗
`tabindex=number`	✗	✗	✗	✗	✗	✗	✗	✗	✓	✓	✓	✗
`title=string`	✗	✗	✗	✗	✗	✗	✗	✓	✓	✓	✓	✗

map

Specifies a collection of hot spots for a client-side image map. **ALL except HTML 2.0**

Attributes	2.0	3.2	4.01	N3	N4	N6	IE3	IE4	IE 5	IE 5.5	IE6	O5.x
`<event_name>=` `script_code`	✗	✗	✗	✗	✗	✗	✗	✓	✓	✓	✓	✗
`class=classname`	✗	✗	✓	✗	✓	✓	✗	✓	✓	✓	✓	✓
`dir=ltr|rtl`	✗	✗	✗	✗	✗	✓	✗	✗	✓	✓	✓	✗
`id=string`	✗	✗	✓	✗	✓	✓	✗	✓	✓	✓	✓	✓
`lang=language_type`	✗	✗	✗	✗	✗	✗	✗	✓	✓	✓	✓	✗
`language=javascript|` `vbscript`	✗	✗	✗	✗	✗	✗	✗	✗	✓	✓	✓	✗
`name=string`	✗	✓	✓	✓	✓	✓	✓	✓	✓	✓	✓	✓
`style=string`	✗	✗	✓	✗	✓	✓	✗	✓	✓	✓	✓	✓
`title=string`	✗	✗	✓	✗	✗	✓	✗	✓	✓	✓	✓	✓

marquee

Creates a scrolling text marquee in the page. **IE3+**

Attributes	2.0	3.2	4.01	N3	N4	N6	IE3	IE4	IE 5	IE 5.5	IE6	O5.x
<event_name>= script_code	x	x	x	x	x	x	x	✓	✓	✓	✓	x
accesskey= key_character	x	x	x	x	x	x	x	x	✓	✓	✓	x
align=top|middle| bottom	x	x	x	x	x	x	✓	x	x	x	x	x
behavior=alternate| scroll|slide	x	x	x	x	x	x	✓	✓	✓	✓	✓	x
bgcolor=color	x	x	x	x	x	x	✓	✓	✓	✓	✓	x
class=classname	x	x	x	x	x	x	x	✓	✓	✓	✓	x
datafld=column_name	x	x	x	x	x	x	x	✓	✓	✓	✓	x
dataformatas	x	x	x	x	x	x	x	✓	✓	✓	✓	x
datasrc=id	x	x	x	x	x	x	x	✓	✓	✓	✓	x
dir=ltr|rtl	x	x	x	x	x	x	x	x	x	✓	✓	x
direction=down| left|right|up	x	x	x	x	x	x	✓	✓	✓	✓	✓	x
height=number	x	x	x	x	x	x	✓	✓	✓	✓	✓	x
hspace=number	x	x	x	x	x	x	✓	✓	✓	✓	✓	x
id=string	x	x	x	x	x	x	x	✓	✓	✓	✓	x
lang=language_type	x	x	x	x	x	x	x	✓	✓	✓	✓	x
language=javascript| vbscript	x	x	x	x	x	x	x	✓	✓	✓	✓	x
loop=number	x	x	x	x	x	x	✓	✓	✓	✓	✓	x
scrollamount=number	x	x	x	x	x	x	✓	✓	✓	✓	✓	x
scrolldelay=number	x	x	x	x	x	x	✓	✓	✓	✓	✓	x
style=string	x	x	x	x	x	x	x	✓	✓	✓	✓	x
tabindex=number	x	x	x	x	x	x	x	x	✓	✓	✓	x
title=string	x	x	x	x	x	x	x	✓	✓	✓	✓	x
truespeed	x	x	x	x	x	x	x	✓	✓	✓	✓	x
vspace=number	x	x	x	x	x	x	✓	✓	✓	✓	✓	x
width=number	x	x	x	x	x	x	✓	✓	✓	✓	✓	x

menu

Renders the following block of text as individual items. Use standard lists instead. **ALL, but deprecated in HTML 4.01**

Attributes	2.0	3.2	4.01	N3	N4	N6	IE3	IE4	IE5	IE 5.5	IE6	O5.x
<event_name>= script_code	x	x	D	x	x	x	x	✓	✓	✓	✓	✓
accesskey= key_character	x	x	x	x	x	x	x	x	✓	✓	✓	x
class=classname	x	x	D	x	✓	✓	x	✓	✓	✓	✓	✓
compact	✓	✓	D	x	✓	✓	✓	x	x	x	✓	x
dir=ltr|rtl	x	x	x	x	x	✓	x	x	✓	✓	✓	✓
id=string	x	x	D	x	✓	✓	x	✓	✓	✓	✓	✓
lang=language_type	x	x	D	x	x	✓	x	✓	✓	✓	✓	✓
language=javascript| vbscript	x	x	x	x	x	x	x	✓	x	x	x	x
style=string	x	x	D	x	✓	✓	x	✓	✓	✓	✓	✓
tabindex=number	x	x	x	x	x	x	x	x	✓	✓	✓	x
title=string	x	x	D	x	x	✓	x	✓	✓	✓	✓	✓
type=button| reset|submit	x	x	x	x	✓	x	x	x	x	x	x	x

meta

Provides various types of unviewed information or instructions to the browser. **ALL**

Attributes	2.0	3.2	4.01	N3	N4	N6	IE3	IE4	IE5	IE 5.5	IE6	O5.x
charset=string	x	x	x	x	x	x	✓	x	x	x	x	x
content=metacontent	✓	✓	✓	✓	✓	✓	✓	✓	✓	✓	✓	✓
dir=ltr|rtl	x	x	✓	x	x	✓	x	x	x	x	x	x
http-equiv=string	✓	✓	✓	✓	✓	✓	✓	✓	✓	✓	✓	✓
lang=language_type	x	x	✓	x	x	✓	x	x	x	x	x	x
name=string	✓	✓	✓	✓	✓	✓	✓	✓	✓	✓	✓	✓
scheme=string	x	x	✓	x	x	✓	x	x	x	x	✓	x
url=url	x	x	x	x	x	x	✓	✓	x	x	x	x

multicol

Used to define multiple column formatting. **N3, N4**

Attributes	2.0	3.2	4.01	N3	N4	N6	IE3	IE4	IE5	IE 5.5	IE6	O5.x
class=classname	✗	✗	✗	✗	✓	✗	✗	✗	✗	✗	✗	✗
cols=number	✗	✗	✗	✓	✓	✗	✗	✗	✗	✗	✗	✗
gutter=number	✗	✗	✗	✓	✓	✗	✗	✗	✗	✗	✗	✗
id=string	✗	✗	✗	✗	✓	✗	✗	✗	✗	✗	✗	✗
style=string	✗	✗	✗	✗	✓	✗	✗	✗	✗	✗	✗	✗
width=number	✗	✗	✗	✓	✓	✗	✗	✗	✗	✗	✗	✗

nextid

Defines values used by text editing software when parsing or creating the document. **HTML 2.0 only**

Attributes	2.0	3.2	4.01	N3	N4	N6	IE3	IE4	IE5	IE 5.5	IE6	O5.x
n=string	✓	✗	✗	✗	✗	✗	✗	✗	✗	✗	✗	✗

nobr

Renders text without any text wrapping in the page. **N3+, IE3+**

Attributes	2.0	3.2	4.01	N3	N4	N6	IE3	IE4	IE5	IE 5.5	IE6	O5.x
class=classname	✗	✗	✗	✗	✗	✗	✗	✗	✓	✓	✓	✗
dir=ltr|rtl	✗	✗	✗	✗	✗	✗	✗	✗	✓	✓	✓	✗
id=string	✗	✗	✗	✗	✗	✗	✗	✗	✓	✓	✓	✗
lang=language_type	✗	✗	✗	✗	✗	✗	✗	✗	✓	✓	✓	✗
language=javascript|vbscript	✗	✗	✗	✗	✗	✗	✗	✗	✓	✓	✓	✗

noembed

Defines the HTML to be displayed by browsers that do not support embeds. **N2, N3, N4**

noframes

Defines the HTML to be displayed in browsers that do not support frames. **HTML 4.01, N2+, IE3+, O5.x**

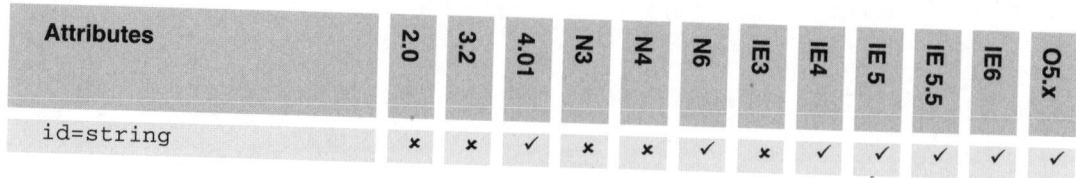

Attributes	2.0	3.2	4.01	N3	N4	N6	IE3	IE4	IE 5	IE 5.5	IE6	O5.x
id=string	✗	✗	✓	✗	✗	✓	✗	✓	✓	✓	✓	✓

nolayer

Defines the part of a document that will be displayed in browsers that don't support layers. **N4**

noscript

Defines the HTML to be displayed in browsers that do not support scripting. **HTML 4.0, N3+, IE3+, O**

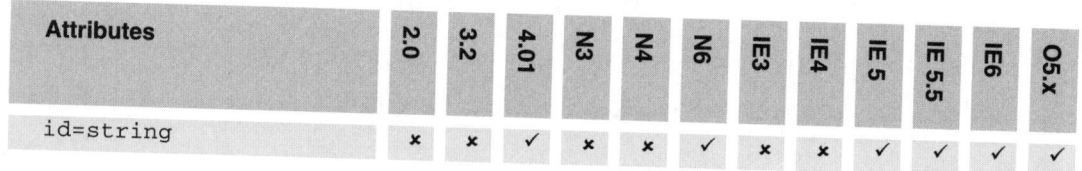

Attributes	2.0	3.2	4.01	N3	N4	N6	IE3	IE4	IE 5	IE 5.5	IE6	O5.x
id=string	✗	✗	✓	✗	✗	✓	✗	✗	✓	✓	✓	✓

object

Inserts an object or other non-intrinsic HTML control into the page. **HTML 4.01, N6, IE3+, O5.x**

Attributes	2.0	3.2	4.01	N3	N4	N6	IE3	IE4	IE 5	IE 5.5	IE6	O5.x
<event_name>=script_code	✗	✗	✓	✗	✗	✓	✗	✓	✓	✓	✓	✓
accesskey=key_character	✗	✗	✗	✗	✗	✗	✗	✓	✓	✓	✓	✗
align=absbottom|absmiddle|baseline|bottom|left|middle|right|texttop|top	✗	✗	D	✗	✗	✓	✓	✓	✓	✓	✓	✗
archive=url	✗	✗	✓	✗	✗	✓	✗	✗	✗	✗	✓	✓

Attributes	2.0	3.2	4.01	N3	N4	N6	IE3	IE4	IE5	IE 5.5	IE6	O5.x
border=number	✗	✗	D	✗	✗	✓	✓	✗	✗	✗	✓	✓
class=classname	✗	✗	✓	✗	✗	✗	✗	✓	✓	✓	✓	✓
classid=string	✗	✗	✓	✗	✗	✗	✓	✓	✓	✓	✓	✗
code=filename	✗	✗	✗	✗	✗	✓	✗	✓	✓	✓	✓	✗
codebase=path|url	✗	✗	✓	✗	✗	✓	✓	✓	✓	✓	✓	✗
codetype=url	✗	✗	✓	✗	✗	✓	✓	✓	✓	✓	✓	✗
data=string	✗	✗	✓	✗	✗	✓	✓	✓	✓	✓	✓	✗
datafld=column_name	✗	✗	✗	✗	✗	✗	✗	✓	✗	✗	✗	✗
datasrc=id	✗	✗	✗	✗	✗	✗	✗	✓	✗	✗	✗	✗
declare	✗	✗	✓	✗	✗	✓	✓	✗	✓	✓	✓	✗
dir=ltr|rtl	✗	✗	✓	✗	✗	✓	✗	✗	✓	✓	✓	✗
height=number	✗	✗	✓	✗	✗	✓	✓	✓	✓	✓	✓	✓
hspace=number	✗	✗	D	✗	✗	✓	✗	✓	✗	✓	✓	✓
id=string	✗	✗	✓	✗	✗	✓	✓	✓	✓	✓	✓	✓
lang=language_type	✗	✗	✓	✗	✗	✓	✗	✓	✓	✓	✓	✗
language=javascript|vbscript	✗	✗	✗	✗	✗	✗	✗	✓	✓	✓	✓	✗
name=string	✗	✗	✓	✗	✗	✓	✓	✓	✓	✓	✓	✓
notab	✗	✗	✗	✗	✗	✗	✓	✗	✗	✗	✗	✗
shapes	✗	✗	✗	✗	✗	✗	✓	✗	✗	✗	✗	✗
standby=string	✗	✗	✓	✗	✗	✓	✓	✓	✗	✗	✗	✗
style=string	✗	✗	✓	✗	✗	✓	✗	✓	✓	✓	✓	✓
tabindex=number	✗	✗	✓	✗	✗	✓	✓	✓	✓	✓	✓	✗
title=string	✗	✗	✓	✗	✗	✓	✗	✓	✓	✓	✓	✓
type=button|reset|submit	✗	✗	✓	✗	✗	✓	✓	✓	✓	✓	✓	✓
usemap=url	✗	✗	✓	✗	✗	✓	✓	✗	✗	✗	✓	✓
vspace=number	✗	✗	D	✗	✗	✓	✗	✓	✗	✓	✓	✓
width=number	✗	✗	✓	✗	✗	✓	✓	✓	✓	✓	✓	✓

ol

Renders lines of text marked with `<li>` tags as an ordered list. **ALL**

Attributes	2.0	3.2	4.01	N3	N4	N6	IE3	IE4	IE5	IE 5.5	IE6	O5.x
`<event_name>=` `script_code`	✗	✗	✓	✗	✗	✓	✗	✓	✓	✓	✓	✓
`accesskey=` `key_character`	✗	✗	✗	✗	✗	✗	✗	✗	✓	✓	✓	✗
`class=classname`	✗	✗	✓	✗	✓	✓	✓	✓	✓	✓	✓	✓
`compact`	✓	✓	D	✓	✓	✓	✓	✗	✓	✓	✓	✗
`dir=ltr|rtl`	✗	✗	✓	✗	✗	✓	✗	✓	✓	✓	✓	✗
`id=string`	✗	✗	✓	✗	✓	✓	✗	✓	✓	✓	✓	✓
`lang=language_type`	✗	✗	✓	✗	✗	✓	✗	✓	✓	✓	✓	✗
`language=javascript|` `vbscript`	✗	✗	✗	✗	✗	✓	✗	✓	✓	✓	✓	✗
`start=number`	✗	✓	D	✓	✓	✓	✓	✓	✓	✓	✓	✓
`style=string`	✗	✗	✓	✗	✓	✓	✓	✓	✓	✓	✓	✓
`tabindex=number`	✗	✗	✗	✗	✗	✗	✗	✗	✓	✓	✓	✗
`title=string`	✗	✗	✓	✗	✗	✓	✗	✓	✓	✓	✓	✓
`type=button|` `reset|submit`	✗	✓	D	✓	✓	✓	✓	✓	✓	✓	✓	✓

optgroup

Creates a collapsible and hierarchical list of options. **HTML 4.01, N6, IE6, O5.x**

Attributes	2.0	3.2	4.01	N3	N4	N6	IE3	IE4	IE5	IE 5.5	IE6	O5.x
`<event_name>=` `script_code`	✗	✗	✓	✗	✗	✓	✗	✗	✗	✗	✗	✓
`class=classname`	✗	✗	✓	✗	✗	✓	✗	✗	✗	✗	✗	✓
`dir=ltr|rtl`	✗	✗	✓	✗	✗	✓	✗	✗	✗	✗	✗	✗
`disabled`	✗	✗	✓	✗	✗	✗	✗	✗	✗	✗	✓	✓
`id=string`	✗	✗	✓	✗	✗	✓	✗	✗	✗	✗	✗	✓

Attributes	2.0	3.2	4.01	N3	N4	N6	IE3	IE4	IE5	IE 5.5	IE6	O5.x
label=string	✗	✗	✓	✗	✗	✓	✗	✗	✗	✗	✓	✓
lang=language_type	✗	✗	✓	✗	✗	✓	✗	✗	✗	✗	✗	✗
style=string	✗	✗	✓	✗	✗	✓	✗	✗	✗	✗	✗	✓
title=string	✗	✗	✓	✗	✗	✓	✗	✗	✗	✗	✗	✓

option

Denotes one choice in a `select` drop-down or list element. **ALL**

Attributes	2.0	3.2	4.01	N3	N4	N6	IE3	IE4	IE5	IE 5.5	IE6	O5.x
<event_name>=script_code	✗	✗	✓	✗	✗	✓	✗	✓	✓	✓	✓	✗
class=classname	✗	✗	✓	✗	✓	✓	✗	✓	✓	✓	✓	✓
dir=ltr|rtl	✗	✗	✓	✗	✗	✓	✗	✗	✗	✓	✓	✗
disabled	✗	✗	✓	✓	✗	✓	✗	✗	✗	✗	✗	✓
id=string	✗	✗	✓	✗	✗	✓	✗	✓	✓	✓	✓	✓
label=string	✗	✗	✓	✗	✗	✓	✗	✗	✓	✓	✓	✓
lang=language_type	✗	✗	✓	✗	✗	✓	✗	✗	✓	✓	✓	✗
language=javascript|vbscript	✗	✗	✗	✗	✗	✗	✗	✓	✓	✓	✓	✗
plain	✗	✗	✗	✓	✓	✗	✗	✗	✗	✗	✗	✗
selected	✓	✓	✓	✓	✓	✓	✓	✓	✓	✓	✓	✓
style=string	✗	✗	✓	✗	✓	✓	✗	✗	✗	✗	✗	✓
title=string	✗	✗	✓	✗	✗	✓	✗	✗	✗	✗	✗	✓
value=string	✓	✓	✓	✓	✓	✓	✓	✓	✓	✓	✓	✓

p

Denotes a paragraph. The end tag is optional. **ALL**

Attributes	2.0	3.2	4.01	N3	N4	N6	IE3	IE4	IE5	IE 5.5	IE6	O5.x
`<event_name>= script_code`	✗	✗	✓	✗	✗	✓	✗	✓	✓	✓	✓	✓
`accesskey= key_character`	✗	✗	✗	✗	✗	✗	✗	✗	✓	✓	✓	✗
`align=center| left|right`	✗	✓	D	✓	✓	✓	✓	✓	✓	✓	✓	✓
`class=classname`	✗	✗	✓	✗	✓	✓	✓	✓	✓	✓	✓	✓
`dir=ltr|rtl`	✗	✗	✓	✗	✗	✓	✗	✗	✓	✓	✓	✗
`id=string`	✗	✗	✓	✗	✓	✓	✓	✓	✓	✓	✓	✓
`lang=language_type`	✗	✗	✓	✗	✗	✓	✗	✓	✓	✓	✓	✗
`language=javascript| vbscript`	✗	✗	✗	✗	✗	✗	✗	✓	✓	✓	✓	✗
`style=string`	✗	✗	✓	✗	✓	✓	✓	✓	✓	✓	✓	✓
`tabindex=number`	✗	✗	✗	✗	✗	✗	✗	✗	✓	✓	✓	✗
`title=string`	✗	✗	✓	✗	✗	✓	✗	✓	✓	✓	✓	✓

param

Used in an `object` or `applet` tag to set the object's properties. **ALL except HTML 2.0**

Attributes	2.0	3.2	4.01	N3	N4	N6	IE3	IE4	IE5	IE 5.5	IE6	O5.x
`datafld=column_name`	✗	✗	✗	✗	✗	✗	✗	✓	✓	✓	✓	✗
`dataformatas= html|text`	✗	✗	✗	✗	✗	✗	✗	✓	✓	✓	✓	✗
`datasrc=id`	✗	✗	✗	✗	✗	✗	✗	✓	✓	✓	✓	✗
`id=string`	✗	✗	✓	✗	✗	✓	✗	✗	✗	✗	✗	✓
`name=string`	✗	✓	✓	✓	✓	✓	✓	✓	✓	✓	✓	✓
`type=button| reset|submit`	✗	✗	✓	✗	✗	✓	✓	✗	✗	✗	✓	✓
`value=string`	✗	✓	✓	✓	✓	✓	✓	✓	✓	✓	✓	✓
`valuetype=data| ref|object`	✗	✗	✓	✗	✗	✓	✓	✗	✗	✗	✓	✓

plaintext

Renders text with no formatting. **HTML 2.0, deprecated in HTML 3.2, N2, N3, N4, IE3+**

Attributes	2.0	3.2	4.01	N3	N4	N6	IE3	IE4	IE5	IE 5.5	IE6	O5.x
`<event_name>=` `script_code`	✗	✗	✗	✗	✗	✗	✗	✓	✓	✓	✓	✗
`accesskey=` `key_character`	✗	✗	✗	✗	✗	✗	✗	✗	✓	✓	✓	✗
`class=classname`	✗	✗	✗	✗	✗	✗	✗	✓	✓	✓	✓	✗
`dir=ltr|rtl`	✗	✗	✗	✗	✗	✗	✗	✗	✓	✓	✓	✗
`id=string`	✗	✗	✗	✗	✗	✗	✗	✓	✓	✓	✓	✗
`lang=language_type`	✗	✗	✗	✗	✗	✗	✗	✓	✓	✓	✓	✗
`language=javascript|` `vbscript`	✗	✗	✗	✗	✗	✗	✗	✓	✓	✓	✓	✗
`style=string`	✗	✗	✗	✗	✗	✗	✗	✓	✓	✓	✓	✗
`tabindex=number`	✗	✗	✗	✗	✗	✗	✗	✗	✓	✓	✓	✗
`title=string`	✗	✗	✗	✗	✗	✗	✗	✓	✓	✓	✓	✗

pre

Renders text in fixed-width type. **ALL**

Attributes	2.0	3.2	4.01	N3	N4	N6	IE3	IE4	IE5	IE 5.5	IE6	O5.x
`<event_name>=` `script_code`	✗	✗	✓	✗	✗	✓	✗	✓	✓	✓	✓	✓
`accesskey=` `key_character`	✗	✗	✗	✗	✗	✓	✗	✗	✓	✓	✓	✗
`class=classname`	✗	✗	✓	✗	✓	✓	✗	✓	✓	✓	✓	✓
`dir=ltr|rtl`	✗	✗	✓	✗	✗	✓	✗	✗	✓	✓	✓	✗
`id=string`	✗	✗	✓	✗	✓	✓	✗	✓	✓	✓	✓	✓
`lang=language_type`	✗	✗	✓	✗	✗	✓	✗	✓	✓	✓	✓	✗
`language=javascript|` `vbscript`	✗	✗	✗	✗	✗	✗	✗	✓	✓	✓	✓	✗

Table continued on following page

Attributes	2.0	3.2	4.01	N3	N4	N6	IE3	IE4	IE5	IE 5.5	IE6	O5.x
style=string	✗	✗	✓	✗	✓	✓	✗	✓	✓	✓	✓	✓
tabindex=number	✗	✗	✗	✗	✗	✗	✗	✗	✓	✓	✓	✗
title=string	✗	✗	✓	✗	✗	✓	✗	✓	✓	✓	✓	✓
width=number	✓	✓	D	✓	✓	✓	✗	✗	✗	✗	✗	✓

q

A short quotation, such as a message. **HTML 4.01, N6, IE4+, O5.x**

Attributes	2.0	3.2	4.01	N3	N4	N6	IE3	IE4	IE5	IE 5.5	IE6	O5.x
<event_name>= script_code	✗	✗	✓	✗	✗	✓	✗	✓	✓	✓	✓	✓
accesskey= key_character	✗	✗	✗	✗	✗	✗	✗	✗	✓	✓	✓	✗
cite=url	✗	✗	✓	✗	✗	✓	✗	✗	✗	✗	✓	✓
class=classname	✗	✗	✓	✗	✗	✓	✗	✓	✓	✓	✓	✓
dir=ltr|rtl	✗	✗	✓	✗	✗	✓	✗	✓	✗	✗	✓	✗
id=string	✗	✗	✓	✗	✗	✓	✗	✓	✓	✓	✓	✓
lang=language_type	✗	✗	✓	✗	✗	✓	✗	✓	✓	✓	✓	✗
language=javascript| vbscript	✗	✗	✗	✗	✗	✗	✗	✗	✓	✓	✓	✗
style=string	✗	✗	✓	✗	✗	✓	✗	✓	✓	✓	✓	✓
tabindex=number	✗	✗	✗	✗	✗	✗	✗	✗	✓	✓	✓	✗
title=string	✗	✗	✓	✗	✗	✓	✗	✓	✓	✓	✓	✓

rt

Contains text to render as an annotation or pronunciation guide for content given by the `<ruby>` element. **IE 5+**

Attributes	2.0	3.2	4.01	N3	N4	N6	IE3	IE4	IE 5	IE 5.5	IE6	O5.x
accesskey= key_character	✗	✗	✗	✗	✗	✗	✗	✗	✓	✓	✓	✗
class=classname	✗	✗	✗	✗	✗	✗	✗	✗	✓	✓	✓	✗
dir=ltr|rtl	✗	✗	✗	✗	✗	✗	✗	✗	✓	✓	✓	✗
id=string	✗	✗	✗	✗	✗	✗	✗	✗	✓	✓	✓	✗
lang=language_type	✗	✗	✗	✗	✗	✗	✗	✗	✓	✓	✓	✗
language=javascript| vbscript	✗	✗	✗	✗	✗	✗	✗	✗	✓	✓	✓	✗
name=string	✗	✗	✗	✗	✗	✗	✗	✗	✓	✓	✓	✗
style=string	✗	✗	✗	✗	✗	✗	✗	✗	✓	✓	✓	✗
tabindex=number	✗	✗	✗	✗	✗	✗	✗	✗	✓	✓	✓	✗
title=string	✗	✗	✗	✗	✗	✗	✗	✗	✓	✓	✓	✗

ruby

Denotes text that has an associated `<rt>` element rendering an annotation or pronunciation guide for that text. **IE 5+**

Attributes	2.0	3.2	4.01	N3	N4	N6	IE3	IE4	IE 5	IE 5.5	IE6	O5.x
accesskey= key_character	✗	✗	✗	✗	✗	✗	✗	✗	✓	✓	✓	✗
class=classname	✗	✗	✗	✗	✗	✗	✗	✗	✓	✓	✓	✗
dir=ltr|rtl	✗	✗	✗	✗	✗	✗	✗	✗	✓	✓	✓	✗
id=string	✗	✗	✗	✗	✗	✗	✗	✗	✓	✓	✓	✗
lang=language_type	✗	✗	✗	✗	✗	✗	✗	✗	✓	✓	✓	✗
language=javascript| vbscript	✗	✗	✗	✗	✗	✗	✗	✗	✓	✓	✓	✗

Table continued on following page

Attributes	2.0	3.2	4.01	N3	N4	N6	IE3	IE4	IE 5	IE 5.5	IE6	O5.x
name=string	×	×	×	×	×	×	×	×	✓	✓	✓	×
style=string	×	×	×	×	×	×	×	×	✓	✓	✓	×
tabindex=number	×	×	×	×	×	×	×	×	✓	✓	✓	×
title=string	×	×	×	×	×	×	×	×	✓	✓	✓	×

S

Renders text in strikethrough type. **HTML 3.2, deprecated in HTML 4.01, N3+, IE3+, O5.x**

Attributes	2.0	3.2	4.01	N3	N4	N6	IE3	IE4	IE 5	IE 5.5	IE6	O5.x
<event_name>=script_code	×	×	D	×	×	×	×	✓	✓	✓	✓	✓
accesskey=key_character	×	×	×	×	×	✓	×	×	✓	✓	✓	×
class=classname	×	×	D	×	✓	✓	×	✓	✓	✓	✓	✓
dir=ltr|rtl	×	×	D	×	×	✓	×	×	✓	✓	✓	×
id=string	×	×	D	×	✓	✓	×	✓	✓	✓	✓	✓
lang=language_type	×	×	D	×	×	✓	×	✓	✓	✓	✓	×
language=javascript|vbscript	×	×	×	×	×	×	×	✓	✓	✓	✓	×
style=string	×	×	D	×	✓	✓	×	✓	✓	✓	✓	✓
tabindex=number	×	×	×	×	×	×	×	×	✓	✓	✓	×
title=string	×	×	D	×	×	✓	×	✓	✓	✓	✓	✓

samp

Renders text as a code sample listing, usually in a smaller fixed width font. **ALL**

Attributes	2.0	3.2	4.01	N3	N4	N6	IE3	IE4	IE 5	IE 5.5	IE6	O5.x
`<event_name>=` `script_code`	✗	✗	✓	✗	✗	✓	✗	✓	✓	✓	✓	✓
`accesskey=` `key_character`	✗	✗	✗	✗	✗	✗	✗	✗	✓	✓	✓	✗
`class=classname`	✗	✗	✓	✗	✓	✓	✗	✓	✓	✓	✓	✓
`dir=ltr|rtl`	✗	✗	✓	✗	✗	✓	✗	✗	✗	✓	✓	✗
`id=string`	✗	✗	✓	✗	✓	✓	✗	✓	✓	✓	✓	✓
`lang=language_type`	✗	✗	✓	✗	✗	✓	✗	✓	✓	✓	✓	✗
`language=javascript|` `vbscript`	✗	✗	✗	✗	✗	✗	✗	✓	✓	✓	✓	✗
`style=string`	✗	✗	✓	✗	✓	✓	✗	✓	✓	✓	✓	✓
`tabindex=number`	✗	✗	✗	✗	✗	✗	✗	✗	✓	✓	✓	✗
`title=string`	✗	✗	✓	✗	✗	✓	✗	✓	✓	✓	✓	✓

script

Denotes a sequence of script code for the browser to execute. **HTML 3.2+, N2+, IE3+, O5.x**

Attributes	2.0	3.2	4.01	N3	N4	N6	IE3	IE4	IE 5	IE 5.5	IE6	O5.x
`archive=url`	✗	✗	✗	✗	✓	✗	✗	✗	✗	✗	✗	✗
`charset=string`	✗	✗	✓	✗	✗	✓	✗	✗	✗	✗	✗	✓
`class=classname`	✗	✗	✗	✗	✓	✓	✗	✓	✗	✗	✗	✗
`defer`	✗	✗	✓	✗	✗	✓	✗	✗	✓	✓	✓	✓
`event=<event_name>`	✗	✗	✗	✗	✗	✓	✗	✓	✓	✓	✓	✗
`for=element_name`	✗	✗	✗	✗	✗	✗	✗	✓	✓	✓	✓	✗
`id=string`	✗	✗	✗	✗	✓	✓	✗	✓	✓	✓	✓	✗
`lang=language_type`	✗	✗	✗	✗	✗	✓	✗	✗	✓	✓	✓	✗

Table continued on following page

Attributes	2.0	3.2	4.01	N3	N4	N6	IE3	IE4	IE5	IE 5.5	IE6	O5.x
language=javascript|vbscript	x	x	D	✓	✓	x	✓	✓	✓	✓	✓	✓
src=url	x	x	✓	✓	✓	✓	x	✓	✓	✓	✓	✓
style=string	x	x	x	x	✓	✓	x	✓	x	x	x	x
type=button|reset|submit	x	x	✓	x	x	✓	✓	✓	✓	✓	✓	✓

select

Defines a list box or drop-down list. **ALL**

Attributes	2.0	3.2	4.01	N3	N4	N6	IE3	IE4	IE5	IE 5.5	IE6	O5.x
<event_name>=script_code	x	x	✓	x	✓	✓	x	✓	✓	✓	✓	✓
accesskey=key_character	x	x	x	x	x	x	x	✓	✓	✓	✓	x
align=absbottom|absmiddle|baseline|bottom|left|middle|right|texttop|top	x	x	x	x	x	x	x	✓	✓	✓	✓	x
class=classname	x	x	✓	x	✓	✓	x	✓	✓	✓	✓	✓
datafld=column_name	x	x	x	x	x	x	x	✓	✓	✓	✓	x
datasrc=id	x	x	x	x	x	x	x	✓	✓	✓	✓	x
dir=ltr|rtl	x	x	✓	x	x	✓	x	x	✓	✓	✓	x
disabled	x	x	✓	x	x	✓	x	✓	✓	✓	✓	x
id=string	x	x	✓	x	✓	✓	x	✓	✓	✓	✓	✓
lang=language_type	x	x	✓	x	x	✓	x	✓	✓	✓	✓	x
language=javascript|vbscript	x	x	x	x	x	x	x	✓	✓	✓	✓	x
multiple	✓	✓	✓	✓	✓	✓	✓	✓	✓	✓	✓	✓
name=string	✓	✓	✓	✓	✓	✓	✓	✓	✓	✓	✓	✓
size=number	✓	✓	✓	✓	✓	✓	✓	✓	✓	✓	✓	✓
style=string	x	x	✓	x	✓	✓	x	✓	✓	✓	✓	✓
tabindex=number	x	x	✓	x	x	✓	x	✓	✓	✓	✓	x
title=string	x	x	✓	x	x	✓	x	✓	x	x	x	✓
type=button|reset|submit	x	x	x	x	x	✓	x	x	x	x	x	x

server

Used to run a Netscape LiveWire script. **N2, N3, N4**

Attributes	2.0	3.2	4.01	N3	N4	N6	IE3	IE4	IE 5	IE 5.5	IE6	O5.x
class=classname	✗	✗	✗	✗	✓	✗	✗	✗	✗	✗	✗	✗
id=string	✗	✗	✗	✗	✓	✗	✗	✗	✗	✗	✗	✗

small

Specifies that text should be displayed with a smaller font than the current font. **HTML 3.2+, N3+, IE3+, O5.x**

Attributes	2.0	3.2	4.01	N3	N4	N6	IE3	IE4	IE 5	IE 5.5	IE6	O5.x
<event_name>=script_code	✗	✗	✓	✗	✗	✓	✗	✓	✓	✓	✓	✓
accesskey=key_character	✗	✗	✗	✗	✗	✗	✗	✗	✓	✓	✓	✗
class=classname	✗	✗	✓	✗	✓	✓	✗	✓	✓	✓	✓	✓
dir=ltr|rtl	✗	✗	✓	✗	✗	✓	✗	✗	✗	✓	✓	✗
id=string	✗	✗	✓	✗	✓	✓	✗	✓	✓	✓	✓	✓
lang=language_type	✗	✗	✓	✗	✗	✓	✗	✓	✓	✓	✓	✗
language=javascript|vbscript	✗	✗	✗	✗	✗	✗	✗	✓	✓	✓	✓	✗
style=string	✗	✗	✓	✗	✓	✓	✗	✓	✓	✓	✓	✓
tabindex=number	✗	✗	✗	✗	✗	✗	✗	✗	✓	✓	✓	✗
title=string	✗	✗	✓	✗	✗	✓	✗	✓	✓	✓	✓	✓

spacer

Used to specify vertical and horizontal spacing of elements. **N3, N4**

Attributes	2.0	3.2	4.01	N3	N4	N6	IE3	IE4	IE 5	IE 5.5	IE6	O5.x
align=absbottom| absmiddle|baseline| bottom|left|middle| right|texttop|top	✗	✗	✗	✓	✓	✗	✗	✗	✗	✗	✗	✗
class=classname	✗	✗	✗	✗	✓	✗	✗	✗	✗	✗	✗	✗
height=number	✗	✗	✗	✓	✓	✗	✗	✗	✗	✗	✗	✗
id=string	✗	✗	✗	✗	✓	✗	✗	✗	✗	✗	✗	✗
size=number	✗	✗	✗	✓	✓	✗	✗	✗	✗	✗	✗	✗
style=string	✗	✗	✗	✗	✓	✗	✗	✗	✗	✗	✗	✗
type=button| reset|submit	✗	✗	✗	✓	✓	✗	✗	✗	✗	✗	✗	✗
width=number	✗	✗	✗	✓	✓	✗	✗	✗	✗	✗	✗	✗

span

Used (with a style=string sheet) to define non-standard attributes for text on the page. **HTML 4.01, N6, IE4+, O5.x**

Attributes	2.0	3.2	4.01	N3	N4	N6	IE3	IE4	IE 5	IE 5.5	IE6	O5.x
<event_name>= script_code	✗	✗	✓	✗	✗	✓	✗	✓	✓	✓	✓	✓
accesskey= key_character	✗	✗	✗	✗	✗	✗	✗	✗	✓	✓	✓	✗
class=classname	✗	✗	✓	✗	✓	✓	✗	✓	✓	✓	✓	✓
datafld=column_name	✗	✗	✗	✗	✗	✗	✗	✓	✓	✓	✓	✗
dataformatas= html|text	✗	✗	✗	✗	✗	✗	✗	✓	✓	✓	✓	✗
datasrc=id	✗	✗	✗	✗	✗	✗	✗	✓	✓	✓	✓	✗
dir=ltr|rtl	✗	✗	✓	✗	✗	✓	✗	✗	✗	✓	✓	✗
id=string	✗	✗	✓	✗	✓	✓	✗	✓	✓	✓	✓	✓

Attributes	2.0	3.2	4.01	N3	N4	N6	IE3	IE4	IE 5	IE 5.5	IE6	O5.x
lang=language_type	✗	✗	✓	✗	✗	✓	✗	✓	✓	✓	✓	✗
language=javascript|vbscript	✗	✗	✗	✗	✗	✗	✗	✓	✓	✓	✓	✗
style=string	✗	✗	✓	✗	✓	✓	✓	✓	✓	✓	✓	✓
tabindex=number	✗	✗	✗	✗	✗	✗	✗	✗	✓	✓	✓	✗
title=string	✗	✗	✓	✗	✗	✓	✗	✓	✓	✓	✓	✓

strike

Renders text in strikethrough type. **HTML 3.2, deprecated in HTML 4.01, N3+, IE3+**

Attributes	2.0	3.2	4.01	N3	N4	N6	IE3	IE4	IE 5	IE 5.5	IE6	O5.x
<event_name>=script_code	✗	✗	D	✗	✗	✗	✗	✓	✓	✓	✓	✓
accesskey=key_character	✗	✗	✗	✗	✗	✗	✗	✗	✓	✓	✓	✗
class=classname	✗	✗	D	✗	✓	✓	✗	✓	✓	✓	✓	✓
dir=ltr|rtl	✗	✗	D	✗	✗	✓	✗	✗	✗	✓	✓	✗
id=string	✗	✗	D	✗	✓	✓	✗	✓	✓	✓	✓	✓
lang=language_type	✗	✗	D	✗	✗	✓	✗	✓	✓	✓	✓	✗
language=javascript|vbscript	✗	✗	✗	✗	✗	✗	✗	✓	✓	✓	✓	✗
style=string	✗	✗	D	✗	✓	✓	✗	✓	✓	✓	✓	✓
tabindex=number	✗	✗	✗	✗	✗	✗	✗	✗	✓	✓	✓	✗
title=string	✗	✗	D	✗	✗	✓	✗	✓	✓	✓	✓	✓

strong

Renders text in bold face. **ALL**

Attributes	2.0	3.2	4.01	N3	N4	N6	IE3	IE4	IE 5	IE 5.5	IE6	O5.x
`<event_name>=` `script_code`	✗	✗	✓	✗	✗	✓	✗	✓	✓	✓	✓	✓
`accesskey=` `key_character`	✗	✗	✗	✗	✗	✗	✗	✗	✓	✓	✓	✗
`class=classname`	✗	✗	✓	✗	✓	✓	✗	✓	✓	✓	✓	✓
`dir=ltr|rtl`	✗	✗	✓	✗	✗	✓	✗	✗	✗	✓	✓	✗
`id=string`	✗	✗	✓	✗	✓	✓	✗	✓	✓	✓	✓	✓
`lang=language_type`	✗	✗	✓	✗	✗	✓	✗	✓	✓	✓	✓	✗
`language=javascript|` `vbscript`	✗	✗	✗	✗	✗	✗	✗	✓	✓	✓	✓	✗
`style=string`	✗	✗	✓	✗	✓	✓	✗	✓	✓	✓	✓	✓
`tabindex=number`	✗	✗	✗	✗	✗	✗	✗	✗	✓	✓	✓	✗
`title=string`	✗	✗	✓	✗	✗	✓	✗	✓	✓	✓	✓	✓

style

Specifies the style properties (that is, the style sheet) for the page. **HTML 3.2+, N4+, IE3+, O5.x**

Attributes	2.0	3.2	4.01	N3	N4	N6	IE3	IE4	IE 5	IE 5.5	IE6	O5.x
`behavior`	✗	✗	✗	✗	✗	✗	✗	✗	✗	✗	✗	✗
`dir=ltr|rtl`	✗	✗	✓	✗	✗	✓	✗	✗	✗	✗	✗	✗
`disabled`	✗	✗	✗	✗	✗	✓	✗	✓	✗	✗	✗	✗
`id=string`	✗	✗	✗	✗	✓	✓	✗	✗	✗	✗	✗	✗
`lang=language_type`	✗	✗	✓	✗	✗	✓	✗	✗	✗	✗	✗	✗
`media`	✗	✗	✓	✗	✗	✓	✗	✓	✓	✓	✓	✓
`src=url`	✗	✗	✗	✗	✓	✗	✗	✗	✗	✓	✓	✗
`title=string`	✗	✗	✓	✗	✗	✓	✓	✓	✓	✗	✗	✓
`type=button|` `reset|submit`	✗	✗	✓	✗	✓	✓	✓	✓	✗	✗	✗	✓

sub

Renders text as a subscript using a smaller font than the current font. **ALL except HTML 2.0**

Attributes	2.0	3.2	4.01	N3	N4	N6	IE3	IE4	IE5	IE 5.5	IE6	O5.x
<event_name>=script_code	✗	✗	✓	✗	✗	✓	✗	✓	✓	✓	✓	✓
accesskey=key_character	✗	✗	✗	✗	✗	✗	✗	✗	✗	✗	✗	✗
class=classname	✗	✗	✓	✗	✓	✓	✗	✓	✓	✓	✓	✓
dir=ltr|rtl	✗	✗	✓	✗	✗	✓	✗	✗	✗	✗	✓	✗
id=string	✗	✗	✓	✗	✓	✓	✗	✓	✓	✓	✓	✓
lang=language_type	✗	✗	✓	✗	✗	✓	✗	✗	✗	✗	✓	✗
language=javascript|vbscript	✗	✗	✗	✗	✗	✗	✗	✓	✓	✓	✓	✗
style=string	✗	✗	✓	✗	✓	✓	✗	✓	✓	✓	✓	✓
tabindex=number	✗	✗	✗	✗	✗	✗	✗	✗	✗	✗	✗	✗
title=string	✗	✗	✓	✗	✗	✓	✗	✓	✓	✓	✓	✓

sup

Renders text as a superscript using a smaller font than the current font. **ALL except HTML 2.0**

Attributes	2.0	3.2	4.01	N3	N4	N6	IE3	IE4	IE5	IE 5.5	IE6	O5.x
<event_name>=script_code	✗	✗	✓	✗	✗	✓	✗	✓	✓	✓	✓	✓
accesskey=key_character	✗	✗	✗	✗	✗	✗	✗	✗	✓	✓	✓	✗
class=classname	✗	✗	✓	✗	✓	✓	✗	✓	✓	✓	✓	✓
dir=ltr|rtl	✗	✗	✓	✗	✗	✓	✗	✗	✓	✓	✓	✗
id=string	✗	✗	✓	✗	✓	✓	✗	✓	✓	✓	✓	✓
lang=language_type	✗	✗	✓	✗	✗	✓	✗	✗	✗	✗	✓	✗
language=javascript|vbscript	✗	✗	✗	✗	✗	✗	✗	✓	✓	✓	✓	✗
style=string	✗	✗	✓	✗	✓	✓	✗	✓	✓	✓	✓	✓
tabindex=number	✗	✗	✗	✗	✗	✗	✗	✗	✓	✓	✓	✗
title=string	✗	✗	✓	✗	✗	✓	✗	✓	✓	✓	✓	✓

table

Denotes a section of `<tr>`, `<td>`, and `<th>` tags organized into rows and columns. **ALL except HTML 2.0**

Attributes	2.0	3.2	4.01	N3	N4	N6	IE3	IE4	IE 5	IE 5.5	IE6	O5.x
`<event_name>= script_code`	✗	✗	✓	✗	✗	✓	✗	✓	✓	✓	✓	✓
`accesskey= key_character`	✗	✗	✗	✗	✗	✗	✗	✗	✓	✓	✓	✗
`align=center| left|right`	✗	✓	D	✗	✓	✓	✓	✓	✓	✓	✓	✓
`background=string`	✗	✗	✗	✗	✗	✗	✓	✓	✓	✓	✓	✗
`bgcolor=color`	✗	✗	D	✓	✓	✓	✓	✓	✓	✓	✓	✓
`border=number`	✗	✗	✓	✓	✓	✓	✓	✓	✓	✓	✓	✓
`bordercolor=color`	✗	✗	✗	✗	✗	✗	✓	✓	✓	✓	✓	✗
`bordercolordark=color`	✗	✗	✗	✗	✗	✗	✓	✓	✗	✗	✗	✗
`bordercolorlight= color`	✗	✗	✗	✗	✗	✗	✓	✓	✗	✗	✗	✗
`bottommargin`	✗	✗	✗	✗	✗	✗	✓	✓	✗	✓	✓	✗
`celpadding=number`	✗	✓	✓	✓	✓	✓	✓	✓	✓	✓	✓	✓
`cellspacing=number`	✗	✓	✓	✓	✓	✓	✓	✓	✓	✓	✓	✓
`class=classname`	✗	✗	✓	✗	✓	✓	✓	✓	✓	✓	✓	✓
`clear=all| left|right|none`	✗	✗	✗	✗	✗	✗	✓	✗	✗	✗	✗	✗
`cols=number`	✗	✗	✗	✗	✓	✗	✓	✓	✓	✓	✓	✗
`datapagesize=number`	✗	✗	✗	✗	✗	✗	✗	✓	✓	✓	✓	✗
`datasrc=id`	✗	✗	✗	✗	✗	✗	✗	✓	✓	✓	✓	✗
`dir=ltr|rtl`	✗	✗	✓	✗	✗	✓	✗	✗	✓	✓	✓	✗
`frame=above|below| border|box|hsides| lhs|rhs|void|vsides`	✗	✗	✓	✗	✗	✓	✓	✓	✓	✓	✓	✗
`height=number`	✗	✗	✗	✓	✓	✗	✗	✓	✓	✓	✓	✗
`hspace=number`	✗	✗	✗	✗	✓	✗	✗	✗	✗	✗	✗	✓
`id=string`	✗	✗	✓	✗	✓	✓	✓	✓	✓	✓	✓	✓

Attributes	2.0	3.2	4.01	N3	N4	N6	IE3	IE4	IE5	IE 5.5	IE6	O5.x
lang=language_type	✗	✗	✓	✗	✗	✓	✗	✓	✓	✓	✓	✗
language=javascript|vbscript	✗	✗	✗	✗	✗	✗	✗	✓	✓	✓	✓	✗
nowrap	✗	✗	✗	✗	✗	✗	✓	✗	✗	✗	✗	✓
rules=all|cols|groups|none|rows	✗	✗	✓	✗	✗	✓	✓	✓	✓	✓	✓	✗
style=string	✗	✗	✓	✗	✓	✓	✓	✓	✓	✓	✓	✓
summary	✗	✗	✓	✗	✗	✓	✗	✗	✗	✗	✗	✗
tabindex=number	✗	✗	✗	✗	✗	✗	✗	✗	✓	✓	✓	✗
title=string	✗	✗	✓	✗	✗	✓	✗	✓	✓	✓	✓	✓
valign=bottom|top	✗	✗	✗	✗	✗	✗	✗	✗	✗	✗	✗	✗
vspace=number	✗	✗	✗	✗	✓	✗	✗	✗	✗	✗	✗	✗
width=number	✗	✓	✓	✓	✓	✓	✓	✓	✓	✓	✓	✓

tbody

Denotes a section of `<tr>` and `<td>` tags forming the body of the table. **HTML 4.01, N6, IE3+**

Attributes	2.0	3.2	4.01	N3	N4	N6	IE3	IE4	IE5	IE 5.5	IE6	O5.x
<event_name>=script_code	✗	✗	✓	✗	✗	✓	✗	✓	✓	✓	✓	✗
accesskey=key_character	✗	✗	✗	✗	✗	✗	✗	✗	✓	✓	✓	✗
align=center|left|right|justify|char	✗	✗	✓	✗	✗	✓	✗	✓	✓	✓	✓	✓
bgcolor=color	✗	✗	✗	✗	✗	✗	✗	✓	✓	✓	✓	✗
char=string	✗	✗	✓	✗	✗	✓	✗	✗	✗	✗	✓	✗
charoff=string	✗	✗	✓	✗	✗	✓	✗	✗	✗	✗	✓	✗
class=classname	✗	✗	✓	✗	✗	✓	✓	✓	✓	✓	✓	✗
dir=ltr|rtl	✗	✗	✓	✗	✗	✓	✓	✓	✓	✓	✓	✗
id=string	✗	✗	✓	✗	✗	✓	✓	✓	✓	✓	✓	✗

Table continued on following page

Attributes	2.0	3.2	4.01	N3	N4	N6	IE3	IE4	IE 5	IE 5.5	IE6	O5.x
lang=language_type	✗	✗	✓	✗	✗	✓	✗	✓	✓	✓	✓	✗
language=javascript|vbscript	✗	✗	✗	✗	✗	✗	✗	✓	✓	✓	✓	✗
style=string	✗	✗	✓	✗	✗	✓	✓	✓	✓	✓	✓	✗
tabindex=number	✗	✗	✗	✗	✗	✗	✗	✗	✗	✗	✗	✗
title=string	✗	✗	✓	✗	✗	✓	✗	✓	✓	✓	✗	✗
valign=baseline|bottom|center|top	✗	✗	✓	✗	✗	✓	✗	✓	✓	✓	✓	✗

td

Specifies a cell in a table. **ALL except HTML 2.0**

Attributes	2.0	3.2	4.01	N3	N4	N6	IE3	IE4	IE 5	IE 5.5	IE6	O5.x
<event_name>=script_code	✗	✗	✓	✗	✗	✓	✗	✓	✓	✓	✓	✓
abbr	✗	✗	✓	✗	✗	✓	✗	✗	✗	✗	✓	✗
accesskey=key_character	✗	✗	✗	✗	✗	✗	✗	✗	✓	✓	✓	✗
align=center|left|right|justify|char	✗	✓	✓	✓	✓	✓	✓	✓	✓	✓	✓	✓
axis=cellname	✗	✗	✓	✗	✗	✓	✗	✗	✗	✗	✓	✗
background=string	✗	✗	✗	✗	✓	✗	✓	✓	✓	✓	✓	✗
bgcolor=color	✗	✗	D	✓	✓	✓	✓	✓	✓	✓	✓	✓
bordercolor=color	✗	✗	✗	✗	✗	✗	✓	✓	✓	✓	✓	✗
bordercolordark	✗	✗	✗	✗	✗	✗	✓	✓	✗	✓	✓	✗
bordercolorlight	✗	✗	✗	✗	✗	✗	✓	✓	✗	✓	✓	✗
char=string	✗	✗	✓	✗	✗	✓	✗	✗	✗	✗	✓	✗
charoff=string	✗	✗	✓	✗	✗	✓	✗	✗	✗	✗	✓	✗
class=classname	✗	✗	✓	✗	✓	✓	✗	✓	✓	✓	✓	✓
colspan=number	✗	✓	✓	✓	✓	✓	✓	✓	✓	✓	✓	✓
dir=ltr|rtl	✗	✗	✓	✗	✗	✓	✗	✗	✓	✓	✓	✗

Attributes	2.0	3.2	4.01	N3	N4	N6	IE3	IE4	IE5	IE 5.5	IE6	O5.x
headers=string	✗	✗	✓	✗	✗	✓	✗	✗	✗	✗	✓	✗
height=number	✗	✓	D	✗	✓	✓	✓	✗	✓	✓	✓	✓
id=string	✗	✗	✓	✗	✓	✓	✓	✓	✓	✓	✓	✓
lang=language_type	✗	✗	✓	✗	✗	✓	✗	✓	✓	✓	✓	✗
language=javascript|vbscript	✗	✗	✗	✗	✗	✗	✓	✓	✓	✓	✓	✗
nowrap	✗	✓	D	✓	✓	✓	✓	✓	✓	✓	✓	✓
rowspan=number	✗	✓	✓	✓	✓	✓	✓	✓	✓	✓	✓	✓
scope=row|col|rowgroup|colgroup	✗	✗	✓	✗	✗	✓	✗	✗	✗	✗	✓	✗
style=string	✗	✗	✓	✗	✓	✓	✓	✓	✓	✓	✓	✓
tabindex=number	✗	✗	✗	✗	✗	✗	✗	✗	✗	✓	✓	✗
title=string	✗	✗	✓	✗	✗	✓	✗	✓	✓	✓	✓	✓
valign=baseline|bottom|center|top	✗	✓	✓	✓	✓	✓	✓	✓	✓	✓	✓	✓
width=number	✗	✓	D	✓	✓	✓	✓	✓	✗	✓	✓	✓

textarea

Specifies a multi-line text input control. **ALL**

Attributes	2.0	3.2	4.01	N3	N4	N6	IE3	IE4	IE5	IE 5.5	IE6	O5.x
<event_name>=script_code	✗	✗	✓	✗	✓	✓	✗	✓	✓	✓	✓	✓
accesskey=key_character	✗	✗	✓	✗	✗	✓	✗	✓	✓	✓	✓	✗
align=absbottom|absmiddle|baseline|bottom|left|middle|right|texttop|top	✗	✗	✗	✗	✗	✗	✗	✓	✗	✗	✗	✗
class=classname	✗	✗	✓	✗	✗	✓	✗	✓	✓	✓	✓	✓
cols=number	✓	✓	✓	✓	✓	✓	✓	✓	✓	✓	✓	✓
datafld=column_name	✗	✗	✗	✗	✗	✗	✗	✗	✓	✓	✓	✗

Table continued on following page

Attributes	2.0	3.2	4.01	N3	N4	N6	IE3	IE4	IE 5	IE 5.5	IE6	O5.x
datasrc=id	✗	✗	✗	✗	✗	✗	✗	✓	✓	✓	✓	✗
dir=ltr|rtl	✗	✗	✓	✗	✗	✓	✗	✗	✓	✓	✓	✗
disabled	✗	✗	✓	✗	✗	✓	✗	✓	✓	✓	✓	✓
id=string	✗	✗	✓	✗	✓	✓	✗	✓	✓	✓	✓	✓
lang=language_type	✗	✗	✓	✗	✗	✓	✗	✓	✓	✓	✓	✗
language=javascript|vbscript	✗	✗	✗	✗	✗	✗	✗	✓	✓	✓	✓	✗
name=string	✓	✓	✓	✓	✓	✓	✓	✓	✓	✓	✓	✓
readonly	✗	✗	✓	✗	✗	✓	✗	✓	✓	✓	✓	✓
rows	✓	✓	✓	✓	✓	✓	✓	✓	✓	✓	✓	✓
style=string	✗	✗	✓	✗	✓	✓	✗	✓	✓	✓	✓	✓
tabindex=number	✗	✗	✓	✗	✗	✗	✗	✓	✓	✓	✓	✓
title=string	✗	✗	✓	✗	✗	✓	✗	✓	✓	✓	✓	✓
type=button|reset|submit	✗	✗	✗	✗	✗	✓	✗	✗	✗	✗	✗	✗
wrap=physical|vertical|off	✗	✗	✗	✓	✓	✗	✗	✓	✓	✓	✓	✗

tfoot

Denotes a set of rows to be used as the footer of a table. **HTML 4.01, N6, IE3+**

Attributes	2.0	3.2	4.01	N3	N4	N6	IE3	IE4	IE 5	IE 5.5	IE6	O5.x
<event_name>=script_code	✗	✗	✓	✗	✗	✓	✗	✓	✓	✓	✓	✗
accesskey=key_character	✗	✗	✗	✗	✗	✗	✗	✗	✓	✓	✓	✗
align=center|left|right|justify|char	✗	✗	✓	✗	✗	✓	✗	✓	✓	✓	✓	✗
bgcolor=color	✗	✗	✗	✗	✗	✗	✗	✗	✓	✓	✓	✗
char=string	✗	✗	✓	✗	✗	✓	✗	✗	✗	✗	✓	✗
charoff=string	✗	✗	✓	✗	✗	✓	✗	✗	✗	✗	✓	✗

Attributes	2.0	3.2	4.01	N3	N4	N6	IE3	IE4	IE5	IE 5.5	IE6	O5.x
class=classname	✗	✗	✓	✗	✗	✓	✓	✓	✓	✓	✓	✗
dir=ltr|rtl	✗	✗	✓	✗	✗	✓	✗	✗	✓	✓	✓	✗
id=string	✗	✗	✓	✗	✗	✓	✓	✓	✓	✓	✓	✗
lang=language_type	✗	✗	✓	✗	✗	✓	✗	✓	✓	✓	✓	✗
language=javascript| vbscript	✗	✗	✗	✗	✗	✗	✗	✓	✓	✓	✓	✗
style=string	✗	✗	✓	✗	✗	✓	✓	✓	✓	✓	✓	✓
tabindex=number	✗	✗	✗	✗	✗	✗	✗	✗	✓	✓	✓	✗
title=string	✗	✗	✓	✗	✗	✓	✓	✓	✓	✓	✓	✗
valign=baseline| bottom|center|top	✗	✗	✓	✗	✗	✓	✓	✓	✓	✓	✓	✗

th

Denotes a header row in a table. Contents are usually bold and centered within each cell. **ALL except HTML 2.0**

Attributes	2.0	3.2	4.01	N3	N4	N6	IE3	IE4	IE5	IE 5.5	IE6	O5.x
<event_name>= script_code	✗	✗	✓	✗	✗	✓	✗	✓	✓	✓	✓	✓
abbr=string	✗	✗	✓	✗	✗	✓	✗	✗	✗	✗	✓	✗
accesskey= key_character	✗	✗	✗	✗	✗	✗	✗	✗	✓	✓	✓	✗
align=center|left| right|justify|char	✗	✓	✓	✓	✓	✓	✓	✓	✓	✓	✓	✓
axis=cellname	✗	✗	✓	✗	✗	✓	✗	✗	✗	✗	✓	✗
background=string	✗	✗	✗	✗	✗	✗	✓	✓	✓	✓	✓	✗
bgcolor=color	✗	✗	D	✓	✓	✓	✓	✓	✓	✓	✓	✗
bordercolor=color	✗	✗	✗	✗	✗	✗	✓	✓	✓	✓	✓	✗
bordercolordark=color	✗	✗	✗	✗	✗	✗	✓	✓	✗	✓	✓	✗
bordercolorlight= color	✗	✗	✗	✗	✗	✗	✓	✓	✗	✓	✓	✗

Table continued on following page

Attributes	2.0	3.2	4.01	N3	N4	N6	IE3	IE4	IE 5	IE 5.5	IE6	O5.x
char=string	x	x	✓	x	x	✓	x	x	x	x	✓	x
charoff=string	x	x	✓	x	x	✓	x	x	x	x	✓	x
class=classname	x	x	✓	x	✓	✓	✓	✓	✓	✓	✓	✓
colspan=number	x	✓	✓	✓	✓	✓	✓	✓	✓	✓	✓	✓
dir=ltr|rtl	x	x	✓	x	x	✓	x	x	✓	✓	✓	x
headers=string	x	x	✓	x	x	x	x	x	x	x	✓	x
height=number	x	✓	D	x	✓	✓	x	x	✓	✓	✓	✓
id=string	x	x	✓	x	x	✓	✓	✓	✓	✓	✓	✓
lang=language_type	x	x	✓	x	x	✓	x	✓	✓	✓	✓	x
language=javascript|vbscript	x	x	x	x	x	x	x	✓	✓	✓	✓	x
nowrap	x	✓	D	✓	✓	✓	✓	✓	✓	✓	✓	✓
rowspan=number	x	✓	✓	✓	✓	✓	✓	✓	✓	✓	✓	✓
scope=row|col|rowgroup|colgroup	x	x	✓	x	x	✓	x	x	x	x	✓	x
style=string	x	x	✓	x	✓	✓	✓	✓	✓	✓	✓	✓
tabindex=number	x	x	x	x	x	x	x	x	✓	✓	✓	x
title=string	x	x	✓	x	x	✓	x	✓	✓	✓	✓	✓
valign=baseline|bottom|center|top	x	✓	✓	✓	✓	x	✓	✓	✓	✓	✓	✓
width=number	x	✓	D	✓	✓	x	✓	x	✓	✓	✓	✓

thead

Denotes a set of rows to be used as the header of a table. **HTML 4.01, N6, IE3+**

Attributes	2.0	3.2	4.01	N3	N4	N6	IE3	IE4	IE 5	IE 5.5	IE6	O5.x
<event_name>=script_code	x	x	✓	x	x	✓	x	✓	✓	✓	✓	x
accesskey=key_character	x	x	x	x	x	x	x	x	✓	✓	✓	x

Attributes	2.0	3.2	4.01	N3	N4	N6	IE3	IE4	IE 5	IE 5.5	IE6	O5.x
align=center|left| right|justify|char	✗	✗	✓	✗	✗	✓	✓	✓	✓	✓	✓	✗
bgcolor=color	✗	✗	✗	✗	✗	✗	✗	✓	✓	✓	✓	✗
char=string	✗	✗	✓	✗	✗	✓	✗	✗	✗	✗	✓	✗
charoff=string	✗	✗	✓	✗	✗	✓	✗	✗	✗	✗	✗	✗
class=classname	✗	✗	✓	✗	✗	✓	✓	✓	✓	✓	✓	✗
dir=ltr|rtl	✗	✗	✓	✗	✗	✓	✗	✗	✓	✓	✓	✗
id=string	✗	✗	✓	✗	✗	✓	✓	✓	✓	✓	✓	✗
lang=language_type	✗	✗	✓	✗	✗	✓	✗	✗	✓	✓	✓	✗
language=javascript| vbscript	✗	✗	✗	✗	✗	✗	✗	✓	✓	✓	✓	✗
style=string	✗	✗	✓	✗	✗	✓	✓	✓	✓	✓	✓	✗
tabindex=number	✗	✗	✗	✗	✗	✗	✗	✗	✓	✓	✓	✗
title=string	✗	✗	✓	✗	✗	✓	✗	✓	✓	✓	✓	✗
valign=baseline| bottom|center|top	✗	✗	✓	✗	✗	✓	✓	✓	✓	✓	✓	✗

title

Denotes the title of the document and is used in the browser's window title bar. **ALL**

Attributes	2.0	3.2	4.01	N3	N4	N6	IE3	IE4	IE 5	IE 5.5	IE6	O5.x
dir=ltr|rtl	✗	✗	✓	✗	✗	✓	✗	✗	✗	✗	✗	✗
id=string	✗	✗	✗	✗	✓	✓	✗	✓	✓	✓	✓	✗
lang=language_type	✗	✗	✓	✗	✗	✓	✗	✗	✓	✓	✓	✗

tr

Specifies a row in a table. **ALL except HTML 2.0**

Attributes	2.0	3.2	4.01	N3	N4	N6	IE3	IE4	IE 5	IE 5.5	IE6	O5.x
<event_name>= script_code	✗	✗	✓	✗	✗	✓	✗	✓	✓	✓	✓	✓
accesskey= key_character	✗	✗	✗	✗	✗	✗	✗	✗	✓	✓	✓	✗
align=center|left| right|justify|char	✗	✓	✓	✓	✓	✓	✓	✓	✓	✓	✓	✓
background	✗	✗	✗	✗	✗	✗	✗	✗	✗	✗	✗	✗
bgcolor=color	✗	✗	D	✓	✓	✓	✓	✓	✓	✓	✓	✓
bordercolor=color	✗	✗	✗	✗	✗	✗	✓	✓	✓	✓	✓	✗
bordercolordark=color	✗	✗	✗	✗	✗	✗	✓	✓	✗	✓	✓	✗
bordercolorlight= color	✗	✗	✗	✗	✗	✗	✓	✓	✗	✓	✓	✗
char=string	✗	✗	✓	✗	✗	✓	✗	✗	✗	✗	✓	✗
charoff=string	✗	✗	✓	✗	✗	✓	✗	✗	✗	✗	✓	✗
class=classname	✗	✗	✓	✗	✓	✓	✓	✓	✓	✓	✓	✓
dir=ltr|rtl	✗	✗	✓	✗	✗	✓	✗	✗	✓	✓	✓	✗
id=string	✗	✗	✓	✗	✓	✓	✓	✓	✓	✓	✓	✓
lang=language_type	✗	✗	✓	✗	✗	✓	✗	✓	✓	✓	✓	✗
language=javascript| vbscript	✗	✗	✗	✗	✗	✗	✗	✓	✓	✓	✓	✗
nowrap	✗	✗	✗	✗	✗	✗	✓	✗	✗	✗	✗	✗
style=string	✗	✗	✓	✗	✓	✓	✓	✓	✓	✓	✓	✓
tabindex=number	✗	✗	✗	✗	✗	✗	✗	✗	✓	✓	✓	✗
title=string	✗	✗	✓	✗	✗	✓	✗	✓	✓	✓	✓	✓
valign=baseline| bottom|center|top	✗	✓	✓	✓	✓	✓	✓	✓	✓	✓	✓	✓
width=number	✗	✗	✗	✗	✗	✗	✗	✗	✓	✓	✓	✗

tt

Renders text in fixed-width type. **ALL**

Attributes	2.0	3.2	4.01	N3	N4	N6	IE3	IE4	IE5	IE 5.5	IE6	O5.x
`<event_name>= script_code`	✗	✗	✓	✗	✗	✓	✗	✓	✓	✓	✓	✓
`accesskey= key_character`	✗	✗	✗	✗	✗	✗	✗	✗	✓	✓	✓	✗
`class=classname`	✗	✗	✓	✗	✓	✓	✗	✓	✓	✓	✓	✓
`dir=ltr|rtl`	✗	✗	✓	✗	✗	✓	✗	✗	✓	✓	✓	✗
`id=string`	✗	✗	✓	✗	✓	✓	✗	✓	✓	✓	✓	✗
`lang=language_type`	✗	✗	✓	✗	✗	✓	✗	✓	✓	✓	✓	✗
`language=javascript| vbscript`	✗	✗	✗	✗	✗	✗	✗	✓	✓	✓	✓	✗
`style=string`	✗	✗	✓	✗	✓	✓	✗	✓	✓	✓	✓	✓
`tabindex=number`	✗	✗	✗	✗	✗	✗	✗	✗	✓	✓	✓	✗
`title=string`	✗	✗	✓	✗	✗	✓	✗	✓	✓	✓	✓	✓

u

Renders text underlined. **HTML 3.2, deprecated in HTML 4.01, N3+, IE3+, O5.x**

Attributes	2.0	3.2	4.01	N3	N4	N6	IE3	IE4	IE5	IE 5.5	IE6	O5.x
`<event_name>= script_code`	✗	✗	D	✗	✗	✗	✗	✓	✓	✓	✓	✓
`accesskey= key_character`	✗	✗	✗	✗	✗	✓	✗	✗	✓	✓	✓	✗
`class=classname`	✗	✗	D	✗	✓	✓	✗	✓	✓	✓	✓	✓
`dir=ltr|rtl`	✗	✗	D	✗	✗	✓	✗	✗	✓	✓	✓	✗
`id=string`	✗	✗	D	✗	✓	✓	✗	✓	✓	✓	✓	✓
`lang=language_type`	✗	✗	D	✗	✗	✓	✗	✓	✓	✓	✓	✗
`language=javascript| vbscript`	✗	✗	✗	✗	✗	✗	✗	✓	✓	✓	✓	✗
`style=string`	✗	✗	D	✗	✓	✓	✗	✓	✓	✓	✓	✓
`tabindex=number`	✗	✗	✗	✗	✗	✗	✗	✗	✓	✓	✓	✗
`title=string`	✗	✗	D	✗	✗	✓	✗	✓	✓	✓	✓	✓

ul

Renders lines of text that have `<li>` tags as a bulleted list. **ALL**

Attributes	2.0	3.2	4.01	N3	N4	N6	IE3	IE4	IE 5	IE 5.5	IE6	O5.x
`<event_name>=` `script_code`	✗	✗	✓	✗	✗	✓	✗	✓	✓	✓	✓	✓
`accesskey=` `key_character`	✗	✗	✗	✗	✗	✗	✗	✗	✓	✓	✓	✗
`class=classname`	✗	✗	✓	✗	✓	✓	✓	✓	✓	✓	✓	✓
`compact`	✓	✓	D	✓	✓	✓	✓	✗	✗	✓	✓	✗
`dir=ltr|rtl`	✗	✗	✓	✗	✗	✓	✗	✗	✗	✓	✓	✗
`id=string`	✗	✗	✓	✗	✓	✓	✓	✓	✓	✓	✓	✓
`lang=language_type`	✗	✗	✓	✗	✗	✓	✗	✓	✓	✓	✓	✗
`language=javascript|` `vbscript`	✗	✗	✗	✗	✗	✗	✗	✓	✓	✓	✓	✗
`style=string`	✗	✗	✓	✗	✓	✓	✓	✓	✓	✓	✓	✓
`tabindex=number`	✗	✗	✗	✗	✗	✗	✗	✗	✓	✓	✓	✗
`title=string`	✗	✗	✓	✗	✗	✓	✗	✓	✓	✓	✓	✓
`type=button|` `reset|submit`	✗	✓	D	✓	✓	✓	✓	✗	✓	✓	✓	✓

var

Renders text as a small fixed-width font. **HTML 2.0+, N6, IE3+, O5.x**

Attributes	2.0	3.2	4.01	N3	N4	N6	IE3	IE4	IE 5	IE 5.5	IE6	O5.x
`<event_name>=` `script_code`	✗	✗	✓	✗	✗	✓	✗	✓	✓	✓	✓	✓
`accesskey=` `key_character`	✗	✗	✗	✗	✗	✗	✗	✗	✓	✓	✓	✗
`class=classname`	✗	✗	✓	✗	✗	✓	✗	✓	✓	✓	✓	✓
`dir=ltr|rtl`	✗	✗	✓	✗	✗	✓	✗	✗	✓	✓	✓	✗
`id=string`	✗	✗	✓	✗	✗	✓	✗	✓	✓	✓	✓	✓

Attributes	2.0	3.2	4.01	N3	N4	N6	IE3	IE4	IE5	IE 5.5	IE6	O5.x
lang=language_type	✗	✗	✓	✗	✗	✓	✗	✓	✓	✓	✓	✗
language=javascript|vbscript	✗	✗	✗	✗	✗	✗	✗	✓	✓	✓	✓	✗
style=string	✗	✗	✓	✗	✗	✓	✗	✓	✓	✓	✓	✓
tabindex=number	✗	✗	✗	✗	✗	✗	✗	✗	✓	✓	✓	✗
title=string	✗	✗	✓	✗	✗	✓	✗	✓	✓	✓	✓	✓

wbr

Inserts a soft line break in a block of nobr text. **N2, N3, N4, IE3+**

Attributes	2.0	3.2	4.01	N3	N4	N6	IE3	IE4	IE5	IE 5.5	IE6	O5.x
class=classname	✗	✗	✗	✗	✓	✗	✗	✓	✗	✗	✗	✗
id=string	✗	✗	✗	✗	✓	✗	✗	✓	✓	✓	✓	✗
language=javascript|vbscript	✗	✗	✗	✗	✗	✗	✗	✓	✗	✗	✗	✗
style=string	✗	✗	✗	✗	✓	✗	✗	✓	✗	✗	✗	✗
title=string	✗	✗	✗	✗	✗	✗	✗	✓	✗	✗	✗	✗

xml

Used to specify XML content that serves as an XML data island in the HTML document. **IE 5+**

Attributes	2.0	3.2	4.01	N3	N4	N6	IE3	IE4	IE5	IE 5.5	IE6	O5.x
id=string	✗	✗	✗	✗	✗	✗	✗	✗	✓	✓	✓	✗
src=url	✗	✗	✗	✗	✗	✗	✗	✗	✓	✓	✓	✗

xmp

Renders text in fixed-width typeface, as used for sample code. Use `pre` or `samp` instead. **HTML 2.0, deprecated in HTML 3.2, N3+, IE3+**

Attributes	2.0	3.2	4.01	N3	N4	N6	IE3	IE4	IE5	IE 5.5	IE6	O5.x
`<event_name>=` `script_code`	✗	✗	✗	✗	✗	✗	✗	✓	✓	✓	✓	✗
`accesskey=` `key_character`	✗	✗	✗	✗	✗	✗	✗	✗	✓	✓	✓	✗
`class=classname`	✗	✗	✗	✗	✓	✗	✗	✓	✓	✓	✓	✗
`dir=ltr|rtl`	✗	✗	✗	✗	✗	✗	✗	✗	✓	✓	✓	✗
`id=string`	✗	✗	✗	✗	✓	✗	✗	✓	✓	✓	✓	✗
`lang=language_type`	✗	✗	✗	✗	✗	✗	✗	✓	✓	✓	✓	✗
`language=javascript|` `vbscript`	✗	✗	✗	✗	✗	✗	✗	✓	✓	✓	✓	✗
`style=string`	✗	✗	✗	✗	✓	✗	✗	✓	✓	✓	✓	✗
`tabindex=number`	✗	✗	✗	✗	✗	✗	✗	✗	✓	✓	✓	✗
`title=string`	✗	✗	✗	✗	✗	✗	✗	✓	✓	✓	✓	✗

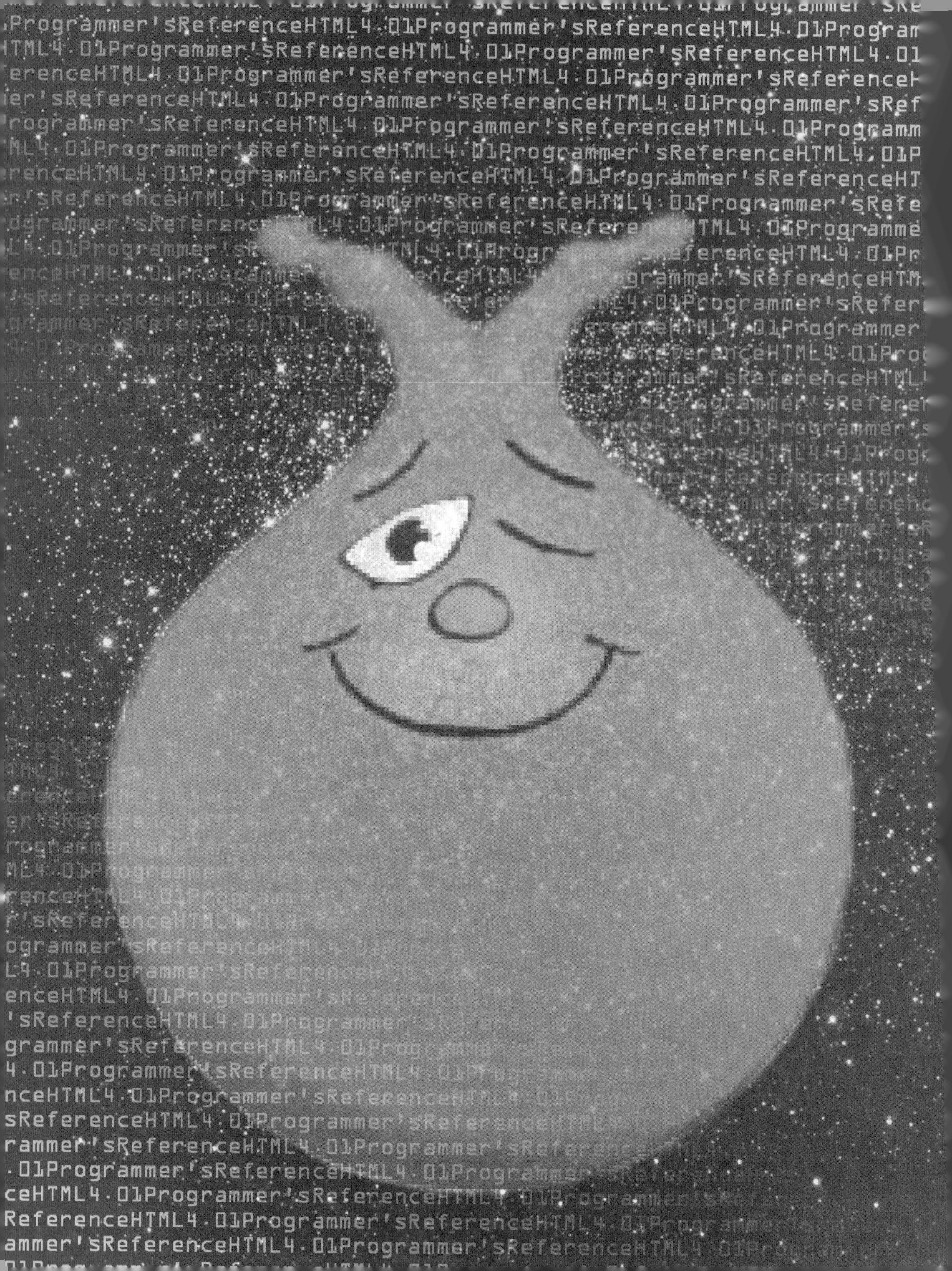

Special Characters in HTML

The following table lists the codes that must be employed in order to use certain special characters in HTML pages. The characters are inserted with either the decimal code or the equivalent HTML mnemonic; so for the registered trademark character you may use either ® or ®.

Character	Decimal Code	HTML Mnemonic	Description
"	"	"	Quotation mark
&	&	&	Ampersand
<	<	<	Less than
>	>	>	Greater than
			Non-breaking space
¡	¡	¡	Inverted exclamation
¢	¢	¢	Cent sign
£	£	£	Pound sterling sign
¤	¤	¤	General currency sign
¥	¥	¥	Yen sign

Table continued on following page

' &#39 Single Quote/Aostrophe

Character	Decimal Code	HTML Mnemonic	Description
¦	&#166;	&brvbar;	Broken vertical bar
§	&#167;	&sect;	Section sign
¨	&#168;	&uml;	Diæresis/umlaut
©	&#169;	&copy;	Copyright
ª	&#170;	&ordf;	Feminine ordinal
«	&#171;	&laquo;	Left angle quote
¬	&#172;	&not;	Not sign
	&#173;	&shy;	Soft hyphen
®	&#174;	&reg;	Registered trademark
¯	&#175;	&macr;	Macron accent
°	&#176;	&deg;	Degree sign
±	&#177;	&plusmn;	Plus or minus
²	&#178;	&sup2;	Superscript two
³	&#179;	&sup3;	Superscript three
´	&#180;	&acute;	Acute accent
µ	&#181;	&micro;	Micro sign
¶	&#182;	&para;	Paragraph sign
·	&#183;	&middot;	Middle dot
¸	&#184;	&cedil;	Cedilla
¹	&#185;	&sup1;	Superscript one
º	&#186;	&ordm;	Masculine ordinal
»	&#187;	&raquo;	Right angle quote
¼	&#188;	&frac14;	Fraction one quarter
½	&#189;	&frac12;	Fraction one half
¾	&#190;	&frac34;	Fraction three-quarters
¿	&#191;	&iquest;	Inverted question mark
À	&#192;	&Agrave;	Capital A, grave accent

Character	Decimal Code	HTML Mnemonic	Description
Á	`&#193;`	`&Aacute;`	Capital A, acute accent
Â	`&#194;`	`&Acirc;`	Capital A, circumflex
Ã	`&#195;`	`&Atilde;`	Capital A, tilde
Ä	`&#196;`	`&Auml;`	Capital A, diæresis/umlaut
Å	`&#197;`	`&Aring;`	Capital A, ring
Æ	`&#198;`	`&AElig;`	Capital AE, ligature
Ç	`&#199;`	`&Ccedil;`	Capital C, cedilla
È	`&#200;`	`&Egrave;`	Capital E, grave accent
É	`&#201;`	`&Eacute;`	Capital E, acute accent
Ê	`&#202;`	`&Ecirc;`	Capital E, circumflex
Ë	`&#203;`	`&Euml;`	Capital E, diæresis/umlaut
Ì	`&#204;`	`&Igrave;`	Capital I, grave accent
Í	`&#205;`	`&Iacute;`	Capital I, acute accent
Î	`&#206;`	`&Icirc;`	Capital I, circumflex
Ï	`&#207;`	`&Iuml;`	Capital I, diæresis/umlaut
Ð	`&#208;`	`&ETH;`	Capital Eth, Icelandic
Ñ	`&#209;`	`&Ntilde;`	Capital N, tilde
Ò	`&#210;`	`&Ograve;`	Capital O, grave accent
Ó	`&#211;`	`&Oacute;`	Capital O, acute accent
Ô	`&#212;`	`&Ocirc;`	Capital O, circumflex
Õ	`&#213;`	`&Otilde;`	Capital O, tilde
Ö	`&#214;`	`&Ouml;`	Capital O, diæresis/umlaut
×	`&#215;`	`&times;`	Multiplication sign
Ø	`&#216;`	`&Oslash;`	Capital O, slash
Ù	`&#217;`	`&Ugrave;`	Capital U, grave accent
Ú	`&#218;`	`&Uacute;`	Capital U, acute accent

Table continued on following page

Character	Decimal Code	HTML Mnemonic	Description
Û	Û	Û	Capital U, circumflex
Ü	Ü	Ü	Capital U, diæresis/umlaut
Ý	Ý	Ý	Capital Y, acute accent
Þ	Þ	Þ	Capital Thorn, Icelandic
ß	ß	ß	German sz
à	à	à	Small a, grave accent
á	á	á	Small a, acute accent
â	â	â	Small a, circumflex
ã	ã	ã	Small a, tilde
ä	ä	ä	Small a, diæresis/umlaut
å	å	å	Small a, ring
æ	æ	æ	Small ae, ligature
ç	ç	ç	Small c, cedilla
è	è	è	Small e, grave accent
é	é	é	Small e, acute accent
ê	ê	ê	Small e, circumflex
ë	ë	ë	Small e, diæresis/umlaut
ì	ì	ì	Small i, grave accent
í	í	í	Small i, acute accent
î	î	î	Small i, circumflex
ï	ï	ï	Small i, diæresis/umlaut
ð	ð	ð	Small eth, Icelandic
ñ	ñ	ñ	Small n, tilde
ò	ò	ò	Small o, grave accent
ó	ó	ó	Small o, acute accent
ô	ô	ô	Small o, circumflex
õ	õ	õ	Small o, tilde

Character	Decimal Code	HTML Mnemonic	Description
ö	ö	ö	Small o, diæresis/umlaut
÷	÷	÷	Division sign
ø	ø	ø	Small o, slash
ù	ù	ù	Small u, grave accent
ú	ú	ú	Small u, acute accent
û	û	û	Small u, circumflex
ü	ü	ü	Small u, diæresis/umlaut
ý	ý	ý	Small y, acute accent
þ	þ	þ	Small thorn, Icelandic
ÿ	ÿ	ÿ	Small y, diæresis/umlaut

The HTML 4 specification defines additional character references beyond the decimal code range of 0-255, primarily for Greek letters and other useful symbols for technical documents, some of which are given below. The full list can be found at http://www.w3.org/TR/html401/sgml/entities.html.

Character	Decimal Code	HTML Mnemonic	Description
Œ	Œ	Œ	Capital OE, ligature
œ	œ	œ	Small oe, ligature
A	Α	Α	Greek Capital Letter Alpha
Ω	Ω	Ω	Greek Capital Letter Omega
α	α	α	Greek Small Letter Alpha
ω	ω	ω	Greek Small Letter Omega
€	€	€	Euro Currency Sign
∷	∝	∝	Proportional to
∞	∞	∞	Symbol of Infinity
≅	≅	≅	Approximately Equal to

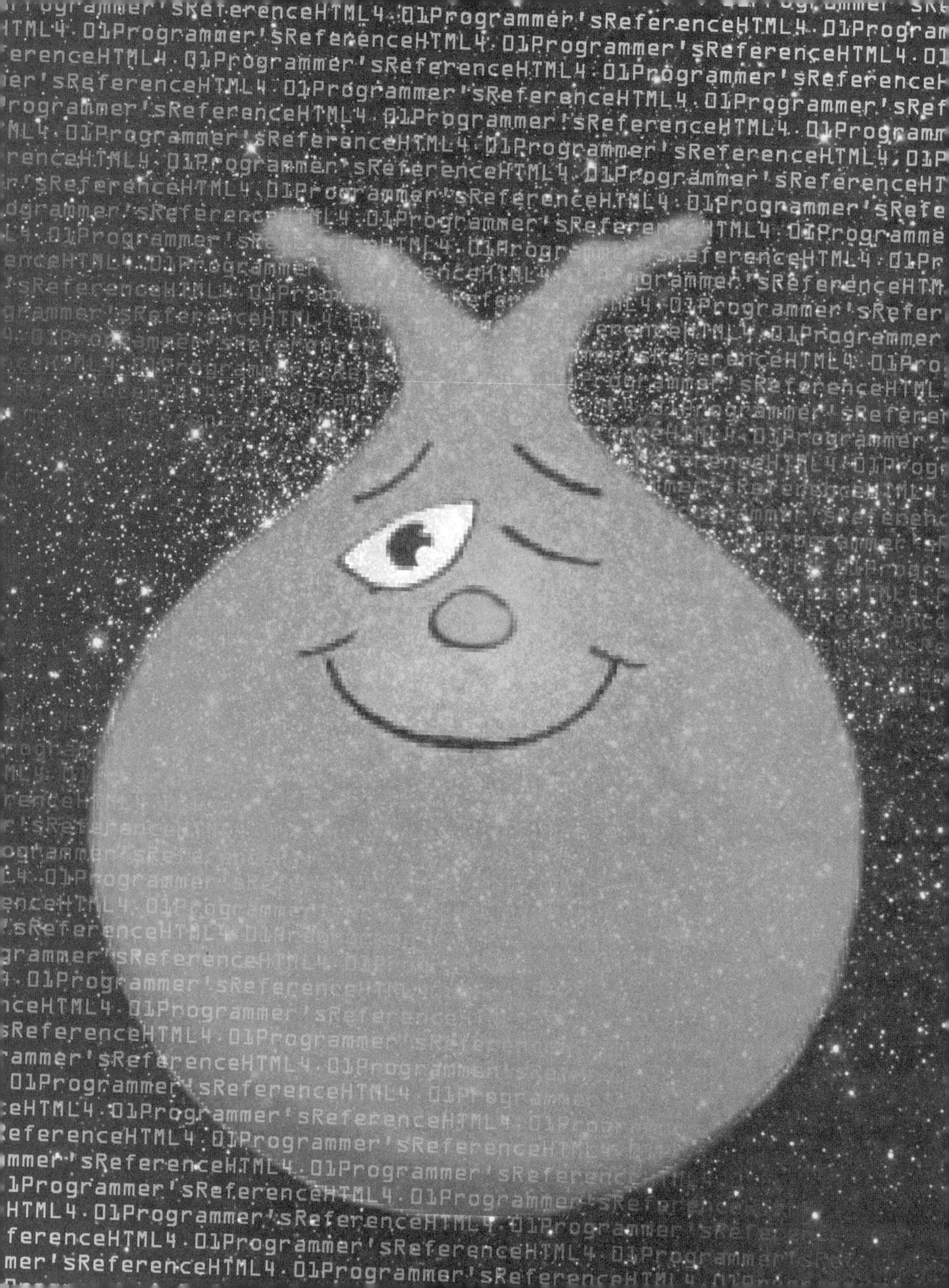
HTML4.01Programmer'sReference

C

HTML Locales and Character Sets

Language Codes

The following table lists the two-letter ISO language codes for many of the world's major languages. The codes may be used to declare the use of a particular language in a document by means of the lang attribute.

Language	Code	Language	Code	Language	Code
(Afan) Oromo	om	Hindi	hi	Russian	ru
Abkhazian	ab	Hungarian	hu	Samoan	sm
Afar	aa	Icelandic	is	Sangho	sg
Afrikaans	af	Indonesian	id	Sanskrit	sa
Albanian	sq	Interlingua	ia	Scots Gaelic	gd
Amharic	am	Interlingue	ie	Serbian	sr

Table continued on following page

Language	Code	Language	Code	Language	Code
Arabic	ar	Inuktitut	iu	Serbo-Croatian	sh
Armenian	hy	Inupiak	ik	Sesotho	st
Assamese	as	Irish	ga	Setswana	tn
Aymara	ay	Italian	it	Shona	sn
Azerbaijani	az	Japanese	ja	Sindhi	sd
Bashkir	ba	Javanese	jw	Sinhalese	si
Basque	eu	Kannada	kn	Siswati	ss
Bengali (Bangla)	bn	Kashmiri	ks	Slovak	sk
Bhutani	dz	Kazakh	kk	Slovenian	sl
Bihari	bh	Kinyarwanda	rw	Somali	so
Bislama	bi	Kirghiz	ky	Spanish	es
Breton	br	Kirundi	rn	Sundanese	su
Bulgarian	bg	Korean	ko	Swahili	sw
Burmese	my	Kurdish	ku	Swedish	sv
Byelorussian	be	Laothian	lo	Tagalog	tl
Cambodian	km	Latin	la	Tajik	tg
Catalan	ca	Latvian, Lettish	lv	Tamil	ta
Chinese	zh	Lingala	ln	Tatar	tt
Corsican	co	Lithuanian	lt	Telugu	te
Croatian	hr	Macedonian	mk	Thai	th
Czech	cs	Malagasy	mg	Tibetan	bo
Danish	da	Malay	ms	Tigrinya	ti
Dutch	nl	Malayalam	ml	Tonga	to
English	en	Maltese	mt	Tsonga	ts
Esperanto	eo	Maori	mi	Turkish	tr
Estonian	et	Marathi	mr	Turkmen	tk
Faroese	fo	Moldavian	mo	Twi	tw

Language	Code	Language	Code	Language	Code
Fiji	fj	Mongolian	mn	Uighur	ug
Finnish	fi	Nauru	na	Ukrainian	uk
Flemish	fl	Nepali	ne	Urdu	ur
French	fr	Norwegian	no	Uzbek	uz
Frisian	fy	Occitan	oc	Vietnamese	vi
Galician	gl	Oriya	or	Volapuk	vo
Georgian	ka	Pashto, Pushto	ps	Welsh	cy
German	de	Persian	fa	Wolof	wo
Greek	el	Polish	pl	Xhosa	xh
Greenlandic	kl	Portuguese	pt	Yiddish	yi
Guarani	gn	Punjabi	pa	Yoruba	yo
Gujarati	gu	Quechua	qu	Zhuang	za
Hausa	ha	Rhaeto-Romance	rm	Zulu	zu
Hebrew	he	Romanian	ro		

These two letter codes can be qualified to explicitly to deal with specific localization issues for a language by the use of one or more subcodes. Such codes should be appended to one of the language codes by a dash or an underscore, where two letter subcodes are understood to denote an ISO3166 country code. The following table lists some common combinations in this format.

Language	ISO Subcode
Danish for Denmark	da_DK
German for Austria	de_AT
German for Switzerland	de_CH
German for Germany	de_DE
English for Canada	en_CA
English for Denmark	en_DK
English for Great Britain	en_GB
English for Ireland	en_IE

Table continued on following page

Language	ISO Subcode
English for the US	en_US
French for Canada	fr_CA
Hungarian for Hungary	hu_HU
Italian for Italy	it_IT
Japanese for Japan	ja_JP
Greenlandic for Greenland	kl_GL
Lithuanian for Lithuania	lt_LT
Latvian for Latvia	lv_LV
Dutch for the Netherlands	nl_NL
Polish for Poland	pl_PL
Portuguese for Portugal	pt_PT

ISO Character Sets

The American Standard Code for Information Interchange (ASCII) is probably the most well known and widely accepted character set for digitally encoding text, and comes from the time of 8-bit computing. The original ASCII set used seven bits for representing the character, leaving one bit to be used for a parity bit to detect transmission errors. For this reason, ASCII codes from 0x0 to 0x7F represent the core set of characters, including the unadorned upper and lower-case Latin alphabet, punctuation, and common symbols. These are the safest characters to use, and should display correctly on just about any computer made since the '70s!

ASCII was later enhanced to use the parity bit to effectively double the range of available characters, extending the range to cover 0x0 through 0xFF, and allowing many accented Latin characters and other neat symbols to be made available.

There was little standardization in the extra characters supplied, and this is where the International Standards Organisation took the baton from the US. The ISO 8859-1 character set, also referred to as Latin 1, was established, and it standardized the extra characters provided by 8-bit encoding. This character set contains the characters used by all the major West European languages, and is also the preferred encoding on the Internet today.

However, there are many flavors of the ISO 8859 standard, in addition to the vanilla Latin 1, that specify alternative characters for the range 0xA0 through 0xFF, in addition to standard ASCII. These alternatives represent national characters, leaving characters in the range 0x20 through 0x7F the same as in US-ASCII (ISO 646). Thus, ASCII text is a proper subset of all ISO 8859-X character sets.

ISO Code	Languages Covered
ISO-8859-1	Latin 1 *North America, West Europe, Latin America, The Caribbean, Canada, Africa*
ISO-8859-2	Latin 2 *Eastern Europe*
ISO-8859-3	Latin 3 *SE Europe, Esperanto, Miscellaneous others*
ISO-8859-4	Latin 4 *Scandinavian/Baltic Additional Characters not covered by ISO-8859-1*
ISO-8859-5	Cyrillic
ISO-8859-6	Arabic
ISO-8859-7	Greek *equivalent to ELOT928*
ISO-8859-8	Hebrew
ISO-8859-9	Latin 5 *as ISO-8859-1, except that Turkish characters replace Icelandic ones*
ISO-8859-10	Latin 6 *Lappish, Nordic, and Eskimo languages*
ISO-8859-15	A more complete version of ISO-8859-1 with several additional characters

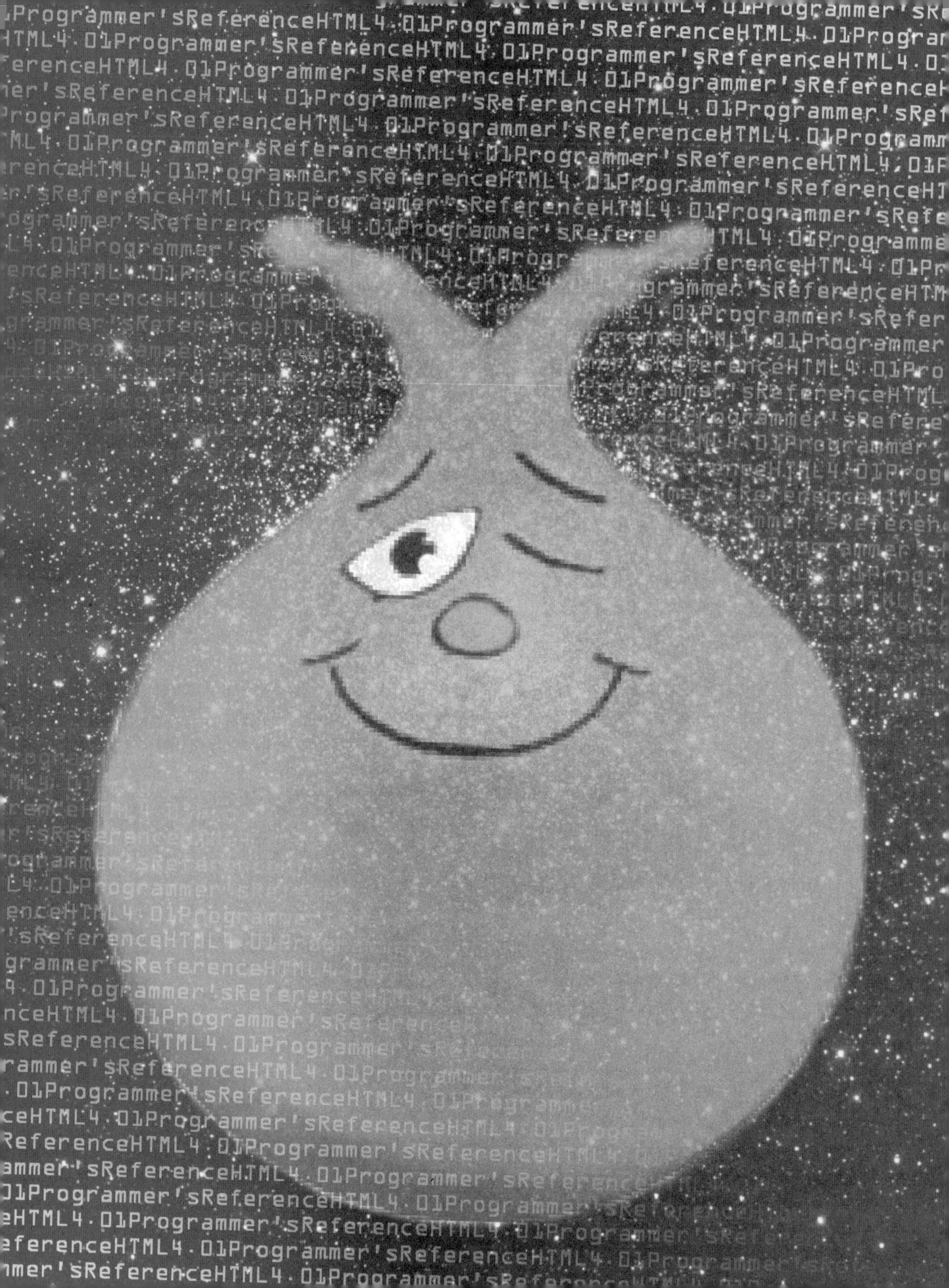
Programmer'sReferenceHTML4.01

D

HTML Color Names and Values

Colors can be applied to HTML elements using either one of a set of descriptive names, or a numeric value indicating the intensities of red, green, and blue required for that color. Each of these three components is represented internally by a single 8-bit byte, meaning that any color may be described by a sequence of six hexadecimal digits. The first two give the intensity of the red component, the middle two denote the strength of the green, and the last two give the intensity of blue in the color. Hence, white is indicated by maximum intensities for each RGB element, or FFFFFF, and conversely zero intensities for each, 000000, will produce black.

A brief word on the **Web-Safe Color Palette** is appropriate at this point. The term is used for a concept originally devised by Netscape in 1994, in an attempt to reduce the problem of colors displaying differently when viewed on different systems. It is a problem that occurs mainly when a browser is running on a 256-color setup, and the Web-Safe palette (or **Netscape palette**) addresses the issue by restricting the range of available RGB hexadecimal values for colors in the palette to 00, 33, 66, 99, CC or FF. So, if your web page must be reliably viewable on legacy systems, make sure you use color values that obey this rule. For example, 99FFFF will produce a light blue on any system that you can be confident will quite closely resemble the color seen on your own screen.

Colors Sorted by Name

Color Name	Hex Value	IE5 Color Constant
aliceblue	F0F8FF	HtmlAliceBlue
antiquewhite	FAEBD7	HtmlAntiqueWhite
aqua	00FFFF	HtmlAqua
aquamarine	7FFFD4	HtmlAquamarine
azure	F0FFFF	HtmlAzure
beige	F5F5DC	HtmlBeige
bisque	FFE4C4	HtmlBisque
black	000000	HtmlBlack
blanchedalmond	FFEBCD	htmlBlanchedAlmond
blue	0000FF	HtmlBlue
blueviolet	8A2BE2	HtmlBlueViolet
brown	A52A2A	htmlBrown
burlywood	DEB887	htmlBurlywood
cadetblue	5F9EA0	htmlCadetBlue
chartreuse	7FFF00	htmlChartreuse
chocolate	D2691E	htmlChocolate
coral	FF7F50	htmlCoral
cornflowerblue	6495ED	htmlCornflowerBlue
cornsilk	FFF8DC	htmlCornsilk
crimson	DC143C	htmlCrimson
cyan	00FFFF	htmlCyan
darkblue	00008B	htmlDarkBlue
darkcyan	008B8B	htmlDarkCyan
darkgoldenrod	B8860B	htmlDarkGoldenRod
darkgray	A9A9A9	htmlDarkGray
darkgreen	006400	htmlDarkGreen
darkkhaki	BDB76B	htmlDarkKhaki
darkmagenta	8B008B	htmlDarkMagenta

Color Name	Hex Value	IE5 Color Constant
darkolivegreen	556B2F	htmlDarkOliveGreen
darkorange	FF8C00	htmlDarkOrange
darkorchid	9932CC	htmlDarkOrchid
darkred	8B0000	htmlDarkRed
darksalmon	E9967A	htmlDarkSalmon
darkseagreen	8FBC8F	htmlDarkSeaGreen
darkslateblue	483D8B	htmlDarkSlateBlue
darkslategray	2F4F4F	htmlDarkSlateGray
darkturquoise	00CED1	htmlDarkTurquoise
darkviolet	9400D3	htmlDarkViolet
deeppink	FF1493	htmlDeepPink
deepskyblue	00BFFF	htmlDeepSkyBlue
dimgray	696969	htmlDimGray
dodgerblue	1E90FF	htmlDodgerBlue
firebrick	B22222	htmlFirebrick
floralwhite	FFFAF0	htmlFloralWhite
forestgreen	228B22	htmlForestGreen
fuchsia	FF00FF	htmlFuchsia
gainsboro	DCDCDC	htmlGainsboro
ghostwhite	F8F8FF	htmlGhostWhite
gold	FFD700	htmlGold
goldenrod	DAA520	htmlGoldenRod
gray	808080	htmlGray
green	008000	htmlGreen
greenyellow	ADFF2F	htmlGreenYellow
honeydew	F0FFF0	htmlHoneydew
hotpink	FF69B4	htmlHotPink
indianred	CD5C5C	htmlIndianRed
indigo	4B0082	htmlIndigo

Table continued on following page

Color Name	Hex Value	IE5 Color Constant
ivory	FFFFF0	htmlIvory
khaki	F0E68C	htmlKhaki
lavender	E6E6FA	htmlLavender
lavenderblush	FFF0F5	htmlLavenderBlush
lawngreen	7CFC00	htmlLawnGreen
lemonchiffon	FFFACD	htmlLemonChiffon
lightblue	ADD8E6	htmlLightBlue
lightcoral	F08080	htmlLightCoral
lightcyan	E0FFFF	htmlLightCyan
lightgoldenrodyellow	FAFAD2	htmlLightGoldenrodYellow
lightgreen	90EE90	htmlLightGreen
lightgrey	D3D3D3	htmlLightGrey
lightpink	FFB6C1	htmlLightPink
lightsalmon	FFA07A	htmlLightSalmon
lightseagreen	20B2AA	htmlLightSeaGreen
lightskyblue	87CEFA	htmlLightSkyBlue
lightslategray	778899	htmlLightSlateGray
lightsteelblue	B0C4DE	htmlLightSteelBlue
lightyellow	FFFFE0	htmlLightYellow
lime	00FF00	htmlLime
limegreen	32CD32	htmlLimeGreen
linen	FAF0E6	htmlLinen
magenta	FF00FF	htmlMagenta
maroon	800000	htmlMaroon
mediumaquamarine	66CDAA	htmlMediumAquamarine
mediumblue	0000CD	htmlMediumBlue
mediumorchid	BA55D3	htmlMediumOrchid
mediumpurple	9370DB	htmlMediumPurple
mediumseagreen	3CB371	htmlMediumSeaGreen

Color Name	Hex Value	IE5 Color Constant
mediumslateblue	7B68EE	htmlMediumSlateBlue
mediumspringgreen	00FA9A	htmlMediumSpringGreen
mediumturquoise	48D1CC	htmlMediumTurquoise
mediumvioletred	C71585	htmlMediumVioletRed
midnightblue	191970	htmlMidnightBlue
mintcream	F5FFFA	htmlMintCream
mistyrose	FFE4E1	htmlMistyRose
moccasin	FFE4B5	htmlMoccasin
navajowhite	FFDEAD	htmlNavajoWhite
navy	000080	htmlNavy
oldlace	FDF5E6	htmlOldLace
olive	808000	htmlOlive
olivedrab	6B8E23	htmlOliveDrab
orange	FFA500	htmlOrange
orangered	FF4500	htmlOrangeRed
orchid	DA70D6	htmlOrchid
palegoldenrod	EEE8AA	htmlPaleGoldenRod
palegreen	98FB98	htmlPaleGreen
paleturquoise	AFEEEE	htmlPaleTurquoise
palevioletred	DB7093	htmlPaleVioletRed
papayawhip	FFEFD5	htmlPapayaWhip
peachpuff	FFDAB9	htmlPeachPuff
peru	CD853F	htmlPeru
pink	FFC0CB	htmlPink
plum	DDA0DD	htmlPlum
powderblue	B0E0E6	htmlPowderBlue
purple	800080	htmlPurple
red	FF0000	htmlRed
rosybrown	BC8F8F	htmlRosyBrown

Table continued on following page

Color Name	Hex Value	IE5 Color Constant
royalblue	4169E1	htmlRoyalBlue
saddlebrown	8B4513	htmlSaddleBrown
salmon	FA8072	htmlSalmon
sandybrown	F4A460	htmlSandyBrown
seagreen	2E8B57	htmlSeaGreen
seashell	FFF5EE	htmlSeashell
sienna	A0522D	htmlSienna
silver	C0C0C0	htmlSilver
skyblue	87CEEB	htmlSkyBlue
slateblue	6A5ACD	htmlSlateBlue
slategray	708090	htmlSlateGray
snow	FFFAFA	htmlSnow
springgreen	00FF7F	htmlSpringGreen
steelblue	4682B4	htmlSteelBlue
tan	D2B48C	htmlTan
teal	008080	htmlTeal
thistle	D8BFD8	htmlThistle
tomato	FF6347	htmlTomato
turquoise	40E0D0	htmlTurquoise
violet	EE82EE	htmlViolet
wheat	F5DEB3	htmlWheat
white	FFFFFF	htmlWhite
whitesmoke	F5F5F5	htmlWhiteSmoke
yellow	FFFF00	htmlYellow
yellowgreen	9ACD32	htmlYellowGreen

Colors Sorted by Group

Color Name	Value	IE5 Color Constant
Blues		
azure	F0FFFF	htmlAzure
aliceblue	F0F8FF	htmlAliceBlue
lavender	E6E6FA	htmlLavender
lightcyan	E0FFFF	htmlLightCyan
powderblue	B0E0E6	htmlPowderBlue
lightsteelblue	B0C4DE	htmlLightSteelBlue
paleturquoise	AFEEEE	htmlPaleTurquoise
lightblue	ADD8E6	htmlLightBlue
blueviolet	8A2BE2	htmlBlueViolet
lightskyblue	87CEFA	htmlLightSkyBlue
skyblue	87CEEB	htmlSkyBlue
mediumslateblue	7B68EE	htmlMediumSlateBlue
slateblue	6A5ACD	htmlSlateBlue
cornflowerblue	6495ED	htmlCornflowerBlue
cadetblue	5F9EA0	htmlCadetBlue
indigo	4B0082	htmlIndigo
mediumturquoise	48D1CC	htmlMediumTurquoise
darkslateblue	483D8B	htmlDarkSlateBlue
steelblue	4682B4	htmlSteelBlue
royalblue	4169E1	htmlRoyalBlue
turquoise	40E0D0	htmlTurquoise
dodgerblue	1E90FF	htmlDodgerBlue
midnightblue	191970	htmlMidnightBlue
aqua	00FFFF	htmlAqua
cyan	00FFFF	htmlCyan
darkturquoise	00CED1	htmlDarkTurquoise
deepskyblue	00BFFF	htmlDeepSkyBlue

Table continued on following page

Color Name	Value	IE5 Color Constant
darkcyan	008B8B	htmlDarkCyan
blue	0000FF	htmlBlue
mediumblue	0000CD	htmlMediumBlue
darkblue	00008B	htmlDarkBlue
navy	000080	htmlNavy
Greens		
mintcream	F5FFFA	htmlMintCream
honeydew	F0FFF0	htmlHoneydew
greenyellow	ADFF2F	htmlGreenYellow
yellowgreen	9ACD32	htmlYellowGreen
palegreen	98FB98	htmlPaleGreen
lightgreen	90EE90	htmlLightGreen
darkseagreen	8FBC8F	htmlDarkSeaGreen
olive	808000	htmlOlive
aquamarine	7FFFD4	htmlAquamarine
chartreuse	7FFF00	htmlChartreuse
lawngreen	7CFC00	htmlLawnGreen
olivedrab	6B8E23	htmlOliveDrab
mediumaquamarine	66CDAA	htmlMediumAquamarine
darkolivegreen	556B2F	htmlDarkOliveGreen
mediumseagreen	3CB371	htmlMediumSeaGreen
limegreen	32CD32	htmlLimeGreen
seagreen	2E8B57	htmlSeaGreen
forestgreen	228B22	htmlForestGreen
lightseagreen	20B2AA	htmlLightSeaGreen
springgreen	00FF7F	htmlSpringGreen
lime	00FF00	htmlLime
mediumspringgreen	00FA9A	htmlMediumSpringGreen
teal	008080	htmlTeal
green	008000	htmlGreen
darkgreen	006400	htmlDarkGreen

Color Name	Value	IE5 Color Constant
Pinks and Reds		
lavenderblush	FFF0F5	htmlLavenderBlush
mistyrose	FFE4E1	htmlMistyRose
pink	FFC0CB	htmlPink
lightpink	FFB6C1	htmlLightPink
orange	FFA500	htmlOrange
lightsalmon	FFA07A	htmlLightSalmon
darkorange	FF8C00	htmlDarkOrange
coral	FF7F50	htmlCoral
hotpink	FF69B4	htmlHotPink
tomato	FF6347	htmlTomato
orangered	FF4500	htmlOrangeRed
deeppink	FF1493	htmlDeepPink
fuchsia	FF00FF	htmlFuchsia
magenta	FF00FF	htmlMagenta
red	FF0000	htmlRed
salmon	FA8072	htmlSalmon
lightcoral	F08080	htmlLightCoral
violet	EE82EE	htmlViolet
darksalmon	E9967A	htmlDarkSalmon
plum	DDA0DD	htmlPlum
crimson	DC143C	htmlCrimson
palevioletred	DB7093	htmlPaleVioletRed
orchid	DA70D6	htmlOrchid
thistle	D8BFD8	htmlThistle
indianred	CD5C5C	htmlIndianRed
mediumvioletred	C71585	htmlMediumVioletRed
mediumorchid	BA55D3	htmlMediumOrchid
firebrick	B22222	htmlFirebrick

Table continued on following page

Color Name	Value	IE5 Color Constant
darkorchid	9932CC	htmlDarkOrchid
darkviolet	9400D3	htmlDarkViolet
mediumpurple	9370DB	htmlMediumPurple
darkmagenta	8B008B	htmlDarkMagenta
darkred	8B0000	htmlDarkRed
purple	800080	htmlPurple
maroon	800000	htmlMaroon
Yellows		
lightgoldenrodyellow	FAFAD2	htmllightgoldenrodyellow
ivory	FFFFF0	htmlIvory
lightyellow	FFFFE0	htmlLightYellow
yellow	FFFF00	htmlYellow
floralwhite	FFFAF0	htmlFloralWhite
lemonchiffon	FFFACD	htmlLemonChiffon
cornsilk	FFF8DC	htmlCornsilk
gold	FFD700	htmlGold
khaki	F0E68C	htmlKhaki
darkkhaki	BDB76B	htmlDarkKhaki
Beiges and Browns		
snow	FFFAFA	htmlSnow
seashell	FFF5EE	htmlSeashell
papayawhite	FFEFD5	htmlPapayaWhite
blanchedalmond	FFEBCD	htmlBlanchedAlmond
bisque	FFE4C4	htmlBisque
moccasin	FFE4B5	htmlMoccasin
navajowhite	FFDEAD	htmlNavajoWhite
peachpuff	FFDAB9	htmlPeachPuff
oldlace	FDF5E6	htmlOldLace
linen	FAF0E6	htmlLinen

Color Name	Value	IE5 Color Constant
antiquewhite	FAEBD7	htmlAntiqueWhite
beige	F5F5DC	htmlBeige
wheat	F5DEB3	htmlWheat
sandybrown	F4A460	htmlSandyBrown
palegoldenrod	EEE8AA	htmlPaleGoldenRod
burlywood	DEB887	htmlBurlywood
goldenrod	DAA520	htmlGoldenRod
tan	D2B48C	htmlTan
chocolate	D2691E	htmlChocolate
peru	CD853F	htmlPeru
rosybrown	BC8F8F	htmlRosyBrown
darkgoldenrod	B8860B	htmlDarkGoldenRod
brown	A52A2A	htmlBrown
sienna	A0522D	htmlSienna
saddlebrown	8B4513	htmlSaddleBrown
Whites and Grays		
white	FFFFFF	htmlWhite
ghostwhite	F8F8FF	htmlGhostWhite
whitesmoke	F5F5F5	htmlWhiteSmoke
gainsboro	DCDCDC	htmlGainsboro
lightgrey	D3D3D3	htmlLightGrey
silver	C0C0C0	htmlSilver
darkgray	A9A9A9	htmlDarkGray
gray	808080	htmlGray
lightslategray	778899	htmlLightSlateGray
slategray	708090	htmlSlateGray
dimgray	696969	htmlDimGray
darkslategray	2F4F4F	htmlDarkSlateGray
black	000000	htmlBlack

Colors Sorted by Depth

Color Name	Value	IE5 Color Constant
white	FFFFFF	htmlWhite
ivory	FFFFF0	htmlIvory
lightyellow	FFFFE0	htmlLightYellow
yellow	FFFF00	htmlYellow
snow	FFFAFA	htmlSnow
floralwhite	FFFAF0	htmlFloralWhite
lemonchiffon	FFFACD	htmlLemonChiffon
cornsilk	FFF8DC	htmlCornsilk
seashell	FFF5EE	htmlSeashell
lavenderblush	FFF0F5	htmlLavenderBlush
papayawhip	FFEFD5	htmlPapayaWhip
blanchedalmond	FFEBCD	htmlBlanchedAlmond
mistyrose	FFE4E1	htmlMistyRose
bisque	FFE4C4	htmlBisque
moccasin	FFE4B5	htmlMoccasin
navajowhite	FFDEAD	htmlNavajoWhite
peachpuff	FFDAB9	htmlPeachPuff
gold	FFD700	htmlGold
pink	FFC0CB	htmlPink
lightpink	FFB6C1	htmlLightPink
orange	FFA500	HtmlOrange
lightsalmon	FFA07A	htmlLightSalmon
darkorange	FF8C00	htmlDarkOrange
coral	FF7F50	htmlCoral
hotpink	FF69B4	htmlHotPink
tomato	FF6347	htmlTomato
orangered	FF4500	htmlOrangeRed
deeppink	FF1493	htmlDeepPink

Color Name	Value	IE5 Color Constant
fuchsia	FF00FF	htmlFuchsia
magenta	FF00FF	htmlMagenta
red	FF0000	htmlRed
oldlace	FDF5E6	htmlOldLace
lightgoldenrodyellow	FAFAD2	htmlLightGoldenrodYellow
linen	FAF0E6	htmlLinen
antiquewhite	FAEBD7	htmlAntiqueWhite
salmon	FA8072	htmlSalmon
ghostwhite	F8F8FF	htmlGhostWhite
mintcream	F5FFFA	htmlMintCream
whitesmoke	F5F5F5	htmlWhiteSmoke
beige	F5F5DC	htmlBeige
wheat	F5DEB3	htmlWheat
sandybrown	F4A460	htmlSandyBrown
azure	F0FFFF	htmlAzure
honeydew	F0FFF0	htmlHoneydew
aliceblue	F0F8FF	htmlAliceBlue
khaki	F0E68C	htmlKhaki
lightcoral	F08080	htmlLightCoral
palegoldenrod	EEE8AA	htmlPaleGoldenRod
violet	EE82EE	htmlViolet
darksalmon	E9967A	htmlDarkSalmon
lavender	E6E6FA	htmlLavender
lightcyan	E0FFFF	htmlLightCyan
burlywood	DEB887	htmlBurlywood
plum	DDA0DD	htmlPlum
gainsboro	DCDCDC	htmlGainsboro
crimson	DC143C	htmlCrimson
palevioletred	DB7093	htmlPaleVioletRed

Table continued on following page

Color Name	Value	IE5 Color Constant
goldenrod	DAA520	htmlGoldenRod
orchid	DA70D6	htmlOrchid
thistle	D8BFD8	htmlThistle
lightgrey	D3D3D3	htmlLightGrey
tan	D2B48C	htmlTan
chocolate	D2691E	htmlChocolate
peru	CD853F	htmlPeru
indianred	CD5C5C	htmlIndianRed
mediumvioletred	C71585	htmlMediumVioletRed
silver	C0C0C0	htmlSilver
darkkhaki	BDB76B	htmlDarkKhaki
rosybrown	BC8F8F	htmlRosyBrown
mediumorchid	BA55D3	htmlMediumOrchid
darkgoldenrod	B8860B	htmlDarkGoldenRod
firebrick	B22222	htmlFirebrick
powderblue	B0E0E6	htmlPowderBlue
lightsteelblue	B0C4DE	htmlLightSteelBlue
paleturquoise	AFEEEE	htmlPaleTurquoise
greenyellow	ADFF2F	htmlGreenYellow
lightblue	ADD8E6	htmlLightBlue
darkgray	A9A9A9	htmlDarkGray
brown	A52A2A	htmlBrown
sienna	A0522D	htmlSienna
yellowgreen	9ACD32	htmlYellowGreen
darkorchid	9932CC	htmlDarkOrchid
palegreen	98FB98	htmlPaleGreen
darkviolet	9400D3	htmlDarkViolet
mediumpurple	9370DB	htmlMediumPurple
lightgreen	90EE90	htmlLightGreen
darkseagreen	8FBC8F	htmlDarkSeaGreen

Color Name	Value	IE5 Color Constant
saddlebrown	8B4513	htmlSaddleBrown
darkmagenta	8B008B	htmlDarkMagenta
darkred	8B0000	htmlDarkRed
blueviolet	8A2BE2	htmlBlueViolet
lightskyblue	87CEFA	htmlLightSkyBlue
skyblue	87CEEB	htmlSkyBlue
gray	808080	htmlGray
olive	808000	htmlOlive
purple	800080	htmlPurple
maroon	800000	htmlMaroon
aquamarine	7FFFD4	htmlAquamarine
chartreuse	7FFF00	htmlChartreuse
lawngreen	7CFC00	htmlLawnGreen
mediumslateblue	7B68EE	htmlMediumSlateBlue
lightslategray	778899	htmlLightSlateGray
slategray	708090	htmlSlateGray
olivedrab	6B8E23	htmlOliveDrab
slateblue	6A5ACD	htmlSlateBlue
dimgray	696969	htmlDimGray
mediumaquamarine	66CDAA	htmlMediumAquamarine
cornflowerblue	6495ED	htmlCornflowerBlue
cadetblue	5F9EA0	htmlCadetBlue
darkolivegreen	556B2F	htmlDarkOliveGreen
indigo	4B0082	htmlIndigo
mediumturquoise	48D1CC	htmlMediumTurquoise
darkslateblue	483D8B	htmlDarkSlateBlue
steelblue	4682B4	htmlSteelBlue
royalblue	4169E1	htmlRoyalBlue
turquoise	40E0D0	htmlTurquoise

Table continued on following page

Color Name	Value	IE5 Color Constant
mediumseagreen	3CB371	htmlMediumSeaGreen
limegreen	32CD32	htmlLimeGreen
darkslategray	2F4F4F	htmlDarkSlateGray
seagreen	2E8B57	htmlSeaGreen
forestgreen	228B22	htmlForestGreen
lightseagreen	20B2AA	htmlLightSeaGreen
dodgerblue	1E90FF	htmlDodgerBlue
midnightblue	191970	htmlMidnightBlue
aqua	00FFFF	htmlAqua
cyan	00FFFF	htmlCyan
springgreen	00FF7F	htmlSpringGreen
lime	00FF00	htmlLime
mediumspringgreen	00FA9A	htmlMediumSpringGreen
darkturquoise	00CED1	htmlDarkTurquoise
deepskyblue	00BFFF	htmlDeepSkyBlue
darkcyan	008B8B	htmlDarkCyan
teal	008080	htmlTeal
green	008000	htmlGreen
darkgreen	006400	htmlDarkGreen
blue	0000FF	htmlBlue
mediumblue	0000CD	htmlMediumBlue
darkblue	00008B	htmlDarkBlue
navy	000080	htmlNavy
black	000000	htmlBlack

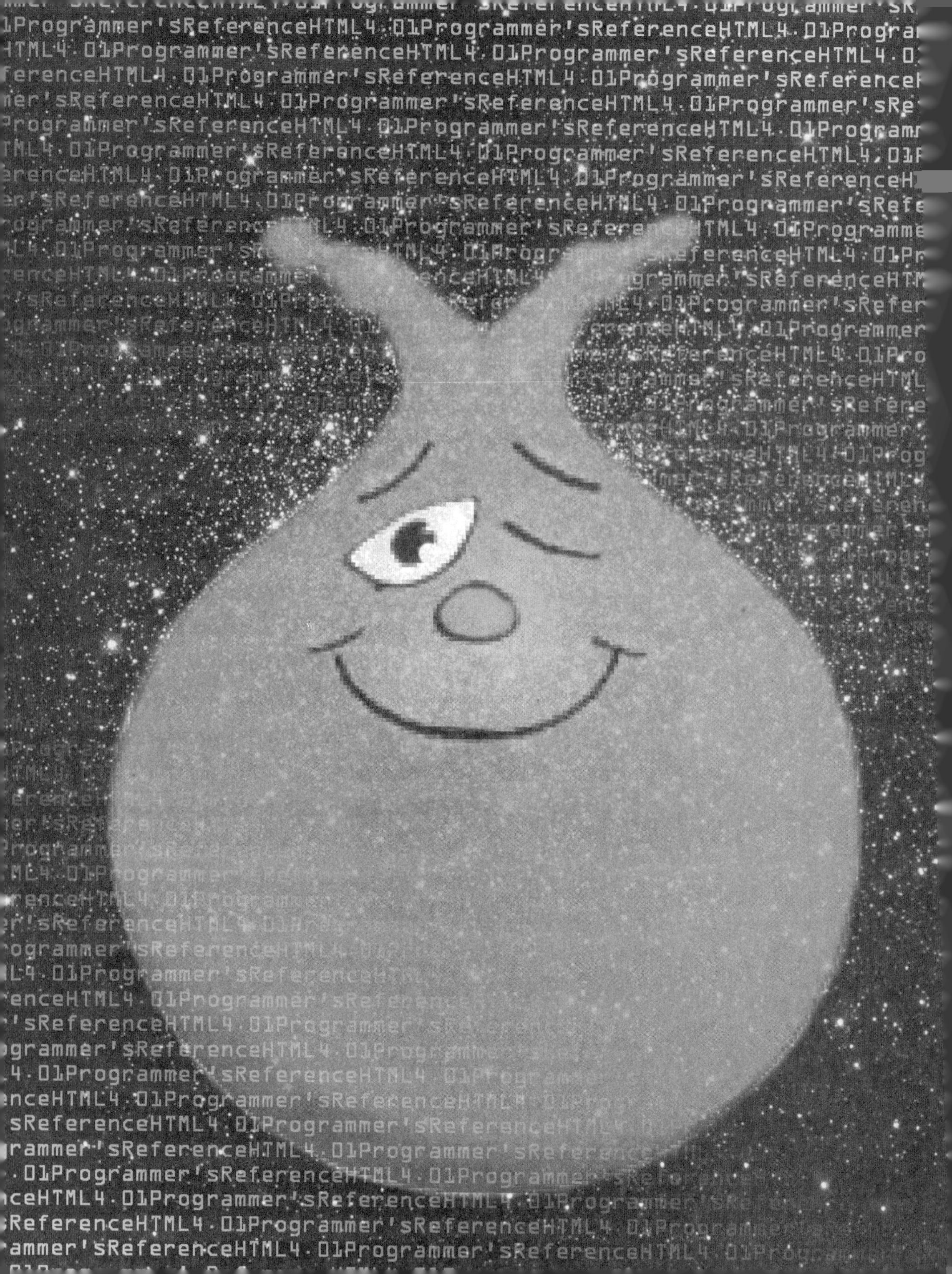

E

MIME Types

Originally devised as a means to declare the type of content contained by Internet mail messages, MIME (Multipurpose Internet Mail Extensions) types have now achieved a much wider range of usage. In particular, they can be specified at the start of any web document so that the server and browser can apply any formatting or further processing as may be appropriate.

There are currently eight main MIME types, namely `application`, `audio`, `image`, `message`, `model`, `multipart`, `text`, and `video`. Each of these is further arranged into a plethora of sub-types, and the most useful of each group of subtypes are listed here.

Each MIME type is made up of a type and a subtype, separated by a /, for example `text/plain`.

Application

activemessage	vnd.dna	vnd.motorola. flexsuite.fis
andrew-inset	vnd.dpgraph	vnd.motorola. flexsuite.gotap
applefile	vnd.dxr	vnd.motorola. flexsuite.kmr
atomicmail	vnd.ecdis-update	vnd.motorola. flexsuite.ttc

batch-SMTP	vnd.ecowin.chart	vnd.motorola.flexsuite.wem,
beep+xml	vnd.ecowin.filerequest	vnd.mozilla.xul+xml
cals-1840	vnd.ecowin.fileupdate	vnd.ms-artgalry
commonground	vnd.ecowin.series	vnd.ms-asf
cybercash	vnd.ecowin.seriesrequest	vnd.mseq
dca-rft	vnd.ecowin.seriesupdate	vnd.ms-excel
dec-dx	vnd.enliven	vnd.msign
dvcs	vnd.epson.esf	vnd.ms-lrm
EDI-Consent	vnd.epson.msf	vnd.ms-powerpoint
EDIFACT	vnd.epson.quickanime	vnd.ms-project
EDI-X12	vnd.epson.salt	vnd.ms-tnef
eshop	vnd.epson.ssf	vnd.ms-works
font-tdpfr	vnd.ericsson.quickcall	vnd.musician
http	vnd.eudora.data	vnd.music-niff
hyperstudio	vnd.fdf	vnd.netfpx
iges	vnd.ffsns	vnd.noblenet-directory
index	vnd.FloGraphIt	vnd.noblenet-sealer
index.cmd	vnd.framemaker	vnd.noblenet-web
index.obj	vnd.fsc.weblaunch	vnd.novadigm.EDM
index.response	vnd.fujitsu.oasys	vnd.novadigm.EDX
index.vnd	vnd.fujitsu.oasys2	vnd.novadigm.EXT
iotp	vnd.fujitsu.oasys3	vnd.osa.netdeploy
ipp	vnd.fujitsu.oasysgp	vnd.palm
mac-binhex40	vnd.fujitsu.oasysprs	vnd.pg.format
macwriteii	vnd.fujixerox.ddd	vnd.pg.osasli
marc	vnd.fujixerox.docuworks	vnd.powerbuilder6
mathematica	vnd.fujixerox.docuworks.binder	vnd.powerbuilder6-s
msword	vnd.fut-misnet	vnd.powerbuilder7
news-message-id	vnd.grafeq	vnd.powerbuilder75

news-transmission	vnd.groove-account	vnd.powerbuilder75-s
ocsp-request	vnd.groove-identity-message	vnd.powerbuilder7-s
ocsp-response	vnd.groove-injector	vnd.previewsystems.box
octet-stream	vnd.groove-tool-message	vnd.publishare-delta-tree
oda	vnd.groove-tool-template	vnd.rapid
parityfec	vnd.groove-vcard	vnd.s3sms
pdf	vnd.hhe.lesson-player	vnd.seemail
pgp-encrypted	vnd.hp-HPGL	vnd.shana.informed.formdata
pgp-keys	vnd.hp-hpid	vnd.shana.informed.formtemplate
pgp-signature	vnd.hp-hps	vnd.shana.informed.interchange
pkcs10	vnd.hp-PCL	vnd.shana.informed.package
pkcs7-mime	vnd.hp-PCLXL	vnd.street-stream
pkcs7-signature	vnd.httphone	vnd.svd
pkix-cert	vnd.hzn-3d-crossword	vnd.swiftview-ics
pkixcmp	vnd.ibm.afplinedata	vnd.triscape.mxs
pkix-crl	vnd.ibm.MiniPay	vnd.trueapp
postscript	vnd.ibm.modcap	vnd.truedoc
prs.alvestrand.titrax-sheet	vnd.informix-visionary	vnd.tve-trigger
prs.cww	vnd.intercon.formnet	vnd.ufdl
prs.nprend	vnd.intertrust.digibox	vnd.uplanet.alert
remote-printing	vnd.intertrust.nncp	vnd.uplanet.alert-wbxml
riscos	vnd.intu.qbo	vnd.uplanet.bearer-choice
rtf	vnd.intu.qfx	vnd.uplanet.bearer-choice-wbxml
sdp	vnd.is-xpr	vnd.uplanet.cacheop

set-payment	vnd.japannet-directory-service	vnd.uplanet.cacheop-wbxml
set-payment-initiation	vnd.japannet-jpnstore-wakeup	vnd.uplanet.channel
set-registration	vnd.japannet-payment-wakeup	vnd.uplanet.channel-wbxml
set-registration-initiation	vnd.japannet-registration	vnd.uplanet.list
sgml	vnd.japannet-registration-wakeup	vnd.uplanet.listcmd
sgml-open-catalog	vnd.japannet-setstore-wakeup	vnd.uplanet.listcmd-wbxml
sieve	vnd.japannet-verification	vnd.uplanet.list-wbxml
slate	vnd.japannet-verification-wakeup	vnd.uplanet.signal
vemmi	vnd.koan	vnd.vcx
vnd.$commerce_battelle	vnd.lotus-1-2-3	vnd.vectorworks
vnd.3M.Post-it-Notes	vnd.lotus-approach	vnd.vidsoft.vidconference
vnd.accpac.simply.aso	vnd.lotus-freelance	vnd.visio
vnd.accpac.simply.imp	vnd.lotus-notes	vnd.vividence.scriptfile
vnd.acucobol	vnd.lotus-organizer	vnd.wap.sic
vnd.aether.imp	vnd.lotus-screencam	vnd.wap.slc
vnd.anser-web-certificate-issue-initiation	vnd.lotus-wordpro	vnd.wap.wbxml
vnd.anser-web-funds-transfer-initiation	vnd.mcd	vnd.wap.wmlc
vnd.audiograph	vnd.mediastation.cdkey	vnd.wap.wmlscriptc
vnd.bmi	vnd.meridian-slingshot	vnd.webturbo
vnd.businessobjects	vnd.mif	vnd.wrq-hp3000-labelled
vnd.canon-cpdl	vnd.minisoft-hp3000-save	vnd.wt.stf

vnd.canon-lips	vnd.mitsubishi. misty-guard.trustweb	vnd.xara
vnd.claymore	vnd.Mobius.DAF	vnd.xfdl
vnd.commonspace	vnd.Mobius.DIS	vnd.yellowriver- custom-menu
vnd.comsocaller	vnd.Mobius.MBK	whoispp-query
vnd.contact.cmsg	vnd.Mobius.MQY	whoispp-response
vnd.ctc-posml	vnd.Mobius.MSL	wita
vnd.cups- postscript	vnd.Mobius.PLC	wordperfect5.1
vnd.cups-raster	vnd.Mobius.TXF	x400-bp
vnd.cups-raw,	vnd.motorola.flexsuite	xml
vnd.cybank	vnd.motorola. flexsuite.adsi	zip

Audio

32kadpcm	telephone-event	vnd.nuera.ecelp4800
basic	tone	vnd.nuera.ecelp7470
G.722.1	vnd.cns.anp1	vnd.nuera.ecelp9600
L16	vnd.cns.inf1	vnd.octel.sbc
MP4A-LATM	vnd.digital-winds	vnd.qcelp
mpeg	vnd.everad.plj	vnd.rhetorex.32kadpcm
parityfec	vnd.lucent.voice	vnd.vmx.cvsd
prs.sid	vnd.nortel.vbk	

Image

cgm (Computer Graphics Metafile)	vnd.dxf
g3fax	vnd.fastbidsheet
gif	vnd.fpx
ief (Image Exchange Format)	vnd.fst
jpeg (Joint Pictures Expert Group)	vnd.fujixerox.edmics-mmr
naplps	vnd.fujixerox.edmics-rlc

png (Portable Network Graphics)	vnd.mix
prs.btif	vnd.net-fpx
prs.pti	vnd.svf
tiff (Tag Image File Format)	vnd.wap.wbmp
vnd.cns.inf2	vnd.xiff
vnd.dwg	

Message

delivery-status	news
disposition-notification	partial
external-body	rfc822
http	s-http

Model

iges	vnd.dwf	vnd.parasolid.transmit.binary
mesh	vnd.flatland.3dml	vnd.parasolid.transmit.text
vnd.mts	vnd.gdl	vnd.vtu
vnd.gs-gdl	vnd.gtw	vrml

Multipart

alternative	form-data	report
appledouble	header-set	signed
byteranges	mixed	voice-message
digest	parallel	
encrypted	related	

Text

calendar	vnd.curl
css	vnd.DMClientScript
directory	vnd.fly
enriched	vnd.fmi.flexstor
html	vnd.in3d.3dml
parityfec	vnd.in3d.spot
plain	vnd.IPTC.NewsML
prs.lines.tag	vnd.IPTC.NITF
rfc822-headers	vnd.latex-z
richtext	vnd.motorola.reflex,
rtf	vnd.ms-mediapackage
sgml	vnd.wap.sl vnd.wap.si
t140	vnd.wap.wml
tab-separated-values	vnd.wap.wmlscript
uri-list	xml
vnd.abc	

A specific character set may be specified for the `text/plain` MIME type using a parameter in the Content-type field, for example `content-type: text/plain; charset=iso-8859-1` specifies the ISO Latin 1 set. Note that the default here is US-ASCII, which is effectively a subset of ISO Latin 1.

Video

iges	vnd.dwf	vnd.mpegurl
mesh	vnd.flatland.3dml	vnd.mts
model	vnd.fvt	vnd.nokia.interleaved-multimedia
MP4V-ES	vnd.gdl	vnd.parasolid.transmit.binary
mpeg	vnd.gs-gdl	vnd.parasolid.transmit.text
parityfec	vnd.gtw	vnd.vivo
pointer	vnd.motorola.video	vnd.vtu
quicktime	vnd.motorola.videop	vrml

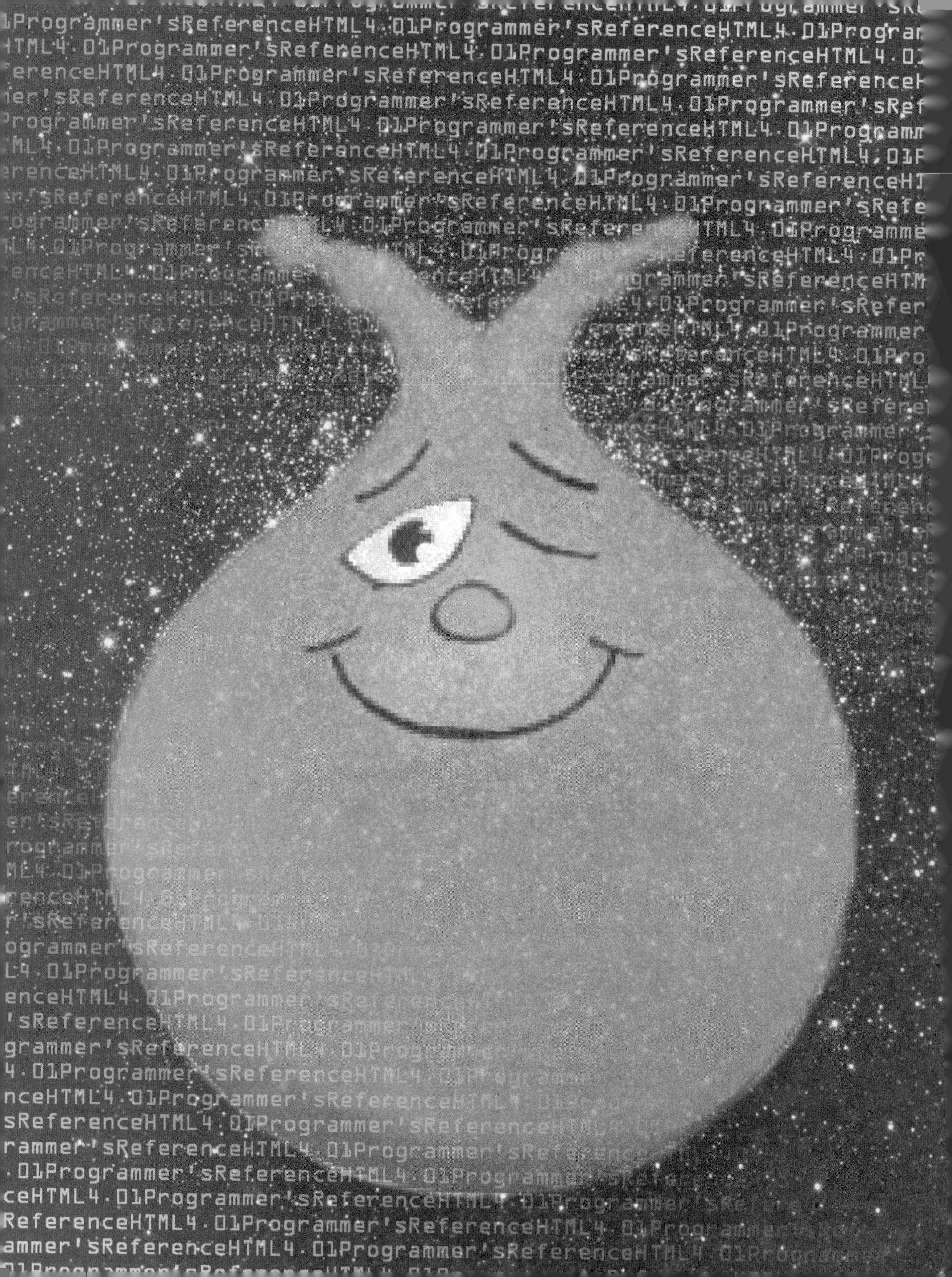

CSS Browser Support Reference

In this appendix we have listed all properties that belong to the CSS 1 and CSS 2 Recommendations, and how they are supported in the most popular browsers. We also include Netscape- and Internet Explorer-specific properties. Support in Internet Explorer 6 has not been included as the relevant information could not be gathered at the time of going to press.

In the following tables each property is shown in **bold,** with its values beneath, for example, `charset`. The CSS column of each table shows which versions of CSS the value belongs to (1, 2, or 1 & 2). This column is also used to show where a value is Internet Explorer- or Netscape-specific (IE or N).

Syntax Properties

Property and Value(s)	CSS	IE3	IE4	IE5	IE5.5	N4	N6	Opera 5
@								
charset	2							
fontdef	2					✓	✓	✓
font-face	2		✓	✓	✓			

Table continued on following page

Property and Value(s)	CSS	IE3	IE4	IE5	IE5.5	N4	N6	Opera 5
import	1 & 2		✓	✓	✓		✓	✓
media	2		✓	✓	✓		✓	✓
page	2							
Inclusion Methods								
Embedded Style Sheets	1 & 2	✓	✓	✓	✓	✓	✓	✓
External Style Sheets	1 & 2	1	✓	✓	✓	✓	✓	✓
Inline Style Sheets	1 & 2	✓	✓	✓	✓	✓	✓	✓
Miscellaneous Syntax								
!important	1 & 2		✓	✓	✓		✓	✓
Comments	1 & 2	✓	✓	✓	✓	✓	✓	✓
Unicode-Escapes	2							✓
Pseudo-Classes								
:active	1 & 2		✓	✓	✓		✓	✓
:first	2							✓
:first-child	2						✓	
:focus	2						✓	
:hover	2		✓	✓	✓			✓
:lang	2							
:left	2							✓
:link	1 & 2	✓	✓	✓	✓	✓	✓	✓
:right	2							✓
:visited	1 & 2	✓	✓	✓	✓	✓	✓	✓
Pseudo-Elements								
:after	2						✓	✓
:before	2						✓	✓
:first-letter	1 & 2				✓		✓	✓
:first-line	1 & 2				✓		✓	✓

Property and Value(s)	CSS	IE3	IE4	IE5	IE5.5	N4	N6	Opera 5
Rule Set Syntax								
Declaration Grouping	1 & 2	✓	✓	✓	✓	✓	✓	✓
Declaration Shorthands	1 & 2	✓	✓	✓	✓	✓	✓	✓
Selector Grouping	1 & 2	✓	✓	✓	✓	✓	✓	✓
Selectors								
Attribute Value	2						✓	✓
Attribute-Hyphen	2						✓	✓
Attribute-Simple	2						✓	✓
Element-Adjacent	2						✓	✓
Element-Child	2						✓	✓
Element-Descendent	1 & 2	✓	✓	✓	✓	✓	✓	✓
Element-Simple	1 & 2	✓	✓	✓	✓	✓	✓	✓
Element-Universal	2						✓	✓
HTML-Class	1 & 2	✓	✓	✓	✓	✓	✓	✓
HTML-ID	1 & 2	✓	✓	✓	✓	✓	✓	✓

Units Properties

Property and Value(s)	CSS	IE3	IE4	IE5	IE5.5	N4	N6	Opera 5
Absolute Length								
cm	1 & 2	✓	✓	✓	✓	✓	✓	✓
in	1 & 2	✓	✓	✓	✓	✓	✓	✓
mm	1 & 2	✓	✓	✓	✓	✓	✓	✓

Table continued on following page

Property and Value(s)	CSS	IE3	IE4	IE5	IE5.5	N4	N6	Opera 5
pc	1 & 2	✓	✓	✓	✓	✓	✓	✓
pt	1 & 2	✓	✓	✓	✓	✓	✓	✓
Angle								
deg	2							✓
grad	2							✓
rad	2							✓
Color								
[#RGB]	1 & 2	✓	✓	✓	✓	✓	✓	✓
[#RRGGBB]	1 & 2	✓	✓	✓	✓	✓	✓	✓
"[rgb(r% ,g%, b%)]"	1 & 2		✓	✓	✓	✓	✓	✓
"[rgb(r, g, b)]"	1 & 2		✓	✓	✓	✓	✓	✓
[UI Name]	2		✓	✓	✓			✓
[VGA Name]	1 & 2	✓	✓	✓	✓	✓	✓	✓
[X11 Name]	2	✓	✓	✓*	✓	✓	✓	✓
Frequency								
Hz	2							
kHz	2							
Relative Length								
em	1 & 2		✓	✓	✓	✓	✓	✓
ex	1 & 2		✓	✓	✓	✓	✓	✓
px	1 & 2	✓	✓	✓	✓	✓	✓	✓
Time								
ms	2							✓
s	2							✓
URL								
absolute	1 & 2	✓	✓	✓	✓	✓	✓	✓
relative	1 & 2	✓	✓	✓	✓	✓	✓	✓

Font Properties

Property and Value(s)	CSS	IE3	IE4	IE5	IE5.5	N4	N6	Opera 5
font								
[caption/ icon/menu]	2		✓	✓	✓			
[font-family]	1 & 2	✓	✓	✓	✓	✓	✓	✓
[font-size]	1 & 2	✓	✓	✓	✓	✓	✓	✓
[font-style]	1 & 2	✓	✓	✓	✓	✓	✓	✓
[font-variant]	1 & 2		✓	✓	✓		✓	✓
[font-weight]	1 & 2	✓	✓	✓	✓	✓	✓	✓
[line-height]	1 & 2	✓	✓	✓	✓	✓	✓	✓
[message-box/small-caption status-bar]	2		✓	✓	✓			
inherit	2						✓	
font-family								
[generic family]	1 & 2	✓	✓	✓	✓	✓	✓	✓
[specific family]	1 & 2	✓	✓	✓	✓	✓	✓	✓
inherit	2						✓	
font-size								
[absolute size]	1 & 2	✓	✓	✓	✓	✓	✓	✓
[length]	1 & 2	✓	✓	✓	✓	✓	✓	✓
[percentage]	1 & 2	✓	✓	✓	✓	✓	✓	✓
[relative change]	1 & 2		✓	✓	✓	✓	✓	✓
inherit	2						✓	
font-size-adjust								
[number]	2							

Table continued on following page

Property and Value(s)	CSS	IE3	IE4	IE5	IE5.5	N4	N6	Opera 5
inherit	2						✓	
none	2							
font-stretch								
[absolute stretch]	2							
[relative stretch]	2							
inherit	2						✓	
font-style								
inherit	2						✓	
italic	1 & 2	✓	✓	✓	✓	✓	✓	✓
normal	1 & 2	✓	✓	✓	✓	✓	✓	✓
oblique	1 & 2		✓	✓	✓		✓	✓
font-variant								
inherit	2						✓	
normal	1 & 2		✓	✓	✓		✓	✓
small-caps	1 & 2		✓	✓	✓		✓	✓
font-weight								
[absolute weight]	1 & 2	✓	✓	✓	✓	✓	✓	✓
[weight scale]	1 & 2		✓	✓	✓	✓	✓	✓
[relative weight]	1 & 2		✓	✓	✓	✓	✓	✓
inherit	2						✓	

Color & Background Properties

Property and Value(s)	CSS	IE3	IE4	IE5	IE5.5	N4	N6	Opera 5
background								
[background-attachment]	1 & 2	✓	✓	✓	✓		✓	✓
[background-color]	1 & 2	✓	✓	✓	✓	✓	✓	✓
[background-image]	1 & 2	✓	✓	✓	✓	✓	✓	✓
[background-position]	1 & 2	✓	✓	✓	✓		✓	✓
[background-repeat]	1 & 2	✓	✓	✓	✓	✓	✓	✓
inherit	2						✓	
background-attachment								
fixed	1 & 2		✓	✓	✓		✓	✓
inherit	2						✓	
scroll	1 & 2		✓	✓	✓		✓	✓
background-color								
[color]	1 & 2		✓	✓	✓	✓	✓	✓
inherit	2						✓	
transparent	1& 2		✓	✓	✓	✓	✓	✓
background-image								
[URL]	1 & 2		✓	✓	✓	✓	✓	✓
inherit	2						✓	
none	1 & 2		✓	✓	✓	✓	✓	✓
background-position								
[(left|center|right) (top|center|bottom)]	1 & 2		✓	✓	✓		✓	✓
[x y]	1 & 2		✓	✓	✓		✓	✓
[x% y%]	1 & 2		✓	✓	✓		✓	✓
inherit	2						✓	
background-positionX								

Table continued on following page

699

Property and Value(s)	CSS	IE3	IE4	IE5	IE5.5	N4	N6	Opera 5
[left|center| right]	IE				✓			
[length]	IE				✓			
[percentage]	IE				✓			
background-positionY								
[length]	IE				✓			
[percentage]	IE				✓			
[top|center| bottom]	IE				✓			
background-repeat								
inherit	2						✓	
no-repeat	1 & 2		✓	✓	✓	✓	✓	✓
repeat	1 & 2		✓	✓	✓	✓	✓	✓
repeat-x	1 & 2		✓	✓	✓	✓	✓	✓
repeat-y	1 & 2		✓	✓	✓	✓	✓	✓
color								
[color]	1 & 2	✓	✓	✓	✓	✓	✓	✓
inherit	2						✓	
layer-background-image								
[URL]	N					✓	✓	
none	N					✓	✓	
layer-background-color								
[color]	N					✓	✓	
transparent	N					✓	✓	

Text Properties

Property and Value(s)	CSS	IE3	IE4	IE5	IE5.5	N4	N6	Opera 5
letter-spacing								
[length]	1 & 2		✓	✓	✓		✓	✓
inherit	2						✓	
normal	1 & 2		✓	✓	✓		✓	✓
text-align								
[string]	2							
center	1 & 2	✓	✓	✓	✓	✓	✓	✓
inherit	2						✓	
justify	1 & 2		✓	✓	✓	✓	✓	✓
left	1 & 2	✓	✓	✓	✓	✓	✓	✓
right	1 & 2	✓	✓	✓	✓	✓	✓	✓
text-decoration								
blink	1 & 2					✓	✓	✓
inherit	2						✓	
line-through	1 & 2	✓	✓	✓	✓	✓	✓	✓
none	1 & 2	✓	✓	✓	✓	✓	✓	✓
overline	1 & 2		✓	✓	✓		✓	✓
underline	1 & 2	✓	✓	✓	✓	✓	✓	✓
text-indent								
[length]	1 & 2	✓	✓	✓	✓	✓	✓	✓
[percentage]	1 & 2	✓	✓	✓	✓	✓	✓	✓
inherit	2						✓	
text-shadow								
[shadow effects]	2							
inherit	2						✓	
none	2							

Table continued on following page

Property and Value(s)	CSS	IE3	IE4	IE5	IE5.5	N4	N6	Opera 5
text-transform								
capitalize	1 & 2		✓	✓	✓	✓	✓	✓
inherit	2						✓	
lowercase	1 & 2		✓	✓	✓	✓	✓	✓
none	1 & 2		✓	✓	✓	✓	✓	✓
uppercase	1 & 2		✓	✓	✓	✓	✓	✓
text-underline-position								
above	IE				✓			
below	IE				✓			
white-space								
inherit	2						✓	
normal	1 & 2					✓	✓	✓
nowrap	1 & 2						✓	✓
pre	1 & 2					✓	✓	✓
word-spacing								
[length]	1 & 2						✓	✓
inherit	2						✓	
normal	1 & 2						✓	✓
word-wrap								
break-word	IE				✓			
normal	IE				✓		✓	

List Properties

Property and Value(s)	CSS	IE3	IE4	IE5	IE5.5	N4	N6	Opera 5
list-style								
[list-style-image]	1 & 2		✓	✓	✓		✓	✓

Property and Value(s)	CSS	IE3	IE4	IE5	IE5.5	N4	N6	Opera 5
[list-style-position]	1 & 2		✓	✓	✓		✓	✓
[list-style-type]	1 & 2		✓	✓	✓	✓	✓	✓
inherit	2						✓	
list-style-image								
[URL]	1 & 2		✓	✓	✓		✓	✓
inherit	2						✓	
none	1 & 2		✓	✓	✓		✓	✓
list-style-position								
inherit	2						✓	
inside	1 & 2		✓	✓	✓		✓	✓
outside	1 & 2		✓	✓	✓		✓	✓
list-style-type								
[bullet types]	1 & 2		✓	✓	✓	✓	✓	✓
Asian	2							
decimal	1 & 2		✓	✓	✓	✓	✓	✓
decimal-leading-zero	2							
E.European/Middle E.	2							
Greek/Latin	2							
inherit	2						✓	
lower-alpha|upper-alpha	1 & 2		✓	✓	✓	✓	✓	✓
lower-roman|upper-roman	1 & 2		✓	✓	✓	✓	✓	✓
none	1 & 2		✓	✓	✓	✓	✓	✓
marker-offset								
[length]	2							
auto	2							
inherit	2						✓	

Size and Border Properties

Property and Value(s)	CSS	IE3	IE4	IE5	IE5.5	N4	N6	Opera 5
border								
inherit	2						✓	
border-bottom								
[border-color]	1 & 2		✓	✓	✓		✓	✓
[border-style]	1 & 2		✓	✓	✓		✓	✓
[border-width]	1 & 2		✓	✓	✓		✓	✓
inherit	2						✓	
border-bottom-color								
color shorthand	2		✓	✓	✓		✓	✓
inherit	2						✓	
transparent	2							
border-bottom-style								
dotted | dashed	2				✓		✓	✓
groove | ridge | inset | outset | double	2		✓	✓	✓		✓	✓
hidden	2						✓	✓
inherit	2						✓	
none	2		✓	✓	✓		✓	✓
solid	2		✓	✓	✓		✓	✓
border-bottom-width								
[length]	1 & 2		✓	✓	✓	✓	✓	✓
inherit	2						✓	
thin | medium | thick	1 & 2		✓	✓	✓	✓	✓	✓
border-color								
[color shorthand]	1 & 2		✓	✓	✓	✓	✓	✓

Property and Value(s)	CSS	IE3	IE4	IE5	IE5.5	N4	N6	Opera 5
inherit	2						✓	
transparent	2							
border-left								
[border-color]	1 & 2		✓	✓	✓		✓	✓
[border-style]	1 & 2		✓	✓	✓		✓	✓
[border-width]	1 & 2		✓	✓	✓		✓	✓
inherit	2						✓	
border-left-color								
color shorthand	2		✓	✓	✓		✓	✓
inherit	2						✓	
transparent	2							
border-left-style								
dotted|dashed	2				✓		✓	✓
groove|ridge|inset|outset|double	2		✓	✓	✓		✓	✓
hidden	2						✓	✓
inherit	2						✓	
none	2		✓	✓	✓		✓	✓
solid	2		✓	✓	✓		✓	✓
border-left-width								
[length]	1 & 2		✓	✓	✓	✓	✓	✓
inherit	2						✓	
thin|medium|thick	1 & 2		✓	✓	✓	✓	✓	✓
border-right								
[border-color]	1 & 2		✓	✓	✓		✓	✓
[border-style]	1 & 2		✓	✓	✓		✓	✓

Table continued on following page

Property and Value(s)	CSS	IE3	IE4	IE5	IE5.5	N4	N6	Opera 5
[border-width]	1 & 2		✓	✓	✓		✓	✓
inherit	2						✓	
border-right-color								
color shorthand	2		✓	✓	✓		✓	✓
inherit	2						✓	
transparent	2							
border-right-style								
dotted|dashed	2				✓		✓	✓
groove|ridge|inset|outset|double	2		✓	✓	✓		✓	✓
hidden	2						✓	✓
inherit	2						✓	
none	2		✓	✓	✓		✓	✓
solid	2		✓	✓	✓		✓	✓
border-right-width								
[length]	1 & 2		✓	✓	✓	✓	✓	✓
inherit	2						✓	
thin|medium|thick	1 & 2		✓	✓	✓	✓	✓	✓
border-style								
[dotted|dashed]	1 & 2				✓		✓	✓
[groove|ridge|inset|outset|double]	1 & 2		✓	✓	✓	✓	✓	✓
[hidden]	2							✓
inherit	2						✓	
[none]	1 & 2		✓	✓	✓	✓	✓	✓
[solid]	1 & 2		✓	✓	✓	✓	✓	✓
border-top								

Property and Value(s)	CSS	IE3	IE4	IE5	IE5.5	N4	N6	Opera 5
[border-color]	1 & 2		✓	✓	✓		✓	✓
[border-style]	1 & 2		✓	✓	✓		✓	✓
[border-width]	1 & 2		✓	✓	✓		✓	✓
inherit	2						✓	
border-top-color								
color shorthand	2		✓	✓	✓		✓	✓
inherit	2						✓	
transparent	2							
border-top-style								
dotted|dashed	2				✓		✓	✓
groove|ridge|inset|outset|double	2		✓	✓	✓		✓	✓
hidden	2						✓	✓
inherit	2						✓	
none	2		✓	✓	✓		✓	✓
solid	2		✓	✓	✓		✓	✓
border-top-width								
[length]	1 & 2		✓	✓	✓	✓	✓	✓
inherit	2						✓	
thin|medium|thick	1 & 2		✓	✓	✓	✓	✓	✓
border-width								
[keyword shorthand]	1 & 2		✓	✓	✓	✓	✓	✓
[length shorthand]	1 & 2		✓	✓	✓	✓	✓	✓
inherit	2						✓	

Dimension Properties

Property and Value(s)	CSS	IE3	IE4	IE5	IE5.5	N4	N6	Opera 5
height								
[length]	1 & 2		✓	✓	✓		✓	✓
[percentage]	2		✓	✓	✓			✓
auto	1 & 2		✓	✓	✓		✓	✓
inherit	2						✓	
line-height								
[length]	1 & 2	✓	✓	✓	✓	✓	✓	✓
[number]	1 & 2		✓	✓	✓	✓	✓	✓
[percentage]	1 & 2	✓	✓	✓	✓	✓	✓	✓
inherit	2						✓	
normal	1 & 2	✓	✓	✓	✓	✓	✓	✓
max-height								
[length]	2							✓
[percentage]	2							✓
inherit	2						✓	
none	2							
max-width								
[length]	2							✓
[percentage]	2							✓
inherit	2						✓	
none	2							
min-height								
[length]	2							✓
[percentage]	2							✓
inherit	2						✓	
min-width								
[length]	2							✓
[percentage]	2							✓

Property and Value(s)	CSS	IE3	IE4	IE5	IE5.5	N4	N6	Opera 5
inherit	2						✓	
width								
[length]	1 & 2		✓	✓	✓	✓	✓	✓
[percentage]	1 & 2		✓	✓	✓	✓	✓	✓
auto	1 & 2		✓	✓	✓	✓	✓	✓
inherit	2						✓	

Margin Properties

Property and Value(s)	CSS	IE3	IE4	IE5	IE5.5	N4	N6	Opera 5
margin								
[length shorthand]	1 & 2	✓	✓	✓	✓	✓	✓	✓
[percentage shorthand]	1 & 2	✓	✓	✓	✓	✓	✓	✓
auto	1 & 2	✓	✓	✓	✓	✓	✓	✓
inherit	2						✓	
margin-bottom								
[length]	1 & 2	✓	✓	✓	✓	✓	✓	✓
[percentage]	1 & 2	✓	✓	✓	✓	✓	✓	✓
auto	1 & 2	✓	✓	✓	✓	✓	✓	✓
inherit	2						✓	
margin-left								
[length]	1 & 2	✓	✓	✓	✓	✓	✓	✓
[percentage]	1 & 2	✓	✓	✓	✓	✓	✓	✓
auto	1 & 2	✓	✓	✓	✓	✓	✓	✓
inherit	2						✓	
margin-right								

Table continued on following page

Property and Value(s)	CSS	IE3	IE4	IE5	IE5.5	N4	N6	Opera 5
[length]	1 & 2	✓	✓	✓	✓	✓	✓	✓
[percentage]	1 & 2	✓	✓	✓	✓	✓	✓	✓
auto	1 & 2	✓	✓	✓	✓	✓	✓	✓
inherit	2						✓	
margin-top								
[length]	1 & 2	✓	✓	✓	✓	✓	✓	✓
[percentage]	1 & 2	✓	✓	✓	✓	✓	✓	✓
auto	1 & 2	✓	✓	✓	✓	✓	✓	✓
inherit	2						✓	

Padding Properties

Property and Value(s)	CSS	IE3	IE4	IE5	IE5.5	N4	N6	Opera 5
padding								
[length shorthand]	1 & 2		✓	✓	✓	✓	✓	✓
[percentage shorthand]	1 & 2		✓	✓	✓	✓	✓	✓
inherit	2						✓	
padding-bottom								
[length]	1 & 2		✓	✓	✓	✓	✓	✓
[percentage]	1 & 2		✓	✓	✓	✓	✓	✓
inherit	2						✓	
padding-left								
[length]	1 & 2		✓	✓	✓	✓	✓	✓
[percentage]	1 & 2		✓	✓	✓	✓	✓	✓
inherit	2						✓	
padding-right								

710

Property and Value(s)	CSS	IE3	IE4	IE5	IE5.5	N4	N6	Opera 5
[length]	1 & 2		✓	✓	✓	✓	✓	✓
[percentage]	1 & 2		✓	✓	✓	✓	✓	✓
inherit	2						✓	
padding-top								
[length]	1 & 2		✓	✓	✓	✓	✓	✓
[percentage]	1 & 2		✓	✓	✓	✓	✓	✓
inherit	2						✓	

Positioning Properties

Property and Value(s)	CSS	IE3	IE4	IE5	IE5.5	N4	N6	Opera 5
bottom								
[length]	2			✓	✓			✓
[percentage]	2			✓	✓			✓
auto	2			✓	✓			✓
inherit	2						✓	
clip								
[shape]	2		✓	✓	✓	✓	✓	
auto	2		✓	✓	✓			
inherit	2						✓	
left								
[length]	2		✓	✓	✓	✓	✓	✓
[percentage]	2		✓	✓	✓			✓
auto	2		✓	✓	✓			✓
inherit	2						✓	
overflow								
auto	2		✓	✓	✓			

Table continued on following page

Property and Value(s)	CSS	IE3	IE4	IE5	IE5.5	N4	N6	Opera 5
hidden	2		✓	✓	✓			✓
inherit	2						✓	
scroll	2		✓	✓	✓			
visible	2		✓	✓	✓			✓
overflow-x								
auto	IE			✓	✓			
hidden	IE			✓	✓			
scroll	IE			✓	✓			
visible	IE			✓	✓			
overflow-y								
auto	IE			✓	✓			
hidden	IE			✓	✓			
scroll	IE			✓	✓			
visible	IE			✓	✓			
right								
[length]	2			✓	✓			✓
[percentage]	2			✓	✓			✓
auto	2			✓	✓			✓
inherit	2						✓	
top								
[length]	2		✓	✓	✓	✓	✓	✓
[percentage]	2		✓	✓	✓			✓
auto	2		✓	✓	✓			✓
inherit	2						✓	
vertical-align								
[length]	2							✓
[percentage]	1 & 2						✓	✓
baseline| middle	1 & 2		✓	✓	✓	✓	✓	✓
inherit	2						✓	

Property and Value(s)	CSS	IE3	IE4	IE5	IE5.5	N4	N6	Opera 5
super|sub	1 & 2		✓	✓	✓		✓	✓
text-top|text-bottom	1 & 2		✓	✓	✓	✓	✓	✓
top|bottom	1 & 2		✓	✓	✓	✓	✓	✓
z-index								
[integer]	2		✓	✓	✓	✓	✓	✓
auto	2		✓	✓	✓			✓
inherit	2						✓	

Outline Properties

Property and Value(s)	CSS	IE3	IE4	IE5	IE5.5	N4	N6	Opera 5
outline								
[outline-color]	2							
[outline-style]	2							
[outline-width]	2							
inherit	2							
outline-color								
[color]	2							
inherit	2							
invert	2							
outline-style								
dashed	2							
dotted	2							
double	2							
groove	2							

Table continued on following page

Property and Value(s)	CSS	IE3	IE4	IE5	IE5.5	N4	N6	Opera 5
inherit	2							
inset	2							
none	2							
outset	2							
ridge	2							
solid	2							
outline-width								
[length]	2							
inherit	2							
thin|medium|thick	2							

Printing Properties

Property and Value(s)	CSS	IE3	IE4	IE5	IE5.5	N4	N6	Opera 5
marks								
crop	2							
cross	2							
inherit	2							
none	2							
orphans								
[integer]	2							✓
inherit	2							
page								
[identifier]	2							✓
auto	2							
page-break-after								
[empty string]	IE			✓	✓			

Property and Value(s)	CSS	IE3	IE4	IE5	IE5.5	N4	N6	Opera 5
always	2		✓	✓	✓			✓
auto	2							✓
avoid	2							✓
inherit	2							
left|right	2							✓
page-break-before								
[empty string]	IE		✓	✓	✓			
always	2		✓	✓	✓			✓
auto	2							✓
avoid	2							✓
inherit	2							
left|right	2							✓
page-break-inside								
auto	2							✓
avoid	2							✓
inherit	2							
size								
[lengths]	2							✓
auto	2							✓
inherit	2							
landscape	2							✓
portrait	2							✓
widows								
[integer]	2							✓
inherit	2							

Table Properties

Property and Value(s)	CSS	IE3	IE4	IE5	IE5.5	N4	N6	Opera 5
border-collapse								
collapse	2			✓	✓			✓
inherit	2						✓	
separate	2			✓	✓			✓
border-spacing								
[length length]	2							✓
inherit	2						✓	
caption-side								
inherit	2						✓	
left|right	2							✓
top|bottom	2							✓
empty-cells								
hide	2							
inherit	2							
show	2							
table-layout								
auto	2			✓	✓			✓
fixed	2			✓	✓			✓
inherit	2						✓	

Aural Properties

Property and Value(s)	CSS	IE3	IE4	IE5	IE5.5	N4	N6	Opera 5
azimuth								
[absolute scale]	2							

Property and Value(s)	CSS	IE3	IE4	IE5	IE5.5	N4	N6	Opera 5
[angle]	2							
[relative scale]	2							
inherit	2							
cue								
[URL]	2							
inherit	2							
none	2							
cue-after								
[URL]	2							
inherit	2							
none	2							
cue-before								
[URL]	2							
inherit	2							
none	2							
elevation								
[absolute scale]	2							
[angle]	2							
[relative scale]	2							
inherit	2							
pause								
[percentage]	2							
[time]	2							
inherit	2							
pause-after								
[percentage]	2							
[time]	2							
inherit	2							

Table continued on following page

717

Property and Value(s)	CSS	IE3	IE4	IE5	IE5.5	N4	N6	Opera 5
pause-before								
[percentage]	2							
[time]	2							
inherit	2							
pitch								
[absolute scale]	2							
[frequency]	2							
inherit	2							
pitch-range								
[number]	2							
inherit	2							
play-during								
[URL]	2							
auto	2							
inherit	2							
mix	2							
none	2							
repeat	2							
richness								
[number]	2							
inherit	2							
speak								
inherit	2							
none	2							
normal	2							
spell-out	2							
speak-numeral								
continuous	2							
digits	2							

Property and Value(s)	CSS	IE3	IE4	IE5	IE5.5	N4	N6	Opera 5
inherit	2							
speak-punctuation								
code	2							
inherit	2							
none	2							
speech-rate								
[absolute scale]	2							
[number]	2							
[relative scale]	2							
inherit	2							
stress								
[number]	2							
inherit	2							
voice-family								
[specific voice]	2							
inherit	2							
male|female|child	2							
volume								
[absolute scale]	2							
[number]	2							
[percentage]	2							
inherit	2							
silent	2							
speak-header								
always	2							✓
inherit	2						✓	
once	2							✓

Classification Properties

Property and Value(s)	CSS	IE3	IE4	IE5	IE5.5	N4	N6	Opera 5
clear								
both	1 & 2		✓	✓	✓	✓	✓	✓
inherit	2						✓	
left	1 & 2		✓	✓	✓	✓	✓	✓
none	1 & 2		✓	✓	✓	✓	✓	✓
right	1 & 2		✓	✓	✓	✓	✓	✓
display								
[table types]	2							✓
block	1 & 2					✓	✓	✓
compact	2							✓
inherit	2						✓	
inline	1 & 2						✓	✓
list-item	1 & 2					✓	✓	✓
marker	2							
none	1 & 2		✓	✓	✓	✓	✓	✓
run-in	2							✓
table-footer-group	2			✓	✓			✓
table-header-group	2			✓	✓			✓
float								
inherit	2						✓	
left	1 & 2		✓	✓	✓	✓	✓	✓
none	1 & 2		✓	✓	✓	✓	✓	✓
right	1 & 2		✓	✓	✓	✓	✓	✓
position								
absolute	2		✓	✓	✓	✓	✓	✓
fixed	2							✓
inherit	2						✓	

Property and Value(s)	CSS	IE3	IE4	IE5	IE5.5	N4	N6	Opera 5
relative	2		✓	✓	✓	✓	✓	✓
static	2		✓	✓	✓	✓	✓	✓
visibility								
collapse	2							
hidden	2		✓	✓	✓			✓
hide	N					✓	✓	
inherit	2		✓	✓	✓	✓	✓	
show	N					✓	✓	
visible	2		✓	✓	✓			✓

International Properties

Property and Value(s)	CSS	IE3	IE4	IE5	IE5.5	N4	N6	Opera 5
direction								
inherit	2			✓	✓			✓
ltr	2			✓	✓			✓
rtl	2			✓	✓			✓
ime-mode								
active	IE			✓	✓			
auto	IE			✓	✓			
deactivated	IE			✓	✓			
inactive	IE			✓	✓			
layout-grid								
[layout-grid-char]	IE			✓	✓			
[layout-grid-char-spacing]	IE							
[layout-grid-line]	IE			✓	✓			

Table continued on following page

721

Property and Value(s)	CSS	IE3	IE4	IE5	IE5.5	N4	N6	Opera 5
[layout-grid-mode]	IE			✓	✓			
[layout-grid-type]	IE			✓	✓			
layout-grid-char								
[length]	IE			✓	✓			
[percentage]	IE			✓	✓			
auto	IE			✓	✓			
none	IE			✓	✓			
layout-grid-char-spacing								
[length]	IE			✓	✓			
[percentage]	IE			✓	✓			
auto	IE			✓	✓			
layout-grid-line								
[length]	IE			✓	✓			
[percentage]	IE			✓	✓			
auto	IE			✓	✓			
none	IE			✓	✓			
layout-grid-mode								
both	IE			✓	✓			
char	IE			✓	✓			
line-edge	IE			✓	✓			
none	IE			✓	✓			
layout-grid-type								
fixed	IE			✓	✓			
loose	IE			✓	✓			
strict	IE			✓	✓			
line-break								
normal	IE			✓	✓			
strict	IE			✓	✓			

Property and Value(s)	CSS	IE3	IE4	IE5	IE5.5	N4	N6	Opera 5
ruby-align								
auto	IE			✓	✓			
center	IE			✓	✓			
distribute-letter	IE			✓	✓			
distribute-space	IE			✓	✓			
left	IE			✓	✓			
line-edge	IE			✓	✓			
right	IE			✓	✓			
ruby-overhang								
auto	IE			✓	✓			
none	IE			✓	✓			
whitespace	IE			✓	✓			
ruby-position								
above	IE			✓	✓			
inline	IE			✓	✓			
text-justify								
auto	IE				✓			
distribute	IE				✓			
distribute-all-lines	IE				✓			
inter-cluster	IE				✓			
inter-ideograph	IE				✓			
inter-word	IE				✓			
newspaper	IE				✓			
unicode-bidi								
bidi-override	2			✓	✓			
embed	2			✓	✓			
inherit	2							

Table continued on following page

Property and Value(s)	CSS	IE3	IE4	IE5	IE5.5	N4	N6	Opera 5
normal	2			✓	✓			
word-break								
break-all	IE			✓	✓			
keep-all	IE			✓	✓			
normal	IE			✓	✓			
writing-mode								
lr-tb	IE			✓	✓			
tb-lr	IE			✓	✓			

Generated Content Properties

Property and Value(s)	CSS	IE3	IE4	IE5	IE5.5	N4	N6	Opera 5
content								
[attr(X)]	2							✓
[counter()]	2							✓
[counters()]	2							✓
[string]	2							✓
[URL]	2							
close-quote	2							✓
inherit	2							
no-close-quote	2							✓
no-open-quote	2							✓
open-quote	2						✓	✓
counter-increment								
[identifier integer]	2							✓
inherit	2							
none	2							✓

Property and Value(s)	CSS	IE3	IE4	IE5	IE5.5	N4	N6	Opera 5
counter-reset								
[identifier integer]	2							✓
inherit	2							
none	2							✓
include source								
[URL]	N					✓	✓	
quotes								
[string]	2							✓
inherit	2							
none	2							✓

Dynamic Content Properties

Property and Value(s)	CSS	IE3	IE4	IE5	IE5.5	N4	N6	Opera 5
behavior								
[behavior object ID]	IE			✓	✓			
[behavior script URL]	IE			✓	✓			
[default behavior name]	IE			✓	✓			
cursor								
[{ dir }-resize]	IE		✓	✓	✓			
[URL]	IE							
auto	IE		✓	✓	✓			
crosshair	IE		✓	✓	✓			
default	IE		✓	✓	✓			

Table continued on following page

Property and Value(s)	CSS	IE3	IE4	IE5	IE5.5	N4	N6	Opera 5
hand	IE		✓	✓	✓			
help	IE		✓	✓	✓			
inherit	IE							
move	IE		✓	✓	✓			
pointer	IE							
text	IE		✓	✓	✓			
wait	IE		✓	✓	✓			
filter								
[blend transition filters]	IE		✓	✓	✓			
[reveal transition filters]	IE		✓	✓	✓			
[visual filters]	IE		✓	✓	✓			
zoom								
[number]	IE				✓			
[percentage]	IE				✓			
normal	IE				✓			

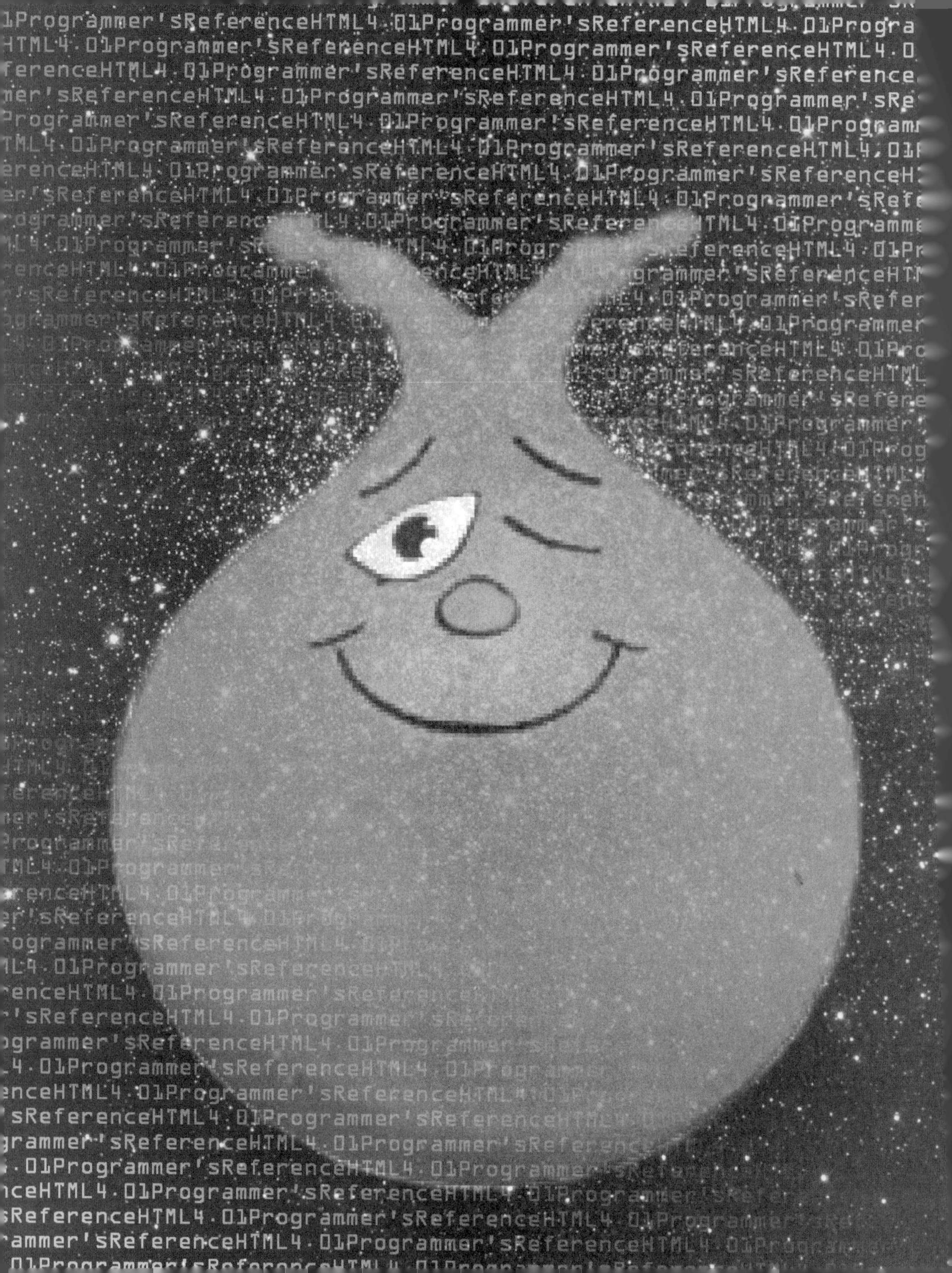

CSS Property Reference

Over 70 Cascading Style Sheets properties are implemented in today's major browsers. Most of them are from the CSS 1 Recommendation, but an increasing number of CSS 2 properties are finding their way into commercial user agents. Here, CSS properties are arranged into several major groups, which indicate those that are from CSS 2, and provide some crucial information for each.

Unless otherwise stated, the following items are supported fully by at least two of the three popular browsers; that is, Internet Explorer, Netscape Navigator, and Opera. Please see the CSS Browser Support Reference in Appendix F for further information about which properties and property values are supported in which browser, along with further information regarding proprietary browser-specific properties and property values.

Units of Measurement

There are two basic styles of measurement: relative and absolute, but in addition to these there is the third approach of percentages. As a general rule, relative measures are preferred, as using absolute measures requires familiarity with the actual mechanism of display (for example, what kind of printer, what sort of monitor, etc.).

Relative Units

Values: em, en, ex, px

em, en and ex are typographic terms, and refer to the sizes of certain display characters. em denotes the height of the element font, and ex (usually) represents the height of the letter x.

px refers to a measurement in screen pixels, which is generally only meaningful for display on a computer monitor, and is affected by the user's display resolution setting.

In IE4, em and ex are the same as pt, and en is the same as px.

Absolute Units

Values: in, cm, mm, pt, pc

in indicates a measurement in inches, cm denotes centimeters, mm millimeters, pt represents a length in typeface points (72 to an inch), and pc is in picas, where 1 pica equals 12 points. These units are generally only useful when you know what the output medium is going to be, since browsers and other user agents may approximate at their discretion.

Percentage

Values: Numeric

When using percentage measures, which may or may not contain a decimal point, the size of an item is given relative to some defined length unit – typically the font size of the current element. Note that child elements inherit the computed value, rather than the percentage value: in other words, a child will not be a percentage of its parent, but the same size as its parent.

Listing of Properties

All properties available in Dynamic HTML are given here together with their JavaScript Style Sheet equivalent, the equivalent scripting property in IE 4, possible values, defaults, and other useful information. The properties are divided up into categories – **font** properties, **color** and **background** properties, **text** properties, **size** and **position** properties, **printing** properties, **filter** properties, and **other** properties.

Font Properties

font

Values:	\<font-size\>, [/\<line-height\>], \<font-family\>, \<font-style\>, \<font-variant\>, \<font-weight\>
Default:	Not defined
Applies to:	All elements
Inherited:	Yes
Percentage:	Only on \<font-size\> and \<line-height\>

This allows you to set several font properties all at once, with the initial values being determined by the properties being used (for example, the default for font-size is different from the default for font-family). This property should be used with multiple values separated by spaces, or a comma if specifying multiple font-families.

font-family

Values:	Name of a font family (for example, New York) or a generic family (for example, Serif)
Default:	Set by user agent
Applies to:	All elements
Inherited:	Yes
Percentage:	No

You can specify multiple values in order of preference (in case the user agent doesn't have the font you want). To do so, simply specify them and separate multiple values with commas. You should end with a generic font-family (allowable values would then be serif, sans-serif, cursive, fantasy, or monospace). If the font name has spaces in it, you should enclose the name in quotation marks.

font-size

Values:	<absolute>, <relative>, <length>, <percentage>
Default:	medium
Applies to:	All elements
Inherited:	Yes
Percentage:	Yes: relative to parent font size

The values for this property can be expressed in several ways:

❑ Absolute size: legal values are xx-small, x-small, small, medium, large, x-large, xx-large

❑ Relative size: values are larger, smaller

❑ Length: values are in any unit of measurement, as described at the beginning of this section.

❑ Percentage: values are a percentage of the parent font size

font-style

Values:	normal, italic, oblique
Default:	normal
Applies to:	All elements
Inherited:	Yes
Percentage:	No

This is used to apply styling to your font – if a pre-rendered font is available (for example, New York Oblique) then that will be used if possible. If not, the styling will be applied electronically.

font-variant

Values:	`normal, small-caps`
Default:	`normal`
Applies to:	All elements
Inherited:	Yes
Percentage:	No

Normal is the standard appearance, and is therefore set as the default. Small-caps uses capital letters that are the same size as normal lowercase letters.

font-weight

Values:	`normal, bold, bolder, lighter` – or numeric values from 100 to 900
Default:	`normal`
Applies to:	All elements
Inherited:	Yes
Percentage:	No

Specifies the 'boldness' of text, which is usually expressed by stroke thickness. If numeric values are used, they must be multiples of 100 (for example, 250 isn't legal). 400 is the same as normal, and 700 is the same as bold.

Color and Background Properties

color

Values:	Color name or RGB value
Default:	Depends on user agent
Applies to:	All elements
Inherited:	Yes
Percentage:	No

Sets the text color of any element. The color can be specified by name (for example, `green`) or by RGB-value. The RGB value can be expressed in several ways; in hex – "#FFFFFF" (or the short hand version – #FFF), by percentage – "80%, 20%, 0%", or by value – "255,0,0".

background

Values:	`<color>, <URL>, <repeat>, <scroll>, <position>`
Default:	`Not defined`
Applies to:	All elements
Inherited:	No
Percentage:	Allowed on background-position

Specifies the background of the element. Transparent is the same as no defined background. You can use a solid color, two colors that will be blended together, or you can specify an URL locating an image to use as a background. The URL can be absolute or relative, but must be enclosed in parentheses and immediately preceded by the `url` keyword, as in this example:

```
body { background: url(http://foo.bar.com/image/small.gif) }
```

It is possible to use a color and an image, in which case the image will be overlaid on top of the color. Images can have several properties specified for them:

❑   <repeat> can be repeat, repeat-x (where x is a number), repeat-y (where y is a number) and no-repeat. If no repeat value is given, then repeat is assumed.

❑   <scroll> determines whether the background image will remain fixed, or scroll when the page does. Possible values are fixed or scroll.

❑   <position> specifies the location of the image on the page, as a horizontal location followed by a vertical location. Values can be given as percentages, by absolute distance in one of the measurement units, or by using one of the following keywords: bottom, top, left, right, or center.

background can be used to set any of the next five properties; it is shorthand for all of them. Individual background properties may be specified separately using the next five properties:

background-attachment

Values:	fixed, scroll
Default:	scroll
Applies to:	All elements
Inherited:	No
Percentage:	N/A

Determines whether the background will remain fixed, or scroll along the page.

background-color

Values:	transparent, <color>
Default:	transparent
Applies to:	All elements
Inherited:	No
Percentage:	N/A

Sets a color for the background. This can be a single color, or two colors blended together. The colors can be specified by name (for example: green) or by RGB-value (which can be stated in hex "#FFFFFF", by percentage "80%, 20%, 0%", or by value "255,0,0"). The syntax for using two colors is:

```
body { background-color: red / blue }
```

background-image

Values:	<URL>, none
Default:	none
Applies to:	All elements
Inherited:	No
Percentage:	No

You can specify the URL for an image to be used as the background. The URL can be absolute or relative, but must be enclosed in parentheses and immediately preceded by url:

background-position

Values:	`<position>, <percentage>, <length>,` top, bottom, left, right, center
Default:	top, left
Applies to:	Block-level and replaced elements
Inherited:	No
Percentage:	Refer to the size of the box itself

Specifies the upper left corner of the background image for the page, and may be given as a percentage, an absolute distance, or by using two of the keywords available. The position is specified by a horizontal value followed by a vertical value. If only one value is given, it is taken to be the horizontal, and the vertical is defaulted to 50%.

background-repeat

Values:	repeat, repeat-x, repeat-y, no-repeat
Default:	repeat
Applies to:	All elements
Inherited:	No
Percentage:	No

Determines whether the image is repeated to fill the page or element. If repeat-x or repeat-y are used, the image is repeated in only one direction. The default is to repeat the image in both directions.

Text Properties

letter-spacing

Values:	normal, `<length>`
Default:	normal
Applies to:	All elements
Inherited:	Yes
Percentage:	No

Sets the distance between letters. The length unit indicates an addition to the default space between characters. Values, if given, should be in units of measurement.

line-height

Values:	normal, `<number>`, `<length>`, `<percentage>`
Default:	Depends on user agent
Applies to:	All elements
Inherited:	Yes
Percentage:	Yes: relative to the font-size of the current element

Sets the height of the current line. Numerical values are expressed as the font size of the current element multiplied by the value given (for example, 1.2 would be valid). If given by length, a unit of measurement must be used. Percentages are based on the font-size of the current font size, and should normally be more than 100%.

list-style

Values:	`<keyword>, <position>, <url>`
Default:	Depends on user agent
Applies to:	Elements with `display` value `list-item`
Inherited:	Yes
Percentage:	No

Defines how list items are displayed. Can be used to set all the properties, or the individual styles can be set independently using the following styles.

list-style-image

Values:	`none, <url>`
Default:	`none`
Applies to:	Elements with `display` value `list-item`
Inherited:	Yes
Percentage:	No

Defines the URL of an image to be used as the 'bullet' or list marker for each item in a list.

list-style-position

Values:	`inside, outside`
Default:	`outside`
Applies to:	Elements with `display` value `list-item`
Inherited:	Yes
Percentage:	No

Indicates if the list marker should be placed indented or extended in relation to the list body.

list-style-type

Values:	`none, circle, disc, square, decimal, lower-alpha, upper-alpha, lower-roman, upper-roman`
Default:	`disc`
Applies to:	Elements with `display` value `list-item`
Inherited:	Yes
Percentage:	No

Defines the type of 'bullet' or list marker used to precede each item in the list.

text-align

Values:	`left, right, center, justify`
Default:	Depends on user agent
Applies to:	Elements with `display` value `list-item`
Inherited:	Yes
Percentage:	No

Describes how text is aligned within the element. Essentially replicates the `<div align=>` element.

text-decoration

Values:	none, underline, overline, line-through, blink
Default:	none
Applies to:	All elements
Inherited:	No
Percentage:	No

Specifies any special appearance of the text. Open to extension by vendors, with unidentified extensions rendered as an underline. This property is not inherited, but will usually span across any 'child' elements.

text-indent

Values:	<length>, <percentage>
Default:	Zero
Applies to:	Block elements
Inherited:	Yes
Percentage:	Yes: relative to width of parent element

Sets the indentation, in units of measurement, or as a percentage of the parent element's width.

text-transform

Values:	capitalize, uppercase, lowercase, none
Default:	none
Applies to:	All elements
Inherited:	Yes
Percentage:	No

- ❑ capitalize will set the first character of each word in the element as uppercase.

- ❑ uppercase will set every character in the element to uppercase.

- ❑ lowercase will set every character to lowercase.

- ❑ none will neutralize any inherited settings.

vertical-align

Values:	baseline, middle, sub, super, text-top, text-bottom, top, bottom, <percentage>
Default:	baseline
Applies to:	Inline elements
Inherited:	No
Percentage:	Yes: relative to the line-height itself

Controls the vertical positioning of any affected element.

- ❑ baseline sets the alignment with the base of the parent.

- ❑ middle aligns the vertical midpoint of the element with the baseline of the parent plus half of the vertical height of the parent.

- ❑ sub makes the element a subscript.

❑ super makes the element a superscript.

❑ text-top aligns the element with the top of text in the parent element's font.

❑ text-bottom aligns with the bottom of text in the parent element's font.

❑ top aligns the top of the element with the top of the tallest element on the current line.

❑ bottom aligns with the bottom of the lowest element on the current line.

white-space

Values: normal, pre, nowrap
Default: normal
Applies to: Block elements
Inherited: Yes
Percentage: No

Sets the spacing between elements. normal indicates that whitespace should be collapsed, pre means that whitespace should be preserved, in the same way as HTML's <PRE> tag, and nowrap means that text should only be broken onto new lines explicitly by <BR> elements.

word-spacing

Values: normal, <length>, inherit
Default: Normal
Applies to: All
Inherited: Yes
Percentage: No

Controls the spacing between words on a web page. Can be specified in all of the normal measurement units.

Size and Border Properties

These values are used to set the characteristics of the layout 'box' that exists around elements such as characters, images, and so on.

border-top, border-right, border-bottom, border-left, border

Values: <border-width>, <border-style>, <border-color>
Default: medium, none, <none>
Applies to: Block and replaced elements
Inherited: No
Percentage: No

Sets the properties of the border element, that is the box drawn around an element. A border is similar in its working to margin settings, except of course that it can be made visible.

❑ <border-width> can be thin, medium, thick, or a unit of measurement.

❑ <border-style> can be none, dotted, dashed, solid, double, groove, ridge, inset, or outset.

The `<border-color>` property specifies a color to fill the background of the element while it loads, and to use behind any transparent parts of the element. By supplying the URL of an image instead, the image itself is repeated to create the border. It is also possible to specify values for attributes of the border property separately using the `border-width`, `border-style`, and `border-color` properties.

`border` is shorthand for all of the above properties.

border-top-color, border-right-color, border-bottom-color, border-left-color, border-color

Values:	`<color>`
Default:	`<none>`
Applies to:	Block and replaced elements
Inherited:	No
Percentage:	No

Sets the color of the four borders. By supplying the URL of an image instead, that image is repeated to create the border.

border-top-style, border-right-style, border-bottom-style, border-left-style, border-style

Values:	`none, solid, dashed, dotted, double, groove, ridge, inset, outset`
Default:	`none`
Applies to:	Block and replaced elements
Inherited:	No
Percentage:	No

Sets the style of the four borders.

border-top-width, border-right-width, border-bottom-width, border-left-width, border-width

Values:	`thin, medium, thick, <length>`
Default:	`medium`
Applies to:	All elements
Inherited:	No
Percentage:	No

Sets the width of the border for the element. Each side can be set individually, or the `border-width` property used to set all of the sides. You can also supply up to four arguments for the `border-width` property to set individual sides, in the same way as with the `margin` property.

clear

Values:	`none, both, left, right`
Default:	`none`
Applies to:	All elements
Inherited:	No
Percentage:	No

Forces the following elements to be displayed below an element, which is aligned. Normally, they would wrap around it.

clip – CSS 2

Values: `rect(<top><right><bottom><left>)`, `auto`, `inherit`
Default: `auto`
Applies to: Block and replaced elements
Inherited: No
Percentage: No

Controls which part of an element is visible: anything that occurs outside the clip area is not visible.

display

Values: `<default>`, `none`, `inline`, `block`, `list-item`
Default: The inherent display type of the element
Applies to: All elements
Inherited: Yes
Percentage: No

This property indicates whether an element is rendered, and if so in what form. If set to `none` the element is not rendered and no screen space is set aside for it. If set to "", it is rendered according to the inherent properties of the element: a block-level element is treated as a block-level element and so on. If a block element selector is set to `display:inline` then it acts as an inline element.

float

Values: `none`, `left`, `right`
Default: `none`
Applies to: All elements
Inherited: No
Percentage: No

Causes subsequent elements to be wrapped to the left or right side of the element, rather than being placed below it.

height

Values: `auto`, `<length>`
Default: `auto`
Applies to: Block and replaced elements
Inherited: No
Percentage: Introduced in CSS 2, based on parent's height

Sets the vertical size of an element, and will scale the element if necessary.

width

Values: `auto`, `<length>`, `<percentage>`
Default: `auto`, except for any element with an intrinsic dimension
Applies to: Block and replaced elements
Inherited: No
Percentage: Yes: relative to parent's width

Sets the horizontal size of an element, and will scale the element if necessary. The value is returned as a string including the measurement type (px, %, etc.). To retrieve the value as a number, query the `posWidth` property.

margin-top, margin-right, margin-bottom, margin-left, margin

Values:	`auto`, `<length>`, `<percentage>`
Default:	Zero
Applies to:	All elements
Inherited:	No
Percentage:	Yes: relative to parent element's width

Sets the size of margins around any given element. You can use `margin` as shorthand for setting all of the other values (as it applies to all four sides). If you use multiple values in `margin` but use less than four, opposing sides will try to be equal. These values all set the effective minimum distance between the current element and others.

overflow – CSS 2

Values:	`auto`, `visible`, `hidden`, `scroll`
Default:	`auto` – user agent dependent
Applies to:	Block and replaced elements
Inherited:	No
Percentage:	No

This controls how a container element will display its content if this is not the same size as the container.

❑   `auto` means that the container will use the default method. For example, as in an image element, the content may be resized to fit the container.

❑   `hidden` means that content that would appear outside the block box is clipped (according to the `clip` property), and will not be available to the user by scrolling.

❑   `visible` means that the content will not be clipped where it overruns the container and will be rendered outside the container's edges.

❑   `scroll` will generate scroll bars so that the entire contents of the container can be viewed by scrolling.

Currently only supported by IE 4.0 or higher.

padding-top, padding-right, padding-bottom, padding-left, padding

Values:	`auto`, `<length>`, `<percentage>`
Default:	Zero
Applies to:	All elements
Inherited:	No
Percentage:	Yes: relative to parent element's width

Sets the distance between the content and border of an element. You can use `padding` as shorthand for setting all of the other values (as it applies to all four sides). If you use multiple values in `padding` but use less than four, opposing sides will try to be equal. These values all set the effective minimum distance between the current element and others.

Positioning Properties

position – CSS 2

Values: absolute, relative, static, fixed
Default: static
Applies to: All elements
Inherited: No
Percentage: No

Specifies if the element can be positioned directly on the 2-D canvas.

- ❏   absolute means it can be fixed on the background of the page at a specified location, and move with it.

- ❏   static means it can be fixed on the background of the page at a specified location, but not move when the page is scrolled.

- ❏   relative means that it will be positioned normally, depending on the preceding elements.

- ❏   fixed means that it can be fixed on the background of the page with respect to one or more sides of the screen, and will not move even when the screen is scrolled.

top – CSS 2

Values: auto, <length>, <percentage>
Default: auto
Applies to: Positioned elements
Inherited: No
Percentage: Yes: relative to parent's width

Sets or returns the vertical position of an element when displayed in 2-D canvas mode, allowing accurate placement and animation of individual elements. Value is returned as a string including the measurement type (px, %, etc.). To retrieve the value as a number, query the posTop property.

left – CSS 2

Values: auto, <length>, <percentage>
Default: auto
Applies to: Positioned elements
Inherited: No
Percentage: Yes: relative to parent's width

Sets or returns the left position of an element when displayed in 2D canvas mode, allowing accurate placement and animation of individual elements. The value is returned as a string including the measurement type (px, %, etc.). To retrieve the value as a number, query the posLeft property.

right – CSS 2

Values: auto, <length>, <percentage>
Default: auto
Applies to: Positioned elements
Inherited: No
Percentage: Yes: relative to parent's width

Sets or returns the right position of an element when displayed in 2D canvas mode, allowing accurate placement and animation of individual elements. The value is returned as a string including the measurement type (px, %, etc.). Currently only supported in IE 5.0 and higher.

bottom – CSS 2

Values:	auto, <length>, <percentage>
Default:	auto
Applies to:	Positioned elements
Inherited:	No
Percentage:	Yes: relative to parent's width

Sets or returns the bottom position of an element when displayed in 2D canvas mode, allowing accurate placement and animation of individual elements. The value is returned as a string including the measurement type (px, %, etc.). Currently only supported in IE 5.0 and higher.

z-index – CSS 2

Values:	<number>, <auto>
Default:	Depends on the HTML source
Applies to:	Positioned elements
Inherited:	No
Percentage:	No

Controls the ordering of overlapping elements, and defines which will be displayed 'on top'. Positive numbers are above the normal text on the page, and negative numbers are below. Allows a 2.5-D appearance by controlling the layering of the page's contents.

Table Properties

border-collapse

Values:	collapse , separate , inherit
Default:	collapse
Applies to:	Table and inline elements
Inherited:	No
Percentage:	No

Selects a table's "border model".

border-spacing

Values:	length, Width ?, inherit
Default:	0
Applies to:	Table and inline elements
Inherited:	Yes
Percentage:	No

Specifies the distance between adjacent cell's borders.

caption-side

Values:	top, left, bottom, right, inherit
Default:	top
Applies to:	Table-captioned elements
Inherited:	Yes
Percentage:	No

Specifies the position of a caption with regards to the table itself.

empty-cells

Values:	show, hide, inherit
Default:	show
Applies to:	Table-cell elements
Inherited:	Yes
Percentage:	No

Controls the rendering of borders around cells that have no visible contents.

table-layout

Values:	auto, fixed, inherit
Default:	auto
Applies to:	Table and inline elements
Inherited:	No
Percentage:	No

Controls the way in which cells, rows, and columns are layed out.

Printing Properties

page-break-after – CSS 2

Values:	<auto>, <always>, <left>, <right>, <avoid>
Default:	<auto>
Applies to:	Block elements
Inherited:	No
Percentage:	No

Controls when to set a page break and on what page the content will resume, either the left or the right. Currently only supported in IE 4.0 and higher.

page-break-before – CSS 2

Values:	<auto>, <always>, <left>, <right>, <avoid>
Default:	<auto>
Applies to:	Block elements
Inherited:	No
Percentage:	No

Controls when to set a page break and on what page the content will resume, either the left or the right. Currently only supported in IE 4.0 and higher.

International Properties

unicode-bidi – CSS 2

Values:	normal, embed, bidi-override
Default:	normal
Applies to:	All elements
Inherited:	No
Percentage:	No

This allows you to create an environment to enable you to change the direction of the text flow.

❑ normal means that no directional embedding will be enabled.

❑ embed lets you use the direction property to set the direction of the text flow.

❑ bidi-override overrides the default directional values of an inline element in order to allow the direction property to set the direction in the element.

Currently only supported in IE 5.0 and higher.

direction – CSS 2

Values:	ltr, rtl
Default:	ltr
Applies to:	All elements
Inherited:	Yes
Percentage:	No

This allows you to set the direction of the text flow either from left-to-right or from right-to-left. This is useful in the case of non-European fonts. In order for this to have an effect the unicode-bidi property's value must be embed or bidi-override.

Currently only supported in IE 5.0 and higher.

Other Properties

cursor – CSS 2

Values:	auto, crosshair, default, hand, move, e-resize, ne-resize, nw-resize, n-resize, se-resize, sw-resize, s-resize, w-resize, text, wait, help
Default:	auto
Applies to:	All elements
Inherited:	No
Percentage:	No

Specifies the type of cursor the mouse pointer should be. This is an IE proprietary property.

visibility – CSS 2

Values:	visible, hidden, inherit, collapse
Default:	inherit
Applies to:	All elements
Inherited:	No
Percentage:	No

Allows the element to be displayed or hidden on the page. Elements that are hidden still take up the same amount of space, but are rendered transparently. Can be used to dynamically display only one of several overlapping elements

❑   visible means that the element will be visible.

❑   hidden means that the element will not be visible.

❑   inherit means that the element will only be visible when its parent or container element is visible.

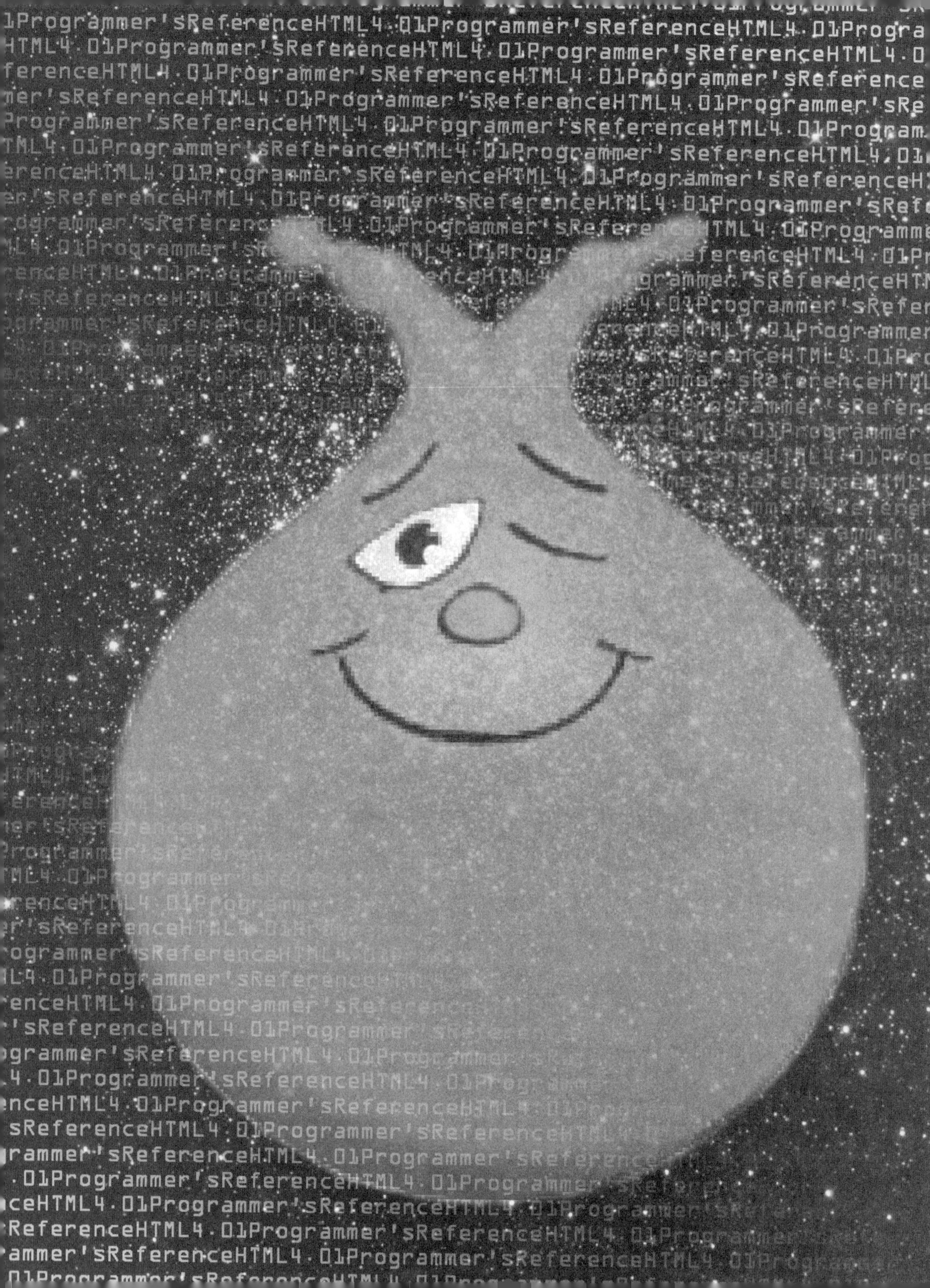
HTML4.01Programmer'sReference

Core DOM Features

What follows is a table of DOM `Document`, `Node`, and `Element` features. Methods annotated with an asterisk (*) have been added in DOM Level 2.

Note: This table does not include XML-only features, most notably those pertaining to namespaces and XML-only node types.

Document Object

Inherits from `Node`.

Method	Description
createElement()	This method creates a node of the indicated type.
createDocumentFragment()	This method creates a node of the indicated type.
createTextNode()	This method creates a node of the indicated type.
createComment()	This method creates a node of the indicated type.

Table continued on following page

Method	Description
createAttribute()	This method creates a node of the indicated type.
getElementsByTagName()	Returns an array of all elements in a document with the tag name used as a parameter.
getElementById()*	Returns the element with the indicated id attribute.
importNode()*	Imports a node from another Document; can be either "shallow" (the node alone is imported) or "deep" (the node's childNodes are copied with it).

Property	Description
documentElement	Document representation of an <html> element.

Node Object

Method	Description
insertBefore()	Inserts a new node before a given childNode.
replaceChild()	Replaces a given childNode with a new node.
removeChild()	Removes the indicated childNode.
appendChild()	Adds a new node to the end of the calling node's childNodes collection.
hasChildNodes()	Returns true if the calling node has any childNodes, otherwise returns false.
cloneNode()	Copies the calling node; if a Boolean true is passed as an argument, it also copies the nodes childNodes collection.
isSupported()*	Allows for testing to determine if a particular DOM feature is supported by this node.

Property	Description
nodeName	Name of the node.
nodeValue	Value of the node; type of value varies with the type of node.
nodeType	Type of node.
parentNode	Parent node of the current node.

Property	Description
childNodes	Collection of childNodes, if the current node has any.
firstChild	First childNode of the current node.
lastChild	Last childNode in the current node's childNodes collection.
previousSibling	Previous node in the current childNodes collection.
nextSibling	Next node in the current childNodes collection.
attributes	Collection of all the attributes of the current node.

NodeList Object

A collection of nodes.

Method	Description
item()	Returns the node of the given index in the collection.

Property	Description
length	Number of nodes in the collection.

NamedNodeMap Object

A collection of named nodes

Method	Description
getNamedNode()	Gets the node of this name.
setNamedNode()	Adds a node with the given name.
removeNamedNode()	Removes the node of this name.

Property	Description
length	Number of nodes in the collection.

Element Object

Inherits from Node.

Method	Description
getAttribute()	Returns the value of the named attribute.
setAttribute()	Sets a named attribute to a new value.
removeAttribute()	Removes the named attribute.
getAttributeNode()	Returns the named attributeNode.
setAttributeNode()	Assigns a value to the named attributeNode; if an attributeNode by name does not exist, a new one is added.
removeAttributeNode()	Removes the named attributeNode.
getElementsByTagName()	Returns a list or collection of all elements with the given tag name that are contained by the current element.
normalize()	Causes there to be no adjacent textNodes in the sub-tree under the current element; all adjacent textNodes are combined and separated only by non-textual (that is, markup) elements.
hasAttribute()*	Returns true if the element has the named attribute.

Property	Description
tagName	Name of the tag corresponding to the current element.

Attribute object

Inherits from Node.

Property	Description
name	Name of the attribute.
ownerElement*	Element to which the attribute belongs.
specified	True if this attribute is present in the original (static) Document before any modification took place.
value	Value of the attribute.

Text Object

Inherits from `Node`.

Method	Description
`splitText()`	Splits a text node into two parts at the index given.

Comment object

Inherits from `Node`.

No additional methods or properties for this object.

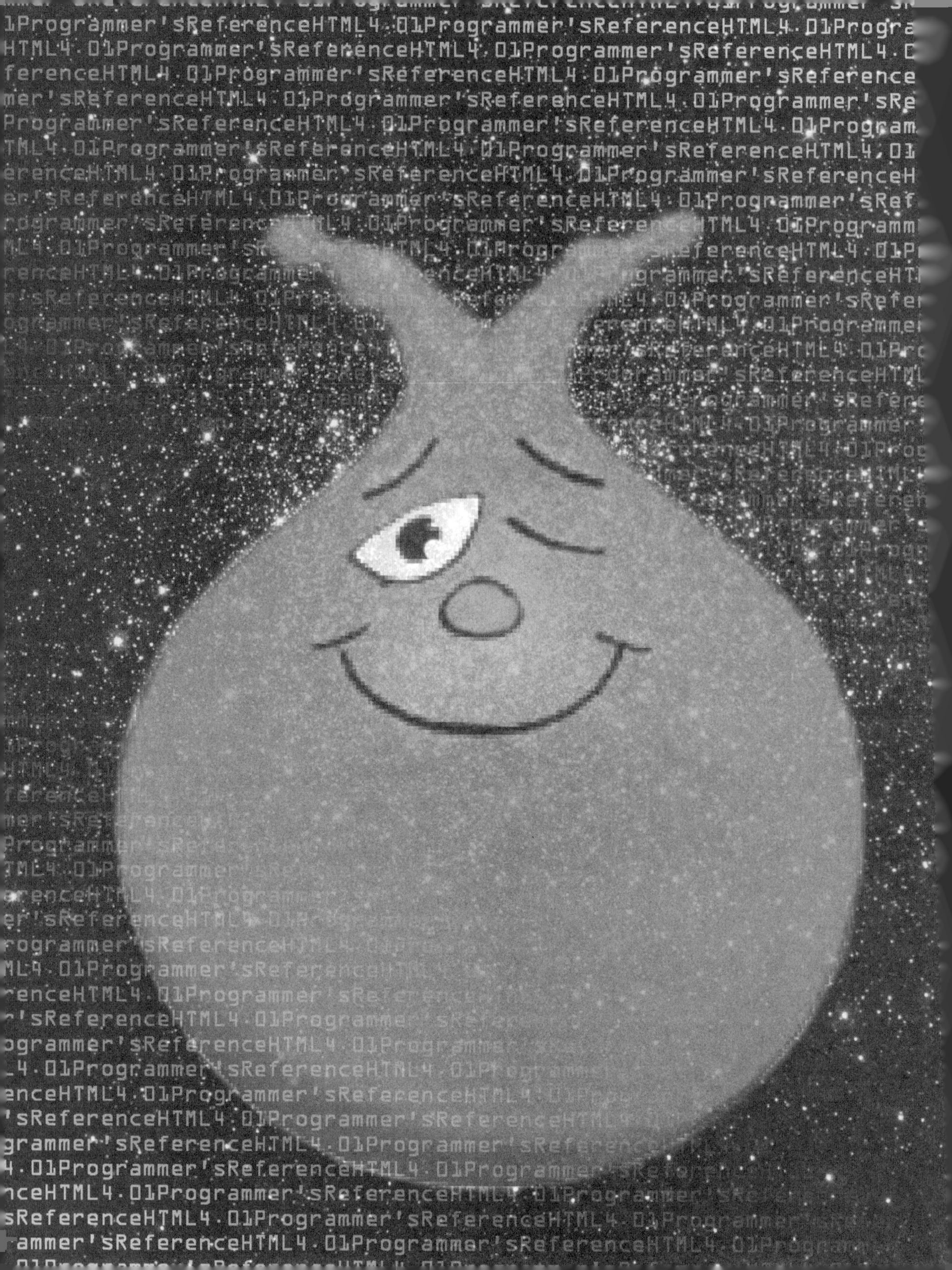
Programmer'sReferenceHTML4.01

Index A - HTML tags

A Guide to the Index

There are two indexes in this book: Index A – HTML tags, and Index B - General. Index A is intended as a quick reference to HTML tags and attributes, while Index B – General has detailed entries arranged hierarchically, covering the entire scope of the book, including tags and attributes.

The general index is presented in alphabetical order, with symbols preceding the letter A. Most second-level entries and many third-level entries also occur as first-level entries. This is to ensure that users will find the information they require however they choose to search for it.

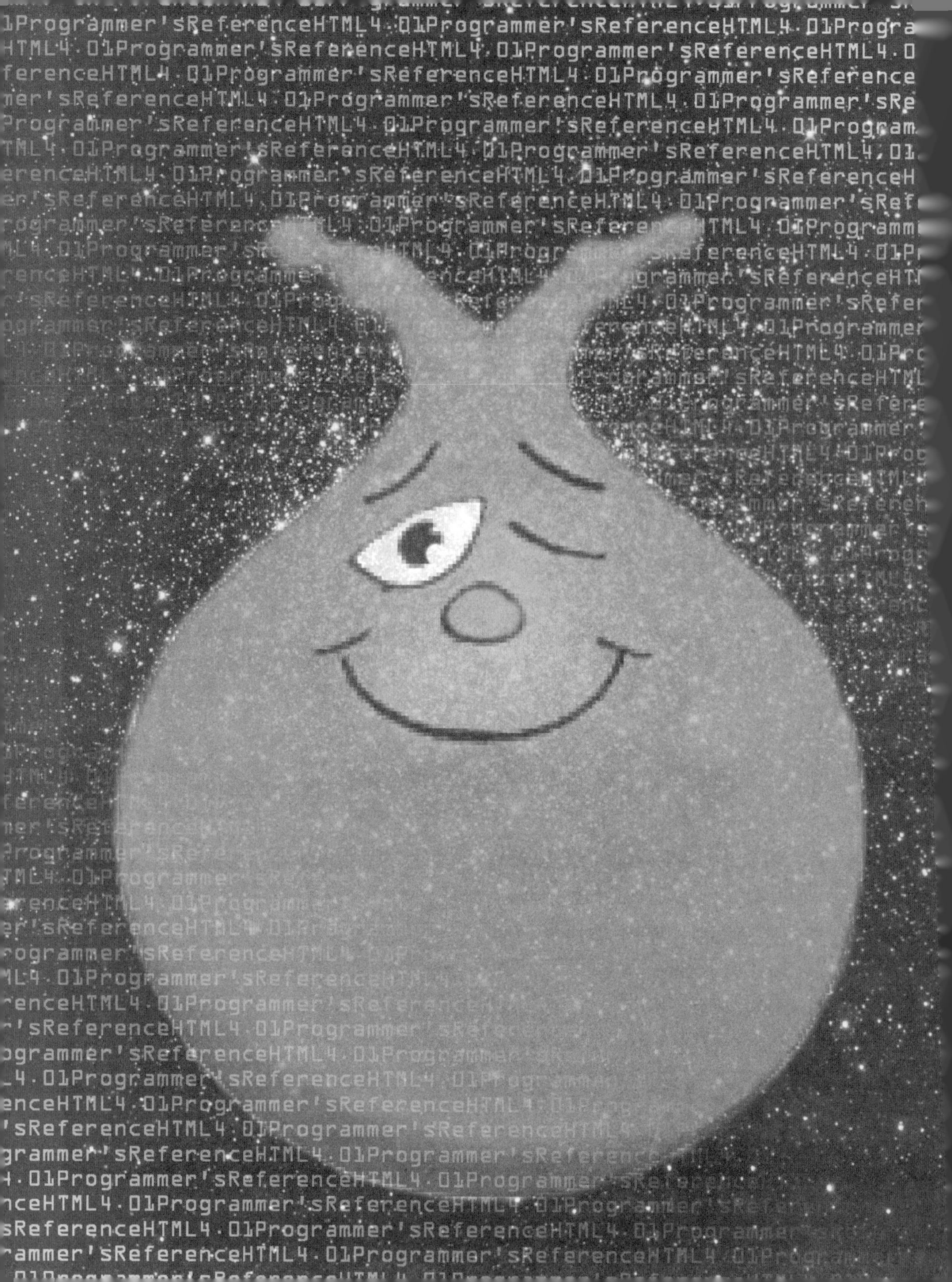
HTML4.01Programmer'sReference

Index B - General

Symbols

@media
specifying multiple media types, 373
<!-- and --> tags
comments, 89
<!> tags, 579
<!Doctype> tags, 579

A

<a> tags, 242
accesskey attribute, 103
active link included between, 101
attributes, 580
charset attribute, 104
coords attribute, 104
hreflang attribute, 104
name attribute, 102
  deprecated, 558
  replaced by id attribute, 560
rel attribute, 104
rev attribute, 105
shape attribute, 105
tabindex attribute, 105
target attribute, 105
type attribute, 105
<abbr> tags
attributes, 581
inline phrasing, 526
absolute URLs, 96
accept-charset attribute, 484
accessibility
see also inaccessibility of web pages, 540
definition, 523
future directions, 541
  adaptive content, 541
  mulimedia, 541
linearizing tables, 530
markup for structure and layout, 530
methods, 529
provide textual equivalents, 528
reasons for
  ease development process, 524
  expand available audience, 524
  moral obligation, 524
repurposability, 529
separate content from presentation, 529
style sheet to add formatting, 530
W Accessibility Initiative, 524

accessibility guidelines
abbreviations and acronyms, 539
animations, 539
color, 540
DTDs and validation, 533
frames, 538
language markup, 534
link mechanisms, 532
longdisc attribute
  use rather than D-Links, 539
metadata, 534
non link printable characters, 537
presentational markup, avoid, 531
provide illustrations, 532
spacer images, do not use, 535
tables, 535
textual alternatives, 531
title links, 532
URLs, 533
accesskey attribute
WAI Working Group guidelines, 526
<acronym> tags
attributes, 581
inline phrasing, 526
<address> tags
attributes, 582
align attribute
tags deprecated for, 406
alink attribute, deprecated, 406
alt attribute, deprecated
<applet> tags, 406
animation, 117
<embed> tags, 269
annotating HTML code, 87
comments, <!-- and --> tags, 89
deletions, <del> tags, 87
insertions, <ins> tags, 87
preformatted text, <pre> tags, deprecated, 89
revision dates, 89
<applet> tags, deprecated, 265, 393
alt attribute, deprecated, 406
attributes, 393, 583
comment attribute, IE specific, 268
examples, 393
mayscript attribute, 444
<area> tags, 107
alt attribute
  accessibility issues in aural style-sheets, 386
alt attributes, 108
attributes, 584
noref attributes, 108
supports same attributes as <a> tags, 108
target attributes, 211
WAI Working Group guidelines, 526

W

X

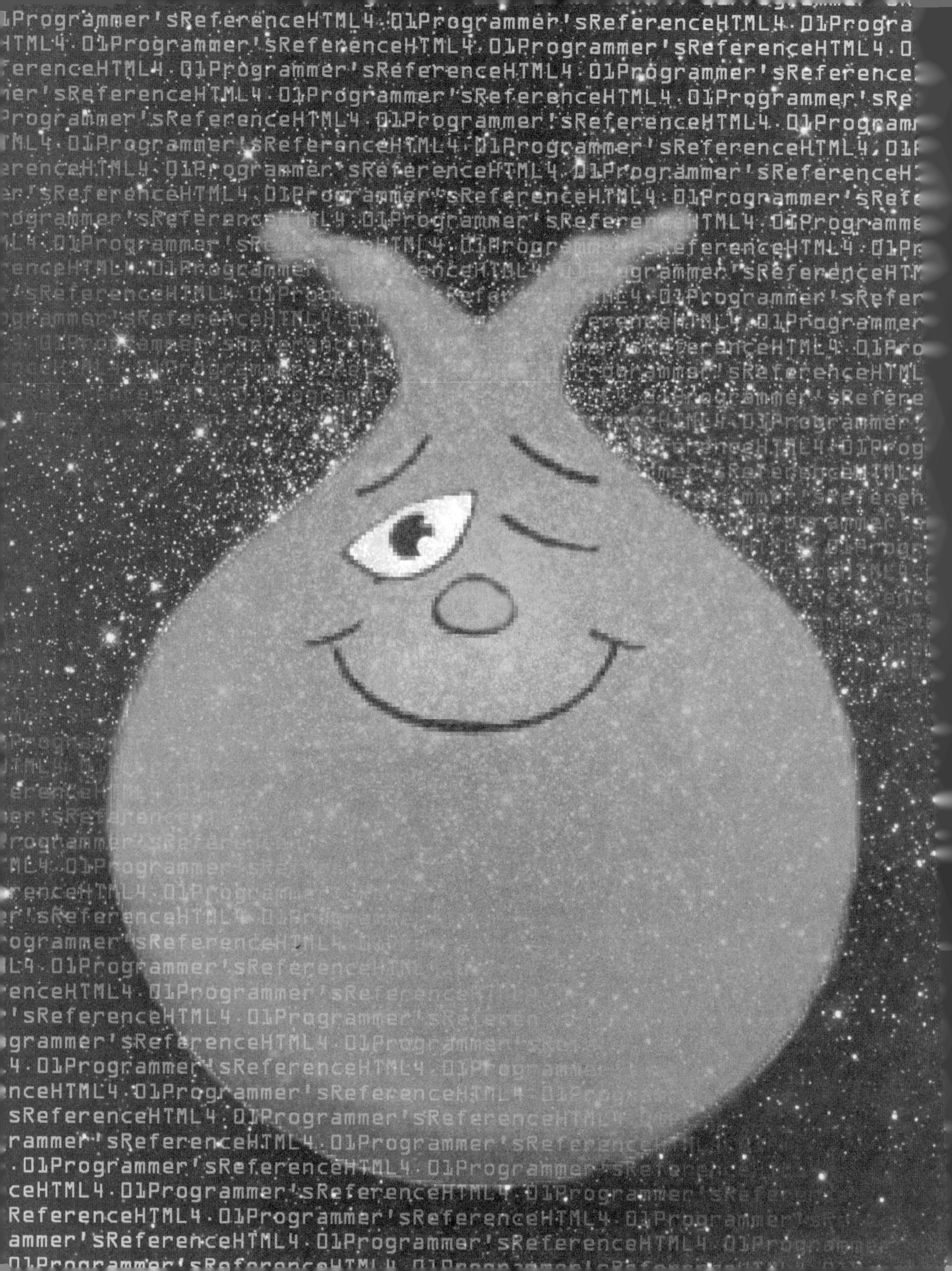
HTML4.01Programmer'sReference

p2p.wrox.com
The programmer's resource centre

A unique free service from Wrox Press
with the aim of helping programmers to help each other

Wrox Press aims to provide timely and practical information to today's programmer. P2P is a list server offering a host of targeted mailing lists where you can share knowledge with your fellow programmers and find solutions to your problems. Whatever the level of your programming knowledge, and whatever technology you use, P2P can provide you with the information you need.

ASP — Support for beginners and professionals, including a resource page with hundreds of links, and a popular ASP+ mailing list.

DATABASES — For database programmers, offering support on SQL Server, mySQL, and Oracle.

MOBILE — Software development for the mobile market is growing rapidly. We provide lists for the several current standards, including WAP, WindowsCE, and Symbian.

JAVA — A complete set of Java lists, covering beginners, professionals,and server-side programmers (including JSP, servlets and EJBs)

.NET — Microsoft's new OS platform, covering topics such as ASP+, C#, and general .Net discussion.

VISUAL BASIC — Covers all aspects of VB programming, from programming Office macros to creating components for the .Net platform.

WEB DESIGN — As web page requirements become more complex, programmer sare taking a more important role in creating web sites. For these programmers, we offer lists covering technologies such as Flash, Coldfusion, and JavaScript.

XML — Covering all aspects of XML, including XSLT and schemas.

OPEN SOURCE — Many Open Source topics covered including PHP, Apache, Perl, Linux, Python and more.

FOREIGN LANGUAGE — Several lists dedicated to Spanish and German speaking programmers, categories include .Net, Java, XML, PHP and XML.

How To Subscribe

Simply visit the P2P site, at **http://p2p.wrox.com/**

Select the 'FAQ' option on the side menu bar for more information about the subscription process and our service.

Programmer to Programmer™

wrox

PROGRAMMER TO PROGRAMMER™

Wrox writes books for you. Any suggestions, or ideas about how you want information given in your ideal book will be studied by our team. Your comments are always valued at Wrox.

Free phone in USA 800-USE-WROX
Fax (312) 893 8001

UK Tel. (0121) 687 4100   Fax (0121) 687 4101

HTML 4.01 Programmer's Reference - Registration Card

Name _____

Address _____

_____

_____

_____

City_____ State/Region _____

Country_____ Postcode/Zip _____

E-mail _____

Occupation _____

How did you hear about this book? _____

☐ Book review (name) _____

☐ Advertisement (name) _____

☐ Recommendation _____

☐ Catalog _____

☐ Other _____

Where did you buy this book? _____

☐ Bookstore (name)_____ City _____

☐ Computer Store (name)_____

☐ Mail Order _____

☐ Other _____

What influenced you in the purchase of this book?

☐ Cover Design

☐ Contents

☐ Other (please specify) _____

How did you rate the overall contents of this book?

☐ Excellent   ☐ Good

☐ Average   ☐ Poor

What did you find most useful about this book? _____

What did you find least useful about this book? _____

_____

Please add any additional comments. _____

What other subjects will you buy a computer book on soon? _____

What is the best computer book you have used this year?

_____

Note: This information will only be used to keep you updated about new Wrox Press titles and will not be used for any other purpose or passed to any other third party.

5334

Check here if you DO NOT want to receive support for this book ☐   5334

wrox
PROGRAMMER TO PROGRAMMER™

NB. If you post the bounce back card below in the UK, please send it to:

Wrox Press Ltd., Arden House, 1102 Warwick Road,
Acocks Green, Birmingham B27 6BH. UK.

———— *Computer Book Publishers* ————